Foundations of Counseling Strategies

Foundations of Counseling Strategies

JAMES R. BARCLAY

Chairman, Department of Educational Psychology
and Counseling, University of Kentucky

John Wiley & Sons, Inc., New York · London · Sydney · Toronto

Library of Congress Catalogue Card Number: 73-158525

ISBN 0-471-04814-3

Printed in the United States of America.

10 9 8 7 6 5 4 3 2 1

Acknowledgments

Many colleagues and students aided me in the preparation of this book: Francis P. Robinson of Ohio State University and Henry B. McDaniel of Stanford University encouraged me initially to write the book. John D. Krumboltz of Stanford University and Nathaniel J. Pallone of New York University read the manuscript and gave many helpful suggestions. Discussions with Sherwin S. Shermis of Purdue University and Margeret McHugh of the University of Victoria, when we were colleagues at Idaho State University, provided many helpful insights into the influence of John Dewey on counseling. Mrs. Sylvia Dost of the University of Maryland shared with me many penetrating insights regarding the role of purification ceremonies in early cultures. Also I am particularly indebted to C. Larry Hagen of the College of Idaho for his continued support of this effort and his permission to abstract and synthesize portions of his doctoral dissertation which were closely related to this book.

Finally, I owe the ultimate completion of the book to the continued urging of many students that I publish it, the unfailing professional cooperation and support of my wife Lisa K. Barclay of the University of Kentucky who argued many points with me (often winning), and the patient forbearance of our children.

JAMES R. BARCLAY

University of Kentucky
Lexington, Kentucky, 1971

Contents

Chapter I FUNCTIONAL AND PHILOSOPHIC
APPROACHES TO COUNSELING 1

Introduction 1
Functional Components of Counseling 4
Counseling and Philosophy: A Model 12
The Present Position in Counseling Toward
   Philosophy 17
Conflicting Positions in Counseling Theory 21
Verification of the Model 28
The Importance of Counseling Theory 31
Summary and Format of the Book 35

PART ONE Cultural Foundations of Counseling 41

Chapter II BEHAVIOR AND CULTURE: A LEARNING
RATIONALE 43

The Nature of Culture 43
Learning the Cultural Transmission 46
The Purpose of Culture 48
Changing Patterns of Cultural Control 49
Methods of Social Learning 55
Value Determination and Deviancy 62
Philosophy, Religion, and Culture 65

Chapter III RELIGION, PHILOSOPHY, AND MEDICINE 67

Primitive Religion 68
Conditioning and Purification in Hebrew Culture 69
Early Medicine 75
The Beginnings of Philosophy 79
Plato and Idealism (427–347 B.C.) 81
Aristotle and Realism (384–322 B.C.) 87

Classical Cultural Transmission and
Behavior Modification   95
Greek Medical Developments   103
Christianity   107
Philosophers of the Christian Era   116
One Thousand Years of Christian Behavior
Modification   123
Summary   131

Chapter IV   PHILOSOPHICAL FOUNDATIONS OF THE
SCIENTIFIC PERSPECTIVE   132

Scholasticism   133
The Mathematical-Philosophical Revolution   139
Dimensions of Psychological Change and
Development   146
The French Sensationists   159
Child Development and Education: Rousseau,
Pestalozzi, Froebel   165
Influences of Associationism and Child Study   174
The Development of Experimental Psychology   178
Summary   182

PART TWO   Philosophical Foundations of Counseling   183

Chapter V   INTENTIONALITY: PERCEPTUAL
FOUNDATIONS OF MODERN
PSYCHOLOGY   185

The Nature of Intentionality and Influence   185
Thomas Aquinas and Scholasticism   187
Themes of Cartesian Thought   200
Spinoza and the Quest for Scientific Ethics   206
Leibnitz and Innate Ideas   211
Reaction and Transition   218
Franz Brentano and the Psychology of Act   220

Chapter VI   SIGMUND FREUD: PSYCHOANALYTIC
THEORY AND CLINICAL DEVELOPMENTS   248
Sigmund Freud: Personality and Influences   249
Philosophic Sources and Influences   251
The Methodology of Freud   255
Theoretical Foundations of Freudian
Psychodynamics   259

The Evolution of Psychic Life   265
Intentionality in Freud   267
Reason and Ethical Determinants   270
Freud as a Redactor and Innovator in
   Intentionality   273
The Influence of Freud   280
Changes in Healing: Healing and Psychotherapy   284
Primary and Secondary Derivations of Freud   286
Summary and Evaluation   299

Chapter VII   PHENOMENOLOGY, GESTALT PSYCHOLOGY
AND EXISTENTIALISM: PROXIMATE BASES
OF SELF-CONCEPT THEORY   302

Phenomenology   302
The Philosophical Basis of Phenomenology   305
German Phenomenology   310
Phenomenology and Existentialism   317
Gestalt and Perceptual Psychology   318
Offshoots of Phenomenology and Gestaltism   325
Existentialism   329
Carl Rogers and Self-Concept Theory   334
Summary   341

Chapter VIII   THE PROBLEM-SOLVING MODEL:
EXPERIMENTALISM   342

Cultural Precursors of Experimentalism   343
Evolution and Science   345
Educational Measurement and Assessment   351
William James: Functionalism & Pragmatism   356
John Dewey   360
Dewey's Theory of Interaction and Counseling   368
Counseling Theorists Related to Interaction
   Theory   371

Chapter IX   LEARNING THEORY AND BEHAVIOR
MODIFICATION   378

An Overview of Learning Approaches: Classical
   and Cognitive   380
Antecedents to Social Learning Theory   385
The Philosophical Basis for Behaviorism   393
Learning Theory and Psychotherapy   399

Application of Behavior Modification Techniques   405
Expanding the Base of Learning Theory   409

Chapter X   EVALUATION AND RESOLUTION:
A FUTURE LOOK   416

Philosophic Reconciliation   417
Methodological Priorities   422
Summary   426

Author index
Subject index

CHAPTER I

Functional and Philosophic Approaches to Counseling

INTRODUCTION

One of the major problems confronting all manner of social scientists today is how to relate the process and goals of change in a technological society to the ideas and conceptual framework of thinking. Briefly stated, how does our thinking relate to our behaving? For urgent human problems as well as common decisions about behavior are solved by planning. The plans of men are usually framed by past history and present and future needs, as well as by the reality of those financial and human circumstances that must be taken into consideration whenever change is desired or needed. Reconstructing the inner city to meet human needs requires not only a definition of those kinds of freedoms and aspects of the good life that are known to relate to man's needs but also a thoughtful attempt to evaluate the problems attending the removal of whole populations, cost factors, and building methods.

Man thinks in ways that may be predetermined by his language and culture. He typically frames up solutions to problems on the basis of his experience or the experience of others. He rehearses various solutions to a problem within his mind, explores his ideas and tentative hypotheses with other people, and attempts to weigh the possible effect of his proposed course of action. As Freud has stated before, thinking is an effort to abbreviate action through vicarious rehearsal. There is an attempt at simulation and at the careful estimate of probable effects. Not only does this approach typify the judgment process of individuals but it is also instrumental in the thinking of policy makers. Programs for change, innovative plans, are usually carefully rehearsed in the minds of the planners, and more recently the use of the computer has been involved in what is known as simulation. Simulation is a full-blown attempt to develop coping skills for dealing with problems. In recent years, intensive group procedures have been initiated to provide small or large groups of individuals with the opportunity to try out their decision-making skills and to gain new experiences in understanding human judgments. Sensitivity training, group simulation projects, and even games such as Monopoly and Life provide the opportunity for actual decision making regarding an array of problems and proposed solutions.

The problem-solving process implicitly or explicitly involves an effort to operationalize attitudes, values, and judgments for some expected or anticipated set of behaviors. Moreover, the process whereby men arrive at priority judgments involves the frameworks of both culture and science. These frameworks, whether cognitive or affective in nature, appear to be by-products of man's experience, whether individual or collective in nature. Moreover, both culture and science can be considered systematic frameworks that are derived from the shaping effect of experience in living and the attempts on man's part to understand and explain his universe.

Man's thought processes appear to be the perceptually moderated medium for coping with reality. Through the ages man has developed a systematic framework for coping with reality. He has observed, studied, categorized, and experimentally tested the phenomena that he perceives operating both within and outside of himself. And this framework, shaped by the living forces of culture, has become his scientific approach to reality. But, in a very real sense, this conceptual framework is a logically distilled fiction. Various groups of men have proposed solutions to not only the problems of forces in the physical sphere but also to the broader notions of reality, values, goals, personal happiness, and truth. These solutions have been tested in the arena of experience, and more than one alternative is usually available to men of reason and experience. These solutions, for example, the philosophy of idealism or realism, are simply the frameworks of thinking and judging, the veritable scaffolding on which man appends his notion of reality, determines what forces maintain certain behaviors, and then, as logically or as consistently as possible, makes judgments about how these forces or ideas can be changed. Historically, man has always been interested in knowing how behavior can be changed. This was the problem confronting Plato, Aristotle, Christ, Darwin, and Marx—to mention but a few eminent individuals—who have been concerned about behavior. In every thoughtful policy decision, as well as in those individual decisions affecting people, the inevitable components are those that relate to man's perception and judgment, as well as to his knowledge of the methods of effecting change in human behavior.

Although today our technological society, through computers, can provide far more data for arriving at judgments and decisions, the decision-making process still resides with human understanding and will. Even though computers can digest, synthesize, evaluate, simulate, and provide expectancy tables with respect to probable behaviors as an outcome of a decision-making process, it is still necessary for someone, either as an individual or a collective entity, to make the final executive decision required to implement a course of action. This is all too clear from the responsibilities and decisions that must be made by the President of the United States on numerous occasions.

The very abundance of information is itself a mediating variable for decision making. The student as well as the expert is confronted with a veritable explosion of knowledge and information. There is so much more to learn and evaluate today than ever before. Moreover, the information is readily available through indexes, summaries, etc. It has been said that 90 percent of the world's scientists who ever lived are alive and producing today. The explosion of knowledge has crammed libraries and other resources to their limit and there is no end in sight. Moreover, pressing unavoidable problems continue to demand the attention of concerned social scientists. There are questions relating to the control of populations, civil rights issues, disarmament, the exploration of outer space, the possible planned genetic alteration of future human beings, and the distinct feasibility of man's control over his own biological and social evolution. These issues challenge many of the older conceptual and affective frameworks spawned over the centuries by man's culture and his rationalizing explanation of himself in relationship to the universe.

These issues tap many areas of ethical and moral concern which have never before been so pressing. There are discoveries and scientific possibilities that were not foreseen in the ideological frameworks of yesteryear. Nonetheless, the frameworks, themselves, are important clues to the range of alternatives that man may have in any given circumstance. Decisions need to be made by both social scientists, conceptualizing and implementing policy, as well as by individuals. And many of these questions, relating to values and what is good and true, cannot be answered by a continual preoccupation with the technical aspects of behavior change. For many years, counselor and psychologist educators have been discussing the goals, processes, and methods of evaluating the products of behavior change. These discussions have invariably been related to techniques and technical procedures. They have less frequently been directed to the crucial areas that form the basis of counselor and client expectations, that is, the perceptual mediation of philosophical, cultural, and human learning bases of judgment and decision making.

This book has been written with the graduate student in educational psychology and or counseling in mind. It is the result of a decade of work in the education of school psychologists and counselors. It bears the imprint of many inquiring discussions by students concerning the big question—seldom verbalized—of how we relate our thinking and judging to the process of implementing change. This book is an effort to provide the graduate student with a cultural and intellectual scaffolding with regard to both the remote and proximate components of decision making that relate to change in human behavior. More specifically, it is an attempt to relate the functional or technical goals, processes, and criteria of evaluation in precipitating change in human individual or group social behavior to both the cultural and philosophical foundations of human judgment and learning. Thus it is a subjective attempt to review and order some of the major cultural and philosophical systems of thought in their historical perspective with an emphasis on the role of the counselor. Moreover, the role of the counselor here is conceptualized in a much broader sense than is connoted by the concept school counselor. By counselor is meant all those who attempt in some way or other, via professional training and experience, to aid their fellow men in the attainment of those unique personal goals that relate to the "good life."

FUNCTIONAL COMPONENTS OF COUNSELING

Counseling can be defined in many ways. It can be looked at as a technique, a function, a corollary of training and placement, or as the by-product of a philosophical structure. Operationally, counseling consists of an array of possible thought processes and behaviors that pertain to a technical process or function. This function is related to problem solving. But it is a special kind of problem solving that is identified culturally by role expectations and professionally by a series of experiences obtained in study and practice. In this broad definition, counseling not only includes the obvious public and private school guidance counselor but also a variety of other functional roles such as the personnel who work in correctional institutions, comprehensive care centers, employment settings, rehabilitation positions, medical clinics, and the like. Obviously, psychiatrists, psychologists, social workers, counselors, and a variety of other professionals utilize the counseling process.

In the past, distinctions have been made between psychotherapy and counseling. Some have viewed these distinctions as relating to whether the counseling process was concerned chiefly with the unconscious or the conscious modes of behavior. Others have distinguished between supportive, insightful, and reconstructive counseling therapy. With these distinctions there have been modifications of training programs, all with the basic notion of preparing students to fill certain roles in society. Distinctions have also been made both in role function and training which relates to the exact specifications of various counseling settings. For example, programs for college student personnel workers differ from the programs provided for elementary or secondary guidance counselors. Programs for clinical psychologists differ from those for counseling or school psychologists. Child welfare, group workers, and psychiatric social workers all show certain differences in training and the societal expectations of what they should be doing. The disparate backgrounds of counselors, psychologists, and social workers contribute to some confusion about the roles of these various specialists in the field of counseling. Roles are related to expectancies. These expectancies have been derived from (1) societal or cultural stereotypes, (2) individual perceptions of the cultural expectancy, and (3) the manner in which these professionals functionally translate the first two principles into an operational framework in their job. In addition, separate historical heritages in counseling psychology and social work have been translated into differential collegiate and university training programs.

Despite the differences in the various roles of professional counselors, there is evidence that similar personality characteristics motivate individuals to seek a career in this area. Holland (1966) has found that counselors, clinical psychologists, and social workers have a relatively high social orientation characterized by a need structure for affiliation, succorance, and nurturance. Halmos (1966) has examined the fundamental postulates which he considers to relate to the motivation and personality characteristics of those who engage in counseling, social work, and psychotherapy.

Halmos suggests that those who enter the helping professions of counseling view this avenue as an approach to effecting change in society. Drawing a parallel to the earlier missionary efforts of clergymen, and the involvement in political activities as an older approach to effecting change in society, he suggests that humanitarian goals can no longer be as adequately fulfilled through either religion or politics as through the counseling profession. He believes that the complexity of social issues, the "mendacity" of grand political generalizations, the stereotyped reduction of politics to expediency, and the loneliness of man in mass society are all reasons for the development of a helping profession in which personal characteristics and relationships become the primary avenue for self-fulfillment.

Certainly, the Church as a vehicle for personal and social salvation has reached a stage of crisis. For it is evident today that there is a considerable amount of controversy within organized religious denominations regarding liberal stances towards social, doctrinal, and educational issues. Although there are many possible reasons for the increasing crescendo of this controversy, it may reasonably be suggested that this is a function of (1) changing attitudes towards social institutions and their role, that is, from a conservation of the cultural tradition to an active force for change, (2) a critical inquiry regarding the functional utility of certain theological dogmas that traditionally have been associated with both Catholic and Protestant Christianity, (3) the emergence of a "new breed" of clergy who are less concerned with the "comfortable pew" and are more prone to preach and advocate a changing social behavior, and (4) the advancement of the cause of ecumenicism, which has tended to level the traditional differences between religious denominations and has emphasized the functional similarities between religious groups.

These observations pertaining to the nature and function of the Church also are reflected in the development of new counselor role and function. For the counselor, considered from an historical perspective, has been generally a maintainer of the "status quo." He has attempted to help individuals who have had problems meet the expectations of others. This has been true very often in the school system where the counselor has been tied—very often not of his own volition—to an adjunct discipline role. In more recent times, with the example of institutional change—albeit slow and labored—as a consequence of impatience and group pressure, counselors have come to view themselves as agents of social change. These role changes appear to be consonant with Halmos' major thesis that the "counselor" is an individual who is dedicated to social reconstruction. And although some do enter into psychological studies as a by-product of a search for self-fulfillment, self-discovery, and meaning, this need not be considered a maladaptive stance, as Halmos has pointed out. One is tempted to suggest that old issues of man's life and future continually are resurrected and reinterpreted in each generation. Those who function in the interpretative role may have been priests and ministers in earlier ages. Today, it appears that some of this former role is subsumed in counseling.

Role expectancies and behaviors are also shaped by functional determinants. Within the broad concept of counseling, there are some functional determinants that need to be stated. Counseling either implicitly or explicitly operates within the limits of some definable goals, methods, and criteria of evaluation. The counseling *goals* of any approach specify more or less precisely the desired outcomes of the counseling process. These goals are formed in the mind of the counselor in response to the judgments he makes regarding the problems of the client. This decision-making process is a complex one based on personal observation, client formulation of problems, test information, the theoretical orientation of the counselor, and above all his individual and subjective evaluation of all the information available for decision-making. Goals are then the product of a combination of multiple information inputs as integrated into the counselor's perception regarding the nature of reality, the conditions of learning, his assumptions about the universe, and the nature of man. Specifically, the manner in which these philosophical and cultural determinants influence the goal evolution in the mind of the counselor is judged to be a function of his own intellectual and emotional perspective. Parenthetically, it is the quality and characteristic determinants of counselor judgment that form part of the basic rationale for this book.

By *methods* or *process* is meant the specific techniques utilized by a counselor to realize the goals specified in his mind and through the mutual decision and consent of the client. Although seldom alluded to in the literature, there are but three major ways in which individuals can be changed. The first of these methods is to bring some kind of psychological pressure on the client to take a course of action, make a decision, or change his behavior. This may take the form of nondirective counseling, directive confrontation, supportive and intentional clarification, as well as the use of technical information. Whatever the manner of approach, in every instance the counselor is utilizing his own cognitive, affective, or behavioral repertory, verbal or nonverbal, to bring to bear the effect or impact of his personality and communication system on the corresponding systems of the client. The second approach is to alter the environment that supports the client's undesirable behavior or to provide those environmental support systems that will promote the emergence of new skills and behaviors. In this approach, changes in the environment may include working with teachers in a specific approach, talking to parents, or a variety of combinations of specific techniques and strategies that are designed to help the client reduce those behaviors or attitudes that he feels are detrimental to him, and to elicit those new behaviors or attitudes that will help him. The third approach is not a distinct one but involves the utilization of the first two by attempts to alter the behavior of the client and to simultaneously restructure some aspects of the environment.

In coping with adult problems, it is often very difficult to effect any practical change in the environment. Thus working with the individual, either privately or in groups, appears to be the most fruitful avenue of approach. With children or adults who function within a structured environment where some environmental control is possible, it is easier to design strategies for coping with environmental systems. In any event, by methods and process in this context are meant whatever direct or indirect procedures are utilized by the counselor as a strategy to effect the changes that are related to the goals and outcomes postulated.

Central to methods and processes is a consideration of the ways and means whereby methods and processes are determined or specified. Obviously, this is a decision-making procedure based on information from various sources. Two major functions take place in this decision-making procedure. One is *assessment* and the other is *strategy making*. Formerly, these two procedures were grouped under three categories that were derived from the medical model in psychotherapy. Diagnosis, prognosis, and treatment were the older terms. Today, in part because of the strictly medical connotation of these terms, assessment and strategy making more adequately represent what actually is desired in counseling.

Assessment is a term that covers both the diagnosis and prognosis phases of the older process. Assessment as well as diagnosis and prognosis are simply terms to cover the method of arriving at a judgment about the problems of another individual. Of course, these terms can also be used in relation to self-assessment or self-diagnosis. In the older medical terminology, diagnosis was used to represent the procedures whereby a clinician arrived at a judgment regarding the causes of a specific ailment. Thus a pain in the stomach might be caused by a variety of malfunctions including heart, liver, stomach, or some combination of these or other unknown causes. Certain clinical symptoms were associated with specific problems. Through the use of observation, physical examination, and clinical laboratory tests, plus the knowledge of pathology which the physician has, he arrives at certain hypotheses relating symptoms and the clinical findings of etiology. Obviously, this includes a host of procedures and methods specific to medicine, neurology, and anatomy. However, the good diagnostician should be able to narrow the hypothesis field to one or two specific hypotheses that he then can test out by differential approaches to determine whether his judgment was correct. Primarily, diagnosis in the medical sense has been concerned with the establishment of the specific causal factors relating to the presentation of symptoms.

Prognosis in the medical sense is an allied judgment to diagnosis. It is concerned with the analysis of medical problems in relationship to the factors of time duration, the progress of the illness, and the general forecast or prediction of the course of the illness both without and with medical treatment. Finally, the treatment procedure itself is obviously designed to eliminate the cause of the symptoms through medication and/or surgery. At the very least in terminal cases, treatment has been related to providing a measure of comfort to the individual through the lessening of pain.

The terms diagnosis and prognosis have been most actively used in clinical psychology. For clinical psychology has been identified as that traditional branch of psychology which has been chiefly concerned with the diagnostic use of testing. The specific training, which has been subsumed generally under the clinical model, has been focused on the development of theoretical personality constructs or systems in which a series of dynamic entities are believed to guide and motivate the behavior of the organism in a cause-effect relationship that is somewhat analogous to the medical one. The operation of this model has tended to focus on the outlining of pathology, clinical symptomatology, and the categorical labeling of clusters of behaviors as derived from observation, interviewing, and testing analysis. The general approach to behavior change has been through either individual or group psychotherapy in which the goals of psychotherapy have been the intellectual assimilation of repressed or emotionally blocked psychic processes. This is done in order to free the individual from those psychological forces which are generally conceptualized to be amoral, blind, instinctive, and above all compelling in their sense of urgency and constraint over the organism.

Consequently, the clinical psychologist, although using other methods such as observation, has tended as a result of his training and the expectancies of his role in medical centers, to search almost exclusively for the *causal* sources of problematic behavior. In the school setting this has led generally to the viewing of maladaptive behaviors, such as acting-out, aggressive, and lack of attending behavior, as evidences of more deep-rooted problems and as being causally related to a host of factors such as inadequate patterns of mothering, intervening variables of ego or superego, varieties of coping mechanisms, and interactive effects. Many of these judgments, moreover, have been inferred from the use of projective techniques in which the basic assumption is that the response of the client reveals in latent fashion the sources of his maladjustment.

The futility of such an exercise in seeking out the causal strands of psychological behavior utilizing the medical model and based on operant modes of behavior is highlighted by Kuo (1967). He indicates that at least five sets of independent and 23 interactive factors must be taken into consideration to determine an adequate theory of behavioral causality. They are: (1) morphological factors, (2) biochemical and biophysical factors, (3) stimulating objects, (4) developmental history, and (5) environmental context. Kuo maintains that every response of an animal organism is the functional by-product of the combined effects of the interactive reactions of these five factoral groups.

A term more preferred by some counseling psychologists is that of *assessment*. Assessment describes the process of observation used by a trained counselor or psychologist in determining the descriptive characteristics of the individual. The emphasis here is to determine the ongoing character-istics of behavior rather than to probe for uncertain causal connections. In addition, assessment is more directly related to treatment alternatives and strategy making. Assessment includes the use of both systematic and occasional observation, interviewing, the study of the environmental "press," the learning contingencies, and the findings of individual and group testing. Each of these separate processes is considered to be a selective method in aiding the counselor in forming his estimate of the cognitive, affective, and social skills of his client. The emphasis is less on the theorized answers to the question WHY? and more on a clarification of the questions: WHAT? WHERE? WHEN? AND HOW OFTEN? Assessment then focuses on the obtaining of as clear and objective picture of the indi-vidual in his various roles and cultural settings as can be gained with the tools and techniques that are available to us. This includes not only the use of observation, interviewing, and test results but also the develop-ment of basal rates of behavior observation in terms of the frequency, duration, extent, and intensity of specific behaviors. In view of the com-plexity of obtaining assessment data, it is even more hazardous to form predictions of what the future behavior will be like. However, in view of the power of habit, and the tenacity with which individual learned behavior is maintained and responses habituated, one can make a judg-ment about the future methods of responding, assuming that environ-mental contingencies are not substantially altered.

Strategy making follows after assessment. Traditionally, the medical model procedures of diagnosis and prognosis were followed by a course of treatment. It is here in this phase of psychological analysis that the profession has been extremely weak. As will be shown in subsequent chapters, global treatment procedures were utilized that were often un-related to diagnosis. The consistency and the strengths of the medical model *for medicine* have been in its long tradition of research and experi-mentation. Medicine has developed a repertory of treatment techniques related to diagnosis. The weaknesses of the psychological assumption of the techniques have been in the short history of scientific exploration of the phenomenological and cultural bases of behavior. In short, there have been weaknesses in the correspondence between diagnostic cate-gories based on hypothetical or intervening clinical states and the actual behavior observations. It is only recently that a number of concrete strategies have emerged that employ one aspect or the other of social learning theory. Catterall (1967), drawing on the work of David Kiersey and William Glasser as well as many others, has developed a com-pendium of alternate strategies of counseling that can be focused *around* the student, utilizing environmental interventions, *to* the student, employing specific installed interventions in which the social or learning environment is altered, *by* the student, in which certain specific assignments are made for the student, and *with* the student, employing individual or group counseling procedures. Teachers, parents, principals, and the student client himself can all be involved in these strategies. One of the basic assumptions of the use of specific strategies is that known principles of learning must be used in relationship to identified basal rates of responding. This entire phase of counseling will be discussed in a later chapter in more detail. Here we point out that strategy making, whether related to global constructs, such as adjustment or mental health, or specific behavioral deficits, such as inattentive behavior in a classroom, is a part of the total functional approach to counseling.

Another pivotal construct in counseling involves the notion of *criterion*. A criterion is a rule or standard of some kind. In counseling it usually refers to a form of behavior. There can be individual criteria of behavior that are reflective of the subjective values and perception of the individual. These are contained implicitly in self-judgments involving self-monitoring introspection, as in conscience. Generally, all human beings have some subjective notions of what constitutes effective behavior for them. This is, in part, a function of their recognition of what is expected of them from others. But in addition to the subjective and personalized criteria of behavior, which may or may not reflect internalized values and cultural norms, all of us are also judged by others in terms of the appropriateness of our behavior in matching the socially accepted criteria of effective human behavior. Much counseling is occasioned by the conflict in criteria of behavior that individuals find between what they themselves consider important and valuable and what others consider important and effective. Formerly, many counselors spoke of adjustment as a criterion for counseling. Unfortunately, this concept was subject to wide differences of opinion. And today we recognize that criteria of effective behavior are contextual, related to the expectations that significant members of our peer group make concerning behaviors of individuals in the group.

There are multiple criteria that most human beings must meet in one way or the other. The expectations of parents, teachers, peers, and others all come to bear on the behavior of a child. Adults must face up to role expectancies that are derived from being a husband or wife, a father, a provider, a member of religious or political organizations, a sportsman, and many other diverse roles. What is considered adequate and expected behavior in one setting may differ considerably from what is expected in another setting.

A recognition then of the multiple nature of the criteria of effective human behavior plus the contextual setting in which these criteria operate provides insight into the problem of evaluation in counseling. If counseling makes a difference in human behavior, it is necessary both for the client and the counselor as well as the profession at large to understand how the process can be judged efficient with respect to outcomes. The evaluation of counseling is dependent on the nature of the goals of the counseling, the process utilized in assessment and strategy making and, above all, the determination of some adequate criterion measures. Specificity in goals, multiple criteria of assessment and the selection of appropriate strategies of intervention in counseling are all prerequisites to the determination of evaluating outcomes.

In summary, the concepts of counseling described here refer to a helping process whereby a professional engages a client in a process relationship. It is imperative that this process involve—either implicitly or explicitly—some goals, methods, and criteria of evaluation. Goals may be specific or nonspecific; methods can include a variety of differential assessment techniques with the strategies of intervention either being related to the assessment or not related. All of this process is evaluated subjectively or objectively or in both ways by the counselor and client as well as by society. This functional description of the work of the counselor is not simply one relevant to the present era, but it may be seen in the role functioning of other individuals in philosophy and religion who were concerned about effecting change in human beings. These pivotal concepts will appear throughout the book in various chapters as the primary structure for describing the alternate approaches to counseling.

COUNSELING AND PHILOSOPHY: A MODEL

The preceding section of this chapter has focused on some of the functional elements of the counseling relationship. This portion of the chapter is concerned with the philosophical framework that undergirds counseling theory and practice. We shall start with an example of approaches that exemplify philosophical frameworks in a school counseling situation.

A familiar scene in most junior high schools is the referral of a student to the counselor because of inattentive behavior, the failure to comply with instructions, learning achievement below potential, sloppy dress, and generally demoralizing behavior in the classroom. Let us watch this student walking idly toward the counselor's office. Furthermore, let us look at the counseling dimensions as they unfold in four typical approaches to this problem.

Counselor A perceives this situation as a common deviation from the goal-centered activity of the school. His approach is typified by an attempt to convince the student that he is taking the "wrong approach" toward the school effort. He may attempt to "reason" with the student, pointing out the complexities of modern society, the need for the development of learning skills, and the apparent reasons why the student's present behavior has brought him into conflict with the school. The focal point of this counseling approach might be termed *object-oriented*. The counselor is taking a sophisticated approach to discipline, attempting to convince the student that he should change his attitudes toward school and teachers through more conformity to the goals of the school effort. This may take the specific direction of a change in dress, a more attentive attitude, studying more, going around with "better" classmates, and achieving at a higher rate.

Counselor B may take another approach to this same situation. He views the student as an individual who is the product of a poor environment. The student is lashing out at society, rejecting the purposes and procedures of education because he has assimilated consciously or unconsciously a host of behavior patterns that represent an inappropriate means of adjustment to reality. In other words, Counselor B sees the problem as one that can be focused on the *subject orientation*. The procedures, methods, and goals of this counselor's approach will be to unscramble the complex unconscious determinants to the poor school behavior which are causing the problems of this student. If the counselor is skillful in unraveling the complex behavioral dynamics of the student—can examine in detail the developmental history of the student—he may be able to help the student develop insights into the causes of his present behavior. Once these insights have been verbalized, the hostilities manifested against the school as surrogate parents identified, and the defense mechanisms that are operative in the student's life properly labeled and integrated into conscious behavior, the student may make the changes that will reduce his conflict with the school personnel.

Still another approach may be taken by Counselor C. This approach assumes that the major problems, perhaps the exclusive problems, of the student stem from learned patterns of behavior that are maladaptive in terms of the task-orientation of the school. The resistant and antisocial behavior of the student are testimony to a pattern of learned behavior that may have been the product of wrong reinforcement contingencies. Furthermore, the student has failed to integrate into the behavioral repertory those internalized controls that are usually reinforced through social intercourse. In this approach, the chief plan is to identify the reinforcement contingencies and to effect behavior change through environmental manipulation and operant conditioning with the end result being a change in behavior patterns. Somewhat similar to the approach of Counselor A, this approach might be called the *object-manipulative* approach.

Counselor D may take still a fourth approach to the problem of the subject. He is concerned with the student as a person, as a unique individual creation whose problems are related to a poor self-concept. He may view the student as an individual who has been bullied and harassed by adults, who has been unable to integrate his feelings about other people, reality, and the school. This counselor focuses his attention on the counselor-client process. He is not engaging in this transaction in order to improve the client's attitude toward school (though this is a hoped for by-product of the process), to probe into the inner dynamics of the student's past life, or to help the student effect new patterns of behavior through learning. His chief concern is to help the student come to terms with his reality, to recognize the need for communication, and the unique nature of an interpersonal relationship characterized by acceptance, nonthreat, and emotional dialogue. Counselor D is engaging in what might be considered a variation of Counselor B's approach, that is, a *subject-manipulative* approach.

These four approaches to counseling represent respectively a realist problem-solving approach, a neo-psychoanalytic approach, a behavioral approach, and a client-centered approach to the same behavioral phenomenon. Counselors A and C represent an approach to interpersonal problems that can be termed an *object*-oriented approach. They are concerned about the force of external reality, that is, the object of perception in their approach to effecting behavior change in the student. Whether the approach be the more direct "reasoning" and "problem-solving" approach of Counselor A or the manipulation of applied learning theory in a social milieu characteristic of Counselor C, the essential intent is to effect those changes through counseling that will bring the subject into a better conformity to the realities of the school situation. This broad approach to effecting behavior change in the school situation may be included under the broad term of behaviorism. Behaviorism includes the older approach of Williamson, the more recent approach of behavioral engineering (Krumboltz, 1964), the position of Meyerson and Michael (1962), the writings of Skinner, Ferster, and others who have attempted to apply principles of experimental psychology to the counseling process, and the behavior therapy approach of Eysenck and Rachman (1965). Although this terminology cannot be said to be strictly behavioristic in the sense of a clear derivation from Pavlovian and Hullian principles, the general grouping of these theorists together suggests a common orientation that this writer has chosen to identify as an *object*-orientation approach.

Counselor B, the neo-psychoanalytic counselor, and Counselor D represent typical approaches to counseling that are *subject*-oriented. In these approaches, the chief purpose of the counseling encounter is judged to be subject-oriented in the sense that the principal efforts of the process are directed towards self-understanding on the part of the client. Despite the variations between the theoretical orientations of Counselor B and Counselor D, the communalities reflect a counselor preoccupation with the internal phenomena of the subject. This approach known as phenomenology emphasizes the *Lebenswelt* or the world of subjective phenomena and facts as contrasted with the world of scientific and objective reality. The *Lebenswelt* is concerned with the everyday sequence of internal phenomena, has its own a priori structure (space-time), and is characterized further by the method of description and comparison as contrasted with the scientific world of the hypothetical-deductive method. Phenomenology includes the humanistic movement in counseling represented by Rogers and Patterson, the existentialist positions of van Kaam, May, and Tillich, as well as the major groupings of neo-Freudians and the adherents of *Daseinanalysis*.

Explanation

The positions that have been sketched in the foregoing pages may not be typical of all the counselors who generally subscribe to one of the theoretical orientations identified therein. They have been thus portrayed to describe counseling theory in terms of a philosophical rationale that may help to understand the mutual relationships between the goals, methods, and criteria of evaluation which are used by counseling theorists in approaching the counseling relationship. In this book, I take the position that counseling as a process of effecting human behavior change is logically related to epistemological and ontological postulates. This means that the goals, methods, and criteria of evaluation developed and utilized by various theoretical approaches to counseling reflect basic assumptions about the hierarchy of knowledge and knowing, and about the nature of reality. Furthermore, that these positions taken toward knowledge and reality do specifically influence the determination of the goals, methods, and criteria of assessment in counseling and the imposition of a theory of man and a value system.

The schema or paradigm that is to be developed here can best be described as one relating to epistemology or to levels of certainty about knowledge. In counseling there is universal agreement that some kind of knowledge is communicated. In any theory about knowledge, there are three central factors to be considered: (1) the one who knows, that is, the subject, (2) the thing he knows, that is, the object, and (3) the act by which he knows, that is, the process. The subject and object are recognizable components in any system of epistemology, but the relative weight given to one or the other depends on the view of the process of knowing. Is knowing an active process involving the prestructure of the subject or is it more a passive process whereby the subject is impregnated from without? The answers to these questions are still not known and have been debated from Plato and Aristotle up through Locke and Leibnitz to the present era. The point, however, is that counseling theories and practices like theories of knowledge may be considered along a two-dimensional plane that involves subject and object at opposite poles on one axis and essence and existence as the polar opposites of process on the other. Figure 1 illustrates the direction of the argument.

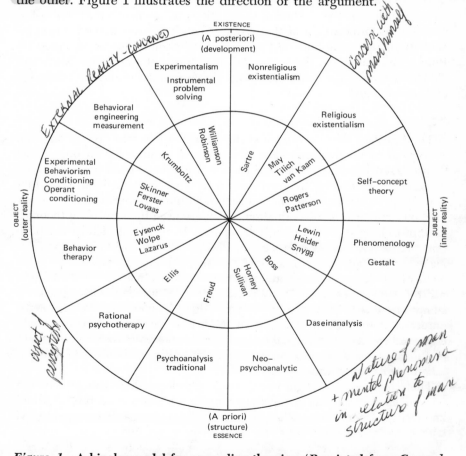

Figure 1 **A bipolar model for counseling theories. (Reprinted from *Counseling and Philosophy: A Theoretical Exposition*, James R. Barclay, Houghton-Mifflin, 1968, Boston.)**

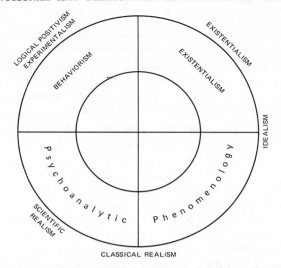

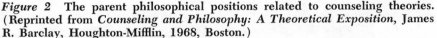

Figure 2   **The parent philosophical positions related to counseling theories.** (Reprinted from *Counseling and Philosophy: A Theoretical Exposition,* James R. Barclay, Houghton-Mifflin, 1968, Boston.)

The diagram identifies four quadrants that represent epistemological and ontological considerations about knowledge and reality. The upper left quadrant contains the counseling positions that emphasize the outer object of perception, that is, external reality, and which are not limited by a priori considerations about the nature of that reality. The lower left quadrant is occupied with theoretical positions that emphasize the object of perception, but superimpose on the nature of external reality philosophical considerations about the nature of that reality. The upper right quadrant represents theoretical positions in which the focal point is less on external reality and is more on the subject of knowledge, that is, man, himself. The lack of identification of a body of a priori or structural considerations about man is met by the existential considerations of man's ongoing and transitory psychic phenomena. The lower right quadrant represents theoretical positions whose focus is on the nature of man and his mental phenomena as determined and related to the structure of man.

These counseling positions can be related to philosophical positions that serve as the parent metaphysical framework. Figure 2 describes this relationship.

THE PRESENT POSITION IN COUNSELING TOWARD PHILOSOPHY

For too long a period, the literature of counseling has seemed to indicate that counselors and counseling theorists are not sufficiently aware of the assumptions that they make regarding human behavior and the methods of changing it. Currently, within the area of counseling psychology there is a growing concern with the exploration of the philosophical dimensions of reality, knowledge, and values. Tillich (1964), May (1958), Beck (1963), McHugh (1964), and the writer (Barclay, 1968) have pointed out the fact that human behavior and the means of changing human behavior involve assumptions and postulates about the nature of reality, the validity of knowledge, and the hierarchy of values that men hold. Specifically, considerations of this nature are related to three areas of counseling theory and practice: (1) the definition of counseling itself, (2) the goals of the counseling process, and (3) the methods or procedures used. In addition, these functional concerns do relate to criteria of counseling and evaluation procedures. As far as the criterion of counseling effectiveness is concerned, it is not unreasonable to assume that all theoretical positions in counseling would agree that a valid criterion of counseling effectiveness must be somehow related to effective human behavior. In other words, if counseling makes a difference, that difference must be evidenced in more adequate and effective human behavior. Where the theoretical positions manifestly disagree with each other is in how to determine the nature and power functions of the criterion as well as the dimensions within which that criterion shall operate.

A genuine exploration into the philosophical frameworks that undergird counseling has been delayed for a variety of reasons. First, counseling developed as an adjunct of guidance and was too often relegated to the position of a technique. For example, Williamson in his earlier works (1939) felt that it was not too important to investigate the assumptions underlying counseling techniques. Second, guidance itself was such an amorphous concept that it eventually connoted the entire scope of in-school and out-of-school experiences. Ultimately, guidance became identified with a general point of view, something akin to the "positive regard for others" enunciated by Rogers. Third, the approach to counseling theory in this country partook of the general Lockean tradition in American psychology, which placed strong reliance on the pragmatic outcomes of procedures, measurement theory, and environmental manipulation instead of on excursions into the analysis of theory. Fourth, the development of psychoanalytic theory, the reliance on a priori conceptions of human nature, unconscious determination, and clinical "art" rather than statistical fact was essentially alien to the predominant trends in American educational thought. Thorndike's measurement approach and Dewey's instrumentalism, which could be rather simply identified in terms of test data and pragmatic problem solving, seemed an ample and easy formula to plug into the guidance program. Fifth, the unfamiliarity with Continental scholarship, the preoccupation with whatever appeared to be new in the book market, the dearth of philosophical training within the ranks of counseling psychologists, and the overly naive statements of counselor educators, who spoke of philosophy as the intellectual justification of our nation's "manifest destiny," all tended to obscure the real issues and questions.

As a result of these problems, counselors and counseling theorists have tended to polarize their approach to counseling, alternating between a dependence on environmental manipulations and an advocacy of perceptual approaches, between a subject-oriented procedure and an object-oriented one. They have shown a reliance on techniques of permissiveness or have cast their lot with problem solving and learning theory in an effort to become more scientific. Often the end result has been an eclecticism, first in practice and then in theory. Although eclecticism fits well with a technique-oriented or "how-to-do-it" approach in counseling and possesses much to commend it by way of flexibility, there are drawbacks to the unconditional acceptance of eclecticism as a philosophical basis for counseling theory. McHugh (1964) has pointed out that, by combining the best of different theories, one may actually be combining that which is conflicting and contradictory. Theory is designed to guide practice. Of course, there is a reciprocal feedback between theory and practice with each confirming or warranting the other. If eclecticism is the ultimate alternative for a theory of counseling, then we must perforce admit that what we do has no consistent theoretical rationale. This is something different from the usual defense of eclecticism in terms of psychological flexibility. Moreover, the argument that most trained counselors do something similar in terms of counseling process is neither a support for eclecticism nor a reason for abandoning the quest for a more comprehensive philosophical basis. For technical aspects of the counseling process can be taught to almost anyone in the absence of theoretical understanding. Even a computer can learn to do effective counseling (Gilbert and Ewing, 1964). Neophytes can easily learn certain response techniques, but it is a far different matter to comprehend the philosophical issues at stake and to engage in the counseling process with some consistent rationale designed to effect change in a predictable manner. It is the argument of the writer that a deeper probing into the philosophical meanings of counseling will actually promote more flexibility rather than rigidity.

Certainly the study of the philosophical meaning of counseling should contribute to the formulation of a consistent set of personal beliefs. Every counselor needs a set of beliefs to give direction to his counseling. As a man thinks, so he should act, and if there is a wide discrepancy between patterns of thinking and acting, one would hope in the case of the counselor or psychologist engaging in counseling practice that this conflict could be resolved either by beginning to think more in accordance with his acts or vice versa. Furthermore, in view of the personal nature of the counseling relationship, the commitment to a process of growth and development in the lives of others, a failure to examine our own beliefs and understandings is a tacit acknowledgment of hypocrisy. Philosophy is a search for the abiding laws and the intellectual justification of the universe. A cosmological inquiry leads inevitably to considerations about our individual responsibility toward either maintaining the universe as it is, or the alternative of reconstruction. One's conception of the universe is incomplete without some questions as to what constitutes reality, that is, what is real? Ontology as a main division of philosophical thinking addresses itself to the nature of experience, the analysis of being and existence. How do we weigh the subjective deeply personal dimensions of reality in the individual against the abstractions of scientific reality, and the cultural "press" of accepted social behavior? What is our responsibility for advocacy or lack of advocacy for a correspondence between individual subjective reality and objective reality? Joined to this question is the search for epistemological certainty and the acceptance of various systems of belief, opinion, and the comparative evidence for belief. What do we accept as truth? How do we arrive at certitude? Ontology, cosmology, and epistemology are all related to axiology or the study of values. What a man believes about the nature of the universe, reality and being, the manner in which he marshals evidence to support his contentions, is in point of fact a decision about ethics and what constitutes the good life.

Some will say that these questions are perennial and cannot be answered. Perhaps so! But the fact that they continue to exist and to challenge man's life show that they are vital and important. For the problems of life in one generation are both similar to and different from those of another era. The search for philosophical roots uncovers relationships and meanings not apparent to ordinary understanding. As Phenix has stated (1958), philosophy . . . "is a disclosure of truths which are hidden from common sight in common perception. It affords insight into the fundamental unities beneath the apparent diversities of the experienced world." And as Dewey remarked earlier (1939, 250):

> Philosophy marks a change in culture; in forming patterns to be conformed to in the future through thought and action it is additive and transforming in its role in the history of civilization. Man states anything at his peril. Once stated, it occupies a place in a new per-

spective, it attains a permanence which does not belong to its existence: it enters provokingly into wont and use; it points in a troubled way to the need of new endeavors.

Unquestionably, philosophical inquiry results in values of importance and worth, affording a vision of ends toward which counseling as a means should be directed.

CONFLICTING POSITIONS IN COUNSELING THEORY

There are conflicting positions and approaches apparent in current counseling goals, methods, and criteria of evaluation. These positions may be arbitrarily identified as those of the humanists and those of the environmentalists. The humanists include the theorists who are generally subject-oriented in their conception of counseling psychology. They emphasize the subjective nature of the process, are concerned with the client as the subject of counseling, and believe that the effects of the counseling process must be essentially registered with client insight and self-report. The humanists include the theorists who are grouped under the label of existentialism, daseinanalysis, self-concept theory, phenomenology, and all others who claim some philosophical kinship with phenomenology, in either its transcendental idealism base or existentialist foundation. Under the general label of environmentalism are those theorists and theories who generally subscribe to the canons of scientific methodology in counseling and who are broadly influenced either by experimental psychology, the Skinnerian point of view, the instrumentalism approach of Dewey, or the earlier logical positivism and realism which influenced Freud and the psychoanalytic school of thought. Certainly, the inclusion of Freudian views along with Skinnerian ideas will cause the arching of some eyebrows, but the emphasis of Freud was definitely influenced by older versions of scientific realism and logical positivism (Tiebout, 1952).

These positions in counseling psychology are not true philosophical positions because, on the one hand, Rogerian theory developed without direct or indirect relationship to the formal philosophical ideas of phenomenology or existentialism (Johnson, 1961) and, on the other hand, Skinner has disavowed any relationship between his methodology and logical positivism (Wann, 1964). Thus the two labels presented here represent positions that the writer is defining in terms of epistemology, that is, the emphasis on either the subject or object of knowledge, or man himself and the environmental adjustment.

Operationally, however, these two major positions do differ from each other in terms of goals, methods, and the criteria of evaluation. In terms of the goals of the counseling process, the humanists differ from the behaviorists chiefly by reason of the specificity of goals. Earlier conceptions of the goal procedure have included a broad spectrum of activities. These activities have included more effective conformity to the goals of the school or community, the adjustment to life problems (whatever they may be), a more realistic attitude toward one's abilities and relationships to others, self-actualization and clarification, more effective peer group relations, and self-reorganization. More recently, the humanist goals in counseling seem to be directed more at the clarification of self-concept, self-understanding, insight, and self-reorganization. In other words, the goals of the counseling process have been directed toward the client in the sense that verbal and nonverbal communication in a nonthreatening setting has been conceived as a major goal of the counseling process. In view of the wide gamut of individual differences, the varieties of problems in a world of multiple values, the humanist approach to counseling has been concerned with the individual and the establishment of a wholesome self-concept. The obstacles to self-growth and fulfillment are postulated to have been found in the environment in the form of defenses and overlays of restrictive behavior. Pine and Boy (1965) state the problem thus:

> He (the client) still has the potential for growth, the capacity to select what is good for the self, the natural thrust toward self-fulfillment, the drive toward self-actualization, the inner-moving dynamic, the will to health. But his inner core is imprisoned, and cries to be released. It is through counseling that the adolescent is able to discover and free this inner tendency. Counseling helps the individual to peel off the defensive layers so that the imprisoned self may again become expressive and exert its thrust toward adequacy (370).

Self-understanding, and self-acceptance are generally conceived to be definable goals of the counseling procedure in the humanist point of view. The writings of Combs and Snygg (1959), Rogers (1951, 1961), Patterson (1959), and May (1958) all tend to document this approach to the goals of counseling psychology.

The environmental approach to counseling psychology differs from the subject-oriented one of the humanist group. The earlier psychoanalytic formulations were concerned primarily with a restoration of the individual to society through the release of specific repressive mechanisms. Although humanistic thought in some aspects still bears a resemblance to traditional psychoanalytic thought, the difference is that psychoanalytic thought had a model of human nature based on sexual repression and neurosis which had to be transformed to conformity with the predominant social behavior. Thus, the emphasis in traditional Freudian analysis was always directed toward the object of knowledge, that is, society, and how the individual can learn to conform and live with this society. As is well known, Freud was not too interested in the individual but, instead, in how that individual could live effectively in the modern environment. Thus, the goals of psychoanalytic therapy were and still are predominantly oriented not to self-understanding but to a correspondence between the individual and society that is marked by the least handicapping mechanisms.

The distinction is more clearly seen in the work of the experimentalists and behavioral engineers who suggest that one of the major problems in present-day counseling is the inability to specify the behavior changes toward which we are willing to work with individual clients. Krumboltz (1964) suggests that self-understanding is a spurious goal:

> The history of science abounds with hypothetical constructs once respected as real entities. Just as chemists have long abandoned the concept of "phlogiston" to account for their observations of fire, and just as physicists no longer postulate "ether" to account for their observations of light transmission through space, so it is time for counselors to re-examine a number of postulated constructs which have been popularly used to account for their observations of human behavior. 'Self-understanding' may be only one of many notions which will prove to have little usefulness in explaining human behavior.

Krumboltz also suggests that very likely self-understanding is seldom the goal desired by the client, and that the presence or absence of self-understanding must be inferred either by the client or the counselor. He wants to be able to determine the answer to a very important question: What specific types of action can a counselor take to help clients achieve the type of behavior they desire? Counseling in this point of view becomes a type of problem solving with the client posing the problem and the counselor *helping* the client probe alternatives and explore his abilities in an effort to help the client with his specific problem. No need is seen here for probing, analyzing, ruminating, or any of the other procedures allied to the goals of the humanist point of view. Humanists, on the other hand, cannot really disagree with this pursuit of individual goals. But they do question the epistemological grounds and the ease with which behaviorists believe that the complex individual subjective world of intentionality can be translated into a problem-solving model. Problems of the subjective world, the humanists would argue, are not always readily reducible in the conscious verbal realm and are, therefore, not always accessible to the scientific problem-solving model.

The contrast between the two approaches to counseling is sharpened even more when process is discussed. The humanists are dedicated to the approach that the way to effect behavior change is to help the client develop insight and self-understanding about himself. This they believe can be obtained through an involvement with the client. Once the client has come to trust the counselor, he will gradually share more and more of his subjective *Lebenswelt* with the counselor. Through this process of verbalization and noncognitive communication, the client begins to change his attitudes and outlook, gain new insights, reorganize his subjective *Gestalten,* and obtain subjective strengths through the verbal definition of the meaning of *his* life and *his* existence. Self-discovery, it is postulated, is a consequence of a dialogue in communication held in a nonthreatening and permissive environmental setting.

The environmentalists, on the other hand, feel that changes in attitudes, self-understanding, etc., do not necessarily result in change of behavior. In other words, they deny the necessary causal nexus between insight, self-understanding, new attitudes, and behavior change. Zax and Klein (1960), after reviewing various criteria for judging the success of psychotherapy, identify the most serious failing of the humanist point of view as a failure to relate intratherapy changes to external behavior change. The environmentalists are impatient with the subjective world of the humanists. It is for this reason that they prefer to *assume* constancy in the subjective world (at least, in terms of large numbers of individuals) and urge the client to identify a problem that can be explored. Relying heavily on learning theory, they insist that once the problem has been identified, the counselor needs to devise ways and means within the scope of his abilities and ethical responsibilities and congruent with present learning theory that will help the client change in the way he wishes. The similarity between some older forms of traditional psychoanalytic thought and modern day behaviorism is transparent here, if one looks closely. Freud's approach to the change of behavior did not depend heavily on insight (despite the verbal deference to this concept) but, instead, on an intensive counter-conditioning approach that, through prolonged contact with the patient, made it possible to actually eliminate certain noxious types of behavior in favor of analyst-oriented behavior. Although the process was one of not too subtle counter-conditioning, the theoretical framework did not include reference to learning theory in an explicit manner.

The approach of Eysenck and Wolpe represents a learning theory interpretation of counseling that is often referred to as behavior modification. This system uses learning principles of desensitization, relaxation, and differential reinforcement techniques both to reduce maladaptive behavior and to promote new behaviors. The work of Krumboltz, Michael and Meyerson, Ferster, Bandura, and others includes some of the procedures used by Eysenck and Wolpe, but with the addition of a strong reliance on Skinner's method of operant conditioning. The behavior modification approach is generally based on the correspondence assumption in epistemology. This assumption holds that the subjective world of individual experience *can* be translated or *can* correspond to the objective world of reality. Unquestionably this assumption holds true as the basis of physical science in terms of the collective perception of masses of individuals. For how else could one have a scientific theory without the assumption of the constancy of perception universally considered? However, the moot point in this discussion is not related to the masses but to the individual. *Can* or *should* the correspondence assumption hold for the one-to-one relationship of counselor and client? If it does, or can be demonstrated then, of course, the behaviorist strategy gains in strength. If it does not, then what guarantee do we have that the client's verbalized statement of his problem accurately represents his subjective state?

The environmentalists according to Krumboltz (1964) can find few documented statistical studies supporting the humanist allegation that self-understanding can lead to behavior change measured by an external criterion. Krumboltz cites Hobbs (1962), for support of this statement. Grossberg (1964), in addition, reviews a host of studies, completed within the behavioral learning point of view, that support the notion that a change in behavior can result in a change of attitudes measurable in the external domain of reality. The process of nondirective counseling is further attacked by Krumboltz as: (1) tending to depreciate the value of self-improvement, (2) promoting an unwarranted degree of inflexibility in human behavior, and (3) promoting a degree of dependency on counselor cues.

If the differences between the humanists and environmentalists are accented in their varying conceptions of the goals and methods of counseling, they clash headlong in the area of criteria of counseling effectiveness. In the past history of counseling, the criteria of effective human behavior were related to whatever one was willing to settle for (Howes, 1961). Unanswered questions were related to whether "success" in counseling could be determined immediately or over a long period of time. Many felt that counseling could be evaluated in terms of the areas of improved student achievement, student feelings and morale, changes in behavior, or personal satisfaction and adjustment. Other criteria, which were often used and still are, related to the differences obtained on testing instruments or longitudinal studies. The use of the Q-sort technique, changes in various Minnesota Multiphasic Personality Inventory scales and indexes, changes in counselor's ratings of clients, and client self-report instruments have all been used as criteria of measuring the effectiveness of the counseling process.

From the humanist point of view there are a wide range of criteria that have been used. Rogers first espoused a clinical and experimental point of view with regard to counseling (1939). At that time he favored personality testing and advocated directive measures as a means of changing behavior. Subsequently (1951 to 1961), he moved away from these approaches, coming gradually to the position that the counseling relationship was a unique and personal experience that was not directly susceptible to the verification of experimental criteria. Considerations of self-understanding, self-acceptance, and insight became the criteria of measuring the effectiveness of the counseling. In view of the focus of the humanist school on the subject of counseling, that is, the individual client, the only real criterion of the effectiveness of counseling, so reason the humanists, must be in terms of the subject himself, that is, his verbal report. The counselor may also judge the effectiveness of the process, but his judging is subject to the bias of the counselor himself. Congruence with the counselor's point of view and outlook on life is very often judged in both humanist and behaviorist camps as a measure of therapeutic reconstruction.

On the contrary, the environmentalist point of view clashes sharply with internal criteria of effectiveness. Michael and Meyerson (1962) state that "observable behavior is the only variable of importance in the counseling and guidance process, and the only criterion against which the outcome of the process can be evaluated." Krumboltz (1964) believes that self-acceptance is not only difficult to measure but can be explained more parsimoniously through verbal conditioning concepts. As an alternative to the description of subjective states and processes, Krumboltz suggests that criteria for counseling should include: (1) the capability of being stated differently for each individual client; (2) compatibility with, although not necessarily identical to, the predominant goals of the society in which counseling is performed; and (3) some observable testimony as to the degree to which the goals of counseling are attained.

In effect then, the contrast between the humanist and environmentalist points of view is focused on the goals, methods, and criteria of assessment in counseling. They may as individual counselors handle cases in similar practical ways, but the difference in the emphasis revolves about the dichotomy of subject and object of knowledge. The behavioral camp generally advocates counseling as a means of bringing about the best possible congruence between the client and his culture. The emphasis is clearly focused on the scientific nature of reality. The clearest perception of how man may most effectively operate in his environment is related to the more comprehensive understanding of that environment with the shaping and molding of the client through learning procedures in order to effect the soundest congruence.

The humanists, on the other hand, do not deny the validity of science or the reality of the encompassing environment. But, they resist the notion that man must be molded or shaped by any other means than his own purposeful action. Although the behaviorists do not deny the existence of the inner world of subjectivity, they do in effect dismiss it as incapable of being subjected to the scientific method. This would appear to be the real nub of the problem. Can we acknowledge the validity of scientific inquiry without denying the power functions of the subjective realm? The humanists are suspicious of the external criterion of counseling effectiveness, feeling that it is not so much the identification of an external criterion but, instead, the specifications of that criterion. There is, for many humanists, an inkling of Skinner's Walden II in the notion of the appeal to an external demographic criterion in the advancement of society. This, despite the apologies for behaviorism presented by Goldiamond (1964), and Krasner (1962). It is not that either the humanists or the environmentalists deny the hope for producing successive generations of better men, but they differ on the determination of the ends toward which the value judgment of "better" is made. Thus the central issue before counseling theorists is really a descriptive model of what constitutes effective human behavior in our present and future anticipated cultural setting.

Although dichotomous comparisons are often misleading, it is probably true to state that the humanists tend to promote movement toward the criterion of effective human behavior through an understanding of the individual, an exploration of the dimensions of inner space or subjective experience, and the development of an individual access to cultural problems of identity and meaning. Although environmentalism makes provision (theoretically) for the needs of the individual, there is the constant effort at reductionism via the procedures of problem solving, the verbalization of internal phenomena in terms of observable external phenomena, and change through guided reinforcement of certain cultural values.

Table 1 illustrates and summarizes the differences between these two major groupings along the subject-object continuum.

Table 1 **Differences between Environmentalism and Humanism**

Item	Environmentalism	Humanism
General orientation	Object-oriented Cultural norms and scientific reality	Subject-oriented Individual understanding and subjective reality
Goals of counseling	Clarification of individual problems through identification, exploration	Clarification of subjective self-concept and understanding
Methods of counseling	1. Understanding through exploration of environment and scientific knowledge 2. Identification of behavioral deficits 3. Change of behavior through operant conditioning, or social learning theory 4. Removal of maladaptive behavior through desensitization, new learning	1. Understanding of environment and relationship to self 2. Supportive dialogue in exploration of both external and internal environment 3. Changes in self-understanding through insight and clarification
Process orientation	Change in behavior leads to change in attitudes. Attitudes, feelings, motivation, etc. are concomitants of behavior and behavior change reinforces reorganization of thinking.	Change in attitudes, feelings, removal of blocks to self-expression and defensive learning leads to freer expression of ideas, and change in behavior.
Criterion determination	Essential reference to external demographic or cultural criteria of assessment. Use of testing information, statistical inference and scientific research design.	Essential reliance on self-report of client and/or evaluation of counselor with some reliance on measurement theory and statistical analysis.

(**Reprinted from** *Counseling and Philosophy: A Theoretical Exposition*, **James R. Barclay, Houghton-Mifflin, 1968, Boston.**)

VERIFICATION OF THE MODEL

There have been other approaches to the organization and to the analysis of counseling functions, psychotherapy, and the like. Most of them have been based on a logical inference position. For example, Ford and Urban (1965) have written an excellent analysis of systems of psychotherapy which compares them in terms of conceptual framework, foundational postulates and propositions, observation and behavioral consequences, and criteria of evaluation. Mahrer (1967) has contrasted various approaches to psychotherapy in terms of the goals of treatment. Both of these approaches to psychotherapy analysis provide a wealth of information about alternate procedures in psychotherapy.

The model that I present in this chapter is based both on an inferential logical analysis of counseling theory as a branch of epistemology in psychology and on some research evidence. In an unpublished study (Barclay, 1964),[1] I devised a philosophical questionnaire that included 12 scales relating to Idealism, Realism, and Experimentalism. Each major scale had subscales on epistemology, axiology, and ontology. These scales together with a semantic differential and a questionnaire tapping four different approaches to teaching methodology (substantive learning, child-developmental, mental-hygiene, and group process) were administered to 30 counselors in an advanced NDEA Institute at Idaho State University in the summer of 1964. The same instruments were also administered to a beginning class of 45 students at California State College at Hayward in the fall of 1964.

The data analysis revealed (1) that advanced counselors differ from beginning students by being more experimentally oriented; (2) that extremist positions in the philosophy of idealism and, to some extent, the philosophy of experimentalism do carry with them quite different evaluations of concepts relating to the family, deity, and knowledge; and (3) that religious affiliation tends to shape strongly the philosophical tenets held by these counselors, with Catholics tending toward realism, Protestants toward experimentalism, and Mormons toward idealism. There were also very definite trends found relating to the age of the subject, with older individuals being more conservative and younger subjects being more liberal. Substantive learning positions in teaching correlated with the age of the subjects, the philosophical position of idealism, and with concepts of family, prayer, father, and deity. The developmental learning approach correlated with specific aspects of realist philosophy and with a number of concepts such as law, knowledge, and mother. The group process approach was strongly related to experimental epistemology and concepts of teacher, father, mother, principal, etc. The mental hygiene approach also showed a relationship to experimental epistemology, the age of the subjects, and the concept of knowledge.

In another study reported in *Changing the Behavior of School Psychologists: A Rationale and Training Method* (Barclay, 1968), I designed two instruments to measure attitudes toward clinical, phenomenological, and behavioral approaches to psychotherapy for psychologists in two NDEA institutes. *The Psychological Practices Questionnaire* was a 14-item instrument with seven items relating to diagnosis or decision making and with seven items relating to strategy formation. Each item posed a situ-

---

[1] The counselor's *Lebenswelt:* An exploration into philosophical dimensions of beginning and advanced counselors.

ation with four alternatives. One was a clinical alternative, a second was a phenomenological or self-concept alternative, the third was a behavioral alternative, and the fourth was a filler or eclectic alternative. Subjects were asked to rank in priority of their judgment each of the alternatives for coping with the example behavior. *The Concept Checklist* was a list of 51 concepts drawn from clinical, phenomenological, and experimental-behavioral terminologies. Subjects were asked to rate these concepts in regard to their efficacy for school psychology practice.

These inventories together with many other behavioral analyses were administered to enrollees and to two groups of controls. Suffice it to state here that the statistical analysis indicated that the theoretical orientation and paper-pencil type measures were significantly related to actual practice in school psychology. Clinically oriented individuals tended to concentrate more on assessment and less on treatment; phenomenological psychologists tended to treat children and teachers as counseling clients, focusing more on process than either assessment or strategy making; and behavioral oriented psychologists were more concerned with the identification of the specific problem and the working out of appropriate contingencies for learning.

The brief analysis given here cannot hope to convey the impact of two years of research on these instruments and the identification of corrolaries in behavior. This research is mentioned, however, to indicate that the model proposed in this chapter does have experimental verification as well as a logical base. (See also Descriptive, Theoretical and Behavioral Characteristics of Subdoctoral School Psychologists in *American Psychologist, 26*, March, 1971, 257–280.)

Another study of specific relevance to this model is an extensive analysis completed by Coan and reported in an article entitled "Dimensions of Psychological Theory" (Coan, 1968). Coan, concerned with the developmental construction of psychological theory, was able to factor analyze the ratings given 54 different theorists by 232 psychologist correspondents, throughout the United States, who at one time or another had taught history of psychology courses and were known to be interested in this general topic. Six major factors emerged from the factor analysis and regression analyses for each factor completed by Coan. These factors bear a marked resemblance to the ones I developed in this present model. Factor 1 appeared to be a subjectivistic, mentalistic, or phenomenological one with the negative pole described as objectivistic, physicalistic, positivistic, or behavioral. Factor 2 appeared to be related to a pattern of holistic, totalistic, or molar approaches versus an elementaristic, atomistic, or molecular one. Factor 3 appeared to be experimental versus clinical, and factor 4 a methodological one characterized on the positive pole by content that lends itself to quantitative treatment versus procedures less readily permitting quantitative treatment. Factor 5 appeared to be a dynamic versus static continuum, and factor 6 a contrast of biological versus social influences. Coan schematically diagrammed the factors and relationships of various theorists to the factors. His figures 1 and 2 are reported with permission (see Figures 3 and 4).

Apart from the importance and interest of his procedures, I was struck with the amazing similarity to my own model that occurred as a result of the statistical analysis of the ratings of theorists. Coan's findings suggest that psychological theorists tend to be divided along continua that relate to subjectivism and objectivism, restrictive and fluid orientations, and biological and social methodologies. This analysis of theorists in accordance with statistical procedures lends considerable support to the validity of the model presented here concerning the analysis of counseling theories.

THE IMPORTANCE OF COUNSELING THEORY

Buford Stefflre and Kenneth Matheny (1968) in a monograph entitled *The Function of Counseling Theory* have admirably addressed themselves to the role and function of counseling theory as it affects the client, the counselor himself, and the training institution. Their remarks are so congruent with the position presented in this introductory chapter that it is fitting they be summarized here as a logical extension and completion of it. "Theories derive from bases which are personal, historical, sociological, and philosophical. In the field of counseling we know so little about the accuracy and usefulness of theoretical formulations that we must look inward to needs and desires rather than outward to data to understand why, from among many, a particular theory is chosen by an individual" (1968, p. 4).

They suggest that a good theory can provide an operational base for counseling, but that the attributes of a good theory are: (1) it is clear, (2) it is comprehensive, (3) it is explicit, (4) it is parsimonious and (5) it generates useful research.

They view counseling practice and outcomes as being derived, at least partially, from the expectations of clients and counselors. "Counseling theory influences the behavior of the client in at least two ways: (1) by partially determining the conduct of the counselor, it indirectly affects the client because the counselor's acts, in turn, elicit behavior from the client, and (2) by determining what the client expects from counseling and how he will act during counseling" (1968, p. 10). Counselors themselves through the effect of their personality, their training, the identifica-

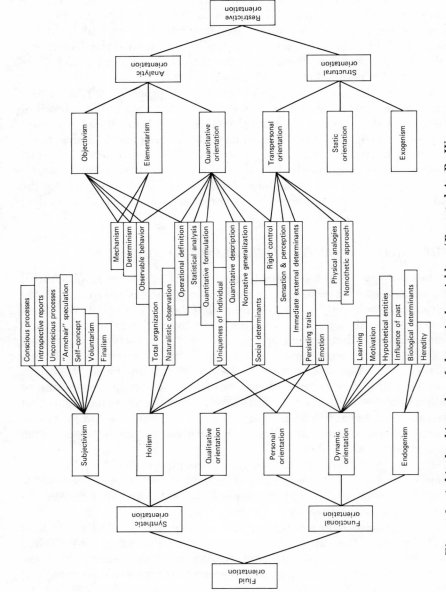

Figure 3 A bipolar hierarchy of theoretical variables. (Reported in R. W. Coan, "Dimensions of psychological theory," *American Psychologist,* 23, October 1968, No. 10, p. 720.)

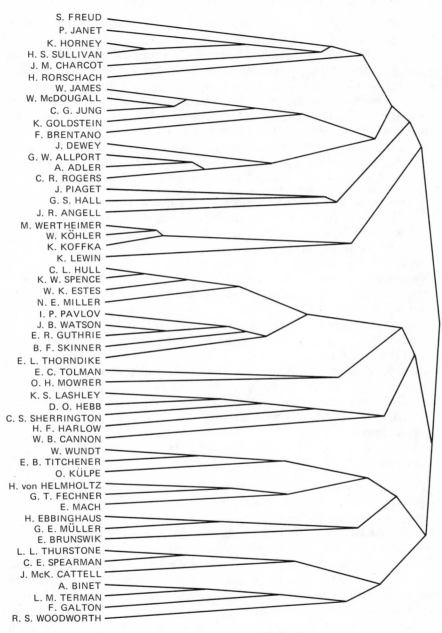

Figure 4 The hierarchical grouping of theorists. (Reported in R. W. Coan, "Dimensions of psychological theory," *American Psychologist,* 23, October 1968, No. 10, p. 721.)

tion with a social class group, and their teaching background do affect the expectations of the client.

Summarizing a considerable amount of literature in the field relating to the influence of theory on counseling procedures, Stefflre and Matheney cite the viewpoint of Shoben (1962) to suggest that the study of theory helps to rationalize the counselor's behavior. They comment on the studies of Fiedler (1950a, 1950b) which tended to suggest that counselors are more influenced by their experience in counseling than by their theory, stating: "However, his (Fiedler's) research has been criticized for not making fine distinctions among positions and thus suppressing the influence of theory" (1968, p. 20–21). They also state:

> However, a new line of research begun by Sundland and Barker (1962) challenges Fiedler's results by showing that a general bi-polar factor called "analytic versus experiential" accounts for much difference between therapists. Therapists at the analytic pole stress conceptualization, training, unconscious processes, and a proscription of spontaneity. Those at the experiential pole stress the personality of the therapist and unplanned approach to therapy. A subsequent study (Wallach and Strupp, 1964) using psychotherapists from a variety of orientations found four factors explaining therapist behavior: maintaining personal distance, preferring intensive therapy, keeping verbal interventions at a minimum, and considering psychotherapy as an art. Orthodox Freudians were highest in maintaining personal distance, preferring intensive therapy, keeping verbal interventions at a minimum, and lowest in considering therapy as an artistic activity. The client-centered group was distinct in considering psychotherapy as an art and in their lack of preference for intensive therapy. The level of experience of the therapist seemed unrelated to reported therapy activity (1968, p. 22).

Finally, Stefflre and Matheney touch on a subject of considerable importance to the student, that is, the influence that counseling theory should have on counselor education. They describe some of the typical stances that have occurred in counselor education. They point out that some counselor educators tend to teach by the critical error method, in which the shaping of students is accomplished through a critical evaluation of his process experience. Rightly they observe that such critical evaluation makes sense only in terms of the value and theoretical system of the professor. Still other institutions provide an overview of theoretical systems and allow students to pick and chose what they will. The problem here is that most theoretical systems are based on a profound analysis of man and his relationship to the universe. As knowledge accumulates, it becomes increasingly more difficult for students to filter out the important features of theory from the unimportant ones.

By way of commentary, the writer believes firmly that the teaching of counseling involves both technical competencies or skills in coping with a variety of circumstances, but it also includes—usually at higher education levels—inquiry into the more substantive assumptions, interpretations, and beliefs that have influenced man in his attempt to change behavior. With the accumulation of knowledge and with the issues that face those who would counsel with others in a rapidly burgeoning technological civilization, it is most important to identify explicitly those central issues that underlie many of the technical problems.

SUMMARY AND FORMAT OF THE BOOK

It is the argument of this chapter that counseling theories may be considered along a bipolar continuum in which the poles represent outer reality versus inner reality and a priori essence orientations versus a posteriori existence orientations. Broadly speaking, the two halves of the schema relate to theories that are outer-oriented versus inner-oriented. Although the outer-oriented groupings are considered here under the generic term of environmentalism, there are distinct differences as to philosophical base, learning orientation, methods, goals, and procedures. The same can be said for the other half of the schema. Here the interrelationships between philosophical ideas, cultural movements, and learning theories all become most difficult to unscramble. Any attempt to filter out the derivation of ideas and to analyze influence relationships is difficult at the very least, since the interreactions that are constantly taking place make it difficult to determine how much the changes in one theory are related to the findings in another. A classic example of this is the modifications to connectionism announced by Thorndike after a study of the new Gestalt approach to learning. The same is true in counseling psychology where positions once held in one way have a tendency to shift and to make modifications as new approaches are formulated. Thus Williamson's original problem-solving approach based on Dewey's philosophical notions, now appears as congruent with some of the contentions of behavior modification theory as enunciated by Krumboltz and the Stanford school of counseling. Rogers, starting out with a base in liberal Christian theology, psychoanalysis, and experimentalist philosophy, has now, for some time, shifted into the existential camp.

These shifts and interrelationships are difficult to assess. However, an attempt to do so is important to the understanding of the total variety of counseling systems and theories which are now characteristic of the field. Moreover, the student needs to be able to synthesize, to some extent, the variations of techniques as well as philosophical points of view. To this end, Table 2 is designed to provide an overall summary of the basic environmentalist and humanist positions. The reader is cautioned that many other noted theorists are not mentioned in this outline. Moreover, it is also important to recognize that the assignment of categories to counseling positions is not always an easy task.

For purposes of clarification, a description of the balance of this book is now presented. It is concerned with both the cultural foundations and the intellectual foundations of counseling theory. Part I describes the cultural phenomena that are related to the development of human behavior in a social setting. The chapters in this portion of the book are concerned with culture and its historical amplification through medicine, philosophy, and religion. Certain core ideas have been selected out of the complex development of civilization to illustrate the early antecedents of the theories of human behavior and behavior change. In conjunction with these developments, certain major historical persons and movements are dealt with in an effort to exemplify how ideas were translated into policy-making decisions. For the most part, the individuals chosen for detailed analysis represent key synthesizers of ideology with implications for innovation in behavior.

Part II is concerned with the specific quadrants of the model given in this chapter as an expansion of the modern intellectual foundations of counseling theory. Each chapter here deals with some of the fundamental assumptions, historical antecedents, and modern developments of this point of view.

It should be understood that an undertaking of this kind requires a considerable duplication of the historical accounts of philosophy and psychology. However, the objective has been to shape the accounts of these philosophical and psychological ideas with respect to their effect on ideology and behavior change. In so doing, certain major concepts have been detailed in great depth, and others have been merely summarized. Good arguments can be made for the inclusion of many other people and movements. But the purpose of this volume is to provide for the beginning graduate student or for the advanced graduate student a detailed analysis of the philosophical and cultural foundations of counseling theory. It is organized along the major quadrants of the theory proposed in this chapter.

This work should not be considered as a review of the most recently reported literature in counseling. Nor should it be considered as a "practical" book endorsing a "how-to-do-it" approach. The writer believes that there are many excellent resumes of counseling literature and

Table 2 Representative Counseling Approaches Environmentalist Approach

System	Antecedents	Human Nature	Learning	Counseling Goals	Counseling Methods	Evaluation
1. *Psychoanalysis* Freud, Ellis	Positivism evolutionism German physiology	Neutral-active contaminated by culture seen through instinct and perceptory-motor	Instinctual energy plus habit formation	Removal of blocks to full psychic integration and reconstruction	Diagnostic evaluation based on symptom formation Treatment through development of insight	Subjective patient reaction plus psychotherapist evaluation
2. *Behavior learning therapy* Eysenck, Wolpe, Lazarus	Psychoanalysis British associationism and British physiology measurement theory, scientific realism	Neutral-passive with innate reflexive drives and needs	Conditioned responses or reflexes	Removal of maladaptive behavior and construction of appropriate behavior	Desensitization and counterconditioning—reciprocal inhibition	Measurement evaluation plus client and therapist evaluation
3. *Experimental behaviorism* Skinner, Ferster, Lovaas	Thorndike-Hull Skinner theory, measurement theory Some sociocultural theory. Logical positivism	Neutral-passive innate reflexes and needs with their drive stimuli	Reinforced or conditioned responses	Successive, systematic changes in learning environment	Classical conditioning, operant conditioning—reciprocal inhibition	Measurement evaluation only
4. *Behavioral engineering* Krumboltz, Meyer Michaelson, Bandura	Skinnerian theory, connectionism, Dewey, experimentalism, social behaviorism	Neutral-active, no drives specified	Problem solving in a learning framework as in No. 3	Same as No. 3 plus emphasis on formation of transference to individual	Nos. 2 and 3 social modeling, social reinforcement	Measurement criteria plus cultural criteria
5. *Experimentalism* Williamson, Robinson, eclectics	Connectionism Dewey's Experimentalism, measurement theory, scientific realism	Good-active drives unspecified but observed in cultural conflict	Problem solving in a cognitive framework	More effective human behavior in a social setting	Problem-solving steps, use of cognitive insight plus learning	Subjective testimony plus measurement and reference to cultural criterion
6. *Neo-psychoanalytic* Horney, Sullivan	Psychoanalysis, phenomenology, existentialism, Gestalt Theory	Neutral-interactive subject to distortions	Habit-formation in sociocultural milieu	Removal of blocks to integration and psychic reconstruction	Diagnosis, insight therapy, environmental change	Largely subjective evaluation of client or therapist

Table 2 Representative Counseling Approaches Humanistic Approach

System	Antecedents	Human Nature	Learning	Counseling Goals	Counseling Methods	Evaluation
7. Self-concept theory Rogers, Patterson, etc.	Dewey's experimentalism, psychoanalysis, liberal Christian theology, existentialism, phenomenology, Rousseau	Good-active to be interpreted through interaction with environment	Through cognitive reorganization based on noncognitive appraisal	Self-fulfillment and integration in a cultural frame of reference	Insight, self-understanding, self-clarification	Subjective evaluation, process not directly susceptible to measurement
8. Existentialism (Nonreligious) Sartre	Existentialism, phenomenology, idealism	Undetermined biological structure	Appraisal of meaning and identification	Self-fulfillment and integration with or without cultural adaptation	Insight, self-understanding, identification with meaning	Subjective evaluation process not directly susceptible to measurement
9. Existentialism (religious) May, Tillich van Kaam	Existentialism, phenomenology, Thomism (in some instances), liberal Christian thought	Biological and spiritual structure seen in dualistic perspective	Appraisal of meaning and values of man in the world and the hereafter	Self-fulfillment and integration in union with dualistic notion of universe	Insight, self-understanding, identification, spiritual evaluation and clarification of meaning	Subjective evaluation process not directly susceptible to measurement

research—many worthy compendia of case studies and comparative techniques. This book has as its direct purpose the provision of an organizing framework for the systematic exploration of the philosophical and cultural assumptions that underly counseling theory, and which are ordinarily inadequately understood by graduate students and even professors in the field of counseling theory. The book is frankly based on 10 years of teaching experience with graduate students in the field. It is literally the product of their kind urging and the sympathetic and encouraging response of many colleagues in the field.

PART ONE

Cultural Foundations of Counseling

CHAPTER II

Behavior and Culture: A Learning Rationale

Man is as thoroughly encapsulated in his social environment as a group of goldfish in their aquarium. Social behavior is the interactive result of physiological structure and social learning. Thus culture, as a series of historical patterns that are transmitted and learned, becomes the chief molder of human life and also is the primary criterion for judging the effectiveness of human behavior. Whatever personal sources there may be for judging relevant human behavior, ultimately what a man does is judged in the context of where he lives and with whom.

THE NATURE OF CULTURE

Man lives in a social environment. He is constantly being affected by the culture in which he lives. This process begins at birth and continues throughout life. By culture is meant not that popular and superficial understanding of the term relating to "good breeding," "finishing schools," or a "society" orientation to manners but, instead, the sum total of man's learned behavior in a social environment. Thus any aspect of our day-to-day behavior is included under the concept of culture. Culture used in this way refers to that which is tangible, such as automobiles, toothbrushes, skyscrapers, and astronauts' capsules. It also refers to intangible behavior and includes wishes, hopes, fears, and ways of thinking. Culture thus used includes the buoyant optimism of Americans to be popular in international politics, and it comprises also the hopes of the young African nations that they can develop a technological civilization.

There are varying attitudes toward culture. One is that culture is an absolute entity. It is seen as a huge, superorganic, all-enveloping constellation of controls that determine everything about a particular society

(Bidley, 1947). In this view, culture becomes a sort of self-generating autonomous force that evolves according to fixed laws. It determines all behavior absolutely. As a corollary, the only possible way of understanding any individual's behavior is by understanding his society. There is another point of view regarding culture that is a more humanistic one. Christopher Dawson (1934) has expressed the view that culture is a spiritual community that owes its unity to common beliefs and a common attitude toward life. A middle position toward culture is taken by Kluckhohn (1945). He sees culture as a series of historically created patterns serving as potential guides for human conduct. This view mediates between the two extreme views in that a determinism is recognized, but it is not considered as absolute. The customs of a group may, at times, be abrogated because of some special circumstances. No one must always absolutely follow all the regulations of his culture. However, if an individual wills to remain with the social setting, he must meet some of the cultural expectations unless he wishes to suffer from exclusion.

The manner in which a culture evolves as well as the purpose of that evolution are centrally related to the development of philosophy. For every culture establishes certain working rules for the behavior of those who live in the culture. These rules appear to have been worked out on a trial-and-error learning basis in the early stages of cultural development. They then form the bases of a philosophy of life. Insofar as cultural anthropologists can agree in their definition of culture, it would appear that culture exists to safeguard the human species in a specific locale. It would seem that the establishment of a series of behavioral expectancies relating to roles and functions in a social group are indispensable anchors for stability and security. Culture, therefore, is simply the code of behavior that grows up in a social group to maintain the security of the group in obtaining a continuing food supply and in perpetuating the group. Leslie White (1949) has analyzed culture in terms of the systematic utilization of energy through technology. He maintains that the evolution of culture is dependent on the systematic development of a technology for controlling nature. White recognizes three stages in the development of culture. The first was the use of tools and language; the second was the discovery of agriculture—new methods of raising food that immediately brought a whole train of social and technological advances, such as the smelting of metals, the development of the wheel, the plow, the loom, the invention of writing, and the organization of cities. The third stage has occurred since the late 1700s and consists of the proliferation of certain basic techniques. First, the discovery of how to get power from heat was a major contribution.

Although the Romans had gears, transmission factors, and the like, they did not have any real conception of how to obtain power from heat. Their main source of energy was, aside from animal and human power, waterpower and, to some slight extent, windpower. Within this latter period, during the 1700s, a second great discovery was the systematic unfolding of the scientific method in applications to the physical sciences. Although the Greeks and the scholastics made valuable contributions to the methodology of science, they reached an impasse that tended to rest on philosophical arguments. Finally, during the 18th, 19th, and 20th centuries, the rapid invention of the steam, gas, and diesel engines plus the harnessing of the atom have altered the course of civilization considerably because of the vast amount of energy now harnessed and available through technology. White proposes the formula $E \times t = C$ (Energy times technology equals culture). He suggests that the great power and prestige of the United States does not rest on any concept of manifest destiny but, instead, on the technological development in which the United States has excelled in recent decades.

Although other anthropologists may not subscribe to White's particular theories, they do recognize the force of his arguments. Moreover, in recent years, the study of the theory of culture has been joined to an understanding of how a culture effects its transmission. Certain cultural control mechanisms exist within every culture. They include the primary mechanism of the family. The family and its extended counterpart, the tribe, has always been the central mechanism in maintaining and transmitting culture. Certain methods of behavior were important to ensure the collective security. These methods included regulations about sexual behavior, roles and functions of the sexes, and an explicit or implicit identification of a body of behaviors that were appropriate to men and women within the group. With the differentiation of economic roles and power roles within the community, certain individuals assumed more responsibility for interpreting or augmenting the behavioral rules. These groups of individuals were identified as the power structure: the chieftains, the council of the elders, and the fathers of the community. The need for differentiating various roles also required that some individuals exert a police or judgmental function, that others take charge of spiritual or religious matters, and that still others be concerned with formal and informal education.

Thus learned behavior which was tried and found to be pragmatically sound in terms of maintaining the primary purposes of the culture became the body of customs that guided the subsequent behavior of members of the group. When these customs became sanctioned by the group in a formal manner, they evolved into a law code. These cultural mechanisms of control became the chief methods for keeping the group together and for meeting certain objectives of security and cohesiveness. Institutions such as the family, customs, law, ethics, religion, priesthood, chieftains, police functions, and educational institutions are very real control mechanisms that maintain the expected behavior of individuals in a group. Moreover these institutions are interpreted very differently from culture to culture, but underlying the peculiar variations are the same basic mechanisms. Every cultural control mechanism exists because it serves—or did serve—the group in some rather practical way. Customs and law appear to have emerged on the basis of a trial-and-error method. Certain ways of behaving were crucial in hunting, farming, domestic relations, order, security, etc. Religion probably arose because early man needed a method of explaining a threatening and insecure existence dependent all too often on forces that he did not understand.

LEARNING THE CULTURAL TRANSMISSION

Since all of us grow up in a culture, we learn cultural behavior by a process of imitation and shaping that is, for the most part, unconscious. We behave in certain ways without really being aware that we are behaving in conformity with our culture. This process of enculturation continues until an individual is unmistakably a Frenchman, an Indian, an American, or a German. We learn our culture by living it. We do not inherit culture through our genes, as we inherit a tendency towards blue eyes or blond hair.

Social behavior is learned in specific ways. One major determinant is the systematic process of shaping human behavior through selective reinforcement procedures. The reward of parents or social peers in response to appropriate behavior reinforces the continuation or repetition of this behavior. Second, the individual's perception of his reality is shaped continually through models, play activities, vocational roles, and imitation. In the earlier cultural systems, as well as our own, the existence of an elaborate kinship system and the sanctioning of certain customs presented a model of behavior that was transmitted to culture. Thus boys learned to identify with certain kinds of behavior characteristic of males in their tribe. They may have envied the status of the older men and looked forward to possessing the same status. They knew that they had to conform to group procedures in hunting and other matters. Deviation could expose both them and the society to the direst consequences and, hence, could not be tolerated.

Much of our early development is structured along the directions of those command phrases that our parents and others are constantly using to shape our behavior. For, as children, we are dependent creatures. We did not choose to be born, nor do we choose when we shall eat or sleep, what clothes we shall wear, or when we may play, sit, read, or study. The reactions to this process of environmental controls have been identified clinically. Some of us apparently internalize the conflicting expectations of our culture and our needs. Others become aggressive and strike back either covertly or overtly at the very controls that force us to behave in certain ways. Often the early control system lasts into later life. We are told as children to eat so that we may grow up strong like daddy. And thus we unconsciously equate food with strength and power and continue to overeat well into our maturity. Early explorations of sexual organs often result in severe indictments with fears of loss of love, sanity, or the threat of ill health. In our emotional life, dirt, black, evil, sin, and sex often become one end of a dichotomy, whereas cleanliness, white, virtue, and repression become the other end.

Thus the criterion of effective human behavior in a given culture emerges as a basic conformity to cultural expectations. We learn that if we are to obtain the approval of others we must learn to make certain kinds of responses to specific social expectations or stimuli. Through the process of operant conditioning, we try out alternate and slightly different courses of action in our behavior. These successive approximations are judged against the criterion of peer and superior reactions. Ultimately, the laws and customs of our society are incorporated into our behavior habits. Thus from our first simple learnings to the more complex processes of discrimination within a social context, we learn how to behave within the cultural setting. We learn both how to generalize our behavior approximations and how to make discriminatory judgments about special circumstances. Patterns are built up. These patterns are called habits, and as the habits become more firmly imbedded in our response repertory, they subtly alter and direct the nature of our perception. The mind is structured in its mode of learning and perceiving by its physiological organization as well as by the cultural contingencies. If the rationale of Berlyne (1960) and Taylor (1962) is correct, the brainstem reticular activating system that spreads its fibres throughout the brainstem and into the thalamus plays a vital part in both learning and perception. For it appears that this system first relays impulses from any sense receptor to any part of the cortex and that later cortical differentiations appear through a process of conditioned responses. It would appear that the child's early perceptual responses are gradually tied down (neurologically speaking) by the social and personal reinforcers of early object relations such as the mother's smile and her approving caressing and familial patterns of reinforcement. Thus culture or man's cultural transmission and responses to living in a group context seem to be the chief generalized reinforcer or patterner of individual social behavior. Effective human behavior is seen to be contextual to the culture and to be expressed by patterns of stable, predictable behavior that are in essential agreement with the expectations of a given culture.

THE PURPOSE OF CULTURE

The purposes of culture appear to be related to the establishment of stable predictable patterns of human behavior. One of the first necessary requisites for existence in a social community are some general prescriptions about behavior. Relationships must be established on a firm and predictable basis. Individuals in a group cannot feel secure unless they know that certain types of stimuli will elicit certain types of responses. Assessment, the prediction of dependable behavior, and the determination of criteria of effective behavior are functions of culture that exist in some form or other in every social group. From the puberty rites and taboos of the upper Paleolithic period to present-day forms of objective testing, the evaluation and the maintenance of behavior have been important functions in cultural control mechanisms. Evaluation as a means of intellectual and personality assessment plays a central role in the transmission of those forms of behavior deemed essential to the survival of a culture. It is the way in which a given society makes sure that individuals promoted to certain roles and trusted with adult responsibilities are, indeed, ready and capable of assuming those roles.

Man has always felt the need of defining certain characteristics that were required for successful functioning. Conforming behavior in a social setting thus became the first major criterion of effective human behavior. And this conforming behavior meant, specifically, that adult men would hunt together in a specified manner, that they would respect each other's women, that they could and would agree on a manner of obtaining a food supply, repelling enemies, rearing children, and placating gods. In short, culture had as its prime purpose the establishment of a repertory of behaviors that would make life secure, would insure a food supply, would effect mutual defense and education systems, and would preserve the species. Predictable patterns of social behavior aimed at the maintenance and sustenance of human life in a social setting have been the avowed purposes of the cultural transmission and patterning.

From the earliest times, it appears that man has identified certain predictors of effective human behavior. Although the early predictors were variously assessed and measured in terms of manliness, hunting prowess, knowledge of sexual mores, battle strategy, and leadership, the constellations of behavior that led to the development of these terminal goals emerged as meaningful dimensions of evaluation and assessment in early societies. Moreover they became the means devised to preserve the characteristics of the culture. These specific criteria of effective human conduct were basically related to stable predictable patterns deemed consonant with the survival of the group. In fact unpredictable and erratic or deviant behavior worked against the survival of the group. Thus stable predictable behavior was invested with a sanction by the group and was related to ritual practices. Eventually, certain kinds of behavior developed into powerful control mechanisms that were used by the culture to control behavior.

The origin of these control mechanisms appears to be found in the attempt of man to relate his own pleasure-seeking propensities to the effects of a social reality. Man learned early that certain stable patterns of behavior were necessary to maintain the security of the group, to engage in collective food-gathering, and to provide for mutual protection. The family, customs, law, ethics, religion, priesthood, chieftains, police functions and education all seem to have been developed as man's unique response to the challenge of his environment. The mechanisms of control thus evolved possessed a basic stabilizing effect that made for psychologic security through a degree of measured predictability of behavior. Through measured experience in a social setting as a criterion of effectiveness, these control mechanisms, stemming from the family, became the chief methods of cultural transmission.

CHANGING PATTERNS OF CULTURAL CONTROL

The impact of the family, a common religion, a common cultural tradition, and specific mores can all be viewed as powerful means to shape the behavior of individuals within a group. However, these traditional mechanisms of control are not as powerful today in American culture as they were in the agrarian culture of decades ago, or the primitive cultures of early man. Many of these traditional cultural control systems vested so heavily in the family and the land have been countered by the phenomenon of mobility that is characteristic of American culture in the 20th century. Even ten years ago, data from the census indicated that one out of five individuals in the United States moved between March 1957 and March 1958 (Burgess, 1961). Observations made on the characteristics of the mobile population suggested that: (1) people living in rural nonfarm areas moved more than individuals living in either urban or rural-farm areas; (2) nonwhites moved more than whites; (3) more males moved than females; (4) the 20 to 24 age group was most mobile and contained the highest proportion of interstate migrants; (5) the population in the Western region of the United States was most mobile and that of the Northeast least mobile.

From these data, it would seem that the following general conclusions could be drawn about geographic mobility: (1) there is a great degree of mobility in our population; (2) there is a trend toward living in metropolitan areas, particularly in the suburbs; (3) the greatest degree of mobility occurs in the young adult period; and (4) the West is the area of greatest mobility.

Mobility certainly is rooted in the peculiar circumstances of American culture. There have been some attempts to predict or to suggest why mobility is a continuing American phenomenon. Tarver (1961), in a study of migration, postulated that mobility among the various subdivisions of the United States is a corollary of the distinctive demographic, economic, and social structure of the country. On the basis of nearly 40 variables, which include density of population, average per capita income, location in relationship to metropolitan areas, percentage of farmland and many others, he claimed to account for approximately 85 percent of the mobility changes.

Svalastoga, in a book entitled *Prestige, Class and Mobility* (1959), suggested that the intersociety determinants relating to mobility may be reduced to four major groups of variables, the first having to do with changes in the distribution of roles in the society primarily under the influence of technological innovations, the second having to do with demographic changes, the third with changes in the distribution of abilities or skills, and the fourth with changes in attitudes as induced through class relationships and education. Beshers (1961) related mobility to a decision-making process wherein individuals of varying strata of society weighed the decision to migrate on the basis of either purposive-rational or hedonistic factors. He made a number of conclusions that shed light on the qualitative nature of our mobility. He found that, in the change of locale, the amount of migration among professionals is greater than among others. He found that college educated people tended to migrate more frequently than others. He also pointed out that individuals with six or less years of education were least mobile, farmers and farm operators were also not as mobile, and young adults move more than any other age group.

These studies tend to confirm what Cole (1950) suggested many years ago about the special characteristics of American culture. He stated that there were certain significant traits in emerging American culture. He listed them as: (1) an abiding conviction in democracy with its principles of individual freedom and social control; (2) a growing secularization of society with the subsequent deemphasis of institutional religion; (3) the technological pattern of American society wherein energy harnessed by technology is consistently resulting in the reshaping of society; (4) the immigration movement and the public school system wherein many disparate elements of our culture were being theoretically neutralized; and (5) a social status system based on middle class values.

There have been many and varied effects proceeding from the mobility phenomenon. The traditional anchors of the land, a religion based on the land, such as in the old European tradition of "whose land, his religion" (Cuius regio ejus religio), and a family of assured social status have all but disappeared in modern American culture. Parenthetically, one might observe that it is no longer "who you are" but "what you do" that is important in American society.

Mobility today means that, in most instances, the family exists alone in a strange area. Very seldom do uncles, aunts, cousins, grandparents and others reside next door or in the same community. Mobility means that the significance of property and of the land as a cultural control mechanism has broken down. Banks indicate that the average length of occupancy of a house with a 25-year mortgage is seven years or less. Changes have resulted in sex roles with women coming to marriage not with cooking ability and a dowry, but with a professional competency such as teaching, nursing, or secretarial work. Mobility has resulted in changes of housing patterns, such as the ones seen in the vast sprawling suburban developments wherein relatively homogeneous groupings are imposed by salary criteria or contracting agreements. Changes in the strength of institutional religion have also occurred. It is a well-known fact that a large group of our population changes its religious affiliation either by marriage or personal preference. Few families can count on a similarity of religious outlook throughout the extended family.

Perhaps the greatest changes of all have taken place in the pattern of child rearing. Urie Bronfenbrenner (1960) has suggested that certain basic trends have been in evidence during the past 25 years. Among these trends are the following:

1. Greater permissiveness toward the child's spontaneous desires.
2. Freer expression of affection.
3. Greater reliance on indirect "psychological" techniques of disciplining, such as reasoning or appeals to guilt, versus direct methods such as physical punishment, scolding, and threats.
4. In consequence of the above shifts in the direction of what are predominantly middle class values and techniques, there has been

a narrowing of the gap between social classes in their patterns of child rearing.

5. In succeeding generations the relative position of the father vis-à-vis the mother is shifting, with the former becoming increasingly more affectionate and less authoritarian, and the latter becoming relatively more important as the agent of discipline, especially for boys.

Bronfenbrenner has suggested that these findings mean that middle class parents, although in one sense more lenient in their discipline techniques, are using methods that are actually more compelling. Moreover, the compelling power of these practices is probably enhanced by the more permissive treatment accorded middle class children in the early years of life. The successful use of withdrawal of love as a discipline technique implies the prior existence of a gratifying relationship; the more love present in the first instance, the greater the threat implied in its withdrawal.

Oddly enough, from a learning point of view, including identification and modeling, this very indulgence or permissiveness of behavior on the part of parents and particularly the father is symptomatic of the lessening of another basic control mechanism, that is, the family. Burton and Whiting (1960) suggest that the process of identification consists of the covert practice of the role of an envied status, and that this identification occurs via the learning of a role by rehearsal in fantasy or in play rather than in actual performance.

Moreover, the job description of many middle class males in our society does not lend itself to rehearsal by children. They can no longer observe their father plowing the field and fixing things at home. Green (1946) proposed that the middle class male is caught up in a lifelong struggle for self-improvement that takes him away from the home for long periods of time and forces him to work long hours in the evening and weekend. Recognizing the feminine role in upward striving, the wife engages in all sorts of socially approved activities, committees, and organizations. As a result, the child's need for individual attention is often shuttled off to television and babysitters. Havighurst and Davis (1955) have also suggested that middle class mothers are more severe in the early critical training of children with the result that this training is likely to produce an orderly, conscientious, responsible, tame, but frustrated child. Investigations of the relationship between social status aspiration and the personality of children have indicated that there were low but significant associations between status and measured personality factors (Sewell and Heller, 1956; Guinouard and Rychlak, 1962).

Bronfenbrenner believes that the differential treatment of children takes place as families move up the social scale. From more direct methods, the family proceeds to indirect methods, boys get less punishment, and girls less indulgence and protectiveness. At the upper levels, girls are not as readily debilitated by parental affection and power, nor is parental discipline as effective in fostering the development of leadership and responsibility in boys. Miller and Swanson (1958) have interpreted these results as an indication that America is moving toward a bureaucratic society that emphasizes, to put it colloquially, "getting along rather than getting ahead." If it is true that certain of our traditional cultural mechanisms of control are breaking down, then it may be that children will conclude that the values or lack of values shown by their parents are not worthy of emulation or identification. Thus presumably, we can look forward to two kinds of reactions: (1) the formation of new militant attitudes that differ strongly from the values of parents as a kind of reaction formation, and (2) the development of an ever-increasing number of equalitarian families who, in turn, will produce successive generations of ever more adaptable, but unaggressive "organization men."

There is, however, mounting evidence that a new reaction is in full swing within American society. New demands for civil rights, a mounting dissatisfaction with the traditional roles of education, the emergence of extremist groups may all be harbingers of a post-industrial society. Toynbee in his *Study of History* has suggested that when a culture falls on what he calls a "time of troubles" creative minorities are often replaced by less educated and enlightened, but dominant minorities who rely on force or coercion in confronting urgent problems. The example of Socrates confirms the reaction that took place in Ancient Greece. Certainly Diocletian's attempt to restore the ancient Roman Empire was another example of this procedure.

If the effects of mobility are assessed correctly, they have resulted in some strikingly new patterns that have, in effect, broken down many of the older social mechanisms of control. By so doing, there has been a felt lack of predictability in behavior, a flux of standards in values, and a fear on the part of many reactionary individuals that our culture is deteriorating. Thus with the breakdown of strong familial controls, land-based religious values, and traditional modeling roles of males and females, a vast degree of social indecision has emerged which may be related to the social and attitudinal characteristics of our population. This has been pinpointed by some as a "lack of commitment." It has been identified by others as a "lack of patriotism"—a tolerance for materialistic and creeping socialistic ideals. Moreover, there has been a decided opposition to new cultural control mechanisms that have assumed a great deal of power in our present society.

The partial disintegration of some of the older control mechanisms, coupled with international pressures and technological developments, has given great power to a new control mechanism that is rapidly becoming one of the greatest of all potential control systems. This is mass communication. Mass media of communication have this in common with other traditional mechanisms of control, that they represent on an unconscious level certain ritual and symbolic processes for warding off evil. Within the traditional mechanisms of control, such as the family, religion, and customs, certain rites or rituals were compulsory. The bases of these rites and rituals may be interpreted as being necessary external significants of the need to ward off evil, and to celebrate the communality of the social group. Thus, indirectly, the family feasts at Thanksgiving and Christmas, and the entire host of traditions focusing on the land and religion have been identified with proper ways of insuring the continuance of the "good life."

Boskoff (1959) has stated that mass communications are standardized stimuli providing a margin of unanticipated stability and cohesion in our society. He states that they do this: (1) by the scattering or diversion of audience attention; (2) by the refocusing of existing tensions and their reduction by the semblance of an expanding scale through myriad contacts with distant places and personages; (3) by the illusion of modernity and the appeal to the latest that is really new as a criterion of value; (4) by providing a sense of confidence in a remote authority derived from the pronouncements of officials, cultural idols, and heroes, and (5) by providing an important element of ritual regularity and predictability vested in expected symbols such as regular TV programs, the daily newspaper, and the weekly magazine.

Thus, it may be concluded that with the rise of mobility and the diminishing influence of traditional cultural mechanisms of control, a number of subtle but distinct differences have occurred in the sex roles of men and women, the attitudes toward land, the family, and religion, the changes in the essential ethnocentrism of racial groups, the patterns of child rearing, and the role of education as a systematic source of cultural transmission.

Both mass media and education have emerged as dominant control mechanisms for the shaping of the future culture. Mass media, and particularly television, exert a tremendous influence on American culture. Television has nearly surpassed the role of the family, since it is the one common link that all Americans share. They can have immediate access to the President as he talks to them in moments of crisis and allays their insecurity, ambivalence, and fears as the supreme father figure of the nation. Their values are shaped continually by an unceasing flow of adolescent violence that is most incongruous in a society which absolutely requires positive peaceful means to survive. Mass communications have resulted in a multiple control mechanism that is as complex as the culture it mirrors and controls. From a psychological viewpoint, it would seem, as Boskoff has stated: "to create a superficial but effective consensus reducing and insulating irritations, imposing a kind of stabilizing order that allows us to maintain a kind of vague optimism about underlying conditions." Of all the effects of mobility and technological change, it is the one that potentially may be the greatest boon or threat to our way of life. Used by social scientists, it can help to accelerate learning; used by greedy commercial interests, it can help to develop a pervasive hedonistic culture, a model for learning all kinds of deviant and maladaptive behavior.

Education has also emerged as a primary control mechanism far in excess of what it traditionally was. For now values and success are strictly contingent on education. The school from elementary through graduate degrees constitutes the central mechanism for transmitting the cultural inheritance as well as the cognitive reservoir of technology and understanding. And it is in this context, and with the need for some humanization of the problem solving of vast numbers of children and young men and women, that the counselor makes his contribution (see Table 1).

METHODS OF SOCIAL LEARNING

In recent years considerable emphasis has been placed on the question of social learning. The importance of this area of research cannot be questioned particularly in terms of its relevance to the cultural transmission and methods used by various cultural control mechanisms in teaching individuals within the group setting. From the previous section of this chapter the argument has been established that cultural control mechanisms based on the need for collective security establish behavioral contingencies for success in a given culture. These behavioral contingencies function in accord with certain implicit or explicit criteria. The criteria of effective human behavior are related to cultural expectations and transmitted through the cultural mechanisms of control. In any society or group of people working together, it would appear that the chief agents of the cultural transmission are the authority group and the peer group. In other words, the power structure of the organization sets the criteria of effective human behavior.

Table 1 Summary of Culture and Control Mechanisms

	Primary Criterion Source	Secondary Criterion Sources		
Definition level	Culture as a series of historical patterns — Related to the enhancement and survival of the individual and group	Family as basic social unit — Related to survival of the unit	Peer group as another social unit — Related to survival of a common age or interest level	Law, custom, church, education, mass media, civil authority; specific control mechanisms — Established by the culture to enhance and maintain the culture
Operational level	A coherent methodology developed by the group — Related to the prediction and control of stable patterns of behavior	A microcosmic control system reflecting the culture — Related to the prediction and control of stable patterns of behavior	A microcosmic control system reflecting the culture — Related to the development of stable patterns of behavior	Coherent methodologies devised by the culture for sustaining appropriate predictable behavior in the individual and group
Behavioral level	A complex chain of behaviors that are shaped, sustained, reinforced, and extinguished by the group — Utilizing past experience and trial-and-error learning	A specific network of behaviors designed to sustain the optimum behaviors of male, female, and minor children — Utilizing a series of learned behavior involving coercive and reciprocal behaviors	A specific network of behaviors formulated and designed to sustain the optimum behaviors of specific interest groups — Utilizing a series of learned behaviors involving coercive and reciprocal behaviors	The development of specific sets of criteria for guiding and controlling individuals and groups — Utilizing reference to a series of criterion behaviors in learning

We can see this operating in business, education, law, medicine, and labor unions, as well as in the family unit. It is most assuredly a major factor in the classroom learning situation. For here, the individual student must somehow come to terms with the behavioral expectations of the teacher—who represents the power structure—and the peer group. For thse two groups, the teacher and the peer group, collectively set the interim criteria of effective human behavior in the classroom. They specify what is acceptable conduct and what is not acceptable. The same situation applies to a business firm or to higher education. Research evidence in social learning theory thoroughly substantiates the impact of the cultural transmission. Examples of some of the specific research supportive of this contention can be found in research relating to: (1) sociometry and peer group pressures; (2) the concept of the environmental "press," and (3) social learning principles.

Research on sociometry or peer nominations has been extensive. The most complete and comprehensive compendium of earlier research is to be found in Gronlund's book *Sociometry in the Classroom* (1959). Although much of the earlier research on sociometry and peer nominations has indicated that this source of measurement of individuals is correlated to numerous dimensions of personality inventories, that it possesses longitudinal prediction strength in terms of dropout status or success factors in leadership, and that it is quite stable in terms of overall reliability, the chief problem connected with the use of sociometry has been the difficulty of devising a technique readily usable between classes of individuals. In a number of studies I have examined sociometric phenomena both from the phenomenological and behavioral points of view. An analysis of the sociometric phenomenon (1966a) has suggested that sociometric choices may not only be interpreted from the phenomenological point of view of older social psychology but may gain strength by a parsimonious interpretation from the social learning frame of reference. In other studies, I have demonstrated that sociometric elections are predictors of school dropouts and possess considerable stability in the absence of interventions (1966b), are associated with distinct interest patterns obtained and derived from the environment (1966c), and are reflective of differential patterns of reinforcement as related to the age and sex of the teacher (1966d). In a study by Barclay and Barclay (1965) it was also found that sociometric choices are related to indexes of perceptual integration. Other studies that have shown the power of the peer group in setting interim criteria of effective behavior are the studies of Backman and Secord and Backman, Secord, and Pierce (1962, 1963) in which there is strong indication that the peer group opinions are important social reinforcers in determining patterns of acceptable behavior and resistance to change. They have demonstrated that the greater number of significantly perceived persons in a group who support the behavior of an individual, the greater his resistance to change. In other words, change can seldom be instituted in a member of a group as long as there are others whom he regards as significant persons in that group who sustain his behavior. Dittes and Kelley (1956) found that among persons who attach equal importance to their membership in a group, those who receive information that they are only minimally accepted by their colleagues, and that this evaluation is subject to change, possibly becoming worse, conform more than persons who receive information that they are highly accepted and that this situation is stable. Lott and Lott (1960) confirmed the hypothesis that if a person is rewarded in the presence of fellow group members, he will develop positive attitudes toward them. In this study, individuals were conceptualized as discriminable stimuli to which responses could be learned. Flanders and Havumaki (1960) in an experiment with teacher praise found that the differential rewarding of students' responses by a teacher resulted in the substantial alteration of the sociometric status of individuals thus rewarded. This evidence would then suggest strongly the importance of both the peer group and the authority power structure in providing reinforcement for the shaping and molding of behavior in a group. The criteria of effective behavior in a given group, then, are obviously a function of the status and characteristics of the power structure in that group.

Still further evidence of the nature of this transmission of social behavior is provided by recent studies in the measurement of the environmental "press." This approach began with the studies of Pace and Stern (1958) and has been followed up by Holland, Astin, and Nichols in studies that started with National Merit Scholars and later extended into groups of students available through the American College Testing Program. Holland, Astin, and Nichols were chiefly concerned with the problem of finding a more adequate series of criterion measures in the college setting. The research effort not only uncovered some very real environmental forces operating in selective college and university environments but culminated in the independent research of Holland establishing a vocational preference inventory that tapped some of these dimensions (1962). The theoretical posture on which the studies are based is explained by Holland as follows:

> The theory assumes that at the time a person chooses a vocation, he is the product of his heredity and a variety of environmental forces including peers, parents, and other significant adults, social

class, American culture, and the physical environment. Out of his experiences, he develops a hierarchy of orientations for coping with environmental tasks; this hierarchy may be referred to as the pattern of personal orientations. Each of these orientations is related to a particular physical or social environment and to a particular set of abilities. The person making a vocational choice in a sense "searches" for those environments which are congruent with his personal orientation (Holland, 1962, 1).

Holland postulated that people who are successful in different occupations tend to differ in basic personality attributes. He has isolated six categories or environmentally associated personality characteristics, that is, Realistic, Intellectual, Social, Conventional, Enterprising, and Artistic. For each type he has developed a model orientation, a theoretical complex of personal traits, coping mechanisms, vocational and educational goals, aptitudes, and previous history. The extent to which a person resembles any model orientation is called his personal orientation for that type. His total pattern with respect to all six model orientations is his pattern of personal orientations.

This research in the matter of college careers and personality attributes would indicate that differential "presses" exist within the university setting. Holland has pointed out that individuals with a certain preference for intellectualism tend to find their way into curricula that express this "press." For example they may be attracted to the biological sciences. They will have certain expectations about what professors may require of them. They also come with some expectations about peer relations. Generally speaking, they are susceptible to a given type of learning behavior that will include a specific kind of reinforcement and certain professor expectations, and will provide certain types of exemplary models for their imitation and emulation. If they enter a curriculum that does not appear to be congruent with their own preferences, they may either decide to alter their behavior to conform to the "press" or eventually to seek another field in which they feel more comfortable.

This selective environmental "press" can be exemplified through the analysis of a university department. A university committee may choose a chairman of a department who represents in their collective judgment the kinds of behaviors and values that they wish to perpetuate in this area. As the chairman of the department and other major professors look for young colleagues they will, of course, be interested in a man's academic preparation, degrees, and the like, but they will also be looking for those characteristics that indicate to them, through verbal and nonverbal cues, that the prospective department colleague is congruent with their own "learning press." What is really being described here are possible means whereby the culture is passed on.

Nor are these environmental "press" characteristics limited to a college or university environment. In studies relating to the secondary school environment (1967) and to the elementary school environment (1967, 1968), I have established the fact that similar type presses clearly compatible with Holland and Astin's collegiate research can be found even in the secondary and elementary school areas.

The meaning of these research efforts regarding criterion determination and the methods of transmitting the environmental "press" is focused sharply by studies relating to social learning itself. Bandura and Walters (1963) have described a number of studies concerned with social behavioral learning. Addressing themselves to the central problem of how behavior is formed and transmitted, they present their own research evidence and logic in connection with other studies. They state that social learning is transmitted by a variety of techniques. These techniques may be summarized under the headings: (1) observational learning; (2) shaping and modeling; (3) imitation, and (4) patterns of reinforcement or reward.

By observational learning is meant the individual's perception of what behavior is expected by others. Children as well as adults continually observe a variety of behaviors. A child's behavior depends, in part, on how he perceives the social contingencies of behavior and, also, on his past experience in reinforcement. Included here as well are judgments regarding the risk-taking involved and the question of value. Closely allied to observational learning is the susceptibility to shaping, molding, and modeling. Social behavior is constantly shaped by the force of verbal and nonverbal interaction relating to cultural criteria. This means that all individuals in a group are to some extent responsible for the formation of social behaviors. Those who are either in power structure functions, or have risen to peer-group power, control the behaviors of those within the group by an implicit or explicit manifestation of appropriate behavior. This can also be said of the shaping and control of deviant behavior. The impact of the shaping force of the environment plus the provision of exemplary models of behavior by the group are unquestionably strong influences on individuals who wish to remain within the group. This has some explanatory force for analyzing the impact of aggressive behavior on a group. When a group is susceptible to an aggressive model, Bandura has pointed out (1963) that the incidence of aggressive behavior increases in that group. Studies with small children who were exposed to aggressive adult models indicated that aggressive responses also were increased.

This also explains how deviant behavior in a family setting can often be transmitted to children and can be very resistant to change. Families who have odd methods of behavior may find other families who support their behavior and reinforce it. Subsequently, an entire enclave of a different pattern of behavior can be established within a culture constituting, in effect, a subculture. This is certainly demonstrable in terms of religious subcultures, for instance, the Hutterites wherein a distinct pattern of behavior has been cultivated, transmitted, modeled, and shaped, and it is also relevant to an analysis of subgroups of racial minorities.

Allied to these methods of social transmission are other techniques, such as imitation. The role of imitation and the vicarious rehearsal of behavior has been underestimated in the transmission of social behavior. Some have thought that imitation in children is initiated by a basic envy of the power of adults or of models. Bandura has suggested that learning takes place even if the child or individual does not overtly rehearse or imitate the model provided. The casual observation that all of us make of children rehearsing roles and playing what they consider to be the appropriate behaviors of adults indicates clearly that imitation is a factor in the acquisition of motor, social, and possibly even academic skills. Imitation with its reliance on the use of motor and sensory modalities may be one way of acquiring appropriate role behavior.

The most important aspect of social learning is tied to the systematic or even desultory reinforcement of certain kinds of responses. As is known from learning theory, there are a number of forms of reinforcement. Most of these reinforcement procedures are dispensed in accord with what Skinner has called schedules of reinforcement. Schedules of reinforcement can be broadly divided into variable and fixed schedules. Variable reinforcement occurs at intermittent stages and can be tied either to a certain ratio of responses or an interval period. Fixed reinforcement occurs likewise in relationship to ratio or interval periods. Essentially, most human reinforcement occurs on a variable-ratio or a variable-interval basis. We do not receive verbal or social approval for everything we do, but certain reinforcements are dispensed by the power structure or peer group at given intervals. Reinforcement can take the form of verbal approval, a concrete monetary or gustatory reward, promotion, or a variety of culturally valued rewards.

Just as important as positive reinforcement can be the effects of disapproval, punishment, and discipline. Obviously, the negative effects do not carry, according to present research, the same shaping power as positive reinforcements, but they do act as deterrents to antisocial or anticultural behavior. When the effects of positive reinforcement are combined with the effects of punishment, it is possible to perceive how human behavior is strongly controlled and shaped by a continual process of social interaction dispensed by the power figures within a cultural setting. Thus it can be stated here that patterns of culture are passed on through specific power groups within the culture by utilizing both systematic and nonspecific techniques of shaping, molding, and modeling appropriate behavior. The obvious argument of this research and the chain of thought to the problem at hand is that, in order to understand how behavior can be changed and altered, it is imperative to understand how it has been sustained and created initially.

VALUE DETERMINATION AND DEVIANCY

Since cultural patterns of behavior are transmitted by power agents within the culture through a process of social learning, it is apparent that the values of a given culture are obviously inculcated. In every culture, no matter how primitive or sophisticated, certain pivotal problems occur. These problems are related to what constitutes the good life, what is truth, what ought to be done in relationship to these two areas, and what ought not to be done. As a society gains in sophistication and security, more intellectual and behavioral deviancy from these cultural norms is permitted. Thus one may state as a kind of general principle that the flexibility of the criteria of effective human behavior operating within a culture is proportionate to the degree of sophistication and security of that culture. The behavioral transmission of the aboriginal cultures is much more rigid and precise in terms of what constitutes effective behavior and what does not than the behavioral transmission of modern American culture. In effect, this is also a function of the mobility of individuals within a group. A tribal culture is much more restricted and, therefore, much less tolerant of deviancy than is a more developed culture.

Sir James G. Frazer in *The Golden Bough* has suggested that the history of man's intellectual development can be compared to a long rope in which there are colored strands: a black one of magic, a red one of religion, and a white one of science. Roche (1958) on a commentary regarding this metaphor states:

> History begins with the black, then moves to black and red, and in time shows a white thread or two. In modern times the white thread imparts a dominance, but the black is still discernible and the red exists in large measure (10).

Magic, religion, and science in its philosophical and methodological components have this in common: that they represent at different stages of development man's efforts to provide a systematic explanation and justification of his behavior. These frameworks have been the basis for systematically attempting to cope with both socially accepted and deviant behavior. They provide a basis for the implementation of a cultural transmission.

Deviant behavior can be considered both as a psychological and a physical problem. From the earliest days these two aspects have been locked together so that treatment for the one has often shaded over into treatment for the other. Insofar as early man and present-day man are both judged ultimately in terms of specific contextual criteria of effective behavior, there has always been a concern on the part of man as to the methods of changing deviant behavior or curing illness.

As far back as five thousand years ago, according to Weatherhead (1951), primitive man was convinced that physical health and disease were dependent on states of mind, the reverence for deities, and/or punishment for deviancy. One can only conjecture about the origins of magic and religion in terms of the control of human behavior. The predominant cause-effect basis of man's thinking plus the reinforcement of certain of his behaviors could be one of the explanations for the rise of magic and religious control mechanisms.

The important fact, however, remains that cultural mechanisms of control have sought some kind of a cognitive justification for differentiating patterns of reinforcement. Illness as a kind of physical deviancy and the failure to behave as a kind of psychological deviancy were both judged in terms of the cultural criteria. Obviously, a sick or ailing person constituted a burden to a tribal unit. Either he needed to be cured or the common good of the group dictated that he be eliminated. We see evidence of this in terms of the Spartan custom of inspecting male children for deformities and abandoning those who did not meet the inspection and health criteria. We observe similar practices in the abandonment of elderly or sick individuals in Eskimo culture. Elimination, exile and, in some instances, execution were commonly recognized as ultimate methods of coping with physical and behavioral deviancy. In the ancient Greek city states one of the most powerful punitive resources was exile. A similar punishment could take place for failure to meet the behavioral expectations of the group. A failure in hunting or the inability to conform to expected behavior in aboriginal culture was dealt with directly, since the entire survival of the group depended strongly on a consistent performance.

With sophistication and the development of religion, a whole host of behaviors were prescribed for the group. Worship, a reverence for religious objects, prescribed rituals, and cleansing procedures are typical of most cultures as they attempt to control their approach to reality with certain definable rituals.

The goals of these behavioral imperatives are obviously related to the survival of the group and to the transmission of the cultural heritage. Dependability and predictability of behavior is a requisite for living within a given culture. Despite the sophistication of modern life, we still remove the deviant from the mainstream of society. We lock people up who demonstrate by their behavior that they cannot be depended on to behave in a predictable and secure (to the group) method. Thus we punish crime by removal from society. We do the same (although presumably not as punishment) for extreme mental illness.

Abstracting from the specifics of both magic and religion, it is apparent that these mechanisms administered by witch doctors, shamens, priests, or physicians have certain common elements. In other words, the priest-physician of early days was a guardian of the cultural transmission and functioned as a resource person for aiding the cultural group to make a determination regarding deviancy in an individual.

A variety of techniques were developed based on the specific assumptions of magic, religion, or later philosophy. These techniques included both cognitive and behavioral approaches. Amulets, charms, the use of ceremonials, herbs, mud-packing, the use of blood, and primitive drug extracts were all used in the process of restoring individuals to health and to maintaining health. Primitive operations such as trephining of the brain were used to release individuals from the power of devils. To some extent, man has always resorted to the use of education to attune members of the group to the spiritual precepts important to the group. Thus cognitive argument and persuasion have been a tool of psychotherapy. The recognition of the power of evil forces has led to the development of specific techniques for coping with the problems of behavioral deviancy.

In ancient Egypt, Imhotep who appears to have been a magician and architect in the Third Dynasty (2900 B.C.) became identified with a cult of healing. Treatment of mental and physical illness included the use of ceremonials, as outlined above, plus the practice of sleeping in the sanctuary of the temple. Early man came to recognize that sleep had curative effects. Sleeping in the temple was designed to allow the god to effect cures or to prescribe remedies in dreams. While the patient slept, priests glided to and fro whispering prescriptions for health. The use of hydrotherapy was another technique practiced extensively both in ancient Egypt and in the Greek and Roman cultures.

Many techniques that are still used to some extent or in modified form were originated in this early period. Babylonian priests used to recite long lists of devils to patients until they came to one where the patient was visibly disturbed. It was then held that this devil was the cause of the disturbance. This is interesting to note in view of later word-association methods. A technique used by Socrates was that of free-association as found in "The Clouds" of Aristophanes. In a dialogue between Strepsiades and Socrates, Socrates is portrayed as searching out the resistance and obstruction to the learning of his system through having Strepsiades stretch out on a couch and freely express his ideas—evidently a precursor of Freudian psychotherapy.

Persistent in all early religious history is the conviction that the failure to obey the gods or religious tenets brings about evil or misfortune. The story of Job in the Old Testament, featuring the recurring attempts of his friends to convince him of some kind of guilt that had been repressed and his denial of such guilt is testimony to the impact of this thinking. Moreover, the Bible itself states: "I will visit the sins of the father unto the sixth generation." The wisdom literature of the Bible conveys the same impression about the relationship between personal illness and deviancy or cultural transgression.

Nor are these older ideas absent in the modern-day world. Although man has progressed scientifically, he is still interested in the forecasts of astrology and in superstition. As jets zoom through the stratosphere, one half of their passengers wear amulets or magic items. Hotels and motels typically omit the number 13. And in terms of psychotherapy we may have substituted for the devil the unconscious, but we are still concerned about methods of extirpating the devil within. We still must rely mainly on intellectual argument and insight formation or patterns of behavioral alteration. The witch doctor, the priest, the physician, the psychotherapist, and the counselor are all links in a chain that concerns problems of deviant behavior and thought. The restoration to physical and mental health and the change of behavioral patterns are linked not only in the historical tradition of man but also in the continuing problems of the determination and transmission of the cultural heritage today.

PHILOSOPHY, RELIGION AND CULTURE

What has been said about the specific techniques of behavior transmission in terms of social learning is applicable throughout the course of man's development of a psychotherapeutic technique. Successful techniques have embodied: (1) certain token symbols of a concrete nature such as amulets and medicines, (2) certain actions that restrict or augment behavior, and (3) the massive systematic application of social learning principles in both sustaining appropriate behavior and in eliminating inappropriate behavior. Although the specific techniques used will be alluded to throughout this book, the predominant emphasis herein is centered on the intellectual development of ideas that have formed the basis of a justification for treatment procedures.

Philosophy does not emerge first in a culture. It is the distilled product of many ages of behavior. Thus, first man learns to behave in a given way through trial-and-error learning. Then he establishes certain kinds of customs, laws, and religious prescriptions to guide behavior. And, finally, he sanctions his cultural behavior by an intellectual framework that expresses and justifies his behavior. For this reason, philosophy has emerged as a consequence of culture and not as an a priori condition for it. From philosophy in the classical and medieval sense has developed a specialized area of philosophy relating to the methodology of science.

What is true of philosophy is likewise applicable to the development of psychotherapy or counseling. It is apparent from the present status of psychotherapy that goals, methods, and criteria of performance have been largely inherited from medicine or from various pragmatic techniques that appear to have had some success. Thus, the profession has grown first from a technique to the status of a discipline wherein some truly philosophical and theoretical frameworks could be developed.

With this observation in mind, we shall now examine the intellectual system that underlies the development of systems of psychotherapy. Our focus will be on the development of the philosophical principles that underlie a major portion of what is called the intentionalistic tradition. The development of the philosophies of idealism and realism involves questions regarding the existence of good and evil in the world, questions regarding the nature of man, truth, falsity, and above all the question of what constitutes the good life. If we look carefully at this latter consideration we shall ascertain what are the behavioral goals of adjustment in the world of that period. Moreover, we shall also be able to identify recurring pivotal problems that man has addressed himself to through magic, religion and, finally, philosophy and science.

CHAPTER III

Religion, Philosophy and Medicine

Two of the persistent mechanisms for the control of man have been religion and philosophy. Religion and philosophy have this in common, that both attempt to explain the basis of man's relationship to the universe. However, religion is more directed to the affective side of man, and philosophy is more directed to the cognitive concerns. Both have offered explanations of the nature of the universe, although religion has attempted more often to find a justification for preexisting supernatural beliefs, and philosophy has sought to identify logical and rational principles based on a naturalistic explanation. Medicine has been developed within the fabric of both approaches, and the interactive effect of religion and medicine and philosophy and medicine has led to a reservoir of opinions and beliefs, mystical and scientific, about health and happiness.

Some of the basic notions that have been spawned in the interactive core civilizations of Ur, Egypt, and India have left their permanent effect on the ideological and language structure of Western civilization. Some of these ideas have existed first within the framework of religion and then have developed into philosophical and scientific notions. For example, consider the notion of illness as a result of sin or evil spirits. In primitive religion much of the substance of ritual was focused on the expurgation of the devil or the atonement for real or imagined guilt because of cultural transgression. This idea, changed in great substance, still lurks within modern psychotherapy under the concept that the unconscious is the devil within which must be expurgated by rational analysis. Certain other core ideas have remained within the entire expanse of psychotherapeutic relationships. Some of these other notions are: (1) that everything exists from natural causes; (2) that virtue is its own reward and brings about happiness, and vice versa for sin; and

(3) that man's state in the world is essentially one of probation wherein he should focus chiefly on the perfection of his spiritual attributes.

The purpose of this chapter is to highlight certain key features in religion, philosophy, and medicine that have shaped the thinking and behavior of Western culture. Encyclopedic works have been written about each of these areas, but the purpose here is to focus on certain key concepts and ideas that will provide a deeper understanding of the persistence of certain thought patterns within Western culture and of the frame of reference in which most counseling is done.

PRIMITIVE RELIGION

Early man was unquestionably overwhelmed by the many unknowns in his life and environment. His need for some kind of answers to the extraordinary events surrounding him together with his associational learning relating causes and effects formed some of the framework for religion. Early man undoubtedly developed rites and rituals of a magic nature from both a superstitious (that is, attributing causal connections to certain spontaneous or accidental behavior occurrences) or a cultural transmission that was passed on to him. Tyler (1871) suggested that early man had an animistic way of thinking in which the objects of nature, both animate and inanimate, were imbued with consciousness. In this sense trees, mountains, stones, and springs all had spirits. Piaget (1952) has confirmed the existence of this primitive epistemology in the thinking of children. Even today, much superstitious and animistic thinking lurks in the subconscious of man. Consider, for example, the way in which individuals will refrain from talking about an anticipated bad event. A man will express the hope that a tire will not blow out and his wife will say: "Don't mention it." References to the dead are sometimes considered in the same way as if to indicate that talking about something or someone will bring about certain consequences. Children will angrily kick a table on which they bumped their heads, and grown men will curse at rugs that they stumble over. In short, there remains within man a kind of animistic thinking that is only slightly glossed over by cultural sophistication and scientific thinking.

Systematic elaboration of magical practices into a religious framework is everywhere in evidence in early man. Charms, good luck pieces, amulets, and other tokens were used as articles that would bring good fortune or that would ward off evil. Places such as sacred groves, mountains, boulders, trees became endowed with religious significance. Later on astrology, almanacs, dream interpretations, phrenology, palmistry, and spiritualism developed as more sophisticated means of foretelling the future and of contacting the spirit world. But in all of them a common thread is evident: these tokens or techniques served as primary means to bring about good fortune and/or ward off evil. Combined with these techniques has been the pervading conviction that man can atone for his personal evil or group sin by some kind of sacrifice. Sacrifice of adult human beings and children eventually gave way to the sacrifice of animals and birds. But the essential belief was that sin was atoned for through sacrifice. The continuation of this conviction is evidenced in the survival of the Hebrew Temple complex into the first years of the Christian era. Sacrifices also were popular in both Greece and Rome and formed an integral part of classical religious ceremonies.

The impact of the environment and life conditions was also an important determinant in the development of early religious practices. Thus, birth, death, and food supply were the most important factors in the cultural evolution of religious practice. Attitudes toward death may have been inspired by a combination of veneration, revivification, and fear of vengeance. The dead were often buried beneath heavy stones, as a method of restricting them so that they could not return to harm the living. The Egyptians provided them with food and tools and often considered dead leaders as gods. Ancestor worship also was practiced in early Greece and Rome where a kind of heroic example of the dead prevailed. Unquestionably, early man believed in an afterlife similar to the life that he lived on earth.

Propagation of the species was also a mystery, and for this reason many religious rituals were associated with fertility cults in order to insure control of the processes of birth and generation. Venus statuettes are found throughout the Middle East with clear accent on the female sexual organs. The food supply was also most important to early man. The more animals available, the more certain man could be of survival and a higher standard of living. In addition, there were the periodic needs for annual flooding such as existed in the Nile River Valley and the Tigris-Euphrates delta. These floods were needed to insure a continual supply of grain. Cave paintings and early art objects often show animals and ritual techniques for the controlling of the forces of nutrition and the propagation of animals.

CONDITIONING AND PURIFICATION IN HEBREW CULTURE

Although volumes could be written about early religion and the methods in which behavior was controlled, the emphasis here is on those central features of thinking and behavior that are related to the existence of our modern Western culture. The Hebrews provide both an historical and relevant example for a central theme in Western culture, that is, purification and atonement.

Because the Bible has played such a decisive role in shaping the ethics and ideology of Western civilization, the attempt to examine critically the historical material within it was delayed until the last century. Even today, any discussion of the ancient Hebrews must strike a careful balance between the Biblical narrative, archeological discoveries, and the conflicting interpretations of both groups of material. Yet like many other nations, the Israelites went through phases of tribal division, national unification, expansion and decline and, finally, conquest by other empires.

Israelite history is the key to the understanding of the Jewish religion for most of the pre-Christian era. As Roland De Vaux, the Biblical archeologist, has stated, "Once more we must insist that Israel's religion was an historical religion and that the faith of Israel was based on God's intervention in the history of his people . . . Whatever may be said of neighboring religions the cult practiced in Israel was not the outward expression of myths, but the homage paid by man to a personal God who made a covenant with his people whom he had saved and who remained faithful to that covenant" (De Vaux, 1961 493,506).

The covenant was first made with Abraham whom God promised to make the father of a multitude of nations. This agreement was handed down to his descendants by the sign of circumcision and the promise in Genesis, 17: 7 ". . . And I will establish my covenant between you and your descendants after you throughout the generations for an everlasting covenant to be from God to you and your descendants after you." The above covenant was subsequently renewed on Mt. Sinai. In accepting monotheism the Jews dedicated themselves to the unseen God whom no image could represent. Besides idolatry, they rejected blasphemy, bestiality, sodomy, and incest. Their law was expressed in a series of codes—some of which date from this time or earlier, and others that were formulated later but were ascribed to this era by religious authorities. Among the earliest codes are the Decalogue or Ten Commandments, a milestone for its ethics and for the institution of the Sabbath. Other laws dating from the desert period are scattered legislative texts in Exodus and Numbers. They form part of the Priestly Code. Most of this code is, however, made up of laws about sacrifice, the priestly installation ritual, the laws of purity, and finally the law of Holiness dealing with rites and the priesthood.

The evolution of Hebrew religion was characterized by phases. The first phase related to the original patriarchal desert society that is still characteristic of many nomads in the Arabian peninsula. Jahweh was the political force that united them through religion, led them out of the wilderness, and fought for them against their enemies, etc. A second phase began with Moses and the formation of the law and priesthood which served as the primary catalytic agent for the religious establishment and the future monarchy. Other phases included the period of the monarchy, the Babylonian captivity when the synagogue was established, and finally the later stage after the return from Babylon when the influence of Greek and Roman culture modified the original religion.

The development of the Hebraic religion was characterized by the use of behavioral learning focused in the extended family or tribe. The Hebraic religion similar to many other religions made extensive use of instrumental conditioning. Within instrumental conditioning four general types have been identified: (1) reward training, (2) punishment training, (3) aversive training, and (4) avoidance training. Hebraic religious behavior involved extensive use of each of these forms of instrumental conditioning. The "good life" was postulated on certain types of behavior. If man obeyed the laws and prescriptions, he was promised life for "three score and ten years." Furthermore, if he refused to obey the law, then he would be punished by any number of a variety of methods.

In the Hebrew tradition there are many examples of this use of conditioning as a method and technique of cultural shaping and control. When Abraham was called out of his homeland, he was given three promises. One was that he would have an heir, the other that his seed would be countless as the stars, and third that his people would inherit the land of Canaan. He obeyed and was rewarded with an heir and the multiplication of his tribal family. On a larger scale, the tribal community was urged to follow the precepts of Jahweh. "If ye walk in my statutes and keep my commandments and do them—then I will give you rain in due season, and the land shall yield their fruits" (Lev. 26: 3,4). Thus the security of the land and the community are tied to certain behavioral actions on the part of the community. Later, when the people of Israel disobey these commandments, they are banished to the land of Babylon.

An example of avoidance training is found in the precepts regarding leprosy. Although an individual leper might be considered healed, he was not allowed to return to the community at once but had to be examined over a period of time by priests who were especially skillful in diagnosing the illness. If he appeared to be healed, he was given a certificate and ultimately readmitted to the society. However, it is apparent that leprosy was considered a punishment for sin and evil. The understanding and control of mental illness and the punishments meted out for sin were based on the premise of the words: "The Lord shall smite thee with madness and blindness, and astonishment of heart" (Zilboorg, 1941, 29). This phrase was not a metaphor; it was meant literally. In the writings of Leviticus it is also stated that "a man or woman that hath a familiar spirit, or that is a wizard shall surely be put to death; they shall stone them with stone; their blood shall be upon them" (Zilboorg, 1941, 29). Thus it was not only to avoid the evil that created physical or mental illness but also to avoid contact with those so afflicted. The law of God was then used to justify exclusions and even executions, since mental and physical illness of certain types were considered deviancy from the law of God. One can surmise that many psychotics and border-line disturbed people were thus disposed of.

Certainly, the use of associational learning, the superstitious ascribing of certain behaviors to causal effects, the systematic instilling of ritual behaviors that were designed to assure good fortune and to ward off evil were primary learned methods of insuring conformity to social and political goals.

Hebrew religion, politics, and medicine were all tied together in the religious codes. There is nothing similar to the emergence of Greek sci-ence in Hebrew culture. For one of the most basic ideas of science, that of exact quantitative measurement, is completely lacking in Jewish rec-ords. All measurements were empirical and pragmatic, whether they be of area, for example, the amount one's ox would plow in one day, or the distance measured by marching. Neither were there exact standards. Length was measured by the limbs of the body, and weight and volume were measured by stones and jugs of varying sizes. In this agricultural society the main concern was to find workable solutions for mundane problems and to see that God had received His just share.

A central theme in Hebraic religion was an ethnocentrism built on the notion that the Hebrews were God's chosen people. This rationale was based on God's covenant with his people, and the notion that if they followed Him, he would make them his chosen nation. But to be a party to the contract with the Spiritual and Holy God, the nation itself had to be as perfect as possible. The followers of Jahweh were to be a spotless host, free of both moral and physical blemishes, unsullied by natural discharges, a living force, untainted by the dead. This entire logic was expressed by the Hebrew devotion to purity.

Not only must they as individuals be free of serious moral offenses and physical defects, but so must all things that touched their lives, the food they consumed, their lands, their houses, even their marriage partners. Foreign influences and intermarriage with other nations defiled the He-brew people. The most sacred institutions of Jewish life, circumcision and the Sabbath, receive their meaning within this framework. The first, because it removed an impurity, was held to be an initial sign of the covenant, and the second because the sacredness of the Sabbath required cleansing and rest.

In allegory as well as law, cleanliness became Godliness. The ideal life was one of temperance, physical and moral purity. The priests, the most holy members of the community abstained from alcohol, married only the virgin daughters or widows of priests, and could show no disfigurement. Even after the Pharisees introduced new religious and medical ethics, this concept of a pure temperate existence still determined the daily regimen. God's reward for his people's faithfulness was health, fertility, and long life for themselves, their crops, and their lands.

The ideal of purification was broad enough to include the concept of God being both the smiter and healer of his people, and of disease being the result of moral transgression, which commentators like Castiglioni and Baruch mention as the underlying rationale of Jewish medicine (Castiglioni, 1947; Baruch, 1964). God indeed punished his people for their transgressions with famine, pestilence, wild beasts, and the sword, but this was only construed as a means to chasten them so that once more they would present themselves holy and perfect before him. Indeed, it is significant that the religious revivals in the Old Testament era involve not only periods and movements of moral purification but a rededication to the physical purity first demanded in the Mosaic Code.

The sweeping effect of this doctrine on Jewish life can only be seen by an examination of the different areas it touched. After the Exodus, the first act of the Jews was to fight and occupy their new land. For this struggle God gave them a holy commission to cleanse Jahweh's land of all people who were "an abomination to him." They were imbued with the idea that soldiers had to be ritually clean (Josh. 3:5) and continent (I Sam. 21:6, II Sam. 11:11) so their camp also had to be cleansed and purified for the expected residence of Jahweh (Deut. 23:10–15).

The equating of sanitation with purification is best seen in the Mosaic Code. Here the prophylactic concept was extended to the land itself, which was to be granted a sabbath every seventh year against the depletion of its mineral resources (Lev. 25:2–7). The Israelite homes and garments were similarly enjoined by these sanitary regulations. Mildew, which discolored walls and clothes, was considered a form of leprosy, requiring a seven-day quarantine and then removal of the affected area or item (Lev. 13:47–49, Lev. 14:33–48). Household objects touched by persons suffering from a discharge were similarly considered as unclean as the persons themselves (Lev. 15:1–13). Not only were certain animals declared inedible but so was the flesh of diseased and dangerous domestic animals (Deut. 15:19–21). Even blemished animals were considered unfit for sacrifice.

The most stringent regulations were reserved for men. The lame, the blind, and those with skin irritations or discharges were as much outcasts as murderers who fled to cities of refuge.

The determination of the state of their impurity was left to the priests, who served as a sanitary police. Although some commentators have attempted to portray the priests as a healing cult, their function was solely to prepare the individual by quarantine and washing to rejoin the rest of the ritually clean community. Where this proved impossible, the individual was banished as were the lepers in Leviticus (13:45), and the blind and lame in David's conquest of Jerusalem (II Sam. 5:8).

If discharges and disease made the individual ritually unclean, then removal of them by washing became symbolic of the removal of sin or moral defilement. Washing thus constituted an important part of the ritual that made priests fit for their office. All of these prescriptions about cleanliness and ritual ablutions were important to the Hebrews as a means of remaining worthy or fit for the holiness of their God. As a direct reward for their adherence to these laws and prescriptions, Jahweh promised his followers their land and their farm animals, health, fertility, and long life. This promise is best expressed in Exodus 23:25:

> You shall serve the Lord, your God, and I will bless your bread and your water; and I will take sickness away from the midst of you. None shall cast her young away or be barren in your land; I will fulfill the number of your days.

Indeed, the Biblical ideal of three score and ten promised in Psalm 90:10 was a remarkable life expectancy for such primitive conditions.

Not only was fertility a blessing but the converse, barrenness, was a curse. Although birth in the family was a reward for purity, death was a defilement. Both the corpse, which was doomed to corruption, and its tomb were unclean as were those who touched these objects. The defilement attached to the corpse prevented the Jews from practicing dissection in the pre-Christian era, although later Talmudists did perform some anatomical experiments (Jakobovits, 1959).

The ritual purification notion exists to some extent in other religions but was clearly highly developed within Hebrew culture. The basic notion is that cleanliness is desired by God and that His people must measure up to this expectation. The same concept is found in the religious significance of sacrifice. Blood was considered the very essence of life, and sin or transgression could only be atoned for by the cleansing sacrifice of atonement. The temple, as the only recognized place for offering this sacrifice, then became the focal point of early Hebrew culture.

The purification ideal, important as it was to the early Hebrews, did not continue in its unmitigated form. Jakobovits (1959) maintains that, since Talmudic times, the predominant ideal has been a respect for life. The transition from the canons of prescriptive and ritual purity to a lesser expectation occurred following the Babylonian captivity when the Hebrews' fundamental institutions were denied them and they were forced to rethink the basis of their faith. Within this time span, the five centuries before Christ, traditionalist Jews were forced to accept two important conclusions about the ideology of the God of national destiny: first, that considering the leadership they had, this idea was no longer politically viable and, second, that the politically run Church could no longer meet the deep spiritual needs of the people or, for that matter, the letter of the law.

The consequences of this evaluation led to a fragmentation of Jewish opinion regarding the laws and the notion of purification. The two reactions most familiar to historians were the development of the monastic Essene community who have been identified with a traditionalist point of view, and the development of a rethinking and interpretation of the scriptures by the Pharisees. Both groups shared a common repudiation of the national Church leaders.

The Essenes practiced a rigid system of discipline, including all of the ritual purification laws such as daily washing, abstinence from alcohol and meat, and the other rituals prescribed in the laws. It was not, however, the Essene monastic strictness which formed the basis for Judaism, but the ideals of the Pharisees. The Pharisaic schism was primarily an attempt to wrest control from the priestly elite and to democratize the religion. In order to succeed, the Pharisees had to deemphasize the idea of obedience to the leadership and to stress, instead, inner controls based on reason and conscience. To do this, their emphasis had to be more on the individual, his civil and spiritual rights, and above all on his right to life. Thus purification became secondary to the persevering and furthering of the physical and spiritual health of the individual. By this logic, later Talmudists were even able to prescribe unclean substances if this aided the patient, and dissection of the dead if it answered an important point in medical research.

EARLY MEDICINE

Among early peoples, as indeed among some today, disease was looked on as having a supernatural origin, the work of an unfriendly demon or angry god. Attempts to rid the body of disease consisted of a variety of techniques, for instance, sacrifices calculated to appease the deity involved, fasting, adherence to dietary laws, and sometimes primitive operations such as trephining. Through accidental and trial-and-error inclinations early man learned that certain herbs, plants, and natural phenomena possessed medicinal characteristics. Mud baths in soil slightly radioactive were encouraged without understanding as to the medicinal properties involved; foxglove, containing digitalis, was prescribed for heart disease.

Both the Babylonians and the Egyptians possessed medical libraries and developed medical "know-how." The Egyptians were advanced in their knowledge of medicine. They knew much about anatomy and used it in their mummification processes. In the temples were medical schools; diseases were catalogued and classified according to symptoms. From the evidence viewed in tombs, we are likewise to believe that they did some surgery, understood much about the properties of various herbs, and even knew that the heart was the center of the circulatory system of the blood.

In the Ebers papyrus of Egypt dating back several thousand years before Christ, we have a wealth of information about early medical science. This papyrus provides information about the variety of Egyptian medicine and drugs. Though a vast number of incantations are given to accompany some of the prescriptions, showing that superstitious and religious formulas were considered prominent factors in disease, there are, nonetheless, more than 900 prescriptions set forth. According to Thorwald (1962), the writers of this manuscript knew and used at least one third of the medicinal plants and herbs listed in modern pharmocopeia.

The ancient Hebrews were unquestionably influenced by Egyptian and Babylonian medicine. Some kind of stay in Egypt by the descendants of Abraham is supported by historical evidence. Also, there is evidence that Moses and his lieutenants were educated in the wisdom of Egypt. De Vaux (1961) believes that there was a considerable medical influence in Hebraic law codes from the fact that there were many Egyptian names among the Levites, the priestly cast of the ancient Hebrews. Furthermore, there is also considerable similarity between some passages of the Hebrew law and the Code of Hammurabi.

In any event the first medical references in the Old Testament are found in texts dating before the Exodus, and archeological evidence and philological analysis have shown that some of the most important aspects of Jewish medicine already existed during the Patriarchal era. Within this nomadic society, healing was generally attended to by the family itself. Physicians were not mentioned in Israelite sources until the 8th century B.C. II Chronicles (16:12) gives the first historical reference to physicians, locating them in the reign of King Asa, in the 8th century B.C. The Israelites' most distinctive operation, circumcision, was done by the father, the head of the clan, and in one case the mother (Exod. 4:25).

The prophylactic regulations of the Mosaic code, which have been extolled as Israel's unique contribution to medicine, were enacted as public health laws to serve a settled people. Most of them were contained within the Book of Leviticus. Besides the rules on the Sabbath, circumcision, and sexual relationships, which predated the Exodus, the code contained provisions dealing with diet, hygiene, cleanliness, and sanitation.

In the light of subsequent discoveries, the Hebrew dietary laws were eminently rational and correct in their formulations of what was potentially clean or safe food. Vegetarianism was permitted except for the fruit of newly planted trees, but among mammals, only herbivorous animals which parted the hoof were considered acceptable (Lev. 11:3–8, Deut. 14:4–8). All insects except locusts, rapacious aquatic and predatory birds, and fishes without fins or scales were forbidden. The beneficial nature of these ordinances is demonstrated by the fact that under subtropical conditions, meat from vegetarian animals is much less likely to contain food poisoning agents than that of the carnivores. Restrictions against swine were especially severe, but for good reasons. The hog is subject to infestation by Trichenella spiralis and tapeworms. The Egyptians also had a prohibition against pork.

Other features in Hebrew medicine were related to hygiene and personal cleanliness. Hebrew laws considered all body discharges as unclean (Lev. 15:1–15). These regulations incorporated into the purification framework extended to both abnormal body discharges as might be found in gonorrhea and normal emissions as semen. Women were subject to special restrictions regarding the blood of their menstrual period and following parturition. Detailed laws existed relating to the removal of wastes, refuse, and the burial of the dead. Very comprehensive regulations existed relating to leprosy and other skin diseases.

In later Biblical literature there are more details regarding specific aspects of medical knowledge. The period of the monarchy that followed Judges was noteworthy for its excellent historical writing. Both I and II Samuel, which dated from Solomon's time, I and II Kings, written after the destruction of the Temple, record battle wounds, blindness, madness, giantism, and supernumerary digits. But, perhaps, the most vivid reporting came in the description of the bubonic plague that afflicted the Philistines after the capture of the ark (I Sam. 5:6–15). The Israelites described the tumors produced and singled out the mice that carried the flea vector as agents for the transmission of the disease [see S. H. Blondheim, "The First Recorded Epidemic of Pneumonic Plague: The

Bible. I Sam. VI," *Bulletin of the History of Medicine* **29** (1955), 327–345].

The books of Kings and the literature of the preexilic period no longer reflected a pastoral society but a state with the resources and organization to afford large engineering works such as the fortresses and waterworks at Gibeon, Megiddo, and Lachish, to field professional armies, and to maintain a large leisure class. During this period the Hebrews developed medical resources consisting of soothing ointments, spices used for embalming, and for ritual purposes. Physicians also appeared for the first time in spite of the fact that the reference in II Chronicles 17 was not complimentary. Surgery had improved to the point where fractures were now reduced and bandaged (Ezek. 30:21). The trephined heads at Lachish (c. 700 B.C.) show that this may have been a recognized practice for treatment of battle casualties (Kenyon, 1965). Two instances of artificial respiration done by Elijah (I Kings 17:17–24) and Elisha (IV Kings 4:32) show a high degree of clinical skill.

After the Babylonian exile the development of Hebrew medicine begins to derive something from the influence of Greece. Philo Judaeus, the Alexandrian Jew, who lived from 70 B.C. to 40 A.D., while making use of an allegorical method to explain the scriptures, could express the ideas therein in terms of both Hebrew and Greek philosophical thought with the result that the Hebrew ideas became considerably modified by Greek influence.

In addition, however, it should be noted that Hebrew literature also records a considerable amount of events related to personality problems and assessment procedures. There is a considerable discussion of the problems of anxiety in Job. Saul's apparent paranoia is described in I Sam. 18:10; 30–34; 28:20, and 31:5. Certainly there are many lasting tributes to mental stages in the Psalms where sequences of inferiority feelings, depression, guilt, expiation, anxiety, release and sublimation are described. There are some evidences of personality assessment and testing provided also. One of these is Eliezer's test of Rebecca for spontaneity of kindness.

> He was resting his camels by a well close to the town, just at the time of evening when women go out to draw water, and he prayed thus: O Lord, who are the God of my master Abraham speed my errand today and show kindness to my master Abraham. I have taken up my post by this well, and the daughters of the citizens will be coming out to draw water. It may be that one of them, when I ask her to let down her pitcher and give me drink, will say, Here is drink for thee, and I will water thy camels as

well. Let this be the bride thou has chosen for thy servant Isaac; if it proves so, I shall know that thou are showing kindness to my master (Gen. 24:12–14).

Other examples are the elimination of cowardly warriors by a test of how men drink from a stream. Those who drank from their hands were selected whereas those who got down and lapped the water were rejected (Judg. 7:1–8). The wisdom of Solomon in deciding the mother of the child is another instance of comparative psychological sophistication (III Kings 3:16–28). But all of these examples serve to reinforce the primary notion that physical illness as well as psychological illness is a function of religious approximation to the law and the prophets. Even as physical illness could occur as a result of not observing the dietary laws, so mental illness could be related to the hidden sin, and the unpurged guilt (see Book of Job).

It is clear from the foregoing that both physical and psychological adjustment were measured in relationship to the individual's conforming to the prescriptions and ritual of the law: consequences that were attributed to God's vengeance but most likely were administered by their own consciences and sense of guilt.

THE BEGINNINGS OF PHILOSOPHY

Philosophy really had its beginnings in Grecian thought. It did not spring up full blown in any one locale or another, but it seems to have developed out of an attempt by many thinking individuals to analyze and to explain the conditions of life and existence. Man has always attempted to justify his behavior and existence in terms of thought. In the earlier civilizations of Sumeria and Egypt, as well as in Israel, the explanation and justification of man's behavior was couched in terms of magic or theology. Whatever was not understood in these cultures found an explanation in religious tradition. Israel came close to philosophy in its Wisdom Literature, but it was the Greeks who first sought to provide a naturalistic explanation for man's environment and behavior.

There are many possible sources for the rise of a philosophical mode of thought in Greece. Some of them are the basic domestic religion with its accent on man's divine potentialities, the geographic and political factors that divided sections of Greece into small compartments, the spirit of individualism and competition that is so manifest in the Olympic meets and athletic games, the rise of a limited but distinctly new form of democratic government, the lack of an organized and strongly entrenched priesthood, and a generalized feeling that "man is the measure of all things."

The earliest Greek speculation in philosophy seems to have been concerned with the quest for understanding the nature of reality. Greek thinkers were searching for a basic substratum or foundation essential to all reality. *Thales,* a citizen of Miletus on the western coast of Asia Minor, is generally considered to be one of the first Greek philosophers. By his prediction of an eclipse of the sun on May 28, 585 B.C., he achieved a degree of distinction among his compatriots. This gave him a standing that encouraged him to express some theories about the nature of the universe. He advanced the idea that the basic element present in everything was water. Thales seems also to have been the first Greek to use and to adapt the Egyptian discoveries in geometry. He had traveled to Egypt and brought back with him much Egyptian knowledge. Thales' geometric teachings consisted of a variety of propositions that were proved by a deductive method—taking them for the first time into the wide realm of universal rather than specific application. He insisted that abstract or general principles of operation existed which formed a basis of empirical observation. He, therefore, approached the nature of empirical phenomena with the idea that there was a universal substratum or principle of operation. This was a quest for the ultimate nature of reality. His conclusions suggested that the universal substance was water. His observations in astronomy, mathematics, geometry, and experience apparently led him to this conclusion.

Thales' successors, *Anaximander* and *Anaximines,* advanced the theories that the universal substance was fire and air, respectively. Later on *Empedocles* was to name the four major elements, earth, air, fire, and water, as the basic substratum. The quest eventually led *Democritus* to state that the ultimate nature of the universe was determined by minute atoms! From these early beginnings, philosopher-scientists began the long unending process of explaining and verifying the nature of reality.

The next philosophical movement took place in the extreme western Greek world—southern Italy. Just as the two schools of thought were separated by a geographic gulf, so also were they far apart in their philosophical viewpoints. *Pythagoras,* the founder of the school, is a rather shadowy and mystic figure who seems to have traveled extensively in the East (580–507). Pythagoras was very interested in mathematics, since he had been the pupil of Thales and had visited Egypt at Thales' suggestion. Pythagoras rejected the pessimism of the Homeric epics and advocated a mystical approach to philosophy. He felt that man was the center of the universe, but that man had an immortal spirit which was entombed in the body. To Pythagoras and the quasi-secret society of followers who accepted his ideas, the chief goal of life was purification from evil and spiritual freedom from the body. Knowledge was the means of this redemption. Religion was a by-product of their philosophic quest for the nature of reality. The studies of Pythagoras further led him to believe that the key to the universe was not to be found in water, fire, or air—as the Milesians had advanced—but, instead, in the mathematical abstractions of numbers. Moreover, he conceived of numbers not as attributes or properties of various substrata but as the ultimate reality in themselves. Hence, the philosophical, religious, and aesthetic ideas propounded by the Pythagorean school were all based on combinations and harmonies of the numbers of Pythagoras; the essential substratum underlying reality was a balanced equilibrium that ordered the universe, imparted health to the body, and the qualities of goodness to the soul. Philosophy was a serious quest for personal sanctification through wisdom.

Many men contributed to the individualization of thought that permeated Greece at this time. *Heraclitus* (500 B.C.) believed that the universe was in a constant change of flux, *Protagoras* (481–411) is known for his famous dictum "Man is the measure of all things, of things that are, that they are, of things that are not, that they are not." This is the famous statement of relativity that spearheaded the sophist movement.

The Sophists were a group of traveling philosophers. They were characterized by a certain spirit of opportunism. Not by plan or intent, but rather by the peculiar circumstances that existed in Greece, they proved to be very important in the development of a spirit of critical individualism. They accentuated the place of the individual in Greek thought and stressed the worth of his ideas and his goals over that of the collective state enterprise. They frankly doubted the existence of the Greek gods and, by asking questions, provoked considerable thought. They acted as yeast that produced the intellectual fermentation characteristic of the golden age of Athenian civilization.

PLATO AND IDEALISM (427–347 B.C.)

One of the persisting philosophies in Western culture has been that of idealism. It still underlies much of contemporary thinking, since it postulates an essential dualism in the universe between ideas and physical matter, spirit and flesh. It places a primary importance on the subjectivity of ideas as against physical matter. Plato's world consisted of a real world of ideas or concepts that constituted the ultimate nature of reality. He considered the everyday life a temporary and transitory existence in which the rational soul longed for previous delights. The world of physical phenomena is deceitful, untrustworthy, and temporary. At best, it is a faint material copy of the world of ideas. Knowledge and learning are illusory unless reason directs them toward the reminiscence of things forgotten.

Plato's Metaphysics[1]

Plato's metaphysical system has often been contrasted with that of Aristotle. Actually, Aristotle refined some of the elements of Plato's system and qualified them. Plato accented a dichotomy between a world of ideas and a world of reality. To understand Platonic thought, it is necessary to reverse our concepts of real and apparent. For Plato, the *real* world was the world of archetypes or ideas and the *apparent* world was the world of our senses. Thus Plato thought that pure ideas constituted the only true reality. The ordinary world of things we see around us is not real; it is, rather, a series of mere shadows cast by the true reality of the idea world. Plato derived this concept from his soul theory. In his *Phaedrus* Plato has Socrates describe the way in which souls move up and down in their preexistent abode. In their movement up and down, which for some strange reason Socrates believed happened seven times, all souls were allowed to catch glimpses of these pure idea concepts. These ideas were the archetypes, the original, primal ideas of truth, beauty, justice, mercy, temperance, etc. The more of these archetypes a soul was permitted to see, the wiser, more temperate, and just would be the person whom the soul inhabited later on. On the contrary, the fewer ideas seen, the less knowledge and wisdom would be manifest in subsequent earthly life. This soul theory, which even in translation reads like beautiful poetry, has had very important consequences for the Western world. In brief, what Plato did was to create two worlds, a real world of ideas inaccessible to ordinary men, and the world of everyday events and things, wherein man was continually being deceived by his faulty sensory perception.

[1] *Note.* The rise of philosophy in the golden age of Athens can certainly be related to the high degree of Athenian individualism. There is an interesting parallel to modern-day problems in the characteristics of this period. First there was military success over the Persians, the rise of a considerable economic security through trade, the gaining of limited democracy through the reforms of Solon and Cleisthenes, the systematic discounting of the older religion of the hearth, and a great reconstruction of public buildings marking a rise in architecture. Art, philosophy, sculpture, and drama were all encouraged and heavily rewarded by the wealthy classes of Athens. Aeschylus, Sophocles, Aristophanes, Euripides, Zenophon, Herodotus, and Phidias are a few of the names associated with this period.

Second, although the account of idealism begins with Plato it should be pointed out that Socrates, Plato's teacher, was the unquestionable stimulus for not only much intellectual probing but also for a method of intellectual and behavioral change. This method will be discussed later in the chapter.

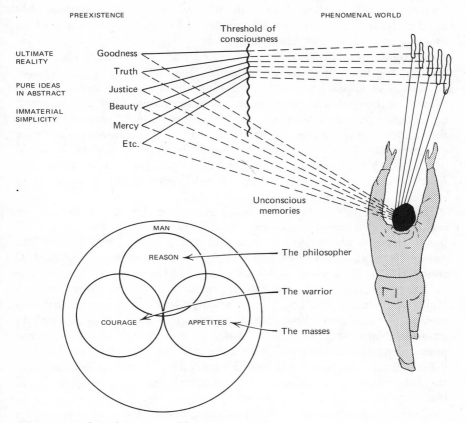

Figure 1 **The Platonic world.**

Unfortunately, Plato had difficulty in relating the world of actual phenomena to the so-called ultimate reality of the idea world. All he could say was that the world of physical phenomena is but a faint and imperfect copy of the spiritual world. In point of fact, he depended on a kind of arbitrary predestination of man's soul for the key to why some people are fit to be philosophers and others are not. Even though Socrates supposedly admonished us to know ourselves first, true understanding of the world of ideas is somehow dependent on an intangible characteristic known in our terms as intuition (see Figure 1).

Psychology and the Nature of Man

Plato's psychology was closely tied to his concept of the soul. If we recall that Plato believed that the soul spent time in the abode of souls between periods of inhabiting a body, his psychology will be more readily intelligible. It was a fundamental premise of Plato's metaphysical outlook that an individual was born *already knowing what he is capable of knowing*. No one can possibly understand and express more than what his soul has been predisposed to learn. Thus, in effect, learning is the elicitation of capabilities and knowledge already stored in the remote corners of the soul. The teacher's role is to lead these faint memories out of the unconscious to a conscious recognition. The teacher effects this through certain questions that are designed to jog this faint reminiscence of a prior life. Strange as this may seem to the modern student, it should not be overlooked that the very word education comes from two Latin words *e ducere*, meaning literally to lead forth or, to paraphrase, to extract.

Even as Plato's metaphysics is characterized by the dichotomy or polarity of idea world versus the phenomenal world, so man as a composite being is characterized by a soul and a body. The soul was the pure essence, the efficient or effective reason for rational and intellectual conduct. The Greeks equated soul with consciousness and breath. The unique characteristic of man was his rationality and his ability to generalize utilizing abstractions. As a result, Plato could reason that this portion of man, generating as it did abstract concepts, was in itself an immaterial pure substance. Since it was pure substance, it was not composed of parts or matter and, therefore, was not subject to mortality or deterioration. This was the essential vital spirit of man that was not only the sole cause of all thinking but also was the ultimate root of all learning.

The body, on the other hand, was composed of lesser vital principles that were characterized by courage and the appetites. All three of the vital principles had a localized residence. The rational principle was anchored to the brain, the spirit of courage was located in the chest, and the appetites in the abdomen or belly. Because of the pure nature of the rational soul, the body tended to blind the soul to the nature of truth and good.

All men, thought Plato, reflect a dominance of one or the other of these three principles of activity. The philosopher was dominated by reason, the warrior by the spirit of courage, and the common man by his appetites. The predominance that Plato placed on reason and the recognition that few, indeed, are capable of governing their life solely by principles of reason showed the nature of man's interminable psychological conflict. Reason was the very essence of man. Although Plato did not question the reality of the lower appetites of man, he suggested that they must be submerged to the primacy of reason. The rational soul of man was the essential cause of reason.

It was the soul that perceived phenomena and formed concepts. In the allegory of the cave, Plato explained how the common man is like a captive chained in a cave in such a fashion that he cannot move but must look at a wall. Light (truth) streamed into the cave from behind the individuals. All that the captive could see of reality was the shadow on the wall (sensory experience and physical phenomena). Sensory processes, then, merely supplied the raw material from which the rational soul digested the essential notes—which should conform to the world of ideas.

Traces of the concept of the unconscious can be readily discerned in Plato. In the *Republic* speaking of the blind movements of the soul, Plato describes the searching of the soul:

. . . which ascends from sole half-night kind of day to the true light of existence, which we will term true philosophy (Davis, 1849, 210).

The very analogy of the cave cited above with man's gradual liberation from darkness hinted strongly of the determinist element of the unconscious:

Behold men, as it were, in an underground cave-like dwelling having its entrance open toward the light and extending through the whole cave—within it persons who from childhood upward have had chains on their legs and their necks, so as, while abiding there, to have the power of looking forward only, but not to turn round their heads by reason of their chains, their light coming from a fire that burns above and afar off, and behind them (202).

Plato's conception of the role of the principles of the human soul showed a striking foreshadowing of the later Freudian conception of id, ego, and superego. As Tiebout (1952) has written:

Plato, as we have said, presents in certain of his dialogues a "medical" psychology and what might be called an "orthopsychiatric" ethic. In his own thought, of course, this prosiad, "medical" analysis is bound up with his "second level" vision of the nature of evil and the way of salvation . . . In his analysis of the nature, the health, and the pathology of the soul, Plato distinguishes three faculties or principles (*dynameis*) in the human psyche: the intellect (*nous*) or reasoning part (*to logistiken*), the contentious or willful part (*to thymoeides*), and the appetitive or desiring part (*to epithymetiken*).

The function of the rational power in the soul is to organize and control the other two powers. The proper function of this power constitutes wisdom or "prudence" (*sophia phronesis*). The reasoning part thus plays in Plato's system a role analogous to the Freudian ego (155–157).

It can be seen from the analysis of Plato's concept of reason and intellection that he weighed this function of the soul as the highest. Similar analysis of the appetitive portion of the soul reveals that Plato conceived the "natural desire of pleasure" (*emphytos epithymis hedonou*) in terms consistent with the Freudian id. For this appetitive principle in man is described as essentially irrational, lawless, and insatiable.

The other principle of vital activity bore some resemblance to the Freudian superego or conscious ego-ideal. Plato conceived man as a creature being driven by many forces. The soul was a principle of movement, and true knowledge hearkened back to a preexistent world of ideas.

Ethical Values and Personality Theory

In his ethical views, Plato conceived the goal of man's moral life to be individual happiness or well-being. This well-being demanded a harmony in the psyche between the vital principle of reason, will or contentiousness, and appetite.

All the Platonic virtues (*aretai*) center in this conception of the well-balanced ordered soul. The key "virtue" is justice (*dikaiosyne*) which means a state in which everything is in its proper place, functioning naturally. The other three "virtues" temperance (*sophrosyne*) courage (*andreia*) and wisdom (*sophia*) refer, primarily, to the proper functioning of each of the three parts of the soul. Temperance signifies the proper moderation and subordination of "desire," courage the properly disciplined "spirited" element, and wisdom the rule of the rational element. It is really reason (*nous*) or the rational principle (*to logistikon*) that is the saving remnant of the psyche, for it is in virtue of the rule of reason that "justice" prevails in the soul (Tiebout, 158).

From the analysis of the three major forces in man, it is then comparatively easy to understand Plato's concept of personality. He believed that each individual showed a dominance of one or other of these aspects of the soul. Those in whom reason dominated were the philosopher-guardians in Plato's conception of government. Those in whom manly courage was uppermost were the warriors and soldiers. And those who were dominated by their belly and who lacked moderation and temperance as well as reason and courage, were the "hoi polloi" or the masses. What

Plato suggested, of course, was a proper proportion between these varied sources of behavior. Since the cultivation of reason and the higher virtues was comparatively rare, the reward for this kind of behavior was obviously statesmanship.

Religion and Aesthetics

Plato identified religion with philosophy. In his opinion, the highest object of philosophical speculation and the object of religious worship are identical. Plato united the practical and theoretical in his design for the state and could not conceive of a world of theory without some practical results. His purpose in writing the *Republic* was to construct a practical theory of government and an education system based on what he considered to be the appropriate theoretical framework. Thus he conceived atheism not only as impious, but as irrational. He believed that there was a God and he deduced this from the order and design that could be recognized not only in animals but in the larger world of astronomy and physics. This kind of an argument is known in philosophy as a teleological argument. He disagreed with the earlier Greek materialists who considered that man had originally evolved from matter. Plato's entire metaphysical outlook centered around the reality of an ultimate idea world, and it supported the notion of the existence of an Absolute Good, or the supreme idea of wisdom. Seldom does Plato mention God as a personal being but, instead, as a guiding principle of providence that is everywhere present. He also mentioned the existence of intermediary deities such as a world soul, the soul of stars, and demons of air and water.

In summary, Plato's metaphysical theory recognized that the highest of the ideas is the *Good*. But the *Beautiful* is more outstanding. Plato conceived beauty as harmony and identified harmony with symmetry. The good, therefore, is beautiful, and phenomena that partake of the good also partake of the beautiful. Art has for its object the realization of the beautiful. Plato accordingly taught that all artistic productions, the works of sculptors and painters as well as the ones of poets and rhetoricians, should be placed at the service of the state and be so organized as to assist the guardians in the establishment of a moral community.

ARISTOTLE AND REALISM (384–322 B.C.)

The greatest of Plato's pupils from a philosophical and historical aspect was Aristotle. Born into a family of physicians, he came from the Stagira, at the age of seventeen, to Athens and attached himself to the school of

Plato. For 20 years he associated with Plato, until the latter's death in 347. After the death of Plato, he left Athens until 335 when he returned and founded a school known as the Lyceum, which was a rival to Plato's Academy. During the interim period between Plato's death and his return to Athens, Aristotle served as the tutor of Alexander the Great.

In his early years, Aristotle seems to have been an enthusiastic Platonist in his views. After he left Athens, Aristotle's views began to change and even his presentation of them was altered. At first, he tended to follow Plato's method of presentation through a dialogue and discussion with several individuals. Later, he abandoned this technique and wrote in a straightforward manner. Although we shall discuss here Aristotle's views and his criticism of Platonic thought, it should be noted that Aristotle was not at all popular in antiquity. He was overshadowed completely by Plato and the Platonic school. Aristotle's real contribution must be reserved for the medieval synthesis of his ideas by Thomas Aquinas. These same ideas are still echoed in the philosophy of Neo-Thomism.

Criticism of Idealism

Aristotle criticized Plato's resort to a metaphysical idealism to explain the nature of reality. Plato had denied the validity of common elements in phenomena and had attached an unjustifiable significance to the abstracted ideas that form ultimate reality. Thus, he had suggested that there is a mystical form of whiteness that exists in a world of pure being. Aristotle denied this concept completely. He said that whiteness inhered in the subject that was white. There was no need to presume or to postulate the existence of a universal idea of whiteness off on a cloud. This was the basic formulation of the realist approach to reality. In this thesis, as Wild (1955, 17) has commented:

> The universe is made up of real, substantial entities, existing in themselves and ordered to one another by extra-mental relations. These entities and relations really exist whether they are known or not. To be is not the same as to be known. We ourselves and the other entities around us actually exist, independent of our opinions and desires. This may be called the thesis of independence.

Aristotle's criticism of Plato is based on empirical grounds. He believed in the world of phenomena as they appear. He assumed the necessity of cause and effect relations and believed that the world was obviously operating under certain general principles. The explanation of the world of phenomena had to incorporate (1) a method of explaining the process of change and becoming, and (2) the elements of ultimate causation and orderly controls. Thus, Aristotle denied that there was some system of mystical ideas or universals that existed over and beyond the actual phenomena of experience. He suggested that universals exist in the human mind alone and that they are abstracted from empirical evidence of experienced phenomena. For example, our notion of whiteness is a universal concept, but this universal idea does not exist in reality; it is simply a mental concoction resulting from our phenomenal experiencing of objects that are white. We see John who has a white shirt, we see Patty with a white blouse. From numerous experiences with the element of whiteness, we create a mental concept of white in our mind. The same process takes place in other universal concepts such as man, woman, house, and the like. This approach to phenomena is termed realism. It postulates that reality is ordered to itself by extramental relations, principles, laws, etc. In other words, that the universe is held together by certain immutable laws and bonds. Man can know these laws and bonds in part as they are, but not necessarily in their absolute sense (that is, as known to God).

Psychology and Theory of Knowledge

Aristotle postulated the existence of phenomena outside the mind as a basic axiom in his theory of knowledge. He considered science and philosophy as equivalent terms and divided all human knowledge into three areas: (1) practical, (2) poetical, and (3) theoretical. By practical science, he meant politics and ethics; by poetic science, he included not only the philosophy of poetry, music, and the study of culture but also aesthetics. By theoretical science he understood (1) physics, (2) mathematics, and (3) metaphysics.

Aristotle's theory of knowledge was based on empirical investigation. He maintained that man's knowledge was dependent on sense knowledge. But he avoided the contention of Locke, made many centuries later, that the sum of all man's knowledge is based on sense experience. Aristotle believed that man had five principles of activity, or faculties. They were: (1) the nutritive principle, (2) the sensitive principle, (3) the appetitive, (4) the locomotive, and (5) the rational principle. He thus conceived man as a being possessed of a number of faculties and the soul as being a vital principle of movement. The substantial attribute of the soul was the power to think and, of course, the ultimate abstraction of sense knowledge and digestion of sense data was ascribed to the intellectual faculty of reason.

Aristotle considered sensation to be dependent on an alteration of phenomena. But, Aristotle maintained that it was the human mind that digested the data of experience and sensation. He likened sensation to some combustible material that was capable of burning but that required intellection for ignition. The sensation of external phenomena requires the presence of the intellectual faculty to recognize, to synthesize, and to establish concepts. Aristotle considered man's five external senses: hearing, smelling, sight, taste, and touch as primary avenues to discern motion and change. The intellect then employed four internal senses to analyze the in-put of sensation, (1) memory, (2) imagination, (3) instinct, and (4) common sense. From the external senses, raw data filtered up to the internal senses wherein it was compared with previous experiences, analyzed, and finally prepared for reconstruction by the intellect into universal or abstract ideas.

Man's knowledge of external phenomena can therefore be compared to the process of coming up from a dark basement into the full light of day. The first steps in the process of knowledge are sensory elaboration of phenomena. Subsequently, higher on the stairs, the action of the internal senses is applied to elementary sensory data. Finally, the intellect of man digests the essential qualities of experience in the form of a universal idea.

Aristotle does not use the term logic in the sense that we do today. He considered logic as an analytic process leading to scientific conclusions. Thus, Aristotle conceived of science and philosophy as one and the same things and insisted that the methodology of natural science was the same as that of philosophy. In a very real sense, Aristotle held that philosophy was the justification of phenomenal relations in the purest and most universal manner.

Aristotle, too, was looking for a universal substratum. He actually conceived it to be being. Thus, the ultimate nature of reality is constituted by being, and metaphysics in Aristotle's view, then, is the knowledge of immaterial Being, or of Being in the highest degree of abstraction. Aristotle saw in the analysis of thought processes the fundamental basis for a logical methodology. In analyzing thought processes and concepts, he concluded that all our thoughts and concepts could be divided into a number of categories. These categories were substantial forms or methods of our thinking about phenomena. They were (1) substance, (2) quantity, (3) quality, (4) relation, (5) activity, (6) passivity, (7) place, (8) time, (9) situation, and (10) disposition. These categories are the classes of things or the framework created by the human mind to analyze phenomena.

Aristotle examined the nature of knowledge and scientific procedure in his *Posterior Analysis*. He pointed out that all knowledge is based on scientific demonstration and certain intuitive premises that the human mind brings to the analysis of phenomena. From the very logic of thought, Aristotle believed there are certain premises: one of them was the *law of contradiction,* that is, that a thing cannot be and not be at the same time. Induction he defined as a reasoning process whereby one proceeded from particular facts to general ones. Aristotle in his discussion on the scientific method developed the syllogism. The syllogism was a tool for logical thinking. It was based on the process whereby individual facts may be deduced from universal laws. Aristotle believed that the first step in any investigation was to determine the object of the investigation. Subsequently, through observation and categorization of phenomena, it was possible to discover hypotheses. Some of these hypotheses may seem absurd from the beginning. All knowledge is based on facts. What cannot be demonstrated as a fact must be accepted as a premise on grounds of immediate self-evidence such as the principle of contradiction or on the witness and testimony of something more secure than science, that is, theology. If these conditions are met, then the truth obtained by demonstrative knowledge will be necessary. Hence, a scientific demonstration, in Aristotle's opinion, was "an inference from necessary premises."

It is this quality of necessary inference that distinguishes fact from opinion. For in Aristotle's philosophy of science, scientific knowledge and its object differ from opinion in that scientific knowledge is commensurately universal and proceeds by necessary connections, and that which is necessary cannot be otherwise. Thus, Aristotle was saying that the first principles of any science cannot be demonstrated in that science, but that principles which are first, absolutely, are indemonstrable. They belong to the classification of facts that are known by rational intuition. Thus, for example, the nature of man's soul is evident as a mover. This inference, Aristotle would deduce from the fact that a thing is or is not. The difference is that in being there is movement, and in nonbeing there is a lack of movement.

It is evident from this analysis that Aristotle differed considerably from Plato in his metaphysics, theory of knowledge, psychology, and scientific methodology. Plato had resorted to a world of universal ideas as the ultimate ground of existence. Aristotle posited the universal only in the mind, but with roots in physical phenomena. Plato enunciated a theory of knowledge strongly dependent on deductive procedures. Knowledge was a sort of guessing game ending in the most satisfactory cases in full reminiscence of the past. For Aristotle, knowledge was based on an essential dependence on sensory processes. But, with great care, Aristotle avoided, on the one hand, the theory of material sensism, namely that the higher processes of the mind are merely agglutinated combinations of primary sensations (for example, Locke) and, on the other, the theory of idealism, in which resort is had to universals outside the realm of the mind.

In his psychology he is closest to Plato. For both Plato and Aristotle recognized the existence of a hierarchy of vital principles and functions in man. Because of the essential immaterial quality of the rational principle, Aristotle was faced with the problem of explaining how the rational principle apprehended individual sensory data. It would never do to have primary sensation directly effect the rational principle, for this would mean that material forces could effect an immaterial spirit of rationality. Thus, through the use of five external senses, four internal senses, and the informing principle of rationality, Aristotle developed a theory of knowledge whereby first sensation is gradually spiritualized through the internal senses and ultimately is assimilated into a universal state by the abstracting power of the intellect.

Metaphysics and Physics

Metaphysics for Aristotle was the inquiry into the highest principle of being. One of the major problems facing any metaphysician is to determine the relationship of becoming or potency to actuality or finalization. Potency and actuality for Aristotle represent the ultimate principles of change and are two states of being. They are metaphysical constituents of reality. But there are also some physical constituents to the nature of reality. Four other constituent factors are involved. These are causes, or that which in any way influences the production of something. The classes of causes are (1) *material*, (2) *formal*, (3) *efficient*, and (4) *final*. All being is composed of *matter* and *form*. Matter is described as the prime stuff of the universe. It is undetermined and unresolved until united with form—which is the determining factor. The universe can thus be considered a cosmic organization in which these four causes are acting on matter. The *material cause* is the raw stuff of which everything is made, for example, in modern terms, atoms; *the formal cause* is considered the exact form that determines the shape or construction of the matter into determinate being; the *efficient cause* is the active force of construction; and the *final cause* can be considered the ultimate purpose for which the other causes were utilized. To take a rather common example, let us consider the question of a salami. The material cause of salami would be bits of meat in an indeterminate mass. The formal cause would be the conceptual notion of the salami as possessed in the mind of the maker. The efficient cause would be his actual molding of the salami into the form possessed in his mind, and the final cause would be his desire to market it for money.

In Aristotle's notion, matter and form characterized the entire range of being in the universe. Matter was the imperfect element, and form was the perfecting element. From matter arose all the imperfections, limitations, and corruptibility of physical phenomena, whereas from form proceeded the specific nature of things. Matter presumed a common denominator to all physical phenomena—this common denominator was *being*—hence, being was the most universal of all concepts.

The central theme of Aristotle's physics was centered on the concept of motion. He distinguished three kinds of motion (1) quantitative, (2) qualitative, and (3) spatial. Space he considered the interval between bodies. Time was a universal concomitant of temporal existence and was the measurement of motion. Both space and time were necessary attributes of physical phenomena and both were conditioned or understood through the mind of man. Without mind, Aristotle thought, there would be no time.

These notions of physics were applied to astronomy by Aristotle. He subscribed to the current views of the earth being the center of the universe. He felt that the earth was stationary and spherical. It was surrounded by a sphere of air and a sphere of fire. These spheres daily revolved around the earth from east to west. Beyond the spheres were the stars, and beyond them the Deity who maintained all in motion.

Ethics and Politics

In Greek philosophy, theory and practical affairs were seldom joined. Nonetheless both Aristotle and Plato deduced applications of the metaphysics and psychological theories to the practical realm of ethics and politics. Aristotle agreed with Plato that the supreme good of man was happiness. Happiness, to Aristotle, was a conforming to the end for which man was made. The end of human existence was that form of good that was distinctly peculiar to man, and this in Aristotle's opinion was good appropriate to a rational being. Since there were two parts to the human soul, and they could be roughly divided into rational and irrational, man ought to live according to the rational principle.

Now the soul of man is divided into two parts, one of which has a rational principle in itself, and the other, not having a rational principle in itself, is able to obey such a principle. And we call a man in any way good because he has the virtues of these two parts. In which of them the end is more likely to be found is no matter of doubt to those who adopt our division; for in the world both of nature and of art, the inferior always exists for the sake of the better or superior, and the better or superior is that which has a rational principle. This principle, too, in our ordinary way of speak-

ing, is divided into two kinds for there is a practical and a speculative principle. This part, then, must evidently be similarly divided.
And there must be a corresponding division of actions; the actions
of the naturally better part are to be preferred by those who have it
in their power to attain to two out of the three or to all, for that is
always to every one the most eligible which is the highest attainable
by him. (*Aristotle, Politics, Book VII, Chapter 14*).

Virtue, for Aristotle, meant the practice of a good in the highest degree
possible for a given individual. Virtue is not just a feeling, or an occasional act, but is rather a fixed quality or habit of mind. Above all,
if virtue is to be truly operative, it is necessary for the lower forces
or passions of man to be subordinate to the higher rational principle.
Since the two major objects of man were considered to be Good and
Truth, there are then two kinds of virtues, moral and intellectual ones.
Moral virtues proceed from the faculty of choice or the rational appetite called the will. Intellectual virtues proceed from perfections of
the intellect itself without relation to other faculties. There are perfections of the scientific reason, such as understanding, science, and wisdom,
which are concerned with first principles, demonstration, and the search
for highest causes. There are perfections of the practical reason, such as
art, and practical wisdom. Justice is merely the observance of the right
order for all the faculties of man. In this sense, it is identical with the
concept of virtue. In a more restricted sense, justice applies to virtue that
regulates man's dealings with other men. It is, therefore, the political
virtue *par excellence*.

In his political doctrine, Aristotle governed his approach by the concept of justice as a political virtue. Man's social life begins with his
family, and the state exists to perpetuate the family intact. He considers
three forms of government: (1) monarchy, (2) aristocracy, and (3) republic. The best form of government for any given people is that which
best meets their needs. Although monarchy seems to be the ideal, an
aristocracy, not of wealth but of intellectual responsibility, seems to
Aristotle to be the best government.

In summary, Aristotle recommended an intellectual approach to education. In his opinion, knowledge is a good in itself and it is better to
know than not to know. Practical and vocational learning has a universal
place, but intellectual formation is the *summum bonum* of education.
The habit of learning and searching for wisdom is intellectual virtue.
The habit of practicing this intellectual virtue toward others is justice,
and the coordination of this entire process must be guided by the state;
and its enlightened philosopher rulers in an effort to develop what is

best in the individual both for himself and for the state. This is the concept of liberal education fully developed by Aristotle remaining as a profound challenge even to this present day.

Because of the complexity of Aristotle's views on the universe and on man, it is helpful to present in chart form some of the essential points of Aristotle's theories. Figures 2 and 3 are designed to summarize the foregoing discussions.

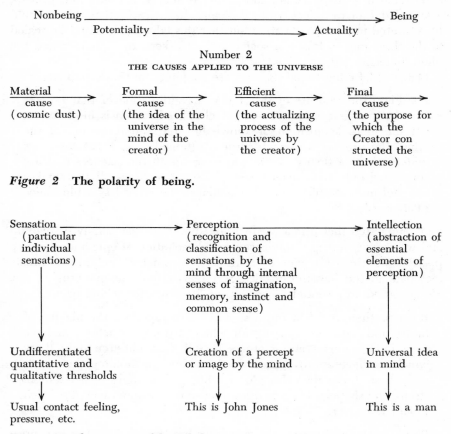

Nonbeing ————————————————→ Being
      Potentiality ————————————→ Actuality

Number 2
THE CAUSES APPLIED TO THE UNIVERSE

| Material cause (cosmic dust) | → | Formal cause (the idea of the universe in the mind of the creator) | → | Efficient cause (the actualizing process of the universe by the creator) | → | Final cause (the purpose for which the Creator con structed the universe) | → |

Figure 2 **The polarity of being.**

Sensation ————————→ Perception ————————→ Intellection
(particular individual sensations) / (recognition and classification of sensations by the mind through internal senses of imagination, memory, instinct and common sense) / (abstraction of essential elements of perception)

Undifferentiated quantitative and qualitative thresholds / Creation of a percept or image by the mind / Universal idea in mind

Usual contact feeling, pressure, etc. / This is John Jones / This is a man

Figure 3 **The process of knowledge.**

CLASSICAL CULTURAL TRANSMISSION AND BEHAVIOR MODIFICATION

Both Plato and Aristotle were very concerned with what can be called behavior formation. Both of them wrote extensively on the subject of learning and education, since they were concerned with the development of a knowledgeable but virtuous populace. Plato conceived education as a tool of the state to be administered by the elite. Plato, more than Socrates, was aware of the fact that all men are not teachable in the same sense. He did not, therefore, agree with Socrates that knowledge was the key to order and virtue. Plato deplored the notion that true knowledge could be dispensed wholesale to all men. Financial success, affluence, and technical skills were not the proper results of learning but, instead, a knowledge of the ideal truth. Basically, he believed that there should be a limited universal education but that this education should be scaled to the three major classes of society—the workers, the warriors, and the philosophers.

Plato's chief educational theories are contained in the *Republic*:

> For Plato the true life of the soul is a continuation of that process by which at first order rose out of chaos; education is information, not the mere acquisition of knowledge, but the formation of the mind, the process by which form is attained. . . . Education thus understood is a theory of life and sums up all the sciences that are concerned only with department of life; it includes all that makes the soul more perfect and all that makes the body less a hindrance (Peters, 1953, 89).

Plato suggested that primary education should consist mainly of reading and writing (grammar), the learning and recitation of epic and dramatic poetry, and the rudiments of arithmetic, geometry, and music. Music included all the humanities such as fine arts, culture, philosophy, etc. He proposed an essential censorship of literature for school use:

> It seems then, our first business will be to supervise the making of fables and legends, rejecting all which are unsatisfactory; and we shall induce nurses and mothers to tell their children only those which we have approved, and to think more of molding their souls with these stories than they do of rubbing their limbs to make them strong and shapely. Most of the stories now in use must be discarded (Plato 1957, 69).

Plato concluded his remarks on censorship thusly: ". . . the first principle to which all must conform in speech or writing is that heaven is not responsible for everything, but only for what is good" (1957, 72).

Plato conceived censorship as necessary, since an essential part of Greek education was composed of mimesis or dramatic imitation. In the imitation of dramatic compositions there was a fundamental identification, and Plato wished to make sure that the identification young men made was with the good and beautiful as he viewed it. Plato believed that education was a serious duty of the guardians and that all care should be exercised in controlling the nature of educational experience:

It will be easy enough, if only they will see to the one great thing, as the saying goes, though I would rather call it the one thing that is sufficient; education and nurture. If a sound education has made them reasonable men, they will easily see their way through all these matters as well as others which we will pass over for the moment, such as the possession of wives, marriage, and child-bearing, and the principle that here we should follow as far as possible the proverb which says that friends have all things in common.

Yes, all should go well then.

Moreover, when a community has once made a good start, its growth proceeds in a sort of cycle. If a sound system of nurture and education is maintained, it produces men of good disposition and these in their turn, taking advantage of such education, develop into better men than their forebears, and their breeding qualities improve among the rest, as may be seen in animals.

That is likely enough.

In short, then, those who keep watch over our commonwealth must take the greatest care not to overlook the least infraction of the rule against any innovation upon the established system of education either of the body or of the mind. When the poet says that men care most for the "newest air that hovers on the singer's lips," they will be afraid lest he be taken not merely to mean new songs, but to be commending a new style of music. Such innovation is not to be commended, nor should the poet be so understood. The introduction of novel fashions in music is a thing to beware of as endangering the whole fabric of society, whose most important conventions are unsettled by any revolution in that quarter . . . it would be harmless, he replied, were it not that, little by little this lawless spirit gains a lodgement and spreads imperceptibly to manners and pursuits and from thence with gathering force invades men's dealing with one another, and next goes on to attack the laws and the constitution with wanton recklessness, until it ends by overthrowing the whole structure of public and private life.

Really, said I. Is all that true?

So I believe, he replied.

Our children's pastimes, then, as I began by saying, must be kept from the first within stricter bounds; if any license be admitted they will catch the spirit and will never grow into law-abiding and well-conducted men. And so, when they have made a good beginning in their play and musical education has instilled a spirit of order, this reverence for law, in complete contrast to the license you were describing just now, will attend them in all their doings and foster their growth, restoring any institutions that may earlier have fallen into decay.

That is true.

As a consequence, they will rediscover rules of behavior which their predecessors have let fall into disuse, including matters supposed to be of little importance; how the young should be silent in the presence of their elders, give up their seats to them, and take dutiful care of their parents; not to mention details of personal appearance, such as the way their hair is cut and the clothes and shoes they wear. It would be silly, I think, to make laws on these matters; such habits cannot be established or kept up by written legislation. It is probable, at any rate, that the bent given by education will determine the quality of later life, by that sort of attraction which like things always have for one another, till they finally mount up to one imposing result, whether for good or ill, for that reason I should not myself be inclined to push legislation to that length (1957, 114–116).

Plato viewed education as the orderly process of imbuing young people in the culture and values acceptable to the state. Following the postulate established by his metaphysics and psychology, he believed that education should concentrate on the formation of those qualities and virtues in students that were desired by the teacher. Once a quality educational system had been established with the primacy of state loyalty and reason employed in the search of wisdom, Plato could see no further need for educational alteration.

For this reason, Plato advocated what can be called today a theory of mental discipline. He believed that arithmetic, geometry, astronomy, and music activities developed the individual's perception. Plato believed that mathematics: "rouses the naturally drowsy and dull and makes him quick, retentive and shrewd—a miraculous improvement of cultivation upon his native parts" (Plato, Laws, 1934, 130). As Kolesnik (1958) has remarked, Plato's theory on education did not seem to guarantee that any one of the subjects in the curriculum would, of and in itself, automatically guarantee intellectual competency. The *quadrivium*, or pursuit of the four liberal arts, arithmetic, geometry, astronomy, and music were necessary preludes to the process of *dialectic*. Through the study of these disciplines the mind was detached from material knowledge and sense impressions and began to rise to the realm of idea, truth, and being.

Here, then, seem to be the roots of the theory which was to grow and develop for centuries, and which was to play such an important part in educational practice in western civilization down to the present day—the theory which holds that the best possible type of education is purely intellectual; that not all men are capable of this great good, but that for those who are cultivation of the highest power of man's soul is the end of education; that this end is attainable through studies having a particular form; that the content of these studies is relatively unimportant, but that what matters most is the efficiency with which they train the mind (Kolesnik, 116).

In Platonic thought, man's intellectual development was a progression through the appetites, spirit of courage, to reason. Education, then, must result in wisdom that is based on a true integration or balance of conflicting desires. In this sense, education was the search for the good life—the reaching out for the true, the good, and the beautiful. This desire was in itself a sign of incompleteness, since man could become complete only by a systematic modification of his inordinate strivings. Aristotle regarded education as a branch of political science. That education was a subject of controversy in his age is shown from the following remarks:

Our age disputes a great deal about the ends and aims of education. There are different opinions as to what is to be learned by the young, either to make them virtuous or happy for life. It is still an open question whether more attention should be given to the development of the intellect or to the training of character. The education prevailing at the present time throws no light on the subject, nor does it decide whether the schools should fit the pupils to meet the needs of practical life, or train them to virtue, or introduce them to higher studies; each of these several views has found its defenders (Politics VII, 2).

Aristotle in his treatise on politics set forth the view that education should be liberal instead of practical. Although he recognized the need for the latter, he saw fit to choose the former as the more practical. He did not deny the fact that useful subjects are necessary and, in fact, ought to be a part of every child's education, but he suggested that this should not mean the inclusion of every possible practical subject.

The subject matter of some of his other treatises suggests the curriculum he may have had in mind: poetic, rhetoric, metaphysics, physics —subjects certainly suggestive of the classical liberal arts. He leaves little doubt, however, regarding the objectives of the liberal education that he proposes. The education worthy of a free man consists essentially in the cultivation of his intellect.

Aristotle reached the same conclusions in his *Ethics*. Here he was concerned with the identification, description and suggestion of means to the supreme good of man. The supreme good of man is that which is sought not for some other purpose, but because it is a good in itself. This is the ultimate message of Aristotle's concept of education. Education is better than no education. Practical and vocational education is a good form of education, but intellectual training is the supreme end of education.

Aristotle treated of the nature of the learning process also. He spoke of the laws of association of ideas and stated that ideas are associated by reason of (1) contiguity in space or time, (2) similarity, and (3) contrast. These laws of the association of ideas were used for many centuries, and were revived by Hartley in the 18th century. In addition, Aristotle recognized the basic concepts of reward and reinforcement as conditions of learning.

Concerning the nature of transfer of training, Aristotle considered the mind as somewhat analogous to the body. He believed that certain subjects in the academic curriculum had an intrinsic value for developing intellectual acumen. This is not to say that Aristotle believed mind was exactly similar to muscle and that training could be accomplished for both in the same manner. In Aristotle's psychology, the commanding principle of man was the rational immaterial soul. Obviously, one could not train an immaterial principle by material exercise. Nevertheless, through the effort made by the mind to learn the rigors of mathematical process, a sound foundation was created for the higher studies of logic and dialectic. Thus, Aristotle laid the foundation of a theory of mental discipline that has lasted to the present day. Aristotle, in keeping with his considerations on moral and intellectual virtue, believed that virtue was established only by long, repeated habits of discipline. He considered education as a form of virtue and believed that no man could possess intellectual virtue without prolonged effort and attempts at self-discipline. He did not state that any particular subject or other would result automatically in habits of mental discipline, but that this was one of the fundamental purposes of his educational theories cannot be denied.

Both Plato and Aristotle saw behavior being formed as the result of a learning process. The notion of learning and the identification of principles of learning underscore the formation of moral habits of virtue.

Aristotle, particularly, provided guidelines for the development of what can be called a balanced and adjusted personality. He suggested that moral virtue is acquired by the repetition, and imitation of habits of prudence, justice, and temperance wherein a moderation and balance is established between the intellectual concepts of good and bodily desires.

Since moral virtue was not an innate characteristic of man, Aristotle thought it had to be taught. It was taught through observation and imitation, and through the example of a community of scholars. For this reason, both Plato and Aristotle established special schools in the form of the Academy and the Lyceum. Both schools relied heavily on the discussion seminar technique that had been founded by Socrates. Both consisted of a kind of continuing seminar series in which scholars worked with a master philosopher in probing the intellectual and moral issues of the day. Learning thus included not only the formation of intellectual habits of reasoning but the systematic development of character and practical wisdom. Aristotle conceived intuition and insight as being basic components to the learning process. And his discussion of how the incontinent man acts against knowledge (Ross, 1954, 163–164) suggests that he advocated a process for evaluating contradictory behavior in an individual. He suggested that one had to decide, first, whether a given behavior was truly a human act, that is, one for which the individual could be considered responsible and, second, as to whether the individual was behaving in a certain way only in relationship to certain objects of knowledge or rather as a habitual attitude.

The goals of the cultural transmission through education and training for Plato and Aristotle were ultimately the contemplation of wisdom. And this wisdom both intellectual and moral was to be used for the services of the state. The methods for this procedure were concerned with a systematic imitation of exemplary behavior, the study of appropriate wisdom, and the use of intuition and logic in the analysis of man's problems. Aristotle speaks of the goal determination process as follows:

> Let us again return to the good we are seeking, and ask what it can be. It seems different in different actions and arts; it is different in medicine, in strategy, and in the other arts likewise. What then is the good of each? Surely that for whose sake everything else is done. In medicine this is health, in strategy victory, in architecture a house, in any other sphere something else, and in every action and pursuit the end; for it is for the sake of this that all men do whatever else they do. Therefore, if there is an end for all that we do, this will be the good achievable by action, and if there are more

than one, these will be the good achievable by action (Ross, 1954 *Ethics* 1.7, 11).

Thus it would appear that Aristotle advocated the determination of goals in behavior as related to anticipated outcomes or subjectively considered goods. Continuing then, he suggests a decision-making process.

And we must also remember what has been said before, and not look for precision in all things alike, but in each class of things such precision as accords with the subject matter, and so much as is appropriate to the inquiry. For a carpenter and a geometer investigate the right angle in different ways; the former does so in so far as the right angle is useful for his work, while the latter inquires what it is or what sort of thing it is, for he is a spectator of the truth. We must act in the same way then, in all other matters as well, that our main task may not be subordinated to minor questions. Nor must we demand the cause in all matters alike; it is enough in some cases that the *fact* be well established, as in the case of first principles; the fact is the primary thing or first principle. Now of first principles we see some by induction, some by perception, some by a certain habituation, and others too in other ways. But each set of principles we must try to investigate in the natural way, and we must take pains to state them definitely, since they have a great influence on what follows. For the beginning is thought to be more than half of the whole, and many of the questions we ask are cleared up by it (Ross, 1954 *Ethic* 1.7, 14).

Finally, Aristotle recognizes the fact that individuals do seek various kinds of happiness and need a clarification of their goals.

The characteristics that are looked for in happiness seem also, all of them, to belong to what we have defined happiness as being. For some identify happiness with virtue, some with practical wisdom, others with a kind of philosophic wisdom, others with these or one of these, accompanied by pleasure or not without pleasure; while others include also external prosperity (*Ibid*, 15).

Methods of inducing certain types of behavior are related to the learning process, including mental discipline, the censorship of the state educational enterprise, and the use of seminar discussion techniques. That understanding and rational acceptance was one of the criteria of effective education is seen in the interesting article by Halpern (1963) on the use of free association by Socrates. This article is drawn from an analysis of Aristophanes "The Clouds." Strepsiades, a rural merchant, has been driven deeply into debt by his son. Searching for a solution to his problems, he decides to enroll in Socrates' school. Stepsiades has no understanding of the socratic discipline of tutoring in the art of self-knowledge and logical reasoning. Although he attends all the routine of education, he exhausts Socrates' patience, and Socrates grows perplexed and angered altering his usual methods to what might be called free association. Socrates instructs Strepsiades to speak his mind freely.

SOCRATES. ... I have never seen a man so gross, so inept, so stupid, so forgetful. All the little quibbles, which I teach him, he forgets even before he has learnt them. Yet I will not give up. I will make him come out into the open air. Where are you Strepsiades? Come, bring your couch out here.

STREPSIADES. (from within): But the bugs will not allow me to bring it.

SOCRATES. Have done with such nonsense! Place it there and pay attention (Cited from Halpern, 424–425).

Socrates then tells Strepsiades to "ponder awhile over matters that interest you." He tells him to cover his head and says: "Come, wrap yourself up; concentrate your mind, which wanders too lightly; study every detail; scheme and examine thoroughly . . . keep still, and if any notion trouble you, put it quickly aside, then resume it and think it over again."

Halpern suggests that the portrayal of Socrates' therapy may not have been accurate because of the satire of Aristophanes, but the point is made here that such techniques were, at least, known and useable in the classical period. It is interesting to observe further that Freud used the same technique sitting behind his patient and even having them keep their eyes closed.

GREEK MEDICAL DEVELOPMENTS

The Greeks in accordance with the principles of empirical observation, which they had, in part, inherited from Egyptian and Hebrew medicine, held the conviction that disease was part of the order of nature, and that its progress could be watched and cured by natural means. In the 5th century B.C. Hippocrates earned the title of "Father of Medicine" by attempting to separate the ideas of a natural medical science from religion. He was the first to teach that some diseases clear up best if very little is done by the physician and that medicine must be separated from magic.

According to Hippocrates the most important practice of medicine was clinical observation itself, a fact that is still recognized as of paramount importance in medicine. He drew conclusions from texture, change of complexion, voice, and the like. Hippocrates' attitude toward treatment was characterized by one of the famous sayings attributed to him: "Our natures are the physicians of our diseases." He admitted that medical skill at its most could never be more than a supplement to the healing power of nature. He strongly opposed the careless use of drugs, and his own prescriptions were relatively few in number. He attached great importance to diet which, he said, should be full in winter but more sparing in the summer. Sedentary people were advised to eat less than active workers.

He also recognized the importance of rest, hot baths, and soothing music in curing individuals. These latter influences were known for many centuries before Hippocrates and were also ascribed to Asclepius, who reputedly founded temple establishments for individuals needing rest and recuperation.

Hippocrates introduced the practice of traction in the treatment of fractures. He was very adept in the use of splints, and his treatment of dislocations does not differ too substantially from methods in use today. He also noted that the surgeon should take care to keep clean fingernails, a fact which was not thoroughly established until Lister in the 19th century.

During the 5th century B.C. a theory referred to as the four humour theory was advanced by both Hippocrates and the Greek philosopher Empedocles. According to this theory, life consisted of vital fluids, the body being the form and basis for the circulation of these fluids. These fluids were affected by four qualities of matter: heat, cold, dryness, and moisture, and disease was considered as a result of a fluid becoming too hot or too cold, too dry or too moist. Antiquity knew the red fluid as blood, the yellow fluid as bile, and the whitish fluid as secretions from the nose and lungs. Finally, a black fluid, bile was discovered adding to the complement of four fluids corresponding basically to the four elements of the earth, air, fire, water, and earth. As Peters has written:

> Considering first the physical structure, we find the basis is the four elements—air, fire, water, earth. To each of these substances corresponds a quality called dry, hot, moist, or cold: and again in correspondence with these a humour, namely blood (warm), phlegm (cold), yellow bile (dry), black bile (moist). Health is defined as a right mixture of these; disease is consequently a disturbance of the relations, usually expressed as a change of ratios (1965, 57).

In the light of the four fluids theory, the patient's reactions were observed to recognize the course of disease. In a common cold, for example, it was noticed that the sick man secreted mucus from the nose and lungs. It was, therefore, considered that colds were caused by an excess of white fluid and that the natural power of the body sought to eliminate this excess. An attack of malaria manifested itself by cold with subsequent immoderate amounts of heat. When the fever abated, it was followed by heavy perspiration. In this sense a recognition took place in a primitive way of the bodily attempts to reestablish an homeostasis.

Galen, a philosopher-physician of the first century before Christ accepted the basic elements of Hippocrates' theories but, in addition, combined the four elements or fluids theory into a series of combinations relating to temperaments. Four major temperaments emerged from his theories in which an inclination to a given temperament is dependent on the particular preponderance of element mixes.

Galen's four major temperaments were melancholic, choleric, phlegmatic, and sanguine. Each of these temperaments represented a series of naturalistic or empirical observations that had been made about individuals. Galen provided one of the first systematic nosologies or classification systems for the analysis of personality. The melancholic individual was considered to be moody, sober, and reserved. The choleric was restless, aggressive, and excitable; the phlegmatic was passive, peaceful, and calm; and the sanguine was sociable, outgoing, lively. Figure 4 outlines Galen's basic temperaments.

The popularity of this system can be seen from the fact that Immanuel Kant many years later maintained a categorical point of view that every

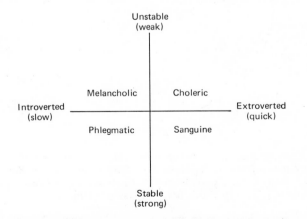

Figure 4 **Galen's temperaments. (Reproduced from H. J. Eysenck and S. Rachman, *The Causes and Cures of Neurosis*, Robert J. Knapp Publisher, San Diego, 1965.)**

person could be assigned some dimension on this categorical system. Wilhelm Wundt discussed these types from the polar dimensional point of view, labeling the one dimension slow-quick and the other strong-weak. He wrote (1903):

> The ancient differentiation into four temperaments . . . arose from acute psychological observation of individual difference between people . . . The fourfold division can be justified if we agree to postulate two principles in the individual reactivity of the affects: one of them refers to the strength, the other to the speed of change of a person's feelings. Cholerics and melancholics are inclined to strong affects while sanguinists and phlegmatics are characterized by weak ones. A high rate of change is found in sanguinists and cholerics, a slow rate in melancholics and phlegmatics (pp. 637–38).

Recently, Eysenck and Rachman (1965, 16) has reported the results of intercorrelations between traits based on modern factor analytic studies by Guilford, Cattell, and Eysenck. The following figure represents

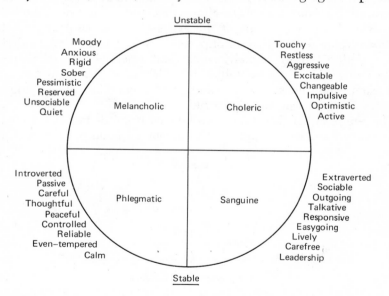

Galen's categories and their dimensions.[2] **H. J. Eysenck and S. Rachman,** *Causes and Cures of Neurosis,* **Robert R. Knapp, publisher, San Diego, Cal.** (Reproduced from H. J. Eysenck and S. Rachman, *The Causes and Cures of Neurosis,* Robert J. Knapp Publisher, San Diego, 1965.)

[2] The dimensions within the circle are those used by Galen. The trait characteristics outside the circle represent the results of modern factor analytic studies of the inter-correlations between traits as reported by Guilford, Cattell, Eysenck and others.

a composite list of traits that are associated with the basic dimensions as reported by Eysenck and Rachman.

Galen's system provided the basis for much personality theory and analysis. It was used in the ancient world and was retained in the medieval synthesis of Christianity. It also was employed by the ancient Arabians.

In summary, the classical development of philosophy and medicine provided an intellectual basis for the Roman and medieval methods of healing which followed. The recognition of a basic dualism in reality and man, the development of reason as a criterion of personal and social excellence, the enunciation of associative principles of learning, the methods of developing intellectual and moral habits of behavior, the development of a methodological tool of reasoning and logic, and the use of a series of prescriptions for medicinal healing are some of the contributions of this period in man's intellectual evolution. Obviously, the development of an insight type of learning, an emphasis on cognitive understanding, the origination of intensive learning-therapy sessions—possibly an ancient counterpart of modern sensitivity training sessions—and specific techniques like the ones depicted by Socrates, Hippocrates, and Galen contribute to an understanding of the ways and means in which healing was applied.

CHRISTIANITY

Tertullian in the second century spoke with challenge the words: "Hesterni sumus" or "We are a people of yesterday, and we have filled every place among you—cities, islands, fortresses, towns, market places, the very camps, companies, palace, Senate, and Forum. We have left you only your temples!" And well he might say this, for the spread of Christianity in the ancient world was phenomenal and unparalleled. The student of history can find explanations for why this took place. The Christian believer takes the view that God prepared the world for the coming of Jesus Christ, and that this coming took place "in the fullness of time." The agnostic looks for an explanation in psychological, sociological, or political reasons. But whatever the explanation may be, the fact of the existence of Jesus Christ cannot be denied. For many millions today, he is the God-man, Redeemer of Mankind, and Saviour of the World. For others, he may be only a model teacher who inspired people. But the reality of his existence, the significance of his teaching, and the tradition that followed it have had a major impact on the development of Western culture.

Christ and His Teaching

For 33 years Jesus lived in Palestine. Only the last three years of his life were dedicated to the preaching and the spreading of his ideas. The New Testament, written by his disciples sometime after his death pictures Jesus as a graceful leader of men who moved among the Jews of his day with conviction and integrity. For his followers, he brought the message of a new life, the fullness of spiritual values, and the friendship of a personal God. He promised a happiness beyond the intellectual sophistication of philosophy. He talked to all kinds of people: philosophers, priests, tax collectors, farmers, shepherds, and prostitutes. And his influence made an impression that was to be felt in every corner of the Roman Empire in less than 100 years.

To understand the impact of Christ's teachings, it is helpful to recognize the peculiar significance of the time and place of his mission. The Jews were a conquered people. They had a glorious past, with scriptural prophecies of a Messiah who was to come and deliver them. Rome's soldiers were garrisoned close to the temple in Jerusalem. The oppression of financial corruption, political dependence, and servitude reminded the Jews constantly of the contrast with their glorious past. Thus, in the Jewish mentality there was a conviction spawned by their own religion and cultural tradition as a promised people, that eventually Israel would achieve greatness under a future superman idealized in the concept of the Messiah. Many hundreds of years had passed, and the Jews were constantly oppressed, first by one foreign rule, and then by another. The Messiah hopes were a predominant feature not only of Jewish religious thought but also of the educational system of the synagogue. Hence, whether we ascribe the willingness of the Jewish people to listen to Christ to a psychological expectancy augmented by political subservience, or to the Christian conception of divine grace, we cannot deny the existence of a will to believe.

Christ did not address his teaching to one group or another. He talked to masses of the common people, along with the Scribes, Pharisees, and doctors of the Jewish law. His sermons or discourses contained *something for everyone*. He taught in a way that met individuals' needs. He spoke of the shepherd tending his sheep—many of the common people were shepherds or farmers. He spoke of making his disciples, "fishers of men," for this analogy was very clear to Galilean fishermen. He constantly engaged in discussions that met the needs of many different kinds of people. He used practical examples, as for instance, when he was summing up his message by stating that the love of God and neighbor fulfilled the Commandments, and a lawyer asked him what was meant by the word "neighbor." Following this question, he told the story of the Samaritan who had fallen among thieves. His message was driven home with complete understanding. Again, when the temple priesthood attempted to trap him on the question of loyalty to God and Rome, he asked them for a coin and stated the well-known "Render unto Caesar the things that are Caesar's and to God the things that are God's." Again, Christ taught with authority. Before the Sanhedrin, when asked if he were the Son of the Living God, he acknowledged it by saying, "Thou hast said it!"

Christ also engaged in considerable healing. Although this is not the place to discuss whether Christ performed miracles, it is appropriate to mention the thought of one Christian theologian (Weatherhead, 1952) who considers many of the healings of Christ to have been based on mechanisms of suggestion. This in his opinion does not deprecate the mission of Christ. Weatherhead suggests that the cures performed by Christ can be classified into three categories, which he mentions as (1) cures that involve the mechanism of suggestion, (2) cures that involve a more complicated technique including touching, the use of spittle, etc., and (3) cures that involve the psychic mechanism of the faith of other people than the patient. Whatever may have been the mechanisms involved, some of the healings reported are indeed spectacular, such as the raising of Lazarus after he had been dead or reported dead for three days.

The Parable as a Behavioral Paradigm: Social Learning in the Early Church

Although parables had been used as a standard approach to teaching by other Hebrew scholars, in the accounts of Christ's teaching the use of the parable is found to be a chief vehicle of the transmission of his thought. Time and again, Jesus responds to a direct question by an extended parable. Consider again, the questions of the lawyer seeking to define what constitutes one's neighbor. In this instance, Jesus replies by the account of the good Samaritan. He thus demonstrates by the parable what constitutes loving one's neighbor, as well as the definition of who one's neighbor is.

The parable provides an immediate *vicarious experience*. Through the format of a story, the imagination of the audience is captured. Moreover, it constitutes *a model* for the hearers to imitate. It is a direct image that can be fixed in the imagination and memory of the individual. As a result, it provides a kind of early *audiovisual aid*. Finally, it nearly always focuses on *action and behavior* rather than intellectual insight and understanding.

Moreover, it is apparent that Jesus himself wished to impress on his hearers the essential priority of behavior in the translation of his message. When asked by a scribe to define which was the first commandment, Jesus answered:

> The first commandment of all is, "Hear, O Israel! The Lord our God is one God; And thou shalt love the Lord thy God with all thy whole heart and with thy whole soul and with thy whole mind, and with thy whole strength."
>
> This is the first commandment. And the second is like it. "Thou shalt love thy neighbor as thyself. There is no other commandment greater than these." And the Scribe said to him, "Well answered, Master, thou has said truly that he is one and that there is no other besides him; and that he should be loved with the whole heart and with the whole understanding, and with the whole soul, and with one's whole strength; *and that to love one's neighbor as oneself is a greater thing than all holocausts and sacrifices.*" And Jesus, seeing that he had answered wisely said to him, *"Thou are not far from the kingdom of God"* (Mark 12:30–34).

Here we see that Jesus reinforces the commentary of the scribe by a direct statement affirming the correctness of the response.

This same theme is directly conveyed by Jesus in his words: "An example have I given you that you should love one another as I have loved you." And St. Paul speaking of the resurrection hinges the entire Christian belief on this major example, this overtly observed behavioral manifestation of the message of Jesus. "And if Christ has not risen, vain then is our preaching, vain too is your faith" (1 Cor. 15:14–16). St. Paul also clarifies precisely in behavioral terms just what it means to love one's neighbor.

> And I point out to you a yet more excellent way. If I should speak with the tongues of men and of angels, but do not have charity, I have become as sounding brass or a tinkling cymbal. And if I have prophecy and know all mysteries and all knowledge, and if I have all faith so as to remove mountains, yet do not have charity, I am nothing. And if I distribute all my goods to feed the poor, and if I deliver my body to be burned, yet do not have charity, it profits me nothing.
>
> Charity is patient, is kind; charity does not envy, is not pretentious, is not puffed up, is not ambitious, is not self-seeking, is not provoked; thinks no evil, does not rejoice over wickedness, but rejoices with the truth; bears with all things, believes all things, hopes all things, endures all things.

Love of one's neighbor then is demonstrated through behavior that provides a model to others. "See how the Christians love one another," was one of the early slogans voiced about the Christians. They were to provide a model for behavior. Moreover, Paul exhorts the Christian community to strive for spiritual gifts, the chief of which he seems to identify as prophecy. Unfortunately, this word in English does not convey the meaning that Paul wished. It obviously refers to one of a number of charismatic gifts. But by Paul's own interpretation, it would appear that prophecy is a special type of extempore preaching that is somehow able to provide meaningful learning for the hearers (I Cor. 14:2–5). Moreover, this type of transmission is especially designated for believers (14:22–24).

Paul's concerns about the utilizing of these charismatic gifts of prophecy, glossalalia, and the like stem from some knowledge that Christian enthusiasm and unbridled attempts at communication and behavioral witnessing can provide a psychological bedlam.

Here again, we observe one of the fundamental characteristics of both Christ's teaching and that of the early Church. Even as Jesus taught a concomitant priority of action to go along with faith, He provided a continual behavioral example for his disciples. They were sustained in their own behaviors by his example, the model that he provided and the reinforcement that he selectively used in shaping their behavior. However, he also utilized methods of extinguishing inappropriate behavior. He pointed out the futility of seeking the foremost place in his Kingdom to James and John: to demonstrate to total inadequacy of their understanding, he washed the feet of his disciples. Once again, we observe the use of a specific behavioral act to demonstrate a spiritual understanding.

The very sense of comradeship, the close union between master and disciples continued at a rapid pace over the years of his ministry. Very likely, the continued association, the modeling effect of his behavior, the shaping effect of his teaching and reinforcement, and the sense of physical unity as well as spiritual unity became a model for the elaboration of the early apostolic ministry. The group of disciples and apostles operated as one continual sensitivity training session in which much individual behavior was subject to the scrutiny of Jesus and to the halting attempts of the others to learn the method of Jesus.

The Early Church and the Dissemination of Christianity

The essential message that was left with the Apostles was one of a method of life and behavior. It was group centered, provided for strong personal attachments to the group, and contained a minimum of academic dogma or novel departures from Judaism. Jesus was considered the

Messiah. He had provided a model for them, instructing the apostles to filter out the essential behaviors necessary for eternal life from those useless formulas, hairsplitting arguments, and the basic formalism of the Pharisees and Sadduccees who emphasized so extremely their own epistemology of priority of theological knowledge over behavior.

It is very apparent from the Acts of the Apostles that the earliest Church organization attempted to reproduce in an artificial manner the communality of the Christ-disciple relationship. Pentecost provides an example of a tremendous group psychological reaction in which an all night prayer meeting, discussion, and policy session resulted in a spiritual manifestation. The pattern was being set here for the Christian method. Prayer, fellowship, the breaking and sharing of the bread and wine, all this resulted in a tremendous surge of common behavior that provided a psychological reinforcement for both modeling and maintaining behavior. It was this physical sense of communality, of sharing, that led Paul later to provide the intellectual justification of the experience in the explanation of the Mystical Body of Christ. It is only through this type of mystical union, the effects of which are clearly related to the psychological phenomena of group therapy, and utilized by the Wisdom of the Holy Spirit, that the spiritual identification with the Master could be maintained.

As a result, the Apostles attempted to model their community even more directly on the Christ-disciple relationship. Thus the Acts of the Apostles tell us:

> And all who believed were together and held all things in common, and would sell their possessions and goods and distribute them among all according as anyone had need. And continuing daily with one accord in the temple, and breaking bread in their houses, they took their food with gladness and simplicity of heart, praising God and being in favor with all the people. And day by day the Lord added to their company such as were to be saved (Acts 1:42–47).

Obviously, the Apostles themselves were convinced that the last times were at hand and that the end was soon to come. This organization seemed to provide them with a continuation of the relationship that they had known with Christ. Their enthusiasm, convictions, and knowledge of their past experience guided them into the establishment of a physical as well as spiritual communism, which possibly provided them with the spiritual internship that was necessary as a first step to test their own behavior.

Thus it is consistent with this rationale to suggest that the development of the early Christian community was tied to a distinctive mark or characteristic that appealed to many people. Surely the groups who joined the early Church found a distinctive appeal in joining a sect such as this. Women, slaves, the military and, later on, the intelligentsia all found some reason for becoming a part of the tradition. An examination of the biblical sources themselves plus the testimony of contemporary historians quoting Roman documents, for instance, Pliny's letters to Trajan, indicate that the characteristic most outstanding was the new behavioral patterns of the converts. The spread of the early Church appeared to be tied directly to the behavioral model that it provided, the sense of community identification in a pluralistic society, and the powerful emotional experiences proceeding from the group settings.

The phenomenal spread of Christianity particularly after the Roman Empire itself became Christian was the result of some highly sophisticated principles of missionary accommodation that embodied thoroughly what we now know as social learning theory. Paul himself set the example of appealing to all kinds of individuals. In speaking to the philosophers of the Agora in Athens, he pointed out to them the fact that he recognized they were a religious people. Noticing an altar marked "to the Unknown God," he used this fact to expound on Christianity. As Newman wrote:

> Instead of uttering any invective against their Polytheism, he began a discourse from the unity of the divine nature; and then proceeded to claim the altar, consecrated in the neighborhood to the Unknown God, as the property of Him whom he preached to them, and to enforce his doctrine of the Divine Immateriality, not by miracles, but by argument and that founded on the words of a heathen poet (Newman, 1871, 67).

Voss has written well on the entire missionary principle of accommodation:

> St. Paul's example was followed and further developed by the early Apologists and Church Fathers. It was from the contemporary literature of the times and even from pagan philosophy that they borrowed the intellectual weapons for the exposition and defense of Catholic teaching. There was first of all the important question of terminology. It was the sacred duty of the Church to teach and propagate the Word of God. To do so, she had to express the revealed truths in human concepts and image. These she did not create, or only rarely so. She was at pains to explain the unfamiliar with the help of the familiar. Because of her world-wide mission, however, the Church retained but few words which bespoke her Jewish origin, like *hosanna, alleluja, amen.* She rather turned, as might be expected,

to the familiar terms and expressions of Greek and Latin literature. Again, St. Paul was showing the way by using words like *soteria, mysterion, psychikos, eulogia,* and others, which were common household words in the language of the mystery religions. Following in his footsteps the early Christian writers soon adopted into the Christian vocabulary terms like *hostia, sacrificum, immolare, sacramentum,* and the like, and even such familiar words as soul, sin, redemption, ascetisism and many others. That these expressions, taken over from the secular and religious pagan literature, signified in their pagan context something altogether different from the Christian concept was no unsurmountable obstacle. The non-Christian words were simply, by a process of definition and education, emptied of their pagan content and filled with a new Christian meaning (Voss, 1946, 6).

Contemporary philosophy was also utilized in the service of the Christian Church. In Stoicism, and above all in Neoplatonism, the early apologists found much truth that could be accommodated to Christian teaching.

It is not surprising to encounter Plato, at any rate his successors, disciples and friends of the Neo-Platonic school, not only in the forecourts of Christianity, but right in its mysteries, in the trinitarian and christological speculations. It was especially in the spirit of Origen and St. Augustine that Plato seemed to have a Christian rebirth (Adams, 1930, 12).

And although the early Church tended to utilize Platonic philosophy as an intellectual vehicle, the Medieval Church in Aquinas' philosophy and theology harkened back to Aristotle.

When later at the opening of the twelfth century the mind of the West began to turn toward Aristotle, and the approaching forces of the monastically-minded Aristotelianism threatened western thought, Thomas Aquinas appeared, the gifted pupil of a great master. By combining Aristotelianism with the most essential elements of Platonic thought and adjusting it to Christian truths, he brought it into the service of the cross of Christ. Despite all opposition he pressed the intellectual weapons of Aristotelianism so completely into Christ's service that even today the theologican can hardly move a step without keeping his eye fixed on St. Thomas and the Philosopher of Stagira (Adams, 1930, 12).

Again, the Church found no difficulty in assimilating the existing rites and customs of the people into the liturgy. Newman pointed out:

The use of temples, and those dedicated to particular saints, and ornamented on occasions with branches of trees; incense, lamps, and candles; votive offerings on recovery from illness; holy water; asylums; holy days and seasons, use of calendars, processions, blessing on fields; sacerdotal vestments, and tonsure, the ring in marriage, turning to the East, images at the later dates, perhaps the ecclesiastical chant, and the Kyrie Eleison, are all of pagan origin, and sanctified by their adoption into the church (Newman, 1920, 372).

Gradually, the Christian Church accommodated itself to the Graeco-Roman culture. The essential key was to assimilate those elements of the culture that were thought to be compatible with Christianity. By superimposing new meanings on old rituals, new learnings were accrued. The same process continued in literature, music, the arts, and in every other aspect of human culture. And if, at first, the converts to Christianity may have tolerated certain aspects of Greek and Latin literature and customs, at a later date, their successors strictly censored all of these things. It is for this reason that the works of Ovid and even Homer were carefully scraped off parchment, and the Bible and other religious works copied over the same writing material. Although this pertains to a much later date, it is illustrative of the principle that guided much of the development of Christianity.

In the early medieval period the same principles of accommodation were continued. Gregory the Great, Patrick in Ireland, Augustine of Canterbury in England, and Boniface in Germany took into account the nature of these primitive tribes. They recognized the patriarchal or tribal unities centering in the chief and the council of elders. Thus, they sought first to convert the chief, his wife, and certain of the elders, recognizing the rest would fall into line. The early monks adopted the dress of the druids, while sacred springs and groves and the custom of dancing around midnight fires were all utilized and preserved but converted to a Christian meaning. Gregory the Great wrote to Abbot Mellitus, a fellow missionary of Augustine of Canterbury, who was striving to convert the English:

Tell Augustine that he should not destroy the temples of the gods but rather the idols within those temples. Let him, after he has purified them with holy water, place altars and relics of the Saints therein. For if those temples are well built, there is no reason why they could not be converted from the worship of demons to the service of the true God. The people seeing that their places of worship are not destroyed, will more readily banish error from their hearts and acknowledge and adore the true God, because they come to places familiar and dear to them. Further, since it has been their custom to slaughter oxen in sacrifice to the demons, they should receive some solemnity in exchange. Let them, therefore, on the day of the dedication of their churchs, or on the feast of the martyrs whose relics are preserved in them, build themselves huts around their one-time temples and celebrate the occasion with religious feasting. They will sacrifice and eat animals not any more as an offering to the devil, but for the glory of God to whom they will give thanks as the giver of all things. Thus, if they are not deprived of all the external pleasures, they will grasp more readily the interior joys of their new faith. For it is quite impossible to efface all at once everything pagan from their stubborn minds, just as it is impossible to climb mountains by leaps and bounds instead of step by step (Venerable Bede, 1896, 1, 64).

Thus, in summary, the final clue to the spread of Christianity is vested in the psychological approach to social learning that included a variety of techniques for the maintenance of a new way of life.

PHILOSOPHERS OF THE CHRISTIAN ERA

The acceptance by the intelligensia and the political forces of Rome of the Christian religion brought about a widespread and continuing attempt to integrate the new with the old. There were no spectacular changes in philosophical and psychological thinking but, instead, a gradual disintegration of classical ideals. Prior to the conversion of certain philosophers to Christianity, the earlier Greek tradition had been effected by a number of movements among which were Stoicism, Epicureanism, Scepticism, and Neoplatonism. A brief discussion of these movements may shed light on the development of Christian philosophy.

Stoicism was reportedly founded by Zeno sometime in the third century B.C. He purported to base his ideas on the principles of Socrates. Although many elements of Aristotelian thought were incorporated into Stoic philosophy, the basic distinction between matter and form was lost. Zeno had a strong Roman following. Accounted as Stoics were *Cicero* (writer and orator, 40 B.C.), *Persius* (a satirist, A.D. 34–62), *Epictetus* (philosopher and writer, A.D. 90), and *Marcus Aurelius* (emperor and philosopher, A.D. 121–180). The basic tenets of this school of thought were pragmatic and utilitarian. Everything was reduced to matter, for God and world were identified. The supreme ethical code was to live according to nature. Happiness was dependent on the knowledge that all nature was subject to law. The goal of man's life was conformity to nature through the utilization of reason. Virtue was the life led in a consistent manner according to nature.

Epicureanism is reported to have been founded by *Epicurus* who lived in the third century B.C. He is said to have been a self-taught philosopher and not too well instructed in the philosophy of Plato and Aristotle. One of the chief followers of Epicurus was *Lucretius,* the Roman poet (95–51 B.C.) who wrote about Epicurean philosophy in his poem *De Natura Rerum* (about the nature of things). For the epicureans the purpose of life was happiness. Happiness was judged by pleasure and pain. The only unconditioned good in life was pleasure. Epicurus denied the existence of an afterlife but recognized that some kind of restraint was needed in the constant pleasure seeking of man. Therefore, he constructed a series of axioms or canons whereby man should judge and weigh his pleasure seeking. No pleasure seeking could be considered a good if it resulted in illness or bad repute. Things that were illicit and harmful should not be sought even if they were pleasurable. Thus Epicurus and his followers suggested a moderation in pleasurable experiences. An hierarchy of pleasures existed for all men. First, pleasure was the enjoyment of knowledge and intellectual pursuits. Only subsequent to this pleasure were other experiences to be sought. In effect, then, each man became his own criterion for what should be sought and avoided.

Scepticism was a kind of reaction to both stoicism and epicureanism. Sceptics considered the stoics as fatalists and the epicureans as opportunists. Both of these schools were corruptions of classical Greek philosophy, and both had certain axioms or canons from which conduct could be deduced. The sceptics, however denied the extension of human knowledge and insisted that all virtue was centered in a placid imperturbability. A product of the discouraging times that accompanied the fall of Greece and the conquest of Rome, scepticism simply denied the efficacy of an attempt to secure valid scientific or moral knowledge.

Neoplatonism of all these variations seems to have had the most lasting effect on the development of the medieval approach to man and philosophy. The philosophy of Plato seemed admirably suited to the synthesis of Judaeo-Christian theology. *Philo* (A.D. 40) was an Alexandrian Jew who attempted to bring the revealed religion of the Old Testament into an agreement with the philosophy of the Greeks. In his works, Philo suggested that revelation is the highest possible philosophy, that the Greeks derived their ideas from the Jewish Scripture, and that the difference between Judaism and Classical Greek philosophy was that the former used symbols to convey truth, whereas the latter spoke openly.

Plotinus (A.D. 205–270) was the true founder of the Neoplatonist school. An Egyptian by birth, he resided in Rome for a number of years where he influenced the Roman Emperor Gallienus. Plotinus' philosophy centered around the three major ideas of *the One, the Nous,* and *the World-Soul.* He conceived of the One as the ultimate reality, God, from whom all good and truth emanate. The Nous was intellect, which for Plotinus was a conglomeration of emanations, in which intellect acted as a mirror to the One. It was, in fact, identified by Plotinus with Plato's world of ideas. The World-Soul was the mirror image of the Nous and included all individual souls as well as matter. In this conception of reality, Plotinus considered light to be the opposite of dark, spirit to be the opposite of matter. Matter was considered to be the source of all evil. Plotinus believed that by reconciling the philosophy of Plato with the religious tradition through the doctrine of emanations, he had bridged the gap between philosophical and theological speculation. Plotinus was a philosopher who was cognizant of the influence of Christianity, and who attempted to meet current intellectual needs without recourse to Christian belief. His ideas persisted many centuries in the last strongholds of pre-Christian Greek and Roman philosophy.

In addition to the Greek and Roman contributions of Stoicism, Epicureanism, Scepticism, and Neo-Platonism, a tremendous amount of literature was produced in the first centuries of the Christian era. The Christian writers have been referred to as Fathers of the Church. Traditionally, the philosopher—theologians of the first five centuries have been divided into two groups: (1) the ante-Nicene writers, and (2) the post-Nicene writers. This division was made on the basis of the Council of Nicaea, which was held in 325 at the order of Constantine. This first great council of the Christian Church was called to discuss certain doctrinal matters. It also marked the beginning of an official recognition of Christianity by the Roman Empire.

The early Christian writers were chiefly apologists. They attempted to convince by logical process and elaboration. Irenaeus, Tertullian, Clement of Alexandria, Origen, and many others wrote on all possible aspects of Christian philosophy and theology. All of these men were concerned with the propagation of Christianity and, hence, wrote explicitly or implicitly about education.

Clement of Alexandria (150–215 A.D.) attempted to establish Christianity as a philosophy. In several of his writings he wrote of educational theory. *The Exhortation to the Greeks, the Pedagogue,* and *the Stromata* emphasized the value of moral education and suggested that Christ was the teacher *par excellence. Origen* (185–255 A.D.) spent his entire life in teaching and writing. He was considered the first real Christian scholar. He wrote prolifically, compiling a large polyglot edition of the Bible wherein the text in Hebrew was compared with Greek versions. Of all these early writers, Origen was the most Platonic in his thought. *Tertullian* (160–240 A.D.) wrote on the subject of idolatry and suggested that Christian parents send their children to the Roman schools, but that they should make sure that their children were thoroughly indoctrinated in their religious beliefs at home.

The period extending from the Council of Nicaea to the end of the 5th century is marked by a tremendous elaboration of theological controversies. There were literally hundreds of divergent opinions expressed about the nature of Christ, the wills in Christ, and the relations of various Christian doctrines to philosophy. To this period belong *Ambrose of Milan* (340–397), *Jerome* (321–420), and *Augustine* (354–430). These individuals witnessed the crumbling of the Roman world. They lived after the great persecutions of the Church and really stood at the threshold of the Middle Ages. Ambrose was an excellent Latin and Greek scholar. By profession he was a lawyer. He became the bishop of Milan and produced a number of treatises on Christian morality. He encouraged the study of ancient literature, wrote many sermons and orations, and served as a model for much of medieval thought. *Jerome* was one of the founders of the monastic movement. He was a member of an old Roman family and spent many years in the desert of Palestine. He engaged in the monumental task of translating the Greek Bible into Latin but found time to write on the education of women. His basic views on the rigid training of women remained as a text for convent-style education.

Augustine is a very important figure in the history of Christian thought. His significance lies in his personality, his varied background and interests, the multitude of his writings extending over a period of 40 years, and his contribution to the Middle Ages. Augustine was born in Africa of a pagan father and a Christian mother. At an early age he adopted the Manichean beliefs, which maintained the reality of a principle of good and a principle of evil in the world. After a long and tortuous self-examination, as told in his *Confessions,* he joined the Christian Church. He later became a bishop.

Augustine witnessed the very crumbling of the Roman Empire. In his *City of God* he spoke of the heavenly city and the earthly city, the world of God and the world of Rome. In an elaborate study he traced the evolution and development of Rome and her inevitable downfall. He produced the first philosophy of history in these analyses. Augustine's writings influenced the whole future course of Christianity. His ideas formed the principle theological vehicle of the next 700 years. Even in the Reformation, Luther returned to the ideas of Augustine once more.

The Augustinian system is essentially a Platonic system. The central ideas of Plato, that is, of a world of ideas and a world of physical phenomena, were incorporated in Augustine's *City of God*. And yet, Augustine was primarily an eclectic. He varied from writing to writing —hence, there are conflicting interpretations of what he really believed and meant. He tried to satisfy his mind with one philosophical approach after another.

His psychological autobiography, the *Confessions*, reveals to us the crises and experiences of his divided self. This book shows him as both sensuous and spiritual minded, a critical analyst and a naive mystic. At times he is a philosopher free to speculate and to push reason to its limits; on other occasions, he is an individual prone to accept abjectly any pronouncement on matters of faith. Sometimes he speaks of evil as a means to good. At other times he exalts reason to absolute heights, but often he insists that faith takes prime priority. The world for him is now good and pleasant—and yet condemned to wretchedness. Good works are encouraged in one place, and faith is declared the only salvation in another context.

The central ideas of Augustine may be summarized under the headings of God, man, and the human soul. God is the source of all truth and all good. He permits evil for a great good. Augustine felt that the great paradox of human existence was the problem of good and evil. This thought reflected the ideas of Plato, the philosophical syntheses of Neoplatonism, and his early training in Manicheism. As a result, Augustine tended to weigh all knowledge in terms of whether it contributed to the good of the soul or to its detriment. In a subtle but significant manner, Augustine insisted that knowledge is not a good in and for itself—as the Greeks had indicated—but, instead, that it is a means to be used for man's salvation. The basic polarity of good and evil permeated all of Augustine's writings. In his *Confessions* is revealed the evolution of the Christian Augustine from the Roman Augustine. In the *City of God* he was constantly manifesting the conflict between his classical and Christian self. The nineteenth book of the *City of God* highlights this conflict. Here he expounds on the need of the Christian to look to the heavenly city for his lasting happiness. He also provides implicitly guidelines for moral counseling.

If you ask us now what the city of God says, first to this question of the supreme good and evil, it will answer you at once: eternal life is the perfection of good, and eternal death the consummation of evil; and the aim of our life must be to avoid the one, and attain the other. Therefore it is written: "the just shall live by faith." For we see not our greatest good, and therefore are to believe and hope for it; nor have we power to live accordingly, unless our belief and prayer obtain help of Him who has given us that believe and hope that He will help us. But such as found the perfection of felicity upon this life, placing it either in the body, or in the mind, or in both": or to speak more plainly, either in pleasure or in virtue, or in pleasure and rest together, or in virtue, or in both: or in nature's first desires, or in both, fondly and vainly are these men persuaded to find true happiness here . . . What is our desire in this perfection of good, but that the flesh should not lust against the spirit, and that there were no vice in us against which the spirit should lust? Which since we cannot attain in this life, however much we try, let us by God's grace endeavor this, that we do not subject our spirit unto the concupiscence of our flesh, and so set our seal unto the bond of sin with a free consent.

So then far be it from us ever to think that we have attained the true happiness whilst we live here. Who is so wise but has now and then divers fights against his own lusts. What is the office of prudence? Is it not to discern between things to be chosen and things to be refused, to the end that no error be incurred in either? This testifies that there is evil in us, and that we are in evil. It teaches us that it is evil to assent unto sin, and good to avoid it. But yet neither can prudence nor temperance rid our lives of that evil which they forewarn us of and arm us against. And what of justice, that gives everyone his due? And the just order of nature is that the soul be under God, the flesh under the soul, and both together under God. Is it not plain that this is rather continually laboured after than truly attained in this life? For the less that the soul does meditated on God, the less it serves Him, and the more that the flesh lusts against the soul, the less command has the soul over it. Wherefore, as long as we are subjected unto this languor and corruption, how dare we say we are safe, and if not safe, much less blessed by the perfection of attained bliss?

. . . For true virtue may not dissemble, in profession what it cannot perform: but it aims at this only, that man's life which being in this world is perturbed with all these extremes of sorrows should in the life to come be made partaker both of safety and felicity . . . Wherefore as we are saved, so are we blessed by hope; and as we have no hold on our safety, no more have we of our felicity, but by hope, patiently awaiting it; and being as yet in a desert of thorny dangers, all these we must constantly endure until we come to the paradise of all ineffable delights, having then passed all the perils of encumbrance. This security in the life to come is the beatitude we speak of, which the philosophers not beholding will not believe but forge themselves an imaginary bliss here, wherein the more their virtue assumes to itself, the falser it proves to the judgment of all others (City of God, London, J.M. Dent & Sons, 1947, vol. 2, pp. 237–240).

Augustine believed that the Roman world was doomed and that nothing could preserve it. He insisted that the Romans had worshiped devils, that their civilization was corrupt, and that God was allowing the fall of Rome as a punishment. He, therefore, urged all Christians to remain aloof from the cause of wickedness and to hope for the eternal happiness of the divine promises.

That Rome's impending doom was a subject of great influence can be seen from the vast numbers of men and women who sought out monasteries as a source of retreat from the world. Jerome, Ambrose, Benedict, and numerous others founded the monastic way of life, which purported to endure this earthly existence in penitential preparation for eternal happiness. The writings of Augustine reveal the mind of a man twisted by contrary emotions. The impact of the later Christian writers is a psychological one. It is the expressed disavowal of the classical Roman education. Augustine points out a number of psychological principles that influenced greatly the future of the Roman world and the development of medieval Christianity. They may be summarized as follows:

1. There is an eternal struggle between good and evil. Evil is permitted so that good may result.

2. The body is accidentally evil, because it is matter. The soul is the immaterial substance that permeates the body. The body is not in itself evil but is the origin of all kinds of lusts and desires that make man evil.

3. Human happiness rests in God and the attaining of the heavenly city. No permanent happiness can be attained on earth.

4. Because everything is changing, and subject to error, man needs something stronger than himself to depend on. Christ is the great hope of man.

5. The idea that contamination with the world leads to sin and eternal ruin, and that only by withdrawal—at the very least participation without ego involvement—can man keep his sights on his eternal destiny.

6. The notion that man himself is prone to evil and sin and his only hope lies in faith, prayer, and grace.

7. The conviction that philosophy is essentially blind without faith. Human knowledge is worthless unless it leads to eternal salvation. Further yet, that certain human knowledge is positively detrimental to salvation.

The basic psychology of Augustine's approach to classical civilization emphasized the priority of faith and religion. The result of the wholesale adoption of this attitude led to an accent of withdrawal from the affairs of the faltering Roman state. Certainly, the fall of Rome cannot be ascribed to Christianity alone, but the Christian approach to the Roman administration was one of apathy and fatalism. Terrible things were happening: the barbarians had overrun the frontiers and raced southward, civil organization was in chaos, fiscal problems were tremendous, inflation, the breakdown of communication, plagues, and internal disorders were apparent everywhere. Augustine provided a philosophy of history that analyzed the foundations of Rome and interpreted her subsequent rise and decline in terms of a final grand punishment meted out by an angry God. These ideas and the guidelines provided became the intellectual basis of medieval asceticism.

ONE THOUSAND YEARS OF CHRISTIAN BEHAVIOR MODIFICATION

In the light of modern research in social learning theory, the analysis of the spread and gradual control of Christian thinking over the social systems of the Graeco-Roman world becomes an interesting and extended example of the manner in which an ideology grafted onto the earlier philosophical and religious traditions is extended into the gradual dominance and control of the social management of behavior.

An early legacy of the Christian Church was the mission of healing. Certainly the Hebraic tradition at that time had been influenced by the Greek practice of medicine. Moreover, Luke, one of the Evangelists, was reported to have been a physician. The New Testament is filled with anecdotal reports about various miraculous healings performed by Christ. Weatherhead (1952) classifies these healings under three major classifications: (1) cures that involved the mechanism of suggestion such as the cleansing of the leper (Mark 1:40–45), and the curing of the man by Bethesda's pool (John 5:1–18); (2) cures that involve a more complicated technique such as the "possessed" man at Capernaum (Luke 4:33–37) and the deaf stammerer (Mark 7:32–37); and finally (3) cures that involve the influence of a psychic "atmosphere" or the "faith" of people other than the patient, for example, Jairus' daughter

(Matt. 9:18–26), the Centurion's servant (Matt. 8:5–13), and the epileptic boy (Mark 9:14–29).

In most of these instances, Christ appears to have used a combination of appeals to Faith plus the use of a symbol such as spittle, the touch of a hand, and the like. Considering these accounts aside from the theological explanation, one can certainly see parallels to many subsequent accounts of miracles and healings at sacred places such as Lourdes and Fatima. Nor is there anyone who will read these pages who has not witnessed declarations of faith and or has not read about cures attributed to faith healers.

In the early days of the Church as well as in the mass groupings of people in revival-type atmospheres, a crucial element appears to be the joining of some kind of faith or conviction to some kind of behavior. It is the touching of the hem of Christ by the woman with the hemorrhage that effects the cure. It is the decision to get up from one's seat and walk to the front of an auditorium to declare one's faith in Jesus as saviour that converts.

Totally apart from the question of whether Christ cured in virtue of his divinity or by reason of psychic suggestion, the fact is that the healing ministry in the Christian Church has had a long history that extends into the present. When the Church became an anchor of society, and particularly when it became the sole maintainer of quasi-Roman tradition and law in the West, it became more and more intransigent as to the role of faith versus medicine in healing. As long as the medical tradition established by the Greeks and continued by the Romans was maintained, there was a recognition of the power of the physician.

But there lurked continuously within the fabric of Christianity, the legacy of the Hebrews as well as of the classical Greeks that illness, whether physical or mental, was the result of evildoing, punishment by God, or the possession of evil spirits. Although the Greeks broke away from this tradition and quietly substituted the beginning of a scientific theory of medicine with Aesculapius, Aristotle, and Hippocrates, the spirit of medical inquiry was tied to the existence of medical school facilities in the ancient universities and, in part, to the independence of those facilities from Christian control. Of the great classical universities, Athens was finally divested of "pagan" faculty under the reign of Justinian (527–565) when the faculty were required to be Christian. Although some limited medical study still continued in the Eastern Empire, the main emphasis of medical science remained in North Africa at Alexandria and only succeeded in developing further under the Arabian and Islamic scholars.

Two major approaches appear to have existed and grown simultaneously within the Christian Church. One was the tendency to dismiss physical illness and medicine and to substitute religious faith as the basis for healing. The other was to establish and to maintain hospitals and infirmaries for the sick and aged. Infirmaries for the care and cure of the sick are found at Monte Cassino and the Hotel-Dieu at Lyons in the 6th century. Later, medieval orders during the crusades, for instance, the Order of St. John of Jerusalem, attempted to provide help for ailing individuals. But there was also a certain hostility to the practice of medicine as far back as the period of Gregory the Great (590 A.D.). White (1955) documents a long sequence of decrees and papal interdicts against the development of medicine. He also points out how the Church systematically opposed the dissection of human bodies from the time of Augustine and Tertullian through Boniface VIII. As late as the early part of the 19th century a Pope, Pius V, decreed that all physicians before administering treatment should call in a "physician of the soul" on the grounds that the "bodily infirmity frequently arises from sin" (White, 1955 Vol. II, p. 37).

The most distressing phase of the opposition of Christianity to medical science came in the High Middle Ages when Innocent VIII exhorted the clergy of Germany "to leave no means untried to detect sorcerers, and especially those who by evil weather destroy vineyard, gardens, meadows and growing crops" (White I, 352). This was an injunction to carry out witch-finding inquisitions and a manual was prepared for use entitled the Witch Hammer (*Malleus Maleficarum*). Space does not permit a full discussion of the events that occurred as a result of this sanction, but suffice it to say that thousands of elderly individuals, recluses, and any one who showed some degree of behavioral deviancy were suspect and often tried and put to death as witches.[2] Moreover, the Protestant reformers were not a bit better when it came to witch-hunting. Both Calvin and Luther encouraged the notion by their explicit preaching and writing that the devil was the source of most illness, and they specifically charged the Roman Church with being the consort of the devil (for example, "the Whore of Babylon"). John Wesley, as late as 1768, declared that "the giving up of witchcraft is in effect the giving up of the Bible" (White I, 363). Moreover, the history of witchcraft in

---

[2] White's documentation of the struggle of science against Christianity in its legalistic and official forms, that is, Catholic and Protestant is extremely detailed. He points out that the Church opposed the use of inoculation, quinine, cocaine, chloroform and nearly every scientific advance relating to human health. Moreover, he points out that in every age, even from the earliest centuries, there were clergymen who were repelled at these extremes and who rejected the popular notion of satanic possession as a unitary explanation.

Salem and the part that the Mathers played in this is a well-known segment of early American history.

In short, the Church generally opposed the development of a scientific discipline of medicine and helped actively to stamp out what existed in the Graeco-Roman tradition. In medieval times, licenses were grudgingly issued to medical schools for the dissection of one body every three years. Moreover, there were endless controversies over issues of why man did not have one rib less than women in accordance with the biblical story. Evil spirits were considered to be able to manipulate the weather, to cause bad fortune, possess individuals, and to take other than human form.

Looking at the existing historical documents regarding the decline of Rome and the development of Christianity, it is apparent that Christianity as a minority sect in its initial stages depended strongly on a social behavioral approach to winning converts. The emphasis on behaving in a new manner, in the conceptual equality of all men, appealed to slaves, women, the military, and finally to the intelligentsia. The appeal to slaves and women is obvious because both had a very inferior position in the Graeco-Roman world. St. Paul always referred to women as his helpers. He mentioned Prisca, Evodia, and Syntiche as fellow-workers, fellow-evangelists. In the Book of Romans he said: "Salute Mary who has labored much among you . . . Salute Tryphaena and Tryphosa, who labor in the Lord . . . Salute Aquila and Prisca, my helpers in Christ Jesus . . . and the church which is their house . . . . Phoebe is our sister in the ministry of the Church . . . she also hath assisted many and myself also" (Rom. XVI, 3–5). St. Paul in particular made use of women in the spreading of his mission. The earliest procedure of Gospel preaching had taken place through the utilization of the synagogues and congregations of the Jewish Diaspora (those Jews living in other lands of the Roman Empire). Coming to a town as a distinguished rabbi from Palestine, Paul would be received and even though his opinions were very often rejected by the Jewish group, courtesy would dictate to the women the obligation of food and shelter. Thus the beginnings of Christianity were tied very closely to a type of underground activity in which groups of men and women, looking for some kind of psychological and religious security in an age when the formal religion had all but been abandoned, were drawn together for common group sessions that included both food and singing along with religious guidance.

The military also was instrumental in these earliest days. A number of soldiers and officers had been involved in the happenings in Jerusalem. The account of Cornelius the Centurion plus the trial of Jesus by Pilate are noted in the New Testament. Speeding along the Roman roads and seaways, the Roman legions moved from place to place. Many of the soldiers witnessing the religious phenomena in Jerusalem were impressed. Many heard the preaching of the Apostles and Disciples. Tertullian, a Christian writer of the 2nd century, was a soldier's son and told of a Christian prayer group in the "Thundering Legion" of the army of Marcus Aurelius. Furthermore, the story of the martyrs who were converted while they were soldiers also demonstrates the fact that the military organization had been infiltrated by Christianity.

Slaves also found the new Gospel appealing. The institution of slavery was widespread in the Roman world. St. Paul wrote in a way that made it clear he viewed slavery as a social stigma. Once a slave, Onesimus, had fled from a friend of Paul's and had turned to Paul. Paul wrote to his friend and urged clemency after he had converted the slave: "I Paul, a prisoner of Jesus Christ, beseech thee for my son, whom I have begotten in my bonds" (Philemon 10). Over a period of five centuries, Christian influence would be brought to bear on the question of slavery, although the system was never abolished. But the influence of slaves in the homes of the Romans was a tremendous factor in the spread of Christianity. The more intelligent slaves were nurses, domestics, and teachers. Celsus, a Roman critic, denounced as the most dangerous missionaries of Christianity the domestic slaves. Augustine ascribed the virtue of his mother Monica to the influence of an old Christian slave.

In addition, the ecclesiastical offices were often held by slaves or former slaves. Many of the early bishops of Rome seem to have been slaves. Callistus was just a Greek name for "beautiful," probably imposed on a young slave by a master. Pius is a name suggesting virtue and in the case of one individual recorded as Pius, it is probable that he had been a slave, since he had a brother Hermias who was also a slave. Along with slaves, descendants of the great Roman families such as the Cornelii, the Pompenii, and the Caecilli, gathered in catacombs and worshiped. Christianity offered to the slaves a hope for the next world. It promised them that God considered them in an equal manner with the rich and powerful. All men were brothers with Christ, all had a common Father who cared for them and loved them.

Finally, the Church appealed to members of the intellectual class. Paul did not confine his preaching to slaves and ex-Jews, but extended it to all who would listen. As the ferment of Christianity spread, teachers, lawyers, and philosophers became interested in the beliefs of Christ. Moreover, the primitive beliefs expressed in the New Testament were elaborated and detailed into a theology by Paul. As a result, some of the uneducated apostles found difficulty in understanding them. Peter is reported to have written:

. . . Paul also according to the wisdom given unto him hath written unto you; as also in all of his epistles speaking in them of these things in which are some things hard to be understood, which they that are unlearned and unstable wrest, as they do also the other scriptures unto their own destruction (II Pet., 15, 16).

Intellectuals, impressed by the personal example of Christians, began to scrutinize their beliefs. Clement of Alexandria, Irenaeus, Origen, and Tertullian were only a few of the many individuals schooled in Greek philosophy and culture who began to work out a systematic intellectual explanation of Christianity. And this intellectual synthesis with Greek philosophy did not always conform to the Christian message. Origen, for example, adopted the Platonic concept of the preexistence of the human soul; others saw a mystery element in Christianity that was fostered by Christ's use of parables. But by the middle of the second century (150 A.D.), the appeal to intellectuals had been clearly established through a number of apologetic writings.

The Church also viewed education as the very heart of the cultural transmission of Christian ideas. In the earliest days an institution called the Catechumenate had been the core of the Christian education effort. The catechumenate had as its purpose the instruction of inquirers or intended converts. The teaching consisted of questions and answers and the course of studies extended over an indefinite time. At first, it would seem that several years were required to complete the studies and to be accepted by the elders of the congregation. This was true because instruction in Christianity embraced not only a body of knowledge or doctrine but a gradual alteration in the individual's moral life and character. To this end, he was provided with an endless list of the examples of martyrs, the Apostles and, above all, the example of Christ. Moreover, the elders of the congregation maintained a close supervision over his progress, noted changes in his behavior, and shaped his progress by their own exemplary models.

Subsequently, the catechetical school was established, very often in relationship to an existing school or university. Here scholars could come and study about Christianity and, particularly, could gain reflective interpretations of their secular studies. Schools were established at Caesarea, Antioch, Edessa, Jerusalem, Carthage, and at many other places. The institution of the catechetical school reached its fullest development in the 4th and 5th centuries just prior to the Roman acceptance of Christianity. Afterward Christianity penetrated into all institutions of learning, including the universities, and there was no further need for catechetical instruction. The system declined and disappeared in the 8th century.

With the formal acceptance of Christianity as the state religion, the former clandestine sect became the core of the power structure in society. Where Church and State remained relatively intact a kind of Caesaropapism grew up and provided the continuing power structure. This was the case in the Byzantine Empire. In the West, the Church gradually absorbed the residue of Roman culture and learning, filtering out of the total cultural transmission those aspects that could be accommodated into the Christian framework.

The Platonism of Augustine, the need for security, and the disavowal of much that was Roman led to the development of a complex system of spiritual advisement. The earlier catechumenate and catechetical schools provided a basis for conversion and the establishment of new intellectual and behavior patterns. The Church, through its schools, devised a complex system of changing behavior and attitudes. The system was premised on the notion that one can grow spiritually through a conformity to and an agreement with the will of God. The Church through its divine guarantees and its reservoir of revelation could not be wrong, and its ministers pointed the way to salvation.

The monastic way of life became extremely popular as a retreat for intellectuals initially and subsequently as a basic institution in Christianity. Vows of poverty, chastity, and obedience, complete environmental control, ritual worship, and confession became the mainstays of the system. Both external and internal controls were stringently maintained in a continual shaping of thought and behavior.

Representative of the basic shaping policy of these monastic organizations, for instance, the Benedictines, Carthusians, Dominicans, and Franciscans, are the following comments of Jeremias Drexelius, a Jesuit of the 16th century, on the subject of the conformity of the human will to the divine will. He provides the following guidelines for the conformity of a human will to that of the divine:

1. "To desire to do all things at the bidding of the divine Will, and therefore, to set about nothing without first imploring the Divine Aid.

2. It is a mark of true devotion towards the Divine Will, not merely not to shrink from sorrows and calamities when they are present, but willingly to seek them when they are absent, and for this reason, because God is far nearer by His Grace to those who are afflicted in various ways, than to those who enjoy uninterrupted prosperity.

3. The greatest possible distrust of self. This is pre-eminently a Chris-

tian virtue, and one which was scarcely known at all to the heathen of old time.

4. Most complete trust in God, whence it comes that when any one is injured or offended he does not immediately plan vengeance, but says to himself—'God has seen and heard this, and He will avenge in His Own time.'

5. To be able to endure all things in noble silence.

6. To attempt for the honour of God things which are difficult, and which are supposed to be scarcely possible" (Drexelius, 1912 110–125).

The system attempted to model humility, self-derogation, self-distrust, and complete intellectual acceptance of religious dogma and authority. Spiritual advisement became a special type of institutional counseling. Monasteries and convents had spiritual directors to whom the religious went for spiritual counsel. Since these directors were nearly always priests who could utilize confession as another of the tools for controlling internal attitudes, they became very powerful in the lives of those whom they directed. Regular monthly days of recollection and semiannual or annual retreats were scheduled for the comprehensive isolation of the individual before a series of religious lectures and experiences designed to reform his life. In later centuries, inspired mainly by the Jesuits and Carmelites, spiritual advising was developed within rules that related to the sequential development of the Christian life through given stages of mystical experience. The Carmelite literature of St. John of the Cross, and St. Theresa of Avila provide other examples of the manner in which spiritual unity with God became the obsessive task of countless generations of men and women. The development of these so-called spiritual qualities and characteristics required primarily an obedience to the spirit and a breaking of the human will. It also required contemplation, silence, penance and, in many many instances, individuals went to great extremes of masochism and sadism.

On the other hand, many spiritual advisors became very adept at guiding the intellectual and affective growth of their advisees. Moreover, when one considers that the monastic or contemplative life is characterized by a preoccupation with ritual routine, a lack of environmental stimulation in the form of verbal contact or normal social activities, one can estimate the great power that spiritual directors had over their advisees in terms of one of the only legitimate sources for social reinforcement. When one couples to this knowledge the general belief that illness—physical or mental—was the product of sin, one can understand the psychological desparation of many people.

Moreover, much of the Church system was built on the establishment and maintenance of guilt over sins real or fancied. The intensity of the system, the fact that convents and clerical offices were often the assigned lots of second or third sons or daughters leads one to understand easily how whole convents of women could begin to cluck like chickens, could show other abnormal symptoms, or come to believe readily and convincingly in all kinds of miracles.

SUMMARY

In this chapter medicine, philosophy, and religion are discussed as three avenues that affect man's behavior. The healer, the philosopher, and the theologian are all concerned with the physical and mental problems of man. Each of these areas devised goals, methods, and procedures for effecting certain kinds of changes in people or social groups. All utilized to some extent moral persuasion, modeling, tokens, rituals, and classical and operant conditioning plus punishment and reward to effect the shaping of human behavior.

Judaism, Christianity, and classical Greek philosophy have been discussed in some detail for the reason that Western civilization is built on many of these ideas as revised or revived at various times. In the extended study of the development of Christianity from a simple set of beliefs to an elaborate theological system that extended both social and individual controls over government and personal lives, there is a lesson for those who would wish to examine the manner in which an ideology becomes a social power force.

CHAPTER IV

Philosophical Foundations of the Scientific Perspective

The history of science in general and the history of psychology in particular is tied to a series of developments that had their remote origins in the ancient world, but their specific development during the past 600 or 700 years. A gap is often noted in modern education in the failure to recognize that styles of thought are crucial to behavior or to the designing of experiments. Asking the right question is often more important than knowing the right procedures. So often, students learn how to interpret confidence levels in statistics and even to perform competently the procedures required in experimentation without realizing that behind the technical operations which they are performing lies an entire approach to psychological phenomena that has been developed over a long period of time.

The purpose of this chapter is to provide an overview of some of the significant developments that occurred from the rise of Scholasticism to the beginning of scientific psychology in the early 19th century. Stemming from the beginnings of Scholasticism in the 12th and 13th centuries, two major traditions have their origin in this period—the empirical tradition of Locke, traced through the associationist school in England and through the French sensationists, and the intentionalist tradition of Leibnitz and his followers. The former becomes an environmentally oriented school of thought in which education plays a crucial role in the conditioning of experience. This is obviously the objectivist tradition that contributed strongly to the foundations of our own American school and psychological tradition. The emphasis in this chapter is on the environmentally oriented or pre-behavioral approach to education, experience, and learning. The other tradition (to be discussed in the next chapter), which incorporated elements of subjectivity into the nature of perception, can be traced into the main currents of German psychology in Herbart, Lotze, Brentano, Freud, and the entire Gestalt psychology of a later era. But it is important to recognize that the inclusion of a given philosopher or psychologist in one or the other chapters does not mean that he was lacking influence in the other area. Descartes, for example, was most influential in the thinking of Locke and Hume, the founders of the English objectivist tradition, while also influential in the later writings of Leibnitz and Brentano. What is important to recognize is the fact that philosophical systems are built on the foundations of prior philosophical thought. Plato's views were related to Socrates, Aristotle's to Plato, and the Arabian Alexandrian school of thought to Oriental mysticism and Neoplatonism. Augustine's views were a synthesis of Neoplatonism and Christian apologetical writing. Through these earlier reactions and counterreactions came ultimately the development of Scholasticism. And as a counterreaction to the overwhelming influence of theology and authority came the Renaissance, Reformation, Enlightenment, and the development of science as we know it today. And yet there is a continual repetition in philosophical thought. This repetition is largely caused by the fact that philosophical inquiry results from a sameness of purpose, subject, and unity in the problems of inquiry, that is, human nature, values, and knowledge. Thus the theme is old, but it is repeated in a thousand variations with adaptation and application to the constant progress of the physical sciences.

SCHOLASTICISM

Scholasticism is the name given to the intellectual movement sparked in the 11th century. It can be said to have started when the expository and dialectical methods handed down in the monastic and cathedral schools of the early Middle Ages came to be applied to theological data, and when rhetoric and logic came to be viewed not only as tools in themselves but as effective instruments for increasing learning. Scholasticism marked the assent of the use of reason as a valid tool in analyzing religious phenomena. It was an effort on the part of philosopher-theologians to analyze the nature of reality, human nature, learning, the physical sciences, and theology no longer according to Platonist ideas such as those of Augustine, but in the light of Aristotelian concepts.

Scholasticism owes its rise to a number of factors. Certainly, the Carolingian revival of learning played an important role in stimulating intellectual activity. Scholars such as John Scotus Eruigena and Roscelin began to systematically question and doubt some of the older dictums of Augustine, Jerome, and the early Church fathers. Political and economic developments also were important in providing an atmosphere that was conducive to the revival of learning. The crusades resulted in large-scale contacts with the Arabian philosophers such as Averroes, and Avicenna. These Arabian philosophers had inherited the Greek manuscripts of Aristotle, and were not hampered by the ecclesiastical censorship of Europe. They based much of their scientific investigations of physical and mathematical phenomena on the guidelines of Aristotle—rather than on Plato. They were not only influential in North Africa but were also influential in Spain where an entire Muslim culture, far in advance of Christian Europe, had sprung up through a liaison of Mohammedan and Jewish intellectual traditions.

A certain amount of political stability had been established in Europe by the beginning of the Middle Ages. France had a comparatively strong central government; England had a relatively stable government. Although central Europe was not as stable and as organized as these countries, it was now possible to live in relative security and to pursue a degree of learning and education outside of monasteries. Roads had been repaired and, although feudal customs still were most powerful, it was possible to travel from place to place. Economic conditions had improved and international banking concerns had developed. The impending doom of the Byzantine Empire (1453) brought flocks of Greek scholars to Italy during the last 100 years of the Middle Ages. In fact, conditions had so much improved that building programs were flourishing all over Europe. This was the period of the building of the great cathedrals and the origin of many technical schools and trade unions known as guilds. During this time Dante composed the *Divine Comedy*. In Spain *the Cid* was written and in France, the *Romance of the Rose*; in England it was the period of Chaucer and the rise of the Arthurian legends, while in Germany it was the era of the Meistersinger. In architecture, Gothic style was developed and, in law, the Middle Ages marks the granting of the *Magna Charta*, the charter of English liberties, and the ultimate foundation of much of English common law, which plays an important role in American law. This is also the time of the rise of the papacy to its greatest power under Innocent III and Boniface VIII. Concurrently, a great revival of learning took place that resulted in the foundation of the medieval universities and Scholasticism.

Scholasticism as a movement may be characterized as an attempt at intellectual and cultural synthesis. It was an attempt to unite philosophy and theology in a hierarchy of learning. Scholasticism originated in the period from 800 to 1000. This was a period of heavy leaning on the early Church fathers. The writings of this era were spotty, often incomplete, and derived fundamentally from Platonic thought. From 1000 to 1200 the

Scholastic movement gained momentum and tackled certain problems concerned with the nature of reality and universals. The introduction of Aristotelian works through the writings of the Arabians and the renewed study of Greek also stimulated new approaches to problems. During the period from 1200 to 1300 Scholasticism reached its peak. The works of Aristotle were freely circulated inasmuch as the Church had reluctantly decided to allow what it could not prevent. This was the time of Aquinas, who is considered the greatest of medieval thinkers. During the century from 1300 to 1400, Scholasticism went into decline and became involved in many senseless and minor details.

The movement of Scholasticism derived its name from the Scholastics, or schoolmen. There is a long series of individuals who contributed to the formation of the medieval system of Scholasticism. Although its beginnings were made in the 10th and 11th centuries, the real formation of Scholastic thought occurred in the 12th century. During this century scholastics tended to divide into two major groups, the rationalists and the mystics. The former were concerned with the development of logic, reason, and science, the latter with the more intuitive approach to faith and reason.

It is not relevant in this survey to dwell on Scholasticism. But is it important to highlight several issues that it raised and that were important to the development of the spirit of inquiry. A few of the chief rationalists should also be discussed in this context. Five individuals will be mentioned briefly. They are Peter Abelard (1079–1142), Roger Bacon (1214–1292), Albert the Great (1193–1280), Thomas Aquinas (1224–1274), and Duns Scotus (1266–1308).

Abelard was one of the early exponents of rationalism. He was a brilliant analytic thinker who produced a work entitled *Sic et Non* (which might be paraphrased as "For and Against"). Essentially, what he did was to take a number of major issues that involved both philosophy and theology and to express opinions for and against these issues. The opinions for often represented earlier thought, and those against his—or other individual's—opinions against traditional points of view. In this sense his negative responses were often more exciting and provoking than the affirmative ones.

Roger Bacon was a Franciscan monk at Oxford. He made one of the first attempts to formulate a scientific methodology by advocating the use of the empirical method, that is, the observation and classification of phenomena. He was most opposed to Aristotle and is reported to have said that he would burn the books of Aristotle if he could. His chief work *Opus Majus* contained many observations about scientific phenomena. He wrote some of his minor works in a code that was not deciphered until many centuries after his death. He observed the sun and stars and evidently had some means of refraction. In summing up for Pope Clement the body of doctrine that he was teaching at the University of Oxford in the 13th century, he started out with the principle that there are four grounds of human ignorance:

> These are first, trust in inadequate authority; second, the force of custom which leads men to accept too unquestioningly what has been accepted before their time; third, the placing of confidence in the opinion of the inexperienced; and fourth, the hiding of one's own ignorance with the parade of a superficial wisdom (James J. Walsh. *The Thirteenth, the Greatest of Centuries,* Catholic Summer School Press, 1913, 41).

Bacon also studied a variety of matters that relate to modern physics and chemistry. He recognized the possibilities of power that exist in certain compounds and theorized about the possible consequences for both warfare and transportation.

> . . . One may cause to burst forth from bronze, thunderbolts more formidable than those produced by nature. A small quantity of pre-pared matter occasions a terrible explosion accompanied by a bril-liant light. One may multiply this phenomena so far as to destroy a city or an army (Walsh, 42–43).

And, again,

> Art can construct instruments of navigation such that the largest vessels governed by a single man will traverse rivers and seas more rapidly than if they were filled with oarsmen. One may also make carriages which without the aid of any animal will run with remark-able swiftness (Walsh, 42–43).

The study of natural science was also pursued by Albert the Great, the teacher of Thomas Aquinas. Albert the Great was a Dominican monk who taught at Paris. He was not only a theologian but also a philosopher and a scientist. An idea of the great industry of this man may be gained from the fact that his completed works consist of 20 volumes containing an average of 500,000 words per volume.

Walsh (46–51) summarizes some of the contributions of Albert the Great. He states that Albert the Great wrote treatises on the origin of metals and minerals; that he listed a series of compounds and analyzed the organic structure and physiology of plants; that he made observations on the dependence of temperature on the latitude and elevation of the sun's rays; that he observed that the Milky Way is nothing but a vast assemblage of stars and that the configurations on the moon are not reflections of the earth but the topological characteristics of the moon itself; and that he was acquainted with a considerable amount of knowledge regarding germination in plants, the periodical and temporary closing of blossoms, and the diminution of sap through evaporation. But of major interest are his observations on geography. Walsh writes (46–51):

> He treats as fabulous the commonly-received idea, in which Bede had acquiesced, that the region of the earth south of the equator was uninhabitable, and considers, that from the equator to the South Pole, the earth was not only habitable, but in all probability actually inhabited, except directly at the poles where he imagines the cold to be excessive. If there be any animals there, he says, they must have very thick skins to defend them from the rigor of the climate, and they in all probability have a white color. The intensity of cold is however, tempered by the action of the sea. He describes the antipodes and the countries they comprise, and divides the climate into seven zones. He smiles with a scholar's freedom at the simplicity of those who suppose that persons living at the opposite region of the earth must fall off, an opinion that can only rise out of the grossest ignorance "for when we speak of the lower hemisphere, this must be understood merely as relative to ourselves." It is as a geographer that Albert's superiority to the writers of his own time chiefly appears. Bearing in mind the astonishing ignorance which then prevailed on this subject, it is truly admirable to find him correctly tracing the chief mountain chains of Europe, with the rivers which take their source in each; remarking on portions of coast which have been raised by volcanic action above the level of the sea; noticing the modification of climate caused by mountains, seas and forests, and the division of the human race whose differences he ascribes to the effect upon them of the countries they inhabit.

The greatest of all the Scholastics was *Thomas Aquinas* (1224–1274). Aquinas' contribution to Scholasticism is unparalleled in that his influence has lasted into the modern period. Aquinas will simply be mentioned in passing here, since a full exposition of his contribution to psychology and philosophy will come logically in the next chapter.

Duns Scotus, also an Oxford monk, was present at the University at the same time as Roger Bacon. He is said to have been influenced in his dislike of authority and Aristotle by Roger Bacon. This appears to be the gist of his contribution: that what may be true in philosophy (science) is not necessarily true in theology, and vice versa. Scotus is best known for his tortuous distinctions that were chiefly applied to theological notions. But one emphasis is important. Scotus stressed the role of the will in man and in God to a very high degree. Whereas Aquinas posited the priority of intellection or knowing in decision making, Scotus posited the priority of willing—and doing. Thus Scotus has been likened to Kant in the fact that both Scotus and Kant accent the role of will or the seeking of good and the avoiding of evil over the purely cognitive approach to knowing. Both Scotus and Kant emphasize the fact that human reason as such cannot demonstrate the truths that most vitally affect the future of man.

Aquinas and Scotus represent polar positions that are forerunners of much later thought. Aquinas placed chief emphasis on intellection and knowledge, believing that both man and God are determined in their behavior, to a large extent, by the knowledge that they have. Thus we see here the cognitive emphasis that Aquinas brought to his resolution of science and religious experience. Although there are different orders of experience and knowledge, it was Aquinas' opinion that the highest order was abstract knowledge and that the lower orders of knowledge related to sensory and perceptual experience. As a result, his entire system was a cognitive synthesis of philosophy (including the entire realm of natural science) with theology. Scotus, allowing for the possibility of distinction between science and/or philosophy and theology, emphasized far more the aspect of subjectivity and will in his system, with the ultimate court of appeal in religious matters being that of divine revelation.

It is interesting to observe that Aquinas and Scotus represent two points of view that were espoused by two different religious orders of teachers and practitioners. The Dominicans were clearly intellectualistic in their approach and followed Aquinas. The Franciscans were much more doers and were followers of Scotus. Scotus did not contribute much to the philosophy of science, but later followers tended to get into very subtle distinctions that then merged with a kind of mysticism which affected other writers such as Tauber who, in turn, influenced Luther.[1]

---

[1] One of the chief controversies that sparked a good deal of argumentation in the Middle Ages was the question of universals. On the surface it may seem that this whole issue was largely "Much ado about nothing." But in point of fact the question is not so irrelevant as may be thought. The basic issue was how does the human mind generalize and handle knowledge—particularly abstract concepts? Four opinions or solutions were voiced in the Middle Ages: (1) nominalism, (2) conceptualism, (3) ultra realism, and (4) moderate realism.

Nominalism was the opinion that an abstract notion such as the concept of chair was only a mental convenience in dealing with individual chairs—in other words—a name. This opinion was later held by Locke and Hume and is the opinion most identifiable with modern science. Conceptualism asserted that the universal idea was the creation of the mind and imposed by the very structure of the mind. Thus the

THE MATHEMATICAL-PHILOSOPHICAL REVOLUTION

It is beyond the scope of this study to describe all of the motivations that entered into the formation of the revolt against authority—political, theological, and philosophical—but this much appears certain that the intent of this revolution was essentially directed at the methodological tools that had been used in the past. Scholasticism had posited a hierarchy of methodological tools that had placed a premium on faith and divine revelations first, logical deduction second, and empirical evidence third. Despite individuals such as Albert the Great, Roger Bacon, and Thomas Aquinas, the system as it existed had no room for science. For the controls and political source of power were in the hands of spiritual authorities, who, as could be expected, sought to maintain the *status quo*.

The beginnings of the new approach are found in the Saracenic culture of Spain and North Africa with the invention of algebra and a new method of utilizing numbers (the Arabic System). In the 15th century

mind has a structure that determines the mode of forming concepts or ideas, and the mind's ability to handle universals is derived from this inherent structure of the mind. This opinion was later voiced by Kant in the 18th century and is very directly related to notions that the phenomenologists have raised about the nature of knowledge, as well as to some of the investigations that Piaget and his group have made in relationship to the categories of thinking that are found in children. In a very real sense, Bruner's stages of thought are also related to this point of view.

Ultra realism was the view that universals really exist outside the human mind. This opinion holds that there is a universal idea or prototype of chair, car, and the like. In a very real sense this is the view of Plato in his conception of a world of reality and ideas that exist independently of the world of phenomena.

Moderate realism was the fourth alternative, which was the approach taken by Aquinas and by the majority of Scholastics. This approach suggests that universal ideas do exist, but effectively only in the human mind. Outside the human mind there are only individual items, but the human mind abstracts qualities from individual items and creates a universal idea that does have an effective human existence as such.

To see more clearly the relevance of this thinking, let us apply these points of view to the concept of adjustment. Adjustment is an abstract idea. In the nominalist point of view it exists simply as a term, a construct or concept referring to certain basic qualities. In the conceptualist framework the notion of adjustment is related to the cognitive and perceptual structure of man's intellect and is determined, to some extent, by the very nature of the receiving organism—the subsuming organism as Ausubel would state. If this is true, then what is meant by adjustment should have some universal meaning. Ultra realism would suggest that there is some kind of modal or criterion analysis of what constitutes adjustment—in other words, an external referent that exists in itself as an abstraction. Moderate realism would suggest that the abstract notion of adjustment is just that, an abstraction, existing in the mind of man, but strongly shaped in its meaning by the nature of individual experience or different individual characteristics of adjustment in the outer world.

astronomy was revived and a number of individuals, for example, George Purbach (1423–61), Johannes Muller (1436–76), and Copernicus (1473–1543), began to study the heavens systematically. This was, in part, stimulated by the fact that the old Julian calendar was becoming out of step with the solar year. Copernicus devised a new physical system for the universe that placed the sun at the center and described the motions of the earth on its daily axis spin, its annual orbit around the sun, and the gyration of the earth's axis; this view of Copernicus contradicted the older accepted theory of Ptolemy that had been held from the Roman period on. The Ptolemaic view held essentially that the earth was the center of the universe and everything orbited around the earth. The position was in accordance with the Judaeo-Christian tradition which placed man at the center of the universe paralleling the account of the biblical creation. Moreover, from a common sense viewpoint, it did appear that the earth was immovable while everything else floated around it. In opposition to this approach, Copernicus held that the point of reference in astronomy was the fixed stars and sun, not the changing earth. He believed that the universe was essentially an enigma that could be solved by the scientist through the application of numbers and geometry. Thus he insisted that whatever was mathematically true was really true in astronomy also. The universe with its ultimate constituents was nothing but limited portions of space, and as a whole it presented a simple, beautiful, and geometric harmony.

Johannes Kepler (1571–1630) carried Copernicus' ideas forward. A German astronomer at Tübigen, he explained the motion of the tides and the moon as well as some of the laws affecting planets. He insisted that the reason why things are as they are is that they have a basic mathematical harmony. God created the world in accordance with the principle of perfect numbers; hence, the mathematical harmonies knowledgeable to the mind of the Creator furnish the cause why the number, size, and motions of the orbits are as they are and not otherwise. He also believed that the knowledge offered to the mind through the external senses was obscure, confused, contradictory and, hence, untrustworthy. Finally, he believed that all certain knowledge must be knowledge of the quantitative characteristic of phenomena; in other words, perfect knowledge is always mathematical.

Galileo (1564–1642) is known for his controversy with the Inquisition. His contribution to science was essentially the same as that of Copernicus and Kepler. He viewed nature as mathematical order and insisted that natural science could not be established on a philosophical basis alone, but that it is dependent on the immutable laws of mathematics. Thus he insisted that mathematics rather than logic based on judgments is the chief means to scientific discovery. He distinguished between what he called primary and secondary qualities. Primary qualities were those absolute objective realities that are fundamentally identified with the universe. They were of a mathematical nature. Secondary qualities were all the other subjective judgments made by the mind of man. His real contribution was toward the formation of a new cosmology or approach to physical phenomena which regarded the real world simply as a succession of motions in a mathematical continuity. He relegated man with his purposes, feelings, and destiny to the position of a secondary quality, that is, as a rather unimportant spectator watching and participating in the great drama.

Rene Descartes (1596–1650) provided the systematic philosophical basis for the observations of Copernicus, Kepler, and Galileo. His real point of divergence from Scholasticism began with his questioning of the hierarchy of methodological procedure advocated by Scholasticism. Although he refrained from calling into question matters of faith as such, he nevertheless insisted that philosophy and logic could not be the methodological procedure of science. Descartes summed up the revulsion of the age for philosophical speculation when he wrote:

> Of philosophy I will say nothing except that when I saw that it had been cultivated for many ages by the most distinguished men, and that yet there is not a single matter within its sphere which is not still in dispute, and nothing, therefore, which is above doubt. I did not presume to anticipate that my success would be greater in it than that of others; and further when I considered the number of conflicting opinions touching a single matter that may be upheld by learned men, while there can be but one true, I reckoned as well-nigh false all that was only probable (Descartes, 1927, 7).

Moreover, Descartes observed that in the beginning all philosophers of note had been mathematicians and that this quality or preparation for philosophical reasoning had been absent in later developments. Attacking the syllogism, the chief tool of the Scholastic form of logic, Descartes stated that it was only a communication of what we already know, and although logic had some excellent methods to commend it, it was so full of superfluous and injurious concepts that the whole fabric must be suspect. When he realized that the then known status of the natural sciences were also dependent on philosophical reasoning, he concluded that they were too subject to error and falsehood to be accepted. As a result, he proceeded to doubt all knowledge that had previously been accepted. He laid down the principle that he would never assume what is false as true, and that he would arrive at a knowledge that would take all things into consideration. He proposed to solve all philosophical problems on the basis of geometric reasoning from apodictic first principles. His method was to be the deductive geometric one in which there would be a reasoning from first truths or self-evident axioms downward to observed facts.

Descartes proposed the following methodology: (1) to admit nothing save clear and unimpeachable evidence; (2) to divide each of the difficulties under examination into as many parts as possible and as might be necessary for adequate solution; (3) to consider all questions in a fixed order from simple to abstruse; and (4) to make sure that nothing essential was omitted.

Descartes believed that mathematics was the key to knowledge and that it alone would unlock the secrets of the universe. His theory of knowledge started with certain self-evident propositions from which other knowledge could be deduced. Propositions such as the principle of contradiction, or that the effect cannot be greater than the cause, were, he believed, the foundation of all knowledge. Unfortunately, he retained a basic dualism, since he ascribed to the soul of man the possibility of grasping these immediately self-evident ideas. Intuition and deduction were the two main tools of his method. The real world possessed certain primary or mathematical qualities that could be understood through mathematical principles. This world he called the *Res extensa,* or the world of extension. This world was interpreted by the *Res cogitans,* the mind of man. It was here that the subjectivity of man misinterpreted the nature of reality. He conceived the extended world to be like a huge mathematical machine extended in space and time. This theory, known as the vortex theory, expressed a philosophical approach to reality that broke with the fundamental dualism of Scholasticism. He stimulated others, particularly John Locke and Gottfried Leibnitz, who both presented varying aspects of Descartes' theories.

Isaac Newton (1642–1727). There were many intermediate philosopher-scientists who contributed to the total sum of knowledge being accumulated during these centuries. Three of them are Francis Bacon with his critical suspicion of older forms of knowledge, Barrow, who observed that the only real object of science is quantity, and Gilbert, who discovered the magnetic qualities of the earth. But Newton in his discovery and formulation of the scientific method of experimentation was a real genius. He was also interested in theology and philosophy and wrote many thousands of pages on these subjects, seeking to find the secrets of the universe. Like many of the early scientists, he believed that the universe was a riddle that awaited only the unlocking by scientists who possessed the key, that is, mathematics. Attacking Descartes' ideas of innate knowledge, he distinguished between mathematical truth and physical truth. Newton held that the safest method of philosophizing seemed to be, first, diligently to investigate the properties of things and to establish them by experiments and then, later, to seek hypotheses to explain them. Hypotheses then, ought to be fitted merely to explain the properties of things and should not attempt to predetermine them except insofar as they aid in experimentation. Science, Newton held, was composed of laws stating the mathematical behavior of nature. These laws were clearly deducible from phenomena and exactly verifiable in phenomena. Everything over and above these procedures was to be swept out of science. Science, therefore, became a body of absolutely certain truth about the nature of the physical world. Once a principle had been established it was to be held as truth.

Newton proposed a conception of the world that included atoms, force, and ether. He believed that all changes in nature were to be regarded as separations, associations, and motions of atoms. These atoms formed masses that were known as bodies. In conjunction with his theory of mass, he enunciated the laws of gravitation, which united astronomy and mechanical physics into one mathematical science of matter in motion.

For the student of this period the flow of names and contributions can be a source of great confusion. For this reason only brief sketches of these great men have been given. But the impact of their collective force is what is most important with regard to its contribution to educational theory and practice. It is appropriate then to suggest what major changes this mathematical approach to science caused in the world view of this period.

Methodology

The first major contribution of this type of thinking was a change in the tools or techniques used to identify and categorize the nature of reality. From logic and philosophical absolutes, the tools of science became mathematics. Copernicus, Galileo, Kepler, Descartes, and Newton all fell back on mathematics as the chief tool of scientific discovery. The earlier scientists tended to regard geometry as a prime mathematical tool. Newton relied more heavily on algebra. But, in essence, the reliance on mathematics as the vehicle of discovery led to all sorts of indirect developments. John Graunt of London wrote a book in 1662 that led to the beginning of the analysis of vital statistics (*Nature and Political Observations made upon the Bills of Morality*). Edmund Halley, in 1693, published the first insurance tables for the development of actuarial computations. Scientific societies were founded for the development of science and particularly of mathematical and physical scientific discoveries. Thus an academy was established in 1560 at Naples and in 1603 at

Rome. The Royal Society of London was organized in 1660, and in the same year an academy was established at Paris. The Berlin academy was founded in 1700. The academies were important since with the developments in science and philosophy they served as the national centers for the collection and dissemination of information and were as important to the scientists of that period as our modern journals and computers are to us.

Changes in the Nature of Reality

Following the use of new methodological tools the old philosophical ideas about universals were not even of academic interest. Most of these scientists-philosophers were familiar with the basic ideas of Scholasticism and saw no reason for positing a foundation to the nature of reality that was other than scientific realism. In other words, they gave phenomena names and treated them as quantitative variables. Thus the scientific philosophy of realism came to substitute for the philosophical position of scholastic realism. A sharp cleavage was made in the minds of these men between the procedures used in dealing with physical phenomena and those metaphysical aspects of reality that were associated with philosophy. The basic idea came to be that reality was composed of primary and secondary qualities. This distinction crops up time and again in the literature of the period. The primary qualities of reality were those physical phenomena that could be interpreted through the use of mathematics. In other words, physical science was concerned with quantifiable data that had weight, volume, and mass. The unverifiable speculations about these phenomena or the higher abstractions of principles based on the previous theology of man were held to be, at best, subjective considerations. Thus many of these scientists held former academic philosophy to be of little consequence in terms of the advancement of science. They were concerned with the assessment of the physical characteristics of phenomena and not with the subjective interpretations of these phenomena. Thus, Descartes, Newton, and others, although privately interested in the philosophical questions of the relationship of the soul to the body (Descartes believed it to be through the pineal gland) (and Newton spent years in his laboratory secretly attempting to solve the riddles of God and the universe) did not publish or attempt to foster their ideas on these subjects and relationships with the same method that they worked on scientific data. Thus the entire beautiful hierarchy of the Scholastics with the subordination of the bodily functions to the spiritual became essentially irrelevant to the ongoing process of scientific discovery.

Changes in Conception of the Nature of Man

Regarding the nature of man, few if any of these early scientists doubted the existence of the soul. Copernicus and Galileo both subscribed to Roman Catholicism. Descartes also subscribed insofar as it was necessary to avoid persecution. Newton refused holy orders in the Anglican church but was unquestionably concerned with problems of spirituality. The existence of a huge trunkful of unpublished manuscripts with which he spent much of his time attempting to ferret out the problems of man's spirituality testify to Newton's ideas. Nonetheless, these men failed to accent this aspect of man because religious controversy had called the nature of man into question and also because of their preoccupation with the methods of science. Man had been relegated to a spectator in a universe of mass and motion. He was no longer at the center of the universe where the Bible and Scholastic tradition had placed him. Now, he was a collection of atoms obeying certain physical laws and was placed in a universe that operated without any essential regard for his needs. This was a profound change, but one that led to profitable inquiry. Physiologists broke with the general authority of the ancient physicians. Hippocrates and Galen, although they were still studied, no longer had the same authority. It was now possible to examine the human body and to do more dissections. In the Middle Ages this aspect of medicine had been most clearly proscribed and regulated. Physicians at some medieval universities could witness the dissection of a male only twice and of a female only once. Vesalius (1514–1564) dissected the human body and published drawings of what he found. Harvey (1578–1657) in 1616 discovered the circulation of the blood. Botany became a part of medical science. Above all, physicians began to search for the material causes of disease. Thus man's role in this universe began to be viewed more as that of a material creature whose mysteries also had to be investigated by a scientific method of experimentation.

Changes in the Nature of Knowledge and Values

A profound change came about as a result of these investigations. The medieval distinction between natural knowledge and supernatural knowledge broke down. The Scholastics had enunciated a principle of dualism whereby the natural world was known through the use of observation and logical classification, and the supernatural world through the use of revelation and theology. The scientists of the 16th and 17th centuries altered this scheme of things. They insisted that knowledge be confined to the scientific method, including empirical observation and the use of the experimental method. They believed that all physical phenomena could be established through mathematical principles and that the ultimate laws of the universe would be tapped by continued experimentation. Thus, they based knowledge on facts that were quantifiable and verifiable by the rigorous application of mathematical principles. With this type of thinking, it is clear why these scientists placed a great deal of value on the scientific procedure and comparatively little on spiritual matters. Subjectively, most of them still held with conventional morals, since the inquiry into science did not extend this far at this period. It was left for individuals like Spinoza to seek out the scientific explanation for morality. And his approach to this question was not accepted during his own period. What actually occurred was that the scientists of the period, although perhaps privately interested in some of these questions, did not spend their prime energies on the problems of spirituality. By default, these matters were left either to the reformed movement in the Roman Catholic Church, or to the state churches of Anglicanism and Lutheranism.

DIMENSIONS OF PSYCHOLOGICAL CHANGE AND DEVELOPMENT

Although it is most difficult to trace the relationship of ideas in this period, three men derived in various ways their basic concepts from Descartes and the scientific movement that was going on all around them. They are John Locke (1632–1704), Gottfried Leibnitz (1646–1716), and Benedict Spinoza (1632–1677). They are important individuals because they represent, in perhaps the earliest form, the basic cleavage that took place in the development of psychological science. Locke is the forerunner of the British empirical school of thought that, as we shall see, developed ultimately into associationism and the behavioristic approach to psychology. Leibnitz represented the European psychology that was later developed by Herbart, Brentano, and ultimately into the Gestalt approach to pyschology. Spinoza represents the first systematic approach to a scientific study of ethics and moral behavior. Although the implications of these men's writings were not completely identified in their own age, the subsequent development of psychology as a basis for educational development and procedures relies heavily on these three great giants of the 17th century.

John Locke was born in 1632, the son of a Puritan attorney. He was basically a tutor living for many years with the Earl of Shaftesbury and writing on a variety of subjects. His particular areas of influence have been felt in philosophy, government, and education. In philosophy his contribution centers chiefly on the question of how man knows. He raised the problem of knowing as a central question. Locke's influence has been extensive not only in the history of education itself but also in the areas of philosophy, psychology, and political theory, all of which have recip-rocally influenced educational practice and theory. Second, it is not easy to find a system of pedagogy that does not claim, or appear, to stem at least in part from Locke.

John Locke lived in a transitional period in which classical Humanism, with its emphasis on Ciceronian Latin, dominated still, but was just be-ginning to lose its battle with scientific realism. Modern languages were becoming important for reasons of travel, commerce, and literature. Dog-matism in religion had been seriously challenged. The direct importance of Locke lies in two books: *Essay Concerning Human Understanding,* and *Some Thoughts Concerning Education.* The essence of Locke's theo-retical approach was his *tabula rasa* theory.

Locke's own words explain best his theory:

There is nothing more commonly taken for granted, than that there are certain principles, both speculative and practical (for they speak of both) universally agreed upon by all mankind; which, therefore, they argue, must needs be constant impressions, which the souls of men receive in their first beings, and which they bring into the world with them, as necessary and really as they do any of their inherent faculties.

. . .

The senses at first let in particular ideas, and furnish the yet empty cabinet; and the mind by degrees growing familiar with some of them, they are lodged in the memory, and the names got to them. Afterwards the mind, proceeding farther, abstracts them, and by de-grees learns the use of general names. In this manner, the mind comes to be furnished with ideas and language, the materials about which to exercise its discursive faculty; and the use of reason be-comes daily more visible, as these materials, that give it employ-ment, increase.

. . .

Let us then suppose the mind to be, as we say, white paper, void of all characters, without any ideas; how comes it to be furnished? . . . To this I answer, in one word, from experience; in all that our knowledge is founded, and from that it ultimately derives itself. Our observation employed either about external sensible objects, or about the internal operations of our minds, perceived and reflected on ourselves, is that which supplies our understanding with all the materials of thinking (Locke, 1928, Chapter 1).

Locke's primary view here is that men are not born precisely equal intellectually but that the empty cabinets may be of different sizes, to continue his analogy, or the "internal operations of the mind" may differ in their dealings with experiences. Locke was simply attempting to eliminate logically the then-current theory that everyone is born with certain innate ideas—and that these innate ideas may be assumed in any discourse, in the same way that the high school student is taught to "assume" certain basic geometrical postulates.

The basic approach of Locke to experience as the source of all knowledge was summed up by his use of the dictum: "There is nothing in the intellect which has not first been in the senses."[2] He applied this basic idea to the psychology of learning and to government itself. What he actually did was to draw some arbitrary limits to the bounds of thinking, ruling out all so-called innate ideas or metaphysical considerations. In this approach he seems to have been attacking the position of Descartes, who grounded the basis of science in certain immutable a priori principles. In view of the fact that men differed only in the capacity of their learning from experience, Locke suggested that all men were born equal:

> All men are born equal, king and slave, rich and poor, the simple-minded and the genius. All begin life at the same point and the vast differences between men are caused by their experience and education (Eby, 293).

This doctrine applied to government suggested to Locke that the so-called "divine right of kings" was fallacious. In his constitution for the Carolinas he advanced the view that there was no such thing as the divine right of kings. In 1690, he issued two treaties on government which stated that absolute monarchy was inconsistent with civil society and that in the state of nature all men were free, independent, and equal. In the area of religion, he held that church and state should be separated and that there should be no restrictions on the right of worship. Thus Locke was the champion of a sense empiricism which held basically that the mind of man was formed by the kinds of experience that it had. True, he did suggest that certain individuals had a greater capacity for experience and thus provided some glint of an attitude toward individual differences.

One may follow the history of Lockean influence through three ped-

[2] Actually, this dictum had been used by Aquinas also and was not original with Locke.

agogical and psychological lines of descent, stemming from his *Thoughts Concerning Education* and from his *Tabula Rasa* doctrine. One such line leads through the French sensationalists (La Mettri, Condillac, and others), then partially through Rousseau and his followers, but more clearly through the French educators of defective children (Itard and Sequin) to Maria Montessori in Italy. These educators stressed the aspect of the theory which implies that all education is gained initially and solely through sense impression.

Another line of descent follows the English associationists, through Hume, the Mills, Spencer, and Bain, to the displacement and absorption of associationism by the evolutionary point of view. The emphasis here was on the operation of the mind, with little stress on the problem of the manner by which the mind received the materials on which it operated. This development affected Herbart and Brentano in the development of their ideas.

The third line is traced rather clearly through Rousseau, Pestalozzi, separately through Herbart and Froebel, and possibly into the implications of Freudian analytic studies as they pertain to the child. This aspect of Locke's doctrine is concerned with the study of the child for his own sake.

It is certainly recognized that any attempt to designate these lines of descent is somewhat of an artifact, since many other factors influenced the succeeding generations. At times, the relationships seem obscure and the similarities between master and student are less obvious than the differences. These difficulties are inherent in any historical study of the evolution of ideas.

The basic contribution of Locke is the idea that experience can mold a person. In this connection then, the doctrine of the innate depravity of mankind, such as held by the Calvinists, has no place. People are morally neutral, they become what they are through their experience. This had profound implications for child-rearing, education, and the psychology of learning. We shall learn more about Locke's specific educational teachings later in this chapter.

The Lockean Tradition in Psychology and Education

The freshness brought about by the expansion westward of the known world, and the fruitless exhaustion resulting from religious wars, brought something of a religious "truce" on minor doctrinal problems. To discuss the West Indies and Newton, Sir Francis Drake, and Descartes became more fascinating than to argue over trans- versus consubstantiation in the sacrament. Some progress was being made in education; in France, the Jesuit revival of learning and the education of girls was receiving increased emphasis. The writing of Mulcaster, the Port Royalists, Comenius, and John Milton showed new insights into methods and some improvement in theory. But no one said: "Let us study the child—for it is the child whom we teach." In actual practice, with rare exceptions throughout Europe, education was of the type that Locke so vigorously combatted: brutal in discipline, sterile in content, and based on memorization in method. There was little education available or even suggested for the poor (except by Comenius and by Luther). Latin, rhetoric logic, and usually Greek were "taught" but rarely learned; no subject we now think of as "practical" was available except in pitiful amounts in a few universities. Locke himself was educated in such traditional schools, and this may account in part for his hostility toward them.

The child as an individual, or as a learner, was given scant attention or consideration. Each child, more or less indistinguishably and indiscriminately, was the recipient of the learning—or of the blows—imposed by the teacher. If he learned, memorized, or wrote in Ciceronian style the assigned Latin composition, well and good; if not, no "individual differences" were considered as a mitigating factor. Both Catholic and Protestant considered the child to have been, in the words of the psalmist, "conceived in sin, and born in iniquity." This tenet was being widely challenged, for the expansion of the world was tending to break down the narrow provincialism and the dogmatic righteousness of the church. Reports by learned travelers to academic societies and by illiterate sailors to the "village folk" on primitive societies, strange religions, and peculiar customs caused Europeans to realize that they did not have a monopoly on the true or only mode of life. Perhaps, some of their cherished beliefs and dogmas were, at the very least, open to discussion and even to question! The comparative studies—of philosophy, religion, and political philosophy, not to speak of the accent on the scientific method—were damaging to absolutism and dogmatism, and broadening and challenging to man's thinking.

The importance of Locke's writings is expressed by Boyd (1952). Prior to 1660, considerable progress had been made in the English school system by the Puritans, utilizing the arguments of Roger Bacon for freedom of inquiry combined with Comenius' "sense realism"—a forerunner of the whole object-teaching method. With the restoration of Charles II in 1660, however, these gains were largely lost and the educational system suppressed. However, writes Boyd:

> The Puritan spirit found expression once again in the last decade
> of the century, in a notable educational work through which much
> that was essential in its philosophy of education could be carried on

into the new age just ahead. This was John Locke's *Thoughts Concerning Education* (273).

Others, such as John Milton, had written on education, but those works carried little influence and affected educational practices only locally. It was the *total* importance of Locke, his recognized stature as a thinker, and the spread of his writings throughout Europe that made whatever he said on education—or on anything else—important.

> Of the leaders of thought during this era, John Locke was by all odds the foremost . . . Coming just when he did and having fresh and sensible views on many of the deepest problems of the age, he became uniquely important. He was a pivotal figure on whose ideas the new epoch turned; for this reason, his life and contributions merit special study (Eby, 1952, 286).

Locke was not an educator primarily, although his profession was teaching. Education seems to have been somewhat a matter of secondary interest to him. His *Thoughts* were written only as a series of letters to a friend and were published under some protest:

> But you know I can truly say, that if some, who having heard of these Papers of mine, had not press'd to see them, and afterwards to have them printed, they had lain dormant still in that Privacy they were design'd for (1902, lxi).

Consequently, the book suffers from a lack of serious editing, from repetitiousness, and from some superficiality and triviality. The latter, of course, is understandable, since it was an "applied" education, written as a guide for use and not as a theoretical approach to education.

Locke's Ideas on the Child

As can be observed above, Locke was in no sense a "democrat" and, as a result, he believed that education should be restricted to the youths who would later be the nation's leaders—that is, to "gentlemen." In the Dedication of his *Thoughts,* he concluded: "For if those of that rank are by their Education once set right, they will quickly bring all the rest into Order" (1902, lxiii). His attitude toward the poor may be gauged by his remarks in the two-page plan he submitted for "Working Schools:"

> The children of labouring people are an ordinary burden to the parish, are usually maintained in idleness, so that their labour also is generally lost to the public till they are twelve or fourteen years old. The most effectual remedy for this that we are able to conceive . . . is . . . that working schools be set up in every parish to which

the children of all such as demand relief of the parish, above three and under fourteen years of age . . . shall be obliged to come (1902, 189).

At these schools, the children were to be fed little except broth and bread and were to gain some schooling, but the primary intent was economic:

This, though at first setting-up it may cost the parish a little, yet we humbly conceive . . . it will quickly pay its own charges with an overplus (190).

The four general aims of education—particularly as applied to the upper class—are, in the order of their importance: virtue, wisdom, breeding, and learning. Locke anticipates and defends against the numerous criticisms he expects to receive for placing learning last in order, and then he attacks his anticipated attackers for all the worthless knowledge with which they cram their pupils. Education is preparation for adult life (as a "gentleman"); Greek and Latin grammar, theme-writing, and Ciceronian style are merely learning that emphasizes imitativeness, grammatic precision, and memorization at the expense of understanding and utility. Only the scholar who wishes to do so should learn Greek; all students, admittedly, should learn Latin but only for its usefulness in communication. Such things as rhetoric and poetry are to be completely discarded.

Individual Differences

With regard to individual differences, although Locke seemed to indicate that all men were born equal, he appeared to contradict himself. On page one of his *Thoughts* he wrote:

I think I may say, that of all the Man we meet with nine Parts of ten are what they are, good or evil, useful or not, by their Education. 'Tis that which makes the great Differences in Mankind. The little, or almost insensible impressions on our tender infancies, have their important and lasting Consequences.

But later he says:

. . . we shall see whether what is required of him be adapted to his Capacity, and any Way suited to the Child's natural Genius and Constitution; for that too must be consider'd in a right Education. We must not hope wholly to change their original Tempers, nor make the Gay pensive and grave, nor the Melancholy sportive, without spoiling them. God has stamp'd certain Characters upon Men's

Minds, which like their Shapes, may perhaps be a little mended, but can hardly be totally altered and transform'd into the contrary.

He therefore that is about Children should well study their Natures and Aptitudes, and see by often Trials what Turn they easily take, and what becomes them; observe what their native Stock, is how it may be improv'd, and what it is fit for . . . For in many Cases, all that we can do, or should aim at, is, to make the best of what Nature has given . . . to prevent the Vices and Faults to which such a Constitution is most inclin'd, and give it all the Advantages it is capable of. Every one's natural Genius should be carry'd as far as it could; but to attempt the putting another upon him, will be but Labour in vain; and what is so plaster'd on, will be best sit but untowardly, and have always hanging to it the Ungracefulness of Constraint and Affectation (1902, 40).

Elsewhere he wrote:

There are not more Differences in Men's Faces, and the outward Lineaments of their Bodies, than there are in the Makes and Tempers of their Minds; only there is this Difference, that the distinguishing Characters of the Face and the Lineaments of the Body, grow more plain and visible with Time and Age; but the peculiar *Physiognomy of the Mind* is most discernible in children. Before Art and Cunning have taught them to hide their Deformities, and conceal their ill inclinations under a dissembled Outside (1902, 82).

Some of the French philosophers, particularly Helvetius, argued from Locke that education provides the *only* individual differences among men, but it is obvious that they were not drawing the same conclusions that Locke did from the *tabula rasa* doctrine.

It was on the basis of these individual differences, here for the first time explicitly stated as one of the principles of education, that Locke recommended the tutorial method of instruction rather than mass education. More than that, he recognized the "readiness" principle currently so important:

. . . they should seldom be put about doing even those Things you have an inclination in them to, but when they have a Mind and Disposition to it. He that loves Reading, Writing, Musick, etc., finds yet in himself certain Seasons wherein those Things have no Relish to him; and if at that Time he forces himself to it, he only bothers and wearies himself to no purpose. So it is with Children. This Change of Temper should be carefully observ'd in them, and the favorable Seasons of Aptitude and Inclination be headfully laid hold of: And if they are not often enough forward of themselves, a good Disposition should be talk'd into them, before they be set upon any thing (1902, 53).

Presumably the "readinesses" differed among children, so that individual instruction was the only plausible type of education.

While it does not necessarily follow from Locke's doctrine that the mind is only a passive recipient of external stimuli (with the active functions of the mind following the sensation, as a mill grinds only the grain poured into it), yet his *Thoughts on Education* tends to assume this to be the case. The child is to be molded, to be trained by habit, to be disciplined, to be "educated" for his life as a man. Unlike Rousseau, Locke has no sympathy with the child *as a child,* but only with respect to his future status as a gentleman. In this respect, it is unfortunate that Locke was not acquainted with Comenius (at least, he does not refer to him in his writings), for Comenius here was in advance of Locke. Locke seems to have accepted quite uncritically the theories of Montaigne, whose *Essays* he quotes with approval.

In reading Locke, one has the feeling that he was a brilliant, rational, and unfeeling person. His attitude on discipline is worth quoting:

A compliance and Suppleness of their Wills, being by a steady Hand introduc'd by Parents, before Children have Memories to retain the Beginnings of it, will seem natural to them, and work afterwards in them as if it were so, preventing all Occasions of struggling or repining. The only Care is, that it be begun early, and inflexibly kept to 'till Awe and Respect be grown familiar, and there appears not the least Reluctancy in the Submission and ready Obedience of their Minds. When this Reverence is once thus established (which it must be early, or else it will cost Pain and Blows to recover it, and the more the longer it is deferr'd) 'tis by it, still mix'd with as much indulgence as they make not an ill use of, and not by Beating, Chiding, or other servile Punishments, they are for the future to be govern'd as they grow up to more understanding (1902, 29).

Despite the harshness or coldness that appears in the above quotation, Locke's discipline, for his time, was relatively mild. The child was to be severely beaten only for obstinacy. However, in *all* things, the father was to be the absolute arbiter; the desires, needs, and emotions of the child were to be considered only on cool reflection by the father, and the first duty of the child was to learn proper awe and respect for authority. Locke was greatly distressed at the increasing disrespect shown to parental and other authority by the younger generation, and he wished to restore that respectful attitude in which *his* generation had been raised. Although Locke did not hold with the severity of the "original sin" doctrine about the innate depravity of children, he nonetheless held that a child is born with certain "natural inclinations," all of which are bad, and that the purpose of education is to erase, or at least to hide, these inclinations. They are not defined as stemming from "original sin" by Locke, but their existence is simply accepted.

> I have often . . . seen People . . . not take sufficient Care to cover that which is the most shameful Nakedness, viz, their natural wrong inclinations and ignorance (1902, 67).

Elsewhere, he also speaks of education as essential for the correcting of natural tendencies.

The primary motives to behavior are the fear of pain and of the loss of pleasure. These fears are, apparently, innate: "The only thing we naturally are afraid of is Pain or Loss of Pleasure" (1902, 67). This hedonistic doctrine was not new with Locke, of course, nor did he stress it as much as did some of his followers, such as Condillac. When a greater amount of socialization had occurred in later years, the two—and only two—motivators were: shame or disgrace, and the approbation of others.

Locke was a thorough-going dualist. The opening sentence in his *Thoughts* is: "A sound mind in a sound body is a short but full description of a happy state in this world." He separates the mind and body and insists on the strengthening of the body so that it may do the will of the mind. About 40 pages are devoted to the hardening of the body: the shoes of the child should leak, he should swim in the coldest water in winter, the body should be lightly covered even in cold weather, the diet must be adequate but very simple, and he should sleep on a very hard bed. Locke devotes very few pages to the education of women; the sum and substances of these pages is that "the nearer they come to the Hardships of their Brothers in their Education, the greater Advantage will they receive from it all the remaining Part of their lives" (1902, 7).

Locke touches not at all on that which the French sensationists made paramount, and which, one may argue, he originated: the training of the senses. Since all knowledge is acquired originally through the senses, it would not be illogical to assume that sense education is *the* educational method *par excellence*. Locke simply assumed that the senses were healthy and operated normally, providing a "true" picture of the outside world. His primary interests were on the operation of the mind on those materials as they were received. The child must be taught to "reason"— and if two young men are taught to reason well and without bias, they cannot possibly reach different conclusions. It is, of course, the secondary source of ideas, that of internal sensation ("reflection") that the French sensationists denied. To Locke, ideas (which he defined loosely as "objects of thinking", and which are comparable to the *Vorstellungen* of Herbart) were available either directly from empirical, sensory experience, or from reflections on these experiences. Reasoning is this second type of operation. Locke stressed the importance of "reflection"; the French sensationists emphasized the prior sensations and ignored or denied reflection.

The mark of the educated man is his virtue and breeding, but Locke spends more time on developing the power to reason than on virtue. He did not distinguish between children and adults in this respect except in their different quantitative ability to reason:

> But when I talk of Reasoning, I do not intend any other but such as is suited to the Child's Capacity and Apprehension. No body can think a Boy of three or seven Years old should be arg'd with as a grown Man (1902, 60).

In one rare passage he recognizes the effects of emotion on reasoning:

> Children's Minds are narrow and weak, and usually susceptible but of one Thought at once. Whatever is in a Child's Head, fills it for the time, especially if set on with any Passion (142).

The power to reason comes by practice; practice and habits are extremely important aspects of Locke's system. In his *Conduct of the Understanding* he wrote:

> We are born with faculties and powers capable almost of any thing, such at least as would carry us farther than can easily be imagined; but it is only the exercise of these powers, which give us ability and skill in any things, and leads us toward perfection . . . As it is in the body, so it is in the mind; practice makes it what it is; and most even of those excellencies, which are looked on as natural endowments, will be found when examined into more narrowly, to be the product of exercise, and to be raised to that pitch only by repeated actions (1823, 213–14).

In response to his own question of why men then do not reason better, he replies:

> Few men are, from their youth, accustomed to strict reasoning, and to trace the dependence of any truth in a long train of consequences, to its remote principles, and to observe its connexion; and he that by frequent practice has not been used to this employment of his

understanding, it is no mere wonder that he should not, when he is grown into years, be able to bring his mind to it (1823, 218).

Locke's Influence and Derivations of His Thought

One of the chief problems in identifying the contribution and influence of a man like Locke is that his writings are mixed with aspects of psychology, philosophy, ethical theory, and scientific method. Thus, for the modern reader, many of the ideas of Locke, and indeed of others of this period, seem confused and mixed up. The philosopher is concerned with the epistemology of knowledge, the manner in which man knows. The psychologist is concerned with the actual process and features of experience as they result in behavior.

Locke moved away from the dualism that had been held by the Scholastics and the continental philosopher, Leibnitz. Although theoretically supporting the mind-body concept (for how could one really oppose this concept at this time?), Locke, like Descartes, gave lip service to the concept and then proceeded to treat mind without too much consideration for dualism. Locke did recognize that there were some "native tendencies" in man and that the capacity which a man had for learning was in some way dependent on his abilities and "natural aptitudes." But he denied that there were innate ideas or necessary logical and mathematical truths that existed in an a priori sense in the structure of the human mind. Central to his whole system was the idea that man is molded by experience and that the experience of the senses creates the reservoir of knowledge. This knowledge system, in effect, reduced higher mental processes to a fairly mechanical system of categorizing sense knowledge. True, he acknowledged the necessity of reflection, but he felt that this was simply a synthesis of previous experience. Upon this whole system he superimposed the necessity of discipline and training in virtue, so that the systematic assimilation of experience might be meaningful in terms of the expected role that "gentlemen" should follow in the society of the "enlightenment."

These ideas persisted in several following schools of thought. One of these schools was typified by the associationist school that developed later in England. Another influence of Locke was evidenced in the writings of French thinkers, eventually finding itself in the psychological developments of Rousseau, Pestalozzi, Froebel, and others. A third influence proceeded from the English associationists, particularly John Stuart Mill to the German psychologist-philosopher, Franz Brentano. This influence, which took place in the 19th century, reintroduced some of the associationist ideas into Act Psychology as developed by Brentano. As Watson (1963) has written:

In a manner reminiscent of Aquinas, Locke referred to reflection as an internal sense. Locke made a distinction between being aware of an idea (reflection) and merely having an idea in itself. The question of how the mind obtains knowledge of its own operations was thus solved; reflections were ideas about ideas, as it were, reflections on the manner of their occurrence. Act psychologists of the nineteenth century made this distinction an important part of their approach in that they distinguished between act or function on the one hand and content on the other. With Locke, some of them stressed that there are two materials of mind (Watson, 177).

The Associationist School

Although the development of the associationist school of psychology came later, it is appropriate to discuss some of the developments that took place in conjunction with Locke. *David Hume* (1711–1776) wrote several tracts that represented the tradition of Locke. Two of them were *A Treatise of Human Nature* and *An Enquiry Concerning Human Understanding.* More systematic than Locke, he also carried some of Locke's ideas to their logical conclusion. If the mind is a *tabula rasa,* and if there are no innate ideas, why resort to the concept of a soul? Feeling that the astronomers and physicists such as Newton had established a scientific procedure for investigating the laws of the universe and of motion and order, he stated that the same could be done for the laws of understanding and mental life. Seeking a basic law to begin with, corresponding to Newton's law of gravitation, he found it in the laws of the association of ideas. Aristotle had enunciated some of these laws of association many centuries before, and Hume simply elaborated on the same laws. For example, he said that the laws of association were based on similarity, contiguity in time or place, and causality. Aristotle had also held the law of opposites. These laws, Hume believed, explained all processes of thinking. Moreover, when it came to the higher processes of the mind, Hume felt that all mental content consisted of two kinds of impressions: strong ones that were the responses to external or internal sensory stimuli; and weak ones that he believed could be called ideas and were nothing but the fainter copies of impressions once felt. Memory and imagination were simply a description of how ideas—or the fainter impressions—recalled, reconstructed, and utilized earlier sensory experiences. The key to the development of the mental content of a given individual was habit in which all experiences were joined together.

Hume was widely read and appreciated on the Continent. Many German philosophers, particularly the idealists, inveighed against him, but his ideas represented the continuation of Locke's thought reducing many of the confused elements of Locke into a coherent system. Thus the empiricism of Locke was transformed into associationism.

David Hartley (1705–1759) did not add substantially to the psychological aspect of associationism, but he did attempt to connect the theoretical formulations of Locke and Hume with physiological phenomena. As Watson has written:

> The doctrine of vibration suggested by Newton's account of motion, Hartley told us, is his starting point. Newton had spoken of physical impulses as vibratory. Hartley held that external vibrations set in motion the white medullary substance of the brain with which sensations are intimately associated. Changes in one entailed corresponding changes in the other. (It will be noted that nerves have superseded animal spirits.) Hartley took pains to insist that the nerves are solid, and not tubes, necessitating his postulating vibration propagated along them as a means of spread of movement.

> The cerebral vibrations and the ideas perform in parallel. One is not the cause of the other. Rather, they show consistent correspondence. Events in one are correlated perfectly with events in the other. As a consequence, Hartley's view may be interpreted as a simple form of what is called psychophysical parallelism (Watson, 190).

Hartley was one of the first individuals in this era to recognize the need for supporting physiological information and exploration in order to tie together the doctrine of associationism and the physiological events of the body. Although the basis of physiology in that period was poor, developments in the 19th century, beginning with Johannes Muller in Germany, and carried on by Henry Maudsley in England and by Helmholtz in Germany, indicated that his contribution to the overall mind-body parallelism was not insignificant.

In a later chapter, we shall trace the further developments of the associationist school of psychology. The impact of the Scottish school, and of the Mills on Alexander Bain who influenced Edward Lee Thorndike is all a part of this story and the unwinding of the history of psychological thought in relationship to the scientific approach to education. It is sufficient here that this connection be identified to justify the reason for the extensive treatment of Locke in this period.

THE FRENCH SENSATIONISTS

In France, two writers of the 18th century illustrate the influence of Locke. La Mettrie is an example of the atheistic gross materialist who extended the doctrines of Descartes and Locke to an extreme; Abbe

Condillac was a sensationist now most famous for his "statue analogy."

Julian La Mettrie (1709–1751) published, in 1748, a small book, *Man a Machine,* by which he antagonized practically every French thinker and the Church by his atheism, materialism, and boorish attack on anyone who attempted to understand human nature without first being trained, like himself, as a physician. La Mettrie denied the need for, and the existence of, a theological soul, and throughout his writings he attributed all behavior to mechanistic principles. For example:

> The human body is a machine which winds its own springs. Nourishment keeps up the movements which fever excites. Without food, the soul pines away, goes mad, and dies exhausted (La Mettrie, 1943, 93).

The soul (l'ame) is merely that part of us which thinks:

> The soul is therefore but an empty word, of which no one has any idea, and which an enlightened man should use only to signify the part in us that thinks (127).

Complex matters such as "the conscience" are merely matters of "a few more wheels, a few more springs":

> But since all the faults of the soul depend to such a degree on the proper organization of the brain and of the whole body, that apparently they are but this organization itself, the soul is clearly an enlightened machine. For finally, even if man alone had received a share of natural law, would he be any less a machine for that? A few more wheels, a few more springs than in the most perfect animals, the brain proportionally nearer the heart and for this very reason receiving more blood—any one of a number of unknown causes might always produce this delicate conscience so easily wounded, this remorse which is no more foreign to matter than to thought, and in a word all the differences that are supposed to exist here (1943, 127).

La Mettrie cites physiological and anthropological reasons to "prove" that man is not qualitatively different from animals, and he uses his ability and training as a physician to show, rather grandly, how nothing will long remain unknown—to the physician. The source of energy for all bodily movements of animals and man is the motive power of the whole body. To La Mettrie, the physical organism—and especially the brain—was the most significant and important element of the person. However, education, imagination, and the senses also were highly important.

If one's organism is an advantage, and the pre-eminent advantage, and the source of all others, education is the second. The best made brain would be a total loss without it, just as the best constituted man would be but a common peasant, without knowledge of the ways of the world. But, on the other hand, what would be the use of the most excellent school, without a matrix perfectly open to the entrance and conception of ideas? It is . . . impossible to impart a single idea to a man deprived of all his senses (109).

Thus, individual differences may derive from different physiological brain structures, or from education, but it is in the difference of imagination that they are expressed. Despite La Mettrie's oft-expressed distaste for philosophers, including both Descartes and Locke, it is apparent that he adopted Descartes' materialism and extended it to man, changed his mathematics to physiology, and eliminated the theological soul, dualism, and all need for God. From Locke he quotes sometimes with approval and sometimes with disapproval. Like most educated Frenchmen of the period, he was well acquainted with Locke's *Essay.* Their agreement on the dismissal of innate ideas and on the importance of the senses was a significant feature of the continuation and expansion of Locke's thought in the materialism of French writers. Boring (1950) writes:

La Mettrie is important because, taking an extreme position, he became a signpost for a trend—the trend toward materialism away from spiritualism, the trend toward the mechanistic and physiological interpretation of the mind. In this way he was both effect and cause, both representing and promoting the *Zeitgeist* of scientific materialism. He fitted in with the empiricism that Condillac was getting from Locke . . . His vigorous insistence thus makes him the first thorough-going 'objective psychologist' whom we have had occasion to consider in this book (1950, 214).

La Mettrie made the "laws of nature" the basis of judgment in all matters of morals and ethics. "Such is natural law," he wrote that, "Whoever rigidly observes it is a good man and deserves the confidence of all the human race" (1943, 127). Unfortunately, nowhere does he specifically touch on the education or nature of children as distinct from those of adults; his iconoclasm was directed toward male adults, and children were outside his purview. Condillac, who is considered next, entered more directly into the sphere of educational influence.

Abbe Condillac (1715–1780). There are some points of similarity between La Mettrie and Condillac, yet the latter managed to remain a cleric in good standing with both church and state throughout his life, whereas La Mettrie was denounced and exiled. Probably Condillac was well acquainted with *The Human Machine* but avoided any mention of it in his own work to save the embarrassment of "guilt by association," or the stigma of having any relationship with condemned writings.

Both men agreed that experience is a source of all knowledge, and that it is gained only through the senses. Neither conceived of any qualitative difference between animals and man, but Condillac attributed a divine soul to both, and La Mettrie to neither. To Condillac, man differed from animals only in the much greater complexity and capacity of his mind; to La Mettrie, the difference was only a matter of "a few more springs, a few more wheels." Boring (1950, p. 204) attributes to Condillac the initiation of the French empiricistic school and attributes to La Mettrie the essential beginning of materialism. While probably it was Condillac's intention to refute materialism and atheism, it was not difficult for some of his followers, notably Diderot and D'Alembert, to extend his doctrines to closer agreement with La Mettrie and, at least, to deism if not to atheism.

A kind of summary of his key book *Treatise on Sensations,* published in 1754 (six years after La Mettrie's, *The Human Machine*) appears in Condillac's "Dedication" to Madame de Vasse. Speaking of the statue he will describe in the book, he says:

> We thought best to begin with smell, because of all the senses it is the one which appears to contribute least to the cognitions of the human mind. We took the other senses in succession and after considering them separately and together, we beheld the statue become a living being capable of caring for its own preservation.

> The principle determining the development of its faculties is simple. It is comprehended in the sensations themselves, for these being naturally pleasant or unpleasant, the interest of the statue will be to enjoy the one kind and reject the other. Now we are able to show that this interest is sufficient to explain the operations of the understanding and the will. Judgment, reflexion, desires, passions, etc., are only sensations differently transformed . . . Nature gives us organs in order to show us, by means of pleasure and pain, what to seek and what to avoid (Condillac, 1930, xxxi–xxxii).

This statue analogy lies at the basis of Condillac's psychology of man. Condillac supports Descartes concept of an immaterial soul, and there can be no direct treatment by mathematics of an immaterial soul. Nonetheless, Condillac felt that the soul could be influenced by experience and knowledge much in the way that a marble statue could come to life as individual senses engrave their special characteristics on the marble. It is a matter of a transformation whereby the marble (soul) gradually is made aware of experience and, although changed perhaps in terms of quantitative characteristics, does not undergo an essential qualitative transformation.

Practically all modern writers who comment on Condillac's statue analogy have referred to it as "absurd," although they do not elaborate. Some understanding of its appeal to modern behaviorists may be gained by noting that Lashley used a very similar analogy—that of a machine constructed on reflex response principles—in 1923 (Lashley, 1923). It is true that Condillac was not a mechanist, but his model, when combined with La Mettrie's mechanism and determinism, fit nicely into the recent concepts of electronic brains and robots. Scientists of mechanistic inclination are not willing to completely give up the idea, even if the whole statue analogy is artificial.

Condillac's idea of instincts resembles that of more modern theories of instinct as acquired habit, explainable in terms of the conditioned response:

> These habits are definite movements which take place in us without our appearing to direct them ourselves; because of having repeated them, we perform them without thought. These are the basic habits which we call natural impulses, mechanical actions, instincts, and which we falsely suppose to have been born with us. We shall avoid this error, if we judge these habits by others which have arisen naturally and the acquisition of which we very distinctly remember (Condillac, *Logique*, quoted in Schaupp, 1926, 41).

Condillac believed that individual differences could be explained on the basis of the association of ideas—which occurs when the same act of attention embraces both ideas. The stronger the associations, the more intelligent the person. Both their strength and their number, however, depend on the bodily organization. Compayre quotes Condillac as saying that "it has been proved that the faculty of reasoning begins as soon as the senses commence to develop; and we have the early use of our senses because we early learn to reason" (Compayre, 1886, 314). Consequently, early education of the child is to be in observation and reasoning. He does not specifically state that the senses must be educated, although this is not an illogical consequence of his belief that the child needs to *learn* to see, hear, and taste.

Condillac believed that the faculties of the understanding are the same in a child as in a grown man, and that all studies appropriate to manhood would also be appropriate to children if properly graded and scaled. A highly practical pedagogical result of this bit of "mental philosophy" was the resulting trend toward the careful grading of learning material to correlate with the age of the learner. A somewhat less desirable consequence was the support which it gave to the theory that the child is but a miniature adult and should be treated (and dressed) as a "man in miniature." By dressing a child as an adult, by requiring of him adult behavior, he would the sooner become an adult mentally. This is the doctrine against which Rousseau protested bitterly later on in his *Emile*.

Condillac wrote on pedagogy when he composed a 13-volume *Course of Study* for the education of the heirs of the Duke of Parma. In this lengthy work, Compayre finds some (but not many) advanced ideas on education. For example, Compayre says:

> . . . with an indiscretion that is to be regretted, he arbitrarily transports into education certain philosophical principles which are not proper to apply to the art of educating man, whatever may be their philosophical truth; thus Condillac, having established the natural order of the development of the sciences and the arts in the history of humanity, presumes to impose the same laws of progress upon the child (Compayre, 1886, p. 312).

The child must duplicate in his own educational development the progress made by the race. This recapitulation theory is met again and again in later educational theory, and its origin is attributed to a number of men. As far as the writers in this field are concerned, however, this is the first expression of the theory applied to education. The influence of Condillac on French education and on the progress of psychological thought was of considerable duration and extent. Schaupp wrote:

> His work was regarded as the standard psychology by those who had charge of the reorganization of education after the revolution; and only with the ascendance of Cousin's eclecticism in the early part of the nineteenth century did his influence come to an end (1926, p. 18).

This evaluation is confirmed by Sturt (1955) also who wrote in the *Encyclopaedia Brittanica*:

> As was fitting to a disciple of Locke, Condillac's ideas have had most importance in their effect upon English thought. In matters connected with the association of ideas, the supremacy of pleasure and pain, and the general explanation of all mental contents as sensations or transformed sensations, his influence can be traced upon the Mills and upon Bain and Herbert Spencer. And, apart from any definite propositions, Condillac did a notable work in the direction of making psychology a science (p. 220).

This quotation may gain added meaning if it is pointed out that Condillac differed from Locke in several respects. He made sensation the only source of ideas, whereas Locke had insisted on "reflection" as a second source. The elementarism that he borrowed from Locke and from contemporary science became much more basic and essential to his system than it was for Locke's. And, finally, Condillac made hedonism the primary motivator of behavior, whereas Locke—after brief mention of hedonism in childhood—emphasized the social motives of esteem and disgrace.

CHILD DEVELOPMENT AND EDUCATION:
ROUSSEAU, PESTALOZZI, FROEBEL

The importance of the philosopher-psychologists of this period is not so much with respect to any specific doctrine about the nature of the child and learning, nor even their contribution to the destruction of the old theological, social, and political conceptions of man but, instead, the fact that they provided a new base for treating children. This base was characterized by a child-centered approach, a concept of the unfolding of the natural development of the child. Although this approach was begun by Comenius in the 17th century and was amplified considerably by Pestalozzi and Froebel in the 19th century, it is primarily to Rousseau that we must look for the fullest explanation of the permissive child-centered approach that has become a guideline of much educational practice and has influenced indirectly forms of therapy such as client-centered counseling. For the permissive unfolding of the natural powers of the adult, as well as of the child, is a tenet of nondirective psychotherapy.

Rousseau's greatest immediate influences were in practical and theoretical politics, in literature, and in child-rearing practices. His style of writing was adopted by some imitators, and his sentimental stance and worship of nature played a large part in the development of the Romantic era of literature, particularly in Germany. Davidson (1898) claims to trace his influence in literature and child development to practically every European writer of note in the latter half of the 18th century. He names 76 such writers, as for example, Goethe, Schiller, Hugo, Balzac, Dickens, Emerson, and Wordsworth. Furthermore, Davidson suggests that the French Revolution was in large part Rousseau's work. However, this uncritical assignation of credit or discredit fails to place sufficient responsibility on the numerous other factors at work—that is, the *Zeitgeist* as Boring refers to it—some of which Rousseau created, but also some of which created Rousseau.

The incredible story of the life of Jean Jacques Rousseau (1712–1778) is well known. He was born in Geneva, of French parentage. His mother died at his birth, and his father deserted the family when Jean Jacques was ten years old. Thereafter followed 23 years of vagabondage, misbehavior, and general worthlessness such as had never before—and rarely has since—been recorded in an autobiography (Rousseau, 1934). The next ten years, beginning with 1750, were his years of triumph, during which he wrote almost all his enduring works.

These writings, on politics, education, and religion, were of such a nature that he incurred the enmity of the clergy, the government, the encyclopedists, and the rationalists. In 1762, at the age of 50, he began his wanderings in exile—to Switzerland, to David Hume in England, and back to France. He antagonized, in turn, each of his patrons and died in 1778, 66 years old, paranoid, and cantankerous—but an idol of the populace.

Rousseau was not a sufficiently deep "thinker" to rank with Locke, Kant, or Hume. His writings were outpourings of his momentary moods, and therein lay the difficulties of its interpretation and the ambiguity with which he is charged. In his *Emile* he often was inconsistent and self-contradictory, but this had the advantage that it made his readers select and quote or use those passages that suited their needs.

The unparalleled appeal of Rousseau to people of all classes lay, first, in his fervent, emotional, and sincere style; he appeared sincere in his frequent insincerities. Rousseau's fervor was an exciting refreshment after the cold, witty satire of Voltaire,[3] or the dry, unimaginative writings of other rationalists. His beautifully stated truths and half-truths were designed to appeal to sentiment rather than to reason; speaking from his own heart, he reached the hearts of his readers of all classes; and his revolutionary doctrines appealed to all who were out of sympathy in one respect or another with the current regime.

Second, while his predecessors and contemporaries were critical and destructive of many aspects of religion, government, and society, Rousseau made some attempts to institute satisfactory replacements or workable changes instead of being merely iconoclastic. He despised "high society," dogmatism, and autocracy as much as did the rationalists and encyclopedists, but his broad aim was to form the "citizen"—an achievable goal, as against the less practical attempts of the rationalists to form the "universal man" (see Dewey, 1916, 109).

---

[3] Voltaire was at the high point of his popularity when Rousseau began to write. They had been reasonably good friends, but Voltaire became envious and bitter when Rousseau's growing popularity detracted from his own.

Peter Gay, in his Introduction to Cassirer's *The Question of Jean Jacques Rousseau*, wrote:

> The influence of Rousseau's doctrines has been immense—they left their mark of the most diverse spirits and movements. Burke execrated Rousseau as the very embodiment of the Age of Reason. De Maistre and Bonald condemned him as the advocate of an irresponsible individualism and as the philosopher of ruinous disorder. Later critics, such as Sir Henry Maine, attacked him for establishing a "collective despot" and for reintroducing, in the *Contract Social*, "the old divine right of kings in a new dress."
>
> Rousseau's disciples contradicted each other as vigorously as his opponents did. The Jacobins established the Reign of Terror in his name; the German romantics hailed him as a liberator, Schiller pictured him as a martyr to wisdom (Cassirer, 1954, 4–5).

Significant in this respect is the emphasis Rousseau placed on feeling, on the affective life. The esthetic qualities of Locke, the bitter satire of Voltaire, the dry "reason" of the Age of Reason, and the humorless trivialities of the theologians fell before Rousseau's call, "Back to Nature!"

In Paris, Rousseau gradually was initiated, even before he became famous, into some of the celebrated salons of the day, and he became friendly with Diderot and with other philosophers. From these associations primarily (but also from the extensive reading he began to do), he became acquainted with the burning questions of the day. These questions concerned the original nature of man—in terms of his freedom or slavery, the social and political relationship between men, the relationship between man and God, and the more immediate social problems such as the poverty and misery of the people. Particularly in France, autocracy was strong and the plight of the people was severe. The philosophic and economic solutions proposed by the rationalists and the encyclopedists were designed to bring to France, at least in part, the greater individual and economic freedom that existed in England, ideas of which were widely circulated in the works of Hobbes and Locke.

The major portion of Rousseau's educational thoughts are expressed in his *Emile*, published in 1762 (eight years after Condillac's *Treatise*, and 14 years after La Mettrie's *Man a Machine*). In *Emile* Rousseau describes how he would raise a high-born orphan (Emile) to young manhood if he, Rousseau, were his tutor and constant companion. Although his educational theories often became entangled in his political and philosophic ideas, as expressed in his other writings, it was his *Emile* that most directly influenced subsequent education. It became one of the most widely read and discussed books of the century.

Boyd (1911) has described succinctly the education against which Rousseau protested, and which was in vogue at the time:

The dressing of the child as a miniature man indicates the view generally taken of childhood and of education at this time. Just as the boy who was made to wear the same dress as his elders, so he was furnished with the same learning. In the theory of the schools, Latin, and Greek were regarded as necessary for the equipment of the men of culture, and so the child was set betime to the study of Latin and Greek. The method followed in instructing him introduced him to the classics by the adult method of formal grammar. That he did not want to learn the grammatical rules, or did not understand them when he did, was a fact to which no one paid any attention. Most people had too much respect for the educational tradition to consider the child's like and dislikes at all; and the few who gave thought to such things found in the crude faculty psychology, with its demand for an appropriate discipline for each faculty, sufficient justification for the compulsory learning of the languages. It was the firm conviction of the pedagogues of the age that the master faculty of reason was best cultivated by the memorizing of the grammar and the reading of the classical authors; and that even if by chance reason were not developed, the memory, which is the faculty that serves all the other faculties was certainly benefited. What more could any one want (304)?

It is not surprising, in light of the contemporary view of the nature of the child, that Rousseau begged his reader, in the second page of the preface to *Emile,* to "begin, then, by studying your pupils thoroughly, for it is very certain that you do not know them." Earlier in the same paragraph he wrote:

We do not know childhood. Acting on the false ideas we have of it, the farther we go the farther we wander from the right path. Those who are wisest are attached to what is important for men to know, without considering what children are able to apprehend. They are always looking for the man in the child, without thinking of what he was before he became a man (Rousseau, 1926, xlii).

Whereas Locke opened the door to the possibility of child study through his *Thoughts* and his *tabula rasa* doctrine, Rousseau actually initiated the study and gave it a raison d'etre.

Rousseau coordinated the education of Emile with his growth. As Emile passes from one stage or age level into another, the educational methods and emphases change. Since the stages are fairly well differentiated, he treats them in separate chapters: ages 0 to 5 years, 5 to 12 years, 12 to 15 years, and 15 to 20 years.

This has brought from many commentators the charge that Rousseau held to a saltatory theory of development, and that the lines he drew between the various age levels were distinct and invariable.[4] The argument is sustained by the following quotation from *Emile:*

> Each age, each period of life has its proper perfection, a sort of maturity which is all its own. We have often heard mention made of a grown man; but let us now consider a grown child (1926, 121).

Therefore, Rousseau was considered less "modern" than some of his predecessors, for example, Comenius.

It seems, for example, more justifiable to argue that Rousseau's "stages" were designed primarily for convenience in dealing with a longitudinal educational program, just as a university today may offer courses in "The Infant and pre-school child," "child Psychology," and "The Adolescent"—with no sharp break intended between them. Our current school system is divided according to age in almost exact correspondence with Rousseau's stages: birth to 5 years, infancy (preschool, kindergarten); 5 to 12 years, childhood (elementary school); 12 to 15 years (junior high school); and 15 to 20 years (senior high school, junior college). The adoption by our educational system of these particular age classifications, after generations of trying different arrangements, indicated that Rousseau may have had insight into its advantages a century before our professional educators adopted it.

Furthermore, a perusal of *Emile* does not justify this criticism of Rousseau. Progressive, continuous growth is envisioned, for example, in his introduction to Book Third:

> Although the whole course of life up to adolescence is a period of weakness, there is a point in the course of this first stage of life when, growth in power having surpassed the growth of needs, the growing animal, still absolutely weak, becomes relatively strong (1926, 131).

In this introduction to the 12-to-15 year period, he emphasizes the preadolescent's rapid growth in size and strength. In the 15-to-20 year period, he stressed the sexual conflict and the socialization of Emile, again, in terms of gradual change:

> The true course of nature is slower and more gradual. Little by little

---

[4] See, for example, Eby, 1952, pp. 338–340; Compayre, 1886, p. 288, and Wilds, 1942, p. 395.

the blood grows warmer, the faculties expand, the character is formed . . . . The first desires are preceded by a long period of unrest, they are deceived by a prolonged ignorance, they know not what they want (1911, 181).

Do you wish to establish law and order among the rising passions, prolong the period of their development, so that they may have time to find their proper place as they arise? Then they are controlled by nature herself, not by man; your task is merely to leave it in her hands (1911, 180).

Similar expressions throughout the book point to a theory of gradual rather than saltatory development.

Rousseau was guilty of considerable misuse of the term "nature." He used it loosely, frequently, and with whatever meaning or lack of meaning—he wished to attribute to it in any particular sentence. Several meanings were current in Rousseau's time (indeed, just as they are now). Vartanian wrote with respect to the term "nature":

This came to mean, for the Enlightenment, the need for treating man as an adjunct of what was called, with a variety of meanings, nature. The term itself was convenient particularly by its vagueness. Nature was the vade mecum in which the philosophers found, diversely their standards of the truth or the good; it was the amorphous concept by means of which the Newtonian deist might commune with God through the spectacle of the heavens, or with which Rousseau and his adepts might hope to reconcile sentiment with logic (1953, 20).

To the rationalists, the term generally was used to refer to the absolutely precise, mathematically—or rationally—determinable course of events and movements of the universe and by extension from the laws of Newton and Galileo—of man.

To Rousseau, the term meant (insofar as he defined it in the first few pages of *Emile*) the sequential and more-or-less invariable processes undergone by living organisms during growth and development. Man and nature are in conflict; we are "drawn this way by nature and that way by man" (1911, 9). The tree normally grows erect; if forces are applied so that it grows other than straight, it will—when these forces are removed —tend to straighten itself. Similarly, man *tends* to grow erect, but society pulls him this way and that, contrary to nature. And only by his removal from society's iniquities will he grow "naturally."

In another sense but related to the first, nature had the meaning of the primitive conditions that exist where civilization has made no inroads.

In the preface to his translation of *Emile*, Payne summarized Rousseau's conception of a "return to nature" as implying, first, a return to simplicity, second, a return to reality (substance and things, not symbols and words) and, third, a resort to personal experience rather than to adherence to authority (Rousseau, 1926, xxx).

In summary, Rousseau believed that nature itself would teach young people how to develop necessary skills. For a long time the only book he would permit Emile to read was Robinson Crusoe, since he believed that ancient civilizations and primitive peoples were nearer to nature than the modern ones, and the American Indian or South Seas islander appeared to be a prototype of Rousseau's ideal of the man of nature. Rousseau's conception of naturalism was a forerunner of the psychological developmentalism of the 19th century. Moreover, Rousseau in his teachings provides the basis for the environmentalist approach to behavior in that he suggests that nature is the great teacher and, by inference, the shaper of character and moral behavior. In this sense, his teachings are a logical extension of Locke's environmental approach and of the French sensationalists.

Rousseau's educational influence extended in three directions. First, it had an extensive "vogue" effect in France, particularly among the cultured groups who often tried to raise their children in imitation of Emile. Second, it was immediately adopted by the German Basedow (1724–1790), who made Rousseau's teaching an integral part of the educational system of the Philanthropinum established by him at Dessau in 1774. The third and most lasting influence came through Pestalozzi and in diluted form filtered through him into Prussia and back into France. Pestalozzianism became popular also in England and in the 1860s in the United States in what is known as the "Oswego System."

Whereas with Locke the key word was reason, with Rousseau it was nature, and with Pestalozzi it was love. Rousseau's practice had reduced the effectiveness of his writing, whereas the writing of Pestalozzi was not nearly as effective as his practice. Rousseau was an unsuccessful teacher but a skillful writer; Pestalozzi was a successful teacher but a mediocre writer.

Pestalozzi's (1746–1827) contribution can be summarized under two headings: one is his system or method and the other is his philosophy. With regard to his system, the keynote is an emphasis on what he termed *Anschauung*, a word that has no really good English equivalent and that was variously used by Pestalozzi. It has been translated as "object-perception," "observation," or "immediate perception." In England it often was translated as "intuition," certainly not an accurate meaning. Essentially Pestalozzi appears to have meant strictly sensory perception, which

Comenius and Basedow emphasized strongly. Driesch (1915) indicates that Herbart expanded the meaning of the word to the more modern connotation of "content of consciousness." Driesch also summarizes the most important fundamentals of Pestalozzi's own interpretation of his method:

> The most essential points from which I start is this: Sense impression of Nature is the only true foundation of human instruction, because it is the only true foundation of human knowledge. All that follows is the result of this sense impression and the process of abstraction from it . . . Thus the art (of teaching) men is essentially a result of physico-mechanical laws, the most important of which are the following:
>
> 1. Bring all things essentially related to each other to that connection in your mind which they really have in Nature.
>
> 2. Arrange all objects in the world according to their likeness.
>
> 3. Strengthen the impressions of important objects by allowing them to affect you through different senses.
>
> 4. In every subject try to arrange graduated steps of knowledge, in which every new idea shall be only a small almost imperceptible addition to that earlier knowledge which has been deeply impressed and made unforgettable.
>
> 5. Learn to make the simple perfect before going on to the complex . . . Before the child can utter a sound, a many-sided consciousness of all physical truths exists already within him, as a starting point for the whole round of his experiences. For instance, he feels that the pebble and the tree have different properties, that wood differs from glass. To make this dim consciousness clear, speech is necessary. We must give him names for the various things he knows, as well as for their properties (Pestalozzi 1915, 200–205).

A major contribution of Pestalozzi was his insistence that the method of nature requires children to learn to "do" as well as to "know." Knowledge and skill are inseparable. "And knowing and doing are so closely connected, that if one cease the other ceases with it" (1915, 173), a doctrine with distinctly modern overtones. Knowledge without the ability to do (*Fertigkeit*) is not harmonious, and Pestalozzi sought the harmonious development of all aspects of growth.

From the philosophical point of view, Pestalozzi insisted on the principle of "love." All who visited his schools were amazed by the attitude of the students—their reciprocal behavior between each other and toward Pestalozzi, the lack of conflict or bickering among them, and the "home-likeness" of the whole atmosphere. Pestalozzi's school was graded in terms of accomplishments to recognize the presence of individual differences. Thus the reciprocal behavior between teacher and students and between the students themselves must have been an integral part of his school policy.

It is not as easy to trace the sources of Pestalozzi's theory of the child as it is to trace his influence. His doctrine of the natural development and the unfolding of the child's mind appears to come directly from *Emile*, but there are practical differences in pedagogy. The emphasis on *Anschauung*, sense-realism, could have come in part from Rousseau and in part from the 18th century French philosophers such as Condillac. Unlike Locke, who cared little what was taught the child until the age of reason, and unlike Rousseau who believed that until the child was 12 years old the mind was like an unfurnished apartment, Pestalozzi recognized that learning begins at birth. He proposed to take advantage of this, first by education at home, then in a homelike school.

Friedrich Froebel should be mentioned here briefly. Froebel (1782–1852) carried further some of Pestalozzi's ideas. Having spent two years with Pestalozzi and being a minister by profession, he tended to see a religious symbolism in the development of educational experiences. Froebel believed that the development of the individual followed so closely that of the race, that the former could be learned from the latter, and vice versa. Both Murray (1914) and Bowen (1894) see in Froebel a forerunner of Darwin, but Froebel's developmental theory was primarily psychological and spiritual instead of biological. His recapitulation theory was somewhat different from the Herbartians or that of G. Stanley Hall (which we shall discuss later). Each child did not arbitrarily repeat by his own experiences each stage from savagery to civilization. Instead, the various instincts and capacities develop, in the individual, in the same order that they develop in the race—with man the highest point of a continuous universal development and "reason" his crowning glory.

Froebel was very concerned about careful and minute observations of the behavior of the infant. He wrote numerous letters to friends asking them to make observations of their children and to report their observations to him. Basing his ideas on some of these accounts and observations Froebel concluded that hearing was the first sense to become active in the infant. Then he believed that the sense of sight becomes active, and that from two to six years of age the infant is concerned with the use and understanding of language.

Froebel believed that children go through stages. The first is a stage of innately self-active powers that must be expressed through sensory modalities. Froebel does not describe its source, but presumably it is a function of the universal law of development, a gift of God. The child is innately restless, active, curious. Second, the importance of language as an organizer of the "self" is stated as a means of bringing order out of confusion. A third stage is that of play and creativity, with the fourth being related to symbol development in which the child seeks to establish laws—which for Froebel had a religious connotation.

Boyd has called attention to one difference between Froebel and Pestalozzi in relationship to their methodology and procedures:

> . . . though Froebel has obviously learned much from his master and has a good deal in common with him, the methods he employs with young children are very different from Pestalozzi's. The main difference is that he avoids the analytical reduction of experience to elements, and makes a beginning of education with whole interests and not mere fragments. The central feature of the scheme is systematic activity, which presents itself to the child as play (Boyd, 1952, 357).

Froebel does not specifically mention Rousseau, but it is probable that he was well acquainted with the *Emile*, which had considerable influence in Germany, and that he was combatting the idea of discrete stages, which Rousseau is supposed to have emphasized. There are numerous differences and similarities between Rousseau and Froebel; they disagreed on negative or the aversive effects of education, on the place of religion in education, and on the rearing of the child within or without society. Yet, they had much in common, either directly or through Pestalozzi; both protested against the current attitudes toward the child as a plastic wax molded by parents or teachers; both emphasized the internal development, the "unfolding" of the individual through nature; both insisted on respect for the reasons and rights of children and pleaded for the importance of freedom in education.

INFLUENCES OF ASSOCIATIONISM AND CHILD STUDY

Lockean and Rousseauian ideas influenced the systematic observation of behavior, the methods of education for the retarded, and had profound influences on American psychology. As we shall learn, G. Stanley Hall developed the recapitulation theory out of some of these ideas. W. Preyer, a German physiologist and embryologist, kept an account of his son's mental development for four years and published the account in *Die Seele des Kinds* in Leipzig in 1882. Darwin also kept a diary of his son, which was published in 1880. The step-by-step learning sequence, the definition of goal behavior, and the adaptation of the inductive method of learning for young children are all environmental advances that stemmed from this period. Still further, Jean Itard (1775–1838), a physician in a Paris institution for the deaf, experimented with a "wild boy" who had been found in the forests of Aveyron and brought to Paris in 1800. Itard saw a chance for testing out Condillac's theory of education that intelligence is derived solely from sense training, and he was also impressed with Rousseau's notion of the "noble savage." Although Itard failed in his attempt to develop intelligence in the boy, his approach is of interest both in regard to the verification of Locke's and Condillac's ideas and to present-day experimentation with sensory modalities. Boyd stated:

> The principle which guided Itard in his second course of experiments was the idea, which he refers to Locke and Condillac, of the potent influence exercised on the formation and development of the intellect by the isolated and simultaneous action of the senses . . . . As hearing, in his judgment, is the sense which most definitely favors the development of the intellectual faculties, he began with a strenuous attempt to reawaken the long dormant sensibility of the ears (Boyd, 1914, 72–73).

Itard failed in his attempt to progress by the auditory approach, so he switched his attention to vision with no better success. He did somewhat better in the training of the sense of touch, teaching the boy to associate between some objects and ideas, and to make known his wants.

The approach used by Itard, although not completely successful, was sufficient for the French government to endorse sensory training procedures for the mentally retarded. Edouard Sequin (1812–1880) continued this method, training the mentally retarded to learn to walk on narrow boards, to climb ladders, to balance themselves, to gain confidence in their motor abilities, and to distinguish between small differences in temperature, sound, and color. Sequin believed that there was an essential unity in the organism and that training in these physical methods were helpful in forming adequate discrimination judgments. Maria Montessori (1870–1952) following in the same line of thought built on the earlier approaches of Itard and, especially, of Sequin in the development of an individualized approach to learning. Didactic materials, in some instances borrowed from Sequin, consisting of form boards, blocks, rings, and building materials were not designed for play or fun, but for educating the sensory and motor apparatus of the child.

These ideas influenced American psychology and education, which in the 19th century still existed as a branch of philosophy. Although the history of American education is not an appropriate topic for this book, the influence of associationism and child development approaches on psychology in the United States came mainly through the attempt to apply these ideas to education. Early American education as established by the Pilgrims and the Virginians reflected English society. The traditional scholastic emphasis on didactic instruction, modeling via examples, and religious orientation was essential to the Pilgrim approach. The Virginians, on the other hand, more closely reflected the Cavalier approach to education and incorporated much of the education for gentlemen that Locke had recommended. The influence of Pestalozzi was felt in Europe both in Prussia and in France. Horace Mann, in the early years of the 19th century, saw the effects of Pestalozzian ideas in Prussian education and attempted to introduce these ideas in the United States. The famous *Report on the State of Public Instruction in Prussia,* written by Victor Cousin in 1831 on commission by the French government, was quickly translated into English and made available in the United States in 1835. Horace Mann's *Seventh Annual Report* (1843), followed his own inspection and resultant admiration of Prussian education, and the reports of other American visitors, helped to establish American schools along Prussian guidelines. Mann stated:

> About twenty years ago, teachers in Prussia made the important discovery that children have five senses—together with various muscles and mental faculties—all of which, almost by a necessity of their nature, must be kept in a state of activity, and which, if not usefully, are liable to be mischievously employed. Subsequent improvements in the art of teaching, have consisted in supplying interesting and useful, instead of mischievous occupations, for these senses, muscles and faculties . . . Nay it is much easier to keep the eye and hand and mind at work together, than it is to employ either one of them separately from the others (Mann, 1950, 85).

After describing the teaching of reading in the Prussian Schools, Mann argued against the common American method of beginning with the alphabet, suggesting that sounds be the basic component for beginning reading. Nonetheless, Mann still maintained a strong belief in faculty psychology, suggesting that the methods used in Prussia trained faculties and developed moral sentiments. Mann recognized, and insisted that teachers recognize the importance of individual differences: "And on the whole, there is so much difference between the natural quickness of perception and of motion in different pupils, that there can be no such thing as a universal standard" (Mann, 1950, 112).

American educators and administrators did not take kindly to Mann's attempts to modify school procedures along Prussian lines. G. Stanley Hall wrote:

. . . when Horace Mann, after a study of European systems, sought to introduce more gradation, supervision, teacher-training, and organization, he met with the most violent opposition from the teachers of his own state, which he was obliged to leave for the presidency of a small Ohio College (Hall, 1923, 495).

Other sources indicate that Mann's efforts had somewhat more effect than is indicated by Hall. Meanwhile, Pestalozzianism had been introduced in a few places in the United States directly by Pestalozzi's disciples and a few Pestalozzian texts. It was not until 1860, however, that Pestalozzianism began to be widely popular under the guise of "object-teaching." E. A. Sheldon visited an exhibit at Toronto of the object-lessons used by the Home and Colonial School Society. He adopted the method for the Oswego (New York) school system, of which he was superintendent, brought a teacher from London, and popularized the method through conferences and publications.

The Oswego System involved no new concept of the child, but only a new method of teaching; it was somewhat more realistic than the methods it replaced but appeared to be based chiefly on memorization, description, and the naming of items.

Calkins wrote a book entitled *Primary Object Lessons,* which went through 40 editions. It was very reflective of the associationist-sensory methods.

Object-teaching has for its purpose a thorough development of all the child's faculties and their proper employment in the acquisition of knowledge (Calkins, 1882, 15).

Summing up his principles of education, he wrote:

The development of the mind begins with the reception of sensations; and is carried forward by perceptions, and the formations of ideas.

The action and reaction between the external stimulants—material objects—and the mind's inherent powers constitutes the process of natural education. The influence of things upon mind, and of mind upon things, educates (Calkins, 1882, p. 367).

Education is the cultivation of all the native powers of the child by exercising them in accordance with the laws of his being, with a view to development and growth. Repeated exercises of bodily organs give ease of action, and produce habits. Proper exercise of the mental powers give clearness of perception and certainty of knowledge. Proper exercise of any bodily organ or mental or moral power, increases its strength (348).

Similarly, J. Baldwin (1892) divides his book, *Psychology Applied to the Art of Teaching* into six parts, the first five of which deal with the education of perception, representation, thought, emotions, and will powers, respectively. Allen (1893) wrote that "it cannot be denied that individual differences come from permanent bodily and mental peculiarities" (p. 28), and suggested that the will is strengthened by repeating one kind of work many times. The McGuffey readers with their exemplary models, the moralizing stories of the 19th century, the object-teaching procedures, and the use of physical exercise in early childhood education are all precursors of Thorndike and Watson. They are even more amazing prototypes of the methods that are being used today in the revival of behavior modification techniques in learning.

THE DEVELOPMENT OF EXPERIMENTAL PSYCHOLOGY

Just as the history of education is a somewhat peripheral, but essential factor in this discussion, so the history of experimental psychology cannot be described in the detail that it deserves. The focus of this section is chiefly on methodology as it is related to the philosophy of science developing during this period.

In Descartes are the intellectual origins of much 19th century German thought regarding psychology. Descartes had propounded an essential dualism of mind and body. He spent a great deal of his efforts discussing the body of man and viewed it as a complex machine. On the other hand, he had also been concerned about mental processes and with the basic question of perception. Thus Descartes had in a very real manner proposed the basic issues that were developed both by Locke in England and by Leibnitz in Germany. Locke emphasized the importance of environmental experience in shaping behavior. Leibnitz agreed, but he indicated that the perceptory apparatus itself was primary; in other words, that perception was a function of inherent structure shaping experience. For this reason, Descartes and Leibnitz will be discussed further in the next chapter, which deals with the development of intentionality.

Physiologically minded psychologists saw the justification for their experimental method in the vortex theory of Descartes (Boring, 1929, p. 159), whereas Leibnitz, accepting Cartesian psychological views of the universe, could insist that activity is the essential attribute of substance, and thus paved the way for a perception oriented psychology. Kant inveighed against Leibnitzean views and stated that psychology could never be a science because it lacked mathematical verification, and because mental phenomena had no measurable extension.[5] In effect, then, Kant pushed forward the drive toward an analysis of psychological phenomena, subject to the innate philosophical categories of mind that he predicated. Herbart opposed Kant and said that psychology could be a science based on a statics and dynamics of the soul. Although he allowed that mathematics could be helpful in the advancement of psychology, he insisted that psychology was bound also to metaphysics.

Johann Friedrich Herbart (1776–1841) was one of the primary sources of experimental psychology. He had been an attentive observer of Pestalozzi and his methods at Burgdorf. But it became Herbart's task to lay the foundations of a scientific psychology. Herbart was influenced by the English associationists, Pestalozzi and, certainly, by Leibnitz. Even though he succeeded to Kant's chair of philosophy at Koenigsberg, he disavowed Kant's contention about the scientific basis of psychology. And yet, Herbart did not divorce psychology from metaphysics. He considered psychology a science, but not in the sense of physiology or of the mathematical method as such.

Although Herbart rejected a psychology based exclusively on physiological investigation or mathematical reductionism, he did believe that psychological phenomena could be analyzed to some extent by mathematical processes and in a way foreshadowed Fechner's psychophysics. Like the psychology of the English school, Herbart's psychology centered on the elementary bits of experience called sensations. Herbart's influence at this point is related chiefly to his methodological approach to psychology, an approach that signaled a transition from the pure speculation of Kant, Fichte, Hegel, and other German philosophers who had essentially denied the possibility of an objective science of psychology to the experimentalism of Fechner, Wundt, and Helmholtz.

Another approach was taken by Johannes Muller (1801–1858), professor of physiology at Berlin. He has been referred to frequently as the father of experimental psychology. Muller was one of those rare geniuses who not only added substantially to the fund of experimentation taking

---

[5] One of the consequences of Kant's point of view was to identify psychological investigation with idealism. Boring remarks that the effect of Kant on psychology was twofold: "He favored subjectivism, keeping alive the faith in the importance of those mental phenomena that cannot be reduced to brain or body processes, and he gave support to nativism in theories of space because he subjectified space and time into a priori intuitions, removing them from the objective external world" (Boring, 1929, p. 247).

place in the field of sensory perception but who systematically collected, collated, and synthesized the work that had been done in physiology. Muller was not a mechanist. He was a Catholic and believed in two principles, a vital and a mental one. In opposition to many of his contemporaries, Muller believed that the mental principle—which he considered distinct from the vital principles—was centrally located in the brain and in the nervous system (Misiak and Staudt, 1954, p. 21).

Many famous German psychologists and physiologists received their initial training in physiology from Muller. Some of them were Wilhelm Wundt, Emil Du Bois-Reymond, Carl Ludwig, Hermann Helmholtz, and Ernest Brucke. As Jones remarked:

> These men formed a small private club which in 1845 they enlarged to the *Berliner Physikalische Gesellschaft*. Most of its members were young students of Johannes Muller: physicists and physiologists banded together to destroy, once and for all vitalism, the fundamental belief of their admired master. Du Bois-Reymond, Brucke, Helmholtz and Ludwig remained lifelong friends. Within twenty-five or thirty years they achieved complete domination over the thinking of German physiologists and medical teachers, gave intensive stimulus to science everywhere and solved some of the old problems for ever (Jones, 1955 I, 40).

These men, primarily Wilhelm Wundt and Hermann Helmholtz, investigated an encyclopedic array of sensory processes, and their impact on the development of experimental psychology and its processes and procedures through the establishment of laboratories cannot be over estimated.[6]

Other movements that contributed to the experimental methodology of psychology were the development of the theory and elaboration of evolution by Darwin, the physiological experiments of Henry Maudsley in England, the philosophy of the scientific method expounded by John Stuart Mill, and Comte's sociological philosophy of positivism.

---

[6] Jones pointed out that it was this school of thought that dominated the medical studies of Freud through Brucke. "From its very beginning this group was driven forward by a veritable crusading spirit. In 1842 Du Bois wrote: 'Brucke and I pledged a solemn oath to put into effect this truth: no other forces than the common physical-chemical ones are active within the organism. In those cases which cannot at this time be explained by these forces one has either to find the specific way or form of their action by means of the physical-mathematical method or to assume new forces equal in dignity to the chemical-physical forces inherent in matter, reducible to the force of attraction and repulsion' " (Jones I, 40).

Positivism itself was a philosophical movement that purported to be the philosophy of science to end all other philosophical inquiries. The term has been traditionally associated with August Comte, who had maintained that the stimulation of science had fundamentally altered the view that man ought to take toward himself. He felt that, if science had produced such a terminology and technology for methodological advances, this method must at last be applied to man, his nature, and his humanity. He believed that man should finally cease asking questions that he could not answer. Moreover, he saw an evolution in knowledge that he defined as the law of the three stages. All knowledge evolved from theological to metaphysical and finally to scientific stages. Positivism was the scientific stage. Comte felt that the final stage could provide a universal brotherhood for man similar to that of Catholicism before it had been challenged. And this brotherhood was to be based on a scientific knowledge of ourselves and our universe. The ideas of Comte and, to some extent, of John Stuart Mill, who sympathized with this approach, influenced both the course of experimental psychology and Brentano's thinking, thereby entering into the philosophy of scientific method and phenomenology.

The impact of physiological psychology was tremendous. Muller identified the specific energy of nerves. Donders, a Dutch physiologist identified and explored with Helmholtz the nature of reaction time. Helmholtz explored the speed of the neural impulse, enunciated a color theory for vision, and investigated space perception and auditory responses. Wilhelm Wundt established one of the first experimental laboratories for the study of psychological investigations. Concerned with some of the same problems that concerned Helmholtz, he pushed forward even further. Wundt became a veritable institution in his own lifetime. He wrote voluminously, focusing generally on the elements of the mind or the basic states of consciousness. Wundt stressed the experimental analysis of sensation, feeling, and their resultant—ideas. He was also interested in the development of folk psychology and can be considered to be one of the early social psychologists. Wundt profoundly influenced the course of American psychology. Among his original students, or among those who came to spend some time with him, were G. Stanley Hall, James McKeen Cattell, Edward W. Scripture, Edward A. Pace, Lightner Witmer, Charles H. Judd, and Edward Bradford Titchener. Cattell will be mentioned later with respect to the development of measurement theory, Scripture was later director of the Yale Psychological Laboratory, Pace was head of the Department of Psychology at the Catholic University, Witmer founded the first psychological clinic at the University of

Pennsylvania, and Judd was an educational psychologist at the University of Chicago. Titchener, who settled at Cornell University, became one of the most dedicated Wundtians in the United States.

SUMMARY

This chapter traces the development of a philosophy of scientific method as applied to psychological phenomena from the beginnings of Scholasticism to the establishment of the scientific method in psychology. The essential thread running through this development is the identification of a methodology based on observation, analysis, and experimentation. The material contained in this chapter shows the manner in which basic ideas enunciated originally in Scholasticism and in the works of Descartes and Locke were expanded to provide a new basis for interpreting and analyzing the impact of the environment on man.

PART TWO

Philosophical Foundations of Counseling

CHAPTER V

Intentionality: Perceptual Foundations of Modern Psychology

This chapter is concerned with the development of certain philosophical ideas that play a central role in those aspects of psychology relating to perceptual organization and structure. Intentionality is a major construct in the psychoanalytic, phenomenological, and Gestalt approaches to psychology and psychotherapy.

Although many influences may be observed that pertain to the development of approaches to psychotherapy, many of these influences are difficult to trace. From the discussion in previous chapters, it is apparent that concepts relating to reason, mind-body, dualism, the struggle between higher and lower forces in man, and the goals of virtue and habit formation, as well as many other notions, are persistent concerns of man expressed differentially in religion, medicine, and philosophy.

This chapter examines the development of an intentional metaphysics as a core of philosophical conceptions which has influenced both philosophers and psychologists in the past and has been a central recurring theme in many forms of psychological practice today.

THE NATURE OF INTENTIONALITY AND INFLUENCE

The general conclusion that I wish to make in this chapter and in some of the following chapters is that there is an intentional metaphysics that underlies Freudian theory, phenomenology, and the early elements of Gestalt theory which, insofar as epistemology, methodology, and the theory of behavior are concerned, find proximate and specific roots in the psychological theories of Brentano and are ultimately related to a whole chain of thought extending from Aristotle and the Scholastics through Descartes, Spinoza, and Leibnitz. The chief burden of this

185

chapter will be the elaboration of the evolving conception of intentionality through its historical antecedents to the completed psychology of act in Brentano. The following chapter will examine the development of intentionality within psychoanalysis. A later chapter will be concerned with Gestalt psychology and phenomenology. Figure 1 summarizes the chains of influence as they will be discussed.

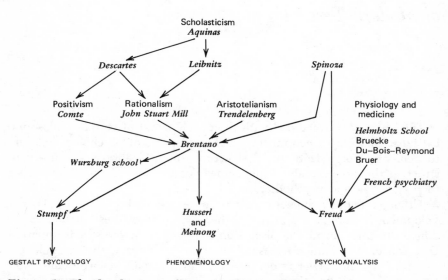

Figure 1 The development of intentionality in 19th century German thought.

Metaphysics has been considered the science of the most general principles. From another point of view, it has been conceived as a theory of the real in contradiction to the theory of the phenomenal that is furnished by the speculative sciences (Külpe, 1897, 22). In this latter sense, metaphysics takes on the shape of a general theory concerning the universe in which general laws explain the roots of individuality which are attained by the several sciences. There have been many metaphysical frameworks suggested in the history of Western man. The Aristotelian metaphysics was concerned with the most general determinations of being itself in order to seek the universal substratum. Kantian metaphysics insisted that, prior to the investigation of most general principles, it was necessary to precede the inquiry by an investigation into the limits of human knowledge and into the innate categories of the human mind. Post-Kantian philosophy sought for metaphysical certitudes in absolutes of a Platonic nature. And England never succeeded in obtaining a permanent commitment to metaphysics.

The school of thought that began, in part, with Aristotle and the Scholastics and was succeeded by Descartes, Spinoza, and Leibnitz represented a metaphysical outlook that was not only an intellectual analysis and recomposition of scientific data but also a system that involved mind in an approach to the data of science. *It was a creation of feeling and will states in the mind which approached sensory data with definite needs and requirements.* This approach to metaphysics was one in which the nature of the mind as an inquiring and enduring principle of vital activity projected itself into the dispassionate inquiry concerning knowledge. This is what is meant in this chapter by intentional metaphysics.

Aristotle and Aquinas both furthered a world view in which man was the center of the universe and man's thought was something that sprang from the inherent potencies of his soul. Not in the same exact sense, but with many of the same implications, Descartes, Spinoza, and Leibnitz developed the position that the problem of metaphysics was the cognition of the self-existent, of that which must be regarded as existing absolutely behind the world of appearances. These same ideas were developed further in Brentano and his students, Freud, Stumpf, and Husserl. Of course, it is true that the *reasons* and in many instances the *methodological tools* devised to explain the self-existent do differ from man to man. But it is my contention that the essential features of an intentional metaphysics can be found uniformly behind the writings of these men.

THOMAS AQUINAS AND SCHOLASTICISM

The epitome of Scholastic thought is found in the writings of Thomas Aquinas. This Dominican monk, who lived from 1224 to 1274, is the very personification of Scholasticism. His life spanned the second and third quarters of the 13th century, a period in which occurred the rise of universities and the flowering of medieval culture. At the beginning of the century, Greek studies were just becoming popular in Northern Italy. Aristotle was still considered by the Church authorities as something to be feared and proscribed. By the end of the 13th century, Aquinas and his monumental work, expressed in his *Summa Theologia* and *Summa Contra Gentiles,* had almost become the intellectual justification for medieval civilization.

Aquinas was born of noble parents in Aquino, Italy. Subsequently, he studied at the newly established University of Naples and decided to become a Dominican priest in 1244. He later was sent to Paris and may have been at Cologne. In either event, he became a student of Albert the Great, the greatest natural scientist of that period.

On completion of his work, Aquinas taught at the University of Paris for three years and then returned to Italy where he taught in various universities for the rest of his life. He died early in 1274 on the way to attend the Council of Lyons. Thomas' writings were very extensive, covering the whole range of Christian theology, philosophy, and many other areas. Medieval Christianity found in Aristotelianism a vehicle for self-expression that was unparalleled. Through a process of accomodation, the early Church fathers assimilated the methodology of the Greek Schools, and soon a plethora of theological formulations and speculations were spelled out. To these early formulations were given the sanction of theology and divine jurisdiction, something that would have been alien to the original Greek philosophers. During the early Middle Ages, much of the rationale behind these decisions had been lost or buried in monasteries. Furthermore, the whole tenor of early Christian and Patristic thought had been Platonic. Thomas Aquinas' great contribution was that he took the work of Aristotle and worked out a synthesis with Christian theology. So great was his work in the opinion of many of the Roman Catholic Church that even today Aquinas has a supraordinary position in Catholic theology.

Science-Faith and the Problem of Methodology

The synthesis of Aristotelian philosophy and Christian theology undertaken by Aquinas was a wedding of two methodological tools. These tools were for philosophy: logic, and for theology: revelation. Logic was the process of reasoning following the principles of induction, deduction, and logical inference as established by Aristotle. Revelation was the reliance on the authority of God or the Church in interpreting God's revelation. The chief sources of revelation were those matters recorded in the Old and New Testaments, and the two major authors of revelation were considered to be Moses and Jesus. The matter of divine revealed truth was considered to be closed with the death of the last Apostle, John, about 100 A.D. Subsequently, the Church was the major instrument of interpreting the ruling on the nature of revealed truth. The Church in the early centuries made such rulings through councils of all the bishops, for example, the Council of Nicaea. Later on, after the split between the Eastern Orthodox church and the Roman church, the position of the Papacy increased strongly and the Popes of the Roman church tended to make these decisions.

With the rise of a body of scientific knowledge and technology, it was apparent that a synthesis between these two methodological criteria was needed in order to relate the body of theological knowledge to the area of natural science or philosophy. It should be noted here that by philosophy the Middle Ages considered all those areas now included in the biological, physical, and social sciences as well as psychology and philosophy in the humanities.

Aquinas divided the entire realm of reality into two parts: the natural and the supernatural. He said that science was concerned with the natural and that the whole body of philosophical knowledge could be examined through the use of logic and reasoning. He thus subscribed to the empirical method of observation, generalization, and categorization. The object of philosophy was natural truth which he believed could be found through the use of the empirical method, experimentation as he knew it, and logical processes. He divided the branches of philosophy or science into three divisions following the prior division of Aristotle. These were the physical sciences, the mathematical sciences, and the metaphysical ones. In the physical sciences he relied most on empirical observation; in the mathematical ones there were the axioms, theorems developed by the early Greeks; and in metaphysics the supreme weapon was logic.

In addition to the domain of philosophy was the deposit of revelation. Science and the tools of science were sufficient for the natural world of reality, but they were essentially inferior to the direct communication of revealed truth. Science and all of its branches was concerned with particular and individual truth. But this knowledge was derived from the products of man's internal and external sensory apparatus, the observation of cause and effect in nature, the application of axiomatic rules, and the general principles of logic. Knowledge revealed by God was supernatural truth and tells man about the second area of reality, that is, the supernatural. The Scholastics, and particularly Aquinas, were convinced that there could be no real contradiction between faith and reason, theology and philosophy, since truth was one, and the author of both realms was God. Aquinas taught that faith was a higher form of knowledge that fulfilled or completed natural knowledge. Where science ends, there faith begins. Faith is the ascent to truth based on the authority of God. Moreover, the truths of revelation may be subjected to the methodology of logic in order to deduce other truths that may be hidden in the original deposit of revelation. Thus Aquinas enunciated a pair of methodological tools that in his opinion covered the entire domain of reality; for natural phenomena, observation, axioms, and logic; for supernatural phenomena, revelation and faith.

The Nature of Man

The entire scheme of Scholastic thinking was based on the nature of man; just as reality was divided between the natural and supernatural, so man was conceived as a creature composed of body and soul. The soul was the form of the human body in the Aristotelian tradition; the body was the matter. The rational soul was defined of itself to be essentially the form of a human body. It was described as a subsistent material substance that informed the body and was its prime mover. All knowledge was knowable in virtue of the action of the soul. The soul, although an indivisible and unitary substance, possessed certain potentialities or inherent powers to fulfill itself. These faculties of souls were divided into vegetative, appetitive, sensory, locomotive, and intellectual.

Aquinas viewed the soul as the energizing agent of the body, and in a very real sense the body was like a television set that was not turned on. Only when the flow of electric energy is present can the instrument work as it is designed to do. Thus Aquinas ascribed all cognition, all learning, all perception, indeed, all functioning whatsoever to the informing principle of the body, that is, the human soul. The balance of the bodily structure served as an avenue for the utilization of the soul. There is no need to consider Aquinas' views on the vegetative level as they are identical to the views of Aristotle. But Aquinas did make some innovations in the area of sensory perception. Aquinas divided the senses of man into external and internal ones, which he termed cognitive sense faculties to distinguish them from the intellectual faculties of mind.

The external senses were those organic avenues of approach whereby external reality instrumentally impinged on the organism. The resulting impression from without the organism activates the sensory organ, and it produces a sensation. The quality of this stimulation is merely expressed as a material and indifferent sign from the sense organ. This is the equivalent of what in modern psychology may be termed "cognitive awareness." Once the awareness had been registered, the internal senses took over to analyze the awareness. Common sense was an internal faculty, not to be identified with the ordinary use of these words. Its purpose, according to Aquinas, was a rather generic one in which the sensations coming from the external senses were sorted out into various categories and were assigned to proper internal senses. To use the analogy of the television set, one might say that common sense in Thomistic use does the unscrambling of the signals received by the set. The imagination is another of the internal senses. This is the internal sense that is capable of reproducing external images after the external stimuli or the original sensation has departed. Its function is to reproduce images of absent objects, and it also plays a creative role inasmuch as it divides and combines many mental images in order to fabricate new mental imagery. The memory was considered the storehouse of previous thoughts. The specific functions of the sense memory, as distinguished from the intellectual memory, were to conserve the images and to reproduce them. It was also concerned with the recognition or identification of relationships of similarity and contrariety between sense images. It is in connection with imagination and memory that Aquinas explained the association of ideas in learning based on reasons of similarity (Plato and Socrates), reasons of contrariety (Hector and Achilles), and reasons of propinquity or contiguity (bread and butter). The final internal sense was known as the estimative sense or instinct. It is the organic faculty by which certain unsensed relations were derived from sensations. This is basically what is known in animals as instinct, for example, the reasons that impel a bird to build a nest in a tree or a female cat to take care of its young.

These external and internal senses were common property of both men and animals in Aquinas' view. All sensitive creatures have in common the appetites that Aquinas called the concupiscible and irrascible faculties. These appetites were basically the faculties of love and hate. Concupiscence was the appetitive desire seeking for pleasure and sensory enjoyment. Obviously, this appetite was concerned with the pleasure of food and sex. The irascible appetite was the faculty of aversion and motivated the organism to varying degrees of hatred. These sensible appetites were directly concerned with the presentation of sensory objects that were viewed as subjectively good or evil; objects toward which the body tends as an end or avoids as a harmful object. Aquinas considered the sense appetites as two opposite ends of the same continuum; the concupiscible appetite inclining the organism toward what might be subjectively harmful or not desirable. Thus the sensory portion of man was similar to that of the animals, consisting of the external and internal senses and sense appetites.

In addition to the sensory apparatus described, Aquinas considered that man had the special cognitive structure that he called intelligence. As a counterpart to the sense appetite, man had a rational appetite that he called the will. The intellectual apparatus of man and the description of it is a remarkable achievement of Thomism. Bearing in mind the fact that the soul activates the organism, it is necessary to explain how concrete sensations as directed from the external senses and mediated by the internal senses are translated into material that the soul can handle. The essential problem that confronted Aquinas was to explain how concrete material sensations and sense images could be acted on by an immaterial subsistent force called the soul. How could a spiritual being without parts be related to material sensations? How could a spiritual soul know concrete things? Aquinas explained the procedure thus: the soul is identified with intellection. Intellection is basically a twofold operation whereby sensory data are transformed by the action of the intellect into abstract and universal concepts. The universal concept is an abstract thing that does not exist in reality as such, but is the product of extraction from sensory data. For example, the senses of man convey certain characteristics about a given individual to the internal senses. A John Brown is six feet tall, he has a sallow countenance, he weighs 200 pounds, and the like. The internal senses compare the sensory data relating to John Brown to other memories of individual men on the basis of previous data accumulated in the memory plus the individual items. The intelligences abstracts those common elements and identifies John Brown as a man in the universal sense. The same application can be made of a chair, a car, or any other object. The immanent act of understanding then is relegated to the higher levels of intelligence. Aquinas recognized two aspects of intelligence—the active aspect, whereby sensory data were stripped of particular elements and translated into universal ideas or concepts; and the passive aspect of intelligence, which was the area in which concepts were formulated and utilized in the actual process of thought production. It is at this highest level that understanding takes place.

Thus, to summarize, cognition proceeds from the immanent act of understanding. Just as there are various faculties in the soul, so there are various orders or levels of cognition. There are cognitive principles that function in the body and cognitive principles that are primarily the function of the soul. Nevertheless, the soul permeates the entire process. To illustrate, one can compare the order of cognition to the case of a man coming out of a dark basement and ascending into the light. The lower senses are relegated to the darker steps and, as the ascent is made through the external senses to the internal senses and, hence, to the active intellect, the awareness of precision of cognition becomes clearer and clearer until basic sensory data can be handled directly by the soul itself at the highest level of intellectual understanding (see Figure 2).

Intentionality

The most difficult part of the entire Scholastic scheme of thinking is the concept of intentionality. Central to this discussion is the importance of realizing that Aquinas considered the soul and the process of cognition not as a passive one, such as Locke later enunciated but, instead, as an active process whereby the soul sought continually to activate the organ-

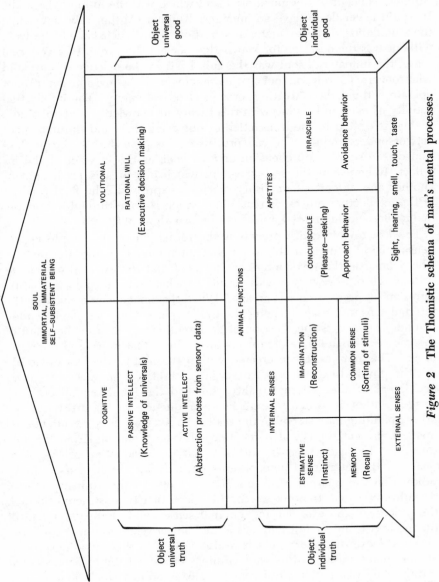

Figure 2 The Thomistic schema of man's mental processes.

193

ism. The stimulus from without was called the instrumental cause of perception, not the efficient cause. This, again, was necessary to preserve Aquinas' concept of the immaterial soul which was the form of the body. It would never do to have an immaterial higher substance be subject to the stimulation of lower material sensation. Thus, such knowledge from without was the occasion for knowledge but not the cause. In a very real sense, the immaterial soul was the only basis for knowledge of any kind whatsoever. To rely on our earlier analogy, the television set cannot operate without the activating force of electrical energy. The intellectual activity of man, in keeping with this theory of knowledge and cognition, is then relegated to the transaction of universal ideas and the immanent acts of understanding. The end process of this procedure is the production of the simple apprehension or idea. This is the first act of the intellect. Judgment is the second act in which one idea is predicated of another and agreement or disagreement is expressed. The final product of the intellectual process is reasoning, which is done through induction, deduction, and inferential apprehension or judgments.

The key to this entire process is the formation of the simple apprehension or idea. It is at this point that intentionality enters the picture. The Scholastic theory of intentionality held that the external object *impresses* the sensory organ with results in what was called in Scholastic terms an "impressed sensory image." When this image is perceived by the internal senses, the act of perception takes place. This act of perception or understanding is the creation of an intentional image on the mind of the knower, which is like the extraorganic object that impressed the sense organ. This new existence created within the mind, which is obviously not the physical existence of extraorganic reality, or the necessary copy and image of that external reality, is called the intentional likeness or image. Rather it is like the realistic production of an artist. As the artist's painting may resemble the reality, so likewise does the intentional image represent the act of perception. However, one important distinction must be made, that is, the fact that the production of the inner image or the intentional perception is not only the result of the sensory production and internal senses but is also *caused* by the explicit power of the informing soul. In other words, the image that is constructed through the process of the external and internal senses, and at the command of the intellect or informing soul, has a dual object relationship. It is related first to the external reality, but it is also related to the intending process of the human mind. In this way, Aquinas explained the differences that certain concepts have for different people. A broiled steak done exactly to our specifications may attract us greatly when we are hungry. The same steak after a large meal may have little or no attraction and may, in fact, repel us. This is not because of some intrinsic quality within the steak itself but, instead, to the secondary object relationship of the mind perceiving it.

In summary, the concept of intentionality is related to the importance of this unity of soul and the relegation of all activity to this vital principle of being. This is of paramount importance in understanding the Scholastic theory of knowledge. The whole process, in a sense, is described in the axiom so widely used in the Middle Ages, *Operatio sequitur esse*. This means simply that the operation of any being in this world must necessarily follow or be governed by the nature or disposition of its essence. A thing does what it ought to do in terms of its basic construction. This position about a priori essence or a given structure must be understood to grasp the present conflict between essentialist philosophies and existentialism. In the Scholastic doctrine and in the position of subsequent phenomenologists (excluding the existentialist), the nature of man in his essential structure governs the functional emergence of his existence and experience.

Epistemology and Ethics

In any theory of knowledge there are three central factors; the one who knows (subject), the thing he knows (object), and the act by which he knows (the process). In Scholastic philosophy the subject of knowledge is man. Since man is a composite being of body and soul, and the form of this composite being begins in the rational soul, knowing must involve the action of the soul in some manner or other. The object of knowledge is whatever impresses the external senses and the results in sensory knowledge. Ultimately, Thomas Aquinas held that all knowledge of the natural order or of natural phenomena is derived through experiencing. As he put it *"nihil est in intellectu nisi prius in sensu"* (nothing is in the intellect unless it is first in the senses). The process of knowledge or the knowing act is the union of the outside that is, the extraorganic object, with the immanent faculty of the soul that is called the intellect. In this process, the sensitive faculties along with the higher intellectual faculties are involved. Thomas Aquinas held to the general doctrines of Aristotle in the sense that he held the concept of causality. As Aristotle before him, Aquinas believed that there was a preexisting order in the universe and that it was the task of man to find out what this order was. Its order was defined by man in terms of laws and of cause and effect relationships. One could be certain about the nature of the natural order or the physical universe through an identification of the essential cause and effect relationships that operate in the universe. Thus, Aquinas would agree with the scientific method, insofar as it is being used today and was used in the past, for the determination of the essential laws that govern natural phenomena. However, in keeping with his basic position about the natural universe and the supernatural, there was another form of epistemological certitude; and this was found in the reliance on faith and revelation. Man could know only in a hazy manner about the existence of God and the ultimate nature of the universe in terms of man's destiny and goals in the hereafter. Essentially, then, Aquinas' point of view may be summarized as holding forth a realistic approach to natural phenomena, the determination of the essential laws that govern the universe, and the framework of its structures through natural observation, testing, and the formulation of laws. He would hold finally for the absolute nature of religious truth and the very real certitude that is attached to faith.

This same dichotomy is found in the ethical teachings of Aquinas. Aquinas believed in the existence of the natural law. This law was known to all men in one form or other. Essentially it relates to order, the golden rule, and the understanding of the fact that the world could not exist as it does without some authorship, and the identification of this authorship as God. However, Aquinas points out that even the greatest minds of early Grecian days were unable to arrive at the accurate understanding of the nature of God. He cites Plato, Aristotle, and Socrates as examples. These men, although great in their own right, could recognize God only as some kind of a first cause or as a first principle behind the nature of the universe. It was necessary for God to reveal himself to man in order for man to understand the nature of the universe, the nature of good and evil, and the moral obligation that man must fulfill the good life in accordance with the dictates of Christianity.

An important consideration of ethics and moral responsibility is Aquinas' teaching on what he called the rational appetite or the will. It will be recalled that according to Aquinas the lower sensory levels of operation, such as the internal senses, seek particular truth: the fact, for example, that a particular statement may be true—that the price on an automobile which is relayed by a salesman is in point of fact, the true price. In other words, the internal senses wish to know whether the particular set of sensations that come to them and are compared to previous memories are true. So likewise, the sense appetite, the concupiscence and the irrascible appetites seek after particular good, for example, what is pleasant for the organism. They seek a sensory gratification in the form of particular individual concrete experiences. This framework for both internal senses and for appetites is common both to animals and to men according to Aquinas. But on the human level, there is a parallel extension of the lower faculties on a cognitive and rational plane. The extension of the internal senses is found in the cognitive plane in intelligence; and the extension of the lower appetite is found in the human or cognitive plane in the rational appetite, which are faculties existing in man alone on the basis of, and because of his rational soul. Just as the internal senses seek particular truth, the intelligence seeks universal truth—the abstract, universal concept of truth. And just as the lower appetites seek particular good, so the will or the rational appetite of man seeks universal good.

These considerations are of importance to the determination of ethics. Aquinas' opinions on the rational appetite are most interesting. He incorporates into it the power of self-reflection or conscience and the final executive power of action over behavior. The will, thus, is the chief executive operation in man, and in this sense it is very similar to what Freud later calls the ego. Although the will may consider the reasons and the logic of the choice, the will makes the decision. However, it should be recognized that Aquinas in his description of the faculties of man, both lower and higher ones, does not suggest a dutiful hierarchy of responses. He recognizes implicitly the existence of strong unruly passions in man. He also submits that the will is besieged by both intellectual reasons, memories, and sense appetites, and is bound by the force of past habits.

From Aquinas' philosophical views on the nature of reality, the nature of man, the nature of knowledge, and the nature of ethics comes the moral theology of the Roman Catholic Church. The general theme that is present throughout Scholastic thought is one of order and synthesis, the unity between diversities. Man is composed of body and soul. The universe possesses both natural and supernatural phenomena. There is an essential unity between these two, and it is the duty of man constantly to subordinate the natural phenomena, the natural appetites, and the lower appetites of man to the supernatural world and to the revelation that shows the path of true virtue. The Church enters into this total situation by providing the means whereby man as a "fallen" creature may arrive at this subordination of lower self to higher self.

Other Contributions of Aquinas

The psychology of man and methodology in science as well as in faith have been discussed at some length in the contribution of Aquinas. These are the aspects of this contribution that are most lasting in terms of even modern Christian educational practice. For they form the basis of one whole segment of education in the United States, the parochial school system. Aquinas' philosophy is still the philosophy of the Roman Catholic Church. Thus, it merits more than a cursory glance in view of the fact that more than one out of five children in the United States attend a school that subscribes to this philosophical approach.

Many of Aquinas' opinions on physics and natural phenomena are basically identical with Aristotle. His theological works, however, are important in the light of the evolution of Christian doctrine. His views on the state and education are of more importance to our concern in this book. In keeping with the basic principles of the natural and supernatural, Aquinas maintained that man is naturally ordained to the society of his fellow man, that all authority, civil and religious, proceeds from God, and that the aim of the state is not merely economical but moral. He argued that the aims of society are better served by the rule of one than by many, but he still maintained that democratic forms of government may be as legitimate as monarchial, aristocratic ones. In the area of education, he considered that the moral and religious education of children held priority over so-called secular knowledge in keeping with the natural and supernatural goals of man.

Aquinas also maintained that man possessed a free will:

> Man has free choice or otherwise counsels, exortations, commands, prohibitions, rewards and punishments would be in vain. Man acts from judgment because by his apprehensive power he judges that something should be avoided or sought, but because of this judgment in the case of some particular act is not from a natural instinct, but from some act of comparison in the reason, therefore, he acts from free judgments and retains the power of being inclined to various things. In that man is rational, it is necessary that he have free choice (Pegis, 1948, 369).

Attitudes Toward Counseling and Adjustment

The essential position toward the change in human behavior and counseling, which may be identified in Aquinas, is one of conformity to the will of both natural rulers and God. Thomas Aquinas has described the basic notions underlying counseling. His emphasis on persuasion as distinct from authoritative direction is of primary importance. The purposes of counseling in the religious sense are twofold: (1) the conformity to the will of God, and (2) the acceptance of the orderly, meaningful nature of the universe. Counseling, implies St. Thomas, is primarily concerned with those methods of skill that facilitate self-directed choices through personal reorganization, furthering thereby the development of the virtue of counsel and ultimately of prudence (Cavanagh, 1958). Virtues that should be clarified stem from habits that are learned. The whole of one's personal life in the Thomistic sense should be a process in self-control; (1) control of passions, (2) a conformity of passions to reason, (3) a conforming of reason to the moral law, (4) and the will to conform to the deposit of divine revelation.

Counseling, then, concerns the entire being. Of central importance is the nature of insight and the development of this. Aquinas felt that from persuasion would come insight, and understanding in the intellect of man.

Summary and Conclusion

The lasting importance of Aquinas in particular and of Scholasticism in general is in the creation of a world order that is conceived to be perfectly harmonized. This world order is one that is essentially teleological and in which the ultimate reality is God as a prime mover and as a redemptive personality. That man is the chief creation of God and, therefore, in a psychological sense, the hub around which the world and the universe rotate symbolically, if not actually, is the central point. The purpose of man's existence is to know God and to serve Him in this life, and to be happy with Him in eternity. Thus over the entire dimension of man's life hang the eternal verities of God and the hereafter. Aquinas could not conceive of any real opposition between faith and reason. He acknowledged that there might be apparent oppositions, but that in cases where such occurred, for example in the Doctrine of the Trinity, where three persons are held united in one God, reason is there suspended and faith takes over.

The extension of this logical world order has many implications for education. If the realities of these dimensions, natural and supernatural, are admitted, then the hierarchy of educational goals that is present in the parochial education of the Catholic Church and in the parochial schools of other faiths has justification. Moreover, if this line of reason is also held, then counseling is a process whereby individuals seek to bring their own behavior into conformity with the will of God. As Cavanagh has said in a modern approach to counseling based on Thomistic theory, "counseling comes about when one individual seeks out another to assist him in his research of reason in the attempt to find the means to the solution of a problem." The Thomistic theory of knowledge and nature of reality, however, ultimately considers man and the resolution of his problems in terms of a conformity by the individual to the nature of the universe. There are, therefore, limitations on the nature of the counseling process as conceived from the Thomistic point of view.

In summary, then, the significant features of Scholastic thought are as follows:

1. The central position of the immaterial subsistent soul as the informing principle of cognition and understanding.
2. The fact that all external objects (extraorganic) and factors exert

only an instrumental causality in the stimulation of cognitive processes.

3. The essential characteristic of the creation of a self-reflective intentional image both on the level of sensible images in the internal sense and of intellectual concepts in the intellect.

4. The positing of an hierarchy of cognitional experience extending from particular sensory apprehension and self-reflective perception and culminating in abstract universal concepts.

5. The positing of an hierarchy of faculties in man in which there is a diversification of object relations, that is (1) the seeking of the external and internal senses for particular and concrete truth, (2) the seeking of the appetitive faculties for particular and concrete good—or the avoidance of evil, (3) the quest of the intellect for universal and abstract truth, and (4) the quest of the will for universal and abstract good.

6. A methodology that is essentially determined by degrees of certitude in which the certitude order extends downward in this ranking: (1) faith and revelation, (2) logical induction and deduction —including axiomatic principles, and (3) empirical sense evidence.

7. A world order that is essentially teleological and in which the ultimate reality is God as a prime mover and a redemptive personality. Man is the chief creation of the universe, and his ultimate end— union with God—is man's chief motivating force.

8. The positing of a free will in man that is determined by and consequent to the intellectual judgment of man concerning the truth of a given object.

9. A fundamental recognition of the strength of passions in man, the struggle that take place in man over the opposition of particular truth or good to universal Truth or Good, and a recognition of the obstacles that impair free will.

THEMES OF CARTESIAN THOUGHT

As pointed out in the previous chapter, Descartes influenced both the environmentalism of Locke and the work of Leibnitz. Descartes' real point of divergence from Scholasticism began with his questioning of the hierarchy of methodological procedure advocated by Scholasticism. Although he refrained from calling into question matters of faith, he nevertheless insisted that philosophy and logic could not be the methodological procedure of science in themselves. Along with the Scholastics he maintained that knowledge was, indeed, conditioned by the question of certitude, but he doubted that logic could be considered a real source of certitude.

Methodology

Descartes observed that in antiquity all philosophers of note had been mathematicians and that this quality or preparation for philosophical reasoning had been absent in later developments. With regard to the syllogism of logic, Descartes stated that it was only a communication of what we already know and, although logic had some excellent methods to commend it, it was so full of superfluous and injurious concepts that the whole fabric must needs be suspect. Moreover, while he recognized that all the natural sciences were also dependent on philosophical reasoning to a large extent, he felt that they too were subject to error and falsehood. When Descartes viewed the then known status of knowledge, he felt that the methodology was primarily to blame. He looked for a new basis for certitude and found it in mathematical and geometric studies. Truth was much clearer in mathematics and geometry than elsewhere because a thing was either right or wrong. Still, he could see why philosophy was preferred by most people because of the freedom in procedure. Descartes stated that the search for truth should begin with mathematics and believed that man should not busy himself about anything that would not afford an object of certitude equal to that found in arithmetic or geometry.

Joined to the methodology of philosophy, Descartes also condemned the adaquation theory of Scholasticism, which had assumed that truth was the adaquation of ideas in the mind with the things that are outside of man (Descartes *Meditations on First Philosophy*, 110). This he considered a gross fallacy and pointed to the obvious discrepancy between sensory perception and objective reality.

Descartes proposed that there were only two ways by which man arrives at knowledge of facts—by experience and by deduction. Experience, he claimed, was primary; deduction does not have the same certitude since, whereas experience involves intuition, deduction includes memory plus the succession of ideas.

His method was to be the deductive geometric one in which there would be a reasoning from first truths or self-evident axioms downward to observed facts. Descartes proposed the following methodology: (1) to admit nothing save on clear and unimpeachable evidence, (2) to divide each of the difficulties under examination into as many parts as possible and as might be necessary for an adequate solution, (3) to consider all questions in a fixed order from simple to abstruse, and (4) to make sure that nothing essential was omitted. Descartes' method consisted entirely in the order and disposition of the objects toward which his mental vision was to be directed. He believed that he must comply with it exactly if he was to reduce involved and obscure propositions step by step to ones that were simpler and then, starting with the intuitive apprehension of those propositions that were absolutely simple, attempt to ascend to the knowledge of all others by precisely similar steps.

Descartes acknowledged that it is impossible for man to know absolute essences. He maintained that all we can know is the appearances, which are relative. This is a marked distinction from Scholasticism where essences were habitually defined absolutely and where operations were thus deduced from the logical definitions. Descartes was proposing that man must take the phenomenological appearances and must utilize them in the quest for knowledge. The importance of this distinction must not be underemphasized, since the Scholastic theory of knowledge depended on the intellect knowing the universal or abstract concept as such. Moreover, the whole Scholastic theory of knowledge was based on the adaquation theory whereby the mind knew truth as universalized and abstracted from sensory images and the universal existed in the reality of the mind itself. Descartes simply denied this. He stated that the universal was just a name, just a term—in effect, he subscribed to the nominalism theory.

The Nature of Man

Descartes taught that man's body and soul, although united, acted as two separate principles. His idea of the relationship between soul and body was based on his attitude toward universals. Descartes considered that the thought of man was the prime attribute or mode of his soul. Mind as the attribute of the soul is the only agent of perception. Again, there is always an intrinsic unity of impression to mental processes, since the soul is an indivisible subject, whereas sensory processes can include a range of impressions, since matter can be divided. Operationally, as well as theoretically, Descartes was careful not to offend traditional Catholic opinion in this area.

Theory of Knowledge

As will be recalled from the earlier discussion, Descartes felt that knowledge had to start with certain self-evident propositions from which other knowledge could be deduced and tested empirically. He ascribed to these intuitive propositions the very basis of all knowledge. Propositions such as the principles of contradiction, or that the effect cannot contain more than the cause were, he believed, the foundations of all knowledge. In this class must also be included the idea of God and of good and evil. Many later philosophers thought that in this doctrine there was present the germ of a theory of innate ideas as an a priori given. This opinion was erroneous as applied to Descartes because what he meant was that these immediate self-evident propositions were contained in the capacity of the mind itself (Hoffding, 1955, I, 221). He plainly stated that the soul has no a priori knowledge as such but depends on its liaison with the human brain for all knowledge. In effect Descartes was saying that the soul had a certain potency—that its chief attribute or mode was the fact of thought. In this sense he retained the medieval conception of potency as activated in the mind and thought process.

These self-evident propositions formed the basis of all knowledge and from them all vital cognizable truth could be deduced. Thus Descartes did not hold with an elaborate inductive process such as the Scholastics outlined for the metamorphosis of concrete sense images into universal ideas through the mediacy of many various soul-informing faculties. Although Descartes took as his starting point the conscious thought process (thus establishing consciousness as a condition for knowledge), he did not hold that the body was simply irrelevant in the process of knowledge.

Descartes viewed the body as a separate substance that had, as its chief attribute, extension. He defined the external sensory processes of reporting as "none other than certain confused modes of thought that are in some way or other connected with extension" (Descartes in Eaton, 153). He recognized the reality of the internal senses of common sense, imagination, memory, and instinct, but he insisted that their cognition is not intellection and does not reside in the same substance as intellectual thought. He accepted the Scholastic interpretation of the function of common sense, to sort out and classify sensory images, and the functions of memory, imagination, and instinct in this same regard. But the important difference in Descartes is that he viewed external objects as causing these images, that is, he saw an efficient causality relationship between extraorganic objects and the resulting organic sense image. This is in marked contrast to the Scholastic view of instrumental causality.

Determinism, Will and Object-Relation

It is apparent from Descartes' conception of man as a cosubstantial being with two essences, united but intrinsically different and really distinguished in virtue of their two principal modes of operation, that is, extension and thought, that he really created a duality in man even greater than the Scholastic thinkers had done. He conceived the soul as an indivisible substance—hence intellect or mind was an operation consisting in thought that was a unitary thing, indivisible in itself, presenting certain immediately self-evident characteristics of which unity of act and consciousness were two essential characteristics.

Descartes spoke of faculties of the mind, and he included under this designation willing, feeling, and conceiving as states of mind. Nevertheless, the above so-called faculties were only modal distinctions in the soul, not real ones.

Descartes stated that the faculty of the will consisted solely in our having the power to choose to do a thing or not to do it:

> The faculty of will consists alone in our having the power of choosing to do a thing or choosing not to do it (that is, to affirm or deny, to pursue or to shun it) or rather it consists alone in the fact that in order to affirm or deny, pursue or shun those things placed before us by the understanding, we act so that we are unconscious that any outside force constrains us in doing so (Descartes, 131).

A number of ideas are present in this quotation that reveal the pattern of thought of Descartes. First, he agreed with the Scholastics that the intellect places knowledge before the will. Second, he stated that the act of will is basically an affirmation or a denial of intellectual presentation. Third, he seemed to suggest determinism in the will through his allegation that we act as if free, but that we are unconscious of determining force from without. From Descartes' conception of efficient causality present in the relationship between extraorganic objects and sensory presentations, and his conception both of the universe and man as a complex machine, it is clear that he conceived of a basic determination of some psychic functions. It is understandable that this should not be explicitly clear because of Descartes' basic desire to get along with the Church. It is also true that he maintained that there was an independence of presentation of self-evident truths which was not in any manner dependent on bodily conditions. But these propositions were of necessity limited. The freedom from sensory process was strictly limited to the higher intellectual modes of thought.

In summary, Descartes broke with Scholastic thinking in a number of ways:

1. He still maintained the central position of an immaterial substance or soul which was the principle of cognition and understanding.
2. He denied a substantial union between body and soul in the sense that the Scholastics had taught it. Rather he affirmed a coexistence of two substances, body and soul.
3. He denied that the substance of soul or body could be known

per se. Instead he maintained that we know the attributes or modes of substance as they manifest themselves in operation or living. The attribute of the soul's substance was thought; that of the body, extension.

4. He considered universals not as things that had a real existence in external reality but as simple terms.

5. He posited an efficient causal relationship between cognition and the objects of cognition, thereby denying the instrumental causality of Scholasticism.

6. He denied the whole Scholastic metamorphosis of sense imagery into universal abstract ideas through the elaboration of various species and faculties as informed by the soul.

7. He emphasized an apodictic intuitive power of the human mind for recognizing certain propositions or axioms as certain and true through insight.

8. He seriously called into question the methodology of logic and based the certitude of knowledge on (1) certain insightful evident propositions, and (2) deductive reasoning.

9. He posited an efficient causal determinism which was connected with extension in all physical bodies, and he implied that there was a determinism in psychic activities that extended up to everything short of those immediate self-evident truths that were known by intuitive reasoning and insight.

10. He explained body-soul relationships in terms of animal spirits, the qualities of the blood, and the dual exchange of body-soul pressures in the pineal gland of the brain.

11. He considered love and hate as related to object-relations of tendency toward or aversion away from a particular object viewed as good or evil.

12. He conceived of thought, God, evil, and good as being self-evident propositions.

13. He recognized the will as a faculty of the soul concerned with affirmation or negation of intellectual knowledge.

Although Descartes broke with the old methodology of Scholasticism and provoked some thought about man's role in the universe and the problems of knowledge, it remained for Spinoza and Leibnitz to complete the line of thought that had been started with their predecessor. Of paramount importance is the philosophy of Spinoza, since in him certain elements of both Scholasticism and Cartesian thought were synthesized in relationship to moral conduct or ethics.

SPINOZA AND THE QUEST FOR SCIENTIFIC ETHICS

Methodology

The fundamental philosophical aim of Benedict Spinoza (1632–1677) was to establish ethics on a thoroughly tested foundation (Ratner, 1927, p. xxviii). His whole system consisted of an expansion of two ideas that were in a sense derived from Descartes—of substance and necessary existence. He took Descartes' dichotomy of mind and matter and united the two attributes of thought and extension under the concept of substance.

Spinoza was convinced that mathematics pointed the rational way to knowledge. Moreover, just as mathematics offers conclusions that are necessary once the given terms have been defined and clarified, so likewise is the universe, God and Nature, a necessary conclusion. Thus he could not accept a teleological explanation of God in which God works for the accomplishment of causes or ends—this he conceived as a manifestation of God's impotence.

Spinoza as a mathematician believed that the truth and validity of our knowledge about man himself and his universe could be established through the same procedure that geometric truth was established, that is, establish the given, the axioms, and then deductively reason to truth. Thus truth for Spinoza did not lie in some external circumstances outside man and his being but, instead, on agreement within man's own mind in which a distinct clearness was present in man's thought because of a perfect consistency (Spinoza, op. cit., p. 299). Man's natural rights were not determined either by nature or by some outside criterion (Spinoza, p. 299). Nature is neither moral or amoral, but is determined by necessity. Man is determined by nature only in that he is a part of nature. In nature there is nothing contingent, but all things are determined from the necessity of the divine nature to exist and to act in a certain manner. Inasmuch as man is a part of nature, he is determined by nature and, although there are certain necessary evils that proceed from nature (evil in the sense that they may oppose the existence of a given individual), man can also improve his own lot through mutual cooperation with nature.

Mind and body are modes of one and the same substance. That which appears under the attribute of extension can also be conceived under the attribute of thought. Spinoza did not conceive of two contrary principles operating in the universe but, instead, two complimentary attributes of one and the same substance. The attribute was merely the way we know the substance of God.

Central attributes in the universe are then extension and thought.

Man's soul is merely a succession of modes of thought that represent his essence as derived from the divine substance as a thinking being. His body is a pure mode or aggregate of forms deriving from extension. Since mental and material existences each have their own laws, within which there is coherence and causality as determined by necessity, they must both be examined according to these separate laws. Nevertheless, there is a unity. How then are the two dependent on each other and how are they connected? Spinoza tied this problem up with free will. He flatly denied that man has free will, rather he suggested that man has consciousness and, because he is conscious of a decision and does not know the reasons that determine this decision, he believes himself to be free. The course of man's existence is determined by a struggle between sensory images and ideas; the former proceed from body and extension and the latter proceed from mind and thought. Spinoza pointed out that both experience and reason taught that thought could not take place adequately if the body was sluggish. Hence, likewise, he avowed that man had no real power over his appetites or his insatiable curiosity and proneness to speak his mind.

Spinoza conceded the all-important role that the emotions or passions played in the determination of individual volitions. He meant by emotion "a modification of the body, by which the power of acting of the body is increased, diminished, helped or hindered together with the ideas of these modifications" (Spinoza, op. cit., p. 203). He distinguished between emotions as actions and as passions on the basis of whether they were present in the mind as inadequate or adequate ideas. An adequate idea was merely one whose effect could be clearly and distinctly perceived by means of the cause, and an inadequate idea was one whose effect could not be understood by means of the cause itself. Thus understanding was central to the problem of individual determination and volition. If the mind could understand adequately the cause of emotional disturbance, then presumably it would see this manifestation as an opportunity for greater fulfillment. If not, then it would be swayed by lack of knowledge, and the emotional reaction would be considered a passion. Paramount to an understanding of this conception is the fact that for Spinoza a thing was good or evil in terms of self-fulfillment.

Moreover, he conceived the entire course of our emotional life as being determined by the quality of the objects our emotions attach themselves to:

All happiness or unhappiness solely depends upon the quality of the object to which we are attached by love. Love for an object eternal and infinite feeds the mind with joy alone, a joy that is free from all sorrow (Spinoza, op. cit., p. 249).

Object relationship is an important factor in man's emotional life. The force and increase of any passion and its perseverance in existence is limited by the power of external objects as compared with our own power. The external object stimulates the emotion that, in turn, creates an idea in the mind along with concurrent modification of the body. Desire and its consequent act, volition, is merely an idea in the understanding—"which takes its rise from emotions which are caused by external causes . . . therefore the strength and increase of desire depends on the power of external causes . . . and this surpasses our own power" (Spinoza, p. 261). As Spinoza remarked, "We see men sometimes so affected by one object, that although it is not present, they believe it to be before them" (Ibid., p. 275).

Theory of Knowledge

Fundamental to an understanding of Spinoza's theory of knowledge are his axioms and presuppositions. He stated that that which cannot be conceived through another must be conceived of itself. This meant that mind and matter, although attributes of God and nature, were totally divorced in reality. Second, he insisted that, from a given determinate cause, an effect necessarily follows. Third, Spinoza declared that the knowledge of an effect depends on and involves the knowledge of the cause. Thus from a clear and precise knowledge of effects, Spinoza felt that it was possible to reason deductively back to the cause.

With regard to bodily functions, Spinoza held that external objects stimulated the sensory organs, thereby causing a twofold effect—in the body, a transmutation of some sort, and in the mind, a confused idea or image that in some part or other is derived and associated with extension. The external object could be considered the efficient cause of the sensory changes and still be considered as proceeding from God, since God and nature were united in one substance and the action of a part is assimilated under the action of the whole. Spinoza recognized the functions of imagination and memory and described the relationship of sensible images to external objects in terms that are very similar to the terms of the Scholastics. Although Spinoza did not refer to the *intentional existence* as such, it is clear that he taught the existence of a sensible image that was the mind's representation of the extraorganic object. Moreover, there is also a parallel in the fact that Spinoza maintained— somewhat more clearly than the Scholastics—that this image in a very real sense involved the basic nature of man as a perceiving agent. He told us that Paul's conception of Peter revealed more about Paul than Peter (Spinoza, introduction, xiv).

Spinoza's theory of knowledge involved both the nature of the affected body, that is, man, and the extraorganic object. Man conceives the nature of many bodies external to himself along with that of his own body. Thus the ideas that we have of external objects indicate and reflect the constitution of our own body. Nevertheless all these images that are conceived as ideas, insofar as they are derived from bodily processes, carry with them the characteristics of extension.

Sensation is the bodily condition corresponding not only to the nature of extended bodies but also principally to the nature of our own body. The general causal sequence or concatenation of the laws of motion as revealed in extended bodies corresponds to the association of ideas or mental laws of nature as revealed in our consciousness. *Thus consciousness, feeling, will, and even reason are determined by the bodily response to external objects. Even further, Spinoza maintained that our very concept of reality is clarified and determined by the inner struggle between sensations and ideas.*

What role then is left for the highest power of thought and mind that Spinoza maintained was a separate dimension of man? Although Spinoza maintained that our conception of reality was determined by external objects, bodily transformations, and a conflict of ideas within us, he nevertheless held that there was a kind of knowledge that was the only truly adequate knowledge, and this was intuitive. This point can be cleared up through a treatment of the hierarchy of knowledge as Spinoza conceived of it.

Spinoza maintained that there were three orders of knowledge: (1) common (based on observation, etc.), (2) axiomatic, and (3) intuitive. He described common knowledge as that sensory basis of all our understanding, axiomatic knowledge as that form of understanding involving the notion of causes, and intuitive, which he reserved for a few individuals. This third form of knowledge Spinoza also called intuitive science.

> This kind of knowing advances from an adequate idea of the formal essence of certain attributes of God to the adequate knowledge of the essence of things (Spinoza 181).

The highest virtue of the mind (and Spinoza equates virtue with power of knowledge) consists in knowledge of God and reality through this third kind of knowledge.

Thus Spinoza conceived of a hierarchy of knowledge and a process whereby extraorganic objects effected transmutations in the body that were represented in the internal senses as an image and in the mind as an idea. Most knowledge was inadequate and confused in that man does not know the causes. In the second and third orders of knowledge, reason and intuition operate on adequate ideas that ultimately must be true (Spinoza said this because he felt that they reflected the nature of God). Nevertheless, there is no exact adequation of ideas either with extra-organic reality, or with the words that we use constantly to express these ideas.

What then did he recommend for men of good will who would live a moral life? First, *responsibility founded on knowledge.* Virtue was nothing less than the power of knowledge. *Second, man should make use of things with moderation.*

> To make use of things therefore, and to delight in them as much as possible (provided we do not disgust ourselves with them, which is not delighting in them) is the part of a wise man. It is the part of a wise man, I say, to refresh and invigorate himself with moderate and pleasant eating and drinking, with sweet scents and the beauty of green plants, with ornament, with music, with sports, with the theater, and with all things of this kind which one man can enjoy without hurting another (Spinoza, op. cit., 276).

In short, Spinoza felt that man should formulate a consistency of approach to his problems.

Spinoza, then, was an elaborator of Cartesian philosophy.

1. Like the Scholastics and Descartes he maintained that man possessed an immaterial substance or soul that was the principle of cognition and understanding.
2. However, he maintained still further that this substance was God Himself and was identified with nature as a sort of vital force.
3. God's two chief attributes were extension and thought and, although the two were separately conceived by man, they were a unity in God himself. This was quite different from what either the Scholastics or Descartes had maintained.
4. Like Descartes he agreed that man could not know simple substances or essences but must rely on phenomenological modes of existence.
5. Regarding universals, Spinoza agreed with Descartes that they were only ideas—with this addition that he considered them confused ideas.
6. Like Descartes, he posited an efficient causal relationship between objects of cognition but, through his concept of God as the primary substance, he understood that God was the efficient cause of knowledge.

7. He too denied the metamorphosis of sensory imagery into universal ideas that alone were known by the intellect.

8. He retained, however, the elaboration of sense imagery in consciousness and in imagination and memory via an intentional existence that was the unique creation of the human mind in and for the human mind.

9. He attempted to place ethics on a scientific basis utilizing truths that he placed on the level of geometric axioms.

10. He recognized the force of the emotions in man and maintained that man's very judgments were determined by forces within or without him.

11. He insisted there were no faculties of the mind as such, that intellection and volition were simple acts of willing and knowing, corresponding exactly to no words or signs, but motivated strongly by desire.

12. Man's only morality is based on his nature—not on some outside criterion. Perfection, power, knowledge, and virtue are all equatable terms.

13. Good is what is conducive to man's preservation of his own body or mind. Evil is what opposes this operation.

14. All sensory knowledge is object-centered to the extent, in some cases, that man is immobilized by the power and strength of this relationship.

15. Free will is a fiction of consciousness. We think we are free because we are aware of our decision. But we know not on what causes we act.

16. Man's supreme knowledge and good is the knowledge of God. This is known through a knowledge of the universe and the laws of nature.

17. He maintained that there are three kinds of knowledge, common, axiomatic, and intuitive. Although he saw determination in each of the first two, he maintained a certain insightful apodictic quality for truths of the highest order that he called intuition.

18. Man is most useful to man; responsibility, moderation, and consistency of action are man's chief ethical rules to the adequate understanding of himself and God.

LEIBNITZ AND INNATE IDEAS

Descartes and Spinoza have this in common that they established a strictly mechanistic conception of nature with regard to the material side of existence. Descartes emphasized the separateness of mind and body characterizing both the attributes of thought and extension. Spinoza reduced these attributes of God to one substance which he identified with nature. Leibnitz both continued this line of thought and stood as a reaction against it.

Gottfried Leibnitz (1646–1716) was the outstanding German philosopher-scientist of the 17th century. He is seldom included in the discussion of educational or psychological thought, and yet he is most important in the historical development of phenomenological thought. A brilliant genius gifted in many areas, including mathematics, he was born in Leipzig in 1646. He traveled widely after completing his education at Altdorf and eventually resided at Hannover where he held the offices of court counselor and librarian until his death in 1716. Leibnitz did not leave an extended exposition of his philosophy, since most of his writings are brief treatises and essays on various scientific and philosophical problems. Leibnitz was inspired by the thought of founding a system of philosophy that would reconcile all the systems of his predecessors and would bring Plato into harmony with Democritus, would demonstrate agreements between Aristotle and Descartes, and would prove that there was no real basic contradiction between Scholastic and scientific thought. This was an ambitious project, but it was not out of line in view of the brilliance of Leibnitz, a man who discovered differential calculus, who ranked among the foremost mathematicians of his day, and was also known as a scientist, philosopher, and religious controversialist. In *Methodology and Science* Leibnitz agreed generally with Descartes and Spinoza on the primacy of mathematical knowledge for affording certainty and arriving at truth. He maintained that science was founded on the demonstration of innate knowledge. In his *New Essays Concerning Human Understanding* he took to task John Locke for his sense empiricism. Leibnitz' opposition to Locke is said to have been summed up in a short interchange wherein Locke is supposed to have said: "There is nothing in the intellect which has not first been in the senses." Leibnitz is said to have responded: "No, there is nothing in the intellect which has not first been in the senses EXCEPT THE INTELLECT." This is the prime focus of the disagreement between the two philosopher-scientists. Leibnitz condemned Locke's *tabula rasa* theory because he believed that there were certain necessary truths that are found in pure mathematics and that appear to rest on other principles, whose proof depends not on experience and the testimony of the senses but on logic itself.

Leibnitz maintained that physics and all natural science have their foundations in metaphysics. Leibnitz took the axioms and insightful reason of Descartes and Spinoza and asserted still further that the ability to recognize these truths was a demonstration of innate ideas in the mind. Because of his position with regard to metaphysics and physics, that is, of the dependency of the latter on the former, he returned once more to a strong emphasis on logic as a methodological tool.

Leibnitz found in the syllogism itself and in mathematical process a close relationship that he identified with innate ideas. Both mathematics and logic were full of truths that could only be appreciated by positing innate principles. The reason that logic had not been utilized well in Scholastic procedures was that the tool had been obscured and confused by words and by the meanings that are associated with language. Leibnitz identified the syllogism—in fact—defined it as a "series of universal mathematics whose importance was not sufficiently known."

Leibnitz considered that evidence was necessary for certitude and that the evidence of experience was not as certain as the evidence of axiomatic propositions. Experience never assures us of perfect universality or of necessity. Experience determines thoughts—but does not furnish ideas as such. "The truths of reason," said Leibnitz, "ground themselves in the necessity of thought." But these truths can be only those propositions which have been reduced to identicals, that is, through the principle of contradiction, and the like.

Man possesses the knowledge of these necessary or a priori truths through identical judgments, that is, those judgments that the subject and predicate can be shown to be and the same concept. Introspection (or what Leibnitz termed self-inspection) gives us a knowledge of these first principles of truth, truths of fact, from which our thought, cognition, and reasoning spring.

Reality and Nature

As will be recalled, Spinoza identified God, nature, and substance. He saw all the attributes of God and nature as proceeding in virtue of the necessary existence of God. There was only one substance that was manifested everywhere. Leibnitz also agreed that ultimately everything could be traced back to God, but he denied that God and substance were identical; instead, he said that there were a multiplicity of substances. He attacked the Cartesian allegation that the real characteristic of matter was extension and motion. He insisted that behind these attributes was the principle of force. Force is made up of small atoms that are not hard and fast but elastic. These components of force Leibnitz called monads. He said that the body was a composite substance made up of a multiplicity of things. The soul was a unity but still reflected multiplicity much as all lines drawn from a periphery meet in the center (Hoffding, I, 354).

The nature of man was formed by the composite of body and soul, which was, in effect, a junction of multiplicity with unity. Leibnitz stated that man's nature required not merely a reasoning soul but something of a figure and the constitution of body. Man is not a machine as Descartes had implied. He is a social being, his speech is at once the instrument and the bond of society. Although man can be defined as a corporeal rational being, this definition is both real and nominal. It is real in that it corresponds to what we know as man, it is nominal in that a rational corporeal creature from the moon would not necessarily be a man.

The soul of man is a unity, a simple substance that has as its characteristic the fact of thought. Nevertheless, this is a wider definition than Descartes', since Leibnitz maintained that the soul was more independent than thought. The thoughts of the soul are not always distinct enough for remembrance or even for recognition by the conscious ego as thought. The soul is an ever-active principle, immortal, possessing dispositions, attitudes, and propensities toward innate truths, and has nothing in it that cannot be expressed by understanding. Leibnitz thus introduced a new concept in regard to the soul and thought, that is, the fact of unconscious mental processes. He maintained that the soul's activities were recognizable and capable of interpretation through the medium of consciousness, but consciousness was not identical with thought.

There were, in his view, three grades of activity in the soul which could be grouped under the category of thought. The first category were those "dark modifications," which were never clear (monads of lowest grade) and which he termed perceptions. When these perceptions had become clearer and memory was present, they had reached the threshold of consciousness. The highest grade of thought was the one that accompanied voluntary attention and reflection; this was known as apperception. Leibnitz suggested that the process of knowledge was very much like a man watching a wave roll in from the ocean and hit the beach. The first stage of thought is the sound of millions of particles of water hitting the shore. This multitude of sounds is there, but is not perceived. The consciousness of hearing this wave will create a certain perception pattern and memory phenomena, but the highest degree of thought will be that which takes place through voluntary attention and reflection concerning the sound of the waves.

The obvious problem of body-soul relationship was met by Leibnitz through his doctrine of monads. Monads were created by God and thus both the monad that comprised the soul and the multiplicity of monads that comprised the body existed in a prearranged harmony. Thus, although both substances were independent, they were both mutually obedient to their Maker. It was very much like two clocks set in a prearranged harmony ticking and striking together.

Faculties and Theory of Knowledge

Leibnitz did not subscribe to the elaborate Scholastic theory of knowledge. He retained the faculties, both sense and rational, but with this distinction that it meant little to state that the soul possessed a faculty or an ability to do something without the conditions for utilizing it. The utilization of a faculty as such requires not only the object or stimulus for activating the faculty but also a disposition toward the object before action can take place. Thus he required as a condition for operation: (1) the inherent and innate potency of faculty, (2) the object or stimulus to action, and (3) the disposition or *intentionality*. Leibnitz retained the concept of intentionality as far as the creation of an intentional existence in the mind was posited, but it was only with regard to the sensible image and not to the universalized intentional existence of the Scholastics. Leibnitz stated:

> . . . I see nothing to hinder our scholastics from saying that everything is done simply by their faculties and from maintaining their intentional species which proceed from objects even to us and find means of entering even into our souls (Leibnitz, 1949, 56).

Nevertheless, he maintained elsewhere that he was referring specifically to sensible images. In line with what he said about faculties meaning nothing unless in operation, he spoke of the intellect thus:

> . . . In my view the understanding corresponds to what among the Latins is called *intellectus* and the exercise of this faculty is called intellection, which is a distinct perception united with the faculty of reflection (Leibnitz, 1949, 178).

It is evident from this quotation that Leibnitz recognized that intellection involves two factors or processes: a recognition of the object of perception, and a self-reflection.

Reason, Volition, and Ethical Determinants

Leibnitz like Spinoza and Descartes was concerned with the ethics of human behavior. He identified reason as a "concatenation of truths." He called it elsewhere man's natural revelation and stated that it was confined to man alone. Moreover, in keeping with his religious orientation, he stated that it was not opposed to faith.

Leibnitz's conception of good and evil are very reminiscent of Spinoza. He defines good as "that which is fitted to produce and increase pleasure in us or to diminish and cut short some pain. Evil is that which is fitted to produce or increase pain or to diminish some pleasure. The emotions are recognized in Leibnitzean philosophy and a distinction is made between desire and the passions. The passions we know by reason of their object. Hence, love is defined as the inclination to take pleasure in the complete perfection or happiness of the object loved. Desire, on the other hand, is characterized by what Leibnitz called uneasiness (*Unruhe*):

> . . . that is to say the little imperceptible solicitations which keep us always in suspense; they are confused determination (p. 117).

The will or volition is closely connected with desire in Leibnitz's view. In fact, he does not consider the will free when desire is present. The will, Leibnitz maintained, had a limited freedom, but he continually pointed out that the very concept of freedom was ambiguous, that it implies spontaneity and deliberateness, and that both of these things are, for the most part, absent from man. There is no freedom of will against the impressions that come from understanding (p. 184). Volition seems to be the result of a conflict between perceptions and inclinations or instincts. The will is thus determined by the result of its tendencies, and yet Leibnitz suggested that the mind itself can employ these dichotomies in order to control influencing tendencies. Sensible images tend to have the greatest control over volition, and it is for this reason that man refuses in many instances to will the greater good, because the greater good idea is not as strongly sensible as others (p. 192). Nevertheless, for all these objections, Leibnitz retained the limited freedom of the will and states that man is free insofar as he is conscious. "They seek for what they know, know not for what they seek," is how he sums up the problem (p. 184). In this view is present a great deal of Spinoza, although theoretically Leibnitz preserves some limited freedom of action —even if conditioned by consciousness of choice—in order to satisfy the requirements of religious ethics. Leibnitz's contribution can be summarized as follows:

1. He reestablished logic and the syllogism as a mathematical tool for science as well as for metaphysics.
2. He declared that physical science in its philosophical notions depended on metaphysics.

3. He suggested that logic had been misused and that it had to be integrated into mathematical models.

4. He insisted that all ideas were the product of thought and, hence, of the soul.

5. He admitted innate ideas or dispositions inherent in certain ways of looking at concepts.

6. He retained the concept of sensory species and intentional existence.

7. He insisted that the soul and body were separate substances, united in a prearranged harmony through monads and God.

8. He explained the nature of thought and reality in terms of a hierarchy of cognition extending from unconscious perception to conscious perception and memory and, finally, to apperception and reflection.

9. He claimed that all truths of reason were grounded in propositions whose termini could be accepted as identical.

10. He claimed the prime attribute of matter was not extension or movement, but force.

11. He admitted and taught the doctrine that the soul could think apart from consciousness.

12. He considered the soul a simple substance, and the body a multiplicity of substances.

13. He required as conditions of thought the innate potency of a faculty plus an external object or stimulus and a disposition toward or intentionality in object-relations.

14. He identified desire with uneasiness and lack of knowledge concerning specifiable object-relations, and he defined passions in terms of object-relations.

15. He retained universal ideas as the essences of things, and not as general terms derived from experience.

16. He distinguished between sense-ideas and ideas of first principles or intellect; the former confused, the latter clear. Truth that was based on sense-ideas he considered inadequate, whereas the truth based on first principles he considered adequate.

17. He viewed good and evil in terms of self-fulfillment or lack thereof.

18. He called reason—man's natural revelation, a concatenation of truths and denied that it was necessarily counter to faith.

19. He recognized that volition was determined in large part by conflicts between sensory perception and the rule of reason.

20. He stated that freedom of will was present only in that we were conscious of making a choice.

REACTION AND TRANSITION

The positions of Thomistic Scholasticism, Descartes, Spinoza, and Leibnitz have illustrated a metaphysical viewpoint in which the mind of man, his feelings, and his emotions not only play an important role in the determination of his perception, but also provide an ethical basis for man's behavior. The Scholastic doctrine of Aquinas first pointed out the nature of intentionality in human experience (although Aristotle may have alluded to it also). All human knowledge was centered on the intentional image that had an object-relationship to both the external stimulus and the internal needs of the mind. Descartes, through his denial of the substantial union between body and soul, tended to emphasize the need for looking at the phenomena of mental experience in a separate manner. The emphasis that he placed on insight and apodictic self-evident truths was grounded on the continuing successive experience of the self as it proceeds through space and time. Spinoza sought to relate these ideas to ethics and to the development of an adequate self-concept through the acceptance and understanding of the emotions. Leibnitz introduced once again the need for a metaphysical framework, the concept of the unconscious as it determines some of the products of perception, and the limited freedom of the will.

Although the positions of Scholasticism, Descartes, Spinoza, and Leibnitz differ on many points, there is a fundamental unity and stress on the intentional character of all man's cognition. These positions have been studied because the intentionalistic frame of reference forms the metaphysical basis of the theory of mind and meaning that ultimately can be traced into psychoanalytic, phenomenological, and Gestalt theories of perception.

It is not relevant here to trace in great detail movements or counter-movements not directly related to the intentionalistic framework, but in view of the fact that Brentano served as the redactor of this approach in the formulation of a modern theory of intentionality, it is pertinent that some other movements that influenced the course of psychology be discussed briefly.

British Empiricism

The whole tendency of British philosophy from Francis Bacon and Hobbes had been toward an environmentalist and pragmatic approach to man, rather than toward a metaphysical or mystical one. Locke proved to be the real exponent of this approach. He simply denied the whole position of an intentional metaphysics. He maintained that there were no innate concepts and principles and that the entire origin and development of ideas could be known through sense experience. He thus did away with rational intuition as a source of knowledge. He said that ideas were known through experience, and he divided experience into external and internal perception. The former he referred to as sensation, the latter as reflection. Sensation was the perception of external objects mediated through the sense; reflection was the perception of the activities of the mind as presented through the senses. Complex ideas such as universals, extension, form, motion, and rest, were merely the result of the combining of many sensory elements. Locke's whole approach was a sensory empiricism based almost exclusively on sensory experience.

Berkeley and *Hume* proceeded much further than Locke, but along two different paths. Berkeley did away with all sensory dependence to form ideas and asserted that ideas are entities independent of the mental activity of the perceiving subject. He became the founder of a British idealism. Hume, proceeding much further than Locke in the environmentalist direction, reduced all mental activity to simple quantitative impressions from the senses which mold or condition the nature of thought.

Kantian Idealism

Immanuel Kant (1724–1804) stands in reaction to both environmentalism and to Leibnitzean philosophy and the intentionalistic metaphysics. Kant's impact on philosophy was great. It was, in reality, a position that avoided the environmentalism of Lockean philosophy, and particularly that of Hume, and that also rejected Leibnitzean rationalism, the position in which Kant had been educated. Kant felt that environmentalism was wrong because it exaggerated the determining influence of sensation on thought. He also disagreed with the intentional metaphysics of rationalism because he did not believe that certain facts or axioms were necessarily self-evident. Turner (1929) paraphrasing Kant puts it this way:

> The whole Wolffian and Cartesian system of psychology he considers to be false in its starting point—the assumption, namely, that we have an intuitive knowledge of understanding. We have, he contends, no such intuition. Thought is a succession of unifications, or syntheses: at the apex of the pyramid, the base of which is the manifold representation, stands the conscious principle; but as the conscious principle is devoid of empirical content, it is, like the

noumenon, an x, an unknown quantity. Descartes says 'I think,' but what, Kant asks, is the I? It is the emptiest of all forms, a psychological subject of conscious states, which never can become the logical subject of a predicate referring to these states or to anything else. Empirical psychology, which alone can extend our knowledge of mental life; does not aim at telling us anything about the ego; rational psychology, which does aim at establishing truths concerning the ego, is wrong in its very starting point and is full of contradictions in the course of its development (537).

Kant's philosophy is an attempt to examine the transcendental characteristics or a priori elements that are the conditions of knowledge and moral behavior. Although Kant commendably attempted to relate his criticism of existing philosophical systems to categories of thinking that are necessary and universal, in the practical sense, he rested his whole system on the analysis by logic and reason of the characteristics of the a priori.

More important than Kant's immediate contribution was the fact that an entire movement of German philosophical idealism grew up as a derivation from Kant. Johann Fichte (1762–1814), Friedrich Schelling (1775–1884), and George Wilhelm Hegel (1770–1831) developed Kantian themes into a vehicle for German romanticism and nationalism. This movement, although certainly related to the development of Marxism, falls outside of the general purvey of influences felt in either environmentalism or intentionality.

Kantian idealism was an important phase of philosophical and psychological thought. Herbart, mentioned in the previous chapter, inveighed against Kant's notion that psychology could not become a science. Brentano, then, becomes the redactor of an intentional metaphysics, or revived rationalism, in which he attempts to develop a new empiricism that is based on perception rather than the sense empiricism of Locke. However, Brentano was much influenced by British empiricism, which he admired, as well as by the physiological studies in psychology by Maudsley, Helmholtz, and Wundt, by the educational writings of Herbart, and by the sociology of Comte.

Because Brentano formed a new synthesis of philosophical realism with a basis in intentionality, we shall now consider Brentano, omitting further discussion of the intervening period.

FRANZ BRENTANO AND THE PSYCHOLOGY OF ACT

In the evolution of psychological thought in the past 100 years, there is scarcely a more fascinating individual than Franz Brentano. Brentano is little studied by contemporary English-reading psychological students because only one of his works has ever been translated into English. Moreover, there is a great deal of misunderstanding about the man and his work. Many of his contemporaries considered his psychological views simply as warmed-over Scholastic speculation. Others rejected him because of his departure from the Roman Catholic Church and considered his writings a kind of tainted Scholasticism. Again, Brentano changed his mind considerably over the period of his productive years and is often misunderstood. Finally, Brentano's earlier work was psychologically oriented, and his later work (for which he is more known) was concerned chiefly with philosophy and ethics. It is also true that Brentano contributed to the confusion about his own point of view in psychology because of his neglect in publishing and his total disinterest in making a name for himself. And yet, today, he is considered to be one of the fathers of *Gestalt* psychology, a contributor to the formation of psychoanalytic thought through his contact with Sigmund Freud, a source of influence on William James, and the teacher of a number of very well-known philosophers and psychologists of the first decades of the 20th century. Franz Brentano taught, among others, Carl Stumpf (the teacher of Koehler in Berlin), Edmund Husserl (the founder of modern approaches to phenomenology), Christian von Ehrenfels, Kazimierz Twardowski, Alexius Meinong, and Sigmund Freud.

Brentano's Background, Life and Personality

Franz Brentano was born in Marienberg on the Rhine on January 16, 1838. He was descended from a famous literary family. He was the nephew of Clemens Brentano, the romantic poet; and his grandfather, Peter Brentano, had been married to Maximiliane Laroche, who had served as an inspiration to the poet, Goethe. His brother was the economist, Lujo Brentano, who is known in the history of politico-economic thought. At an early age, Franz Brentano decided to study for the priesthood. He therefore went to Berlin where he resided with an uncle and took courses at the University of Berlin. There he fell under the influence of Adolf Trendelenberg, who was an Aristotelian. This influence was to result in a lifelong friendship with Trendelenberg.

In 1856, Brentano went to Munich where he studied with Döllinger, the Catholic theologian and historian. After completing his theological studies in 1864, he was ordained a priest and entered a Dominican convent. Two years later, in 1866, Brentano left the convent and became a *Dozent* at the University of Wurzburg. Here he distinguished himself by his attacks on *Naturphilosophie* and the derived idealism of Schelling, so popular at the university at that time. He lectured on philosophy and the history of philosophy and soon drew enthusiastic crowds of students about him. Among them were Carl Stumpf, who much later succeeded Wilhelm Wundt at Berlin and was the teacher of Wolfgang Koehler, Herman Schell, who was to become a champion of German modernism, and Thomas Masaryk, the founder of the Czechoslovakian Republic.

During his years at Wurzburg, Brentano published several articles on Aristotle and church history. He was particularly interested in the development and history of science in the Catholic church. It was, however, during these years at Wurzburg that Brentano began to entertain some serious doubts about matters of faith in the Catholic church. Not only were his mind and conscience beset with doubts, but there was the precipitating factor of the convening of the Vatican Council to discuss the proposed definition of papal infallibility. Brentano was commissioned to prepare an historical and philosophical refutation of the proposed dogma. Brentano thus became, along with Döllinger, the avowed leader of the liberal party that opposed the definition of infallibility, partly on the ground that it was philosophically untenable, and partly because it was considered inopportune.

Brentano, from his first days at Wurzburg, had been much interested in the work of the English philosophers and psychologists. In 1872, after being promoted to the rank of professor extraordinary of philosophy, he left Wurzburg and traveled to England in order to acquaint himself still more with the psychological literature which was appearing in England. He spent time visiting with Herbert Spencer, W. Robertson Smith, and Cardinal Newman. John Stuart Mill, for whom Brentano had a lively admiration, was absent from the country and hence they did not meet. The following year, 1873, was a crucial year for Brentano. Tortured by his doubts about papal infallibility, which was now a defined dogma of the Catholic church, he sadly resigned his professorship at Wurzburg. A month later, Brentano donned secular clothes and left the priesthood. He was now unemployed. Not just technically was he without a teaching position, but worse, he was a man without any defined allegiance. Döllinger invited him to join the "Old Catholic" movement, but Brentano refused. His own brother, Lujo Brentano, wrote to him and advised him at least to join a Protestant church, for then he would certainly be offered a teaching position at one of the Protestant universities. But Brentano refused to compromise his position.

During the following year, he had neither church nor university to occupy his time, so he wrote his *Psychologie vom empirischen Standpunkt* (Psychology from the Empirical Viewpoint). Before the book was actually finished, Lotze appealed to the liberal Austrian Minister of Education, Stremayer, on Brentano's behalf. Over the objection of both emperor and cardinal, Brentano was appointed as professor in the University of Vienna in January 1874. Six years later, he was demoted to the rank of *Privat Dozent* because of his marriage. In Austria, it was not possible for a former priest to be legally married, so Brentano went off to Saxony for the ceremony and thereby lost both his Austrian citizenship and his position. But he continued to teach at Vienna until 1894, when his wife died. The tragedy of his wife's death was coupled with failing eyesight. Brentano resigned his university position and settled in Florence. Finally, when the First World War broke out, he went to Zurich because of his confirmed pacifist convictions. He died there at the age of 79 in 1917.

In comparison with some of the other psychologists and philosophers who were his contemporaries, Brentano did not publish a great deal. His greatest contribution to psychological thought was his *Psychologie*. His later interests were centered more about philosophical questions of epistemology and ethical value theory. At his death, there was a great mass of unpublished manuscripts, many of which were edited by Oskar Kraus and Alfred Kastil and subsequently published.

Brentano's influence on German psychology and the subsequent developments in phenomenological and Gestalt thought is a unique one. Coming at about the same time as Wilhelm Wundt, Brentano's influence seems to have been felt mediately through his students and the force of his personality instead of through his written works. He was well-loved by his students. The composite picture they give us is of a scholar and master teacher of sterling integrity. Although he was led to reject revealed religion and nonrational faith, he remained convinced that reason brought man to God. This quality of impartial integrity, joined to sincere scholarship, seems to have been one of the chief characteristics of Franz Brentano. In his writing and lecturing he often attacked the ideas of other people but carefully distinguished between a man's ideas and his person. In his lecture, he followed outlines very carefully and possessed such a lucid style that he forced his students to participate mentally in his argumentation. He would first state the question, then proceed to one opinion after the other, and finally offer his own solution. Students would be convinced of the truth of each opinion as he argued for it, and then he forced them to change their minds when the next one was given. In this manner Brentano forced much student participation in thinking. A testimony to the challenging nature of his lectures is the fact that students would often follow him home from the lecture hall and stay late into the evening discussing philosophical and psychological issues.

As a person, Brentano was soft-spoken and considerate. When he first came to Vienna, the lecture hall was packed with a crowd of students who were planning to heckle him. However, they were so impressed by his fairness in argumentation, his brilliant manner of exposition, and his manifest sincerity that they gave him a standing ovation at the conclusion of the lecture (Kastil, 1951, p. 13). After his death, Oskar Kraus joined Carl Stumpf and Edmund Husserl in the writing of a testimonial volume to the memory of their friend and teacher. Meinong and von Eherenfels also testified in their written works to the great influence that Brentano had had on their own intellectual formation.

The Evolution of Brentano's Thought

Franz Brentano as a philosopher and psychologist passed through a personal evolution in his thinking processes. Originally he was an avid Aristotelian realist even prior to his assumption of priestly orders in the Roman Catholic Church. Although a priest and professor at Wurzburg, his interest centered on the history of science in the Catholic Church. He lectured on the history of philosophy in general and particularly stressed the writing of the English empiricists Hume, Bentham, and the two Mills.[1] Actually, he was considering these men quite seriously in his classes when Kantian idealism and Naturphilosophie was the strongest philosophical current in German speaking countries. He seems never to have been affected by Kant or Hegel; in fact, he had posted as his fourth

---

[1] *Note.* The fact that Brentano was always in favor of the approach to psychology taken by Locke and Mill as well as Bentham is a factor to be considered in the influence relationship between Freud and Brentano. Merlan observed that Brentano had recommended Freud for some translation of John Stuart Mill (*Journal of the History of Ideas,* vol. 6, 1945, pp. 375–377). Jones stated that Freud had avidly read English authors for a period of ten years in his youth. Andrew Watson writing in the *International Journal of Psychoanalysis* ("Freud the Translator," vol. 39, Part V., September 1958, pp. 326–327) suggests independently that Freud had gained some of his philosophical ideas from Bentham. The various suggestions of similarity to Bentham, Mill, and even Maudsley, the English physiologist, could be explained through the catalytic agency of Brentano. Brentano was in the habit of discussing many current topics of interest in his seminars. Unfortunately, there is no knowledge now of what subjects Brentano pursued in the years 1873 to 1876 when Freud was attending them. There is, however, a record of a conference held for German students in the year 1876 in which Brentano took up the subject *"Was für ein Philosoph manchmal Epoche macht* (What kind of a philosopher sometimes makes an epoch). This conference was primarily concerned with the subject of Plotinus (See Lucie Gilson, *Methode et Metaphysique,* p. 33, footnote 2, J. Vrin, Paris, 1955). From Husserl's recollections ten years later (1884–1886) a list of topics probably representative of Brentano's selection include Hume's *Inquiry Concerning Human Understanding and Principles of Morals,* Helmholtz's speech on the "Facts of Perception," and Du Bois-Reymond's "Limits of Natural Judgment." Certainly these selections indicate that Brentano was not narrowly circumscribed by philosophical titles (Marvin Farber, *The Foundations of Phenomenology,* Cambridge, Mass., Harvard Press, 1943, p. 9).

thesis to be defended for his *venia docendi* (a medieval custom of presenting a paper or thesis as a license for teaching) at Wurzburg "That the True Method of Philosophy Is None Other Than That of Natural Science."[2] In following this thesis, it is possible to detect the strong influence of Trendelenburg and Aristotelian thought on Brentano. Trendelenburg (a teacher of Brentano and an Aristotelian) had maintained that observation was an important method in arriving at experimental verification. He said that the validity of every postulate of natural science was dependent on logic because each segment of science followed a definite method that flowed over into the logic of thought itself.

Brentano's original position at Wurzburg was that of moderate realism. In this view he was espousing the doctrine of Aristotle and the Scholastic developments. Thus he held that there was an objective world of reality that could be known, in part, by man. There was a teleological explanation of man, his purpose, his origin and destiny. Truth was the correspondence of the intellect to the reality that existed outside the mind. Values and ethics as well as the theory of knowledge which he held were those of the Church, that is, Thomas Aquinas. Brentano held both the indeterminist view in psychic life and the correspondence theory. Gradually, he became convinced of psychic determinism and also of the untenability of the correspondence theory of knowledge. By 1911 he had changed his ideas radically from those of his earlier days.

The Doctrine of the Four Phases

One of the first articles published by Brentano appeared in a three-volume work by J.A. Mohler called *Kirchengeschichte*. He wrote a chapter entitled: "The History of Science in the Church." In this article, Brentano proposed his doctrine of the four phases of philosophy. He saw in the history of philosophy a repeating phenomenon in which the course of philosophical thought passed through a series of periods, (1) a period of research inspired by theoretical interest, (2) a diminution of this theoretical interest, (3) scepticism, and (4) mystical reaction. Stumpf pointed out that Brentano had held these ideas from about the year 1860 (Gilson, *Méthod et Metaphysique*, 1955, 26).

Along with this article there were several articles that Brentano had written about August Comte. Brentano seemed to take a special interest in the difficulties that are present in Comte's analysis of the stages or phases of scientific thought. Comte had suggested that mankind's thought

[2] Carl Stumpf, one of Brentano's earliest students at Wurzburg, and a later teacher of Koehler at Berlin indicated his tremendous excitement at the presentation of Brentano's position at Wurzburg. He was then a young law student, but later was Brentano's successor at Wurzburg (Spielberger, 1965, I, p. 54).

passes through three phases, (1) theological, (2) metaphysical, and (3) positivistic or scientific. Brentano analyzed Comte's thought and surmounted the difficulties by taking the view that there was an internal unity of thought in elements that appear to be irreconcilable. He believed that it was possible to believe in the positivistic approach without renouncing theism.

Brentano's doctrine of the four epochs provides the key to his whole methodological approach in philosophy and psychology. Gilson (1955, 31) poses the problem of whether Brentano was influenced by Comte and positivistic thought. She notes that Brentano had abandoned the word epoch and used instead the word state, which was the word that Comte had utilized—thus differing from his earlier thesis. Nevertheless, she concludes that Brentano had accommodated Comte's ideas to his own for the purpose of clarity. Whatever the situation was, there can be no doubt that much of Brentano's approach to philosophy and psychology was positivistic.

Brentano perceived similar patterns in ancient, medieval, and modern philosophy. He believed that Aristotle had marked the apex of original philosophical interest. Subsequently, the Stoics and Epicureans had marked a decline from original interest. Scepticism had been the third stage of development and, finally, Neoplatonism had represented the mystical stage of development. The same order had persisted in medieval philosophy where Brentano saw the genuine theoretical interests as having been stimulated by Anselm and the introduction of Aristotle to Western civilization. The culmination of this period was the work of Thomas Aquinas. Nevertheless, he blamed the Scholastics and particularly Duns Scotus for having contributed to the period of decadence and scepticism that followed through their overly "subtle" distinctions. The final stage of medieval thought was a mystical reaction represented by Nicholas of Cusa and Raymond of Lully.

In the modern period, Brentano viewed Francis Bacon, Descartes, Leibnitz, and Locke as the originators of a new theoretical interest in philosophy. Subsequently, there was a decline in that many philosophers attempted to expound and to improve the systems of these modern greats. Brentano saw Hume, Kant, Reid, and their disciples as being caught up in the meshes of scepticism—regardless of how they resorted to common sense or a priori categories. And finally, he conceived the whole course of Hegelian metaphysics and the Romantic literary movement of *Naturphilosophie* as a mystical reaction akin to Plotinus' Neoplatonism and to Lully's mysticism. In the 1870s, Brentano turned to the study of psychology. There can be little question that, in his own mind, he conceived of himself as standing at the threshold of a new era in philosophy and as the founder of a *philosophia perennis*. He returned, in part, to Aristotelian ideas, but his work can never be considered simply as rehashed Scholasticism. His approach to science, reality, and methodology was one that in many ways combined some features of Aristotle's thought with Cartesian and Leibnitzean themes as well as elements of British empiricism and positivism.

Experience and Logic

Brentano turned to an examination of psychology because he believed that psychology played an important role in all science and knowledge. With words reminiscent of Leibnitz, he maintained that natural science was based on sensory contact with the environment and thus was of questionable truth (Brentano, 1873, I, 25–26). Experience never assures us of perfect necessity causality or universality. It determines our thoughts, but it does not furnish us our ideas. On the other hand, psychic phenomena as represented by thought remained as a sort of existential given that Brentano along with Descartes, Leibnitz, and Spinoza accepted as unquestionably real.

Psychology, in that it was the investigation of these internal psychic phenomena, was extremely important to science, because all science is based on logic, that is, conclusions are obtained via induction and deduction. And consequently, if we are to understand logic, it is necessary for us to understand the basis of logic, which is thought. Brentano recognized a basic dichotomy of sensible knowledge based on experience and noetic knowledge of the intellect as early as 1867 (Brentano, *Psychologie des Aristoteles*, 1867, 113). Although he later altered many of his ideas, at the time of the writing of the *Psychologie* he still maintained that psychic knowledge was dependent on sensory knowledge or images. Thus he held originally to Leibnitz's axiom that nothing was in the intellect that was not first in the senses—except the intellect. The analysis of Brentano's theory of knowledge will be treated later, but for this present discussion suffice it to say that Brentano believed that there were two kinds of judgments made: *vérites de fait* and *vérites de raison*. The former are of the nature of the Cartesian *cogito*, that is, we know we exist and think—but this type of judgment is a general recognition—only to be developed and clarified with time. There is no guarantee that judgments made concerning the existential existence of the ego or self have anything but a subjective value. Hence, they cannot be the basis of knowledge as Descartes asserted. *Vérites de raison*, however, are the real basis of all truth. They are immediate insightful conceptual combinations of object-images or words presented to the mind. Empirical experience is the basis of these concepts.

Brentano insisted that the *truth of judgment* on which all knowledge was based did not lie outside the human mind, but is a matter of the apodictic certainty of insightful knowledge. There are thus two elements to truth: (1) the ebb and flow of empirical experience, (2) the act of the mind whereby certain evidential judgments are apprehended as true. Bear (1954) describes this process:

> . . . Inner perception . . . unlike the outer reports involves no onto-logical leap, calling for speculation about the nature of the external world. It holds its phenomena well in hand so that the existence of the latter is certain. The elaboration of conceptual synthesis from this theater comes easier. The inner data function as ground for perceptually intuited unified concepts which for that reason are ensconced with evidence . . . Perception of acts of conscious moti-vation such as representing, loving, judging, hating, etc., are not only conspicuous here, *but also make manifest causal connections so that they really are the perceptual foundations for the causal con-cept.* The premises of an argument can induce one to draw a con-clusion or for the accomplishment of a definite end certain means may be selected. In both cases inner perception uncovers causal connections (1954, 23).

Thus it is the flow and ebb of experience itself, the congenital bias on the part of nature of informing all minds in virtue of perception with certain concepts which are capable of being organized and recognized by the human mind into causal strands that are the basis of all human knowledge.

The implications of this view are important for obtaining a clear idea of why Brentano placed a high premium on the investigation of psycho-logical phenomena. For him, the very basis of all science and philosophy was to be understood through a knowledge of psychological processes. The substantiation of the causal concept is based on empirical experience. But the recognition of this causal connection resided in the basic power of the mind itself. Here lies the foundation of Gestalt psychology. More-over, Brentano saw in perception the logical justification of the syllogism.

This whole position is similar to that of Leibnitz who had reinstated the syllogism and logic as the true method of science, but who had insisted that it be based on mathematical and geometric models. Through the act of perception, Brentano believed that he had arrived at a certitude analogous to mathematical certitude. But it was only analogous, since mathematics deals with phenomena that are simple and most independent of empirical data, that is, once the concepts and terms are recognized, they are accepted, and axioms derived from them follow logically

(Brentano, *Psychologie*, I, 39). But in the case of psychic phenomena the matter was more complicated.

Psychology and its Methodology

Because Brentano felt that psychology was the key to man's knowledge of himself and of science, his *Psychologie* is concerned with the clarification of the nature, methods, and possibilities for mankind that were inherent in a scientific study of psychology. He was convinced that to do this it was necessary to formulate correct notions about psychology and its subject matter before any real progress could be made. It was because of all the false conceptions of what psychology was or was not, thought Brentano, that there could be no agreement on a proper methodology (*Psychologie*, I, 36). Although Aristotle had defined psychology as the science of the soul, Brentano thought that this term was suspect because of theological connotations. Rather than equate the soul with the term substantial bearer of ideas, Brentano employed the concept of psychic phenomena:

> This is why we shall define psychology as the science of psychic phenomena in the sense and meaning that we have previously mentioned (*Psychologie*, I, 8).[3]

Brentano thus substituted the concept of psychic phenomena for the term soul. In this sense, psychology was defined as the science of mental experiencing. But the experiencing of psychic phenomena differs greatly from the experiencing of external physical phenomena. No man in his right mind doubts the validity and effective existence of his own psychic phenomena. A man knows and feels, loves and hates, with a basic self-knowledge that testifies to the effective reality of his own psychic phenomena. Nevertheless, psychic phenomena pose some new problems for research because they cannot be similarly quantified and observed as are physical phenomena. Brentano felt that the point of departure for psychological thought as well as the other sciences of nature was always experience. As he stated in his introduction to the *Psychologie*:

> The title of this work is indicative of the object and method. My place in psychology is at the empirical viewpoint. My only master is experience (P.E.S., I, 1).

Brentano's psychology followed naturally from his observations about natural science. He felt that the basic method must be experience, and in psychology this experience is based on perception rather than on

---

[3] Hereafter *Psychologie vom empirischen Standpunkt* will be abbreviated as P.E.S.

sensation. Although the raw elements of the psychic act were derived in part from sensory experience, to say to Brentano that sensation was the basis of experience was like saying to the anthropologist that in the beginning was the grammar rather than the speech. It is true that Brentano changed the meaning of empirical experience away from the connotation that Locke had placed on it. Brentano argued that all science and scientific experimentation is ultimately based on the assumption of the validity of our own internal processes (Gilson, *Méthode*, 1955, 22). If man cannot rely on the validity of his own internal senses, his mental perceptions and observations, as well as the faculty of memory, then he is immediately enmeshed in the most profound scepticism. Nevertheless, experience in psychology poses new problems, since it cannot be equated with the observation and experience of physical science. The principal source of our knowledge is the internal perception of our own psychic phenomena. That this basis is lacking in the objective nature of physical certitude is plainly evident. By comparison with mathematics, psychology is plainly at a disadvantage:

> These two sciences are at opposite poles. Mathematics considers phenomena which are simple and most independent, psychology those which are most dependent and most complex. Therefore, mathematics manifests with a certain basic clarity principles which are the foundation of all true scientific research (P.E.S., I, 39).

Nevertheless, psychology reveals itself personally in a richness and complexity that is difficult to translate into the scientific mind-set. Inner perception, therefore, must be the source of psychological experience. But in positing perception as a source of psychological experience, Brentano insisted that a fundamental distinction be made. When he said that perception is the fundamental source of psychic interpretation, *he referred specifically to perception as differing from internal observation.* We can apply external observation to physical happenings, employing our full attention in order to apprehend these phenomena as exactly as possible. This is not true with regard to internal observation. All internal observation reveals to a man is that he is perceiving a phenomenon, but when he gives his attention via internal observation to the object of his perception, he can never be sure of his results. Brentano cited the example of an individual attempting to observe or to analyze his own internal anger. When he manages to give his attention to his own anger, he is no longer really angry.

However, Brentano believed that it was possible to construct legitimate principles about psychic phenomena by a careful observation of the manifestations of psychic phenomena in others, particularly as these phenomena externalize themselves. Even when they do not reveal themselves in words, the psychic phenomena of others can be observed in their actions and conscious modes of doing things. The inferences, which these manifestations offer for diagnosing the inner conditions from which they derive, are often a more sure means of indicating their bases than are the subsequent verbal justifications. Other than those conscious activities, there are also unconscious physical changes that accompany certain psychic conditions or follow upon them. For example, sudden fear makes one pale, embarrassment makes one blush.

To learn more about psychic conditions, Brentano advocated the study of earlier stages of psychic development through either the less developed psychic life of children or of people for whom certain classes of phenomena are completely denied, for example, the blind or aborigines. Brentano thought that experimentation with animals would yield great results (P.E.S., I. 57). Brentano also thought that a potential source of information, particularly about mental states, was revealed through the laws of the association of ideas.[4]

Brentano felt that through patient observation and through experimentation with animals and primitives it would be possible to accumulate a body of factual data concerning the nature and variety of psychic phenomena. But rather than to be too concerned with the raw material of mental life, that is, sensations, *he felt that the true research material of psychology was in the analysis of higher mental processes.* Thus he would rather have the researcher admit forthwith *that the laws of psychic activity have a certain inexactitude and vague character.*

When the body of experimentally derived evidence had been assimilated, then psychology could use in its empirical domain some of the methods of logicians, for example, deduction and induction, providing that both could be confirmed experimentally (Brentano P.E.S., I, 104–105).

Thus the methodology of Brentano as applied to psychological investigations is perfectly consistent with the method he advocated for philosophy. Experience was of prime consideration; but, since psychic phenomena could not be verified either by mathematical procedures or laboratory techniques, indirect methods of observation were necessary.

---

[4] Brentano also dealt with strange phenomena such as vivid dreams, somnambulism, and bizarre occurrences in fever and insanity. He spoke of the influence of foreign or alien experiences on dreams, the peculiar association of sensations in dreams and the exploration of prophetic dreams as instances of recurring memory phenomena. Again, he suggested that individual differences might predispose some individuals toward certain kinds of associations because of temperament or character differences. These would be seen in differentials of judgment and will.

When the results of these findings were subjected to the scrutiny of logical analysis, psychologists could arrive at general laws of psychic behavior. To be sure, Brentano recognized the weakness of these methods. He acknowledged the inexactitude of laws formulated in this manner, but he pointed out that the laws of Kepler were valid even before Newton gave the logical explanation and verification for them.

In setting forth his own methodology, Brentano opposed the abuses of the physiological method. Henry Maudsley, the English physician, had attacked John Stuart Mill for his use of introspection. Maudsley had asserted that any psychology that was not based on physiology was doomed a priori to failure. Brentano expounded Maudsley's views and then pointed out that after this attack on other methods of psychological procedure, Maudsley admitted that physiology could not explain processes of the mind either. The laws of the succession of psychic phenomena are no final laws, said Brentano. They are only theoretical constructs that await a physiological explanation.

Finally, Brentano believed that, since altered physical conditions apparently result in individual psychic differences, *it would be well that a special psychology—perhaps, a psychology of men and women, not to mention an individual psychology—be postulated* (P.E.S., I, 91). Just as there are universal descriptions of zoology and botany in which no individual is completely similar to another, so likewise there ought to be universal and approximate laws of psychic phenomena that could be applied to individuals through a psychology based on individual needs.

The Nature of Psychic Phenomena and Their Characteristics

By the term phenomenon, Brentano usually meant a state or event in consciousness. Physical phenomena, presumably (since their perception is contingent on our awareness of them through consciousness), are based on real existences that are characterized by spatial and temporal extension. They are ordered to each other by means of extramental relations that are grounded in the inherent nature of external reality. Through the psychic act of consciousness, man becomes aware of these physical phenomena—or, at least, of their appearances as signified by sensory perception. Thus it is through psychic phenomena that one understands physical phenomena, since even the felt intensities of sensory processes are only "functions of extensive changes in the primary spatio-qualitative continuum" (Bear, 18).

The proper study of psychology is then the study of psychic phenomena. What are some of the characteristics of psychic phenomena? Brentano thought that this question could best be answered by showing how psychic phenomena differ from physical ones. *First, psychic phe-*

nomena do not have extension. They thus differ from physical phenomena, which are characterized by being localized in space (Brentano, P.E.S., I, 121). Second, *psychic phenomena are always based on representations.* Representations for Brentano were the dynamic first acts of the mind. By themselves, they are simply grammatical terms, nominalistic concepts that indicate the psychically constructed object of perception. In the continuum of psychic consciousness, they form the foundation of all activity. Originally they are formed by the action of the mind on the raw material of sensory experience:

> We need hardly remark again, that by representation we mean not that which is represented, but the act of representing. This act of representing forms the basis not only of judgment, but also of desire as well as all other psychic acts. Nothing can ever be judged, nothing can be desired, nothing can be hoped or feared, unless it has first been represented (P.E.S., I, 112).

Hence, at the basis of all psychic activity, of all psychic phenomena, lies the *Vorstellung* or representation. However, in Brentano's psychology the representation was not a passive image concept caused by the quantitative intensity of sensory experiencing but, instead, was caused by the active process of perception itself. The sensory process provided the stimulation—perhaps, what might be termed the content—but it is the mind itself that invests this elementary sensory stimulation with the quality of meaning. Titchener clarified this concept thus:

> . . . the object to which a mental phenomenon refers is not an object in the outside world, a physical object in our sense, though Brentano would make it a physical phenomenon, but rather what we should term mental content. Brentano splits up idea, judgment, interest, into act and content; the act is psychical, the content physical (Titchener, 1909, 44).

What exists before the representation is merely the quantitative index of sensory stimulation. Once it is received in the act of conscious perception, this stimulation is invested with the psychic quality that constitutes representation by reason and in virtue of the psyche's perception of an object-relationship.

The third characteristic of all psychic phenomena is *their relationship to an object* (Brentano, P.E.S., II, 255). Brentano based his whole classificatory system of psychic phenomena on their essential reference to an object. All psychic activity is characterized by a relational mode to *the object of perception.* Brentano believed that there were only three relational modes to the object and, hence, only three classes of psychic phenomena. They were representation (*Vorstellung*), judgment (*Urteil*), and affective states (*Gemütsbewegung*).

But of paramount importance to the correct understanding of object-relations as developed by Brentano is his concept of consciousness. He maintained that psychic phenomena could be perceived only *through the medium of inner consciousness.* The act of experiencing has a distinct character of its own; it presents immediate evidence, unquestionable and unimpeachable, of the reality of psychic phenomena. In the psychic continuum of consciousness there is a continual flow of primary object-relations based on representations. But, concurrently, there is also a secondary awareness of the self perceiving. Thus a man is not only conscious of the smell of fried chicken but he is also aware that he is conscious and doing the smelling. All perception is related directly or indirectly to the very concept of self, and self-awareness or cognizance is a product of consciousness. This is not to state that Brentano limited the extent of mental life to consciousness. He did not subscribe to the Cartesian *Cogito*, for he recognized that psychic and mental were not equivalent terms. He recognized that the vast majority of our conscious experiencing is at any given time stored away in the memory. What he did insist on was that consciousness, and particularly the secondary consciousness relating all perceived objects to the ego, was an indispensable condition of the psychic act. This means that the very quality of our perception, the very nature of the construction of psychic representation, and the manner in which all sensory experiencing will be interpreted and vested with meaning *is determined by that secondary consciousness.*

The explanations of the nature of consciousness and the psychic act are all integral parts of Brentano's concept of *intentionality.* Intentional existence is still another distinguishing feature of psychic phenomena:

> That which characterizes all psychic phenomena is that which the scholastics of the Middle Ages have called the intentional (as well as mental) presence. . . This intentional presence seems exclusively to relate to psychic phenomena . . . We can then define psychic phenomena by saying that they are phenomena which intentionally contain an object in themselves (P.E.S., I, 124–125).

Brentano's view on intentional existence is not the same as the Scholastic view whereby sensory species were transformed into universal concepts. He did not view the intentional image as the exclusive means whereby knowledge was transformed into universal ideas. His particular purpose in defining the intentional existence was, in part, an attempt to avoid the confusion resulting from Descartes' teaching, in which the sensory content tended to be confused with the immanent act of understanding in the mind. Brentano wished to differentiate between the mental or intentional existence of an object in the mind, and that effective existence independent of psychic phenomena. He thus made a distinction between *effective* and *intentional*. An effective existence was a real existence in extraorganic reality. This physical phenomenon could exist in the mind only as an intentional object. Nevertheless, although the effective existence of extraorganic reality could exist in the mind only intentionally, this very intentional existence was *for the mind* an effective existence. And because the intentional existence was an effective existence—the only truly effective one for the mind—all psychic activity was directed toward intentional images. *And these intentional creations were the mind's version of reality.*

It is best to understand this teaching in relation to sensation. Brentano distinguished only three classes of sensible phenomena characterized by the formation of primary objects; (1) the color phenomenon, (2) the sound phenomenon, and (3) the trace-sense. Every sensory phenomenon participates in local spatial determination. But for every sensation there is present a corresponding psychic continuum. Whereas sensory phenomena are characterized by multiplicity, the psychic equivalent is always a unity (thus constituted by the mind itself). And sensory representations are thus reduced to a unity through reference to the secondary characteristic of consciousness (Ego).

At the time that Brentano wrote his *Psychologie* he was convinced that primary and secondary consciousness were identical in content at any given moment of waking life. He maintained that all psychic activity embodied an emotional tonality and that the creation of the intentional existence was directly connected with the emotional affects of ego or self-involvement. In other words, the sensory stimulation has no meaning until a psychic equivalent—the intentional existence—is created by the mind through an essential relationship to self. It was, then, this self-involvement or reflection, based on emotional tonality and vested in secondary consciousness, that determined the meaning and constitution of psychic life.[5]

---

[5] One of the difficulties in tracing Brentano's thought and influence is the fact that he changed his mind on certain matters. In later years he did change his mind on emotional involvement in the psychic act, but in his *Psychologie* this is the correct approach as he wrote it in 1873.

. . . . It is generally admitted that all psychic activity embodies what has been called an emotional tonality; that is to say that all psychic activity which contains a representation of self and an evident assertion concerning self would be equally the object of an internal affective relation. I myself rallied to this point of view in my Psychology from the Empirical Viewpoint. Since then, however, I have changed my mind and

Still another set of circumstances, Brentano believed, distinguished psychic phenomena from physical ones. Psychic phenomena manifest themselves *successively*, whereas physical phenomena are simultaneous (P.E.S., II, 176–180). There is always a unity of perception in the psychic act. This does not mean that there can be only one object present in consciousness at a time *but, instead, that the simultaneous representations are invested with a unity or Gestalt of meaning.* By unity, then, Brentano did not mean simplicity. Representations may be multiple, but a basic unity of consciousness is manifested in the psychic act. It is the total situation that is comprehended and vested with meaning. For instance, one may be dining in a fine restaurant, enjoying a good steak, sipping a choice wine, and conversing with friends. Although there are a variety of sensory inputs with consequent representations, there is still only one psychic act at a time, and the meaning is not only in terms of the separate representational elements but in reference to the total situation.

The Unconscious

Brentano spent a considerable amount of space discussing the concept of the unconscious in his *Psychologie*. He reviewed the opinions of Leibnitz, Aquinas, Herbart, Fechner, Wundt, and Hartmann as favoring the admission of an unconscious principle of behavior determination. But then he pointed out that Lotze, Alexander Bain, Herbert Spencer, and John Stuart Mill did not appear to be in favor of it. He stated his own objection to the concept on the basis of scientific grounds. He did not think that psychologists should resort to the hypothesis of the unconscious unless certain conditions could be met: (1) that the fact demonstrated in experience could be explained in no other manner, (2) that this fact could not have proceeded from a concomitant but unaware consciousness, (3) that the line of argumentation utilized did not contradict known laws of conscious psychic phenomena (Brentano, P.E.S., II, 143–148).

Brentano did not deny the fact that all psychic life depends on the organic energy of the body. In fact, he felt that there was no doubt at all that material conditions formed the substratum of all psychic life and activity. But he was primarily interested in a description of psychic processes and believed that, at that time (1873), the unconscious hypoth-

---

I now believe that many sensations do not present any affective relationship and do not intrinsically contain either pleasure or displeasure (P.E.S., III, p. 139).

For individuals acquainted with the later Brentano, his views then do not appear particularly congruent with Freudian ideas or even some of those of James or the phenomenologists, but the earlier Brentano differs from the later one.

esis was not in the best interests of scientific psychology. Because of Brentano's very description of psychic phenomena as possessing an object-relationship in consciousness, such a thing as an unconscious psychic process seemed to be a contradiction of terms. As has been indicated previously, Brentano did not state that psychic and mental were the same thing. Hence, likewise, he admitted the distinct possibility of such a thing as the psychic determination of intentional objects proceeding from the organic base of the brain (P.E.S., I, 133). Kraus, commenting on Brentano's acknowledgement that there might well be such a thing as unconscious determination of psychic life, stated that Brentano's ideas are thus in no way opposed to Freud's unconscious (P.E.S., footnote 2, 272).

Hence, it is important to realize that Brentano opposed the hypothesis of the unconscious not because he was absolutely convinced that there was no such thing, but because at the time of his writing, the evidence presented in favor of the unconscious did not meet the rigorous standards of scientific procedure. The unconscious was far from being a novel and unique concept. There were many hypotheses about the unconscious in the philosophical and psychological literature of the day as well as that of past eras. There was more than a hint of the unconscious in Thomas Aquinas' treatment of the instincts, acquired tendencies, *habitus* (states of capability), and inner perfections (Maritain, in Nelson, 1957, 232). Leibnitz formulated a theory of apperception that established a continuum extending from unconscious perceptions to direct conscious reflection with a graded clearness and degree of psychic involvement. It was this conception of the threshold of consciousness that seemed to influence the discussions of Herbart, Fechner, James, and others (Levine, 1923, pp. 14–15). There was also the metaphysical principle of universal will enunciated by Schopenhauer, and Hartmann's assertion that even the simplest phases of mental activity require the concept of the unconscious.

The Evolution of Psychic Phenomena

Brentano had originally planned to extend his *Psychologie* considerably beyond the length at which he left it. He made numerous notes that he used in his teaching. In a teaching manuscript of 1873, references are made to Brentano's conception of the evolution of psychic life.[6] Brentano

---

[6] During the preparation of my doctoral dissertation on Freud and Brentano I made the acquaintance of Dr. John Brentano, the only son of Franz Brentano. Dr. Brentano lived in Highland Park, Illinois and was a retired professor of physics at Northwestern University. Believing that Dr. Brentano might have some unpublished material relating to the influence of ideas between Brentano and Freud, I was astonished to learn that Dr. Brentano had 13 trunks full of unpublished material. In a number of

wondered why it was that all just noticeable differences according to the Weber-Fechner law did not have equal psychic effect on individuals. In fact, in the *Psychologie* he took Wundt to task for insisting that all these just noticeable differences had equal effects (P.E.S., I, 10–12). Brentano discussed Mill's hypothesis that there might be associations or relationships based on peculiar psychochemical forces. This might be a solution, thought Brentano, but he suggested that the reason might be in the nexus of the chain of association of ideas, a nexus that was probably due to the physical stimulus of a given idea remaining below the threshold of consciousness (Brentano, "Plan für das Psychologiekolleg." See appendices manuscript page 54008, No. 15 and following for the original remarks).

Agreeing with Mill, Brentano, asserted in language reminiscent of Hume, that certain processes in the mind are analogous to physical forces and that others are analogous to a possible mental chemistry. Particularly is this true with belief and desire. *They are the possible products of this mental chemistry and the fusion of representations from physical extraorganic forces.* It is the task of the psychologist to uncover the bases of the processes of belief and desire whether chemical or not. To do this, it is necessary to ascertain, first, what are our immediate beliefs and, afterward, the laws whereby the beliefs of one influence another. Regarding desire, it is imperative that man seek to find out what are the primitive and natural objects of our desires, to determine the causes which force us to desire some things that are primitive, indifferent, or even disagreeable (P.E.S., I, 17–21).

In the *Psychologie* Brentano does not answer the question of what forces man to desire some things that are basically disagreeable to him. But in his manuscript outline, in discussing the question of how we assume an exterior world and past temporal states, he sheds light on the evolution of psychic processes as he conceived it. He stated that instinctive inclinations in comparison with judgment are stronger. Instinctive inclinations: (1) are not based on inferences or deductions, but (2) on the original inclination of the organism to assent to each mental image. How does this occur? Brentano answered:

1. We are born with instinctual propensities that assume the validity of our own psychic acts.
2. Later we distinguish other psychic beings.

visits and through the cooperation of Dr. John Brentano, I reviewed numerous unpublished manuscripts and teaching materials. These documents now repose in microfilm at the University of Minnesota and Harvard University, plus, perhaps, some other institutions.

3. Finally, we distinguish bodily beings in accord with our sensory images (Brentano, op. cit, p. 54010).

To quote Brentano directly:

> The correct view is that originally we instinctively agree to all mental images; and that eventually our trust becomes more limited in sphere, but develops from an instinct one to an insightful one. Something similar happens in the realm of memory (Ibid).

Thus Brentano's teaching on the developmental process of knowing reality was that instinctual propensities first identified with psychic imagery. The early organism naturally assumes the validity of its own acts. Subsequently, through experience and development, the primitive reliance on instinctual images is altered through the process of distinguishing other psychic beings and of indentifying them in accord with our sensory memories.

The reason judgment is not as strong as these instinctual propensities, and the reason for so many of man's judgments being based on instinctual and prejudicial assertions is that judgment develops only gradually. It is for this reason that Brentano insisted that judgments pose another relationship to the object-image in the mind—changing it would seem—the modal structure. In conscious more mature life as soon as the representation is present in consciousness, almost instantaneously, the ego either affirms or denies the representation in comparison with the memory traces of reality. Judgment is a necessary prerequisite to facilitate action.

Phenomena of Love-Hate

In the developmental plan of psychic life, phenomena of love-hate (*Gemütsbewegungen*–also classified as emotional states) play an important role in determining behavior. Affective states posed a third relationship to the original representation. Brentano identified with affective movements the faculty of will, since he could see no further relationship to representation that demarcated will from affective movements in general (p. 54011 Nos. 1 and 2). Affective states, just as representation and judgment, must always relate to the intentional object. Man is always glad about *something*, angry about *something*, and the intentional object partakes in the feeling tones toward the external object. Hence, the intentional image or representation of a loved object would incorporate elements of the extraorganic object.

Affective movements of the psyche range over a whole continuum, from mild interest to extreme desire, and from mild distaste to utter hatred. There is, moreover, a great complexity in the sequential order of affective movements. Whereas Brentano was comparatively certain that judgment followed representation, he was not sure that affective movements could be so construed.

What is the relationship of love-hate phenomena to the will? Brentano defined the will only as the prime subject of the moral and immoral (Brentano, *Origin of Knowledge of Right and Wrong*, 1902, 3). The matter of whether an act was to be considered moral or immoral was determined by the nature of representation and judgment. He further wrote in his manuscript that the will develops in reference to its own psychic phenomena. It is the essential regulator of all thought and feeling and operates primarily with regard to the movements of the body and of external objects (*Plan fuer das Psychologiekolleg*, p. 54011, No. 10). The end result of this discussion of the phenomena of love-hate and their relationship to the act of will would seem to be that phenomena of love-hate are the motivating agents behind will activities, and that these will activities are originally motivated with a desire for pleasure and for incorporation of the image in the mind which is first identified with reality and later differentiated through the force of this same reality.

Psychic Determinism and Ethics

Brentano's conception of the causal sequence of psychic acts has real implications for ethics and the philosophy of values. He began as a believer in indeterminism. The Roman Catholic Church has always maintained the freedom of the will in making choices that involve man's ultimate destiny and his cooperation with the Grace of God. Brentano began his career at Wurzburg holding the indeterminist view, but by virtue of his psychological studies he was gradually led to the position of determinism in psychic life. His conception of the intending process of the act of perception reveals, implicitly, psychic determinism. Brentano strongly suggested that affective movements influence the very act of perception.

Although Brentano held that there were some insightful judgments that were independent of psychic determination, he did not identify these judgments with any natural law or *Jus Gentium*. Rather did he seem to indicate that the very act of perception of the ordered structure of reality tended to impinge in a somewhat universal manner on man's psychic apparatus, thereby giving rise to the concept of causality. There was, as Bear observed (1954), "a congenital bias on the part of nature to insure the realization of those desire objects conducive to their (man's) survival" (104). An implicit corollary of this teaching would then be that the very perceptual process contained within itself the seeds of a certain *Gestalt* of insightful reason, so that all men of integrity and self-reflection would apprehend or could apprehend the basic principles of reality.

The fundamental question in ethics for Brentano is not whether an act is good or evil in comparison with an outside standard or criterion, as in the adequation theory of the Scholastics, but whether an act is right or wrong, that is, in conformity with insightful reason or not:

> In what then lies this special superiority which gives to morality its natural sanction? . . . The real logical superiority is no mere aesthetic appearance but a certain inward rightness which then carries with it a certain superiority of one particular act of will over another of an opposite character; in which consists the superiority of the moral over the immoral. The belief in this superiority is an ethical motive, the sanction which gives to ethical law permanence and validity (Brentano, 1902, 10).

Brentano's ethical theory then places a priority on the discernment of right and wrong over good and evil. This follows logically from his declaration that judgment was consequent to representation. For all practical purposes, Brentano is stating that even though there may be affective object-relations that would tend to obscure and color the nature of judgment, nevertheless, in the final resolution of complex ends, and means to these ends, action is predicated on a judgment of rightness or wrongness which is derived from the causal strands of perception. Thus man may really be seeking a pleasure good, but he defers a course of action toward that goal until a judgment has been made concerning the rightness or wrongness of the particular act.

Brentano realized that, practically speaking, few men ever rose above the level of blind and prejudicial judgments, but for men of thoughtfulness and self-reflection, insightful judgment must be the sole criterion for choosing appropriate moral ends and the means to these ends.

The moral act is then that act which is perceived with right reason and is known as an insightful judgment. Immoral conduct would be the product of a vitiated judgment condoned by the will. By his failure to distinguish affective movements from the will, and by his identification of the acts of judgment, that is moral responsibility with the will, it would seem that *Brentano considered the will as the coherent, conscious representative of self*. It is for this reason, namely the relativity of Brentano's ultimate court of ethical appeal, that some individuals have thought that he opened the door to a complete ethical relativism. The act of perception, however, not only determines our response to the outer world of reality through the intending process of psychic involvement but it is the ultimate source of morality as well. Little wonder then that Brentano placed so much emphasis on the analysis of psychic phenomena.

Summary and Recapitulation of Brentano's Thought

To focus the material discussed in the preceding pages, we present the following outline.

I. Methodology

1. Brentano's teaching was that philosophy and science are identical in their method. By his doctrine of the four phases, he illustrated the degeneration of philosophical thinking through the inordinate use of logic.

2. He proposed the fundamental methodological axiom that all knowledge was based on experience, but that experience whether in the mathematical sciences or psychology required an analysis of the psychological conditions of knowledge.

3. All experience is known through psychic phenomena, and they provide an apodictic immediate evidence that is effectively real in the mind.

4. Nevertheless, the immediate reality of psychic phenomena may be classified into two categories: (1) *vérites de fait*, which are phenomena similar to the Cartesian *cogito*, that is the continuing sequence of psychic experiencing, and (2) *vérites de raison*, which are those insightful judgments obtained and derived from the very act of perception.

II. Psychology

1. An investigation of psychic phenomena is paramount to all knowledge because all knowledge depends on perception.

2. Perception involves (1) the perceiving apparatus or structure, and (2) the force of extraorganic reality as an impinging agent.

3. The perceiving apparatus is the soul, by which is meant the substantial substratum of representations and all other psychic activities. This substratum adheres to and is dependent on the organic energy system of the body while it is extensive with the body.

4. Neither sensation nor internal perception reveals to us anything about the nature of this substratum. All that perception reveals to us is a consistency of structure both within and without us whereby the same laws operating in extraorganic reality work psychically in us, that is, causal connections and forces in nature have their psychological counterparts.

5. Thus in psychic phenomena and in the analysis thereof are the causal strands that are the foundation of science, as well as the basis of logic and thought.

6. Nevertheless, the experiencing of psychic phenomena cannot be equated with external observation.

7. The chief tool for the investigation of psychic phenomena is external observation of others: (1) of extreme emotional states, (2) of primitive stages of development, (3) of the psychic life of the mentally disturbed, (4) of the association of ideas, dream phenomena, hallucinations, and other instances of bizarre phenomena.

8. Although psychology is the science of psychic phenomena, nonetheless, psychic phenomena observed in this manner and categorized by logical deduction and induction provide laws of only a vague character.

III. The Nature and Characteristics of Psychic Phenomena

1. Psychology is concerned with psychic phenomena; these phenomena lack extension.

2. Psychic phenomena are always based on representations.
   (a) Representations are merely the psychically constructed objects of perception.
   (b) They are comprised of content from the stimulus of external reality and the form or meaning is given by the dynamic act of the mind.
   (c) They are not passive responses but active agents.
   (d) They may be in the form of either an image or mental word, either individual or abstract.

3. Psychic phenomena are always characterized by a relationship to an object. By object is meant the intentional existence or image created in the mind. This object is a mode of perception.

4. There are three primary relational modes of perception, (1) representation, (2) judgment, and (3) affective states.

5. All psychic phenomena are characterized by an intentional existence that is either an image or a mental word.
   (a) The intentional existence is the focal object of all psychic phenomena.
   (b) The intentional existence is always affectively toned and conditioned.
   (c) There is an intentional order or motivational process whereby present objects may be considered the working out of distant goals.

6. All psychic phenomena possess an intrinsic unity of meaning, follow each other successively, and derive their ultimate energy source from the organism.

7. All psychic processes are conscious, inasmuch as secondary consciousness is an essential part of the psychic act. Nevertheless, there are unconscious determinations that remain below the threshold of consciousness.

IV. Psychic Development

1. The task of the psychologist is to explain the mutual relationships of just noticeable differences in the psychophysical continuum. Primitive desires should be explained, and the association of ideas provide some insight here.

2. Instinct is the original inclination of the organism to assent to a mental image.

3. Original instinctual propensities are modified through contact with reality.

4. Judgment is another mode of relationship to an object.
   (a) The determination of action depends on judgment.
   (b) Judgment affirms or denies the reality of representations in accordance with the memory traces of reality.
   (c) Most of man's judgments are instinctive, that is, swayed by primitive object images and emotional involvements.
   (d) Negative judgments include more possibilities than affirmative ones.
   (e) Instinctual judgments acquire the force of mathematical axioms through habit.

5. Affective movements (phenomena of love-hate) add another modal relationship, the object of perception.
   (a) Love-hate relations are always related to something concrete.
   (b) A wide continuum of feeling tones are present in love-hate relations.
   (c) The operation of affective movements may be nothing more than the purely mechanical way of working out teleological goals.

6. The will is the object of the moral and immoral.
   (a) It is undifferentiated from the affective movements.
   (b) It develops in reference to its own psychic phenomena.
   (c) It operates primarily in regard to the movement of the body and external objects.

      (d) Love-hate phenomena are the motivating agents behind will acts.

7. The psychic act is determined by the process of perception and internal psychic movements.

V. Ethical Theories

1. There is no *Jus Gentium* or natural law as such but, instead, we can say that the external world impinges uniformly on the psychic structure of man, effecting the strands of a concatenated universal causality.

2. Action is always predicated on a judgment of rightness. A judgment of rightness is an affirmation prior to activity.

3. Action should be deferred until a judgment of rightness has been made.

4. A thing is true when the recognition and judgment relating to it are right, and it is good when the love relating to it is right.

5. Pleasure when not corrupt, whether spiritual or material, stands on an equal value footing.

6. The highest practical good embraces everything that is subject to our rational and insightful operation.

7. Although psychic activity is determined, this does not deny the concept of responsibility.

Philosophical Implications

The intentional metaphysics developed from Aquinas through Descartes, Spinoza, Leibnitz, and Brentano forms a philosophical basis for later phenomenological, psychoanalytic, and Gestaltist thought. The application of this philosophical rationale to the problems of human behavior and behavior change can be traced in the development of both psychoanalytic and phenomenological approaches to counseling. The specific connections between this philosophical approach to the problems of knowledge, the object of knowledge, and the subject of knowledge are of concern here. The manner in which many of these ideas have found translation into actual procedures is the subject of a later chapter. The following discussion summarizes the philosophical implications of this approach.

The Problem of Knowledge

In the intentional position the knowledge of reality is essentially a psychological problem. In a real sense, science and logic are dependent on psychological factors of perception. This means that the only really sure kind of knowledge, from an epistemological point of view, is the fact that human beings experience a stream of thought in which they themselves are the self-conscious center of experience. A knowledge of psychology is then viewed as a central key to education, social science, and understanding—both on a personal and international scale. Psychological phenomena are also related to the analysis of language. The role of sensory information-receiving is considered essentially secondary in terms of the process of concept formation. Knowledge of the external universe, as well as of man's internal processes, depends not only on the quantitative flow of experience being registered within man but on the quality of meaning that is attributed to this experience. Furthermore, man has the power, in this position, to analyze and to intuit knowledge that is locked within the very structure of the human mind. This apprehension of ideas or of truth by the human mind is known as intuition. The ability to lay hold of these ideas is essentially tied up with the uniformity of perceptual structure that exists in all men. In virtue of this uniform biological and psychological structure communication takes place. It is also because of this uniformity of structure that man's thought process becomes the basis of logic.

The Object of Knowledge

Although no single philosopher in this school of thought ever denied the validity of the external world of reality, it is apparent that the general teaching of this school maintains that every cognition of man refers to a real and existing thing, and that this object is simultaneously related to both external reality and internal reality. Descartes, Leibnitz, Spinoza, and Brentano all held that empirical experience played a major role in the formation of cognition, but they denied the position of Locke. They also believed that all psychic activity was meaningful, intentional in the sense of self-involvement, and is cognitively known through the medium of consciousness. Again, they all held that the focal point of psychic activity was the intentional image. The intentional image was the production of perception impressed and guided by self-involvement.

The Subject of Knowledge

The intentional point of view maintained that the basic structure of human existence was subjectivity or intentionality and that the perceptory act of the mind is characterized by an immanent power of self-reflection. In this sense, the cognitive structure of man was considered to be permeated or ensconced with emotional tonality. The self-concept is identified as a product of consciousness which ideally possesses a capability for unity of action and control. The power of immanent reflection (conscience), the analysis of subjective experience in terms of social criteria of behavior, and the application of insightful reason make it possible to attain what can be called later on, personal adjustment.

Finally, the proponents of this approach to man and his reality recognized that man is the normative measure of reality; and that man's judgment as informed by insightful reason is the ultimate criterion of ethical conduct. Although psychic determinism is strongly accented throughout the development of the intentionalistic framework, it is apparent that the determinism spoken of is a relative one rather than an absolute one. It is recognized, for example, that man's behavior is dependent on his perception, and that he may make what appear to him to be free decisions, but the unconscious factors relating to this decision-making process may not be known and, thus, may be determinants to the decision. Nevertheless, there is also a strong reliance on the need to regard decision making as a moral and responsible process.

The intentionalistic point of view is marked by an epistemology in which subjective experience ranks high on the hierarchy of knowledge. It conceives of reality in terms of both outer and inner dimensions. Although it recognizes the validity of sensory knowledge and scientific investigation, it insists that psychic phenomena must be comprehended in order to establish the world of science. In terms of values, there is an almost aristocratic cherishing of principles of reason, insight, self-understanding, and moral responsibility. This philosophical framework can be traced into (1) psychoanalytic thought, (2) later phenomenological thought, and (3) Gestalt psychology.

CHAPTER VI

Sigmund Freud, Psychoanalytic Theory and Clinical Developments

Sigmund Freud has had a tremendous impact on the course of psychology and psychotherapy. Although much of his thought has been translated into the specific areas of psychotherapy, he has also influenced the worlds of philosophy, history, and literature. No individual who, in any sense, practices psychology can be ignorant of the impact of Freud on this field. Gardner Murphy (1957) evaluated the impact of Freud on various fields of American psychology and suggested this scale:

Freud's Impact on the Divisions of Modern Psychology.

Physiological psychology	0
Intelligence	0
Learning	1
Thinking	1
Perception	1
Comparative psychology	1
Vocational psychology	1
Drive, feeling, and emotion	2
Child and adolescent psychology	2
Social psychology	3
Industrial psychology	3
Imagination	4
Abnormal psychology	5
Clinical psychology	6
Personality	6

He set up this index: 0 = none, 1 = slight, 2 = limited, 3 = moderate, 4 = considerable, 5 = great, 6 = very great. Whether or not one agrees with this rating, it is indicative of how one renowned individual has evaluated the worth of Freud's ideas in terms of his influence.

SIGMUND FREUD: PERSONALITY AND INFLUENCES

Freud's life spanned 83 years. He was born on May 6, 1856 in the small town of Freiberg in Moravia and he died on September 23, 1939 in London. Born into a Jewish family, he was strongly conditioned by membership in this minority group. He was Jewish to the core, extremely sensitive to the slightest hint of anti-Semitism, and made few real friends among people who were not Jewish (Jones, 1953, I, 12). His Jewish background played an important role in his determination of a profession since, according to Jones, Jews were restricted in the choice of a profession to either business, law, or medicine (Jones, I, 27). Although Freud chose medicine, it was merely the most appetizing of the choices afforded him. As he wrote:

> After forty-one years of medical activity, my self-knowledge tells me that I have never really been a doctor in the proper sense. I became a doctor through being compelled to deviate from my original purpose and the triumph of my life lies in my having, after a long and roundabout journey, found my way back to my earliest path (Jones, I, 28).

The original purpose of Freud's writing obviously refers to his interest in the psychology of human behavior. His education documents it. He had a real passion for collecting books, was an excellent student who was at the head of his class in the Gymnasium six out of eight years, and showed a great gift for languages. Not only did he become a master of German prose—for which he won a Goethe award—but he had a complete mastery of Latin and Greek, was thoroughly at home in English and French, had been taught Hebrew, and taught himself Italian and Spanish. He was particularly interested in English and, according to Jones, read almost nothing but English books for a period of ten years (Jones, I, 16). When he entered the University of Vienna in 1873, every indication points to his basic indecision as to the final choice of a profession. It took him three years longer to complete his medical studies than the ordinary student. The reason for this seems to have been that Freud had a wide range of interests and could not decide into what field he should go. He took courses in anatomy, biology, mineralogy, microscopy, zoology, and philosophy.

Philip Merlan discovered (1945, 1949) that during these years, Freud took a total of five courses from Franz Brentano. These courses were taken by Freud in his third, fourth, fifth, and sixth semesters at Vienna (winter 1874 to 1875, summer 1875, winter 1875 to 1876, and summer 1876). Most of them were entitled: "Readings of Philosophical Writings," but he also took logic in his fourth semester and "The Philosophy of Aristotle" in the summer of 1876. Although Jones tends to make light of this exposure to philosophy, it is a fact that philosophy courses were not required at that time, and it may reasonably be assumed that any student who voluntarily takes many courses from the same professor, while ostensibly pursuing another curriculum, must have more than a passing interest in the professor, the curriculum, or both.

Later on, in 1880, Brentano recommended Freud to Theodore Gomperz, who was looking for a translator for the works of John Stuart Mill. This was four years after Freud had taken his last seminar with Brentano, and in view of the large number of students Brentano had had in the intervening years, it is reasonable to assume that he had a close knowledge of Freud. In point of fact, Dr. John Brentano, the only son of Franz Brentano, confirmed the interest that his father had in Freud's work and the mutual friendship that existed between Breuer and Brentano.[1]

Jones gives us a revealing picture of Freud as a young man closely relating to his professors. There is evidence that he was extremely dependent on Bruecke, the medical advisor, on Breuer, his first collaborator, and on Charcot, with whom he studied in Paris. The details of these close friendships are recorded in Jones' biography of Freud. It is sufficient here to point out that Freud was recognized as a bright student who tended to form strong relationships with his teachers. But just as he identified with these individuals, he also rejected them. He later referred to Bruecke's laboratory in deprecating terms, strongly resented Breuer, and publicly dissented from some of Charcot's opinions. Nor was it only with his teachers that Freud perpetuated this ambivalent friendship pattern. Later, he had similar difficulties with Jung, Fliess, Adler, and Stekel.

Freud's life was filled with writing, research, study, and psychoanalytic analyses. He was perhaps less well known in Vienna than in the rest of the world. As an old man, he was exiled from his native land to die in England. This occurred when the Nazis invaded Austria. His contribution to psychology was immeasurable, and the entire course of psychotherapy has been molded by his formulations. He wrote voluminously, but with a characteristic impatience for detail. His influence has been felt in literature, anthropology, sociology, and religion.

---

[1] Personal communication from Dr. John Brentano, 1956.

PHILOSOPHIC SOURCES AND INFLUENCES

Students of the history of ideas have for many years speculated concerning the philosophical derivation of Freud's ideas. How much, it is being asked, did Freud owe to Helmholtz, Fechner, Herbart, Meynert, Du Bois-Reymond, and other representatives of a strongly positivist emphasis? To what extent was he affected by philosophy, a subject the relevance of which to his work he appears to have constantly minimized? Furthermore, to what extent does Freud owe a debt to the teachings of particular representatives of philosophical and humanistic traditions, such as Plato, Spinoza, Brentano, Schopenhauer, and Nietzsche?

The present argument is an effort to clarify the nature and extent of Freud's connection with his own great teacher of philosophy, Franz Brentano, whose life and work are being intensively studied at the present time, because of his role in establishing phenomenological psychology, and because of his influence on another student of his, the foremost phenomenologist of the 20th century, Edmund Husserl. An effort will be made here to carry forward the work in this area by Philip Merlan (1945, 1949), Herbert Spiegelberg (1965), and John Sullivan (1959). It is argued that the account of Freud's sources provided by Ernest Jones, and most other historians of psychoanalysis, requires serious modification. Freud's recurrent refusal to abandon an intentionalistic perspective, his profound awareness of the importance for psychology of man's symbolic acts of referring and meaning, are strong testimonies to the influence that the too-soon-forgotten Brentano probably exerted on the young Freud.

If these developments are not now as well known as they ought to be, it is in part due to Freud himself. The facts are that Freud on two separate occasions, 1885 and 1907, burned his earlier diaries and manuscripts. Moreover, he did so deliberately to disguise the origin of his ideas. He wrote:

> Let the biographers chafe; we won't make it too easy for them. Let each one of them believe he is right in his conception for the development of the hero; even now I enjoy the thought of how they will all go astray (Jones, I, xii).

It is apparent that Freud succeeded in his intent, since there have been many efforts to analyze the sources of Freud's thinking. It is impossible to discuss all of these efforts comprehensively here, but in view of the importance of Freud to the development of psychotherapy, it is essential that a summary evaluation be attempted.

Freud did not originate most of the ideas in his system. His skill would appear to have been in a novel synthesis of older ideas into a framework that utilized the language and thinking of physics. He was, therefore, a great redactor of older knowledge that resulted in a creative new approach. This is not to negate the contributions of Freud himself in working out new theoretical explanations, but simply to state that without his prodigious reading, his creative insight, and his dogged determination, the course of psychology would have been different.

Let us review some of the studies that have been made to evaluate the sources and influences of Freud's thought. Ernest Jones in his biography tends to minimize philosophical influence. He prefers to place Freud in the camp of the Helmholtz school of thought, although he recognizes that Freud, by bringing back the concept of will, was squarely opposing the teaching of Helmholtz, Bruecke, and Du Bois-Reymond, the leaders of the antivitalism movement in physiological psychology. Jones acknowledges that Freud had some exposure to Herbartian ideas in the Gymnasium (I, 374), and sees a certain parallel between the pleasure principle of Freud and the stability or constancy principle enunciated by Fechner (III, 270–271). With regard to Brentano, Jones acknowledges that Freud did take several courses from him, but palliates this fact by asserting that half of Vienna did likewise (I, 56). In part, Jones' critique must be taken in light of the later development of both Brentano's thought and psychoanalytic progress. A complicating factor in discussing Freud and Brentano is the fact that many scholars who are familiar with Brentano are not as familiar with Freud and vice versa. Furthermore, those who know Brentano are usually thinking of his later writings, which differ considerably from some of his ideas in 1874 (Barclay, 1959). Conversely, Freudian scholars, knowing Freud's abjuration of philosophy, cannot understand how Freud could have been influenced by a philosopher of phenomenology. The period that pertains to a possible influence relationship is the early 1870s, when Brentano was a professor at Vienna, and Freud an impressionable young student. At this time, Brentano was interested in empirical psychology and in the establishment of a proper methodology for the study of psychic phenomena. He later disavowed many of the views he expressed in *Psychologie vom empirischen Standpunkt* (Brentano, 1924, *Psychologie*, vol. III, 139).[2] Again, Freud's earlier views were not always the same as his later ones. Thus, in terms of Freud's sources, it is necessary to look at his earlier period rather than his later period.

[2] For example, Brentano changed his notion about the determinism of psychological phenomena, stating that earlier he had believed in psychic determinism and that he had changed his mind in later years.

In contrast to Jones, however, other psychoanalysts have seen a pervading philosophical motive in Freud's writings. Wittels (1924) suggested that Freud had a powerful bent toward speculative abstractions and was afraid that this would master him. He thus suggests that Freud countered this tendency by studying concrete scientific data. Jones states that once he asked Freud how much philosophy he had read, and Freud answered:

Very little. As a young man I felt a strong attraction towards speculation and ruthlessly checked it (Jones, I, 28).

This answer does not seem to square with the facts, since we know that Freud was familiar with Brentano's thought, the philosophy of Aristotle and Plato, and that he translated John Stuart Mill. Tiebout (1951, 19) in an unpublished doctoral dissertation, however, points out that Freud meant by philosophy something different from what Brentano and John Stuart Mill were advocating.

Philosophy is, for him, generally synonymous with idealism, supernaturalism or non-naturalistic philosophy—and philosophical inquiry generally means non-empirical, mystical and intuitional.

It is through this basic clarification that we understand in what sense Freud meant that he was not interested in philosophy. He was not concerned with idealistic and intuitional forms of abstracting, but he was vitally concerned with realistic and empirical investigations. For this reason it is possible to observe the young Freud taking courses from Bruecke and Brentano simultaneously without any real contradiction. Brentano had stated repeatedly that the method of psychology (and his philosophy) was none other than that of natural science, and that experience was his sole master.

Others have seen connections between Freud's thought and a variety of other sources. Tiebout (1951) and Georgiades (1954) have pointed out the similarities between Freud's conception of the role of the unconscious and conscious behavior to Plato. Zilboorg (1953) and Schwartz (1954) have found similarities between Freud and Aquinas. The latter writer studied the relationship between Freud's concept of ego and superego as compared to Aquinas' concept of conscience and synderesis. Knight (1920) detected a certain similarity between Freud and Plotinus. This latter observation is particularly interesting in view of the fact that Brentano sponsored a seminar on Plotinus entitled: "What kind of a philosopher sometimes sets the tone for an era."[3] This was a seminar

[3] "Was fur ein Philosoph manchmal Epoche macht" in Lucie Gilson, 1955, p. 33.

offered for Brentano's German students at Vienna in 1876. Brentano saw Plotinus as a great redactor or synthesizer of older Greek and Roman ideas. Kaplan (in Nelson, 1957) suggests that Freud was influenced by the Jewish philosophers Maimonides and Spinoza. Maimonides was concerned with Aristotelian philosophy, and Spinoza developed far ahead of his time a scientific approach to ethics. Tiebout (1951), aside from seeing the relationship between Plato and Freud, suggests that there are definite evidences of the influence of positivism, materialism, and determinism in Freud. Watson (1958) has suggested a relationship between Bentham and Freud.

It is my contention that there is a great deal of evidence to support the notion that Freud was influenced by a variety of philosophic sources in the development of psychoanalysis. Rather than specify one or the other sources for this influence, it is more likely that Freud drew selectively from a number of sources and that his five semesters of work with Brentano constituted a major influence in his acquaintance with philosophic sources. Brentano's works and lecture notes reveal that he treated in depth the work of Aristotle, Plato, Comte, John Stuart Mill, Spinoza, and a variety of other philosophers. Barclay (1959) has suggested that Brentano constitutes the major direct source of contact with philosophic sources in Freud's early education.

Freud's philosophical approach may be broadly subsumed under the intentionalistic philosophy that had preceded him. The concept of will, the development of a theory of unconscious determination, the notion of the cathexis, are all found in earlier philosophical literature. But Freud converted some of these older philosophical notions into more modern terms and cast his theory in the language of physics. Furthermore, he incorporated a basic positivism in his thinking that was not incongruous with Descartes' mechanistic universe, in which the real world was considered as extended and quantitative, consisting of mass, energy, and motion. If it be asserted that positivism is a philosophy that accepts science as the only method of knowledge, then certainly Freud was a positivist as were John Stuart Mill and Brentano. Even as Brentano compared Comte's ideas concerning the evolution of science to his own conception of epochs of philosophical development, so Freud revealed something of this same ideology in *Totem and Taboo*, where he distinguished the evolution of man's conception of the universe as passing through three stages, the animistic, the religious, and the scientific. Brentano maintained that philosophy was to use the methods of natural science, and that knowledge arrived at in philosophy was then as valid as other scientific data. Freud, approaching the same problem from a different viewpoint, insisted that the only valid knowledge for man was that of empirical science. The positivistic element in both men's thought finds a common issue in the methodology prescribed for psychology.

THE METHODOLOGY OF FREUD

Freud felt strongly about the importance of psychology in the realm of the sciences. Once he said: "My life has been aimed at one goal only; to infer or to guess how the mental apparatus is constructed and what forces interplay and counteract in it" (Jones, 1953, I, 45). When he returned to Vienna from his study under Charcot, he settled down to using the usual methods of electrotherapy, hydrotherapy, and medical diagnosis in his practice of medicine. But his association with Joseph Breuer, their experiments in hysteria phenomena, and Freud's basic conviction of the inadequacy of conventional methods led him to abandon the unilateral approach of physiology in these problems. Implicitly, and perhaps unconsciously, both Breuer and Freud came to the same conclusions that Brentano had voiced: that physiology at that time could not provide all the answers to the analysis of psychic phenomena. They arrived at this conclusion in a different manner from Brentano. Their convictions were based on the clinical evidence that they had amassed which testified to the insufficiency of the existing approaches to hysteria phenomena. This is not to say that Breuer and Freud disavowed the conventional laboratory means of the scientific method but, instead, that they were convinced that there were other methods—equally scientific—of arriving at valid and scientific conclusions regarding psychic phenomena. What had happened in Freud's thinking was that he had come to the conclusion that the scientific method had to be extended instead of being limited to the laboratory. This is manifest in his assertion that there were only two forms of science, psychology pure and applied, and natural science (Freud, 1933, 229).

Freud insisted that psychoanalysis must treat the psyche as an independent entity. He realized that it was not possible at that time to erect more than a superstructure for psychoanalytic doctrine and that it would be necessary at some future date to explain the ultimate organic foundations of psychic activity. Freud's change in thought was marked by a change in technique. As Erikson (1955, 89–90) stated:

... he offered them (his patients) a conscious and direct partnership, he made the patient's healthy, if submerged, part his partner in understanding the unhealthy part. Thus was established one basic principle of psychoanalysis, namely, that one can study the human mind only by engaging the fully motivated partnership of the observed individual, and by entering into a sincere contract with him.

Moreover, the specifics of Freud's altered method were closely related to the association of ideas and particularly to the process of free association—the same technique that Brentano had predicted would provide important insight into psychic processes. Coupled with the association of ideas, Freud employed introspection. In fact, he proclaimed that self-perception and a knowledge of one's own processes was the indispensable prerequisite for genuine psychological insight.

Psychoanalysis is learned first of all on oneself, through the study of one's own personality. This is not exactly what is meant by introspection but it may be so described for want of a better word (Freud, 1954, 23).

Freud was clearly aware that, in departing from the laboratory method, he was charting a course into the unknown hinterland of psychic phenomena. And he realized that by utilizing what has since become the clinical approach to human behavior, he was incurring the wrath of the entrenched opposition. It was so tempting to try and explain psychic activities in the exclusive terms of natural science.

All of these advances and discoveries were related to the physical side of man, and it followed as a result of an incorrect though easily understandable trend of thought, that physicians came to restrict their interest to the physical side of things and were glad to leave the mental field to the province of the philosophers whom they despised. . . . (Freud, 1953, 7, 284).

Not only did Freud depart from the viewpoint that all psychic phenomena were merely the manifestations of physiological processes, but he insisted on the active importance of the mind on somatic processes. In his article on *Religion and Cures,* Freud spoke of the great power of the mind and of mental processes over somatic ones. He conceded that miracles in holy places may actually have been the result of great collective concentrations of unconscious psychic powers. He reminded his readers that psychotherapy seems to be a most ancient form of therapy in medicine.

It is not a modern dictum, but an old saying of physicians that these diseases are not cured by the drug but by the physician—that is by the personality of the physician—inasmuch as through it he exerts a mental influence (Freud, 1953, 2, 284).

Why then, was this hypothesis of the influence of psychic processes on somatic ones ignored in the erection of a scientific methodology for psychology? Freud thought that it was because of the fear of being unscientific:

The relation between body and mind . . . is a reciprocal one; but in earlier days the other side of this relation, the effect of the mind upon the body found little favor in the eyes of physicians. They seemed to be afraid of granting mental life any independence, for fear of that implying an abandonment of the scientific ground on which they stood (Freud, 1953, 7, 259).

From his investigations in the area of hysteria phenomena, Freud became convinced that psychic life was determined in large part by unconscious and instinctual tensions. From the reluctance of patients to cooperate in their cures, he likewise felt that there was some internal resistance operative. This resistance could not be isolated in the test tube, nor was it plausible to assume a physiological basis. Freud therefore made the momentous decision to utilize a new approach to psychic phenomena. He believed that by the careful analysis of the conscious manifestations of unconscious processes it would be possible to elaborate some general theoretical principles about the nature and meaning of psychic phenomena. To this end he employed introspection and the systematic observation of patients. He also employed the analysis of dreams to interpret the latent basis of behavior. But he warned that investigations in one area of psychic life might well have to wait until some other areas catch up and corroborate the original findings (Freud, 1913, 405).

Through a process of careful systematic observation, Freud accumulated a great deal of data that he used to formulate the theoretical principles of psychoanalysis:

One dislikes the thought of abandoning observation for barren theoretical discussions, but all the same we must not shirk on attempted explanation . . . Speculative theory of these relations of which we are speaking would in the first place require as its basis a sharply defined concept. But I am of the opinion that that is just the difference between a speculative theory and a science founded upon constructions arrived at *empirically*. The latter will not begrudge to speculation its privilege of a smooth, logically unassailable structure, but will itself be gladly content with nebulous *scarcely imaginative conceptions, which it hopes to apprehend more clearly in the course of its development or which it is even prepared to replace by others* (Freud, 1953, 4, 34–35).

Freud believed these theoretical observations, arrived at through an empirical process, were extremely important in the development of a scientific knowledge:

For these ideas are not the basis . . . of the science upon which everything rests—that on the contrary is observation alone. They are not the foundation stone but the coping of the whole structure and they can be discarded and replaced without damaging it. The same thing is happening in our day in the science of physics, the fundamental notions of which as regards matter, centers of force, attractions, etc., are scarcely less debatable than the corresponding ideas in psychoanalysis [Murphy, 1957 (Nelson, ed.), 119].

Thus Freud based his methodology in psychology on the careful observation of phenomena. Through this observation he drew inductive and deductive conclusions that he framed into what we know as psychoanalytic theory. At the time, however, Freud was thoroughly condemned for his "speculations." Yet, today, the validity of his clinical approach to human behavior has been acknowledged by almost everyone. Gardner Murphy writes:

It is my suggestion that the capacity to observe with open eyes and to test empirically had been part of Freud's approach from the beginning, and that despite many premature conclusions the entire system can be pushed gently in the direction of science. . . . While I think the experimental testing of psychoanalytic hypotheses will have some value, it has become evident by now that the experimental is only one of several and by no means necessarily the most suitable method to be used in the development of such a science [Murphy, 1957 (Nelson, ed.), 119].

The use of the unconscious hypothesis was not a popular one among scientists. It was felt that to resort to the unconscious hypothesis was to admit scientific defeat. These concepts were fuzzy and lacked precision. Freud wrote:

The view is often defended that sciences should be built upon clear and sharply defined basal concepts. In actual fact, no science not even the most exact one begins with such definitions. *The true beginning of scientific activity consists rather in describing phenomena and then proceeding to group, classify and correlate them* (Freud, 1953, 4, 60–61).

Freud's essential contribution to psychology was the development of a methodology that has become known as the clinical method. It is sometimes forgotten that Freud did a tremendous amount of personal work that furthered the entire cause of psychology as a science. One great criticism of psychoanalytic doctrine is the fact that theory, speculation, and empirical evidence are all mixed up in Freud's work. The work of Dollard and Miller, as well as many others, has helped to begin an experimental verification of psychoanalytic doctrine. It is, however, unlikely that a sufficient verification of psychoanalytic doctrine can ever be made to satisfy the psychologists of the behaviorist persuasion. The reason is really one of general psychological aim. *Both psychoanalytic findings and modern German phenomenalism have as their general raison d'être the task of teaching mankind to know itself better and to promote the cause of progress.* Although the superficial student of Freud may feel that psychoanalysis is an invitation to libertine activities, nothing could be further from the truth. Freudian concepts ring with an old-fashioned respect for the central role of reason in human affairs. It is Freud's whole contention that through insight and understanding man can obtain a more rational existence. Thus underneath the methodology of psychoanalysis is a real ethical and philosophical motive. Freud was in so great a hurry to develop his theory to explain human behavior and to augment the process of psychotherapy, that he failed to pause long enough to attempt a rigorous experimental justification.

THEORETICAL FOUNDATIONS OF FREUDIAN PSYCHODYNAMICS

The keystone of Freud's psychological system is his theory on the nature and extent of unconscious determination in psychic phenomena. Freud's recognition of the unconscious as such an important determinant in mental life has been a central component in the clinical approach to behavior, including both the process of psychotherapy and the assessment of personality. Much of the rationale of Freud's own psychotherapy system, plus those systems derived from his thinking, has been centered on the notion that somehow repressed material must be brought to conscious attention, with the implied result that the recognition of heretofore unconscious material will alleviate certain aspects of maladaptive behavior. Freud was certainly not the first to think of the concept of the unconscious, but he was unquestionably the popularizer of it. The entire course of psychotherapy has been centered, until recently, on this key notion.[4] Freud's initial theory of mind in relationship to the concept of the

---

[4] The word unconscious has multiple meanings. James Miller in a book on the subject gives no less than 16 different meanings for the word (Miller, 1942, 21–44). It can mean inanimate, incapable of discrimination, absent-minded, anesthetized, unresponsive to stimulation, nonmental, conditioned, unsensing, unnoticed or unattended, unremembering or unremembered, instinctive, innate or inherited, unrecognized and involuntary, incommunicable and unaware of discrimination, etc. The word is used in so many senses that philosophers and psychologists must define their meaning before understanding is possible. The confusion is augmented by the addition of similar con-

unconscious seems to have been worked out jointly with Joseph Breuer. In the book *Studies on Hysteria* (1957), Breuer and Freud presented a theory of mind that was based on psychic determinism and organic cerebral tensions. Breuer believed that there was a physiological substratum which existed as the basis for conscious activities (1957, 185). In Breuer's view the whole organism, physical as well as psychical, is subject to one energy system:

> We shall be safe from the danger of allowing ourselves to be tricked by our own figures of speech if we always remember that after all it is the same brain, and most probably in the same cerebral cortex, that conscious and unconscious ideas alike have their origin. How this is possible we cannot say. But then we know so little of the psychical activity of the cerebral cortex that one puzzling complication the more scarcely increases our limitless ignorance (228).

Breuer's whole theoretical proposal might be called the theory of intracerebral tonic excitation. Breuer proposes the analogy of an electrical system with energy being supplied by a dynamo. Breuer views the brain as behaving like an electrical system of restricted capacity in which either there is light or transmitting power, but that if one is used greatly, then the other must of necessity be diminished, since there is only a limited amount of power available. Conversely, when the energy is not used, it stores up and produces intracerebral excitation that results in a tension or sense of unpleasurable unrest (195). Such tension always builds up when one of the organism's needs fails to find satisfaction.

cepts such as Janet's "subconscious," Prince's "coconscious," and Jung's "collective unconscious."

Historically, the concept can be traced back to Plato in his discussion of the rise of man's knowledge from darkness to light. Plato in his *Republic* speaking of the movements of the soul describes the blind seeking of the soul:

> . . . which ascends from some half-night kind of day to the true light of existence, which we will term true philosophy (Davis, II, 1849, 210).

Aquinas also spoke of the power and force of the unknown in man and left the door open for the hypothesis of the unconscious through his theory of the functioning of the internal sense (common sense) (Maritain in H. Nelson, 1957, p. 232). Brentano inveighed against the philosophical notion of the unconscious in terms of the metaphysics of Schopenhauer (Brentano, II, 1924, Chapter 3) and suggested that psychologists should not resort to the unconscious hypothesis until all other alternatives had been exhausted. Fechner following Leibnitz spoke of the threshold of consciousness, and Poincare believed that the unconscious or sublimal ego enjoyed a prime role in the invention of mathematical hypotheses. These individuals are mentioned only as a representative sample of the range of thought concerning the unconscious which already existed prior to Freud.

This explanation not only applied to the physiological organism but also to the nervous system and psychic phenomena (201). Thus all disturbances of mental equilibrium are somehow connected to an increase in excitation. Breuer regarded hysteria as a clinical picture "which has been empirically discovered and is based on observation" (187). He considered the sexual instinct as the most powerful source of persisting increases of excitation within the cerebral cortex. These increases were very unevenly distributed over the nervous system and, when they reached a certain intensity, created disturbances in the system akin to electrical overloading.

Freud always maintained that the theoretical presentation, which had been mostly the work of Breuer in their joint studies of hysteria, was very important to psychoanalysis. Even as late as 1923 to 1925 he repeatedly called attention to the importance of these studies for the future of psychoanalysis and regretted that they had not been used more widely (Bernfeld, 1944, 341). Certainly, Freud elaborated on the concept of the unconscious in his later works, but he remained in essential agreement with the theoretical considerations of the *Studies on Hysteria.*

Freud was convinced that the association of words, the choice of names, simple errors of speech, and nervous fiddling were all indicative of the determinism of psychic life (Freud, 1956, 4, 15). He thus placed a high premium on very close observation of conscious processes for, although he postulated the existence of the unconscious, he insisted that we must rely on consciousness to give us clues as to the nature of the unconscious:

> Now all our knowledge is invariably bound up with consciousness.
> Even knowledge of the unconscious can only be obtained by making
> it conscious (Freud, 1956, 4, 100–104).

Freud never maintained that the unconscious operated a thought process exactly parallel to that of consciousness. As to what state the unconscious was in, he speculated and used terms that were also used to describe conscious mental processes (Jones, 1922, 18–19). Jones says:

> Freud's conception of the unconscious . . . is a purely inductive one
> built up step by step on the basis of actual experience without the
> introduction of any a-priori speculative hypothesis. It may therefore
> be called the scientific conception in contradistinction to the philo-
> sophical one. Instead of starting with any notions, whether precise
> or nebulous, of what the unconscious ought to be, he investigated the
> actual mental processes that were inaccessible to his patients' intro-
> spection, and which were only to be reached by means of some

technical procedure, such as the psychoanalytic one. As a result of these investigations, he acquired a gradually increasing knowledge of the nature of unconscious processes, of their content, meaning, origin, and significance, and was therefore placed in a position of being able to formulate some general statements on these matters (Jones, 1922, 147).

Thus Freud arrived gradually at the concept of the unconscious as a topological area of the psyche characterized by its dynamic nature, its relationship to primary instinctual energy, its infantile fixation on primary objects of instinctual desire, its basic illogical and amoral character, and its predominant, but by no means exclusive, sexual motivation.

With the acceptance of this primary postulate Freud's approach to behavior differed considerably from earlier systems. For it was within the realm of conscious behavior that most psychologists prior to Freud had looked for the interpretation and understanding of human behavior. What could not be explained through conscious processes of self-analysis and observation was, for all practical purposes, meaningless to them. By insisting that consciousness was the exclusive dimension of psychic reality, Freud essentially shifted the epistemological basis of psychological investigation. Now all behavior was considered meaningful *in terms of the psychological-physiological organism* rather than in terms of logic. The order that existed was indeed a cause and effect order, but in terms of the logic of the unconscious as well as conscious phenomena. Everything which could be observed in mental life had meaning in terms of the intention, direction, or sequence that it held in relation to tension reduction. Mind for Freud was an apparatus for the reduction of free-flowing energy from unstable to stable forms. *All psychic processes, contents, and thoughts of an individual psychic life are meaningful and their meanings are mutually and intimately related* (Gimbel, 1949, 3). Thus behavior is the resultant function of the organism and environment in interaction. In Freud's thought there is no categorical separation between the interpretation of the individual psychic life and its contents, and the understandings of the events of that psychic life. If man is to be completely understood, he must be interpreted as a psychophysical unity of which physical environment is closely related to psychic activity. In the interchange, all psychic processes, causes, and contents have understandable relationships with each other. The physical is the first cause and the primary meaning. *Thus the products and contents of psychic life must be interpreted in terms of the purposes or goals which they represent with special reference to unconscious determination.*

A second major aspect of Freud's system is his approach to instinct. In

Freud's thinking the whole psychic apparatus evolves from a simple neural reflex arc, which is the most elementary of behavior mechanisms in coping with the complex interchanges between needs and drives and external reality. At first, bodily needs are simply answered through reflex mechanisms. A certain complex of reflex mechanisms combine and form an instinct. He wrote:

> An instinct appears to us as a borderline concept between the mental and the physical, being both the mental representative of the stimuli emanating from within the organism and penetrating to the mind, and at the same time a measure of the demand made upon the energy of the latter in consequence of its connection with the body (Freud, 1913, 431).

An instinct then, is a quasi-physical, quasi-biological concept. It is the biological substratum of all thought processes. The source of instinctual activity is excitation or tension in the organism. The purpose of the instinct is the quelling of this unrest through direct motor activity. In other words, as certain needs become apparent in the body chemistry, these needs are translated into tension that is elaborated in the form of an instinct. The instinctual drive is then directed toward the reduction of tension and the restoration of bodily equilibrium.

> By an instinct is provisionally to be understood the physical representative of an endo-somatic continuously flowing source of stimulation as contrasted with the stimulus which is set up by a single excitation come from without. The concept of instinct is thus one of those lying on the frontier between the mental and the physical. The simplest and likeliest assumption as to the nature of instinct would seem to be that in itself an instinct is without quality and so far as mental life is concerned is only to be regarded as a measure of the demand made upon the mind for work (Freud, 1953, VII, 170).

The chief tool of instinct is the pleasure-pain principle. It is through the desire for pleasurable experience and the avoidance of pain that the basic tensions of the physical organism are translated through instinct into action.

The Structure of the Mind

Freud divided the mind of man into two areas: (1) unconsciousness, and (2) consciousness-preconsciousness. The infant is born with no real sense of consciousness, since consciousness entails self-perception and the perception of outer reality. The unconscious stands for all psychic life that is not directly perceived through conscious perception. It is the part of the mind that stands closest to the instincts. At first, it is merely the medium through which instinctual needs are manifested, but subsequently, when conscious perception arises, it becomes the repository for all repressed ideas, that is, ideas that conflict with ego ideals and external reality. It is not a passive area, but a dynamic region where the most active functioning goes on. It is timeless, since time is a dimension of consciousness. It is infantile and wishful in its designs, since it knows no reality, and it is amoral in its seeking because it knows no law but itself. All unconscious processes are only indirectly subject to the reality principle. The ideas in the unconscious are free floating and contain no idea of negation, therefore, they show no mutual contradiction. Sometime in the first year of life there is a splitting between the unconscious and a new segment called consciousness. This occurs as the infant remains awake for longer periods and begins to become accustomed to outer reality.

The second major portion of the mind is the perceptual apparatus. The distinguishing factor of this area is perception. This system is directed toward the outer world; it serves as a mediator of phenomena that occur either as a result of external stimulation or internal tension. The special principle of operation in consciousness is called the reality principle. The reality principle is concerned with the mediation of immediate pleasure-seeking in terms of the conditions imposed by reality. Freud's earliest recognition of the reality principle can be said to have occurred through his development of the notion of repression. In his early studies of hysteria, he recognized that whenever a patient interrupted the continuance of an interpretation and analysis of dream content, repression was present. From the testimony of numerous observations and case histories, Freud concluded that the earliest instrument of organic tension reduction, that is, the pleasure principle, had been subjected to modification through the effect of environmental forces, that is, the reality principle.

> . . . The mental apparatus had to decide to form a conception of the real circumstances in the outer world and to exert itself to alter them. A new principle of mental functioning was thus introduced; what was conceived of was no longer that which was present, but that which was real, even if it should be unpleasant. This institution of the reality principle proved a momentous step (Freud, 1953, 4, 15).

The reality principle was characterized by consciousness, and it developed a special function called *attention* whose activity was "to meet the sense-impressions half way, instead of waiting for their appearance." In connection with this function of attention, there was also a system of *notation* devised for memory purposes. It is together with the concept of memory that the system of preconsciousness is best understood. Freud believed that the perception system of the psyche possessed no capability for preserving memories. He spoke of the preconscious as a system placed near the motor and of the psychic apparatus and in a somewhat intermediary position between the unconscious and consciousness. The unconscious had no direct access to consciousness except through the preconscious. During the day the path leading to the preconscious from the unconscious is closed by the resistance of the censor. The preconscious serves as a repository for memory traces proceeding from the perceptual act of consciousness, and it is likewise subject to the more dynamic instinctual wishes proceeding from the unconscious. Although the path from the unconscious to the preconscious is closely guarded during the day, during sleep unconscious instinctual energy can "charge" certain memory traces with a force that is instrumental in the process of dream formation.

The third characteristic of consciousness is the process of *judgment*.

In place of repression . . . there developed an impartial passing of judgment which had to decide whether a particular idea was true or false, that is, was in agreement with reality or not; decision was determined by comparison with the memory traces of reality (Freud, 1913, 429).

Attention, notation or memory, and judgment are the three characteristics of the psychic state of consciousness. Perception involves all these three functions. Attention seems to be conditioned by an intensity threshold of presentational "quanta." Presentational content may arise from either inner or outer stimulation. The psychic act of perception is the full conscious experiencing of presentational content when they have attained the attention threshold. The notation of conscious memory traces together with judgment are also characteristics of the state of consciousness —although memories in themselves are stored in the preconscious.

THE EVOLUTION OF PSYCHIC LIFE

Freud's original question had been, "what was the nature of psychic life?" This led him to a close examination of the process whereby the psychic organization developed. Freud believed that the whole process of psychic development, ideation, image conceptions, and object-relations were all related to the central goal of the organism, that is, the reduction of tension. But the force of reality on the organism, and the constant anxieties proceeding from the conflict between internal tension and instinct and external culturation processes resulted in all sorts of variations in the psychic structure.

The original instinctual tension of the organism is reduced through the attempt at incorporation. The infant through sucking attempts to incorporate the object of his libidinal desire. Recall that the earliest needs of the infant are for nutrition. Thus in the beginning the sexual instincts possess what Freud called an anaclitic characteristic, that is, they lean up against the ego instincts or need for self-preservation (Freud, 1949, p. 60, footnote one.) The basic nutritional needs of the infant are tied up in the object of his mother's breast, and his earliest relationship is one of identification or emotional tie with his mother. This earliest object-relationship based on the instinctual need for self-preservation is reinforced through pleasure-pain reactions. All his pleasurable experiences are identified with this object, his mother. She allays his hunger by feeding him, she changes his diapers when he is wet, warms him with her caresses and showers on him the first emotional feelings. *Thus she becomes the primary object of his instinctual tension reduction.* To this object, the infant attaches his first cathexis. A cathexis in Freudian terminology "refers to the idea of physical energy being lodged or attaching itself to mental structures or processes somewhat on the analogy of an electric charge . . . it refers to a sum of psychic energy, which occupies or invests objects or some particular channels" (Fodor, 1950, 20). Thus the first object-cathexis in psychic life proceeds from instinctual needs. It is a primary process in Freud's conception of the psychic life.

The whole of infantile life is characterized by object-cathexes based on primary identification or incorporation. Gradually, the infant distinguishes between objects. He builds up an organization of experiences and distinguishes between himself and extraorganic reality. Identification with the object through a process of cathexis is the original form of emotional tie (Freud, 1949, 65).

What is the source of this image that is constructed by the psychic apparatus of the infant? Freud answers this by stating that all images originate from the perceptory process. The image that is constructed by the mind is the joint result of the primary processes and the stimulus of external reality. Originally, the image or psychic equivalent of the object desired is identified in the infant mind with the extraorganic reality. As Freud stated, "the contrast between what is subjective and what is objective does not exist from the first" (Freud, 1953, 5, 184). Through the process of attention, memory notation, and judgment, the infant ego gradually learns to distinguish between what is imagery and what is real. Hall and iLndzey (1957, 42) explain this point thus:

... In order to satisfy a need, he must learn to match what is in his mind with its counterpart in the external world by means of the secondary process. This matching of a mental representation with physical reality, of something that is in the mind with something that is in the outer world, is what is meant by identification.

Thus the difference between internal reality (as vested in the subjective image cathexes and primary process) and external reality (secondary process) is distinguished on the basis of the conscious phenomena of attention, memory, and judgment.

INTENTIONALITY IN FREUD

A short article written by Freud in 1925, entitled "Negation," reveals most accurately Freud's concept of intentionality (Freud, 1953, 5, 181–185). Freud had observed that individuals when relating the association of ideas frequently stated an association and then denied that it was really an association at all. They would say, for example, that it was not their mother about whom they dreamed. Freud remarked that *the negative judgment was the intellectual substitution for repression.* Although the individual might deny it was his mother, Freud observed that it most likely was.

The analysis of this article on judgment provides an insight into Freud's use of the intentional image. He stated that judgment was an intellectual and conscious perceptory act. But below the conscious intellectual function was a deeper psychological meaning that he interpreted as being the freedom of thought from the limits of repression.

> The function of judgment is concerned ultimately with two sorts of decision. It may assert or deny that a thing has a particular property; or it may affirm or dispute that a particular image (*Vorstellung*) exists in reality (Freud, V, 1953, 103).

Freud believed that the original pleasure-ego tried to introject itself into everything it *judged good* and to eject or avoid everything that it *judged evil,* and the basic criterion was, of course, the pleasure principle. Thus the first function of judgment was to affirm or to deny that an object perceived was to be incorporated or avoided. The second function of judgment was to decide not whether a thing should be incorporated or avoided but, instead, whether something already perceived and existing in the consciousness can be rediscovered in reality.

Here, then, is a real description of Freud's conception of intentionality. Freud explains best himself:

Experience has taught that it is important not only whether a thing (an object from which satisfaction is sought) possesses the 'good' property, that is, whether it deserves to be taken into the ego, but also whether it is there in the external world, ready to be seized when it is wanted (Freud, 1953, V, 183).

From this quotation it is possible to observe that Freud conceived the "good" as that which has a property that will satisfy the pleasure ego. Now obviously a "good" that is illusory is not a real good for the ego. Hence, it is necessary that the ego through the process of judgment first adjudge the *reality* of the supposed "good." This is tantamount to saying that for an object really to be good, it must exist and that, implicit in the judgment of "good," is the judgment of existence or nonexistence, affirmation or denial in reality.

This comment also reveals what Freud thought of the nature of reality and intentional imagery. The sense image is originally our only guarantee of reality:

In order to understand this step forward, we must recollect that all images originate from perceptions and are repetitions of them. So that originally the mere existence of the image serves as a guarantee of the reality of what is imagined (Freud, 1953, V, 184).

Freud is thus stating here that perception itself creates an image of the sensory data and that recognition as perception involves the ego systematically conditioning the nature of perception by the criterion of subjective incorporation or expulsion.

There is no confusion in the reality that is present while the extraorganic object is present to the senses. In other words, Freud assumes that the image present in the mind does correspond with outer reality, that it is a psychic representation of the extraorganic object of perception. "The contrast between what is subjective and objective does not exist from the first" (Freud, 1953, V, 184). This contrast:

. . . only arises from the faculty which thought possesses for reviving a thing that has once been perceived, by reproducing it as an image without its being necessary for the external object still to be present (Ibid).

In effect, Freud is thus stating that the only effective reality is the intentional image. *We know the image exists; what we don't know is whether it corresponds to anything in reality, or whether we can find the object in external reality which corresponds to our psychic image.* Freud's position is thus in agreement with the theory of intentional existence as elaborated by Brentano. Through the distinction that Freud made concerning the image as present and as recalled by memory, there is an even closer tie to Brentano and scholasticism, since it will be recalled that the scholastics considered the intentional sensory production *as the product of imagination and memory,* and pointed out that there was a difference between the sensory image as present and concurrent with the extraorganic object and the intentional existence of that representation in the mind when the extraorganic object was not present.[5]

Freud clarifies his own position further:

> Thus the first and immediate aim of the process of testing reality is not to discover an object in real perception corresponding to what is imagined, but to rediscover such an object, to convince oneself that it is still there (Ibid).

Freud recognized the synthetic power of imagination and memory and insisted that an essential feature of judgment was the attempt to clarify and reduce to a unity the confused elements of imagination and memory as portrayed in the intentional image.

> The differentiation between what is subjective and what is objective is further assisted by another faculty of the power of thought. The reproduction of a perception as an image is not always a faithful one; it can be modified by omissions or by the fusion of a number of elements. The process for testing the thing's reality must then investigate the extent of these distortions. But it is evident that an essential pre-condition for the institution of the function for testing reality is that objects shall have been lost which have formerly afforded real satisfaction (Ibid., 185).

[5] The whole intentional process can be understood in relationship to what occurs in the taking of a picture with a camera. This example is not exactly parallel, but it may explain the differences. The unexposed film is, of course, blank and passively receives the image cast upon it. When it is developed, a likeness appears that is a more-or-less accurate representation of the reality itself. Both Freud and the Scholastics, however, realized that man is different from the blank film. His perception of outer reality is emotionally toned by unconscious influences. Thus what he recalls in memory is a subjective creation and not identical to the actual reality. The scholastics referred to sensory presentations as the instrumental causality for the construction of the intentional imagery. They did this because they posited a spiritual substance, the soul, as the ultimate cause of the intentional image. It was not appropriate that an immortal spiritual soul could be influenced by sensory data, thus the intentional creation partook both of the sensory data and the involvement of the spirit. Freud simply substitutes the entire range of unconscious needs and organic tensions as the mediating instrumentality. Once the philosophical terminology of scholasticism and the physiological terminology of Freud have been cleared away, the concepts emerge as relatively parallel and equivalent.

Judgment, says Freud, is the intellectual action which decides the choice of motor action that puts an end to the procrastination of thinking. Thought itself is a substitute for action, and it is the attempt of the ego to "try out" various courses of action intellectually before proceeding to motor implementation. Freud believed that this thought process had its origin in the sensory end of the mental apparatus in connection with sense perceptions and the valuation of reality. Freud insists that there is a continual intending process by the ego:

> For upon our hypothesis *perception is not a merely passive process;* we believe rather that the ego periodically sends out small amounts of cathectic energy into the perceptual system and by their means samples the external stimuli and after each such groping advance draws back again (Ibid., 185, italics the writer's).[6]

The study of judgment, states Freud, affords insight into the intellectual substitution or derivation of intellectual functions from instinctual and primary impulses. He sees *affirmation* in judgment as the intellectual counterpart of union or ego incorporation, and *negation* as a symbol of repression and as derived from the primary action of expulsion. This short article contributes a wealth of insight into Freud's ideas concerning imagination, memory, perception, intentional images, and the active role of the ego in the formation of intellectual *judgment.*

REASON AND ETHICAL DETERMINANTS

Contrary to the opinion of many, Freud was not indifferent to moral values. But Freud's ideas concerning ethics and the formation of moral character spring from his observation concerning the quality and characteristics of psychological experience in reference to the criterion of social behavior. In Freud's elaboration of the reality principle, he spoke of the ego, roughly equating it with reason and circumspection (Freud, 1933, 105). The ego is that part of the id that is modified by contact with the outside world; its conscious elements are the result of the conscious perceptual system, and its primary function is to modify the demands of instinctual drives in terms of the conditions of outer reality (Fairbairn, 1954, 9). It serves as a coherent organization of mental processes— some of which shade into the unconscious—that act as the chief psychic means for personal adaptation and adjustment to the pressures of life in a social environment.

---

[6] This active intending force (of ego or soul) is the distinguishing characteristic of the intentionalistic school as against the passive environmentalist approach of Locke and his modern followers.

Along with the ego, Freud spoke of the superego, to which he allocated the activities of self-observation, conscience, and the holding up of ego ideals (1933, 94). The superego develops out of the original residue of unconscious motivations and early behavior patterns and from the subsequent action of the ego. It thus combines both instinctual and rational elements. Both the ego and the superego play an important role in Freud's conception of ethical behavior.

As has been pointed out, Freud tended to identify the ego with reason. Zilboorg (in Nelson, 1953, 89) observed that Freud had hardly enunciated the pleasure principle before he mentioned that men had to rise above this through the reality principle. The chief way of doing this was through the use of reason. Yet reason can be a very deluding criterion utilized by the ego as a defense against the truth. For not only the perceptive elements of outside reality enter consciousness but also the emotionally toned elements of the unconscious. Both factors are present in the conscious logic called reason. Hence, Freud warned against assuming that what was reason in appearance was, therefore, reason in reality. Kaplan has observed on this point:

> Reason becomes effective only when it draws upon energies not themselves abstractly intellectual and shapes materials not of its own substance. *Psychoanalytic therapy, as well as theory, makes central the employment of reason called insight. It has a quality of irresistible immediacy which contrasts with the psychic distance of the purely discursive intellect* (Kaplan in Nelson, 1953, 213, italics the writer's).

Freud was definitely concerned with truth and goodness, but he realized that it was extremely difficult for man to reach these goals. Tiebout (1951) mentioned that Freud had a love for humanity and a crusading zeal together with an altruistic impulse, somewhat corresponding to Aristotle's conception of true friendship.

Freud's attitude toward reason was not only colored by his epistemology but more deeply shadowed by his conception of the nature of man. It is because of the inadequacy of man's real knowledge of himself that Freud held no brief for *unaided* human reason. Freud did not hold that man is innately good, nor did he believe that man is essentially wicked. Man, to Freud, was morally neutral. Freud viewed man as the end product of evolution, and throughout his life he manifested a belief in the promise of the ultimate evolution of man (Tiebout, 1951, 41). Freud remained convinced of the essential dualism of Cartesian thought, identifying the unconscious with the physiological, and the conscious with limited self-knowledge. Man is to all purposes a physiological machine in which the urges and motivations of the biological organism are expressed in the thought processes, wishes, and emotional drives of the conscious ego.

Freud, therefore, could not accept the traditional theological explanation of man. He saw that some of the forms of organized religious ritual could cater to the neurotic in man and could ally themselves with both unconscious need and overweening superego. In this sense, religion acted as a reinforcement of the irrational in man. Sometimes, too, it posed as a substitute for genuine counseling and interpretation as manifested in psychoanalytic therapy. The psychoanalytic condemnation of religion is extended chiefly to that form of religious zeal that would substitute faith for therapy. For Freud believed that the counseling or psychotherapy process could aid reason in making the best possible intellectual justification for behavior. It was for this reason that the indispensable tool in counseling is the interpretation of the psychoanalyst or counselor. The counselor with his superior knowledge of dynamics is able to see how the early behavior of the individual has led to his present situation. Moreover, the development of skill in diagnosing the logic of the unconscious requires considerable training. If the logic of the unconscious were "reasonable," individuals could analyze their own behavior. It is precisely *this point, that is, the layman's inability to see the chain of unconscious logic that determines his behavior, which necessitates the process of therapy.*

Freud was under no illusions as to what psychoanalysis could do for man. He did not claim that it was a sovereign remedy for man's woes, but he did think that it offered a better solution than either philosophy or religion. Freud's condemnation of religious ritual and totem was leveled against the religious element of mysticism, that mysterious kind of third knowledge which is somehow independent of experimentation and cognitive intuition (Kaplan in Nelson, 1953, 228). But in his view man need not be bound forever to the forces of the irrational and the relentless drive of fate. Insofar as man can grasp through insight the nature of reasonable goals that he may achieve, he will be happy. Freud advocated that man should seek not the absolutely best goal possible but, instead, the best goal attainable that would meet and serve his own individual needs. It is the power of blind irrational drives reinforced by ignorance, fear, and prejudice that causes maladjustment and unhappiness. It is for this reason that Freud thought that psychoanalysis offered the greatest promise to humanity for acquiring true rational insight into psychic problems. Psychoanalysis is no universal remedy, it cannot always offer the solution to individual's problems, since its use is restricted to certain groups of people who can benefit by rational insight into the hidden sources of their problems.

In summary, then, Freud's conception of the role of psychoanalysis was as both a therapeutic technique helpful to certain kinds of people, and as a research technique. His outline of the psychic apparatus was constructed on the model of an electrical system in which there were two ends, a perceptual conscious one and a motor one. The primary instinctual tensions of the organism seek object-relationships or cathexes. At first this cathexis process is ordered to the motor end of the apparatus, later it is subsumed in ideational form by the perceptual system. There is an evolutionary development present in the life of every individual, from behavior controlled primarily by the pleasure principle through the systems of unconsciousness and preconsciousness, which lie close to the motor segment of the psychic apparatus, to behavior that is governed by the reality principle and the ego during the conscious act of perception. The flow of psychic enervation during consciousness is primarily from the perception end to the motor segment, whereas during sleep the direction is reversed. The end of psychoanalytic therapy is rational insight achieved through an understanding of human behavior. The process includes the skillful observation of consciousness and the interpretation of the products elaborated by a psychoanalyst in such way that the individual will understand the causes of his behavior. The goal of this process is more effective behavior through understanding and rational insight. Although psychoanalysis is no universal remedy, Freud thought it offered the best opportunity both for understanding psychic phenomena and for altering human behavior.

FREUD AS A REDACTOR AND INNOVATOR IN INTENTIONALITY

In a previous chapter it was observed that Aquinas, Descartes, Leibnitz, and Brentano all contributed to a philosophical approach that has been labeled intentionality. The essential features of the intentional metaphysical concept of man seem to be: (1) that man has a vital principle of activity; (2) this principle is essentially characterized by rational operation; (3) its purpose is to extend personal dominion over self and environment by means of symbolic manipulation of what is known as thought; (4) this principle is exclusive to man, distinguishing him from all other forms of life, and bears within it the seeking for omnipotence or immortality.

Now in Freud these same essential features are present. Freud recognized man as possessing a vital principle of activity. Naturally he identified this with energy and force—two scientific terms to explain operationally the basic substantive life process. Moreover, he agreed also that the mature goal of man was rational insightful behavior. In his elaboration of the development of psychic life, he showed amply his belief that thought and the subsequent operational modes of the reality principle were the chief means of the ego (which he especially identified with reason, circumspection, and conscious self-perception) to control behavior. He considered a sense of omnipotence, a quasi-hallucinatory wish-projection of grandeur, an early trait of the pleasure-ego that was incapable of development and never completely lost. From a philosophical viewpoint, this teaching of Freud squared very well with the more explicit definition of man's central hierarchical position in earlier Aristotelian-scholastic thought. It is man's inescapable wish to be omnipotent that actually substantiates this position philosophically.

The similarities are even more pronounced in comparing the nature of the body and bodily processes. Aristotle and the scholastics had recognized the body as possessing a principle of activity also. This doctrine of the body was present in Plato and was developed by Aristotle. The body sought pleasure and wished to avoid pain. It was always or most always in conflict with the rational principle of man. It was capable of the most heinous crimes in order to satisfy its needs. Aquinas referred to the concupiscible appetite whereby man was seeking pleasure on a subjective basis. The motions of concupiscence were always directed toward the fulfillment of pleasurable desires. The irascible appetite was the result of frustration of pleasure-seeking. Just as the concupiscible appetite was seeking to incorporate pleasurable objects, so the irascible appetite was attempting to remove unpleasant objects. The object of the concupiscible appetite and the irascible appetite was the quest for subjective good or the avoidance of subjective evil. In their constant quest for good, the sense appetites of man employed the internal sense of imagination, common sense, aestimative force (instinct), and memory as well as the rational appetite of the will. All desire was sparked by the imagery that existed through the sensory process in the internal senses of man. A thing could not be desired unless it were first known. And, thus, in a very real sense, perception was the cause of the particular means chosen by the appetites to satisfy their desires.

Both Aristotle and the scholastics recognized the vast depths of the motivating instinctual nature of man and the manner in which these basic instincts could turn and twist man's rational activities to their own use. But the real difference in the psychology of scholasticism as contrasted with that of Brentano and Freud is the criterion of effective behavior represented by reason. The scholastics held a divinely inspired criterion of revelation and ecclesiastical regulation as the norm toward which man should direct his rational behavior. For Brentano, the norm was informed reason, and for Freud it was informed reason shaped by environmental influences. Freud's views in this matter more directly approximate the views of Spinoza. Spinoza denied the necessity of there being sin between objective and subjective goods. Since he identified the two under the concept of substance, the only evil was a lack of knowledge. Man acts according to instinctual drives because of his nature. His nature is not inherently evil or inherently good, but indifferent. Evil is when man's rational operation is overcome by instinctual drives without a knowledge and control of these drives. When man knows the relationship between his own desires and the rest of the world, he may not be able to abrogate these desires but, at least, he can modify them through knowledge.

Thus the position of intentional metaphysics regarding the body as variously represented in the scholastics, Spinoza, and Brentano was that (1) there is a principle of pleasure-seeking in man which is variously termed appetites, passions, sensual movements or instincts; (2) this principle strives to seek pleasure and to avoid evil by incorporating objects it desires and avoiding objects it rejects; (3) this principle holds subjective good as the ultimate end and is frequently in conflict with the rational principle in man; (4) the control of this principle is dependent on knowledge which is chiefly gained through a correct appraisal of reality.

Freud's teaching on these points is explicitly similar. He held that there was an all-pervading pleasure principle in man. He identified this pleasure principle with the fundamental process of the organism whereby object-cathexes would reduce the internal tension of the organism. This fundamental primary process, proceeding from unconscious substrata of the psyche, was a quasi-biological, quasi-ideational force of energy which he termed instinct. Instincts constantly sought to allay internal tension through the incorporation of objects. He further insisted that the pleasure principle was always seeking subjective good and was frequently in conflict with reality. It thus had to be controlled, and the whole evolution of psychic through processes of memory, attention, and judgment represented the ideational means for control that had been evolved over countless generations. And finally, through self-realization in psychoanalysis, it was possible to arrive at a moderation, if not complete control, of the pleasure principle.

The similarities that have been identified in this chapter between Freud and the intentionalistic teaching of Brentano are made simply to establish the philosophical and intellectual continuity that existed between these two individuals. Obviously, there was a good deal of this common knowledge within the *Weltanschauung* of this period. Moreover, the comparisons that have been made do not suggest that Freud simply translated older ideas into new forms but, instead, indicate that, building on a basic philosophical approach, Freud developed a technique for therapy. No one before Freud had worked out a system of therapy equivalent to psychoanalysis. The genius of Freud resided in his unique ability to translate older concepts into a dynamic system of psychotherapy.

From a philosophical viewpoint, however, the specific similarities between Brentano and Freud may be delineated under four categories: (1) the problem of knowledge, (2) the object of knowledge, (3) the subject of knowledge, and (4) the use of knowledge. It is appropriate here to present some concluding propositions for the purpose of focusing the specific and unique similarities that exist between Brentano and Freud.

The Problem of Knowledge

1. *Brentano and Freud both maintained that the knowledge of reality is a psychological problem and that in a sense all knowledge and science is dependent on psychological factors.*

2. *They both insisted that psychology is a bona fide branch of science and that the true methodology of psychology is that of natural science.* Of course, they differed on the extension or degree to which this natural knowledge could be extended. Brentano insisted that through philosophy, which he identified with natural science, it was possible to deduce the existence of God and the immortality of the human soul. Freud denied this possibility. But both of them agreed that there was only *one* kind of knowledge, and this was the knowledge of science. There was no second or third kind of higher knowledge that was to be known through intuition, innate ideas, or theology.

3. *They both maintained that psychology had profound implications not only for man individually but for the progress of civilization.* Much in both Brentano and Freud recalled Spinoza's statement that there was nothing so useful to man as man himself, and that through knowledge and understanding men could live together with a community of ideals and goals. Brentano felt that a knowledge of psychology was the key to education, social science, understanding on an international scale, and to language itself. Freud also realized the importance of psychology in all these areas. He maintained that psychoanalysis could not provide a universal remedy, but he indicated emphatically that it was better than idealistic philosophy or religion.

The Object of Knowledge

1. Brentano and Freud both maintained that *every cognition of man refers to a real and existing thing, and is object oriented or goal centered.* Neither Brentano nor Freud denied the validity of an external world of reality. Both of them held with Descartes, Leibnitz, and Spinoza that empirical experience played a major role in the formation of cognition. But if Brentano and Freud denied the innate ideas of Leibnitz, they also denied the *tabula rasa* of Locke. Brentano and Freud both assumed the efficient causal connection between extraorganic reality and the sensory stimulation of man's external and internal senses. Brentano acknowledged the external senses and also the faculties of memory and imagination. But these were not distinct faculties in the sense of the scholastic philosophy. Nor were they innate potencies in the sense of Leibnitz; they were simple acts of conscious perception by which man recognized the sensory stimulations effected by external objects. Freud held a similar view. He spoke of memory and imagination, of the faculty of notation whereby man screens the products of external reality. He provided the preconscious as a receptacle for memory and sense images. But in both men there was no question of the existence of internal faculties as such.

2. *All psychic activity is meaningful, intentional in the sense of self-involvement, and is cognitively known through the medium of consciousness.* Thus Brentano and Freud never agreed with the passive concept of experience enunciated by Locke. Theirs was a dynamic and active empiricism as contrasted with Locke's passive empiricism. For Locke's theory results in a concept of passive impregnation of meaning by experience. In Brentano as well as Freud it is the inherent capacity of the receiving mind reaching out toward external objects that contributes the *factor of meaning.* Meaning in intentional metaphysics refers to a subjective phenomenon whose content may be based in part on experience, but whose form is distinctly subjective and individual.

3. *Again, Brentano and Freud both taught that the focal point of psychic activity was the intentional image.* Brentano saw the intentional image as the production of perception impressed and guided by a secondary consciousness (consciousness referring to the recognition of one's own involvement in perceiving). *The psychic image was what it was because of the soul's constant participation or involvement.* Freud's theory of perception, particularly his notion of

energy and object-cathexes, is essentially a physicalistic explanation of a philosophical doctrine. Freud uses energy in terms that, in some ways, could be interpreted as synonymous with soul, that is, in the Aristotelian sense of prime mover. For Freud, energy in the bodily system was the basic force of the human body. It is directed in many ways, but it never completely ceases as long as life is present. Hence, it is in reality the basic substratum of the psychic processes as well as the bodily ones. It is the focus of a specific quantity of energy on an object-cathexis that produces the particular motivational attraction of the object-image. In both explanations, perception is conditioned by inner needs.

The Subject of Knowledge

1. *Brentano and Freud both maintained that the basic structure of human existence was subjectivity or intentionality and that the perceptory act of the mind is characterized by an immanent power of self-reflection.* Although Brentano held that the soul or psyche was the vital principle of psychic energy, and Freud held that physical energy was this source, both agreed that the whole structure of human existence was created by perception that mirrored both the subjective drives of man and the reaction processes evolved to cope with the pressures of reality. Brentano spoke of instinct as the first and most predominant drive of man. He reviewed how man first possessed a hazy self-concept and how this was developed through the gradual introduction to reality. Freud spoke in a similar vein, producing the topological divisions of the psyche into id, ego, and superego. Freud endowed the ego with certain volitional characteristics, maintaining that it was the coherent organization of self-concepts—concepts that in many individuals were impaired by the conflicting demands of instinct, superego, and external reality. Moreover, this coherent organization of the self, which possesses a capability for unity of action and control, is strikingly similar to the notion of the rational will.

Again, with regard to the superego, Freud stated that its functions were self-observation (or the power of immanent reflection), conscience, and the holding up of ego ideals. Thus both in Brentano and Freud the subjectivity of the human mind is mirrored in certain immanent powers of the mind for reflection and self-guidance.

2. *Brentano and Freud also maintained that the cognitive structure of man was permeated or ensconced with emotional tonality.* This is to say that in the progressive evolution of the psychic structure, instinctual force or emotional tonality is present in each and every

psychic act. It is present, first, in the original production, the intentional image or object-cathexis. And second, this object-cathexis is always subject to the operation of secondary consciousness—or in Freud's terms—ego and superego functions.

The Use of Knowledge

1. *Both Brentano and Freud recognized that man is the normative measure of reality; and that man's judgment as informed by insightful reason is the criterion of ethical conduct.*

2. *They also recognized that ethical conduct depended on the analysis of the psychic processes.* Thus the character of reasonable judgments, as distinguished from prejudicial ones, is above all a question of psychological apprehension and self-determination. Neither Brentano nor Freud held any brief for a universal natural law that was a priori cognizable by all men. They held rather with Spinoza that man's fulfillment of his own being was the highest ethical imperative, and that everything that contributed to this was good, everything that stood in the way of it, evil. Furthermore, they maintained that knowledge was power and virtue and that if man could but know the origin of his instinctual drives, and could understand them, then, he could take measures to cope with them. Finally, they were both in accord that the essence of ethical conduct was *responsibility*, a responsibility that forced the individual to forego his own immediate gratification for the cause of humanity.

3. *Brentano and Freud were both determinists with regard to psychic phenomena, but this was only a relative determinism not an absolute one.* Although there is plenty of evidence to affirm the contention that both men supported psychic determinism, neither the one nor the other maintained that man was thereby absolved of moral responsibility. Although man was determined by his instinctual needs and the demands of reality, he could through proper self-knowledge, through the equalization of contrary desires, and through the utilization of scientific knowledge arrive at a balance where a limited amount of free choice was available. But it was only at the highest level of sophistication that this choice and consequent responsibility revealed itself. In this aspect of their teachings they both resemble Leibnitz, who had said that we are free only insofar as we are ignorant of the deepest necessities that underly our "free choices." Thus determinism in psychic life can be squared with moral responsibility. Otherwise, law is meaningless.

These similarities between Brentano and Freud would seem to indicate some kind of a relationship. Since influence cannot be documented, it is most likely that the relationship was a student-teacher one. What seems to have happened is that Brentano left with his students the intellectual seeds of ideas to be developed. His students cultivated these ideas and produced both new variations and new creations. Through Stumpf evolved one current of *Gestalt* psychology, through Husserl phenomenology. Certainly, no argument is made here that Freud did not develop psychoanalysis but, instead, that many of the ideas of his teacher were susceptible to reworking in the theoretical formulations of psychoanalysis. Brentano's orientation was philosophical, Freud's couched in the terminology of physiology and physics. Although neither *Gestalt* psychology, phenomenology, nor psychoanalysis were the creations of Brentano, it would seem that they are, nevertheless, concrete testimonials to the intelligence, creativity, and teaching of a great and usually underestimated man.

THE INFLUENCE OF FREUD

The impact of Freud on the course of modern civilization has been great. An acquaintance with Freud's thought has become one of the hallmarks of a college education. Whether this acquaintance comes through a study of literature, sociology, psychology, or education, it is usually found in one or more collegiate fields of study. More specifically, there are three areas of influence that should be detailed here: (1) Freud's influence on the practice of psychotherapy, (2) his influence in psychology itself, and (3) his influence on clinical and counseling psychology.

Freud and Psychotherapy

Although the theoretical framework for much of Freud's concept of psychotherapy came from philosophical sources, it should be recognized that Freud also derived a considerable reservoir of information with regard to scientific procedures from his physiological studies. Although Freud was never much of a success in experimental research, according to Jones and, had to be prodded by Bruecke to complete his medical degree, it is a fact that the system of psychotherapy that Freud initiated was based on medical technology. Medical practice called for a step-by-step procedure in the approach to pathology. These steps entailed diagnosis, prognosis, and treatment. Through observation of the patient it was possible to form a working hypotheses about the patient from a combination of observation and clinical tests. Thus medical doctors were then and still are trained to observe carefully the presenting symptoms of the patient. Subsequent tests could provide further information that would help the physician to form his working hypothesis regarding the nature of the physical disorder. Essentially, it is the skilled know-how of the physician who can determine what a pain in the chest means. On the basis of the verbal report of the patient, his past history, and the clinical or laboratory tests that may be available, the physician makes a diagnosis. He also includes in this judgmental process a prognosis that estimates the possible alternative ways in which the problem may be terminated. On the basis of accurate diagnosis and prognosis a treatment procedure may be administered that is designed to relate to the diagnosis and prognosis. If one treatment procedure does not effect the expected outcome, another may be tried. If all treatments fail, it may be an indication that the original diagnosis was inaccurate. This calls for further exploration and a new diagnosis.

This approach was adopted by Freud in the development of psychoanalysis as a therapy or treatment vehicle. His theoretical framework regarding the unconscious, the role of instincts, and personality dynamics was the basis for the diagnostic probes, the prognostic speculations, and the treatment procedures.

At first Freud made use of hypnosis, but subsequently he abandoned this approach in favor of a relaxation procedure in which individuals free-associated and revealed their thoughts and attitudes. Closely allied to this procedure was dream analysis. Thus Freud utilized the raw material productions of the patient to gain insight into the underlying causes of their problems. Once the psychoanalyst had made a diagnosis and prognosis, he could proceed to the treatment, which was basically related to an interpretation process. The psychoanalyst interpreted the basic dynamics of the patient in terms of the resistances and repressions that were creating the problems experienced by the patient. The ultimate aim of this treatment, despite varying diagnoses, was to help the patient understand the causes of his problems, to provide a clinical insight into behavior disorders and deficits that, it was assumed, would help the patient to make the necessary cognitive changes. Insofar as the analyst could help, he was expected to reinforce the patient in his efforts to change his thinking *and* his behavior.

Freud's basic ideas and technology have been widely disseminated. Whether one focuses on the early collaborators of Freud, such as Adler, Jung, and Rank, or the later neo-Freudians, such as Horney, Ellis, and Sullivan, the essential procedures of psychotherapy do not differ very much. There is a basic recognition of the central role of the analyst in the diagnosis, prognosis, and treatment phase of the procedure. Insight is postulated as a goal of the treatment procedure, and the end result in mind is a change in the behavior of the patient or client that will take into consideration the understandings provided by the therapist. For this reason, a discussion of the particular varieties in treatment is not initiated in this chapter.[7] As Munroe has stated:

> There is much more common ground among psychoanalytic schools as regards therapy than the outsider realizes as he listens to theories of treatment. Perhaps there is more common ground than the analysts themselves realize since they have a tendency not to talk to one another informally once a serious rift in approach has occurred, and the patient who goes to an analyst of a different school after unsuccessful treatment is very often recriminative and unfair (Monroe, 1955, p. 12).

Freud's theories influenced several generations of psychoanalysts and psychiatrists. Although Alfred Adler, Carl Jung, and Otto Rank were contemporaries of Freud and had their own theories, their contact with Freud certainly can be considered as a source of influence in their writings. Karl Abraham, Sandor Ferenczi, Wilhelm Reich, Wilhelm Stekel, Paul Federn, and Ernest Jones are also famous individuals in the Freudian galaxy. They are considered primary deviations from Freud. In a further generation, and more known to contemporary psychologists, are Harry Stack Sullivan, Albert Ellis, and Karen Horney. According to Monroe (1955, 13), Sullivan was influenced by Ferenczi's approach and by the approach of Franz Alexander. Abraham influenced Erich Fromm and Melanie Klein. There are differences between each of these authorities as to what they retain from Freud and what they add to Freud's approaches. Some of the more liberal psychoanalysts emphasize interpersonal relations and self-concept theory, whereas others emphasize the roles of instinctual drives on sex and aggression. The differences in emphasis do, of course, lead to differences in treatment, but these differences would appear to be more related to the personality of the specific school of thought and its leader than to actual definable differences in techniques.

In keeping with the basic medical approach of diagnosis, prognosis, and treatment, psychoanalytic theory is typically characterized by a detailed analysis of childhood history, the home, parents, and environment,

---

[7] A complete discussion of the varieties of Freudian and Neo-Freudian theory and treatment procedures is not appropriate to the purpose of this book. As will be recalled, the primary purpose of this work is to delineate the philosophical foundations of counseling theories. The differences that exist between Freud and his followers are found more in relationship to specific emphases and treatment than in basic philosophical assumptions.

an exploration into neuropathic traits such as depression, nail-biting, thumb-sucking, enuresis, truancy, and sudden emotional reactions, and a complete family and personal history. Physical diseases, physical symptoms, and present complaints are all integrated into the diagnostic process. The patient's behavior during the interview, his movements, speech, mood, and emotional lability are all looked at carefully in order to infer the question of present conscious functioning. Conscious thought processes and particularly dreams are scrutinized to determine the nature of repressed concepts. Over a period of time, other test findings have been added to psychoanalytic therapy, including the results of the Rorschach test, word associations, and the analysis of defense mechanisms.

A complete literature has developed that spells out the nature of defense mechanisms and the categories of neurosis. The most elaborate and comprehensive of all the compendiums of Freudian investigations is still to be found in Otto Fenichel's *The Psychoanalytic Theory of Neurosis* (1945).

The traditional mainstream of psychoanalytic thought has tended to continue within the practice of medicine. An overwhelming number of those Neo-Freudians who have modified Freud's system have been medical practitioners. Although Freud himself endorsed the notion of lay analysis, this has not been the case in the United States. The elements of Freud's basic system, including the hypothesis of the unconscious, some degree of reliance on instinct theory, intentionality, and the concepts of intra-psychic conflict are present in all of the variations. For the most part, psychoanalytic therapy views the patient as suffering from a disability. The therapist functions as a doctor, utilizing both clinical methods of medicine and psychoanalytic theory to effect the proper treatment. Aside from the direct psychiatric involvement, the vast majority of medical practitioners have absorbed a considerable amount of information about defense mechanisms, psychosomatic disorders, and the like.

Freud and Psychology

Freud's influence on psychology has been considerable. This influence has been felt chiefly through the areas of personality theory, abnormal psychology, and clinical psychology. The theory of intentionality together with the hypothesis of the unconscious and unconscious determinism becomes the theoretical basis for the explanation of defense mechanisms such as repression, rationalization, and projection. Although Freud did not enunciate all of the defense mechanisms outlined in textbooks today, he did present the framework from which they could be developed. Defense mechanisms assume an intra-psychic conflict that is resolved by some kind of goal-alteration, goal-repression, or use of force. Freud's theoretical framework also provided a considerable basis for the development of projective techniques. Although Freud did not invent the Rorschach, it can be said that his psychodynamics have consistently provided the rationale for the development of projective psychology. The *Id-Ego-Superego* test (I. E. S.) and the *Blacky Picture Test* are two recent examples of testing instruments that have been based chiefly on Freudian psychodynamics.

Clinical psychology and, to a large extent, psychiatric social work have become the direct heirs of psychoanalytic theory and therapy outside of the medical field. Clinical psychology traditionally took as one of its bases of operation the application of psychology through the professional relationship to problems of abnormal psychology. Drawing heavily on psychoanalytic theory, clinicians also utilized the correlative procedures of Charcot and Kraepelin in order to collate the behavioral symptoms of similar-type patients and to generalize these behaviors into diagnostic syndromes. Clinical psychology incorporated into the repertory of psychoanalytic procedures a strong reliance on projective techniques and test interpretations. With the need for clinical psychologists after the last world war, governmental subsidies created an impetus for the training of clinicians. Clinical psychology came to represent both an art and a science, with a heavy emphasis being placed on the clinical learnings that took place in dealing with actual patients.

CHANGES IN HEALING: HEALING AND PSYCHOTHERAPY

Two separate movements are worthy of note in the development of a scientific approach to healing and to the problems of mental disturbance. They are the development of a recognition of the power of man's mind over illness, and the changes that took place in the custodial treatment of mentally disturbed and retarded children.

The first of these movements was tied in originally to pseudo-psychological ideas. In the 16th century and thereafter certain individuals became aware of the fact that the mind has a great deal to do with predisposing individuals toward illness. Of course, even Plato and Aristotle, and especially the infirmary-type treatments of Hippocrates and Galen, had recognized this principle to a large extent and thus had developed places of rest with running water, hot baths, music, and other relaxing activities. But this kind of bodily indulgence was not in accord with the medieval Christian assumption about mental illness, wherein mental illness had been considered a punishment from God, the result of sin, to be exorcised with elaborate religious ritual. Moreover, some of the medieval religious practices also included medical practices, such as the use of leeches to draw blood, and other remedies that more often killed than cured. In last extremes, the mentally disturbed were chained, restrained in dungeons, and treated with cruelty. These are generalizations that summarize in the main much of the treatment accorded to the mentally ill. There were, of course, many hospitals and infirmaries run by nuns or brothers under religious auspices that attempted to provide for the poor, the senile, and the physically and mentally infirm. From what we now know about spontaneous remission of mental illness, it is more than likely that there was some limited success in these institutions.

The recognition of the effect of the human mind on mental and physical illness became more evident during the 17th and 18th centuries. Baptista Porta about 1600 was known to have used a magnet that had some healing properties. He was stopped by the Roman Rota from practicing medicine. Moreover, it was most probable that he was utilizing some form of hypnotism. Mesmer (1733–1815) perfected some of these techniques. Mesmer believed that the planets exerted some type of magnetism on the body. Utilizing a salon with background music, flowing robes, and magical passes at individuals, he allegedly cured many people. Although Mesmer was considered a fake by many, his methods did lead to the development of hypnotism as a method for coping with the mental and physical problems of patients. James Braid in 1841 read a paper to the British Medical Association in which he claimed to have cured under hypnosis many diseases, for example, rheumatism, paralysis, and epilepsy. These observations were noted by Charcot and others who continued some of these methods with considerable success.

The second movement is the systematic development of psychiatry. Philippe Pinel (1745–1826), influenced by the liberal ideas of Rousseau and contact with Itard, tried new methods. Unchaining many patients he achieved such success by providing them with better food and talking with them that he was appointed to take over the Salpetriere. As the 19th century progressed, considerable progress was made within psychiatry. W. Griesinger (1817–1868) in accordance with the predominant physiological school of thought stemming from Müller insisted that mental diseases were diseases of the brain. This is the same influence that Freud felt under Bruecke at Vienna. Considerable support was provided for this position in the discovery of the effects of morphine, Sergei Korsakov's study of alcoholism, and Richard Krafft-Ebbing's experiments relating to syphilis.

Emil Kraepelin (1855–1926), an early student of Wundt, summarized what was known of psychiatry in a textbook first published in 1883. He divided mental diseases into those that were caused by external circumstances or conditions and those that were related to internal factors. Krapelin's manual provided the standard basis for psychiatric treatment for many years.

In the examination of hysterics, an area in which Freud was interested, Jean Martin Charcot (1825–1893) pioneered in the use of hypnosis. Freud studied with Charcot for some months and initially used some of Charcot's methods. Pierre Janet (1859–1947) continued some of the work of Charcot, but he integrated it with the ever-increasing flow of clinical evidence regarding the complexity of mental illness.

It became evident, however, that psychiatry alone would not be able to guide the entire mental health movement. Freud's great contribution, though he was a medical doctor, was to provide a systematic nonmedical framework for approaching many problems of mental health. The approach that he generated was not a complete one. The theory on which it was based was partially empirical, and partially physiological. Working with cases that interested him, he did not systematically exclude other hypotheses, and he knew comparatively little about learning theory as such. As a result, he tended to ascribe considerable influence to the unconscious determinants of man, to consider symptoms the visible effects of repression, and to retain a certain amount of medical methodology in his effort to extirpate the causal roots of problems rather than to treat the symptoms. His followers took his theoretical framework, changed elements of it, and emphasized other features, but essentially they remained with his basic philosophical outlook. Assumptions that tended to guide the whole movement were related to the need for personal psychoanalytical experience, the primary position of cognitive understanding as a priority for behavior change, the recognition and dependency on defense mechanisms, symbolic interpretation, and the recognition of the essential illogical associationist approach of basic primary drives in symptom formation.

PRIMARY AND SECONDARY DERIVATIONS OF FREUD

Many continuing contributions were made to the clinical method begun by Freud. A host of scholars, researchers in psychotherapy, and teachers succeeded Freud's efforts. But essentially, the ideological framework of Freud, the assumptions of methodology and attack, and the philosophical framework remain intact. The contributions of these individuals are so important to the development of a clinical framework for the nonmedical practitioner in psychology that they can each be studied as scholars in their own right. For summary purposes here, their contribution will be noted, but the reader interested in detailed analyses of their ideas and specific variations from Freudian theory should consult works that more specifically treat of them. Conceptually and methodologically, I believe that they belong with Freud.

Three individuals are identified as primary derivations from Freud. Actually, two of them can be considered as original sources of alternative approaches which, to some extent, impinge on and were influenced by Freud. These three primary individuals are Alfred Adler, Otto Rank, and Carl Jung. In addition, there are three other individuals who are considered today as Neo-Freudians or, possibly, as secondary derivations of Freudian thought. They are Albert Ellis, Karen Horney, and Harry Stack Sullivan.

Alfred Adler (1870–1937)

Alfred Adler cannot really be said to have been a disciple of Freud. He was never a student of Freud, but he was invited to attend Freud's discussion group—not as a student—but as an equal. Adler was hesitant to join this group because of obvious differences in belief, and after a stormy 10 years he withdrew.

Adler's approach to psychotherapy appears to be summed up by the concept of movement. He believed that all movements were goal directed, that psychic life as such was determined by goals. The actions necessary to achieve the goal are inevitable, but man is free to change his goal, therefore, he has free will. Only living, moving organisms have a soul or free will, but environmental influences form the attitude that man has toward life (Adler, 1957). Since to Adler the psychic life is a "complex of aggressive and security-finding activities whose final purpose is to guarantee the continued existence . . . of the human organism, and to enable him to securely accomplish his development" (1957, p. 8), these two forces, the movement to develop an attitude toward life, become goal-directed behavior. This is in contrast to the sexual basis of behavior so strongly asserted by Freud.

The Adlerian movement in the United States has recognized that behavior is subject to "environmental press" considerations, and that consequences of behavior should be taught to individuals. The popularity of the movement in counseling circles may be ascribed to the fact that Adler and his disciples did grasp some very real contingencies regarding learning, but the adulation that Adlerian followers have had for their founder has sent them back continually to find chapter and verse in the writings of their founder, instead of seeking for newer scientific explanations of the empirical phenomena that Adler fairly intuitively grasped rather than defined.

The psychology of Freud is frequently referred to as tough minded and deterministic, while that of Adler is tender minded and individualistic. This would lead us to question whether the Neo-Freudians are not really Neo-Adlerian, since they too tend to be tender minded and individualistic. The similarities between Adler's life plan, Gestaltist wholeness of life, Lewin's field theories, and existentialist spontaneous life are also quite obvious. Truly, the number of commonly accepted psychological concepts that can be traced to Adler is astonishing.

One of Adler's main contributions to thought was his concept of the natural or universal inferiority complex. Since the human infant is dependent long after he becomes aware of his helplessness, all children develop inferiority feelings. The movement of life goal then becomes one of compensating for these feelings of inferiority. Although organ defects can complicate the inferiority feelings, these too can be overcome or even compensated for by the efforts of the individual. This is the beginning of the life plan.

Another contribution, the family constellation, is the basis of many child guidance centers today. The first born is usually independent, conventional, authoritarian, and law abiding. Sometimes the arrival of a second child can dethrone the first born and can cause a reversal of these qualities. The second child is expected to be a rebel, unconventional, a discoverer, and sometimes even extremely naughty. Or if the first born sets too high a standard, the second may become apathetic and a daydreamer. The youngest child may become a buffoon or family pet and may suffer from work or career difficulties. Or not being threatened by another arrival, he may become the most successful family member.

A third contribution was a rather different interpretation of neurosis. Adler interpreted it as an exploitation of a shocking or threatening experience to justify avoiding life's duties. Although both Freud and Adler used detection and unmasking in the treatment of this malady, Freud would sometimes accomplish it by laying the patient on a couch and by probing deeply into his unconscious, but would confront the patient with his self-deceptive tendencies in a face-to-face situation, compelling the patient to take full responsibility for his own actions.

A fourth contribution was the concept of masculine protest. Since men and women are equal in their ability, much human resource is being wasted by a false evaluation of women. Cultural control has discouraged women and has hampered their achievement of compensation for their supposed inferiority. Resentment and a deep sense of deprivation often cause women to become frigid and unsatisfactory sex partners or to refuse marriage altogether. Also, some men overstress their masculinity to prove their superiority over women if they have no other satisfactory means of achievement. This may be the cause of slavery, war, and hate.

A fifth contribution, social interest, remains a fairly evasive one, but is inherent in most of Adler's philosophy. It means about the same as "love thy neighbor," and is a natural component in each man's goal. It is a continuum from much to none. The neurotic lacks in amount and the criminal may be without any. This is why the criminal may be difficult to cure. The idea of social interest crystallized during Adler's war duty and has certain religious and political connotations, although Adler diligently guarded against any alignment or infiltration of either of them into his system of psychology.

Another contribution that should be mentioned here relates to delinquency. A delinquent child tries to get his own way by hurting others, a neurotic child by making himself a burden; dreams are a way of spurring one's self on toward one's goal or are a warning of obstacles; the choice of earliest memory is an indication of life plan.

Since Adler believed in every individual's right to a creative life, he viewed with deep apprehension any attempt to standardize or to force the minds of human beings into a mold, or to take away from them their personal responsibility for every act. However, life goals and, therefore, character and personality are to some degree controlled and changed by society. It is our job, then, to make sure that these influences are conducive to the maximal development of each individual. The implication seems to be that schools and counselors have a grave responsibility in the formation of the life style of each child, since education can and does affect and condition it.

Otto Rank (1884–1939)

Otto Rank, an Austrian psychoanalyst, was born in 1884. He was not a medical doctor but was trained in philosophy, psychology, history, engineering, and art. Rank was a student of Freud and was assigned to explore the analytic theory in the area of culture. After 20 years, Rank left Freud to develop his own techniques, which he called "psychotherapy" instead of "psychoanalysis." He severely criticized the fundamental concepts of Freud.

Rank's break with Freud brought a new approach to personality development. Of the Freudian theories, Rank advanced the birth trauma. There is little proof that Freud's position influenced Rank. Rank's research however may have led Freud to publish his major book on birth trauma.

The birth trauma is the decisive concept in Rank's approach to personality. Munroe states (1955, 576):

Rank felt that the change from the encompassing, effortless bliss of the womb to the painful hurly-burly of postnatal conditions requiring initiative from the infant—a change during which the infant experiences mortal fear—was actually determining for life: as a consequence of it, the most normal among us carry a load of primal anxiety. The human goal is reinstatement of embryonic bliss—the greatest human terror is separation. The overwhelming trauma of birth experience is repressed.

According to Rank the crucial stage occurs when the child is first separated from the mother. The infant experiences fear and reacts in two basic ways: (1) he may try to reinstate the close bond with his mother. This reaction is the major factor in the etiology of the infant's needs. (2) The reaction may cause future attempts to achieve further separation.

The conflict that develops from these two basic reactions is the need for dependence versus the will to grow and become independent.

Rank considered the separation and union as partialization and totality. To grow, a person must break down the image of totality as a means of adaptation to reality. The totality is broken down into partialization along lines that are meaningful for the child.

From Munroe's writings another influential force is explained. As a child, the integrative power of personality as a whole is the "will." Rank believed "will to be the consequence of being born and living, a necessary development of human organism."

The will becomes important as a means of individualization. As the will develops, feelings of guilt are aroused. According to Munroe, Rank believed that the resolution of this guilt becomes the human ideal and goal for psychotherapy. The person must regain a unity with the world in which he lives similar to the unity that existed before birth. This reintegration is best accomplished by love. The parent with love and understanding accepts the will of the child as the child uses it to identify his individuality in an external world. The will can be accepted even more fully in the loving sexual partner. Because of mutual love there is no feeling of guilt.

Rank thought of the person who gained a reintegration as an "artist." Those who failed to achieve were normal men or neurotic. A normal man or a neurotic adapted widely to the demands of society. No conflict exists because the average man or the neurotic never thought of doing anything but conforming to a set pattern. The relationship to society is the same as the unborn to the womb. Rank's choice of the term "artist" is to convey a sense of creative integration as the highest goal of man. The neurotic cannot bring together his strivings for individuality and the demands inflicted by the external world. He has tried harder than the average man but has failed, perhaps because one or more of his drives was mishandled. The neurotic may choose one of two means of adapting. He may throw his whole ego into every experience with which he comes in contact because he fears separation. The dominating force is the fear of differentiation. His other choice is to try to keep his ego apart from life experiences. Fearing separation and individualization, he becomes detached from the world in which he lives.

The main source of emotional disturbances stems from the child's confusion as to his own identity. To aid the child in adjustment, the therapist assumes the role of the permissive, understanding adult. Major emphasis is placed on the child's feelings, and attempts are made to help him to accept the responsibility for his actions. Only then is he able to overcome his anxieties and feelings of guilt which are rooted in the separation at birth.

The major impact of Rank's theory on American psychological thinking has been through the field of social work. In the late 1920s, his theories were being used in social work for helping troubled families to adjust. Rank lectured in New York and Philadelphia. His views had a profound influence on the development of psychotherapy, counseling, education, and other nonmedical fields in which psychological insight is required.

Carl G. Jung (1875–1961)

Carl G. Jung took his medical degree at the University of Basel after abandoning his plans to be an archeologist. After studying under Pierre Janet in Paris, he joined the Psychiatric Clinic at the University of Zurich. At that time he gave his first series of lectures in America. He was later to become associated with Freud. Jung was the first president of the International Psychoanalytic Association. In 1916 as a result of differences in Jung's and Freud's theories, Jung broke with the psychoanalytic group.

Jung changed his early approach and became one of the most "antiscientific" analysts. His "libido," life energy or life, is the underlying principle of the human soul or psyche. Sexuality is one of its manifestations. Essentially it is a creative force. After sexual (genital) distinction has taken place, no longer is sex essential to all libidinal expression. There are three stages of development: first, the nutritional or sucking; second, the presexual period; and third, the puberty occupation of the sexual zone. There is gradual transition from one stage to the next that requires a sacrifice of the child-self or "hero" who has deep longings. The sacrifice is followed by the rebirth of the hero as a full man. The parent is the chief object of love, and the mother becomes a symbol of the source of life. Since the child must go into the real world but does not want to do so, there is a certain and varying amount of nostalgia for the mother, often identified as the Good Mother, Witch, or Divine Harlot.

With this progress into maturity the libido may take one of two directions: the introversive (concerned with the inner world), and the extroversive (outgoing). Both of these are present, but one direction is more dominant than the other. If a person were an extrovert, he would adjust to his environment easily. His nature is extensive but not intensive, and he never searches his soul. He resists anything that introspects and does not want to know anything about that side of himself. His unconscious is full of repressed tendencies that are infantile because of lack of expression. The extroverts think but do not feel; they construct and are impersonal. Feeling is repressed. But life is not all logic, and at times this repressed feeling may force itself out, and then we get the infantile reaction. The introvert keeps so many thoughts and feelings within himself that external objects may fill him with fear. However, he *wants* to maintain his freedom of action, but the dominance of the external object may force repression, resulting in possible panic. The thoughts and ideas of the extrovert arise from the external objects; those of the introvert arise from within himself.

Jung felt that there are four basic functions of activity, namely, thinking, feeling, sensation, and intuition. *Feeling* is the appreciation of values and sometimes a mood; it is subjective. Intensity of feeling may result in emotion. *Thinking* tells us what the thing is, *sensation* tells us that the thing is, and *intuition* what it may be. These work in pairs: feeling and thinking, sensation and intuition. One of these pairs is dominant in the individual; the other is repressed. This, again, is not conducive to good health.

Jung believed in symbols in one's life which may be in dreams, visions, fantasies, and art. These symbols may actually reflect the feeling of the individual and may indicate his major trend for the future. Jung even goes farther to advance that these symbols may refer to remote past events, far removed in time, that relate to the present. He calls this the "collective unconscious." These events, he thinks, are powerful psychological trends rooted in man's biological makeup even to ancient experiences of the race.

Munroe writes (1958, 548):

> The shadow represents the unconscious . . . the dark side, the unconscious obverse of whatever trends the person has emphasized in his ego consciousness, in the active trend of his living . . . our shadows are intimately related to us as the dark reflection of our conscious

efforts . . . It reflects the universals of human experience and is "personal" only in so far as each individual draws differently upon the primitive human within all personalities.

Also deeply concealed in the unconscious, Jung believes, are found a sexual contra part—anima in the man, animus in the woman. These contra parts are essential to wholesome living and are shown in personality by such as the loving, nurturing principle in the male and the domineering, dictatorial tendency of the woman. Too much identification with or too great denial of these two factors may cause neurotic disturbances.

To develop fully one's personality or "self" is a real achievement which Jung feels to be heroic. He believes that heroes are made of common stuff but that a hero has the courage to go his own way and to be faithful to the law of his being, which includes dark forces of the shadow and the collective unconscious (Jung, 1954).

Jung reports (1954, 92–96), "Our aim is the best possible understanding of life as we find it in the human soul." This expresses well a learning technique many use, the understanding of the individual for what he actually is. Jung's philosophy aids one to understand better many traits in character such as feminine traits in the male. The question may arise if these traits such as introversion may not be changed. The answer is in the negative; the type remains the same, since it is fundamental, even biological. Sometimes a false identification of type may be made, and the child may have been twisted against its nature into the opposite type.

As for society, Jung believes that it is very much like a mask, making an impression on the outside and concealing the true nature of the individual on the other. One tries to play the part assigned to him by society as perfectly as possible, for example, one assigned the role of minister must always try to play this in a flawless manner. What goes on behind the mask one calls "private life," and many times there is a drastic contrast between the public and private lives of an individual that is bound to have repercussions on the unconscious. Too often, one may try to imitate some outstanding society figure not in conformity with the true self—the result being the loss of identity and enslavement to surroundings.

The value of Jung's philosophy as related to psychotherapy is still not fully analyzed. Certainly, Jung had some very penetrating cultural insights that may as yet provide an explanation as to why certain types of learning experiences can be assimilated more quickly than others. His concept of the collective unconscious may well be the cultural key to reinforcement patterns.

Albert Ellis (1913–)

According to Albert Ellis, a rational therapist in New York City, the main purpose of psychotherapy is to enable the individual to alter his neurotic behavior. All human emotion is caused and controlled by thinking. All thought can be expressed in terms of "good" and "bad" dimensions. Emotional disturbance results from "bad" thoughts. Bad thoughts (emotional disturbance) must be converted to "good" thoughts (rational thinking). Toward this end, the rational therapist emphasizes "self interest." With the aim of developing a rational approach to living, the rational therapist attempts to attack irrational thoughts and to replace them with rational ones. The system as proclaimed widely by Ellis and his disciples makes great use of intellectual confrontation to force the client to discard the so-called "irrational" or "bad" thoughts (as judged by the therapist) in favor of the "rational" or "good" thoughts (as judged by the therapist).

Ellis believes that our culture is the cause of many irrational ideas, and that the child is subjected to them before he is old enough to reason for himself. Some of these irrational ideas are as follows:

1. It is necessary for an adult to be loved or approved by everyone for everything he does.
2. It is catastrophic when things are not the way one would like them to be.
3. Certain acts are wrong or wicked and severe punishment should always result.
4. If something is, or may be dangerous or fearsome, one should be terribly concerned by it.
5. It is easier to avoid than to face life's difficulties.
6. One needs something stronger than oneself on which to rely.
7. Anyone should be thoroughly competent in *all* areas.
8. If something once affected one's life, it should always affect it to the same degree.
9. We should make every effort to change other people to conform to our ideas.
10. Happiness can be achieved by inertia and inaction.
11. One has virtually no control over one's emotions and one cannot help feeling certain things (Albert Ellis, 1958, 40–42).

Ellis' fundamental philosophy stems from the beliefs of Freud. Ellis, in his "Operational Reformulation of Some of the Basic Principles of Psychoanalysis," attempted to revise Freud's theories into a lower-order level of theorizing. In this process, Ellis eliminated certain of the original principles that have little or no reference to conditions as they exist today. Some of the revised concepts in brief are as follows (Feigl, 1956, 140–151).

Concept of nature of man: Human beings have certain basic needs or drives, such as hunger, sex, and thirst needs, toward the expression of which they inherit tendencies, but which can be modified by experiential reinforcement or social learning.

Concept of values and ethics: When an individual's perception of himself is threatened, he frequently tends to perceive reality in such a distorted way as to convince himself that he is still a "good" or socially approved individual and that his behavior is justified.

Rational behavior under Ellis' interpretation would tend toward social conformity. The definition of rational, as he uses it, is action based on a maximum of undistorted information. Ellis feels that it is desirable for people to think "rationally." A rational philosophy must lead to a more satisfying life than an irrational one. The therapy involves an attempt to show the individual by logic and reason that he is starting with wrong premises and is drawing wrong conclusions from them. Therapy involves a "teaching" and "learning" situation in which the patient is to adopt more rational modes of behavior. It is termed a corrective emotional experience, not technically a therapeutic technique.

Unfortunately, the truths that appear to be present in Ellis' approach to teaching therapy rely heavily on the definition of reason. Commendable as this may be, it tends to place the therapist in the position of defining what is reasonable and what is not reasonable. Inevitable confrontations occur between therapist and client. With practice—and reinforcing success—the therapist becomes more and more convinced that he possesses the truth, the sum of "reason," and inevitably with this conviction he waxes dogmatic, apostolic in his fervor, and ultimately functions as a dogmatic criterion of adjustment excellence.

Karen Horney (1885–1952)

Karen Horney was trained as a Freudian analyst in Germany and came to the United States in the early 1930s. She made a break with the classical psychoanalytic movement and founded a separate association and training institute. Although she considered her theories "corrective" of Freud, she rejected both his instinct theory and his structural theory of the mind (id, ego, superego).

The underlying determining principle for human behavior, according to Horney, is not Freud's instincts of sex and aggression, but the need for security. When the security of the child in relation to his parents reaches unmanageable proportions, he develops an all-pervasive feeling of the world as a hostile and dangerous place. This feeling is what Horney calls "basic anxiety" (Harper, 1959, 63).

Going against Freud's specific biological needs (sexual), Horney places her entire emphasis on the process of adaptation to life situations (mainly interpersonal). Horney feels that her approach is less "pessimistic" than Freud's. She proclaims her belief "that man has the capacity as well as the desire to develop his potentialities and become a decent human being . . . that man can change and go on changing as long as he lives" (Horney, 1945, 19). Especially in her spoken lectures, man's natural wish to enjoy and to expand comes to the fore, in deliberate contrast to the exclusive wish to avoid suffering.

> We believe that inherent in man are evolutionary constructive forces, which urge him to realize his given potentialities. This belief does not mean that man is essentially good—which would presuppose a given knowledge of what is good or bad. It means that man, by his very nature and of his own accord, strives toward self-realization, and that his set of values evolves from such striving (Horney, 1950, 15).

The qualities of the decent human being, the normal person, THE REAL SELF, the "man" in whom one may have faith, are indicated in many pages as the obverse of the neurotic trends that Horney analyzes very carefully. "Neurosis, it may be said, is always a matter of degree—and when I speak of a neurotic I invariably mean a person to the extent that he is neurotic" (1945, 27).

The anxious person develops various strategies to cope with his feelings of isolation and helplessness. Horney speaks of 10 neurotic needs: (1) for affection and approval, (2) for a "partner" who will take over one's life, (3) for restriction of life with narrow borders, (4) for power, (5) for the exploitation of others, (6) for prestige, (7) for personal admiration, (8) for personal achievement, (9) for self-sufficiency and independence, and (10) for perfection and unassailability. Inner conflicts result from the interplay of these neurotic needs.

These 10 neurotic needs, Horney believed, fall under three general headings: (1) moving toward people, (2) moving away from people, and (3) moving against people. The normal person also has a degree of conflict among these three broad categories of needs, but he achieves a considerable degree of balance and integration among them. The neurotic person, however, tends to create an idealized image of himself in which the contradictory trends presumably disappear (but are actually only repressed).

The mainspring of neurotic manifestations is seen by Horney as a basic anxiety. By this term she means "the feeling a child has of being isolated and helpless in a potentially hostile world" (1945, 63–64). The neurotic patterns are considered primarily as the means of handling this anxiety, which is "the most painful experience man can experience." Anxiety tends to be all-pervasive. It is "hidden and subjective." It covertly determines the behavior of the person, regardless of the real dangers, and is therefore often highly injurious.

The infant's helplessness leads not so much to a focused sense of inferiority, with compensation drive to become superior, as to an exacerbated need for security. This is the need that becomes paramount in all neuroses.

Hostility plays a basic role in Horney's thinking. She repudiates any notion of an independent instinct toward death and destruction. The realistic frustration of normal desires directly awakens feelings of hostility. More important for her view of general psychodynamics is the idea that neurotic frustrations self-imposed in the interests of security also awaken feelings of hostility. In both instances, the hostile feelings themselves arouse anxiety.

Horney considers her approach essentially optimistic, with faith in the natural creative potentiality of man at birth and at any stage of his life cycle. The "real self," the central inner force of the individual, which she believed to be the source of free, healthy development of personality potential, is what the actual self can become by the therapeutic overthrow of the idealized self.

Horney's main idea of therapy, therefore, became that of giving the disturbed individual help in fighting the idealized self-image (including all the neurotic needs tied in with this image), in realistically facing the actual self (seeing himself as he now is), and in releasing the real self (that is, replacing the obstructive forces of pride with healthy growth). The idealized image offers a major stumbling block in therapy, according to Horney, because the recognition of these needs as neurotic trends means for the patient a collapse of what he perceives to be his integrity as a person. Yet it is only by putting the patient therapeutically through his "disillusioning process" and thus weakening the obstructive forces, that the therapist helps the patient to release the constructive forces of the real self for healthy growth.

Horney, of course, believed in a more directive and active therapeutic role for the analyst than did Freud and his classical followers. She felt that the various strategies in relation to neurotic needs, the neurotic trends, the glory seekings and pride systems of the idealized self-image, should be interpreted to the patient.

Harry Stack Sullivan (1892–1949)

Harry Stack Sullivan, psychiatrist of Washington, D. C., profoundly influenced psychiatrists, psychologists, and other social scientists in the 20 years before his death in 1949. Sullivan is considered the protagonist of the interpersonal theory of psychiatry. He was chiefly influenced by Adolph Meyer and William Alanson White. Adolf Meyer is believed to be the first psychiatrist in America to deny the separation of mind and body and to conceive personality in functional terms. William A. White was one of the early advocates of Freudian psychology. He had a broader point of view and was more synthetic than either Freud or Meyer. Sullivan felt that White had carried psychiatry from the treatment of the mentally sick to the encompassing study of processes that involve, or go on between people.

Sullivan developed in his years of practice, particularly with schizophrenics, the major thesis that the primary concern of psychiatry is the study of interpersonal relations. He definitely rejected the dividing of the whole person into mind and body, ego, id, superego, or any other fractionizing. He believed that man must be studied as an entity in his environment. But there are two classes of persons in his descriptions of these environmental interactions: the overt or "real," and the eidetic or "imaginary." These classes are not only self-images but real and imaginary "others" that one interrelates with. They include the "good mother" (tension reduction) and the "bad mother" (anxiety experience) concepts carried over from infancy. Another concept, this time of self, developed in infancy is "good me," the self-personification of the aspects of behavior which elicit satisfaction and rewarding increments of tenderness from the important persons in his environment. "Bad me" involves those aspects of behavior which are reacted to by others in such a way as to induce anxiety in the child. Later, there evolves the "not me," the product of intense anxiety, not often communicated with but present in nightmares and in other feelings of primitive horror, which in normal people remain beyond discussion. All of these, along with the sum of learned things, become incorporated into the self system (Sullivan, 1953).

According to Sullivan, experience occurs in three significantly different modes—prototaxic, parataxic, and syntaxic. Prototaxic includes all the experience of the infant's life up to the time he develops a distinctive self. The experiences that one accumulates without conscious effort and that are not necessarily logically thought out, including dreams, are considered parataxic. Syntaxic experience is characterized by "consensual validation," observation, and analysis. Learning is the organization of experience. To learn, one must have the capability, appropriate and useful experience, and a goal to address the learning activity toward. Learning is first caused by anxiety. The gradient of anxiety is important, since severe anxiety obstructs learning. Early learning is a sublimation process. Later it becomes award seeking and punishment avoiding. Other early learning behavior is trial and error by or from human example, for instance, smiling in an infant. This is important because it becomes part of the content of consciousness.

Sullivan felt strongly that man by himself was meaningless. He believed that one becomes a person oneself only in relation to other people, not just as a consequence of what one is by virtue of instinctive drives. Man's acquisition of cultural equipment pertains most closely to his pursuit of security. This includes prestige, wealth, and power. The ultimate success in the cultural evolution brought on in the individual by this drive is the acquisition of self-respect; and, of course, respect for others follows.

> If there is a valid and real attitude toward the self, that attitude will manifest as valid and real towards others. It is not as ye judge so shall ye be judged, but, as you judge yourself so shall you judge others; strange but true so far as I know and with no exception (Sullivan, 1933, p. 15).

One does not find Sullivan using terms like "adjustment" or "conformity." One of his favorite phrases was "interpersonal cooperation," which indicates the dynamic, positive attitude he had toward this subject. His basic hypothesis was that man is healthy only insofar as he is a satisfactorily functioning social being.

SUMMARY AND EVALUATION

Psychoanalytic theory in the model of counseling theories presented in this chapter has been described in terms of the objectivist side of the schema, and with an essentialist frame of reference. It has been placed on the objectivist side because Freud was very much concerned with the modification of man's internal behavior to conform with his public or social behavior. He believed that man's behavior was a result of a balance or a lack of balance between multiple instinctual and internalized forces. His entire course of treatment in psychoanalysis was designed to provide a more rational frame of reference for man in coping with his own instinctual drives in relationship to society.

In addition, Freud posited a number of postulates about the nature of man. Man was determined by a complex series of instinctual drives. Freud observed and explored the nature of the unconscious in man, the clear distinction between fear and anxiety, which most psychologists today still make. He also contributed strongly to the analysis of personality, the evolution of object-relations as they effect the imagery and thinking of man. But, perhaps one of his major contributions was the development of the defense mechanisms in which he posited that various techniques are devised and used by the ego of man to protect itself. He identified the mechanisms of physical and psychic withdrawal, negativism, explored the phenomena of the conversion of mental ailments and problems into physical ones, identified regression as a withdrawal to an earlier stage of behavior more satisfying to the individual and, above all, labeled and explored as fully as he could, the mechanism of repression. Repression, or the unconscious thrusting down of threatening experiences, Freud thought to be at the root of most neurasthenic symptoms such as nervous breakdowns, phobias, obsessions, tics, hysteria, amnesia, paralysis, and other similar phenomena.

Perhaps, the most comprehensive compendium of psychoanalytic theory is *The Psychoanalytic Theory of Neurosis* by Otto Fenischel (Norton Co., New York, 1945). Every student of counseling theory ought to read sections of this book or all of it. Fenischel summarizes the entire development of psychoanalytic theory and cites the studies that have been done to develop the system. Fenischel, particularly, adequately summarizes the literature of psychoanalysis regarding defense mechanisms and the motives of defense. According to Fenischel, the motives of defense are rooted in external reality. Frustrations and barriers occur because of the clash between social forces of civilization and the basic goal-centered pleasure-seeking propensities of the human organism. The three major agents of the conflict as interpreted by psychoanalytic theory are: (1) anxiety, (2) guilt, and (3) shame-disgust.

The identification of these intra-psychic components and their reality to the shaping of human behavior are lasting contributions of Freud's whole effort in psychology. Even though today, psychoanalytic theory has been recognized properly as a preliminary explanation of human behavior; not adequately tested out as a consistently formulated theory, with some limitations stemming from a too close identification with medical practice, subjective interpretation, and characterized by a preoccupation on overt behavior as symptomatic of historical experiences, the contributions of Freud and the psychoanalytic movement have been of inestimable worth to the development of a comprehensive approach to counseling.

Empirical experience with cases strongly suggests that defensive mechanisms do exist, that anxiety, guilt, and shame are all present in most normal behavior as well as abnormal manifestations of behavior. What may well be, however, is the fact that defense mechanisms are learned behaviors. They are adaptive responses in a social setting that have been learned through modeling, imitation, the observation of others, and trial-and-error experiences. Although Freud appears to have rightly identified many of the manifestations of bizarre thinking and behavior as related to internal or external conflict between the needs and drives of individuals and societal expectations, his explanation of their etiology may, most likely, be faulty. A more parsimonious explanation of much of defense-building behavior may be found within a framework of learning theory, without reference to the extensive instinctual conceptions of the father of psychoanalysis.

CHAPTER VII

Phenomenology, Gestalt Psychology and Existentialism: Proximate Bases of Self-Concept Theory

In this chapter we again take up the thread of intentionality. In the earlier chapters the metaphysics of intentionality was discussed as it was conceptualized by Aquinas, expanded by Descartes, Leibnitz, and Spinoza, reformulated by Brentano, and translated into the scientific model system of Freud. To understand more fully the later developments of phenomenology, Gestalt psychology, and existentialism, we must recognize the manner in which some of the earlier ideas regarding the nature of psychic phenomena, the subject matter of psychology as the dynamic intending act of the mind, and a special methodology permeated separate but related developments in psychology and philosophy. This chapter will deal separately with the following: (1) phenomenology, (2) Gestalt psychology, (3) existentialism, and (4) self-concept theory.

PHENOMENOLOGY

Phenomenology is a philosophical movement. Spiegelberg (1960) acknowledges the difficulty that exists in posing an adequate definition of the movement as it has permeated both German and French philosophy and psychology. It was characterized by Husserl as a genuine positivism and even as a radical empiricism (Edi in Thevenez, 1962, 19). It is radical in the sense that it departs from the approach of Locke and Russell, whose definition of empiricism made the assumption that philosophy was a science of objects and that experience was just another object among objects. As Edi has written:

Phenomenology is neither a science of objects nor a science of the subject. It is a science of *experience*. It does not concentrate exclusively on either the objects of experience or on the subject of experience, but on the point of contact where being and consciousness meet. It is, therefore, a study of consciousness as *intentions* as directed toward objects, as living in an intentionally constituted world (19).

Spiegelberg tends to see phenomenology as a loosely arranged group of intellectuals with a moving spirit in contrast to a specific and stationary philosophical outlook. He notes some common origins, such as the philosophy and psychology of Franz Brentano, but identifies component branches that spread out in different directions (1960, I, 2). He believes that the movement in general is characterized by a need to look for direct intuition as the final test for philosophical knowledge. Insight into essential structures becomes a correlative need in philosophical knowledge.

Phenomenology would appear to be a philosophical framework that represents not only an intellectual analysis and recomposition of scientific data but also, as Külpe mentioned (1897, 22), "the creation of feeling and will of a mind which approaches these data (sensory and perceptual) with definite needs and requirements." It is both a philosophy of such experience and a rigorous methodology. Phenomenology outlines a broader role for philosophy than logical positivism in that the latter philosophy restricts itself to the products of the scientific method, while the former is concerned with a metaphysics of human perception and inquiry regarding the structure of consciousness. Thus phenomenology defines philosophy in a context that is much broader than the objective and methodological limitations of a philosophy of science. A phenomenological criticism of the present nature of science is that science remains essentially unclarified, that is, unaware of its own ontological and epistemological foundations. A philosophy based exclusively on scientific findings then becomes a philosophy based on abstractions several stages removed from the primary world of living experience.

Fundamental to an understanding of phenomenological thought is a recognition that phenomenology makes an arbitrary division between what is termed the *Lebenswelt* and the world of scientific composition. The *Lebenswelt* is characterized by world facts of conscious experience as contrasted with scientific facts. The sensations of my right hand in typing are facts in my own *Lebenswelt*. The explanation of the neurological reactions necessary for such activity and the chaining principles of learning that explain the phenomena may be derived from scientific explanations. The *Lebenswelt* has its own particular sense of being, is characterized by universal a prioris of subjective structure, and is open to different modes of experiencing truth and certitude than the world of science, which is chiefly concerned with phenomena that can be measured within dimensions of space and time.

Phenomenology, of course, is not alone in recognizing the subjective world of experience as a major component in man's life. Science, too, recognizes this aspect of man, but it does not find the content of mental life susceptible to the methodological procedures of science. This, then, is one of the central points in phenomenological thought, that is, it is not only a philosophy concerned about the ultimate grounds of reality but a method for the examination of these basic grounds. In terms of method, the approach of science relies heavily on the hypothetical-deductive method, whereas the method of phenomenology uses the descriptive-empirical method. Husserl believed that the theoretical basis of science is found in the logic of thought itself and that an understanding of logic is predicated on the understanding of the psychic contents of thought. Thus, to use an example, Newton's law of gravitation may be considered as an idealized fiction with a basis in the reality of experience (Farber, 1962, 109).

Phenomenology is a philosophy that is basically concerned with the subjective grounds of human experience. The initial core concept was that of intentionality, the specific doctrine of Brentano which stated that the psychic act of man was directly constituted by the content aspect received from sensory stimulation and the formal aspect of the intending mind. Though sensory data may impress the human mind, it is the mind itself that invests that experience with individual meaning. This concept, which was discussed in relationship to the Freudian notion of cathexis, was also a core supporting notion in Koehler's formulation of the theory of isomorphism.

Although Edmund Husserl is considered the founder of phenomenology as a formal movement, Spiegelberg mentions a number of specific instances where the term was used earlier. He indicates that Kant used it in 1786, that it can be found in the *Encyclopaedia Britannica* of 1788 in an article on philosophy, that it was used by Johann Heinrich Lambert, one of the followers of Christian Wolff, and that it was used by Hegel, Hartmann, William Hamilton, and Charles Peirce, the originator of pragmatism (Spiegelberg, 1960, I, 8–20).

Spiegelberg sees phenomenology emerging as a movement in reaction to the idealism of Hegel and the transcendental German Romanticists, and to the equally brusque and scientific justification of physiological psychology by positivism. It had some of the notion of a conversion attempt, that is, to bring back some of the mainstream thought of psychology into philosophical channels. There was also the attempt to look at some of the abandoned ideas of Neo-Thomism and, to some extent, of Neo-Kantianism. And all of this took place in years of extremely fertile philosophical and scientific ferment. If we join to this crisis orientation the thinking of individuals like Kierkegaard, Martin Buber, and Karl Marx, as well as Friedrich Nietzsche, we capture some of the flavor of the desparate struggle that was going on with regard to an interpretation and understanding of man's role in the world of science.

Edmund Husserl, Carl Stumpf, and Martin Heidegger are three of the major contributors to the development of phenomenology. Interestingly enough, all three are connected vitally with Franz Brentano. Both Husserl and Stumpf were students of Brentano and took his philosophical point of view as their starting point. Martin Heidegger, as a Jesuit student, was much impressed with Brentano but took his starting point from the philosophy of Duns Scotus, a philosophy of individual distinctions contrasting with the Thomistic point of view. Both Husserl and Stumpf acknowledged publicly their dependence on Brentano in the shaping of their original thinking. Subsequently, Husserl, Stumpf, and Heidegger all departed quite radically from the generalistic point of view, expressed by Brentano, and explored many specific points of concern.

THE PHILOSOPHICAL BASIS OF PHENOMENOLOGY

The philosophical derivations of phenomenology could compose a volume by themselves. Essentially, the basic notions in phenomenology can be traced back to Platonic sources. Aristotle's concern with phenomena was basically oriented toward outer reality and objectivity. He was concerned with an explanation of the physical phenomena that he saw about him. Surely, this generated some theorizing about the nature of mind and soul also, but the approach that Aristotle took toward reality was substantially a scientific one—outer-oriented instead of inner-oriented. Plato, on the other hand, was concerned about the true realities, that is, those realities that existed in the world of ideas and that were reflected in life through concrete phenomena. A similar dichotomy can be observed in the opposition of Thomas Aquinas to Duns Scotus, that is, an objective-subjective emphasis. It is also repeated again in the opposition of Lockean-associationist thinking, as represented by David Hume, to the subjectivist conceptualism of Kant. Still further oppositions can be seen between positivism as an objective philosophy of science and Hegelianism as a subjective approach.

Franz Brentano perceived himself as the founder of a synthesis, a philosophy that would provide an over-arching justification for both scientific exploration and subjective investigation.

This theme of Brentano's formed the basis of Husserl's approach to phenomenology, which is called by Husserl, himself a transcendental idealism. Others have referred to it as a radical positivism, but this much is certain that the philosophy in itself is concerned with the subjective grounds of human experience, the structure of consciousness, and those a priori contentions that constitute the subjective grounds of experience. This approach to human nature varies widely from one phenomenologist to another, and it is for this reason that it is very difficult for individuals in psychology or in the applied aspects of psychology, such as counseling, to come to grips with the basic notions of the movement. At the risk of incurring the wrath of one or the other phenomenologists, I have attempted to abstract from the varieties of individual philosophical theorizing the core ideas that characterized much of the movement. These philosophical considerations will relate to (1) epistemology or the theory of knowledge and certitude, (2) ontology or the nature of reality, and (3) axiology or the nature of values.

From the epistemological point of view, the basic tenet discernible in phenomenological thought is the *Cartesian cogito*. Descartes stated that the source of his philosophical rationalizing began with the apodictic knowledge that the only thing man can know for sure is that he is experiencing a stream of thoughts and feelings. This subjective world is the world of the *Lebenswelt*. It is a world in which I as an individual must cope. All of my conscious life I am confronted with a stream of phenomena relating to my thoughts and feelings. This life includes also my contacts with the outer world of reality, the people and forces that impinge on me. The world of science is only a small portion of that outer reality; it is essentially a derived fiction in relationship to the reality of my own experience. The manner in which I come to relate to the outer world is determined by my own psychic structure and by the complex interaction of past and present experiences. This structure of the mind is not immediately aware of basic determining principles, but nonetheless these principles do exist. They are part of the very structure of the mind itself, a part of my being. Thus there exists in the structure of the mind a basis for our reasoning, our logic, and the means whereby meaning is conveyed in the act of perception.

Perhaps an analogy may make the situation clearer. The phenomenologists are saying that man's mind possesses a structure that is an a priori given. It is very much like the computer with all its elaborate circuits. Through the modalities of time and space the mind is programmed by experience, just as the computer is programmed by a set of instructions. However, the data of the human mind are accumulated in accord with man's basic physiological and psychological structure. To carry the analogy still further, just as the computer by reason of its structure digests the data fed into it, analyzes it, and reports it, so the mind of man ingests the sensory data of the environment, organizes it, analyzes it, and invests it with meaning. Meaning is analyzed specifically in the act of judgment. Although meaning is a subjective phenomenon for all men, there exist principles of uniformity, i.e. essential structural components that provide a uniform psychological approach to the data of experience and knowledge. There is, however, one great difference; the computer can handle only what it is programmed to do within its basic structure. It can retain an almost infinite number of facts and variables always open to analysis. The human mind analyzes phenomena presented in consciousness or recalled in relationship to on-going experience, thereby acting in a successive manner.

The mind's structure, then, analyzes the congruence of one set of data against another. It recalls, imagines, reconstructs, and in other ways uses the data of experience. Because of the basic biological and psychological communality of structure, certain phenomena are ordered to each other in a causal-effect manner. Here, some phenomenologists see the emergence of logic as a derived set of principles which can be compared in some ways to part of the essential structure of the computer. The conscious emergence of these principles constitute what is known as logic. The accumulation of principles of logic form the ultimate cognitive formulation of what has been called reason.

The analogy ends here, however, since another possible feature of the human mind is the grasping of new concepts and the creation of new facts and ideas. Central to the emergence of this ability is the notion of innate power that is termed intuition. Intuition is the creative, analytic, and synthetic potential that is innately present in all truly human cognitive structures. Intuition, or the apprehension of innate principles of being and knowing, represents an aspect of mind that is preconscious or, at least, not directly available to the consciousness. Husserl and Heidegger both felt that a deeper investigation of the nature of consciousness and the nature of being would bring into focus some of the hidden principles of structure, some of the a priori structures that lie hidden behind the facade of man's conscious experience. Thus the epistemology of phenomenology centers on human experience, an experience that is the derived product of *both* sensory input and structural formation. This human experience is valued as apodictically certain, that is, immediate and self-evident. Thus this kind of experience, although not susceptible to the canons of external phenomena in the scientific sense of physics, is nonetheless valued highly in the hierarchy of certitude.

This epistemological position then leads to a derived position of phenomenology in the area of ontology. Reality is conceived to consist of both internal and external dimensions. Man is held to know best the internal dimensions of reality and to know least the external dimensions. These internal dimensions of reality are known first on a felt or experience level, a subjective and noncognitive plane rather than a cognitive one. Moreover, the dimensions of external reality are experienced only indirectly through the mediation of internal experience. Thus what man knows about outer reality, that is, the world of scientific investigation and factual knowledge, is filtered through the mediation of his internal experiencing. Phenomenology, in general, conceives the ultimate nature of external reality to be essentially unknowable. What ultimate reality may be, phenomenology suggests, may concern not only the external findings and probings of outer reality, but an intimate look at the structural components of inner reality.

Phenomenology, particularly the phenomenology of Husserl, suggests also that behind the principles and laws of natural science may lie even more precise laws that are also found within man's mental structure. These general laws and principles are very similar to what the Scholastics called "universal ideas." In a sense, they also reflect some of the earlier notions of Plato. Thus there is the flavor of an immanent transcendentalism, the evidence of whose existence is found within the conceptualization process of the human mind. The emergence of the meaning of internal reality within the individual through the evolution of noncognitive to cognitive feelings and conceptualization is analogous to a man coming out of a dark basement walking up the steps towards the light. Even as man in his scientific endeavors has sought to push further and further toward the light, so man must make an attempt to probe the nature of the structure of consciousness (Husserl) and to explore further the nature of existence (Heidegger).

These epistemological and ontological considerations then lead to the axiological or value orientation of phenomenology. Logically, if one pursues the notion of a priori structure back far enough, one comes to the ontological argument for the existence of God. Anselm in the Middle Ages enunciated the ontological argument for the existence of God which held basically that the greatest universal idea that we could conceive of was God. Despite the theological or conceptual problems that point out the shortcomings of this argument, it is this kind of conclusion that lies behind the transcendentalism of phenomenology. God becomes the ultimate ground of Being, the ultimate ground of our experience and existence, the core substructure that informs the essence of consciousness. Although this line of thought is pursued more by the religious existentialist derivations from phenomenology, exemplified by Paul Tillich and Martin Buber, it is nonetheless present in the works of Husserl, and certainly to some extent in the thought of Heidegger, although Heidegger always stopped short of this conclusion.

Questions of good and evil, truth and falsity, are thus related to the consciousness of experience. Brentano felt that the judgment of rightness versus wrongness preceded the judgment of goodness versus evil. He did not subscribe to a natural law that governs all men and provides some kind of criterion for men, except in the sense that he felt the collective judgment of many renowned, thinking, and rational men of integrity had some reflective weight. As far as phenomenology proceeds in the direction of ethics, it would appear that the judgment of what is good must be determined from what can be known about the nature of the ultimate and universal principles or ground of human existence, as reflected in self-consciousness. This apprehension of the canons of ethical conduct is thus obscure and cannot depend either on a kind of subjective pragmatism or on scientific expediency. It is, in fact, based strongly on the intuition of certain moral insights that, one may reason, emerge from within the structure of the mind much in the manner of cognitive awareness. Ultimately, then, man should conduct himself according to his own informed insights based on personal maxims of freedom, attempting continually to clarify in his own thinking the obscure universal laws of nature. In this sort of judgment lies the basis for continued self-probing and self-searching for identity and meaning. Unquestionably, the ethical conclusions of some of the phenomenological thought seem to have been foreseen in the ethics of Spinoza who, with less philosophical sophistication, saw man and nature united in God as the ultimate ground of meaning and existence.

A general interpretation of the philosophical tenets of phenomenology is difficult in view of the individualistic personal opinions of many philosophers. Just as there are many points of view toward client-centered therapy and Freudian theory, so there are many forms of phenomenology. If, however, the tenets that represent the phenomenological movements can be subject to some tentative generalizations, there is at least, a more common agreement on what phenomenology does not hold. Farber (1962, 567) points out that phenomenology (1) does not deny or reject the external world of science, (2) does not try to answer all the questions of human existence, (3) is not an all-inclusive method for dealing with all phenomena, (4) is not intended as a substitute for other methods, (5) does not deny inductive truth or fail to distinguish between various types of truth, and (6) is not intended as a shortcut to spiritualism in metaphysics. Phenomenology asserts that individual subjective experience must be taken seriously and must be given at least equal attention to that area of man's external reality known as science.

Phenomenology as a method has a wide range of applications. Some of this has been discussed earlier in relationship to Brentano. Phenomenology begins with observation and description as does the scientific method. It utilizes both external observation and, to a limited extent, the analysis of internal phenomena. As Brentano pointed out, intuiting as such, should not be confused with introspection. Introspection in itself is a valid personal experience. Intuiting, however, is concerned with the deductions that are based, at least minimally, on the observation of the internal phenomena of others.

Phenomenology is concerned with the mode of appearance of phenomena, of the nature of causality, and spatial and temporal dimensions. As a method, it resists the reductionism of physical phenomena as well as psychic phenomena to the paradigm of stimulus and response. It is primarily a descriptive and analytic procedure utilizing observational techniques and drawing inferences and conclusions about the characteristics of phenomena causally related to phenomena. But because the observing person is also determined in his very observation by internal phenomena and by his reaction to external events, the steps in scientific induction and deduction are considerably more tedious than within the framework of science.

We shall see later how Gestalt psychology utilized some of these observations in psychological method, and particularly how the French-Swiss school of Phenomenological-Genetic psychology in Piaget has amplified these steps of method.

GERMAN PHENOMENOLOGY

In this section we shall discuss briefly the contributions of certain selected German phenomenologists. They are Carl Stumpf (1848–1936), Edmund Husserl (1859–1938), Max Scheler (1874–1928), and Martin Heidegger (1889–   ).

Carl Stumpf was an early student of Franz Brentano at Wurzburg. He was particularly impressed with Brentano's beginning defense of his thesis at Wurzburg, identifying the method of philosophy with the method of natural science. He became Brentano's successor at Wurzburg and later moved to Berlin where he had a continuing influence on many of the Gestaltists. Spiegelberg states:

In particular Stumpf's approach permeated the work of the Gestaltists (chiefly through Wolfgang Köhler, Max Wertheimer, and Kurt Koffka) the group dynamics movement (through Kurt Lewin) and indirectly the new phenomenological psychology of Donald Snygg and Arthur W. Combs (I, 54).

Stumpf also had a lasting relationship with William James, who as a young man had made the acquaintance of Stumpf and had come to respect Brentano through the contact with Stumpf.

Stumpf from the psychological point of view was much interested in the relationship of music to internal phenomena. But his chief contribution lies in the fact that he insisted phenomenology was a neutral science or pre-science that was relevant to all investigators of natural science. He insisted that phenomenology had as its task the analysis of the contents and states of perception which relate to the investigation itself, preparatory to the investigational procedures of science. He argued that phenomenology as a prescience had to provide information about the distinction between substance and attribute—what was of the core or essence of a thing as against what was related and causally dependent on the thing. He also believed that a search for causal connections between phenomena and the use of deduction from empirical experience were both valid procedures for arriving at conclusions and laws of operation.

Finally, Stumpf was concerned with what might be called feeling tones or various bodily sensations. Stumpf's contribution to the continuation of phenomenological method was felt primarily through the Gestaltists and William James. Stumpf of all the German philosopher-psychologists was most oriented to Brentano's earlier phase of concern with psychology.

Edmund Husserl is chiefly responsible for the development of the philosophy of phenomenology. His starting point was with the philosophy and psychology of Brentano, although his own doctoral work was chiefly in mathematics. He was concerned with what he considered to be a crisis in European intellectual life, a crisis that tended to discount reason and to look for external causes for man's life and existence. His approach to phenomenology was first related to method. Only later did philosophical notions begin to be advanced beyond his methodological considerations. The crisis in European science, Husserl thought, was related to the methods of science as well as the findings of science. The evidence of science is directly related to the method of science and, in fact, on the method of science. Husserl thought that some of the presuppositions of science about reality needed to be examined. He was specifically questioning the scientific assumption that reality consists exclusively of an extended world in space and time wherein space is three-dimensional, and the assumption that all change is subject to physical force without the recognition of the impact and meaning of human force in consciousness.

Husserl was convinced that man had to look beyond the methodology of science for those principles that made it possible for man to devise the scientific method in the first place. This led him back to an examination of the immanent relations and structures of thought, the search for a series of a priori structures that underly all knowledge. Although, at first, Husserl seemed to have taken off from Brentano's methodology and conceived his studies in terms of a rationalist psychology, ultimately, he recognized that the real object of his search was for a transcendental first philosophy. A philosophy of this nature was concerned with first principles, and Husserl felt that all knowledge about the *objects* of reality must be reflected ultimately to the *subjects* of reality. What we know about science, then, is in virtue of a methodology that we have created out of the fertility and ingenuity of the human mind. To understand fully the implications of our science, Husserl reasoned, it is necessary for us to comprehend the a priori structures that made it possible for us to be scientific in the first place.

Thus Husserl placed the beginning of his investigations back at the *Cartesian cogito,* but proceeded further in the analysis of what it means to know. He was obviously influenced by Descartes and John Stuart Mill. He also considered himself as a fulfiller of the Leibnitzean promise, that is, to reconcile disparate philosophical systems. Although he admired Lotze and William James along with Brentano, he was not interested in the empirical descriptions of natural phenomena in the sense of John Dewey. Rather was he concerned with the investigation of subjectivism as a basis for reconciling both the world of the individual and the world of science.

Early in Husserl's career he became embroiled in a conflict known as psychologism. This conflict was started with Theodore Lipps, who held that psychology was the basis of epistemology—in short, that the nature and certitude of our knowledge depends on psychological phenomena. Brentano seems to have inclined in this direction also, although he later denied it. Although the controversy remained unsettled, it does seem clear that Husserl's concern with the subjective grounds of experience and with the a priori structures of the mind as a basis for the organization of thinking would lead one to the psychologism position. To some of the opponents of psychologism, it appeared that Husserl and others were simply suggesting that introspection is the basis for the scientific method. Although this may be oversimplifying the controversy, Benjamin Whorf in more recent times has advanced the hypothesis in anthropology that language forms, syntax and grammar, reveal distinctive ways of looking at reality that are formed and molded by a given culture. At issue basically was the answer to the question: Where is the theoretical basis of science? John Stuart Mill, Lipps, and others had suggested that logic is a branch of psychology and that the rules of correct thinking are identical to the natural laws of thought. In this sense, logic then becomes the physics of thinking. Husserl claimed that the basis of logic resided not in the psychology of thought, so much as in the intuitive understanding of the psychic contents of thought. Absolute knowledge could not be obtained from empiricism but from insight and apodictic self-evidence.

Insight and apodictic evidence, Husserl thought, were derived not from the phenomenon itself, but from the meaning given to the phenomenon. Although the phenomenon gives rise to meaning, meaning itself is conveyed by the mind. Thus we see the concept of intentionality once more present. Husserl views psychological acts as experiences of meaning in consciousness. Consciousness not only refers to the total phenomenological existence of the ego but also to the inner becoming aware of one's own experiences. The phenomenological ego or self then is identical with its own basic unity. The forms of the phenomenological ego are based not only on the phenomena presented by sensory experience but by the investment of meaning, the accumulation of meanings, and the total intentional memory of meanings.

This leads us to one final consideration of Husserl, namely his concern with intuition and representation. Husserl meant by representation that psychological act of perception whose content was provided by sensory experience and whose form was provided by the mind in the form of subjective meaning. Intuition was described as that particular concern of the mind which sought to grasp and to comprehend the meaning of phenomena that lie hidden behind those appearances. Thus intuition is regarded as a difference in the mode of consciousness instead of a difference in content.

The analysis of the a priori nature of the structure of conscious experience leads, then, to the reduction of consciousness to the absolute ground of philosophy. The question here is what is the structure of experience? Husserl pursued the question into the area of universals and essences. Are there universal structures that underly the dimensions of subjective experience. Husserl believed that universals were not eternal, changeless, or in any way superior to particular data or experience, but that they had their origin in subjectivity as related to consciousness.

Spiegelberg suggests that Husserl changed or modified Brentano's doctrine of intentionality, conceiving of it as a relational property of having an intention or being aimed by this property, not as an object's immanency in consciousness. Husserl also felt that intentionality was not a necessary or continuous property of all psychic phenomena. Instead, he saw sensory data as forming along the poles of meaning. The stream of consciousness notion, then, suggests a synthetic function for intention:

> I might sum up the account of Husserl's intention by describing it as that component of any act which is responsible not only for its pointing at an object but also for (a) interpreting pre-given materials in such a way that a full object is presented to consciousness, (b) establishing the identity between the references of several intentional acts, (c) connecting the various stages of intuitive fulfillment and (d) constituting the object meant (I, 110).

Husserl felt that the chief investigation of psychology as such should be focused on the intentional structures of consciousness. He felt that psychology lacked a systematic framework for the interpretation of psychic foundations.

Max Scheler is a phenomenologist who has appealed in some senses more to American audiences than to other German phenomenologists. Perhaps, in part, this is because of the fact that he has been preoccupied with many sociological and cultural issues that have a more immediate and practical concern for pragmatic-oriented psychologists and philosophers. Ethics and the implications of sociology and anthropology are the persistent concerns of Scheler.

Scheler focuses much of his phenomenological work on the question of knowledge. He sees knowledge as first being concerned with mastery and achievement in the pragmatic sense. Here he agrees substantially with much of American pragmatism, rejecting only the inadequate metaphysical base, or the lack of such a base. He then conceived of a second form of knowledge, which might be termed self-understanding, and a third form of knowledge that he refers to as knowledge of salvation, suggesting a mystical component or search for higher order understanding.

Scheler in his studies of ethics and phenomena related to value shows the relativity of morality, customs, and beliefs, and he points out that knowledge of social processes and people shape the individualistic form of ethics that proceed from these sociological and anthropological bases. Concerned with methods of knowing other people and the relationship between external appearances and feelings, Scheler emphasizes social interaction as a method of phenomenological experience in which individuals come to know each other, and sympathize, value, and clarify the meaning of experience. Scheler was a prolific writer, as was Husserl, but he was not a rigorous philosopher of science in the sense that Husserl was. Some of Scheler's ideas, particularly the ones related to the investigation of sympathy and modes of knowing, as well as the function of symbols as knowledge, appear to establish him as a quasi-bridge between the more direct phenomenological philosophy of Husserl and Heidegger and the applied psychological system of Freud.

Martin Heidegger

Martin Heidegger's contribution to phenomenology is still incomplete in the sense that all of Heidegger's work and thinking is not yet available or, at least, analyzed. Although in some ways Husserl is the towering source of original phenomenological thought, Heidegger contributed much, too, and may have influenced others more than Husserl. According to Spiegelberg (I, 271, 272), Heidegger had some influence on John Dewey, who expressed an interest in Heidegger's works, and he certainly influenced Paul Tillich in the 1920s.

Heidegger, early in his career, was a Jesuit novice in Freiburg. Here he first came in contact with Franz Brentano's doctoral dissertation on the multiple meanings of being in Aristotle and was affected deeply by it. He taught at Freiburg and submitted a thesis on Duns Scotus' Doctrine of Categories and Meanings. This early emphasis on Scotus betrays Heidegger's interest in individuality and in the question of subjectivity that had been foreshadowed in Scotus' ideas. Although Husserl and Heidegger were acknowledged generally as the giants of phenomenology, Heidegger gradually moved away into an approach that was more existential. Heidegger did not precipitate a rupture with Husserl but, in fact, this appeared to be in evidence long before Heidegger became associated with the Nazi movement. This latter association appears to be the one attempt that Heidegger made to attempt to influence social behavior. He felt, apparently, early in the Nazi movement that his notion of subjectivity and the force of will were compatible with Nazi ideology, and he believed that he could influence the course of the political development. Although this liaison resulted in his being nominated and confirmed as chancellor of the University of Berlin, he resigned subsequently when it became evident what direction Nazi politics was to take. Nonetheless, this association has cast somewhat of a shadow on Heidegger.

Although some, for example, MacLeod (Wann, 1964, 51), state that Heidegger is as deadly as Hegel, it is clear from his earlier writings that he attempted to push the examination of a priori structures of consciousness further than Husserl. An evolution is discernible in the growth of the phenomenological movement from Brentano's early descriptive analyses and categories into the prescience notions of Stumpf, the analyses of consciousness by Husserl, and the subjectivity of Heidegger as he sought for an identification of those subjective roots of consciousness in the ontology of being itself. His preoccupation with the nature of being led him to an examination of nonbeing and to a definition of reality as *Dasein*, the "to be there, or the thereness of the to be there." Heidegger attempted to map out the transcendental categories of life-in-the-world, which he called *existentials*. In an effort to separate his own existential categories from the object-oriented ones of Aristotle and the subject-oriented ones of Kant, he turned to the phenomenological existentials.

As Spiegelberg has stated in reference to Heidegger:

> The historicity of human being consists primarily in the individual's fate based on his own resolvedness within an inherited yet chosen frame of possibilities (I, 338).

And, again,

> . . . The center of gravity of historicity lies in the future. For human being is oriented towards the future ultimately toward man's only authentic possibility death.

Heidegger's analysis of being conceives of man as standing in the clearing of his own being surrounded by a darkness and confusion. Being as related to the subjective self is characterized first by what Heidegger calls ipseity. This can best be expressed simply by the modern notion of "doing one's thing," although this connotation carries something more than what Heidegger meant. What he appears to mean essentially is that each individual's own being is a subjective but very real thing. Being is always characterized by the fact that it is in a context that is the world. The components of the world involve the world itself, the subjective being of man, and the relationship between the two.

Being and world are also affected by the impersonal (people). Both world and people as such constitute threats to the authenticity of individual being. Keeping one's proper distance and relating to others in the world can force the authenticity of the self into roles that are not authentic, not genuinely reflective of man's unique subjectivity. The reactions of man in his subjective being and relationship to people in the world give rise to moods, especially fear and anxiety, that reveal something about the nature of the burden of being itself. Even elated moods do reflect some freedom, temporary or permanent, from the burden of being.

Fear and anxiety have a direct relationship to this problem of being. Fear is a reaction against something. Anxiety, Heidegger conceives of as a fear against nothing in the sense that not being, not doing, and not becoming effects an anxiety noticed in talk, curiosity, and in many typically human relationships. Anxiety, says Spiegelberg, is a pulling away from nothing, a desire not to get caught in the moods of one's own existence (I, 332).

Other characteristics of being are concern, which reflects the fact that most human existence in the world must be related to an involvement in daily activities, looking forward or to the future, and being confused by this continual lack of personalized focus. Death and temporality are other such existential qualities of being. Death is the one certain event that all men face. Temporality is a tendency for all individuals to look to the future, to interpret the present and even the past in relationship to a future state, goal, or plan.

According to Thévenaz (1962) the existential bent of Heidegger was really a distortion of the older phenomenology of both Brentano and Husserl. For Heidegger's pursuit of nonbeing led him to discover that man reveals the nature of being instead through the fundamental anthropological orientation of human concern. Surely Heidegger's analyses, although moving away from certain aspects of phenomenological thought, provided some penetrating analyses of what it means to be and not to be. These ideas have been operationally developed by many individuals today as they seek a genuine sense of being in the world.

PHENOMENOLOGY AND EXISTENTIALISM

One of the chief reasons for the obscurity that attends the study of phenomenology and the attempts that students might make to understand the movement is the manner in which the movement has been fractured and disseminated in a hundred different directions. For this reason I have chosen to dwell chiefly on the contributions of Brentano, Husserl, and Heidegger as the founders of the movement and of the mainstream thrust of phenomenology rather than attempt to trace the movement further. One difficulty of such tracing is that certain ideas become the property of the *Weltanschauung*. This has been particularly true with notions such as the phenomenological approach. They become widely diffused and form the general base for much prolific philosophizing that, at best, sometimes has only a tenous relationship to the originators of the movement or to the basic underlying ideas of phenomenology. Even with Heidegger, it is possible to trace the development and transition from phenomenology to existentialism.

This fragmentation and proliferation is one of the reasons for the active confusion that exists in the minds of many regarding phenomenology and existentialism. Phenomenology, in a sense, is a kind of revived but intensified and modern approach to Scholasticism. It is concerned with the nature of the a priori components of man's structure. It is thus an essentialist philosophy, but one that is subject-oriented. Existentialism, as we shall soon learn, abandons this quest for a determination of the a priori nature of structure and substitutes the more global concept of existence in experience. Phenomenology attempted under Brentano and Husserl to apply as rigorous a methodology to the examination of "inner reality" as experimentalism and behaviorism had shown in relationship to outer reality. In terms of counseling theory and practice it should be reflected as a concern for a deeper understanding of those possible invariant structures that both channel and determine the meaning of psychic phenomena as against the more existential concern with being and experience as such. *Phenomenology in its purest form is a study of subjectivity which is characterized by the transcendental thesis that existence is the result of constitution or structure joined to experience.* It is, therefore, an essentialist philosophy whose method and goals are designed to probe into the inner structure of man.

The works of Sartre, although often grouped with phenomenology, do not fit the above criteria and place him chiefly in the existentialist tradition. Merleau-Ponty also represents a point of view that might be better grouped under existentialism. Closely allied to phenomenology might be considered the German *verstehende Psychologie* represented in the writings of Dilthey, Scheler, Spranger, and Jaspers.

For those who wish to study phenomenology further, perhaps the best exposition of Husserl's philosophy may be found in Farber's work: *The Foundations of Phenomenology* (1962), and the most comprehensive analysis of the entire movement with its many facets can be found in Herbert Spiegelberg's *The Phenomenological Movement* (1960).

GESTALT AND PERCEPTUAL PSYCHOLOGY

Many of the philosophical ideas of phenomenology have found a more eloquent and meaningful expression in the perceptual or cognitive psychologists than in philosophy. Beginning with the Wurzburg movement in German psychology in the latter years of the 19th century, the nature of perception became the focal point of much German psychology. It was at once both a reaction against the introspectionism and "brick-and-mortar" associationism of Wundt, and the physiological studies of the Helmholtz school. Many names are associated with Gestalt psychology. Max Wertheimer, Kurt Koffka, and Wolfgang Koehler are traditionally associated together in the beginning of the movement. Kurt Lewin, although often considered in the second generation of the movement, studied at Berlin only a few years after Koehler. His students, Zeigarnik, Ovsiankina, Lissner, Hoppe, and Frank continued the essential social psychology bent of Lewin.

Although Gestalt psychology had its origins in the first decade of the 20th century, it was swept into American psychology in the late 1920s and 1930s when Wertheimer, Koehler, and Koffka all came to the United States in protest against the Nazi regime. Lewin, too, chose to live in the United States. Koffka went to Smith College, Koehler to Swarthmore, Wertheimer to the New School for Social Research, and Lewin spent time at Stanford, Cornell, Harvard, Iowa, and the Massachusetts Institute of Technology. At about the same time, several American psychologists were also producing works that contained the flavor of Gestalt psychology even if they were not directly related to the movement. In 1932, Wheeler introduced what was termed organismic psychology, and Tolman published his *Purposive Behavior,* which made extensive use of the concept of molar attitudes toward behavior as contrasted to the assumed molecular approach of the behaviorists.

Thus the 1930s marked the rise of a new approach to psychology that emphasized the nature of perception, the unifying principles of insight, figure, and ground in contrast to the specific reductionism of Watson's behaviorism and the atomism of Thorndike. The movement remained popular in the United States through the 1940s and in educational circles seemed to fit well with the Dewey problem-solving model as well as with the growth and maturational studies that were being pursued by Willard C. Olson and others. Both Boring and Hilgard (1950, 1964) have analyzed the present status of Gestalt psychology. Boring said that it died of success and should have resisted the temptation of incorporating behavioral data into its theory (1950, p. 600). Hilgard, citing Koehler's address to the American Psychological Association in 1959 (1964, p. 58), agrees with Koehler that Gestalt psychology had not really been assimilated into the mainstream of American Psychology, but had been neglected and bypassed.

For the most part, this rationale seems to be accurate with respect to American pure psychology studies. But the application of some of these principles has filtered down and has been transformed and extended chiefly into areas of social psychology and educational psychology as a theoretical base for dealing with human behavior in social settings. This is indicated by the tremendous Gestalt emphasis that appeared in text-books on educational psychology after the appearance of Gestalt psychology. This approach of Gestalt psychology, emphasizing the role of insight, configuration, whole- versus part learning, and the like, tended to fit well into the Dewey problem-solving model of learning that had been so extensively propagated in educational circles. Lewin's work, particularly, seems to have been an inspiration, if not a causal link in the development of the achievement-motivation construct of McClelland, the cognitive dissonance of Festinger, and the cognitive balance theory of Heider. More recently, the work of Snygg and Combs, and the writings of Bruner and Ausubel have tended to extend the original Gestalt and Lewinian inheritance to the areas of learning and self-concept formation.

In 1912, three German psychologists who had been research students at Berlin were living near the city of Frankfurt. They were Max Wertheimer, Kurt Koffka, and Wolfgang Koehler. They had all contributed to research relating to perception. Wertheimer had shown how a free association test could be used for the detection of a person's hidden knowledge. He had also studied the *phi phenomenon* and had invited Koehler and Koffka to serve as subjects. The problem was to explain the apparent motion that took place as a series of still pictures was presented rapidly on a screen (the motion-picture effect). Koffka had done work in imagery and thought, and Koehler's original research was related to the problems of hearing. Each of these individuals was concerned with problems of perception, as were a number of other psychological investigators. Stumpf, Koehler's teacher at Berlin, had long been interested in the psychology of music in relationship to the problems of perception. From these studies of perception, and from the friendship that existed between the individuals in the group, came Gestalt psychology.

Gestalt means form or shape. Another word that might express it is configuration. Koehler in *Gestalt Psychology* (1964) makes it clear that Gestalt psychology is a reaction against both the introspectionism of Wundt and Titchener and the behaviorism of Watson. He argues eloquently that these approaches to human behavior are atomistic and are built up on a spurious approach to behavior which mimics but does not approximate the approach that physics takes to physical phenomena.

Perhaps, the core notion of Gestalt psychology is Koehler's doctrine on isomorphism. Koehler stated: "experienced order in space is always structurally identical with a functional order in the distribution of underlying brain processes" (1964, 39). This is to state that whatever is experienced in the spatio-temporal continuum of our life experience has a counterpart in the structure of the brain. There is then a trace in the brain that corresponds to the ordering of sensory experience.

Nonetheless, the manner in which this trace takes place is related to the act of perception. Thus the Gestaltists developed their basic theory of isomorphism into a number of postulates about the nature of perception. They said, for example, that phenomena that are experienced manifest a form. A number of dots on a piece of paper do not have form in themselves, but it is the organization of the dots which provides the basis for the structural form that is present in the act of perception. Form then, is the organization of parts into a whole. This led them to consider the agent that provided the form, and they recognized that events or phenomena took place within a frame of reference that was essentially personal. However, they did discover that sensory experiences tended to be organized in a way that made use of certain principles of parsimonious grouping. In the *Law of Prägnanz* they suggested that perception tends to follow simple configurations or organizations rather than complex ones, that is, that experiences are organized according to the greatest simplicity, regularity, and completeness.

This process of perceptual organization then required a further explanation as to how the act of perception filters out some material that is extraneous and seeks to find a unity or whole in perceiving. This they explained by the *figure* and *ground* concept. When one looks steadily at a tree across the street, one can also observe peripheral vision of cars in the background, people moving, and the like. This example illustrates the figure-ground principle with the tree constituting the figure and the peripheral background the ground.

Learning is explained in terms of changes in perceptual processes, new ways of looking at phenomena. The Gestalt hypothesis for learning is that a psychological or experienced whole is more than the sum of its parts. Learning does not take place on the basis of transfer of training in identical elements but, instead, on the basis of reorganization, and the use of generalization. Insight, or the sudden awareness of new configurations, then plays an important role in the Gestalt approach to learning.

Kurt Lewin (1890–1947), although an associate of the other Gestalt founders, gave his attention to the question of motivation and to the question of learning. It is, therefore, through Lewin that educational theory and practice appears to have received the chief transmission of Gestalt psychology. Hilgard (1964, 67) explains the gradual transition of Lewin's thinking from the field of motivation and human learning to that of social psychology through the historical accident of Hitler's rise to power and World War II. Not only through Lewin's students but also through Tolman's students can the influence of Lewin be felt. The transmission through Tolman seems to have come from the fact that Tolman was quite impressed with Lewin's views. Lewin's students included Zeigarnik who discovered what has been termed the *Zeigarnik* effect, that is, tasks left incompleted are remembered better than tasks that are completed. Ovsiankina, who determined that when individuals have a desire to complete later a task left undone, new tasks are selected at the completion of the previous one, and Hoppe who developed the concept of level of aspiration.

Lewin intended to describe human action in terms of what he called field theory. He pictured a person in his environment in what he called "life space." This life space was a psychological construction that does have some correspondence with the physical space in which an individual lives. He felt that individuals had different life spaces as they fulfilled different roles. Hence, a man could have one life space pertaining to his work, another to his home, and another to his recreation. Essentially, congruence between the physical and the psychological life space was considered a sign of "adjustment." Thus mentally ill individuals could have quite a distorted life space in comparison with the realities in which they live.

Just as individuals move from one physical place to another, so Lewin conceived the psychological life space to include movement toward goals, blockings, frustrations, and alternative ways of solving problems of frustration. Lewin's theories fit well with the defense mechanisms originally referred to by Freud and provide a schematic medium for a discussion of the movement toward goals. In conjunction with this same notion, Lewin mentioned the possible conflict situations that may arise from approach-approach sources, avoidance-avoidance sources, and approach-avoidance sources. These three positions have been discussed often in the literature. In the first one, the approach-approach conflict, an individual is drawn to two goals simultaneously. In the second, he may attempt to avoid two problems simultaneously, and in the third, he is both drawn toward and repelled by the same goal. This latter conflict has been the subject of much investigation by Dollard and Miller.

To explain the movements within the life-space more concretely, Lewin resorted to the use of mathematical terms such as vector to express drive, and valence which was used to explain the attractiveness of certain aspects of the life-space and the repulsion from other areas. Lewin's concept of life-space has had two important implications in educational theory. The first is related to the concept of growth and to the progressive differentiation of the ego, a notion that has been enhanced by Piaget's studies in growth and development with their accent on accommodation and assimilation. Piaget's theory could suggest that the life-space of the infant, at first closely restricted, gradually expands and develops as the perceptory apparatus matures. Typical mechanisms of accommodation and assimilation help to determine the flexibility of that life-space. The other concept that has had wide-spread application is that behavior is determined by the conditions that exist in the life-space. Later psychologists, for example, Snygg, have tended to state that the determinants of behavior are controlled by the experiences in the phenomenal field. A further assumption drawn from the former one is that knowing how an individual perceives a situation will make it possible to predict how he will behave.

Unquestionably, Lewin's contribution to counseling theory and the formation of what is known as a perceptual approach to learning were monumental. He died suddenly before revisions could be made in his theory. Hilgard (1964, 69) in summarizing the evaluations of Lewin points out that mathematical attempts to quantify some of Lewin's mathematical constructs, that is, valence and vector, have proven unsuccessful. But the impact of his thought even in its incomplete stage has been the greatest and possibly the most enduring of the Gestalt tradition.

Hilgard suggests that the Gestalt movement has now fragmented into many separate areas. The theory itself may not have been sufficiently viable to continue in the original direction of the founders. In a manner analogous to what occurred in phenomenology, the original movement started in the area of theory by investigating the central question of whether psychology is or is not the investigation of direct experience or mediated perception. This reminds one forcefully of Brentano's contention about perception and not sensation's being the basic ground of psychological focus. But even as Koehler moved to the demonstration of insight in the chimpanzees (a demonstration that Harlow suggests could be more parsimoniously explained through old or even one-time new learning), so Lewin hastened on to applications in social psychology that enhanced the acceptance of his theories, but decreased the chance for experimental verification.

What has resulted, for better or worse, is a loosely knit group of theorists who not only combine some elements of Gestalt psychology with Freudian modifications but draw on earlier elements of phenomenology or current existentialism. Moreover, in this reciprocal exchange of ideas, the *Weltanschauung* of the modern scholar has been expanded and accelerated by the volume of publications and the continual cross-fertilization of ideas. Counseling practice itself has provided a feedback to some theorists, for example, Snygg and Combs. Two current directions that can be observed are (1) those theorists who consider the most direct application of these ideas to be in counseling and interpersonal relations, and (2) those theorists who provide an additional theoretical basis for learning out of the treasure trove of phenomenology and Gestalt psychology. Representative of the latter class are Gordon Allport, Floyd Allport, Fritz Heider, and George Kelly, who appear to this writer to represent theorists who are concerned with the application of Gestalt-field theory and phenomenology to interpersonal behavior. Gordon Allport has contributed much in the expansion of personality theory into this area. His brother Floyd Allport has pursued the roots of alternate personality theory systems. Fritz Heider was not only closely associated with Lewin but was also a one-time pupil of Meinong who, in turn, was a pupil of Brentano and the founder of the first psychological laboratory in Austria. Fritz Heider has pursued the phenomenological aspect of earlier thought and has incorporated it with Lewinian concepts in the most purist sense of all current theorists. His explanation of cognitive balance and the psychological nature of words and meaning (*Psychology of Interpersonal Relations,* 1958) reflects an important current contribution that is largely overlooked by most counseling theorists because of the rigorous examination of the philosophical nature of language and the concepts discussed. George Kelly and his construct theory also comes close to the mainstream of Gestalt thought, particularly Lewinian notions, and some of the older phenomenologists. His major postulate: "A person's processes are psychologically channelized by the ways in which he anticipates events" (Kelly, 1963, 46) not only illustrates the affinity to Gestalt psychology but also expresses in modern language the classical hypothesis of Brentano regarding intentionality.

Donald Snygg and Arthur Combs reflect both a concern with learning and an adaptation of phenomenological-Gestalt thought to counseling. Johnson (1961) in a study of Rogers' thought wrote to Arthur Combs and asked him about the relationship of phenomenology to his psychological notions. Combs indicated that he had not read the phenomenologists to any extent but thought that certain ideas tend to be generalized out of various disciplines and to lose their identity. A further letter to Donald Snygg was answered together with a copy of a letter sent by Snygg to Spiegelberg. Snygg traced the evolution of his own thinking about phenomenology to an awareness of Lewin in 1935 "by way of his Aristotelian and non-Aristotelian frames of reference," and "to a systematic course at Toronto in 1933 on Brentano and Husserl." Snygg concluded his letter by writing:

The outline shows clearly that you are right in attributing any

German influence to the Gestalt people and through them Stumpf. The basic concept as I see it, antedates Lewin or at least my acquaintance with his work, but his discussion of frames of reference, an obviously phenomenological concept, has been very stimulating to me" (Johnson, 1961, 214).

Combs, in an article (February 1954), mentioned the variables of perception that he felt were central to the counseling process:

1. Perception is a function of the state of the physical organism in which the perception occurs. Perception both affects and is affected by the physical organism which serves as the vehicle for perceiving.

2. Perception takes time. Effective perception requires sufficient exposure to make perceiving possible.

3. Perception cannot occur without opportunity for experience. This opportunity for perceiving may be of a concrete character or may be purely symbolic. In any event, there must be some form of opportunity provided for perceiving to happen.

4. Perception is a function of the individual's values and goals. The values and goals of the individual have a selective effect upon the individual's field of perceptions. Other factors being equal, people perceive more sharply and effectively those aspects of themselves and of life which have greatest value for them.

5. Perception is a function of the self concept of the perceiver. The concept of self has a selective effect on perceptual field. People perceive that which is appropriate for persons with their concepts of self to perceive. . . .

6. Perception is seriously affected by the experience of threat. These effects seem to be of two kinds (a) when a person feels threatened his field of perceptions is reduced to the object of threat producing the well-known effect of tunnel vision; and (b) when threatened, the individual seeks to defend his existing self-organization. Both of these effects seem to have extremely important bearings upon the counseling process.

These quotations from Combs reveal that later phenomenological thought has been influenced by the development of counseling practice, particularly that of Rogers.

OFFSHOOTS OF PHENOMENOLOGY AND GESTALTISM

Phenomenology and Gestalt psychology have this in common that both represented not only a body of information about the nature of perception and cognitive structure variables but also provided a methodological basis for such investigations. Unfortunately, the methodological framework of phenomenology and Gestalt psychology has had little chance to survive within American Psychology and education, with its basic positivistic approach toward scientific method, that is, one of reductionism to manifestly evident observable differences within the stimulus-response model.

The effects of phenomenology and Gestalt psychology can be traced in three major areas: (1) in the methodological studies of French psychologists concerned with child behavior and genetic psychology, (2) in the work of the cognitive theorists of recent years within the United States, and (3) in the broader more diffused area of personality theory and construct theory.

From a methodological point of view, a number of circumstances that relate to the observation of children have been focused in French psychology. Building on the observation techniques of Wilhelm Preyer (1842–1897), the method of clinical examination utilized by Pierre Janet, and the conversations with children used by members of the Wurzburg school, the French movement in psychology was sparked by Alfred Binet (1857–1911) in testing young children, and by Edouard Claparede (1873–1939), who developed a method of observing the thinking and problem solving of children. Claparede was particularly interested in observing the effect of problems on the overt thinking of children. Placing a child in a problematic situation, the observer would simply observe, taking pains not to interrupt or shape the thought process of the child. This psychogenetic method has evolved a series of experimental studies that focus on the ontogeny or origin of logical thinking as possible indices of genetic development. Jean Piaget has been tied to this movement through Barbel Inhelder who collaborated in many of Claparede's experiments.

The influence of both phenomenological methodology as incorporated into psychology and Gestalt theory is evident in Piaget, although this was certainly not his original direction. But the contention that genetic psychology as such is concerned with both an experimental and descriptive phase of research, and the observation that the evolution of logical process is related to a set of spatial-temporal foci, shows the obvious connection. Piaget's theory developed as a descriptive rather than as an experimental system, was based primarily on the observation of child behavior. He has stated that particular sets of principles of organization become operative at particular stages and are replaced as the child matures further. Hence, increasingly complex hierarchies of cognitive structures are developed through which the child reacts in different ways to his environment. Cognitive growth is thus not merely a systematic accumulation of knowledge of self and environment but is, instead, an interactive process between existing or accumulated structures and the environmental stimulation of the learning situation. Specific learned functions are, therefore, the end process of a complex interaction between structural capacity and environmental stimuli that are explained through an accommodation-assimilation process (Flavell, 1963).

While the original Piagetian formulation operated independent of the environment, that is, postulating that the particular stages through which a child developed would occur relatively independent of environmental conditions, it is apparent today that some experimental studies of recent years have modified Piaget's original formulations. Piaget states that although learning cannot explain development, development can, in large part, explain learning (Almy, Chittenden & Miller, 1966).

Piaget views early cognitive development as arising from the perceptual structure, and this perceptual structure is characterized by a development sequence in logical operations. Piaget's method tends to characterize children by their basal level of responding, or typical mode, rather than the ceiling notion so common in the development of intelligence tests. The method itself calls for systematic observation including a dialogue between the observer and the child, using neutral language as much as possible in order to avoid shaping the behavior of the child in relationship to the questioning of the observer. This approach is basically phenomenological in nature, attempting to infer the qualitative nature of developmental logic by typical methods of attack to given problems.

Another area in which phenomenological thinking and Gestalt psychology has had an influence is the area of the cognitive approach to learning among American theorists. Jerome Bruner and David Ausubel are representative of this point of view. Bruner, like Piaget, holds to a sequential development of cognitive functions, but whereas Piaget tends to accent more the invariant developmental structures, Bruner tends to accent the effect of the nurturing environment in the development of cognitive concepts (Elkind, 1967). Bruner, instead of postulating relatively distinct stages through which children pass in order, postulates the emergence of three modes of representation, representation here meaning ". . . the end product of . . . a system of coding and processing . . ." (Bruner, 1964). He feels, however, that although these modes are sequentially developed, the person keeps on using the modes learned earlier even after later ones have been learned. Contrary to Piaget, who feels that human reasoning activities are closely bound to maturational levels, Bruner states that children can learn any highly skilled activity provided that it is broken down sufficiently into its component parts. Maturation is the combining of these component sequences, "orchestration" as he refers to it, into an integrated sequence. The three modes of representation, the enactive, iconic, and symbolic, posited by Bruner, develop sequentially, each one out of the previous one, yet retaining the previous one within the repertoire of the person throughout his life. Enactive representation refers to the mode of representing past experience through a motor response, such as shoe-tying or bicycle-riding. The iconic representation is the organization of percepts and perceptual structures into the corresponding mental images, as for example a picture of an object standing for the object in question. Finally, symbolic representation includes the use of symbols that may not resemble the things represented, may be arbitrarily chosen, and that may not have spatial or temporal proximity to the object in question. This, of course, entails the use of words, either written or spoken, to represent objects, that is, language. Thus through the use of language a person becomes able to represent experience, to draw it from memory, and also to transform it by transforming the patterns by which one expresses it. In a very real sense, language and the logic inherent in it come to control reality with all the attending intentionalistic connotations.

Ausubel's (1963) approach suggests that the primary skill in learning, including school learning, is centered on concept formation. Opposing the traditional, Dewey-based assumptions regarding learning that are given preference in most schools, that is, abstract concepts are built on a long chain of inductive experiences with concrete phenomena, he boldly states that this experience is time-consuming and ignores the fundamental components of concept formation.

He says that "most of the understandings that learners acquire both in and out of school are presented rather than discovered" (Ausubel, 1963, 16). He defines reception learning as the kind of learning in which ". . . the entire content of what is to be learned is presented to the learner in final form" (Ausubel, 1963, 16). Thus the learner is not left to discover for himself everything by trial and error, but he has to internalize the presented material or subsume it into his existing cognitive organization.

Ausubel says that in discovery learning the learner must independently discover the principal content of what is to be learned before it can be internalized, while in reception learning his task is to internalize what is presented; thus the beginning processes of the two are quite different. He suggests that all discovery learning is not necessarily meaningful, and that, although rote learning is, indeed, a form of reception learning, reception learning should and can be meaningful.

Ausubel places chief emphasis on the necessity of adequate cognitive organizers, which he considers the intellective scaffolding on which concepts are subjectively organized by the thought processes. Concept formation is related directly to two major factors: (1) the clarity of the organizer, which he defines as the scaffolding of the verbal structure, and (2) the psychological readiness of the subsumer, that is, the receiving organism. Finally, he argues that meaning itself is a subjective phenomenon and is conveyed in part by the organizer variable. But the precision of psychological meaning is related to both the organizer and the subsuming organism.

These examples of modern developments in both phenomenological method and cognitive theory illustrate what has happened to the phenomenological bases of Gestalt psychology.

EXISTENTIALISM

The other philosophical position that underlies the humanistic approach to counseling is existentialism. Whereas in phenomenology, meaning is prior to or at least embedded in the nature of being, existentialism is a philosophy that focuses on experience and experiencing. While phenomenology is concerned with the emergence of meaning as an already existent potential within the structure to be activated by the environment in some kind of logical sequence of experiences, existentialism bypasses considerations of genetic psychology and development and tends to leap to the concept of experience itself. In a very real sense, existentialism abandons the search for objective philosophical reality in science, and it likewise considers an analysis of the philosophical constituents of a priori structure somewhat fruitless. It concentrates on the transitory nature of human experience itself. Rollo May, reminiscent of Heidegger, calls attention to the term "human being" by explaining that being is a participle, a very form implying that someone is in the process of being something (1958). May defines existentialism as "the philosophical trend of thought which takes as its focus of interest the consideration of man's most immediate experience, his own existence" (1958, 11). More to the point of this discussion, he also defines existentialism as "the endeavor to understand man by cutting below the cleavage between subject and object which has bedeviled Western thought and science since shortly after the Renaissance." Thus existentialism focuses on the immediate experience of man in his living and being. There is an emphasis on the transitory immediate self-evident nature of life experience in which questions of essential structure or nature are to be bypassed in lieu of an examination of the unique characteristics of experience. Sartre carries this trend still further by suggesting that man does not have an a priori being but is, instead, the product of what he wills to be and his experience (1947).

Existentialism is not so much a philosophy as it is a movement. The philosophical roots might be traced to Soren Kierkegaard, a Danish philosopher who opposed vigorously Hegelian idealism. Martin Heidegger seems to be a contributor to the movement also, bringing into the movement the later philosophical thought of phenomenology. But essentially Existentialism is a frame of reference that is shared by philosophers, some theologians, poets, counselors and nonconformists. It is a reaction against formalistic philosophy. It manifests a weariness with the traditions of our culture, the objectivity of science as well as the subjectivity of philosophy. The existentialist is concerned with the matter of existence, the here and now of on-going daily experience. Therefore, he rejects the notion of essences, universals, a priori structures, academic rationalism, and learning theory behaviorism. He is not interested, for example, in the why of behavior, but the fact of behavior. Behavior is or is not. There is little to be gained in seeking for the reasons why behavior occurs. In a sense, existentialism attempts to go to the very roots of man's inner world and to grasp a new concept of reality. It is a reality pictured in direct honest and vital relationship to the primary experience of man as he lives with himself and with others. It attempts to express the feelings of the human mind even though this may result in a description of despair, loneliness, and emptiness.

Insofar as existentialism has a philosophical basis, epistemology plays an important role in the determination of the existentialist ontology and axiology. The emphasis on existence or the transaction between subject and object leads to the observation that man is alone in the universe of his experience. I am the self-conscious center of my own experience. However, this "aloneness" also provides a bond of common union with other men and the epistemological basis of existentialism. For all men not only share the common experience of being but also the ever-present threat of nonbeing. It is the ever-present knowledge of the imminence of nonbeing that May considers at the very core of existentialism. It is the existentialist "categorical imperative," the one absolute that all men share. The fact that death is not relative but absolute, is precisely the reason why men can savor and enjoy the existence that is life. Furthermore, all other knowledge and certitude pale in comparison with the immediate self-evident and apodictic nature of individual experience.

This epistemological imperative then leads to ethical alternatives in terms of action. Man has a choice of two ways in which he can face his problem of nonbeing. He can face the alternative of nonbeing by accepting his existence or running away from it. If he chooses to accept it and to utilize it in a constructive way, he can attain a measure of happiness and can fulfill some commitment to his fellow men. If he chooses to avoid the inevitable nature of death he does not live up to his potentialities. The result is often anxiety and guilt. May also speaks of dimensions of reality, and they follow chiefly from the epistemological framework of existentialism. He refers to them as the *Umwelt*, the *Mitwelt*, and the *Eigenwelt*. The first represents contact with the world of external and material reality which may be identified with scientific findings and other knowledge. The *Mitwelt* is conceived as the world of interrelationships with other human beings, not "herd" relationships in which the individual is forced to conform to the group, but mutual relationships characterized by involvement. The *Eigenwelt* is the world of uniquely personal individual experiences. This is the world of self-relatedness and self-awareness, the basis for our relationship with the other two worlds. These three worlds are not independent, but so interact that they constantly affect each other. They are but three modes of being-in-the-world which, according to existentialist thought, are necessarily interrelated if an individual is to operate efficiently.

Sartre probably represents the existentialist who is most concerned with ontology and who most precisely emphasizes the difference between the phenomenological and existential points of view. For Sartre sees man as first coming into the world and then, through his existence, determining what his "essence" is. Sartre's well-known aphorism sums up his point of view: "Existence precedes essence." Moreover, he says of man:

> . . . . man, first of all, exists, turns up, appears on the scene and only afterwards, defines himself. If man as the existentialist conceives him, is indefinable, it is because at first he is nothing. Only afterward will he be something, and he himself will have made what he will be . . . Not only is man what he conceives himself to be, but he is only what he wills himself to be after his first thrust toward existence. Man is nothing else but what he makes of himself. Such is the first principle of existentialism (Sartre, 1947, 3–4).

Existentialism has not influenced American thought to any extent until approximately the last decade. Within the past few years, an increasingly large number of American psychologists and counselors have been drawn to this particular philosophical camp. Gordon Allport (1960, 1963), Carl Rogers (1961), George Kneller (1961), Franz E. Winkler (1960), Katherine Carroll (1960), Adrian van Kaam (1962), Carlton E. Beck (1963), Paul Tillich (1964), Richard P. Vaughn (1964), and Ted Landsman (1964) are among the authors who have either written on existentialist views or have produced educational and guidance literature in which they have expressed ideas that have a strong existentialist flavor without attaching a label to them. Perhaps, the existentialist emphasis on the importance of the goals and the values of the individual, the opposition to forced conformity, and the idealization of group-membership account for the increasing interest in this philosophical basis for counseling. Harper (1959, 77) explains the matter thus:

> Existential philosophy represents an European trend away from positivism, functionalism, instrumentalism, pragmatism, and operationalism . . . all of which tend to be close to the center of the value system of the scientist and of many American therapists. This is one reason for the lack of popularity of existential analysis in this country. Another reason is that existentialism is a philosophy of crisis. In an environment of desparation, man, as the existentialists see him, is striving for his forgotten power to be; man's plight is one of despairing for his spontaneous existence.

Existentialism, then, is still another basis of the humanistic approach to counseling. It represents a subject-oriented philosophy that emphasizes the existence or the transaction between subject and object rather than any essentialist point of view about the a priori conditions of human nature. In this particular point lies the difference between phenomenology on the one hand and existentialism on the other. There is, of course, much overlapping in both phenomenology and existentialism in beliefs. Within both frames of reference there are Christian or religious orientations as well as nonreligious. Kierkegaard, for example, believed in a "blind leap to faith" as a solution to man's despair and unhappiness. Tillich considers God as the Absolute Ground of our experience and being. It is by really accepting and involving ourself with others that we come to understand more fully the nature of our life and reality within an eternal framework. Both Brentano and Husserl represent general theistic approaches to phenomenology. Heidegger did not. Van Kaam and Vaughn represent Catholic positions in which existentialism is considered as a modern extension of some of Thomistic psychology and philosophy. Sartre obviously represents a nonreligious form of existentialism.

Before going on to Carl Rogers and self-concept theory, it might be well to provide a short critique of the foregoing movements. Phenomenology has lost much of its original momentum. The grand strategy that Husserl planned for an assault on the nature of consciousness and the development of a rigorous methodology for investigating subjective phenomena has never really materialized. Somehow the analysis of conceptual thinking led into all sorts of blind alleys. However, in American psychology Fritz Heider has continued in the clearest phenomenological direction. Thus, likewise, the methodological bent of phenomenology is definitely observed in the work of Piaget.

Gestalt psychology was born with great fanfare and has equally gone into decline. It continues to survive through perceptual theorists and takes its main transmission through Lewin and field theory. Strikingly enough, both phenomenology and Gestalt psychology were first concerned with theory and theoretical principles. Much of the original formulation of Gestalt theory was related to observational studies—awaiting full experimental verification. But as the years passed, these principles became more and more the postulated intellectual framework of certain ideas in education and counseling. And they have survived there more as apodictic canons of behavior rather than as rigorously demonstrated principles. They have become the substance and woof of the faith that men have in counseling. And some of this criticism, at least, can be laid to the failure of those who espoused these theories to test them rigorously and to proceed with due regard for the rigorous methodology to which the leaders subscribed, but which has been largely dispensed with by the second and third generations of followers.

Of prime importance in the decline of phenomenology and Gestalt psychology has been the inadequate understanding that American psychologists have had of the phenomenological method. It is only in very recent years, that the failure to assess more accurately within the traditional scientific frame of reference has caused some researchers to look more closely at the method of Piaget. Moreover, the rise of existentialism as a kind of antiscientific bias has caused behavioral scientists and even true phenomenologists to lose patience. Koch (1963) states that there are "woolly revivalist overtones" in the current interest in existentialism in American psychology. He decries what he considers meaningless slogans, the love of paradox and cryptic yet somehow "pregnant slogans." Of chief concern is the sloppy methodology (as compared with traditional rigorous scientific experimentation), the use of philosophical language in a vain attempt to communicate meaningful psychological knowledge, and a tendency that he describes as "headlong assaults on the ineffable . . ." He is further dismayed by existentialist students whom he describes as "off in some realm of epigrammatic nuance, or ardent association chasing, before a problem even gets started, whether by themselves or others." These criticisms, of course, are voiced by individuals who do not believe or subscribe to the positions outlined in this chapter. That these views are fairly common within the behavioral circles of psychology needs no further documentation. That phenomenological,

Gestalt and particularly existentialist thought have been deficient in the defining of even their own unique methodology is the admission of some existentialists such as Landsman (1964).

CARL ROGERS AND SELF-CONCEPT THEORY

Carl Rogers' counseling approach has been one of the most concrete, albeit watered-down outcomes of the phenomenological tradition. Rogers did not devise his counseling technique in relationship to these philosophical bases as such, but they have become the *post factum* intellectual justification for his techniques. Essentially, Rogers' approach has been that of a technique in search of a theoretical base. This is in accord with Rogers' conviction that theory proceeds from practice—a notion that bespeaks the pragmatic influence of Teachers' College (Rogers, 1951, 15). Rogers' technique of client-centered counseling has enjoyed a widespread acceptance in counseling circles. In fact, its success and widespread adoption is probably one of the most significant events in psychology during the 1950s.

Such phenomenal success for a technique demands an attempt to explain it. There would appear to be at least five reasons why Rogers' approach spread the way it did. First, the approach directly or indirectly did away with the need for the diagnosis and intensive study of clinical entities. It denied in a word the efficacy of the medical model in psychotherapy and challenged the assumptions on which much earlier psychotherapy had been founded. Although Rogers originally cautioned that he would accept only certain kinds of cases who appeared to be able to profit from client-centered therapy, he later opened the door to all kinds of cases. The impact of Rogers' approach was to suggest something *de novo* to the counseling profession, that is, a method which works with a minimum of training. This was very important in a period in which counseling and guidance personnel work were increasing at a phenomenal rate and there were many kinds of demands for experienced and trained counselors. Training in client-centered therapy seemed to make sense to many counselor educators. Even where it did not receive wholehearted support, it was conceded by many privately that the least harm could be done to clients through this approach which stressed acceptance and nondirective responses.

A second reason for the acceptance of client-centered therapy was the fact that it catered to a fundamental American pragmatism and to the Horatio Alger myth, namely, that man can make of himself what he will—not necessarily by dint of hard work as the older version went but, instead, by a concentrated effort at self-understanding. Third, Rogers' approach, summarized in his 19 propositions, contained elements of almost every psychological system or theory. There were fragments of Freud, bits of Lewin, the social aspects of James' functionalism, and Dewey's interaction theory, something from Sullivan's theory of dissociation, as well as principles derived from Snygg and Combs, Goldstein, Maslow, and Allport. Moreover, the nondirective alternative of Otto Rank's therapy approach was made the keystone of the technique. Thus Rogers' propositions formed a good "eclectic" approach to personality theory and counseling. A fourth reason for the success of the approach may be traced to the overzealous pronouncements of the clinical approach, the reaction of many against authoritarianism of any form, and the basic desire to find something concrete in counseling that worked. Finally, and perhaps most important, Rogers' approach had something of the charisma of a new missionary movement. This was tied to some fairly spectacular results in applying the listening technique and nondirective approaches. Nearly all counselor educators have witnessed the almost evangelical enthusiasm and recognition that occurs when a counselor in training learns how to apply some of Rogers' techniques in counseling. Interpreted from another frame of reference, this is the greatest kind of operant conditioning in that counselors are immediately reinforced by their attempt to apply these principles. This kind of reinforcement tended to build up an avid coterie of followers who felt that the technique could work in any place and with any kind of individual. It is a tribute to the real work of Rogers that his approach to nondirective therapy has been formulated so loosely but has generalized beyond his expectations and cautious considerations.

Carl Rogers has had a wide variety of educational experience. He started his education at the University of Wisconsin in the field of agriculture and then switched to Union Theological Seminary to study for the ministry. He spent two years there, then started in the field of psychology at Teachers' College, Columbia University. He derived some of his educational philosophy from William H. Kilpatrick who was a follower of John Dewey in certain aspects of his philosophy. He also studied Freud and absorbed a good deal of Freudian psychodynamics. After graduation and the completion of his advanced studies, he became a psychologist at the Child Study Department of Rochester, New York, where he first developed some of his ideas of client-centered therapy. Since then, he has taught at a variety of university settings, including Ohio State University, the University of Chicago, and the University of Wisconsin. He now resides at La Jolla, California.

Rogers' thought can be traced through his writings as well as from other sources. He himself states:

The development of the writer's own thinking in regard to therapy may be observed by considering the sequence of writings, *Clinical Treatment of the Problem Child,* "The Clinical Psychologist's Approach to Personality Problems," *Counseling and Psychotherapy,* "Significant Aspects of Client-Centered Therapy," and the present volume, *Client-Centered Therapy* (Rogers, 1951, 18).

In his earlier works, Rogers showed a traditional approach to clinical psychology. He favored personality testing, used diagnostic tests, and advocated modification of the environment to effect changes in behavior. Subsequently, he tended to substitute the use of the word "remediation" for diagnosis, and moved toward a more Rousseauian attitude in regard to child behavior (Walker, 1956). Still later, most of the traditional diagnostic procedures were discarded. The case history and active diagnosis were held to be important only for some individuals who were severely handicapped in their ability to cope with their environment (Rogers, 1942). Subsequently, in 1951, Rogers moved to his most nondirective approach, emphasizing the quality of the relationship between counselor and client almost to the exclusion of the other methods of approach. In more recent writings (Rogers, 1961, in Wann, ed., 1964), he appears to be moving toward a rapprochement with existential thinking and to be searching for demonstrable research approaches to evaluating objectively the subject changes in self-concept.

Johnson (1961) in a study of Rogers' thought and its relationship to existentialism wrote to Rogers regarding the similarities between self-concept theory and existentialism. Rogers answered as follows:

> The main contact I have had with the phenomenological existential point of view has been through the work of Kierkegaard and Buber. I do not think it would be correct to say that they had any particular direct influence on my thinking. It was more that some of the theological students at Chicago told me the ideas that I was developing were very much similar to some of the existentialist ideas. It was this that led me to read them and I felt much rewarded by my reading. I have not found Sartre particularly helpful to me. My acquaintance with others in this field is quite limited (Johnson, 209).

Johnson concluded that there was a similarity between Rogers' approach and existentialism on four points:

1. Both schools advocated that experiences and phenomena preceded theory.

2. They both emphasized the importance and worth of the individual.

3. They both placed great emphasis on the individual's phenomenal
or perceptual world of experience.

4. And finally, both theories recognized a force within the individual
directed towards self-actualization and maturity (Johnson, 1961,
19).

Rogers has never felt that it was necessary to bind oneself to a theory
and adhere rigidly to that theory. For this reason it is difficult to depict
accurately what have been the specific influences in his thinking. Certainly, his initial training for the ministry with the obvious idealism that
accompanies this approach found a suitable outlet in both progressive
education and clinical psychology. The influence of Freudian psychodynamics, Lewin's field theory, the therapy approach of Otto Rank, and
Snygg and Combs in perception are all factors in his original approach.
Subsequently, as Rogers has practiced, written, and thought, it would
appear that his approach is, in fact, combining some elements of
phenomenology along with existentialism. Undoubtedly, one of Rogers'
greatest contributions was his early recognition of the weakness en-
gendered in clinical approaches to therapy, and of the overwhelming
effect of the personality of the therapist in the outcomes of therapy.

Rogers' Concept of the Nature of Man

One of the invariant (as far as can be determined) structures of client-
centered therapy, is the notion of the nature of man. Walker (1956)
pointed out that Rogers' concept of the nature of man differs radically
from the Freudian point of view. Freud did not place a direct value
judgment on the nature of man, such as that it is evil and needs to be
reformed (like the Christian doctrine of original sin, and particularly the
extremes of Calvin and Luther), but he felt that its essentially neutral
character had been vitiated by the effect of society itself. Walker quotes
Freud in *The Future of an Illusion* and *Civilization and Its Discontents*:

> It seems more probable that every culture must be built up on
> coercion and instinctual renunciation; it does not even appear certain
> that without coercion the majority of human individuals would be
> ready to submit to the labour necessary for acquiring new means of
> supporting life. One has, I think, to reckon with the fact that there
> are present in all men destructive, and therefore anti-social and
> anti-cultural tendencies, and that with a great number of people
> these are strong enough to determine their behavior in human
> society (Freud, *Future of an Illusion*, 1949, Hogarth Press, 10–11).

And again Freud writes:

> Civilized society is perpetually menaced with disintegration through this primary hostility of man towards one another . . . Culture has to call up every possible reinforcement in order to erect barriers against the aggressive instinct of man. . . Hence . . . its ideal command to love one's neighbor as oneself, which is really justified by the fact that nothing is so completely at variance with original nature as this (Freud, *Civilization and Its Discontents*, New York, Jonathan Cape & Harrison Smith, 1930, 86–87).

When this position is taken toward human nature, then Walker suggests that "the neutral role of the counselor may not be justified by the assumption that all will turn out well if the counselee is permitted to follow his basic impulses." In fact, it is more likely that without active intervention and directive help from the counselor that the client will make a mess of things.

On the contrary, if one assumes that human nature is basically good as may be inferred from the teachings of Confucius, Christ, and the psychological theory of Rousseau, then nothing need be added or coerced. Nondirection then becomes an important tool in helping the individual to grow and develop. Walker concludes that in Rogerian psychotherapy: "the problem of aims and goals in counseling becomes peripheral . . . Goals are of importance only as signposts by which to identify stages of development during the counseling process" (Walker, 1956, 90).

It is for this reason that Rogers places so much emphasis on the counselor approach to the counseling process. The notion of the basic worth of the individual is derived from a fundamental evaluation that man's human nature is good—not neutral, but good, and needs to be allowed to develop in its most natural manner. All of this leads to the conclusion that the counselors must have a positive regard for the client, that a conscious effort must be made not to prejudge others or to devaluate them. Diagnosis is avoided not so much because Rogers could not accept the power potential of judgment but because he recognized diagnosis in the traditional clinical sense as a form of prejudgment that actually created a selective perception on the part of the counselor, a closeness of mind. But in some sense of the word, one of the by-products of this approach was to view Rogers' counseling theory as somehow equivalent to a secular version of the Christian sacramental system. Even as the sacraments are considered avenues for the distribution of God's Grace and help, so the client-centered counselor tended to view the process of counseling as the prime means to self-awareness and understanding. Many client-centered counselors sought to help the client become aware of himself, to recognize his own unique qualities as a person, much in the way that a religious advisor is concerned with the saving of souls. The anchor or fundamental organizer of client-centered therapy seems to be rooted in an approach to man's human nature as essentially good.

Toward a Science of the Person

In recent years, Rogers has tended to define more precisely the philosophical bases of his counseling approach. In *Behaviorism and Phenomenology* (1964), a volume of the Rice University Semicentennial Series, Rogers spells out his basic epistemology. In this address he characterizes the psychology that he identifies with the terms phenomenological, existential, self-theory, self-actualization, health-and-growth psychology, being and becoming, and science of inner experience. He suggests that these terms represent a third force in psychology as distinct from the "objectivist" and "subjectivist" approaches. In terms similar to the existential *Umwelt, Mitwelt,* and *Eigenwelt,* Rogers distinguishes between three epistemological modes of knowing: subjective knowing, objective knowing, and interpersonal knowing. He suggests that all three kinds of knowing involve the formation of hypotheses that we check. Thus, for example, when one tastes a foreign dish, to use Rogers' example, one asks one's self if it is really liked.

> Do I like it? It is only by referring to the flow of my experiencing that I can sense the implicit meanings and conclude, 'I like its flavor but not its consistency.' Or in a very different situation after studying a large body of data I ask, 'What is the unit, the central principle, which I sense in all these varied and seemingly disparate events? Again I turn to my experiencing to try to determine what it is that gives me this sense of commonality (111).

Rogers suggests that all knowledge, even that of objective science, has its beginning as an inner subjective hypothesis that must be checked out. He sees a parallel between an individual searching for the right word that will precisely convey his feelings and the manner in which an individual tackles a new job or a complicated problem in research.

> At first his knowledge of the task is global, imprecise, undifferentiated. Then he begins to sense pattern—that these events or these facts seem to go together, that these other events or facts, while they loom large on the surface, are probably not important. He acts tentatively to test these inner hypotheses, moving forward when the

pattern is sensed as becoming stronger or correcting his direction when his sense of the pattern fades (111).

Just as internal feelings are checked by the self, so objective facts are checked against a reference group or criterion. But even in these instances, where scientists are looking at stimuli and responses in the outer world of facts, Rogers points out that they must agree that the simple world fact is, indeed, this. A judgment of this nature then falls back on the congruence of the subjective judgments to the criterion group. Thus Rogers points out the fact that even objective data are subject to:

> . . . a fallible and human way of knowing, depending basically upon an intelligently intuitive personal selection of the hypothesis, adequate operations for testing it, the wise selection of a reference group, and the empathic understanding of the experiences of that reference group when they actually (or more often in imagination) repeat the operations of the experimenter (115).

Rogers feels, furthermore, that psychotherapy is, indeed, a kind of epistemological testing of hypotheses between two individuals. The one individual may learn about another by asking him directly, or by observing indirect cues, but the essence of psychotherapy is to create a climate that makes it "psychologically safe and rewarding for you to reveal your internal frame of reference" (p. 115). Thus, ultimately, counseling becomes an epistemological transaction, a communication in understanding.

Rogers believes that the psychologically mature person can communicate and can test his hypotheses on all three levels, that is, in terms of his own self-concept, in terms of interpersonal relationships, and in terms of objective data. He feels that it is a great mistake to limit the testing of our knowledge to the objective domain alone. The self-imposed canons of the behaviorist, according to Rogers, limits his creativity and forces him to ignore the whole domain of personal feelings. Nor does Rogers think that the opening of psychology to the new variables of meaning, self-concept, and psychotherapeutic interaction will demean the cause of science or will reduce it to the "pseudoscience" of Freudian insights. Rogers ends his discussion with an impassioned plea for the freedom of man.

> It is my judgment, as I try to understand the vigorous thrust of this phenomenological-existentialist movement in a variety of other fields, as well as in psychology, that it represents a new philosophical emphasis. Here is the voice of subjective man speaking up loudly for himself. Man has long felt himself to be but a puppet in life— molded by economic forces, by unconscious forces, by environmental

forces. He has been enslaved by persons, by institutions, by the theories of psychological science. But he is firmly setting forth a new declaration of independence. He is discarding the alibis of *un*freedom. He is *choosing* himself, endeavoring, in a most difficult and often tragic world, to *become* himself—not a puppet, not a slave, not a machine, but his own unique individual self. The view I have been describing in psychology has room for this philosophy of man (p. 130).

From this vantage point, then, it is clear how client-centered therapy includes in its goals, insight, self-understanding, self-awareness, and self-acceptance. Moreover, it is also a logical consequence of these goals that the client and not the counselor sets the terms of the therapy. Furthermore, since counseling is a very personal process, there is no necessary need for searching for external criteria of meaningful change. Not that Rogers is opposed to such endeavors but, rather, he refuses to limit the efficacy of his method and technique to a set of external criteria, which in his judgment, ultimately depend on subjective judgment also.

The counseling approach of Rogers unites in a practical approach the philosophical notions of phenomenology and existentialism, and the tradition, if not the substance, of the personality variants of Gestalt psychology. This is the approach that emphasizes the subject of knowledge. Although there are distinctions between phenomenology, which posits an a priori essence, as against existentialism, which emphasizes transactional experience, nonetheless, the goals, method, and criteria of counseling have a close unity, a unity that emphasizes man as the measure of reality rather than reality as the measure of man.

SUMMARY

This chapter has focused on the philosophical implications of phenomenology. Phenomenology has been depicted as both a metaphysical frame of reference, including specific views about the nature of reality, knowledge, and values, and as a methodology for the investigation of subjective phenomena. The movement itself is related to, or concurrent with, the development of Gestalt psychology. Both phenomenology and Gestalt psychology have played an important role in the development of cognitive approaches to learning and personality, of methodological approaches to child study within genetic psychology, and have overflowed into existential philosophy. Rogers' counseling theory is seen as one further extension of personality theory within the basic subjective frame of reference of phenomenology, Gestalt psychology, and existentialism.

CHAPTER VIII

The Problem-Solving Model: Experimentalism

Experimentalism as a method and a philosophy tends to be the overt or covert basis for the problem-solving technique in counseling as well as the eclectic approach. Experimentalism has been identified with the philosophy of John Dewey and represents a social relativism that is distinctly characteristic of American culture. Experimentalism was not just translated from Europe and grafted on to American culture, but it is a distinct American development that tends to cast problems of epistemology, ontology, and axiology into a subordinate role, weighing philosophy against the criterion of social experience. Specifically, it tends to emphasize technique, weighing its results in terms of pragmatic utility. Experimentalism is an American phenomenon that evolved as a consequence of the American frontier spirit, of the expansion of the public schools as a vehicle of cultural integration, and as a result of the appreciation of the worth of social evolution.

Even as experimentalism became the *de facto* philosophical basis for progressive education, so its influence was felt in the expansion of the guidance function in education. It became the implicit justification for introducing guidance personnel into the schools. For experimentalism has its philosophical roots in social psychology and pragmatism and is specifically concerned with social adjustment and adaptation. Counseling and guidance were viewed in this light as an adjunct of larger education policy. For the problem-solving emphasis in education seemed a most appropriate one for guidance also in: (1) coping with the adjustment problems of large numbers of students, (2) providing a systematic vehicle for curriculum change and alteration, and (3) developing a specific technique for the maximum utilization of a large number of neophyte guidance workers.

This approach in guidance and counseling tended to ignore questions of philosophy. Philosophy was often relegated to an after-the-fact justi-fication. The predominance of this point of view in counseling can be seen by the dearth of early concern with philosophy in counseling ap-proaches in the United States.

Edmund G. Williamson may be identified as a chief proponent of this point of view. Although currently he manifests a lively interest in philosophical issues, his original bent was related to the problem solving of educational-vocational problems of students (1939). Clifford Froelich (1958) viewed every teacher as a counselor and attempted to expand the guidance function in terms of all teaching. But, perhaps, the greatest support for this point of view comes from those who refer to their orientation as eclecticism. Francis Robinson (1950) has identified himself with the eclectic approach. Eclecticism, although purporting to draw the best elements from every form of counseling theory, tends in virtue of this methodological assumption, that is, that methods should have the first priority rather than philosophical speculation, to relate counseling to a technique level instead of to a philosophical plane. This very logic or rationale of eclecticism is in itself the strongest argument for relating this approach to Dewey's experimentalism. Eclecticism suggests strongly that results are what matter and that the development of a technique must precede philosophy. This is specifically what Dewey suggested about philosophy, and it constitutes the argument in this chapter for the link between experimentalism and eclecticism.

This chapter will argue the point of view that experimentalism as a philosophy and method constitutes an object-oriented culture-sensitive approach to reality and to knowledge. The results of the method and approach are judged in terms of pragmatic consequences, cultural evolu-tion, and a better standard of living and adjustment. The approach is essentially concerned with man's adjustment to reality, and although cer-tainly not omitting a concern for man's subjective feelings, tends to emphasize the outer adjustment of man to his society, and the array of problem-solving skills that he needs to use in making his own individual adjustment to reality. This chapter will develop the historical back-grounds of experimentalism, and outline the essentials of Dewey's philos-ophy as applied to education and counseling, and will conclude with some representative guidance orientations that are derived from this approach.

CULTURAL PRECURSORS OF EXPERIMENTALISM

Since experimentalism is considered here as the by-product of Ameri-can historical experience and cultural evolution, it is necessary to identify some of these movements. The following sections will relate to: (1) cultural dimensions, (2) evolution and science, and (3) measurement theory. These three major factors have all contributed to the development of experimentalism as a unique American philosophy.

The 19th century American was confronted by two major currents in his life. These currents revolved around the changing social system in the United States and the open frontier. As we telescope the voluminous history of that era, it is possible to see these major movements reflected in a variety of psychological and philosophical writings. The development of a free public school system, the expansion of this system, and the rationale for this system are defended and expounded by the works of Dewey. The psychological awareness of conflict between science and religion, the nature of man's existence and humanity, are treated by William James and Edward Lee Thorndike. Measurement theory becomes an important technical tool for evaluating the individual differences that have been modified somewhat by an emerging new social order. And counseling and guidance practice becomes another method of utilizing the school's resources better and of meeting human needs more efficiently.

These movements must be considered in light of what have been termed historical currents in American culture (Lee, 1957). One of the most significant might be called the "frontier syndrome." This is the almost compulsive trend to travel west. The East-to-West movement that began with the Puritans helped spark the Revolutionary War, resulted in the destruction of our Indian population, and ended only as recently as the 1890s. From 1607 to 1900, the American nation was never without a frontier. The impact of 300 years of exploration and new frontiers is still with us today. It has been described in one way by historians, for example, Frederick Jackson Turner (1958), as a means whereby restless and dangerous elements of the culture were siphoned off.

Another factor that has greatly influenced American culture has been the transition from a rural agrarian to an urban industrial economy. While this book is being written, many states are in the throes of legislative reapportionment in response to demands brought about by this transition. The wealth and population of the United States are in the cities and suburbs but because country-dominated legislatures have refused to surrender control to the city representatives, overcrowded slums, poor traffic control, inadequate support for schools, racial discrimination, and air pollution have continued to plague the largest segment of our population. Very often, states have refused to equalize this situation in terms of voting, and it is for this reason that the Supreme Court has ordered the states to begin the task of reapportionment.

Unquestionably, the matter of land and land expansion also has had an important role in American culture. Although there were other reasons for immigrating to America, such as the desire to avoid criminal punishment or military conscription, adventuring for quick wealth, or religious freedom, free land was the chief incentive for immigration. This was related originally to the Enclosure Acts in 16th century England. These acts took place in part because of the redistribution of land by Henry VIII and his successors, and in part because of the advance of commerce and mercantilism. It was cheaper to cultivate sheep and to send the wool to Flanders than to allow large groups of peasants to live on the land. Later, the immigration of Scandinavians, Germans, and Southern Europeans was initiated chiefly by a desire for land and freedom from the economic constraints of European culture. Individuals who would leave their homeland for an uncertain country with many unknown obstacles, such as Indians and wild animals, were often nonconformists and rugged individualists. They helped both to build the rural-agrarian culture and to contribute to the evolution of the cities.

Another significant trend has been the conflict between sectional independence and federalism. The original 13 colonies considered themselves as sovereign states, forming a mutual protection agreement under the Articles of Confederation. Although Independence from England and the Constitution signaled the beginning of a nation, the quality of the Union was tried again and again, culminating in the Civil War. Many of the fears and rivalries of the original 13 colonies have, in a sense, lasted to present days. The doctrine of interposition of state sovereignty has been tried even in recent years because of the integration conflicts in the South. And, although isolationism as a political doctrine was supposed to have died when the Japanese bombed Pearl Harbor in 1941, there are still strong echoes of isolationism in demands for higher tariffs, and in the opposition to financial support of the United Nations and similar issues. These historical trends are reflected in the continued development of American culture. Moreover, they are also reflected strongly in the psychological and philosophical developments of the late 19th century and early 20th century. It is with regard to this background that the historian of ideas must evaluate the rise of pragmatism and measurement theory.

EVOLUTION AND SCIENCE

Against the social and cultural movements of the American scene in the 19th century must be weighed the developments of science in both Europe and America. For during the 19th century there were more changes in conceptions about the nature of the learning process and of the child as a learner than in the entire 3000 preceding years of formal educational development. The causes for these changes are not easy to delimit, but several major factors should be considered.

The first was the post-Civil War economic, technological, geographic, and population growth of the United States with its correlative demands on the educational structure, the changes in outward form, and the search of European science for pertinent insights into the psychology of behavior. A second factor was the dissemination of the Darwinian theory of evolution which presented a new approach to the nature of man. The development of teaching as a paid profession brought demand both from within and without the ranks of educators for the better training of teachers, more teacher-training institutions, and a more clearly specified set of professional standards for those who identified themselves as members of the teaching profession. Then, too, educators were becoming acquainted with the German psychological studies and were particularly impressed by the procedures being utilized in the nationalized school systems in many countries of Europe. Parallel developments in psychology, sociology, and statistical methodology brought about many changes in thinking, even though these changes were slow in being adapted to the school situation.

A hundred years ago, it was assumed that children were basically much alike in needs and capacities, and that the differences which existed were due to good or bad habits, to laziness or to "natural orneriness," or to differences in discipline. The significance of individual differences in a variety of learning situations was recognized by only a few individuals, such as Froebel and Horace Mann, and was hardly ever a factor in educational practice. The school curriculum was under the sway of faculty psychology. The then current point of view was that learning, to be effective, had to "try" the mind and make it work. The assumption was much like that relating to somatic muscles, that is, drill, work, and memorization were the essentials of the training of the mind. Mind and body were considered to be separate but interdependent. Payne (1887) suggested that "a faculty of whatever kind grows by exercise" and that "exercise involves repetition, which as regards bodily actions, ends in habits of action, and as regards impressions received by the mind, ends in clearness of perception."

The classical languages—Latin and Greek—were still being taught in many schools, but were involved in a losing battle. More and more practical subjects were striving for a place in the crowded curriculum. The defenders of the classics based their arguments on the principle of formal discipline, bolstered by arguments like this one by Fitch in 1880:

. . . The study of language is the study of humanity; the forms of language represent the forms of human thought; the history of language is the history of our race and its development; and great command over the resources of language is only another name for great command over the ideas and conceptions which make up the wealth of our intellectual life (1897, 211).

Meanwhile, the influence of evolution theory was being felt in the United States under three major movements: (1) Social Darwinism, (2) Child Study Method, and (3) Recapitulation Theory.

Social Darwinism

One of the strongest educational links to Darwinism came through the writings of Herbert Spencer. During the 18th century, there had been a recurring optimism that, by the use of pure reason, man could lift himself by his boot-straps and could create a Utopia on this earth. Subsequent disillusionment did not prevent the dream from reappearing 150 years later in another guise: that of a slow, evolutionary process to perfection, inexorable and inevitable, unaffected by man's personal intervention or effort. To Spencer, the "survival of the fittest" referred to the survivors of an intraspecies struggle, whether on a physical, social, or economic level. As the fittest among men would survive in every generation, progress toward the ultimate in fitness would be inevitable. The struggle is between individuals; any intervention by social or governmental agencies constitutes an interference with this conflict and, thus, interference with the wisdom of nature. Men should submit to this "natural law," for to control or circumvent it is impossible. Inferior men (and races) are crushed, but the superior ones thrive and perpetuate an improved race.

Spencer was popular in the United States, since his philosophy satisfied the individualism of some of America's economic and intellectual leaders. Hofstadter (1955, 31–32) writes that the reason for Spencer's popularity was his philosophy which:

. . . was scientific in derivation and comprehensive in scope. It had a reassuring theory of progress based upon biology and physics. It was large enough to be all things to all men, broad enough to satisfy agnostics and theists. It offered a comprehensive world-view, uniting under one generalization everything in nature from protozoa to politics. It made Spencer the metaphysician of the homemade intellectual, and the prophet of the cracker-barrel philosopher.

Although Social Darwinism had little influence among psychologists, it exerted considerable impact on American sociological theory. It justified as "Natural Law" the laissez-faire attitudes in law, government, and economics. The corrupt business practices in the late 19th century and early 20th century were considered to be merely individualism at its best. Andrew Carnegie wrote regarding the law of "survival of the fittest":

> It is here; we cannot evade it; no substitutes for it have been found; and while the law may sometimes be hard for the individual, it is best for the race, because it insures the survival of the fittest in every department. We accept and welcome, therefore, as conditions to which we must accommodate ourselves, great inequality of environment, the concentration of business, industrial and commercial, in the hands of a few, and the law of competition between these, as being not only beneficial, but essential for the future progress of the race (Carnegie, 1889, 655).

In such a competitive atmosphere, it is understandable that children were not encouraged to plan for social improvement or human betterment. Since social evolution was considered to be a slow but inexorable and unmodifiable process, the child should be taught to fit into the social pattern by being himself one of the "fit" survivors. The status quo of society should be maintained. Conditions as they were should be accepted, but each individual should make the effort necessary to become successful. This could be accomplished by his working harder, being more thrifty, shrewd, and independent than the other person, and his competing, rather than cooperating, with the other fellow. The popularity of the Horatio Alger series attests to this attitude.

Toward the end of the century, Social Darwinism began to decline because of a number of social, cultural, economic, and legislative factors. Furthermore, the exposure of abuses and graft in government and business circles, labor discontent and strife, plus the informed opposition of individuals such as William James and John Dewey led to its gradual demise. However, the important point to note is that Social Darwinism emphasized a Lockean environmentalist position that appeared to be justified by biology. As we shall learn later, William James, although not as deeply concerned with social problems as was Dewey, appropriated much of Darwinian biology to combat Spencerian individualism by demonstrating that the individual mind does not operate in a social vacuum. Mental activities involve the active interrelationship of a person with a dynamic environment as may be seen in James' concept of the stream of consciousness.

Child Study Method

The second major development of this period relates to the child-study movement. One of the ardent evolutionists in the late 19th and early

20th centuries was G. Stanley Hall. His contributions to both psychology and education have been enormous, although his methodology and conclusions have been subject to justifiable criticism. Foremost among Hall's many ventures into pioneer fields was the child-study movement, which he initiated in Massachusetts in 1893. Soon, other child-study associations were formed in Iowa, Illinois, Nebraska, Kansas, and England. By 1901 societies had also been formed in Poland, Germany, and France. Child study made use of two methods; observation and the questionnaire. "At the peak of its popularity, enthusiastic teachers and parents announced with the utmost finality the results of their hasty excursions into the field of mental development," wrote Bradbury (1937, 35). Baker (1955) observed that science in this movement meant observation of individuals and painstaking record-keeping, with the consequent massing of data that could be sifted and analyzed in search for a law. John Dewey, who was on the advisory board of the Illinois Society for Child Study, objected to the procedure as one that involved the mere collection of facts, unguided by any working hypothesis.

Although a number of contributions emanated from this movement, for example, the discovery of the law of physical development from mass activity of large muscles to a more intricate and specific function in small muscles, the movement as such became discredited in the early 20th century and gave way to more scientific organizations for child study. Bradbury (1937) considered the contributions of this movement to be: "(1) an increased recognition of the importance of an empirical study of child and of educational psychology, (2) a realization of the necessity for a critical evaluation of methods, and (3) a comprehension of the importance of childhood *per se*."

Recapitulation Theory

Another major contribution of Hall is his recapitulation theory. Various forms of the "recapitulation theory" had previously been promoted by educators such as Condillac, Rousseau, Pestalozzi, Froebel, Herbart, and Spencer. All of them had proposed (in one form or another) to tie in methods of education of the individual with the development or evolution of the human race. The Herbartians, for example, had attempted to correlate the total curriculum of the schools with the cultural development of the race. However, it took the zeal for evolution and the genius of G. Stanley Hall to conceive of an educational system founded entirely on the biological evolution of the race. Hall's recapitulation theory stated that the individual, in the course of his development, repeats in encapsulated form the development of the race from earliest savagery to modern civilization. It is based on the "biogenetic law" generally attributed to Haeckel in 1866.

Haeckel's generalization is, in effect, that an animal in its development passes through stages representing the ancestors it had during the evolution from lower animals. This doctrine is termed recapitulation or the biogenetic law, and was epitomized by Haeckel in such phrases as "ontogeny recapitulates phylogeny," and "phylogeny is the mechanical cause of ontogeny," etc. (Hyman, 1955, 981).

The development referred to was embryological only; Haeckel proposed no implications for postnatal life. It was Hall who, like Freud, made the extension, both in time to the adult life of the human and in content, that is, extension to include mental and behavioral life as well as physiological development. Thus Hall wrote (1904):

The boy is father of the man in a new sense in that his qualities are infinitely older and existed well-compacted untold ages before the more distinctly human attributes were developed.

Hall's recapitulation theory is presented in greatest detail in his two-volume *Adolescence* (Hall, 1904). This was a work that "coming at the time when psychology was supposed to be about to unlock the door to scientific education, had a tremendous vogue" (Boring, 1950, 522). In it, Hall attempted to relate the four stages of a child's growth to their appropriate educational methods, using the levels of man's evolution as the criterion. The infant and young child to about age five, according to Hall, relives the infancy of the human race. For example, the grasp reflex is related atavistically to man's arboreal life. During this period the child is undergoing his most rapid growth and is acquiring the fundamental activities that man has acquired: bipedal locomotion, verbal communication, and the like.

From about five to eight years of age, the child is highly imaginative, and loves myths, stories, and poems. This is reportedly the myth-making and poetic period of savagery. During the period of age eight to eleven, the child is repeating the humdrum period of savagery and is more inclined to memorization, showing a plasticity for training. In adolescence, the child is seen as being interested in history, literature, languages, art, and the like with a correlative desire to read, to construct, to use the muscular and sensory apparatus, and to think and do on a large scale. In Hall's theory, the child must live through each stage of development in its proper sequence, since each stage is the proper stimulus for the next. Failure to achieve orderly expression in each stage may result in abnormalities, either mental or social. There is, at least, a surface resemblance here to Freud's theories of psychosexual development for both appear to be rooted in recapitulation theory.

The reasons for the disappearance of the theory are not difficult to analyze. Probably they involved the lack of experimental and pedagogical verification, as recapitulation theory was displaced by the more adequate "new education" proposed by Thorndike and substantiated philosophically by Dewey. Dewey frequently criticized Hall's work contending that:

The business of education is rather to liberate the young from reviving and retraversing the past than to lead them to a recapitulation of it (1916, 84).

Thus, the distinctive cultural traits of American society and the social psychology implications of evolution were factors in the American scene that are unquestionably related to the emergence of Dewey's philosophical system.

EDUCATIONAL MEASUREMENT AND ASSESSMENT

Another important factor in the evolution of experimentalism was the development of a scientific approach to educational measurement and evaluation.

From the puberty rites of the Paleolithic period to present-day forms of objective testing, evaluation has played an important part in cultural control. Evaluation as a means of intellectual and personality assessment plays a central role in the transmission of those forms of behavior that are deemed essential to the survival of a culture. It is the way in which a given society makes sure that individuals promoted to certain roles are, indeed, ready and capable of assuming those roles. Man has always felt the need of defining certain characteristics that were deemed necessary for successful functioning. Conforming behavior in a social setting became the first major criterion for this assessment. Certain present or past characteristics were deemed to be predictors of future congruence to the criterion. Although the early criteria were variously assessed in terms of manliness, hunting prowess, the knowledge of sexual mores, and the recognition of authority, they emerged in early societies as meaningful dimensions of evaluation or assessment. The more specific criteria of effective human conduct were basically related to stable, predictable patterns of behavior that were judged consonant with the survival of the group. Thus stable, predictable behavior was detailed in a ritual routine and was sanctioned by community authority. Eventually, certain kinds of behavior developed into powerful means of education. Thus early man, through a process of trial-and-error, identified certain characteristics that were considered to be reliable predictors of stable group behavior.

In order to insure the criteria of effective and predictable human behavior, a number of cultural mechanisms of control emerged. These mechanisms had as their goal the collective security of the group. They are identifiable as the family, customs, law, chieftains, religious beliefs and leaders, and education. To early man, they represented the concrete framework whereby the cultural heritage was transmitted and the survival of the group was insured.

The earliest form of assessment or evaluation was global in nature. Although no attempt was made to separate intellectual functioning from personality, the behavior patterns of the individual were subjected to the criterion of group collective security. The behavior repertory of the individual was examined and was scrutinized by those in a position of authority to determine whether it represented identifiable patterns of predictable and stable behavior.

The oral examination is a good example of the methods used by early men in evaluation. This, plus feats of courage and prescribed social behavior, served as a predictor of effective behavior. Later, as formal education developed, the degree of memory recall and conformity to school expectations became a part of the evaluation procedure. For whether observation was used alone or as a part of a selection questioning procedure, this technique possessed power functions for prediction in the sense that it provided certain behavioral cues that could be detected and identified, even in the absence of a logical rationale to explain the procedure.

But it was not long before a theoretical framework was joined to the observation procedure. Plato, in his hierarchy of society, demarcated certain kinds of behavior expected of various levels of society. He expected the philosopher-rulers to manifest verbal ability and intellectual wisdom, the soldiers and warriors to evince courage and manliness, and the vast masses to be concerned only with bodily functions. Hippocrates discerned differences in men's constitutional makeup, suggesting that all individuals fell into the categories of phlegmatic, choleric, sanguine, or melancholic. The oral examination, used either by itself or in conjunction with a philosophical position, emerged as an important part of the medieval university, where a student was not compelled to attend any number of regular lectures. The essential burden of evaluation or assessment in medieval education was placed on an elaborate variation of the oral interview, in which a candidate for a degree was examined by a group of university masters before his peers. This took the form of defending a thesis in which the full complement of the young scholar's abilities was brought to bear during the process of presenting an argument and defending it against the attacks of his superiors and peers. The advantage of this type of assessment of behavior, from the evaluation point of view, was that it provided not only an index of the personal knowledge of the candidate but also an idea as to how well a given individual could think on his feet in providing opposing arguments to the charges made against his thesis and in dealing with the general stress of the situation. This form of oral examination, too, is still with us in the modern university where it is used extensively both in foreign and American institutions to determine competency of master's and doctoral candidates.

The use of personal observation and interviewing has always been structured by the needs of the cultural group. These needs provide the point of view or the frame of reference. Even as in early cultures the assessment of men related to personal skills and prowess in hunting and warfare, so later, in medieval and reformation times, monks were scrutinized to determine whether they possessed the kinds of characteristics needed in the monastic life. For example, Ignatius Loyola and his followers developed systematic means for assessing the spiritual life of Jesuits and for evaluating the characteristics of their neophytes. But in all of these periods, the generalized observation applies that means for the assessment of men were always directed by the frame of reference relating to the survival of the group. Deviation has always been considered dangerous because it indicates divergent thinking, and divergent thinking cannot be related to predictable and stable patterns of behavior.

During the 19th century further developments took place in the assessment of behavior. An extension of the oral examination was developed in the essay examination. Used extensively in the developing universities of the 19th century, it still remains as one means of evaluating student ability in a more global manner. A given topic is provided for discussion, evaluation, comparison, and other purposes. The student is expected to marshal his whole knowledge of the subject and his ability to organize concepts in the answer that he writes.

In the middle of the 19th century it was not yet possible to measure much behavior scientifically. Herbart, in the first half of the century, made some abortive attempts to cast psychological data into mathematical form, hoping to derive an equation for the formation of the apperceptive mass. Although the results were not appreciably successful, the attempt led or contributed to later work in psychophysics. The latter, in turn, was a part of the heritage that Cattell brought to this country from Wundt's laboratory. However, Herbart's work did not have any real effect on the measurement movement in England.

Sir Francis Galton

The phrase "survival of the fittest" was applicable to either the species or, as was stressed by Spencer, to individuals within the species. This led a few individuals to envisage the probability that differences of various mental traits and acquired characteristics exist among people, and that they may be measured. Since these differences are factors in survival of the fittest, and since they are transmissible to one's offspring (by Lamarckian inheritance), there should be greater similarity between parents and children in mental traits and acquired characteristics than between unrelated persons.

Galton was the first to perceive that such differences, instead of being the nuisance they were then considered to be, actually presented interesting challenges. Goodenough (1949, 24) points out that "Galton was the first man to see clearly that the only way of reducing the mass of chaotic impressions derived from observation of human beings to systematic order is through a quantitative approach." Galton was interested primarily in the problems of heredity but found that he needed to measure human characteristics to obtain evidence. He measured both the physical and mental characteristics of thousands of persons at his anthropometric laboratory in London and systematically quantified the data. With the assistance of statistical devices already developed (the curve of probability derived by the Belgian Quetelet in 1846), he formulated the principles on which correlation technique is based. Furthermore, Galton was fortunate in having a younger co-worker, Karl Pearson, who was as theoretical in his mathematical approach as Galton was practical. "It would be hard to overestimate the contribution of these two men to the development of the theory and methodology of mental measurement," Goodenough observed (1949, 26).

J. McKeen Cattell, Binet, and Simon

In the United States, Cattell shared Galton's interest in reasons for and the extent of individual differences. Trained in Wundt's laboratory, Cattell showed his independence of the master by working on problems concerned with deviations from norms and differences among subjects, rather than with the norms themselves as Wundt wished him to do. In the early 1890s, he measured sensory-motor and psychosensory differences among college students at the University of Pennsylvania by tests such as dynamometer pressure, rate of movement, reaction time for sound, and digit memory span. Boring referred to Cattell as "the prime mover" of the American mental testing in the 1890s (Boring, 1950, 561).

Both Galton and Cattell assumed that the more complex mental processes were simply higher levels or combinations of the elementary mental processes. Numerous attempts were made to measure higher functions by utilizing the lower ones, but no valid findings or conclusions were obtained. Correlations between results of their psychometric tests and either teachers' estimates of intelligence or students' grades were negligible. In the United States, something of a reaction set in, so that between 1895 and 1910 few attempts were made to measure "intelligence" by any procedure.

In France, Binet and Simon were charged with the task of developing an objective measurement instrument in the area of intelligence. They criticized the studies of Galton and, by extension, Cattell for being too narrowly psychological in nature. They were concerned with the two principal problems of assessment in differential psychology: (1) the need to determine the nature and extent of individual differences, and (2) the need to discover the interrelationships of mental processes within the individual. With the measurement data that Binet and Simon obtained, a variety of rapid developments took place. Cattell coined the term mental test in 1890. Goddard translated the Binet scale into English in 1908 and used it at the Vineland Training School. In his studies of the Kallikak family, he arrived at the notion that the measurements were, indeed, providing an assessment of hereditary differences. Stern, the German psychologist, provided a rationale for the testing results on the basis of mental age and chronological age. Terman in 1916 revised the earlier Binet-Simon instrument and popularized its usage.

J. M. Rice and Achievement Tests

Within the field of education itself, a new approach to the problem of individual differences was instituted by J. M. Rice. Needing objective evidence to support some of his comparisons of different school systems, he developed a list of spelling words that he asked children in various cities to spell. This first tangible effort to measure objectively the "product" of education aroused considerable consternation and opposition when presented at an educational conference, since Rice reported his findings that children who spent 15 minutes per day studying spelling did as well on his test as those who spent 40 minutes per day (in another district). The position of educators was, in part, that they were "developing the mind," and that the measurement of spelling achievement had no meaning. The mind was too ethereal, spiritual, and unmeasureable to be converted to scales or units, so they argued.

Although the presentation of these results brought Rice almost unlimited attacks from educational circles who denounced his findings as foolish, reprehensible, and indefensible, little by little thoughtful men began to appreciate the value of what Rice had demonstrated. Thorndike's development of a volume called *Mental and Social Measurement* in 1904, plus a test for the measurement of handwriting in 1909, led to an acceptance of achievement testing.

Before ending this section, it is relevant to comment briefly on the development of the study of statistics as a tool in psychology and education. The foundations of statistical procedures used in psychology must be related to the findings regarding probability. Bernoulli (1654–1705), LaPlace (1749–1827), and Gauss (1777–1855) laid the foundations of modern probability theory. These individuals explored the method of the least square and demonstrated the value of the normal curve. Quetelet (1796–1874), who was royal astronomer to the king of Belgium, became one of the earliest promoters of record-keeping in relationship to the weather and various social phenomena. Galton with his anthropometric measurements gave an even greater impetus to the study of human measurement, devising additional statistical tools such as the method of correlation, standard scores, median, and various rating-scale approaches.

In addition, the application of mathematical procedures to psychological phenomena also increased tremendously during the 19th century. Kant had felt that psychology dealt with phenomena not susceptible to measurement. Herbart disagreed with this and attempted to formulate some mathematical formulae for the expression of the apperceptive mass notion. Weber, and after him Fechner, developed the entire psycho-physical measurement tradition, which was concerned with the concept of just noticeable differences and the law that the just noticeable increment in a stimulus is proportional to the stimulus. Wundt's laboratory in Europe, Cattell's work in this country, and a variety of contributions from both measurement theory and psychophysics led to a confluence of knowledge that provided a basic technology for the development of test scales. The names of Terman, Otis, Thorndike, Spearman, Thurstone, and Karl Pearson are all prominent in this development. Moreover, in research design and the design of experiments, R. A. Fisher, at an experimental agricultural station in England, did much to develop the notion of controlled experimentation. Fisher found that agriculture allowed for the control of variability through the use of randomization of planting procedures and the blocking of known disturbing sources of variation. Much of his work has been incorporated into the planning of psychological and educational research, particularly as it relates to the analyses of variance and covariance.

WILLIAM JAMES: FUNCTIONALISM AND PRAGMATISM

If a single influence could be determined that might be considered pivotal in the development of experimentalism, it might well be the influence of William James. James' straightforward style of writing, his multiple interests, and his stimulation of his students and colleagues certainly played an important and central role in the unfolding of this particular American tradition. William James, the oldest of five children, was born in New York on January 11, 1842. He came from a well-to-do family in which travel was considered an important part of education. His father was dissatisfied with the American schools; hence, he took all the children to Europe to study in 1855. William James attended various schools in Europe between 1855 and 1858. He studied in London and Paris under tutors and in a private school, enrolled at an academy in Geneva, and obtained a good knowledge of German, Latin, French, and a reading acquaintance of Italian. He dabbled in the arts and humanities. Although he started in the field of chemistry at Harvard in 1861, he later changed to the medical school and obtained his doctorate of medicine in 1869. During 1867 and 1868 he wandered about Germany, Switzerland, and France hearing lectures, reading voluminously in philosophy as well as physiology, and attempting to improve his health. James seemed at the point of committing suicide on one occasion and appeared to be depressed greatly at times. He returned to the United States in 1869, completed his medical degree, and accepted an offer from President Eliot to teach physiology at Harvard.

James advanced through the ranks, becoming a professor of philosophy in 1885 and professor of psychology in 1889. He founded the first laboratory for experimental psychology in the United States in 1875. James' real contribution, however, was felt through the publication of his three books in the 1890s. They were his *Principles of Psychology*, published in 1890 in two volumes, the *Briefer Course* in 1892, and *Talks to Teachers* in 1899. By 1911, tens of thousands of students had read one or more of these works. There were 20 editions of James' *Principles*, 35 of his *Briefer Course*, and 12 of the *Talks to Teachers*. The importance of William James to the historical development of modern ideas on education and childhood lies in his contributions both to a philosophical theory of behavior, pragmatism, and in his psychological approach, which has been termed functionalism.

James grounded his philosophy in empirical experience. He considered pragmatism as a philosophy that placed stress on the part, the element, and the individual, as against rationalism that tended to emphasize universals, and to establish a priori wholes prior to parts in the order of logic, as well as being. He thus grounded the reality of the universe in what was experienced. The parts of experience needed no external connection or linking system based on metaphysics, but were strung together in a coherent whole that was itself forged by experience.

From this epistemological canon, James concluded that the intellectual life of man consisted almost wholly of a process whereby perception is gradually changed into cognition. This process has its ground in experience and even its cognitive determination in the same kind of experience. James' approach has its later parallels in Tolman's work on cognitive mapping, since James felt that concepts and conceptual thinking play three distinct parts in human life:

1. They steer us practically every day, and provide an immense map of relations among the elements of things, which, though not now, yet on some possible future occasion, may help to steer us practically;

2. They bring new values into our perceptual life, they reanimate our wills, and make our action turn upon new points of emphasis;

3. The map which the mind frames out of them is an object which possesses, when once it has been framed, an independent existence. It suffices all by itself for purposes of study. The 'eternal' truths it contains would have to be acknowledged even were the world of sense annihilated (Kallen, 91).

This epistemological approach to knowledge, in turn, shaped James' conception of reality. James considered reality "whatever we find ourselves obliged to take account of in any way." James considered activity to be the basic ground of experience. He could see no need to postulate an extraorganic or supraorganic reality under some kind of gigantic monism but, instead, thought that reality was pluralistic. In terms of the nature of truth, James taught that truth is what a man finds is most beneficial to him, and denied that there were a series of absolute verities. In connection with religious experience, James pointed out that there was a universal religious sense in man while there are many varieties of religious experience. In keeping with his epistemology and ontology, James did not deny the individual reality of religious experience or the meaning that that experience might have for an individual. What he did not accept was the concept of a supernatural world order imposed on man. This he rejected under his consideration of a rationalist world versus an experience world. James considered religious experience a part of the experience world, not the anchor by which all other experience is judged.

Much of what James wrote on philosophy had a "common-sense" ring. He advocated what was then called pragmatism. But he was concerned over the fact that many people mistook what he was talking about. He disagreed, for example, with the allegation that pragmatism was simply a reediting of positivism. He pointed out that truth is greater than scientific fact. He disagreed with the view that pragmatism was simply an appeal to action or that it ignored the theoretical approach. In substance, what he was stressing in his whole philosophical approach was a philosophy opposed to intellectualism and rationalism, in the sense of a narrowing philosophical frame of reference. He contended that man was, indeed, the measure of things, but through experience itself. As James wrote: "The whole originality of pragmatism, the whole point in it, is its use of the concrete way of seeing. It begins with concreteness, and returns and ends with it. Dr. Schiller, with his two practical aspects of truth, (1) relevancy to situation, and (2) subsequential utility, is only filling the cup of concreteness to the brim for us. Once seize that cup, and you cannot misunderstand pragmatism" (Kallen, 1953, 196).

The other major contribution of James relates to his part in establishing a rather unique American psychological system, that is, functionalism. Although functionalism did not long survive as a separate system, it did make a major impact on the development of American psychological thought in the early years of the 20th century. Functionalism was concerned with mental processes, not in terms of introspection but, instead, in relationship to muscular activity. It represented in the works of James, Dewey, Angell, and Judd a reaction against what was then termed structuralism. Structuralism was represented by the Wundt-Tichener school of thought and, generally, assumed that the neurological counterpart of psychological elements was related to the excitation of the particular points in the cortex. Consciousness, itself was considered not in direct but in inverse ratio to the openness of the pathway from sensory to motor elements in the cortex.

James enunciated some of the core notions of this functionalist approach in his concept of the "stream of thought." He believed that consciousness could not be conceived as a union of disparate but identifiable elements but, rather, had to be considered as a unitary whole that occurs at one point in the spatiotemporal continuum. Functionalism attempted to view the operations of consciousness under real life conditions. It opposed the notion of introspective analysis of conscious life and was really a precursor of Gestaltism, which, in fact, soon reinforced the Chicago Functionalism group.

William James provided a broad definition of psychology and a meaning to the concept of mind in which mind became an active, inquisitive, selecting, and adapting process rather than a passive recipient of information derived through the senses. Thus, James' approach to psychology partook of many of the dynamics of the Act Psychology of Brentano. For similar reasons, that is, opposition to the older sense empiricism of Locke, and the advocacy of a dynamic intending procedure in the acquisition of conscious knowledge, these two psychological theorists show similarity of outlook. James also tied in man's mental activities to his biological and physiological heritage by showing that affective and conative aspects of life were also related to cognitive functioning.

The implications of functionalism in relationship to the emergence of a problem-solving stance toward guidance is apparent. William James, together with Edward Lee Thorndike, put the final torch to the tree of faculty discipline. Although it lived on in countless graduation sermons, it was discredited as a theory of learning. In educational theory and practice, functionalism resulted in an increasing use of biological concepts of adaptation and adjustment to the environment. This, then, led by easy steps to the epistemological notion of pragmatism, that is, one learns not by assimilating some absolute or universal notion of truth, but by the very experience of learning itself. Truth—not the absolute truth of the rationalist, but the relative subjective and individually unique truth of the learner, then becomes the object of a controlled experience. It then becomes the responsibility of the school to provide those kinds of experiences that will lead to the maximum utilization of the self through understanding and the cognitive abstraction of this experience into relevant concepts. With this notion of knowledge, it is easy to understand how the axiology of pragmatism, supported by functional psychology, could lean heavily on a value system that encouraged individual experiencing under controlled settings and a concept of good as a function property of experience.

JOHN DEWEY

All of the preceding material of this chapter has led, by way of background, to the consideration of John Dewey. Dewey, like Freud, led a long professional life spanning nearly 65 years. There was little that occurred in the realms of psychology, education, science, labor, politics, international events, or philosophy that did not in some way find itself reflected in his thought and writings. Receiving his doctorate from John Hopkins University in 1884, he turned to an intensive examination of philosophy, first of the Hegelian variety and later of the British empiricist tradition. But though he contributed some thought to the understanding of these philosophies, he later directed his thinking toward William James and Charles S. Peirce. Thus, although he studied other forms of philosophy, even Aristotelianism, he decided at a comparatively early period in his development that pragmatism fitted his concept of an American philosophy best.

In the last years of the 19th century, Dewey taught first at the University of Michigan and then moved on to the University of Chicago, where he became one of the contributors to the functional psychology that emanated from there. Becoming interested also in education, he began a laboratory school to try out some of his ideas. Subsequently, he moved to Columbia University to assume the chairmanship of the department of philosophy. As the 20th century developed, Dewey's own interests expanded. He became interested in the question of social reform, social legislation, and labor. His interests led him to become a founder of organizations such as the American Federation of Labor's teacher union, the American Association of University Professors, and other groups desiring to democratize society. All of this occurred while he continued to be involved in philosophical and psychological thought. He also was elected president of the American Psychological Association in 1900. Meanwhile, he continued to expand on the pragmatism of James and Peirce, extending the areas of investigation into aesthetics, metaphysics, social philosophy, and education.

From the beginning of the 20th century until the late 1940s, Dewey published a book every two or three years and dozens of journal and magazine articles. It is estimated that his books contain 17,000 pages and his journal articles about 5000 pages. Most of his writing was of an even, extremely high quality. However, in view of the complexities of modern society, and the fact that he wished to mirror these complexities in his writing, many readers of Dewey experience difficulty in understanding his thought.

Background of Dewey's Thought

As Dewey himself admitted, he was influenced by a wide variety of events and philosophical systems. First, both in chronology and in importance, is idealism. Dewey's philosophical teachers were idealists. William Torrey Harris, one of the leading idealists of his day, influenced the philosophy of the period toward idealism. German idealism seemed to be a major force in late 19th century America. Although Dewey was to repudiate idealism and the philosophical absolutes that accompanied it, there was, nevertheless, one element of idealism that was incorporated into pragmatism. Idealism, with its emphasis on mind and perception formed a part of Dewey's thinking. The life of the mind, the systems of logic and rationalism, the emphasis on introspection, were all converted into suitable forms in pragmatism. Even though Dewey was hostile to religious idealism, with its accompanying mysticism, he remained convinced of a major tenet of idealism, that ultimately all we know as reality is our interpretation of the world around us.

Another influence was philosophical realism, especially those branches dealing with science and empiricism. Dewey grasped the significance of

Peirce's theories of science and of the scientific method. He consciously attempted to formulate a philosophy of science introducing the innovation of problem solving as a process ancillary to hypothesis making. He also believed that the ultimate test of science was confirmation in the world of experience.

Naturalism, the scientific study of childhood, and evolution also exerted a profound influence on Dewey's thought. Although he rejected Spencer's political formulation of Darwinism, Dewey viewed human beings, their problems, values, and development in terms of a constant, ever-developing and changing process. He dismissed as unverifiable a host of ancient philosophical frameworks, including first principles and first causes, transcendental beings, eternal life, absolutes, perfection and unchanging reality. All of this seemed to be drawn together into an evolutionary social concept that he termed interaction. The young science of ecology pointed to a different way of looking at organisms and environments. Instead of an organism that lived *in* an environment, biologists began thinking in terms of an organism living in and *of* an environment. As the organism affected its environment, the environment affected the organism.

The significance of this biological theory for Dewey was that it pointed toward a resolution of an old problem in philosophy relating to the individual and his social environment. Traditionally, either the social environment was seen as preceding or more important than the individual, or the individual was seen as metaphysically superior to his environment. This, said Dewey, was a dualistic, absolutistic, and inaccurate way of looking at a complex relationship. What is more true is that organisms depend for their existence on their environment. There are aspects of an environment that assist and help an organism as well as elements of an environment that are detrimental to that organism. What must be done is to examine the interaction that takes place. This is no simple task, but is a necessary one requiring the scientific study of all aspects of an organism's mutual, interactive relationship with its environment.

Two more philosophical movements influenced Dewey's thought. The first was humanism and the second utilitarianism. Humanism, broadly conceived, is a philosophical attitude that is oriented toward man. Since the Renaissance, humanism had come to be equated with literary and artistic movements. Many individuals think of humanism as equated to painting, poetry, music, literature, and philosophy. Without being hostile to these manifestations of humanism, Dewey identified himself with another aspect of humanism, the scientific. As Dewey saw it, the purpose of philosophy was not speculation for its own sake, but the giving of direction to man's political, social, economic, and cultural life. Dewey broadened the concept of humanism to mean a philosophical insistence that man could and should make his life on this earth better, richer, and more satisfying in all respects.

Utilitarianism, essentially the contribution of English philosophers in the 18th and 19th centuries, also had a major influence on Dewey. Although he criticized the formulations of English utilitarians, such as Bentham and John Stuart Mill, he nonetheless appropriated the basic core of utilitarianism, that is, the belief that the end good of life was the greatest good of the greatest number and the belief that the value of an idea could be found in asking how beneficial this idea was in improving the life of man. Employing Charles Peirce's theory of meaning, and blending it with this aspect of utilitarianism, Dewey attempted to justify his own concepts by reference to the actual good they would accomplish in this world.

In summary, Dewey and his thought represented an intellectual synthesis of many strands of current 19th century thinking into a new socially oriented philosophy that was proposed as *the* philosophy and intellectual justification of democracy in a world of change. The system itself, with its rather loose and sometimes incomplete aspects, reflects most basically the philosophy of change and problem solving in an evolving social culture.

The Metaphysics of Dewey

Metaphysics, as has been mentioned earlier, is the overarching theory about theory. John Dewey's metaphysical theory contrasts sharply with the intentionalistic metaphysics that was discussed earlier. Intentionality was tied to a basic rationalism, a rationalism that had become identified with science and the scientific method. Dewey did not accept this concept of metaphysics and has been blamed by many philosophers for bringing about a systematic neglect of metaphysics. Although it has been asserted that Dewey was anti-metaphysical, it is more proper to say simply that Dewey ignored some of the traditional concerns of metaphysics.

Implicitly or explicitly, metaphysical systems tend to search for absolutes. These absolutes may relate to questions of first principles in logic or the hierarchy of being, or to absolutes in the community of experience. Dewey did not deny the *possibility* of the existence of absolutes but, instead, questioned: (1) whether it was possible to identify them; (2) whether it was possible to verify them; and (3) whether they were relevant to the concerns of science and of experimentalist philosophy. Dewey suggested that the desire to establish absolutes reveals much less about the nature of absolutes than it does about human beings. Human beings have a strong tendency to want to know something in a secure and unchanging way. Questions dealing with intimate and crucial issues, such as the existence and nature of God, life after death, and the essential meaning of life, have called forth answers that are seized on as being timeless and perfect.

In place of metaphysical systems that established first causes, self-evident truths, divinely revealed axioms, or the leap to the supernatural, Dewey proposed one that was based on the operation of the scientific method. The function of his metaphysical system would be a kind of analysis of: (1) how knowledge is discovered in the real world; and (2) what it is that man ought to do. The most salient features of this metaphysical outlook were its contextual relativity and its dissolution of dualisms. In regard to the first, Dewey saw himself as a philosopher expressing the continual personal and social revolution in human culture:

> . . . It follows that there is no specifiable difference between philosophy and its role in the history of civilization. Discover and define some characteristics, some unique function in civilization, and you have defined philosophy itself. . . . But in any case, there is a certain intellectual work to be done; the dominant interest working throughout the minds of masses of man has to be clarified, a result which can be accomplished only by selection, elimination, reduction and formulation. . . . The life of all thought is to effect a junction at some point of the new and the old, of deep sunk customs and unconscious dispositions, brought to the light of attention by some conflict with newly emerging directions of activity. Philosophies which emerge at distinctive periods define the larger patterns of continuity which are woven in effecting the longer enduring junctions of a stubborn past and an insistent future (Dewey, *Modern World,* 249–250).

Dewey's approach to metaphysics did away with concepts such as supernatural and absolute. He considered that all of the relevance of these terms could be subsumed under what was natural for men. He did not formally posit the denial of such universals (for he recognized this would in itself be an absolute), but he felt that they had no real connection with the world of everyday experience. Thus, Dewey's basic approach to metaphysics can be summarized as: (1) an ignoring of the role of philosophy as a search for absolute truth, (2) a reduction from absolute laws or axioms promulgated once for all time to tentative guidelines to be reexamined constantly, and (3) the identifying of man as a part of nature, a part of social evolution, as a being whose goals and purposes must be considered grounded in the context of his environment.

Dewey further castigated the notion of a dualist universe in which there are two worlds, one the property of science and the other the possession of religion. In this sense, he agreed with the contention of Freud regarding the priority of scientific fact. Dewey pointed up the conflict that took place in epistemology when science and religion clash. As long as science dealt with technical subjects, with classification systems, and the like, there was no necessary conflict with religion. However, in Dewey's approach the method of science, loosely construed, could and ought to be applied to the social problems of man. What could and should be done, Dewey emphasized, was to assume that the entire universe of experience belongs to the natural realm, and that all within it, including man and his beliefs and values, are equally subject to objective scientific scrutiny. Thus, Dewey disposed of dualisms, whether between the natural and supernatural, mind and body, or good and evil.

These metaphysical canons, anchored firmly in an epistemology of knowledge and by experience, obviously influenced Dewey's conception of reality. His ontology contained no room for essences or a static conception of being. Reality, to him, was interaction; the interaction of man with his environment. Reality was continually becoming something greater than it was initially. As Gutzke (1956, 63–64) has written:

> Out of the welter of interaction, as a result of the way the organism reacts and responds, an individual existence emerges as a matter of course . . . . Whatever may be the source of the unifying principle and however the origin of the self may be understood, it seems clear that man as an event in this pluralistic universe does arrive at an awareness of himself as one, that he identifies his own career as the career of that one person he is.

Thus, if there be a metaphysical anchor to all of Dewey's writings, it is found in the concept of interaction. This concept is at the core of Dewey's thought and specifies a natural process in which man engages in a transaction with the universe from which his own self-concept and reality emerges as a distinctively unique composition of perceptions. There is obviously here a close link to James' theory of consciousness and the emergence of self-concept.

Thinking, Values, and Education

The applications of Dewey's metaphysics can be found in his analysis of thinking and problem solving, the emergence of values, and the role of philosophy in education. In line with his basic notion of interaction theory, Dewey suggested that all thinking originates in problematic situations. Thinking itself is just one form of experiencing interaction with the environment:

> All reflective inquiry starts from a problematic situation, and no such situation can be settled in its own terms. It evolves into a resolved situation only by means of introduction of material not found in the situation itself (Dewey, *Experience and Nature*, 185).

Thus, Dewey suggested a problem-solving approach to reality and experience which was not built on a prearranged epistemology. Dewey's five steps to problem solving include: (1) a felt difficulty, (2) its location and definition, (3) the suggestion of possible solutions, (4) the development of reasoning related to the suggestion, and (5) further observation or experimentation leading to the acceptance or rejection of the suggested approach.

From Dewey's approach to problem solving it can easily be seen that values emerge as the product of this problem-solving process and are essentially judgmental.

> Values are not traits of rare and festal occasions; they occur whenever any object is welcome and lingered over; whenever it arouses aversion and protest; even though the lingering be but momentary and the aversion a passing glance toward something else (Dewey, *Modern World*, 261).

Nor do values have any necessary connection with standards or arbitrary criteria:

> In its precise signification a standard is unambiguous. It is a quantitative measure. It is not a value . . . things measured are not values . . . . Yet it does not follow because of absence of a uniform and publicly determined external object that objective criticism of value-objects is impossible . . . . What follows is a judgment and like every judgment it involves a venture, a hypothetical element; that is directed to qualities which are nevertheless qualities of an object (266).

Thus Dewey distinguishes between truth and meaning. Truth, he feels, can only be extended to the records of events and to the description of experiences. Meaning is subjective for man and is a product of the interaction of man with his environment, a product specifically of a problem-solving approach to reality in which values are emerging as experience becomes more clearly distilled and anchored in subjective meaning.

Finally, Dewey was continually concerned with education because it was in education that he felt the products of a philosophy or intellectual rationale could be tested.

> The reconstruction of philosophy of education and of social ideals and methods thus go hand in hand. If there is special need of educational reconstruction at the present time, if this need makes urgent a reconsideration of the basic ideas of traditional philosophic systems, it is because of the thoroughgoing change in social life accompanying the advance of science, the industrial revolution, and the development of democracy. Such practical changes cannot take place without demanding an educational reformation to meet them, and without leading man to ask what ideas and ideals are implicit in these social changes, and what revisions they require of the ideas and ideals which are inherited from older and unlike cultures (260).

Dewey attempted to resolve the ancient dualism in education between knowing and doing. The former was supposed to be reserved to true "knowers," that is, passive spectators of reality. The latter was a somewhat ignoble task. As Dewey regarded it, learning involved "doing something" to things, by this he meant that learning involves an experience. Experiences are composed of two aspects: first, there is the passive doing, the undergoing of something in which things may happen, but in order for this doing and undergoing to be a meaningful experience, it must involve an active consideration of what the experience *meant*. That is, it must involve realizing the consequences of the doing. Thus, doing and realizing needed to be linked. We do not (despite one half century of belief to the contrary) "learn by doing," we learn by *doing and realizing what came of what we did* (Shermis, 1958).

Thus, Dewey proposed an educational system that would unite cognitive learning with experience. The end of education as Dewey saw it was to produce an individual who not only knew how to learn, but who could continue to reform his experience as a consequence of learning. The way in which subject matter, curriculum, ought to be presented to children is for them to deal with it not as facts to be learned or ground to be covered, but as information to be utilized. As a consequence, the extension of the cognitive domain, the investment of meaning, and the process of education becomes a unitary whole. Dewey suggested that early education should begin with experience and the concrete phenomenon. Unfortunately, many of his followers came to construe this as indicating that all knowledge had to be concrete. Dewey did not deny the importance of conceptual thinking and the grasping of high-order abstractions. But as is the case in many theories of learning and human behavior, an inadequate grasp of the total theory may lead to a reductionism that is absurd, for example, the common view that psychoanalytic thought is related only to sexual gratification and the equally absurd contention that Dewey's thinking is only a matter of simple problem solving.

One of the major difficulties that many individuals have with Dewey's entire conceptual scheme of problem solving and the metaphysics of his approach is the lack of absolutes in one form or another. To understand Dewey, it is imperative to realize that he is advocating a philosophy of cultural relativism in which man has the continued obligation to adapt his culture and his personal experience to the reality in which he lives. This is not easy for those who wish to have some canons of behavior and education that exist as criteria. Dewey does not provide any relief for this kind of anxiety, but he suggests that it is simply part of the universe as we know it, judge it, and live in it. Dewey suggested that asking the right questions about the nature of man and the universe was the continuing, besetting problem of mankind. There could be no lasting answers for man, but the process of asking, the process of inquiry, the method of problem solving, and the continual revision of man's thought in terms of the reality of his culture would provide the best means for continued survival in a changing world.

DEWEY'S THEORY OF INTERACTION AND COUNSELING

Dewey's philosophical approach to the problems of education had a profound impact on the first approach to counseling in this country. Directly or indirectly, Dewey provided a rationale for a problem-solving approach to education, and saw education as a process of social accommodation. The notion of improvement of self-understanding through interaction with the environment is a substantive postulate in most counseling approaches. Human activity is viewed as a natural process that functions to modify existence, and self-consciousness is significant in the reconstruction or regeneration of the self. As Gutzke stated:

> Individuality itself is originally a potentiality and is realized only in interaction with surrounding conditions. In this process of intercourse, native capacities, which contain an element of uniqueness are transformed and become a self. Moreover, through resistance encountered the nature of the self is discovered. The self is both formed and brought to consciousness through interaction with the environment (65).

Dewey's theoretical framework provides a basis for approaching counseling from what might be called the American eclectic point of view.

Since his entire theory is really based on the notion of interaction, this does not preclude other theoretical orientations but really seems to be a justification of what Fiedler reported (1950) in terms of a comparison of psychoanalytic, nondirective, and Adlerian therapy relationships.

Self-Concept

Certainly, Dewey's approach to reality placed heavy stress on the development of a realistic self-concept. Although there are elements of idealism in this approach, Dewey felt that through an interaction with the environment the individual would arrive at a coherent cognitive understanding of himself. This was to be accomplished through the utilization of problem-solving activity and through an anchoring of meaning. Once an individual begins to involve himself in a helping-relationship, this ordinarily involves some reorganization of self structure. What is being alluded to here can most likely be explained more parsimoniously under the learning theory approach. Through a process of operant behavior, the counselor becomes more sensitive to the needs of others, more aware of goals, aspirations, values, and process. As a result, this is a kind of operant conditioning that can often relate to other aspects of the counselor's personal and individual life. It can only be made here as an empirical generalization, but many counselor educators have found that the didactic courses in counseling may effect relatively little behavior change in counselor trainees. However, when practicum work is undertaken, and critical analysis of tapes are accomplished, the result is often striking. Individuals appear to undergo a kind of transformation in which they realize in a very direct way how insensitive they have been to cues and how little they have really understood what was going on in the process of counseling. Even as Dewey has stated, experience needs to be integrated or subsumed into the self. It can also be put another way, that is, the repertory of behavior that an individual has at his command must represent appropriate forms of behavior for which he is reinforced. The "success" of counseling is not only something felt by the client, but also by the counselor. As a result, interaction leads to operant learning on the part of the counselor. And success in this aspect of life can often generalize or transfer into other areas.

Substantively what appears to happen is that the perception of the client as an individual, unique in his own right, leads the client to consider the counselor as a person who is responsible and has some personal status. Both mutually reinforce each other for the altered perceptions occurring in both individuals. Interaction of this nature leads to the hypothesis that one might try out these new role perceptions on others. This is of course the weak point in the entire problem-solving approach, that is, there is little research proof to establish the relationship between altered perception in the interview and altered behavior in the outer world. Nonetheless, interaction theory provides a plausible basis for changing perceptions of self-concept on the part of both client and counselor.

Goals of Counseling

From an interaction theory point of view, the goals of counseling should be related to the solving of individual's problems. McHugh (1964), in an analysis of interaction theory as it relates to counseling, has pointed out that security itself seems to be based on the counselee's ability to relate to the world, and that this, in turn, is dependent on the degree to which individuals can develop a method for obtaining adequate answers to problems that confront them.

This means, in a sense, that counseling in the interaction point of view places much emphasis on the method of problem solving. Values, dimensions of outer reality, epistemological concerns, and even concern about guilt can be approached from a problem-solving method. There is not, in Dewey's system, any set of values that must be accepted, other than the importance of an intellectual method for solving the problems of existence. Consideration of alternative courses of action, exploration of ways and means, thus become the central goal for counseling procedures. Since the world is continually evolving, and society does provide an implicit criterion for effective human behavior, Dewey lays great stress on the need for the individual to come to terms with his environment. This means, in point of fact, that alternative courses of action can be explored cognitively, but that eventually there must be a plan of action.

Such interaction with the environment following a new plan of action should provide verification of the soundness of the decision. This soundness of decision is felt within the individual and can be related to the termination of counseling. For when a felt problem has been solved, and counseling is viewed chiefly in this light, then the anxiety, self-conflict, and emotional strain are no longer present. If the solution does not result in some lessening of anxiety and reinforcement from new patterns of behavior that have been instituted, then obviously a new and further solution is to be sought.

In summary, Dewey's interaction theory provides a basis for a problem-solving approach to counseling. Although few theorists may have stated directly that they were following an experimentalist rationale in the establishment of their counseling procedures, there is little question that this philosophical approach has influenced a considerable segment of counseling and guidance theorists in the past few decades.

COUNSELING THEORISTS RELATED TO INTERACTION THEORY

Dewey's interaction theory may be traced in three counseling approaches. The first and earliest adaptation of Dewey's thought seems to have been formulated in the writings of Williamson. Another facet of Dewey's philosophy has been incorporated into Rogers' self-concept theory, and a third derivative influence can be seen in the more recent work of Krumboltz, who most likely reflects Williamson's interpretation of Dewey.

Counseling Theorists and Interaction

Although no cause and effect relationships are postulated regarding the origin and development of guidance and the emergence of Dewey's philosophy, it may be justified to state that the factors that led to Dewey's philosophy were also operant in the development of guidance. Frank Parsons is considered one of the founders of the vocational guidance movement from which educational guidance sprang. The bent of this early vocational counseling was in the direction of the conservation of human talent. Both Sears and Williamson, according to Hutson (1958, 14–15), advocated educational guidance for the same reasons that Parsons had mentioned in vocational guidance, that is, for the conservation of human talent. Sears felt that guidance would help to reduce wasted time and energy, and Williamson suggested that no amount of excellent lecturing, student abilities, and the like would result in good learning without some reduction of the emotional distractions that lead to poor learning. Thus the goal of adjustment or social integration was an early focus in guidance. Koos in 1928 wrote:

> It will help . . . to think of guidance under such categories as discipline, social conduct, and quality of work as *adjustment,* in the sense of effecting a better adjustment of the pupil to the school situation, and guidance under such categories as curriculum guidance, vocational guidance, placement, and follow-up as *distribution,* in the sense of distributing the pupils as advantageous as possible to the curriculum and vocational opportunities at hand . . . .
> . . . I should like to emphasize the great desirability of our seeing that *both* these elements of adjustment and distribution are kept in the concept of guidance that should dominate the practices in guidance in our schools (cited in Hutson, 1958, 15).

Hutson (1958, 20–22) in a review of statements drawn from the history of guidance illustrates some of the assumptions on which guidance was based initially. They may be summarized as (1) relating to the notion that vocational choice is a personal matter of growth and development; (2) that self-knowledge is a gradual growth in self-discovery; and (3) that wise decision making is related to social progress in a democracy.

Edmund G. Williamson

Williamson's influence on the development of guidance and counseling has been monumental. His writing spans a period of well over 30 years and has served as an anchor in the development of guidance services in the school together with their applications to student personnel services and vocational counseling. Williamson became involved with the counseling and guidance movement at a time when no real distinction was made between the two functions. Counseling seemed to be only an adjunct of guidance or a specialized function. The guidance approach consisted of a variety of tools, techniques, and intracurricular and extracurricular activities. It was a comprehensive approach to problems of social concern in the schools.

With the expansion of guidance services, the need for training masses of teachers in the tools and techniques of guidance became apparent. Williamson provided a straightforward approach to counseling which was essentially problem-centered. In his book, *How to Counsel Students* (McGraw-Hill, 1939), Williamson was chiefly concerned with the variety of educational-vocational problems that students manifest. He summarized these problems as:

1. Unwise choice of college, curriculum, and specific courses.
2. Differential scholastic achievement.
3. Insufficient general verbal and scholastic aptitude.
4. Ineffective study habits in terms of organizing, time budgeting, concentration, and resistance to distraction, and persistence.
5. Reading, writing, and speaking disabilities.
6. Insufficient scholastic motivation.
7. Overachievement of the occasional student who by dint of hard work finds himself in a situation that he cannot permanently function in.
8. Underachievement by reason of a variety of causes.

Williamson suggested that counselors follow a number of steps which included: (1) analysis, (2)synthesis, (3) diagnosis, (4) prognosis, (5) counseling, and (6) follow-up. The analysis process referred to the collection of data and test results, the examination of cumulative records, the talking to teachers and parents, and a study of family history, health records, school history, vocational and work experiences, and social and recreational interests. Specific tools recommended for the process of analysis were the cumulative records, the interview process itself, auto-biographies, anecdotal material, and tests having some pertinent relationship to the case problem.

On the basis of information and impressions, the counselor could then proceed to a diagnosis. Williamson viewed diagnosis not as an expert evaluation but, instead, as a hunch based on the information available. In fact, Williamson's approach to diagnosis is much more like Dewey's formulation of a possible hypothesis for investigation in the problem-solving method than the differential diagnosis of etiologies. For this reason, Pepinsky, in his formulation of diagnostic categories, ruled out Williamson's approach on the basis that the categories were not true diagnostic categories and possessed little power potential for differentiating treatment procedures (1948).

Another departure from the medical model is seen in the fact that Williamson advocated explaining the counselor's diagnosis and prognosis to the student. This strongly suggests Dewey's interpretation of meaning within the concept of interaction. Finally, Williamson discusses the technique of counseling as falling within the framework of interaction between client and counselor. He suggested that changes in the client come about by changes in the environment, the learning of needed skills, the change of attitudes, explanation, didactic instruction, and a variety of other procedures. Williamson advocates a position in the counselor-client interaction in which the counselor helps the client to actively set about solving his problems. He thinks diagnosis is important and that the counselor should not pose as a "buddy" of the client but, rather, should preserve his own identity within the school situation. This means that, on occasion, the counselor will have to tell the client certain things, that he must preserve some outward semblance of knowing what he is doing, and that he will actively manipulate the client into situations where a new approach to solving his problems may be tested. In short, Williamson advocates the use of suggestion, encouragement, advice, reassurance, explanation, instruction, and a variety of other tools and techniques, provided that these procedures lead to a process whereby the client begins to solve some of his own problems.

Thus Williamson's approach represents a quite direct translation of Dewey's central philosophical tenets into the counseling-guidance situation. Williamson was quite cognizant of the practical problems that educators have in coping with problem-solving behavior in the schools. Although he was understanding both of the impact of learning on behavior, and of the dynamic nature of the individual in working out his own behavior, he felt that a problem-centered approach to guidance and counseling, stressing steps and outlining processes, was the most direct method of influencing teacher-counselors. This approach fit in well with a technique-oriented need in counseling activities. Nor did Williamson think, at this time, that the validity of counseling procedures had to be demonstrated:

> The validity of the present techniques is assumed and few counselors worry about dependable evidence of this validity (1939, 526).

Williamson did not hesitate to advocate directive methods in counseling. He did not say that all counseling should be directive any more than it should be nondirective. But he recognized the importance of the social criterion in determining the methods to be used in counseling.

> Counseling may be thought of as a method of freeing individuals from their limitations and thus facilitating their development. But the process of freeing does not follow upon unrestricted self-development of inner forces nor by the elimination of self-deficiencies . . . Counseling in a democracy is seen as one of many instrumentalities for aiding individual members to achieve an appropriate and relevant equality of opportunity—educational, vocational, emotional, and social. . . . Thus counseling is individualized, personalized, and permissive assistance in developing skill in attaining and reattaining socially enlightened self-understanding and self-direction (526).

Williamson's approach to counseling reflects in many ways the translation of Dewey's philosophy into a counseling dimension. Dewey himself was not a follower of permissive nondirective methods. He believed in positive leadership from the school in coping with the problems of acculturation and individual meaning. The extremes that followed Dewey in the development of the progressive movement under Kilpatrick do not represent Dewey's approach to education. It would appear that Williamson has indirectly captured the major theme of Dewey's thinking and applied much of it to the guidance and counseling movement.

Eclecticism

Although Williamson has been cited as an example of a counseling theorist who appears to have translated Dewey's thought quite directly to counseling, it is also the argument of the writer that many other counseling theorists and counselor-educators have been indirectly influenced by Dewey. This may have occurred as a by-product of their doctoral education and their exposure to philosophy of education thought, which was cast chiefly in the experimentalist light, or to a more underlying kind of pragmatism. In either case, Dewey contended that philosophy was a product of action, tested empirically and pragmatically before it was enunciated as an intellectual justification of a given set of dynamics. This is precisely the position of the eclecticists. For if Dewey's notion about the emergence of philosophy be applied to the guidance and counseling movement, it is apparent that practice must be built up, techniques tried out, before philosophical principles are enunciated. Possibly the many early (and continuing) conflicts in psychology, that is, between realism and functionalism, client-centered versus directive approaches in therapy, behaviorism versus humanism, has tended to effect a basic pessimism in the minds of many counselor educators as to the genuine relevance of philosophy to counseling.

In general, the eclecticism school has focused on the problems faced by the client. Bixler (1948) states:

> Regardless of the method of counseling employed, success in treatment bears a close relationship to the problem confronting the client. . . . One possible interpretation: it is the client rather than the type of therapy that determine treatment success (1948, 211–214).

Bixler states that because of this problem-centered focus, the counselor must be flexible enough to use an appropriate technique at the appropriate moment, and to select an appropriate therapy from an "armament of therapies." Bixler suggests that there is still a lack of evidence to indicate the superiority of one method over the other. Although this was written in 1948, the situation has not substantially altered since then. He believes that, since therapy is largely a nonintellectual process, it is much more important what the counselor feels toward the client than what he says.

Not all eclectics would agree with Bixler. F. C. Thorne (1955) for example, although insisting that his system is eclectic, states that the counselor must represent an intellectual resource in the counseling setting, that is, he must bring to that setting a reservoir of knowledge and skill in coping with the problems of the client. This emphasizes the role of skill in diagnosis and the need for assembling a good case history. Francis Robinson in his work *Principles and Procedures in Student Counseling* (1950) avoids any real discussion of the theory of counseling and shifts his entire approach to the techniques used and to the criteria of effectiveness. Clifford Froelich (1958) also promoted a position in counseling that tended to emphasize the technical aspects of the guidance function and included the teacher as a part of this function. Froelich's influence was felt in the movement that tended to view guidance as a part of the curriculum in which teachers were directly involved. This position sometimes referred to as "the every teacher is a counselor" movement, although possessing excellent intentions, tended to dilute the nature of counseling services and to make the role of counseling just one of a series of guidance activities. Recent developments in the profession would appear to suggest that the profession is moving away from this approach and toward a specialization of the counseling function.

Some counseling theorists have focused on the problem-solving method, relating it to decision making. Henry B. McDaniel (1959) at Stanford University reflects this approach. Somewhat eclectic in his approach to theory, he recognized early the importance of decision making as a central component in the counseling process. In the sense that Mc-Daniel has used decision making, this may be considered a forerunner of the behavioral engineering approach currently utilized by Krumboltz. Dewey's concern with socially learned behavior, as reported in *Experience and Education* (1938, 1959), seems to be a logical predecessor for much of the current social behavioral learning theory, as described by Ferster, Bandura, and Krumboltz. Dewey saw the influence of environmental circumstances, including the force that other people exert on individuals, when he wrote:

> An experience is always what it is because of a transaction taking place between an individual and what, at the time constitutes his environment . . . The environment, in other words, is whatever conditions interact with personal needs, desires, purposes, and capacities to create the experience which is had (1959, 41–42).

And again he wrote:

> It is then the business of the educator to see in what direction an experience is heading. There is no point in his being more mature if, instead of using his greater insight to help organize the conditions of the experience of the immature, he throws away his insights. Failure to take the moving force of an experience into account so as to judge and direct it on the ground of what it is moving into means disloyalty to the principle of experience itself . . . A primary responsibility of educators is that they not only be aware of the general principle of the *shaping of actual experience by environing conditions, but that they also recognize in the concrete what surroundings are conducive to having experiences that lead to*

growth. Above all, they should know how to utilize the surroundings, physical and social, that exist so as to extract from them all that they have to contribute to building up experiences that are worthwhile (1959, 32–35).

Furthermore, Dewey saw no inconsistency between social control and individual freedom, since the individual is a part of the social group:

No one would deny that the ordinary good citizen is as a matter of fact subject to a good deal of social control and that a considerable part of this control is not felt to involve restrictions of personal freedom . . . Now, the general conclusion I would draw is that control of individual actions is effected by the whole situation in which individuals are involved, in which they share and of which they are cooperative or interactive parts (1959, 54–57).

He drew an analogy to the playing of a game, in which there is agreement on the rules and in which an individual feels unhappy only if he feels that the rules have been broken. Dewey concluded that this ". . . illustrates the general principle of social control of individuals without the violation of freedom" (1959, 58). Thus, it would appear that as long as the individual is participating willingly in social interaction, control by forces in that interaction does not diminish his personal freedom.

In summary, then, this section has discussed the relationship of the eclecticists in counseling to the philosophical tenets of John Dewey. The argument is that a number of influential counselor educators and theorists have directly or indirectly related their approach to counseling to the philosophy of education advocated by Dewey. It is suggested that most of this influence has been indirect and transmitted through the professional education background that unquestionably contributed to the training of these educators themselves.

This chapter as a whole advances the hypothesis that guidance and counseling in its distinctly American manifestation has been closely related to the psychological, educational, and philosophical movements that effected profound change in the extension of the American school system. The writings of Williamson most directly reflected the tendency of American education, in general, and of guidance, in particular, to develop a series of techniques capable of coping with the problems of adjustment and change in a rapidly evolving technological culture. The shortcomings of the movement may be seen in the desire of many educators and counselors to reduce a complex psychological interaction to a methodology that can work in almost all cases.

CHAPTER IX

Learning Theory and Behavior Modification

Virtually no one disagrees that learning is a central factor in human behavior. Learning theory has always exerted a prime influence in American psychological studies, but the emphasis of learning theory in applied fields such as education, special education, counseling, and school psychology has been mediated by philosophical frameworks and training programs. Counseling theory as a derivative of educational training programs and applied psychological thought has been particularly susceptible to educational influences. For example, the early educational thought preceding the emergence of counseling programs was dominated by the theory of formal discipline in which learning was tied into the exercise of mental faculties. Methods of teaching were related to the organization and presentation of information, memorization, and recitation of these items. Goals of the process were aimed at the formation of a truly "Renaissance" man. Later on, with the expansion of public education horizons, Thorndike emphasized habit formation and skill development using classical approaches to association of ideas and skills. Simultaneously, Dewey emphasized process and problem solving. From this dual thrust came a reliance on testing procedures as a means to understand individual differences and on the formation of steps to problem-solving as a basic rational alternative. The consequences of this emphasis led to goals and methods designed to create the truly "democratic" man. With the influence of Lewinian field studies, psychoanalytic thought and mental hygiene approaches, education switched to a concentration on interpersonal processes with the goal being a "well-adjusted" person. More recently, there has been an emphasis on accountability, performance objectives, behavior modification, and flowcharts which are designed to individualize learning and to emphasize responsibility.

All of these approaches use learning theory in a direct or indirect manner. Few teachers or counselors would deny that the presentation of ideas and the process of learning should result in some form of internalized mental discipline in the sense that learning should make it possible for man to organize and mobilize his personal resources and thinking more effectively.[1] Again, few will deny that processes involve the perception of others, social interaction, and that they are mediated by affective states. Problem solving is certainly needed in a culture that is rapidly changing its goals and values. Personal and social adjustment also require a consideration of ways and means to increase personal effectiveness and happiness. But the counselor in training may have difficulty in integrating the disparate cultural streams. It is difficult to know what kind of terminal skills or outcomes can be expected from a series of professors who are "doing their own thing."

For example, students may be exposed to a traditional behavior-modification educational psychology course in which stimulus-response theories are considered in logical steps according to Gagne's paradigm (1965). They may have difficulty in squaring this with a developmental psychology approach in which Piaget's studies form the basis. Subsequently they may study counseling theory in a Freudian and clinical emphasis, and they may do their practicum in a phenomenological group-sensitivity approach. All of this has to be fitted into a work setting that is characterized by a mental discipline framework in a traditional school setting.

During the last decade there has been a rising tide of research to support a learning theory framework as a basis for education, psychotherapy, and counseling. The approach has been centered both on a specific technique called behavior modification and a generalized theory referred to as social learning. Neither of them is really new, but the accumulation of research and the synthesis with older learning systems does constitute something new. The technique of behavior modification has been found to be relevant to a variety of social settings and has bridged in large part the gap between earlier laboratory studies in learning and social contexts. Behavior modification can be considered an operational transformation of much that was earlier known in both cognitive and stimulus-response theories. Social learning theory has provided the integration between cognitive and social approaches to learning on the one hand, and stimulus-response models on the other.

By way of preamble to the consideration of both behavior modification, specifically, and social learning theory, in the larger sense, a brief

[1] Possibly Carl Rogers would not accept the transmission of knowledge by another person as a valid form of learning. It is difficult to take really seriously his contention that everything taught by one person to another "is relatively inconsequential and has little or no significant influence on behavior" (1961, p. 276).

discussion of cognitive theorists and stimulus-response advocates is in order. Cognitive theorists tend to emphasize the process of perception as the central determinant to learning. Stimulus-response theorists tend to emphasize the effect of antecedents to specific responses and the manner in which the simple stimulus-response paradigm is integrated into habits and skills. They have traditionally differed in their level of specificity, dependence on observable and measurable differences, and the control of outcomes.

AN OVERVIEW OF CLASSICAL AND COGNITIVE LEARNING APPROACHES

The oldest formalized classical approach to learning was enunciated by Aristotle. He defined the laws of association of ideas in his principles of contiguity, contrast, and similarity. The first of these principles held that events which occurred in proximity either in space or time tended to be associated together. His principle of contrast indicated that events or phenomena which were highly contrasted also tended to be associated, for example, black and white. His third principle of similarity suggested that events or items which were alike or similar tended to be associated together, for example, bread and butter.

Aquinas continued the thinking of Aristotle and developed an elaborate conception of the psychology of learning recognizing a hierarchical process of sensory input, perceptual resolution, and abstraction. The classicists stressed verbal and cognitive learning. But they also recognized the importance of character formation. This was the province of the philosopher guardians in Plato's ideal republic and the area of theological expertise in the middle ages. Learning took place in Aquinas' view as a consequence of the indwelling of the human soul. Perception and abstraction were essentially the by-products of a metaphysical substance. Grammar, rhetoric, logic, mathematics, and music were the essential vehicles in which learning was developed, and the by-products were mental discipline in the sense of the development of orderly habits of virtue, discipline, and moral character.

These ideas formed the essential components of a mind substance family of learning that was characterized by elements of a religious mental discipline, the use of what has become known as the liberal arts tradition in curriculum. It is also the basis of a theory of transfer of learning in which the application of knowledge, the development of skills and habits, as well as attitudes and ideas, transfer from one set of learning tasks to another. Certainly the classical approaches to learning relied heavily on physical discipline, memorization, and environmental control systems that operated within the learning environment. The basic content of learning was intellectual and consisted of a transmission of a substantive body of facts, principles and knowledge which did not have an exclusive pragmatic "payoff." In later centuries Christian Wolff, a disciple of Leibnitz, applied this approach to what was called formal discipline. This was a theory widespread in its adoption then, and later, that the mind was like a muscle and needed to be exercised vigorously. It was held that man's intellectual capabilities were similar to an open field that needed to be plowed up generously to produce anything but weeds. This approach can also be observed directly in Locke's notion about learning.

The basic core of this learning approach was that the best education is intellectual in nature and that not all men are capable of this great good. In the 19th century Matthew Arnold argued for the classics as being the best knowledge available to man and a prelude to all other knowledge. Herbert Spencer suggested that scientific studies effected rigor in thinking and logic, and Cardinal Newman argued that liberal education was chiefly concerned with intellectual perfection alone, and not the acquisition of knowledge for pragmatic purposes, or even the training in moral virtue. In more modern times, Mark Van Doren, Mortimer J. Adler, and Robert Hutchins have expressed this liberal arts point of view. Gilbert Highet had taken this view of teacher education suggesting that teaching is an art and a skill developed in some individuals and not in others. The characteristics of a good teacher are then more dependent on innate personality characteristics instead of on something that can be developed through specific training. Classical learning theory has tended to respond to the question WHAT is learning? by the answer—intellectual development. It has answered the question HOW can it be assessed? by judging progress in learning primarily in terms of cognitive growth and development joined to verbal abilities. This can be readily seen in terms of the assessment devices used. Oral examinations, essay examinations, the ability to think on one's feet and to defend ideas were all considered methods of evaluating the product of education. Theses, dissertations, term papers, and the passing of extensive examinations also provided indices of assessment. The purpose of this learning was to provide an intellectually developed individual who presumably would be able to solve new problems on the basis of his knowledge of older problems. Certainly a by-product of this education was mental discipline as well as some degree of virtue defined either in terms of humanistic qualities or in terms of supernatural attributes.

A distinction should be made here between mental discipline and formal discipline as a basis for classical learning theory. Kolesnik (1960) in a thorough discussion of this matter suggests that mental discipline usually refers to the notion that man's capabilities can somehow be trained to be more efficient, and to the philosophical notion that such training constitutes one of the chief purposes of schooling. Formal discipline, on the other hand, refers to a position that education consists of the strengthening or development of the powers of the mind by exercising them, preferably on difficult, abstract material such as Latin, Greek, and Mathematics. For disciplinary purposes, the content of the curriculum is judged to be secondary in relationship to the form that is thought to be especially efficacious in the creation of minds able to operate well in any field of endeavor.

The distinction between mental discipline and formal discipline should be made because of the errors that so often are attributed to the former by the attacks on the latter. Mental discipline, as related to transfer of learning, suggests that the study of Latin, for example, might reasonably be expected to improve one's command of English or French; that vocabulary or principles of grammar learned in one subject could be used in another similar setting. But formal discipline would suggest that the study of Latin actually increases mental capacity, with the effort being put into the memorization of verb forms aiding the mind in its formal development.

The error of this judgment is seen readily in the consideration that if this were true, then philosophy should have the effect of making one more logical, and ethics the consequence of making one more alert to forms of morality, etc. It is formal discipline that influenced much of the 19th century education and that was blasted by William James' memory experiments and the subsequent research of Thorndike. Unfortunately, many generations of educators have lambasted mental discipline rather than formal discipline.

A second major component in what might be called the cognitive emphasis in learning is that found in the Gestalt school of thought. Gestalt psychology has been treated in an earlier chapter, but a summary of this cognitive approach to learning is appropriate here. Bigge (1966) contends that the currents of cognitive learning theory fall under the headings of Gestalt psychology, configurationalism, and field theory. In all of these approaches, a neutral-interactive or naturally-active organism is postulated. In the Gestalt theory the focus is on perception or the internal process whereby the brain structures experience. The emphasis in learning is on global structure and the promotion of insightful learning. Transfer of training is assumed on the basis of proper structure and organization within the mind. Although this position was detailed by Koehler, Wertheimer, and Koffka, it has enjoyed comparatively little success in really influencing the course of American educational learning theory. Configurationalism, which is sponsored by Bayles, Bode, and

Wheeler, tends to be a hybrid of Dewey's problem-solving approach cast in the mold of phenomenological thought. Here the emphasis is on aiding students to solve problems through a trial-and-error goal-directed learning. The cognitive field theorists take their origin from field psychology and the earlier work of Kurt Lewin. In more recent times Bruner, Combs, and Bigge tend to be identified with this approach to learning.

Piaget represents a new thrust in cognitive learning theories. Piaget's central research interests have been in the development of theoretical and experimental investigations of the qualitative development of intellectual structures. He has built an interpretation of cognitive development that relates both content, structure, and function into a continuing equation. He views cognitive functioning as related to biological characteristics, to modes of responding to environmental stimulation through assimilation and accommodation, and to schema (organizational or structural systems). His theory, certainly a part of the earlier phenomenological thrust of 19th century science, identifies stages of development that proceed from sensory-motor reflex-oriented behavior through preoperational, concrete operations, and formal operations with typical kinds of thought and behavior patterns characteristic of each stage. Flavell (1964) suggests the following as a capstone of Piaget's cognitive approach:

> Intelligence is said to originate within a biological substrate, a substrate beyond which it soon extends. At its core are the invariant attributes of organization and adaptation, the latter including the two interacting functions, assimilation and accommodation. Through the continued operation of these last, structural units called schemas are born, developed, and eventually form interlocking systems or networks . . . changes in the assimilation-accommodation relationship occur both within and between stages of development and these operations are crucial in determining the nature of cognition (64).

Another modern cognitive theorist is David Ausubel. Ausubel has suggested that the primary skill in school learning is centered on concept formation. Opposing the traditional assumption regarding learning, that is, abstract concepts are built on a long chain of inductive experiences with concrete phenomena, he boldly states that this experience is time-consuming and ignores the fundamental component for concept formation, which is organization (1963). He says that "most of the understandings that learners acquire both in and out of school are presented rather than discovered" (Ausubel, 1963, 16). He defines this type of learning as reception learning in which ". . . the entire content of what is to be learned is presented to the learner in final form." That is, the learner is not left to discover for himself by trial and error what is to be learned but instead internalizes the material and subsumes it into his own cognitive organization.

Ausubel does not deny the efficacy of the inductive method in learning, that is, learning through experience, problem solving, and drawing generalizations from that experience. But he insists that far too seldom do teachers recognize the importance of cognitive organizers in providing the adequate intellectual scaffolding necessary in the combining of thought elements. Furthermore, he states that reception learning is appropriate for children as well as adults, if it be recognized that abstraction must constitute the core of concepts on which most systematic studies are built. He suggests that concept formation is related directly to two major components: (1) the clarity of the organizer, which he defines as the scaffolding of the verbal structure, and (2) the psychological readiness of the subsumer, that is, the receiving organism. Ausubel strongly advocates that teachers concentrate on the major "big" ideas and then systematically explain the portions of each of these ideas until each becomes an organized unit within the mental structure of the learner.

The work of Ausubel and Piaget are complemented by another theorist, Vygotsky (1962). Vygotsky has maintained that verbal behavior is a necessary prerequisite for social or motoric behavior. Children are often observed in a task telling themselves verbally what they must do and then proceeding to action. Vygotsky states that, while initial experiences are largely sensory, as language develops it comes to mediate both thought and action. Thus speech, oral or internalized, ". . . becomes an instrument of thought in the proper sense—in seeking and planning solutions to a problem" (Vygotsky, 1962, 16).

Both the classical and cognitive approaches to learning focus primarily, although not exclusively, on the internal processes of the learner and on those cognitive structure variables that determine the nature of perception. As we shall see subsequently, the problem of perceptual organization and integration is an important factor in susceptibility to alternate reinforcement procedures.[2]

---

[2] This brief discussion of cognitive approaches to learning has not included the entire Freudian and Neo-Freudian approach to learning, and has not accented the affective dimension in learning. There are many terms within typical psychoanalytic theory that have implications for learning, including such as psychic energy, repression, and defense mechanisms. To some extent, the psychoanalytic interpretation of learning theory is represented by the bridge that Dollard and Miller attempted to make some years ago. This will be discussed under the stimulus-response learning approach. The entire question of interaction and process is, indeed, a relevant one, but the earlier solutions of McDougal and the functionalist school of thought appear generally to this writer to be global impressions. To some extent, the same criticism can be made of the derivatives of Gestalt theory who did, in fact, identify process variables but,

ANTECEDENTS TO SOCIAL LEARNING THEORY

In contrast to the classical and cognitive theorists in learning, stimulus-response and conditioning approaches to learning have been more specific in nature, more precise in their definition of antecedent and consequent changes and, until recently, less applicable to human learning. The stimulus-response approach to learning is most clearly demonstrable in terms of response variables. By response variables is meant the observable differences that occur in human behavior as a consequence (presumed) of a given stimulus. Modeled on the reflex phenomenon, stimulus-response theorists have been concerned with those observable and measurable stimuli that bring about or effect observable differences in response. This is not to state that stimulus-response theorists have denied the value of the intervening perceptual processes directly but, instead, to state that in their opinion intervening variables are less susceptible to direct measurement and evaluation. This approach to learning has been conceptualized first in terms of physiological studies and, then, in laboratory studies of infrahumans. An entire vocabulary has been developed that refers to the phenomena of learning as grouped under the stimulus-response and conditioning theorists.[3]

The stimulus-response theorists in learning tend to view learning as what happens between antecedent independent variables and consequent dependent variables. Learning in this sense then refers to the intervening unobserved variables that link the two (stimulus and response) together as, for example, in the following items.

Independent Antecedent Variables	Dependent Consequent Variables
Repetition, activity, behavior, practice, training, observation, modeling, etc.	Trends and changes in behavior, incremental modification of behavior

by comparison with the efficacy of social learning theory today, were dealing chiefly with impressionistic constructs that were global in nature, undifferentiated, and confusing in terms of measurement and the assessment of change.

[3] For example, *reinforcement* refers to stimuli that effect the behavior upon which they immediately follow. Positive reinforcement refers to any set of conditions that strengthen the behavior they immediately follow, and negative reinforcement are stimuli that will diminish the future occurrences of the behavior that they follow (Staats and Staats, 1964, 44). *Extinction* is defined as any set of conditions that result in the decrease or cessation of a learned response. *Learning repertory* refers to a set of learned responses that have generalized into a system of habituated behaviors as a consequence of reinforcement.

The history and development of the behaviorist approach to learning is deeply dependent on the life and work of Edward Lee Thorndike. He influenced the development of this approach in a monumental manner. Hilgard wrote:

> For nearly half a century one learning theory dominated all others in America, despite numerous attacks on it and the rise of its many rivals. It is the theory of Edward L. Thorndike . . . (1956, 15).

And Tolman wrote in 1938:

> The psychology of animal learning—not to mention that of child learning—has been and still is primarily a matter of agreeing or disagreeing with Thorndike, or trying in minor ways to improve upon him . . . All of us here in America seem to have taken Thorndike, overtly or covertly, as our starting point (cited in Hilgard, 1965, 11).

Thorndike, while studying with James at Harvard, began experimentation with children and later on with animals. Some of his earlier studies had been with children, and he had used candy rewards to effect the kinds of changes in which he was interested. However, because of criticism leveled at him for utilizing children, he switched to chickens.[4]

The beginning point in Thorndike's theory of learning was his conception of the original nature of man. Thorndike looked on man as a biological organism that had evolved to his present state. He considered that the acts of man's future behavior are largely determined at the point of conception. "His intellect and morals, as well as his body organs and movements, are in part the consequences of the nature of the embryo in the first movement of life" (Thorndike, *Educational Psychology*, Vol. I: *The Original Nature of Man*, 1913, 1).

Following logically from this basic premise, Thorndike always suggested that the basic task of education was to make use of the given

---

[4] One cannot but speculate on what would have been the consequences of continued experimentation with children had Thorndike continued these studies. It is similar to the report that Lashley made about the experiments he and Watson conducted in 1914 on the Dry Tortugas Islands. Lashley and Watson had been observing instinctive behaviors of the noddy tern and the sooty tern on this barren island. Lashley reported that they stopped their observations once they ran out of cigarettes and whiskey. Lashley commented that if only Watson had taken more cigarettes and whiskey to the Dry Tortugas, the history of psychology might have been very different (Harry F. Harlow, "William James and Instinct Theory," p. 26, in *William James: Unfinished Business* (Robert B. Macleod, ed.), American Psychological Association, 1969).

properties that man has, to develop them, and to shape man for the better in relationship to the knowledge and characteristics desired. This was in marked contrast with the position of Dewey who assumed an almost limitless evolution of potentiality in man, a kind of natural unfolding, and a more congruent equalitarian approach to learning (as it was judged by most educators).

In view of Thorndike's position regarding the nature of man, it was logical that he would view learning primarily as a physiological phenomenon tied in closely with evolution. He postulated a neurological substratum of preformed connections existing within the cortex. These he called S—R bonds and, although he sometimes referred to the neurological correlate, he more often, in practice, referred to the external observable behaviors. Thorndike explained learning chiefly in relationship to three principles: the *law of exercise,* the *law of effect,* and the *law of readiness.* Actually, exercise and effect were the two primary ones, and readiness was enunciated more as a corollary.

The importance of exercise had been recognized in all kinds of learning for centuries before Thorndike formalized it. The drill and repetition that was typical of Chinese education, the Lancastrian school effort, and much of elementary education in the United States during the 19th century demonstrated this fact. *The law of exercise* stated generally that the more a particular neurological connection or bond was exercised, the stronger it became. However, Thorndike demonstrated in a series of experiments that simple exercise alone was not enough, and he made a series of postulates or conditions that were important for the law of exercise, for instance, belongingness, polarity, fatigue, disuse, and effect.[5] *The law of effect* stated that responses which lead to annoying states of affairs tend to be obliterated, and those which lead to a satisfactory state of affairs tend to be confirmed. Thorndike also noted that a satisfying aftereffect seemed to be the crucial aspect of the law of effect and labeled this the "OK" reaction. He observed this particularly in relationship to his experiments where he said "right" or "wrong" immediately after a correct or incorrect response. The law of readiness involved both exercise and effect and stated simply that when a neurological unit was in readiness to conduct, conducting was a satisfactory experience; conversely, the lack of readiness produced an aversive effect. Thus Thorndike suggested that

[5] Belongingness simply refers to contiguity in the sense that certain items tend to be associated together such as bread and butter. Polarity tends to refer to items on a continuum which can be reversed such as learning 9×7 and then knowing what 7×9 is. For a further explanation of these terms, see William Clark Trow, *Educational Psychology,* 2nd edition, Houghton-Mifflin Co., Boston, 1950, 421–427.

the neural connections within the cortex were molded by experience, and that by reason of practice and concomitant states of satisfaction or dissatisfaction the neurological connections within the brain were strengthened or weakened.

Thorndike's influence in learning theory was great at the time he experimented and influenced students of education. But in retrospect it seems even greater today when much of what he actually envisaged appears to be confirmed in the confluence of anthropology, social psychology, and educational theory in social learning. In addition, Thorndike developed and standardized a number of testing instruments and demonstrated their value to school systems. Thorndike believed in a theory of education that placed key emphasis on hereditary individual differences. He felt that the major difference in education was the variable of sex. Boys and girls differ in their ability to excel at various skills. He felt that this extended to questions of reaction time, school grades, and attending behavior. He believed, for example, that accuracy was an hereditary trait, and his conception about the fixed nature of intelligence did much to promote the individualized and group intelligence tests. He also believed that it was the duty of the educator to determine the nature of learning experiences, the selection and rejection of bonds to be formed to meet specific learning situations, etc. The purpose of education, he thought, was to determine the manner in which the basic laws of learning could be fully utilized to promote the student through a course of knowledge comprehension and utilization. This, Thorndike believed, could be best effected through a skilled use of the laws of exercise and effect.

> Try to form certain bonds rather than others, to form them in a certain order, to identify more easily the bonds he is trying to form, to be more satisfied at the right bond, and more unready to repeat the wrong bonds, to be more satisfied by the general exercise of the function, and to be more satisfied by general improvement in it (Thorndike, *Educational Psychology: Briefer Course*, 1914, 219).

Perhaps the greatest contribution of Thorndike to psychology was the fact that he first pulled together, in a systematic manner, the principles of learning that had been surmised or stated in philosophical ways earlier. Trow (1950, 426–427) points out that Herbert Spencer, in explaining evolution, suggested that man tends to substitute for the hedonistic pleasure principle that regulates behavior a conscious feeling of liking which man tends to wish to continue, and vice versa for the avoidance of pain. This naturalistic pleasure principle, thought Spencer, was a guiding factor in evolution. Trow views Thorndike as breaking out of the philosophical and moralistic issues into the preamble of behaviorism.

Thus the transition has occurred. First came the consideration of the hedonistic influence of the conscious experiences of pleasure and pain, and as a consequence varied efforts to parallel them with theories of increased or decreased nervous activity or vital energy and to find analogies in beneficial and injurious actions. Later came the behavioral view, which sidesteps the problem of hedonism and which leaves the ultimate question of why some states of affairs are sought and some avoided still unanswered, but which opens the way to experimentation in order that the effect of various states of affairs may be explored and their influence on learning determined (Trow, 427).

In education, Thorndike's influence has been felt chiefly through testing, mainly because of the emergence of Watson's theory of conditioning, and because of the perception of others that Thorndike was too inflexible in his theory of intelligence and hereditary limitations. Watson's stark statements about behaviorism appeared to turn many educators to the more equalitarian approach of Dewey and Kilpatrick.

The second major component in the development of the behavioral approach to learning was begun in Russia with the studies in physiology done by Ivan P. Pavlov (1849–1936) and V. M. Bekhterev (1857–1927). Both Pavlov and Bekhterev worked in the field of physiology and reflexes. Somewhat independently, they investigated the effects of unconditioned and conditioned stimuli on responses. Beginning with observations of behavior in movement as a clue to what the organism is learning, Pavlov studied the reflex action and the chain of neural connections known as the reflex arc. The results of Pavlov's work and of Bekhterev's studies became known first in German and French translation, but they confirmed the views of John Watson (1878–1958), who had earlier rejected the functionalism of John Dewey, had studied experimental psychology, and who had conducted a number of observations with Lashley and others. Under the stimulation and confirmation of the Russian studies, Watson embarked on an attack against introspection, consciousness in psychology as a mediator of learning, and boldly set forth to create a psychology of behaviorism. Pavlov's ideas appeared to support the bridge that broke down completely the distinction between mind and body and made mind a process that could be explained in physiological terms. This had been the earlier goal of the Helmholtz school of psychology and physiology also. But where the Russians had proceeded with caution in generalizing the effects of conditioning and the mind-process problem, Watson and some of his followers boldly asserted that all learning could be explained through conditioning of one form or the other, and that even consciousness was a spurious notion for interpreting learning.[6]

The connectionism of Thorndike and the behaviorism of Watson had similarities, but they also had a number of differences. Each had the benefit of simplicity; stimuli are presented, and correct responses are stamped in through either reinforcement or the law of effect. In terms of educational policy there were some indirect implications. As far as schoolmen were concerned, both Thorndike and Watson's approach to human behavior was obnoxious. For individual differences were either the function of initial hereditary components or were subject to various learning experiences and, hence, there was little variability in the matters of individual differences (except as reflected in learning curves). The curriculum in the schoolmen's view was reducible to factual data suitable to associative and conditioning learning. Practice, repetition, and drill were considered fundamental and, since transfer cannot be counted on, the training is on specific items rather than on whole concepts. The doctrine of formal discipline, of course, is outmoded, and "training of the mind" a meaningless term.

Unlike Thorndike, however, Watson began without benefit of instincts in the child (something he did apparently believe in earlier); hence, he

---

[6] Classical conditioning is the pairing of a conditioning stimulus to an unconditioned stimulus with the result that the conditioning stimulus will effect the conditioned response. This process might be explained as follows:

1. *Unconditioned stimulus* (UCS). A stimulus which, at the outset of an experiment, evokes a regular and measurable response (for example, the presentation of food to a dog).
2. *Unconditioned response* (UCR). The regular and measurable response to the unconditioned stimulus just referred to (for example, salivation in the dog).
3. *Conditioning stimulus* (CS). A stimulus which (a) does not evoke the UCR, in this respect being neutral, and (b) is paired with the UCS for experimental purposes (for example, a buzzer).
4. *Conditioned response* (CR). Sometimes, as a result of the pairing of CS and UCS, a response resembling the UCR follows the CS, either on test trials with the UCS omitted or in anticipating the UCS. Such a response is the conditioned response.

The conditioning stimulus may generalize from a buzzer to other stimuli, for example, the entrance of the dog into the cage or even the entrance of the experimenter into the dog's kennel. Conditioning in this sense has a wide range of applications. It is most likely that all human behavior has some relationship to conditioning in terms of initial learning patterns. The pairing of the mother's voice and the nursing bottle with the child's hunger, the wide range of feelings about school, and very many personal habits all have their origin in conditioning procedures.

is not concerned with native tendencies that are "wrong" or for that matter "right." Watson thought that he could demonstrate in the laboratory a neural substratum of learning, while Thorndike could only assume the existence of neural S—R bonds. Another difference is that Watson clothed his psychological events in physiological terms, whereas Thorndike often used mentalistic terms. To Watson, an idea was a response, an emotion a measurable response of muscle and gland, and a sensation a neural process. But teachers have found it much easier to continue talking about ideas, sensations, and emotions. Watson's notions had a widespread acceptance in areas other than education, for example, pediatrics. During the period of the 1920s and early 1930s, the mothering patterns recommended by pediatricians included the rigid scheduling of feeding for infants, the avoidance of any show of affection, and stern efforts against bad habits.

Following Thorndike and Watson, a host of other learning theorists began to make modifications and elaborations of the earlier theories. Edwin R. Guthrie (1886–1959) emphasized the adaptation aspect of learning. By learning, Guthrie meant those behaviors that will assist the organism in making necessary adaptations to the environment. Guthrie placed much emphasis on the relationship of ideational concepts to physiological states. He suggested that both habit and motivation were derived from successful responses. Cognition to Guthrie was, in part, a response to physiological states of tension. Clark L. Hull (1884–1952) probably had more recent influence on the development of behavioral learning than anyone else. Reflecting his early training in engineering, he attempted to develop a comprehensive system by utilizing a logical structure of postulates and theorems. Hull's system of learning is by far the most complex of modern stimulus-response theorists. Hull, impressed with the evolution hypothesis, was convinced that the psychological factors of man were the means by which man's adaptation to the environment had been made possible. It is his thesis that the survival of the species had been the result of the appropriate measures that organisms have been capable of manifesting, measures which are directly dependent on organic needs. Hence, survival and learning are mutually dependent. According to Hull, habits result from reactions set into motion by needs and involving physiological changes within the organism that become progressively strengthened in proportion to their use. Reinforcement to Hull has reference to the general action of the organism that strengthens, selects, and establishes those habits that insure man's survival.

In recent years B. F. Skinner (1904–   ) has been considered the most outstanding spokesman for the behavioral approach to learning. Although certainly not a disciple of Thorndike, there are similarities in that they both emphasized reinforcement as the basic factor in learning. Moreover, both Thorndike and Skinner are accorded the testimony of their peers as being extremely creative and innovative psychologists. Skinner has contributed a wealth of research to the modern status of conditioning theories. Of specific importance is his identification of a new type of conditioning called instrumental or operant conditioning. In the tradition of Thorndike rather than of Pavlov, Skinner has focused on the effects or consequences of responding instead of on the contiguity of stimuli. In short, it is what the organism does *to* the environment instead of what the environment does *for* the organism that is important.

The distinct characteristics of operant conditioning are that behavior is emitted by the organism itself, within an environmental context, and the response so emitted is reinforced. Thus the relatively spontaneous response becomes the basis for shaping through reinforcement procedures. For example, Skinner has shaped the behavior of many birds and animals simply by reinforcing one or the other of their spontaneous responses. The example of shaping pigeon behavior to turn in circles is a well-known illustration of instrumental or operant conditioning. What is more important to human behavior is the fact that individuals are continually making responses within environmental settings and are receiving a variety of reinforcements. In human social interaction this means colloquially that nothing succeeds like success or fails like failure. When an individual makes a response to some kind of a social stimulus, he awaits the reinforcement that he will obtain. This may be satisfying or dissatisfying, and in either case the nature of the reinforcement will tend to shape his future responses.

Another specific contribution of Skinner is his development of schedules of reinforcement. Skinner has found that different kinds of reinforcement schedules or sequences can sustain and can shape behavior differentially. For example, if the frequency with which reinforcers are given is related to the rate that responses are emitted, this is termed a *ratio* schedule. If the reinforcement depends simply on the passage of varying lengths of time, it may be termed an *interval* schedule. Each of these two kinds of reinforcement schedules can be combined into either *fixed* or *variable interval* schedules. In the *fixed ratio* schedule the subject is reinforced at a specified number of responses—such as every fourth, tenth, or "*nth*" response. This would be the schedule used for a workman who is paid in relationship to units of work produced, for example, for each twenty items produced he would obtain three dollars. A *variable ratio* schedule differs from the former in that the reinforcement may come at any time—perhaps after the second response, perhaps not until the twentieth. Hence, for example, a pigeon might receive a reinforcer every second or tenth response and then occasionally two successive responses would be reinforced. The other two forms of scheduling reinforcement are also widely used. The *fixed interval* schedule is the schedule in which reinforcers are given at intervals of perhaps five minutes, or a day, or in many cases a month. An example of this kind of reinforcement is the monthly paycheck. The *variable interval* schedule is the schedule used to sustain most human behavior. This is reinforcement at various periods of time which are not planned. Most of human behavior is shaped or molded by variable interval reinforcement schedules. We are not rewarded for everything we do, but occasional reinforcement is necessary to sustain our behavior. Variable interval schedules often result in an even rate of behavior performance and are more resistant to extinction than are other types of schedules of reinforcement.

THE PHILOSOPHICAL BASIS FOR BEHAVIORISM

In earlier chapters of this book the evolution of a philosophy of science has been traced from the studies of Copernicus, Kepler, and Galileo to the systematic philosophical framework that Descartes initiated. It was Descartes more than anyone else who set the stage for the development of an objective philosophy of science. Although refraining from calling into question matters of faith and religion as such, he nevertheless insisted that philosophy and logic itself could not be the methodological basis of objective science. Instead he substituted: (1) systematic observation, (2) certain apodictic mathematical propositions, and (3) deductive reasoning. Of great importance to the development of a philosophy of science was Descartes' distinction between the inner world of thought, which he referred to as the *Res Cogitans,* and the world of external phenomena, which he called the *Res Extensa.* This latter world of extended quantifiable phenomena was the only world in which a philosophy of science could meaningfully operate.

Descartes' distinction between physical and mental phenomena and his development of a philosophical rationale for the exploration of the world of external phenomena led to changes in the concept of (1) the nature of reality, (2) the nature of man, and (3) the nature of knowledge. Descartes' influence was felt in Locke and, through Locke, in Hume. Reality came to be described in terms of external phenomena, forces, and laws. Man was considered the product of his environment, possessing no a priori characteristics other than his biological structure. Knowledge became identified with the product of science. All other forms of epistemological certainty were placed lower on the hierarchy of certitude.

In the 19th century, the methodology developed earlier was applied to questions concerning the nature of man. August Comte's conception of the four stages of man's intellectual development placed science at the final stage. The doctrine of evolution and the identification of psychology with physiology by Helmholtz, Dubois-Reymond, and Bruecke is particularly important in that this was a conscious attempt to stamp out, once and for all, any conception of man as anything more than an evolved animal whose functions and behavior would ultimately be understood in terms of physicalistic forces or conditions. Building on this foundation, Watson, Hull, and Skinner have continued this approach in more contemporary American psychology.

The formal philosophies that have supported this view of reality, knowledge, man, and values may be identified as scientific realism, logical empiricism, and experimentalism. Although there are obvious variations among these approaches, they all represent attempts to create a scientific philosophy. Scientific realism is ultimately derived from classical realism and provides a more essentialistic orientation than the other two, that is, the acknowledgment of an a priori structure. Both logical empiricism and Dewey's experimentalism incline more in the direction of operational definition of existing structures, that is, the existentialist end of the continuum represented by the polar opposites of essence and existence (see Chapter VI). Logical empiricism inclines more to the paramount problem of definition of terms and clarity of language than does experimentalism (a fact well known by those who have studied Dewey's system).

A review of some of the basic principles of these philosophical positions is in order here. The following principles are drawn from various primary and secondary philosophic sources to illustrate the basic philosophic stances of these approaches toward knowledge, reality, and values. Certainly not all realists will agree with my wording of these principles, nor will all experimentalists. The variation in philosophical thought is almost endless, and these principles are presented as representative statements about knowledge, reality, and values, not as absolute, precise formulations of specific philosophers.

As can be seen from the comparison of statements contrasting the older scientific realism with Dewey's conception of experimentalism, there has been a gradual transition from a realist position, which focused on structure and on a-priori essence, to a scientific approach to problem solving, centered on experience. Logical empiricism, which represents a more scientific approach to the older form of realism, is considered by some to be the most precise of all philosophies. It has been presented as "the philosophy to end all philosophies" (Feigl, 1955) and is an attempt to place the findings of science in precise mathematical and logical order.

Table 1   Philosophical Bases of Behaviorism[7]

Epistemology (Knowledge)	
Scientific Realism	*Experimentalism*
There is no knowledge in the mind that is not first in the senses.	Experience is the ultimate ground of human existence.
The world of our sense experience as perceived by us corresponds with the world of physical phenomena. Man understands the functioning of the universe by an accurate correspondence of concepts in his mind to the operating principles of the universe.	Experience is the key to knowing. It includes not only reflection but doing, and does not require a transformation into some metaphysical system that is out of touch with experience.
Knowledge is based on an organized and systematic methodology of perception, which includes careful observing, checking results, and systematically enunciating generalizations and principles.	True reality is what we have here in front of us: oak trees and doorknobs; mothers-in-law and ice cream. There is no need to conjure up an artificial reality beyond this. The whole thing, just as we experience it, is the way it is.
The laws of the universe are discovered through systematic observation, generalizations, and scientific testing. Truth is the tested and verified principle that explains cause and effect relations.	The ultimate test of truth is whether it works. To the degree that a solution solves a problem in the real world of experience, it may be said to be true.
Reality, as it is in itself, can be known in part by the human mind.	Meaning is determined by experience.
Meaning is based on the correct adequation of symbolic content in the subject's knowledge with the external reality.	

Ontology (Reality)	
The physical world is made up of matter which is in motion. The primary structural units of matter are constantly undergoing changes of a physical, biological, and chemical nature.	What the ultimate nature of reality is we shall never know. Moreover, it is of very little concern to us, since all our experiences are in the forms of transactions between ourselves and the outer reality.
No universal idea or prototype of existence exists absolutely in space and time. The universal idea or abstraction is essentially the creation of the human mind through the synthetic process of pooled perceptions.	The reality we live in—the world of sensation of change, of growth and death is the only world we can intelligently manage in human discourse.
Reality exists in itself without reference to human plans, motivations, or purpose.	How the machine runs is less important than that man be capable of controlling the laws for his own development.

[7] *Note.* Scientific realism is used as an example of object-oriented philosophy charac-

Table 1 (Continued)

Axiology (Values)	
Scientific Realism	Experimentalism
The ultimate basis of morality is informed reason. This informed reason is based on the best scientific insights available.	Problems of good and evil must always be weighed in the contextual setting of social consequences.
The knowledge of the real world of existence through man's logical and scientific endeavor constitutes the only reliable guide to human conduct, individual and social.	We relinquish a certain amount of our human dignity when we cravenly slink off to put our lives and fortunes under the protection of an Absolute. For once we do this, we must give up thinking about our values. Absolutes are not subject to inquiry. They cannot be questioned or looked into; they can only be obeyed.
There are certain immediate self-evident truths that form the basis of logic, reasoning, and morality, and lie in the very structure of man and the pattern of social evolution.	
There is a moral law or natural law which is intrinsically contained in the ordered nature of external reality. This law, though often unwritten and unspoken, exists and can be found through the scrutiny of external reality (Scholastic Realism).	The question of what you should do depends on what ends you have in view, on what circumstances you wish to prevail in this corner of reality, and on what arrangements of the situation would be an improvement on what you have already done at this moment.

terized by an essentialist point of view. Experimentalism is included as an object-oriented philosophy with an existentialist point of view.

Feigl views logical empiricism as the philosophy of science effort ". . . to abandon the dogmatic, other-worldly, super-naturalistic, tender-minded, rationalistic, parochial pre-conceptions and to replace them by critical, worldly, naturalistic, fact-minded, empirical, experimental, and universally applicable ways of thinking" (Feigl, 306).

Logical empiricism as applied to scientific thinking calls for definition of terms and precise meanings. It suggests a polarity between accuracy and error, form and chaos, regularity and randomness, pattern or form and formlessness. It defines outcomes in terms of improbability and probability, predictability and unpredictability. The role of the observer in science is one of careful specification and limitation of the conditions of observation, with the ultimate outcome being the promotion of a complete isomorphism or external-internal congruence between theoretical frameworks and concrete systems. The philosophy of science is dedicated to the clear specification of logical terminology in the description and analysis of phenomena. When this is applied to psychological phenomena, and particularly to those of learning, it results in a necessary reduction of complexities to definable and observable phenomena such as stimuli and responses.

The identification of philosophy with the methodology of science, and the particular stance taken by the logical empiricists toward other philosophical positions, has been one of generalized intolerance. Consciously or unconsciously, the identification of science with philosophy has tended to place the scientific method as the supreme criterion of philosophical clarity. Simultaneously, the restrictions of science circumscribe logical empiricism and force it to bypass the more perennial (but less definable) problems in philosophy. Logical empiricism appears to focus more and more on detailed analyses of logic and language with the ultimate intended desideratum, the establishment of an absolute objectification of communication. As O'Neil has stated (1964, 3):

> In a sense, of course, one of the more or less invariant characteristics of any really rigorous analytic approach is what the psychologists have become fond of referring to as an "intolerance of ambiguity" . . . There is perhaps a certain irony implicit in the fact that it is precisely the analytical philosopher who is frequently the first to condemn the authoritarian excesses of the old-fashioned metaphysician and yet who, of all contemporary philosophers, seems to be most fervently committed to the establishment of a sort of neo-absolutism based upon purely methodological criteria, a sort of tyranny of technique.

In summary, the philosophical constructions of scientific realism, experimentalism, and logical empiricism tend to provide a frame of reference for the behavioral learning approach. Good as they might appear in terms of the precision of scientific thinking, there are some limitations. First, the methodology of the philosophy of science is based on the findings of science and is, therefore, an abstraction of science itself. The methodology of science, as defined by behavioral learning studies, tends to discourage the empirical-inductive method so typical and fruitful in the investigations of Brentano, James, and other early psychologists. There has been a gradual emergence, accelerated in the 1930s and 1940s by Hull, in favor of the hypothetical-deductive method. This approach, instead of considering the empirical basis of psychic phenomena through the use of analysis of behavior, has tended to emphasize a reductionism to the stimulus-response concept. Koch and Zener have pointed out

(Wann, 1964) that psychology is tremendously handicapped by a conception of behavior that is circumscribed by the global terms *stimulus* and *response*. Zener has put it this way:

> In no other science is there a single, unqualified noun referring to the totality of events studied by that science, comparable to the term behavior. There are optical, mechanical, magnetic, intro-atomic events all of which are physical events; there are a variety of biological events—metabolism, growth, reproduction, contraction, secretion; but no single, unqualified term exists in either science comprehending all of the events which constitute its subject matter. Furthermore, there are no biological laws comparable in generality to stimulus-response laws—no such physical or chemical laws. No other science handicaps itself with the incubus of a term which so discourages analysis and encourages over-generality of interpretation of obtained functional relationships (K. Zener and Gaffron, M. "Perceptual Experience: An Analysis of its Relations to the External World through Internal Processings," in *Psychology: A Study of a Science*, S. Koch (ed.), IV, 515–618, New York: McGraw-Hill, 1962).

Testing theory and statistical models have profited from the scientific approach to behavioral phenomena. Illustrative of this are statistical levels of confidence, correlational coefficients, factor analysis, and a host of other mathematical manipulations that have been made possible through the philosophy of science and psychological reductionism. However, it should be pointed out that all of these statistical operations *assume* an isomorphic relationship between the category of responses obtained and the real phenomena, a correspondence of felt attitudes or concepts with this reduction, and the accuracy of responses. These are big assumptions.

A second major conclusion about the philosophical basis of traditional behaviorism can be found in the attitude toward reality or being. Reality testing and the examinations of the parameters of reality have been confined to external physical phenomena that can be characterized by quantity and measurability. The approach here follows clearly a line of philosophical thought originated by Descartes, followed up by Locke and Hume, and expounded in modern times by a variety of philosophers of science. Undoubtedly, this method has yielded tremendous fruits, but any honest appraisal of the method would have to suggest that in fact, rather than in principle, reality is limited to those externally defined phenomena that are viable in a world of experimental manipulation and statistical inference.

A third fact about the philosophical bases of behaviorism relates to the epistemological hierarchy that it has established. When the method is one of rigorous science, when the conception of reality is circumscribed by external phenomena then, obviously, the hierarchy of epistemology is affected. At the apex of credence is the scientific fact or principle, and in descending order are other forms of knowing, including opinion, subjective personal knowledge, and beliefs.

Fourth, axiology or values are dependent on epistemological positions as is true in other philosophical systems. This means that premium value is placed on the scientific fact as fact. When this scientific fact is extended to social behavior, it holds that science should be able to provide the answers to what constitutes ethical and moral human behavior. This obviously requires a definition of what constitutes good and evil as well as truth and falsity. In short, the traditional philosophy of science bases have tended to result in what can only be termed a behavioral ethnocentrism that polarizes the canons of scientific method, the objective findings, epistemological "fact," certitude, cosmological inquiry, and scientific values at the "good" end of the continuum, and mental phenomena, the phenomenological method, metaphysical inquiry, subjectivity, and the "indefinite" intervening variables at the "bad" end.

LEARNING THEORY AND PSYCHOTHERAPY

Learning theory and the philosophy of behaviorism have also been applied to psychotherapy. This development is comparatively recent in psychotherapy literature, and it came about by a recognition that psychotherapy is a form of verbal and nonverbal interaction and is not substantively different from other forms of social learning. Behavior is subject to modification through responses of either client or psychotherapist, and certain habits are inevitably reinforced or subject to extinction procedures in the process.

The first real attempt to apply learning theory to psychotherapy was an attempt by J. C. Dollard and N. E. Miller (1950) to integrate psychoanalytic theory with learning. Although their approach was carefully couched as a theoretical one that was subject to research verification, they attempted what can be summarized as a bridge between Hull's reinforcement approach and Freudian theory. They broadened the notion of both stimulus and response as defined by Hull and also acknowledged the existence of primary or innate drives such as pain, thirst, hunger, sexual excitement, and the like. They believed that there are innate response hierarchies that are shaped via the principle of reinforcement. They also view the learning process in terms of four conditions: (1) an event that must initiate the sequence of behavior (drive), (2) a particular stimulus event that relates to the kind of response to be effected (cue), (3) a response to the situation (response), and (4) a reduction in the intensity of the drive (reinforcement). Dollard and Miller believed that a number of human behaviors are initiated through the association of certain responses—possibly randomly developed—that are tied in with innate drives.

Behavior disorders or maladaptive behaviors often have as their base a conflict between innate physiological drives and an environmental situation. They conceived this source of conflict as residing in the person more primarily than in the circumstances. Conflict generally results in relationship to sex, fear, anger, and other emotional responses. The specifics of this conflict usually center on or around two major categories, that is, approach and avoidance. Borrowing from Lewin these concepts, they expanded on them in terms of learned behavior and psychotherapy. The approach-approach conflict reflects one in which behavior toward two divergent objects is elicited, and the individual cannot move in both directions at the same time. In the avoidance-avoidance reaction, the individual attempts to avoid two situations simultaneously, and in the approach-avoidance set of circumstances he is both drawn and repelled simultaneously.

With these kinds of conflicts, neurosis is often learned and reflects conflicts that are inaccessible to verbal awareness. Dollard and Miller considered symptoms in the more or less orthodox Freudian tradition, that is, as responses which symbolically demonstrate the unconscious conflict. They thus conceive psychotherapy in its goal as a removal of the underlying conflict rather than as a removal of the symptom. Of course, the patient or client should help in making these conflicts conscious and subject to conscious manipulation. It would appear that the therapist's role in psychotherapy is one of identifying and of modifying the various elements of the avoidance sequence of behavior, while the client attempts to explore alternative responses to drive reduction. Dollard and Miller recognized the importance of new verbal learning and new behavioral responses in the elimination or extinction of conflict. The process of psychotherapy involves both the conscious elaboration of the client, the acquisition of new verbal responses, and the interpretation by the psychotherapist. But fundamental to the entire system of Dollard and Miller is the notion that the core of psychotherapy should be viewed from the learning analysis of behavior.

Another contributor to learning therapy is Joseph Wolpe. Wolpe originally adopted Freud's view of human behavior, but after reading the Russians and through an exposure to Hull, he came to reject most of the former influence and to question a good deal of the latter influence. He has developed a learning psychotherapy entitled reciprocal inhibition. Wolpe considers the neurosis as a persistently maladaptive form of learned behavior with a prominent anxiety component acquired in anxiety-generating circumstances. Anxiety plays a central role in his system and almost always is considered causally related to some antecedent events. The most prominent feature of Wolpe's system is the notion that any behavior that has been learned can be unlearned. Wolpe suggests that there are two forms of unlearning or extinction. The one is simply a fatiguelike state varying with response frequency. Though the response may not be emitted over a period of time, the fact is that it still remains as a part of the behavior repertory and may reoccur in a spontaneous recovery. The second form of unlearning is what Wolpe terms reciprocal inhibition. Most of his therapy procedures are based on this process, which involves associating a response antagonistic to the response to be extinguished. Since both responses cannot exist simultaneously, the older response will be extinguished. For example, in the case of an alcoholic, a painful shock is administered every time a bottle of alcohol is flashed on a screen. Or in the case of a phobic movement, a more painful response is associated with it. For example, a child who shows a phobic reaction in a classroom is forced to leave the room. There are many varieties of this approach, but the general intent is to produce a response associated temporally and spatially to the maladaptive response, with the end in mind that the maladaptive response will be weakened and finally extinguished.

Wolpe's theory bears considerable resemblance to Eysenck and Rachman's views of neurosis (1965). Eysenck tends to view behavior in terms of two major categories: (1) maladaptive overlays that are learned, that is, neuroses, and (2) behavioral deficits or appropriate behaviors that have not been learned. In the former case, the problem is to eliminate behaviors that are causing problems to the individual or to the society in which he lives. In the latter case, the problem is to help the individual effect new learnings that are more appropriate. Neurotic behaviors fit into the first category and behavior disorders, such as aggression, fit into the second category. Both Wolpe and Eysenck tend to agree that the therapist should treat the symptom itself directly without worrying about the underlying root of the behavior. As Eysenck writes (1965, 10):

> The point, however, on which the theory here advocated breaks decisively with psychoanalytic thought of any description is in this. Freudian theory regards neurotic symptoms as adaptive mechanisms which are evidence of repression; they are the visible upshot of unconscious causes. Learning theory does not postulate any such un-

conscious causes, but regards neurotic symptoms as simply learned habits; there is no neurosis underlying the symptom, but merely the symptom itself. *Get rid of the symptom (skeletal and autonomic) and you have eliminated the neurosis.*

The treatment procedures then relate to both the extinction of maladaptive responses and to the building up of missing appropriate responses.

From the point of view of learning theory, treatment is, in essence, a very simple process. In the case of surplus conditioned responses treatment should consist in the extinction of these responses; in the case of deficient conditioned responses treatment should consist in the building up of the missing stimulus-response connections.

Eysenck hastens, however, to add that the simplicity of the system does not infer that it can be easily administered by those who are unaware of the total complexities of the situation. Eysenck summarizes in a very comprehensive manner the differences that exist between learning therapy and psychoanalytic thought.

The approach to psychotherapy represented by Eysenck and Wolpe is also supported, in general, by a variety of other social behavioral learning theorists, for example, Bandura, Krasner, Ullman, and Gerald Patterson. This approach essentially blasts some of the old assumptions about counseling and psychotherapy. Some of them are: (1) the notion that changes in verbal behavior are necessary prerequisites for improvements in other maladaptive behaviors, (2) the conviction that it is important to talk about things you do not want to talk about or to make more affect statements, or to recall early memories, and (3) the assumption that maladaptive symptoms are really indicative of underlying unconscious conflicts.

A considerable amount of research evidence has been accumulated in support of the behavioral learning approach to psychotherapy. Eysenck (1965), in reviewing the studies of the recovery rate from neurotic disorders that are claimed for psychoanalysis and other dynamic psychotherapies as compared with custodial treatment and/or nonspecific treatment, could see no real evidence that these recovery rates were better than the ones that could have occurred by a spontaneous remission of symptoms. Grossberg (1964) provided an extensive survey and review of the research findings related to behavior modification and behavior therapy. According to Grossberg's review, behavior therapy has been found to be successful in a variety of treatments for phobic reactions such as fear of small animals, fear of the dark, fear of height, fear of cars, agoraphobia, fear of injections, and public speaking. Desensitization has been used to allay undue anxiety reactions such as feelings of guilt

Table 2 **Differences between Psychoanalytic and Behavior Therapy According to Eysenck[8]**

Psychotherapy (Psychoanalytic)	Behavior Therapy
1. Based on inconsistent theory never properly formulated in postulate form.	Based on consistent, properly formulated theory leading to testable deductions.
2. Derived from clinical observations made without necessary control observations or experiments.	Derived from experimental studies specifically designed to test basic theory and deductions therefrom.
3. Considers symptoms the visible upshot of unconscious causes ("complexes").	Considers symptoms as unadaptive conditioned responses.
4. Regards symptoms as evidence of *repression*.	Regards symptoms as evidence of faulty learning.
5. Believes that symptomatology is determined by defense mechanisms.	Believes that symptomatology is determined by individual differences in conditionability and automatic lability, as well as accidental environmental circumstances.
6. All treatment of neurotic disorders must be *historically* based.	All treatment of neurotic disorders is concerned with habits existing at *present*.
7. Cures are achieved by handling the underlying (unconscious) dynamics, not by treating the symptom itself.	Cures are achieved by treating the symptom itself, that is, by extinguishing unadaptive C.R.s and establishing desirable C.R.s
8. Interpretation of symptoms, dreams, acts, etc., is an important element of treatment.	Interpretation, even if not completely subjective and erroneous, is irrelevant.
9. Symptomatic treatment leads to the elaboration of new symptoms.	Symptomatic treatment leads to permanent recovery provided autonomic as well as skeletal surplus C.R.s are extinguished.
10. Transference relations are essential for cures of neurotic disorders.	Personal relations are not essential for cures of neurotic disorder, although they may be useful in certain circumstances.

[8] H. J. Eysenck (ed.), *Behaviour Therapy and the Neuroses*, Pergamon Press, New York, third impression, 1967, p. 11.

and devaluation as well as exaggerated startle responses resulting from war experience. Sexual disorders have not always responded to treatment as well through behavior therapy techniques. The use of aversive drugs has been partially successful in coping with homosexual behavior and cases of transvestites. One study reports the successful treatment of two homosexual males by a process of verbally reinforcing assertive and masculine behavior.

Conversion reactions such as hysterical paralysis, functional blindness, and anorexia (failure to eat) have been reversed through reinforcement procedures and, in one case, by making other reinforcements such as visits, books, music, and television watching contingent on eating. Obsessive compulsive reactions have also been treated successfully through these techniques. Desensitization has been used in successfully eliminating obsessive thoughts of world destruction, illness, and compulsive handwashing. Jones (cited in Grossberg) mentioned a review of 15 studies in which bell-conditioning techniques were applied to 1446 enuretics with a total of 76 percent success. Other studies report the cure of speech disorders through desensitization, the extinction of bedtime tantrums through operant conditioning, and the gradual development of speech in autistic children who had been subjected to many kinds of traditional therapies prior to the behavioral treatment.

Although there are a number of specific techniques associated with learning therapy, such as (1) aversion therapy, (2) operant conditioning, (3) reinforcement withdrawal, and (4) desensitization, Ullman and Krasner (1965, 29) believe that they can all be subsumed under the general rubric of the knowledgeable utilization of environmental contingencies to alter the subject's response to stimuli.

We should make it clear that while there are many techniques, there are few concepts or principles involved. In terms of techniques, Bandura (1961) ordered his review around extinction, discrimination learning, methods of reward, punishment, and social imitation. Grossberg (1964) organized his material around the procedures of aversion, negative practice, positive conditioning, reinforcement withdrawal, and desensitization. Mowrer (in press) comments aptly that the techniques reduce to extinction and conditioning, and while we will present our review of techniques following the general outline of Wolpe's (1954) review, we wish to agree with Mowrer's point and elaborate on it. Despite differences in approaches and techniques, we would propose that all behavior modification boils down to procedures utilizing systematic environmental contingencies to alter the subject's response to stimuli. There are two points that are crucial. The first is the systematic or programmatic nature of the arrangement of the stimulus environment. The second, and more important to the immediate discussion, is that it is the response to stimuli and not the specific response, *per se,* that is the focus of treatment.

APPLICATIONS OF BEHAVIOR MODIFICATION TECHNIQUES

The accumulation of literature that relates to applications of behavior modification has been astounding. McReynolds (1969) listed a partial bibliography of 465 items accumulated in recent years. The contributions have been in different areas, but center around a fairly consistent methodology that is grounded in learning theory generally and in behavior modification specifically. For example, a consistent child development theory has been developed by Sidney W. Bijou and Donald M. Baer (1961) in their works on *Child Development* (1961). Arthur and Carolyn Staats in *Complex Human Behavior* (1963) have covered similar ground. Arthur Staats in *Learning Language and Cognition* (1968) has extended learning theory to cover typical cognitive construct variables.

In the areas of preschool education and of special education, Siegfried Engelmann and Carl Bereiter have published a number of research studies concerned with disadvantaged children (*Teaching Disadvantaged Children in the Preschool,* 1966). Frank Hewitt (*The Emotionally Disturbed Child in the Classroom,* 1968) has developed a behavioral learning strategy for educating children with maladaptive behavior, utilizing a task-analysis of skills and a carefully planned environmental control system. Barbara Bateman (1967) has specified in clear detail approaches to diagnosis and educational planning for children with learning disabilities.

In the area of classroom learning, learning theory and behavior modification techniques have spurred the development of a variety of other specific techniques. For example, prescriptive teaching and the determination of specific behavioral objectives in learning have been accelerated by Larry Peter (*Prescriptive Teaching,* 1965) and by Robert F. Mager (*Preparing Instructional Objectives,* 1962). The relationship of alternate learning steps in classroom procedures has been spelled out by Robert R. Gagne (*The Conditions of Learning,* 1965). In addition, learning theory has influenced the development of a methodology of observational techniques to determine the antecedents and consequences of specific problem behavior in the classroom (Patterson and Harris 1968, Hamerlynck 1968, Montgomery, 1968). Joseph A. Cobb (1970) has described how behavioral observations relate to the prediction of achievement variables in fourth graders. Moreover, the entire attempt to utilize computers in the programming of educational objectives and in the approximation to criteria established is indirectly related to developments in learning theory (Frank B. Baker, 1971) as conceptualized by the Program for Learning in Accordance with Needs (PLAN), the Teaching Information Processing System (TIPS), the Individualized Mathematics Curriculum Project (IMCP), and others.

In the area of family relationships and working with disturbed families, G. R. Patterson and his associates (Patterson and Reid, 1967, Patterson, Cobb, and Ray, 1970, Patterson, Ray, and Shaw, 1968) have identified patterns of reciprocity and coercive behavior which exist in the family, methods of observing interaction between members of the family, and procedures for working with these families to effect changes. Some of the recent work has been concerned with the development of probability indices for predicting the eruption of aggressive behavior in response to differential stimuli.

The role of the school psychologist as a learning consultant has been studied and reported by Barclay, Goodwin, Garvey, and Montgomery (Barclay, 1968, 1971, Goodwin, Garvey, and Barclay, 1971, Barclay and Montgomery, 1971). When working with school psychologists who attended two NDEA sponsored institutes, an effort was made to teach methods of coping with maladaptive children, the increase of learning skills in children with learning deficits, and consultation procedures with teachers and parents. The reinforcing value of the school psychologist in shaping and maintaining the behavior of teachers was discussed in an article by Brown, Montgomery, and Barclay (1969).

In the area of counseling, John D. Krumboltz has published a number of studies relating to the application of learning theory to counseling (1964, 1965, 1966, 1967). Many other studies have been shared with some of his students (Ryan and Krumboltz, 1964, Krumboltz and Thoresen, 1964), (Krumboltz and Goodwin, 1966). The sum impact of these studies has been referred to by both Krumboltz and Hosford (1970) as a revolution in counseling.

Krumboltz's starting point is essentially this—that counseling theorists and practitioners have not been asking the right questions. They have consistently sought to ask questions about changes in self-concept, or attitudes, or internalized states which may or may not have a clear and unambiguous relationship to behavior. Krumboltz believes that counselors are in the business of changing behavior and that their entire focus ought to be on this matter. In this approach the psychotherapy procedures used in behavioral therapy have been scaled down into what Krumboltz considers a more practical and intelligible approach to public school counseling. They have in point of fact taken on somewhat of a problem-solving cast in the behavioral frame of reference.

Krumboltz defines counseling as: "whatever ethical activities a counselor undertakes in an effort to help the client engage in those types of behavior which will lead to a resolution of the client's problems" (1965). He thinks that in the future counselors will be specializing in specific areas such as personal adjustment, vocational decision making, and the like. In a monograph entitled *Stating the Goals of Counseling* (1966), Krumboltz spells out in detail his rationale for counseling. He states that any set of goals for counseling should meet each of the following criteria.

1. The goals of counseling should be capable of being stated differently for each individual client.
2. The goals of counseling for each client should be compatible with, although not necessarily identical to, the values of his counselor.
3. The degree to which the goals of counseling are attained by each client should be observable.

The important implications of these goals are that counseling should be attuned to the conscious level of problem formation of the client rather than be interpreted in terms of a framework of theory. In this sense, in order to work with a client there is a need that the counselor establish a basic rapport with his client. This does not mean that both must have similar values but, instead, that a given counselor cannot help an individual consider alternative solutions to his problem which are diametrically opposed to the counselor's values. Finally, Krumboltz states that the evaluation of effective counseling, the criterion, must be observable in terms of overt behavior. This suggests that the older criteria of insight, self-report, or counselor judgment are too subjective to serve as real criteria of counseling effectiveness.

The behavioral goals of counseling reflected in this approach have been identified as (1) altering maladaptive behavior, (2) learning the decision-making process, and (3) the prevention of problems. Krumboltz feels that many clients are unhappy about some aspect of their behavior or the subjective feelings which spring from that behavior. For example, an individual may feel lonely because he has never learned to interact effectively with other people. In this instance the counselor's task is to determine what kinds of behavioral goals may be important to the client in terms of behavior change. This is no easy task, but with the use of learning theory and the techniques that have been developed in behavior modification practice, Krumboltz believes that it will be possible, in most cases, to arrive at a plan of action behavior that will effectively begin to act as an operant.

A major factor in the arriving at alternative forms of behavior is a consideration of the decision-making process. The counselor here acts as a means or catalyst to effect decision making on the part of his client. This implies that the counselor may have to acquaint clients with the fundamentals of the decision-making process, the consideration of liabilities, assets, and alternatives in order to reach a sound conclusion about a course of action. Finally, Krumboltz suggests that the systematic teaching of decision-making skills would be an excellent manner of helping individuals solve their own problems.

A most comprehensive review of behavioral counseling has been authored by Ray E. Hosford (1970). In this review, Hosford traces some of the foundational assumptions of the approach and points out that behavioral techniques do not supplant but, instead, supplement many of the traditional approaches to counseling. He spells out that there are four crucial elements in the strengthening of new behaviors: (1) that the reinforcements chosen be powerful enough to motivate individuals to continue the behavior being reinforced, (2) that the reinforcements be applied systematically, (3) a knowledge on the part of the dispenser of reinforcement when to dispense and when not to, and (4) that the counselor or reinforcer be able to elicit the behavior that he plans to reinforce. Hosford also points out that the specific reinforcement history of the individual is important in determining appropriate reinforcers. Drawing heavily on social learning theory, he points up the effect of models, in imitation and social prestige. For example, reinforcement dispensed by a high-status person counts more than when the same reinforcement is dispensed by a low-status person. Finally, he singles out the effects of peer models and peer reinforcement as being most important in effecting certain kinds of changes in children and adolescents.

In summary, behavior modification techniques have been incorporated into the framework of learning theory and have been applied with many outstanding results to a host of problems that involve children in preschool, special education, and the regular classroom, where deviant or underachieving children are present; and it has influenced developments in programmed instruction, computer-assisted instruction, and training programs involving counselors and school psychologists, as well as service programs for parents. These examples of the consequences of the extension of learning theory into the applied fields of education and social relations have been cited simply as testimony to a set of studies that have occurred in recent years. Some obvious assets that have been derived from this movement are: (1) the development of both behavioral observation technologies and the sharpening up of methodological considerations in applied research; (2) the development of a set of viable concrete operational criteria to measure changes in behavior; and (3) the growth of a number of new problems that have emerged into the asking or formulation stage as a result of the research findings.

EXPANDING THE BASE OF LEARNING THEORY

Hosford in his review of behavioral counseling pointed out that behaviorism does not supplant other techniques in counseling, but supplements them (1970). Those who have accepted behavioral learning techniques do not suddenly change their behavior in relationship to clients. And increasingly, those who use the technology of behavior modification are aware of the important inner dimensions of reality that the technology does not appear to touch.

There are some real difficulties with behavior modification as the core notion in a philosophy of counseling. First, behavior modification is a technique that is morally neutral. It can be used for a variety of end products and by a variety of individuals. Moreover, learning theory itself appears to be grounded in a philosophy of science that is tied to the development of science itself and is thus circular. This is particularly true of the behavioral learning theories. There has been a preoccupation with the S—R model and with the consequent demonstrable and observable behaviors. The word, deemphasis, may be the right term to describe the behavioral stance, since few behaviorists deny the reality of intermediate sets of phenomena that mediate learning and the acquisition of skills, for example, perception and intentionality. But this deemphasis, rather by omission than intent, is an important deficiency in the behavioral approach to learning, since it tends to ignore the interactive effects that, indeed, may be the consequences of the engineering of adjustment skills.

This deemphasis also extends to the utilization of observation. External observation of behavior is certainly an important dimension of evaluation of change, but it requires many trained observers who have achieved a reliability in their agreement on what constitutes a behavioral phenomenon, and it also assumes that these observers are alert to what is going on and are not occasionally "wool gathering." In addition, behaviorists have tended to ignore the use of testing. To a large extent the reliance on test changes as a criterion of change in counseling has been extensive. Moreover, tests that have been used have not been appropriate to the dimensions to be measured. The whole attack on testing that has taken place during the last decade and the sensitivity that schools have developed to this problem have been the result of much irresponsible testing of children. On the other hand, testing is an objective form of observation that can supplement the accumulation of knowledge about individual characteristics. New tests appropriate to the measurement of the environmental "press" and consonant with learning theory could well be developed for this purpose.

Finally, the criteria of behavior change provide some difficulties. It is possible that responses in the S—R paradigm may be too atomistic, even as constructs such as "adjustment" or "good self-concept" are too molar. Perhaps, an intermediate phenomenon, for instance skill, should be considered as a terminal objective of behavioral intervention.

These objections are not truly criticisms but, instead, are shortcomings in the learning framework, which I believe are currently being corrected by the emergence of a larger social learning theory framework that encompasses literature from social psychology, anthropology, psycholinguistics, and other sources, as well as learning theory. The wide parameters of this body of information and research suggest that a set of canons or assumptions should be determined to provide structure. The logical requirements of a comprehensive model for social learning practice are fivefold: (1) the phenomena of the model must be empirically observable, definable, and classifiable; (2) the interpretation of the phenomena must be noneclectic, that is, describable in terminology corresponding as accurately as possible to the simplistic empirical fact; (3) the ordering of the phenomena must be logically consistent and parsimonious, yielding adequate discriminatory judgments; (4) the model must possess power functions for assessment and evaluation of differential phenomena within the model, and (5) the model must be philosophically sound and compatible with the scientific approach.

The Empirical Base of Social Learning Phenomena

One of the first tasks in the development of a comprehensive theory is to define the basic phenomena that will serve as the focus for investigation. By way of consideration, one may look at either global constructs that have been used to refer to learning or at very specific concepts. Examples of the former are learning as an "art," wherein learning was considered a product of personality, ego development, motivation, formal discipline, or problem solving. These global constructs represent humanistic notions, intervening variables or an array of complex skills. Although, on the other hand, learning can be defined in terms of responses, habits, and skills in fairly precisely defined terms, there is mounting research evidence today that perceived expectations as manifested in both nonverbal, verbal, and behavioral communications may function as a chief source of variance in both achievement and social learning. There is evidence that internal phenomena can be examined more rigorously than before. Methodological concerns about the top-ography of internal events, the availability and control of reinforcers for internal events, and the unreliability of internal introspection, have generally foreclosed intentional phenomena from further exploration and tended to polarize theorists into cognitive and behavioral camps. Homme (1965), however, denies that private events are not susceptible to anal-ysis. He has suggested that it is possible to obtain reliable scientific data about the occurrence or nonoccurrence of an internal response. Believing that the topographical locus is less important than the occurrence-non-occurrence dichotomy, he states that a subject knows and can discrim-inate occurrence and nonoccurrence. Utilizing the Premack principles (Premack, 1965), that is, the differential probability hypothesis—that for any pair of responses the more probable one will reinforce the less probable one, and the indifference principle—that the same rules hold regardless of the responses' topography, Homme states that internal events can be controlled and shaped through the proper use of contin-gency arrangements within the individual. If getting a cup of coffee is a high probability behavior, an individual concerned with writing a paper can say to himself: "as soon as I think about that paper I am to write, I will get some coffee."

There would seem to be ample research evidence to support the notion that phenomenological events covary with physiological conditions. Kuo (1967) has spoken of the term behavioral gradient to express the dif-ferences in intensity and extensity of the involvement of different as-pects of the body in the animal's response to the environment, with the most essential feature of the behavioral gradient concept being that in any given response of the animal to its environment—internal or external —and in any given stage of development, the whole organism is involved. Hebb's analysis of imagery (1968) suggests strongly that imagery is a physiological correlate of sensory input, central excitation, and motor output. This fits nicely with the theory of personality stated by Eysenck and Rachman (1965) in relationship to the introversion-extroversion and the stable-unstable dimensions of behavior being related to the central excitation and inhibitory aspects of the nervous system. Jacobson (1964) states that he has never encountered a verbal report of a mental state without a concomitant and characteristic efferent pattern, for example, neuromuscular activity recorded electromyographically. He has con-cluded that mental events are composed of both epiphemeral and central activation occurring in a reciprocal manner. Evidence of the substantia-tion of this contention has been provided through a series of studies re-ported by Bergum and Lehr (1966, 1967) and Koff and Hawkes (1968). The former investigators utilized a differential set of measurements to identify the physiological correlates of differential stimuli. They found capillary pulse pressure and time differentials to be among the best physiological measures of perceptual reactions. Koff and Hawkes, in a study of pupillary responses, demonstrated that pupillary dilation appears to be related to interest-disinterest relationships and found, in an analysis of 27 sixth graders, that significant differences in pupil dilation occur in response to the viewing of pictures of friends versus nonfriends. There was significantly more pupillary dilation on the average to pictures of friends than there was to pictures of nonfriends.

That intentionalistic imagery, as such, can be utilized in achieving both changes in attitude, perception, and behavior is a contention of both desensitization studies and of studies that have been concerned with the role of expectation in mediating learning. Cautela (1969) has described therapeutic approaches to behavior modification through the use of an hierarchy of reinforcing events and of systematic desensitization procedures. Susskind, Franks, and Lonoff (1969) have written about the improved outcomes in teacher class-management as a result of a desensitization program with third and fourth grade teachers, indicating that teacher imagery and fears regarding noisy, fidgety, and inattentive children were a substantial component in the actual classroom expectations of these teachers. Teachers as a consequence of systematic training in desensitization procedures were able to maintain more control in the classroom and to cope with disruptive influences more effectively.

Explicitly or implicitly, the message from much recent research on classroom learning appears to be centered on the phenomenon of expectation and its impact on behavior. Expectation can be defined as a derivative of judgment, and judgment is based on perception. Thus Perception—Judgment—Expectation—and Behavior fit together and it would appear impossible to ignore the role of these intermediate variables on learning. Bloom (1969) writes, "Each teacher begins a new term (or course) with the expectation that about a third of his students will adequately learn what he has to teach. He expects about a third of his students to fail or to just get by" (p. 1). Through such expectations grounded in the school policy of grading, beliefs about poor home conditions or low IQ, the teacher enters into a series of relationships that more or less confirm his expectations. Thus Brophy and Good (1970) analyzed the processes by which teachers communicate differential performance expectations to different children and found that better performance was expected from children who were liked. These children were more likely to be praised than children not liked. Beez (1968) reports a study in which biased psychological reports were distributed randomly to two sets of elementary teachers who were working with 60 Head-start children. Each teacher was asked to teach a few simple operations to children randomly assigned to her. Independent observers rated and evaluated the performance without knowing anything about the experimental treatment. The results indicated that teachers who have been given favorable expectations about a pupil (as indicated in the psychological report) tried to teach more symbols than did teachers given unfavorable expectations.

These studies relating to the differential effects of expectation and group cohesiveness, taken in conjunction with the intentionality-behavior equation, support the notion that the phenomena of social learning must include not only responses and skill phenomena but also the intentionality based phenomena of perception that can be related to measurable physiological dimensions.

Characteristics of the Social Learning Model

If a model is to conform to canons of parsimony it should try to stay close to the empirical and observable inferences that relate to behavior. But there are many constructs in psychological literature that need to be more fully probed in terms of answers to the questions WHAT, WHERE, HOW OFTEN, AND WHEN, rather than to the question WHY. Causal relationships in complex human interactions are most difficult to trace and are often questionable in their resolution. But the operational characteristics of the construct of need as it relates to cognitive structure, alternate models, social interaction, and personal achievement should be further investigated. This, one may surmise, could lead to an understanding of those cognitive structure variables that mediate the products of perception.

In relationship to criterion determination, it would appear that multiple criteria of differing epistemological significance need to be integrated into the outcomes of leading interventions. Achievement, whether in academic learning or in behavior change, if it is to be truly meaningful in terms of the individual's self-competency judgments, must involve not only some demonstrable behavior manifestation, but it must be related to that individual's personal sense of worth, dignity, and sense of accomplishment.[9] Moreover, value determination in terms of subjective

[9] Unfortunately, some of these terms do not lend themselves to typical behavioral precision. But they are—a phenomenological fact which cannot be ignored by social learning theorists. The existential absolute of the certainty of death, and the limitedness of human existence, the fruitlessness of vain striving against social forces make it imperative that individuals come to a sense of their own worth and dignity and integrate their experience into a perception of self-competency which involves personal meaningfulness. Group consensus such as in extended sensitivity training

worth and destiny are simply too important to be ignored in making judgments about the progress of any type of treatment.

In effect, the task for social learning theorists is to determine what multiple criteria of effective human behavior can be ascertained that include not only self-competency judgments but peer and authority judgments. For example, in the case of school achievement the inputs of what constitutes meaningful achievement should be drawn not only from parents and school personnel but also from individuals themselves. Criteria should be meaningful, relative to expectations, and tailored to community needs. Treatments involving counseling, modeling, or other procedures need then to be related to these criteria. Our task is essentially a monumental "goodness of fit" relationship that will consider individual differences, mediating variables, for instance, expectation, and differential reinforcement, against multiple criteria of assessment. This is obviously easier said than done. With the use of new forms of testing, computer technology, and performance objectives, data should be accumulated that will make it possible both for Johnny to know what is expected of him and what his reasonable progress might be, and for his teacher to know what specific strategy might best be selected to develop cognitive or affective aspects of his achievement. The same paradigm can be fitted to differential aspects of counseling with students at different levels, using alternate techniques.

Philosophical Expansion of Behaviorism

I venture a personal opinion that scientific realism, experimentalism, and logical positivism are inadequate bases for a true philosophical foundation for social learning theory. Epistemologically, an adequate philosophy will have to consider a variety of knowledge inputs. Moreover, behavior in this approach would be looked at as an interactive effect and, therefore, the product of both cognitive structure variables and perception, and learning. Thus intentionality would be inferred from behavior itself and the physiological correlates. Empiricism must include not only externally viable observational phenomena but those internal correlates. This position differs from earlier conceptions of intentionality as a long-lasting causal strand, and it suggests viewing behavior and intentionality as simultaneous phenomena.

From the point of view of axiology or value determination, the priority

simply cannot substitute for personal meaningfulness, nor can the acquisition of hollow social criteria in some behavioral paradigm. Value determination is a personal and individualistic phenomenon—albeit related to personal competency, but not absolutely tied into social conformity.

for value judgments would be shifted to the locus of the individual himself. This means, of course, that counselors may find themselves in value conflicts with clients and will have to recognize ways and means of relating their judgment to the expectations of clients. What this means possibly in terms of a philosophical position is the development of a *behavioral phenomenology*. Such a behavioral phenomenology would possibly effect a bridge between those cognitive structural determinants to expectation and judgment and the observable simultaneous presentation of behavioral phenomena.

In summary, this last section of this chapter is not a criticism of what learning theory has provided to the development of new and effective ways of coping with human problems, but is, instead, a subjective plea for an extension of the parameters of the evaluation of learning to a broader philosophical dimension that will include internal phenomena, the reordering of certitude priorities, and the development of a methodology for appraising simultaneous internal phenomena as they covary with external manifestations of behavior.

CHAPTER X

Evaluation and Resolution: A Future Look

The purpose of this final chapter is to provide an evaluation and perspective for the preceding chapters of this book. One of the major reasons for writing this book has been a conviction that students majoring in the helping professions, particularly counseling, social work, and psychology ought to be able to provide for the future in the social and cultural perspective of the past. If we are to believe Heidegger, much of our thinking in the present, and our interpretation of the past, is altered by our judgment of the future and its expectations.

It is apparent that in every age there have been individuals who by constitutional inclination, training, or cultural role have functioned as counselors. For the most part these individuals, whether they have been witch doctors, priests, philosophers, or kindly teachers, have attempted to aid individuals in the assimilation of the cultural perspective. To a large extent, their functional role was to support and buttress the existing cultural framework, to aid in the transmission of learning. But it is likewise apparent today that man's cultural evolution calls for not only an enhanced personal awareness and creativity in his own identity quest but also for the systematic utilization of technology in the prediction and control of social behavior. The increasing secularization of society, the reduction of the need for hard labor, and the shrinkage of the world—both psychologically and physically in terms of travel—the ever-threatening forces of environmental pollution, overpopulation, and fear of extinction will require absolutely that man exert strict controls over his environment, and at the same time program sufficient freedom and personal involvement to allow for growth and development.

Within our society we perceive both the demands for more personal and group involvement via group training sessions, personal and humanistic concerns for alienation and methods of coping with narcotics, drugs, and alcohol, and the simultaneous demands by government, science, and

416

education for accountability in politics, technology, and learning. The pall of heavy smoke that clouds the noonday sun over our large cities, the accelerated heartbeat of the commuter as he fights his way through crowded and clogged freeway arteries, the constant press for achievement, money, and power, force a realization on all of us that life is becoming increasingly unbearable.

Some have thought that the way to solve this problem is to "drop out" of society by drugs or other means. Others have ordered us to return to the "golden Jerusalem" of yesteryear with superordinary patriotism and insular conservatism. Still others have thought that salvation rests in the development of new approaches that utilize systems analyses, technological objectives, computer assessment procedures, and monitored feedback on the nature and progress of social experiments. But the facts would seem to suggest, taken in a cultural and historical perspective, that man has increasing needs both for individualization and humanization, and for technological prediction and control over his environment. Can these two contrary forces of individuality and technological development be integrated? Will the counselor or social worker or psychologist of the near future be able to synthesize, reconcile, and mediate between these two important thrusts? I do not propose any easy compromise or superarching metaphysical stance to reconcile these approaches (although it does appear that a behavioral phenomenology may make progress in this direction). It does appear, however, that some kind of reconciliation must take place on three levels—at least. These levels are philosophical, methodological, and personal.

PHILOSOPHICAL RECONCILIATION

From the previous chapters of this book it is apparent that the philosophical bases of the two major strategies for effecting change in human behavior have long been identified and utilized. The humanistic-idealistic tone in human behavior has been identified and regenerated anew in almost every generation. Plato represented this view in Greek society. Duns Scotus with his theory of individuality struggled for recognition in the medieval period. Rousseau with his naturalism represented another effort. In similar fashion, Aristotle, Aquinas, and the physiologists of the 19th century attempted to set up an environmental control approach based on a science approach. These differences are most sharply seen, however, in the area of epistemology. The hierarchy of beliefs and of acceptable evidence that humanism is willing to settle for constitutes some logical priorities that contrast with the philosophical base of environmentalism. In more recent counseling approaches, humanism in its component philosophical systems of idealism, phenomenology, and existentialism is willing to extend a greater degree of epistemological confidence to the subjective realm than is behaviorism. The conflict that exists philosophically appears operationally between the goals, processes, and criteria of counseling.

It is, perhaps, unrealistic to assume that these disparate points of view can be united at present or in the future under one philosophical system. But earlier attempts did not conceptualize the pluralistic nature of society that exists at present, nor were the communication vehicles and resources available to them that are now available to us today. In a way, the relationship of humanism to behaviorism and vice-versa is somewhat analogous to the relationship of faith to reason in the Middle Ages. Faith and reason were considered to refer to two distinct epistemologies. Although they might be opposing each other on some specific issues, they were held to be compatible and not absolutely contradictory. This type of solution will admittedly not satisfy extremists on either side, but it should be attempted. Let us look briefly at the evaluation of the strengths and weaknesses of these two major strategies that exist in counseling practice today, and then let us focus on some possible alternative solutions to major points of difference.

First, what are some of the strengths and weaknesses of both major strategies toward counseling? Humanism has as one of its strengths a recognition of the subjective nature of man, his internal states, feelings, and concerns. Its preoccupation with the individual as an individual makes counseling a highly personal kind of encounter that focuses on the individual communication or transaction that takes place between counselor and client. In a very real sense, this kind of counseling process reveals a kind of mystical relationship that, in its highest form, approaches a spiritual and charismatic quality. This meets one of man's greatest human needs, the need for communication—and for reassurance and forgiveness. Whether we like the concept or not, counselors often function in the role of a priest. They mediate on the conscious level, and whether or not they recognize their conciliatory role, they often deal with guilt, anxiety, and fears that need psychologically to be forgiven.

This very characteristic of human relationships underscores the weakness of the humanistic strategy in counseling—and some would dispute that it is a weakness. For the very notion of transaction makes it difficult to specify precisely what are the goals, procedures, and criteria of this strategy in counseling. Although replete with a richness of personal involvement, the imprecision of the independent variables used in effecting change, together with the variety of possible change criteria, render any objective assessment of change very difficult.

In the efforts to assess the quality of changes in counseling (whether nondirective or directive), earlier results are ambiguous. Ohlsen, Proff, and Roeber (1956) reviewed 400 papers in their analysis of 25 years of counseling research without arriving at any definite conclusions. Tyler (1961) evaluated approximately 150 studies relating to counseling effectiveness and observed that work had only begun in answering the question: Does counseling do any good? On the other hand, Campbell (1965) followed up 768 students who had participated in a study of Williamson and Borden in 1940, wherein a matched control was compared with an experimental group who had been seen by the college counseling service during their freshman year. Criteria used in the original study included an interview relating to educational and vocational adjustment along with first quarter grade-point averages. Campbell, in his 25-year follow-up found that counseled students generally received better grades, obtained more advanced degrees, showed a tendency to have a higher income and to rate higher on a global evaluation of contribution to society. Although not a factor in the study itself, it is interesting to note that 87 percent of the counseled students recalled the interview and many could give a precise description of their reactions to the counseling even after 25 years. This fact alone could indicate that even short contacts in counseling may have a much greater effect on the lives of individuals than counselors are aware of. More recently, Hosford and Briskin (1969) find more significant evidences of changes because of counseling, largely because of better experimental design features and more rigorous behavioral criteria.

Perhaps, the more positive findings reflect a gradual transition from more global efforts at criterion determination to more specific ones, with increasing sophistication regarding research methodologies. For earlier attempts at measurement of humanistic counseling effectiveness typically included client verbalization, movement from rigidity to flexibility of outlook, adjustment test scores, and changes in self-concept estimation. But these approaches lack the precision that is typical of behavioral strategies in counseling. Nonetheless, the greater depth of involvement, and the "personalistic" nature of the art of humanistic counseling may require exemption from such externalized criteria.

The more recent behavioral approach to counseling together with the psychotherapy reports that have stemmed from the application of learning theory to the counseling process may be characterized as a process in which a set of individual goals in counseling are related to specific behavioral objectives. In this sense, behaviorism is task-oriented in that the goals and procedures of counseling are related either to the reduction of certain behavioral deficits or maladaptive behaviors, or the building up of a set of new and appropriate behaviors. It is also closely attuned to the characteristics of the culture, the need expectancies and the conformity requirements of society. In some instances, the goals of counseling are subsumed under more adequate information-seeking or decision-making behaviors. But this could be one somewhat covert means to have the client come to terms with the reality of what he must possess or must do, if he is to meet his own expectancies in this culture. In nearly all cases, behavioral counseling seems to work best in a setting where the behaviors desired can be precisely identified. Although interim criteria may be defined in terms of the frequencies of information-seeking behavior, or more adequate decision-making, very often the interim criterion is shaped by the ultimate criterion derived from some social expectations. In other words, the behavioral counselor often brings to the counseling process a more precise idea or notion of what constitutes effective human social behavior in a given setting, and this judgment, rightly or wrongly, appears to be referenced in relationship to cultural expectations.

Possibly, humanism is less likely to fall into the trap of singling out some initial statements of the client as the verbal conceptualization of his problem. Van Kaam (1962) has pointed out the importance of not prejudging the direction of therapy by jumping to unwarranted conclusions based on the cognitive verbalization of the counselee or client. For example, Van Kaam suggests that both higher aspirations of a client and the whole realm of emotive feelings are often difficult to verbalize, and a counselor taking a cue from the initial client verbalization of a problem may be reacting to the wrong set of concerns. This appears to be a very important point in adjustment counseling or in personal identity counseling. The outcomes by the very nature of the client's inability to verbalize his feelings sometimes cannot be specified within a behavioral frame of reference. On the other hand, Krumboltz (1966) has pointed out that very often clients want help with specific problems and not more insight into the nature of their feelings about these problems.

Whereas on the one hand the behavioral counselor ought to be less impatient in the determination of the problem to be solved, the humanist ought to recognize that very often individuals do want help with specific problems. On the question of normative-type criteria toward which the counseling process is directed, behaviorists should be cautious not to become *de facto* maintainers of the social status quo, and humanists should be aware of the devastating consequences that can occur from marathon group "sensitivity" sessions. In this latter category of group activities, it is apparent that "confession" can become a normative behavior. The sharing of experiences can help probe depths of feelings and concerns, but the group can also become a tremendously effective force to induce conformity—even if the conformity is supposedly individualistic in nature, that is, "doing your own thing."

Humanism, in my opinion, has tended to gain something from its identification with phenomenology and to lose something through its liaison with existentialism. The earlier intent of phenomenological thought was to develop a rigorous methodology, the counterpart to objective science, for the investigation of the nature and quality of psychic phenomena. Unfortunately, this original bent, seen in the works of Brentano, Husserl, Heidegger, Koehler, and James, has never been fully recognized or utilized in American counseling theory and practice studies. The few (and excellent) exceptions to this have been found in the writings and studies of Heider, Osgood, and Kelly. Concentration on the richness of internal experience and on the search for more descriptive information relating to the subjective grounds of conscious experience could yield a harvest equal or superior to some behavioral research. On the contrary, the abandonment of this quest, that is, the fairly unqualified conversion to existentialism has tended to reduce this aspect of humanistic counseling to a kind of secular mystical experience. Experience in and of itself can be rather meaningless (as many testify). It is the quality of experience and not the quantity of experience that is important. Where an experiential relationship can be joined to a quest for meaning in either a spiritual or societal community, the transaction can be meaningful in the larger sense of that word. For example, in problems of personal identity and of understanding, such as those that touch on religion or the quest for self-understanding, phenomenological inquiry can be a contributing factor toward personal growth. Tillich (1964, 7) has spoken of religion as the aspect of depth in the totality of human experiencing. In the recent and overdue theological probing into the meaning of religious experience, the phenomenological, psychological, and anthropological concepts of meaning are merging. Religious experience has now been conceptualized as a general instead of a special function of the human spirit. The harsh stereotype of church bazaars and teas, the notion of an asocial religious ethnocentrism, has begun to yield to goals of spiritual community and identity exemplified in a concern for freedom, equality, and personal growth with social obligations in personal behavior.

The behavioral approach, however, has singular power potential for coping with specific kinds of client needs. In the school setting as well as in the collegiate setting, where a task-oriented achievement is important, school counselors are often faced with the need to determine the answers to some very important questions, for instance: (1) what constitutes effective learning behavior in various classrooms, curricula, or social settings? (2) How can ineffective (either from the client's view or the social setting) behavior be changed? Aside from the issue of what should be the goals of the school learning process, the function of the school in our society has been operationally related to the transmission of a body of learning skills and information which are deemed to be valuable in our society. The schools, as other cultural agencies, do advocate values, processes, and criteria to be used in the learning process whether or not they are defined specifically.

Effective human behavior in our culture is described in terms of expectations and differential environmental "presses." These cultural "presses" are transmitted through cultural mechanisms such as the family, law, religion, mass media, and education. They are transmitted in the concrete and specific ways in which parents, law enforcement officials, ministers, teachers, television models, and peers reward, punish, and shape behavior. Moreover, learning theory in its aspects of reinforcement, punishment, shaping, and modeling of criteria, implicitly or explicitly is used by all kinds of people to sustain and augment desirable behavior. Behavioral counseling in its method and technology can make a great contribution in the identification of operational methods of identifying researchable criteria and techniques for reaching these criteria. There is also a largely untapped potential in this strategy for combining the various streams of performance-contracting, computer utilization, and self-pacing achievement procedures to individualize learning outcomes, using newer technology.

METHODOLOGICAL PRIORITIES

The argument that has been developed in this chapter thus far has focused on the distinctive advantages which humanism and behaviorism have for dealing with various counseling phenomena and goals. There are, however, specific points of controversy between the two major strategies that must be explored further. These points of contention are related to the priorities of emphasis that the two strategies make. Three areas need to be mentioned: (1) the question of the priority of thought or verbal elaboration over motor behavior in change; (2) the question of diagnosis in understanding behavior and directing treatment alternatives, and (3) the question of freedom of will and personal responsibility.

The first question relates to the priority of thought over motor behavior in effecting change. Generally, the humanistic approaches to counseling have supported the procedural notion that the counseling process must first focus on the elaboration and exploration of an appropriate verbal behavior on the part of the client through self-understanding, insight, and progressive reduction of resistance and fear to others. The priority of verbal behavior and cognitive realignment is viewed as a causal factor in changing overt and external behavior. Hence, the humanistic approach has tended to emphasize verbal exchange, insight, and cognitive-affective reconciliation as an a-priori condition to the restructuring of actual behavior in social or education settings. The behaviorists have emphasized an opposite priority, falling back on the principles of operant conditioning. In this approach, a strategy for a new behavior is designed either through role playing, modeling, or prescription. The client is supported in taking steps to initiate this new behavior with the implied assumption that once a new mode of behavior has been developed, appropriate cognitive and affective changes will take place within the client as an operant of his new behavior.

At stake is the question of self-concept and how it relates to behavior. There is also the question of how it can be changed. Perhaps no other area in educational or counseling psychology has been so studiously researched as the area of self-concept. Many hundreds of studies have been reported that have been concerned with the correlation of measures of the self-concept with sentence-completions, word-associations, Q Sorts, and inventories of all kinds to measure what has been called the self-concept or perception that an individual holds of himself (Wylie, 1961; Viney, 1969). Essentially, self-concept research has attempted to measure the phenomenal field, drawing heavily on the theoretical assumptions of intentionalistic psychology, psychoanalytic, neopsychoanalytic, phenomenological and, more recently, existentialist psychology. The rationale has been represented by Fromm (1939), Horney (1937), Maslow (1954), Rogers (1951), and Snygg and Combs (1949).

Wylie (1961), in one of the most comprehensive surveys of self-concept research, points out that the measurement of self-concept as a phenomenological set of constructs presents an entire array of methodological problems in which judgments of what constitutes self-concept are related to estimates of social desirability, response set, and acquiescence, not to mention the need to establish construct validity in accordance with Cronbach and Meehl's rationale (1955) and the triangulation procedures of Campbell and Fiske (1959).

Recent research in the self-concept and allied areas has tended to provide a new view of the self-concept in relationship to the emergence of skill competencies and behavior. Shulman (1969) pinpointed a crucial area in self-concept studies when he noted that most measures of self-concept are based on what individuals say about themselves and less often on how they behave in particular settings. These perceptions are then mediated strongly by reference to a criterion situation and to the estimate of self-competency. Shulman believes that the self-concept, as such, is tied strongly to feelings of self-competency and, as self-competency changes, aspiration levels will change accordingly. Soares and Soares (1969) sought to confirm or deny the overwhelming impression from the literature on the disadvantaged that these children have a lower or impaired self-concept (Kohn, 1959; Coleman, 1966; Levine, 1968). Results of their comparisons of disadvantaged and nondisadvantaged elementary children indicated that disadvantaged not only evidenced positive self-perceptions but had higher self-perceptions than advantaged children. This situation changed somewhat in the secondary level where disadvantaged children appeared to have somewhat lower self-concept scores (1970). Similar findings were reported in a study by Trowbridge (1970) using Coopersmith's Self-Esteem inventory.

These findings appear to be confirmatory of what Skinner (1964) has suggested about the self-concept. He denied the causal effect of self-concept on behavior, labeling it rather an epiphenomenon, that is, a set of self-descriptive verbal behaviors that follows rather than causes crucial behaviors. If we are to accept the findings of Shulman, Soares and Soares, and Trowbridge, the self-concept emerges as a socially derived by-product of competency and experience moderated considerably by the criterion of social desirability in the classroom universe. What a child can do is probably important in what he thinks of himself. What an adult is capable of doing and of eliciting reinforcement for is probably a significant part of his self-concept. Thus, although the literature is not clearly indicative of the relationship between cognitive conceptualization and behavior, it does support the notion of an interactive effect between cognitive structure variables and ongoing behaviors. There does not appear to be evidence to support in an unqualified manner either the contention that a priority should be placed on verbal and cognitive elaboration of feelings as a means of changing self-concept, or on the exclusive use of behavior. Probably they interact in a unique and individualistic manner, and counselors should be able to judge when one or the other needs to be used in counseling.

A second question is related to the problem and role of diagnosis. Both humanism and behaviorism tend to deemphasize diagnosis in the traditional medical sense of that word. Perhaps too much reliance has been placed in clinical psychology on the role of testing in diagnosis. Moreover, there have been some assumptions regarding the relative emphasis of the unconscious and repressed material to the determination of ongoing behavior. The humanist strategy in counseling, while often rejecting the use of testing, does generally hold that early childhood behavior, methods of child-rearing, early experience, and parental acceptance or rejection play an important role in shaping present and future behavior. Rogers' own client-centered theory includes a number of propositions about self-actualization based on the assumption of unresolved "visceral tensions" and the like. Thus, although retaining many of the elements of psychoanalytic theory in relationship to symptomatic behavior and repression, humanism has tended to reject the clinical testing procedures that were designed to evaluate personal functioning.

Behaviorism has tended to downgrade the efficacy of this clinical approach on the grounds that it is time-consuming and that many tests are not related to the problem behavior at hand but, instead, are related to dynamic constructs that are related to a theoretical system with few behavioral correlates. Behaviorists have tended to rely more heavily on the immediate antecedents of problem behavior and the learned or reinforced consequences of such behavior.

Although diagnosis based on the use of clinical testing instruments has been compared to a task that is in "some way similar to measuring a floating cloud with a rubber band—in a shifting wind" (Schneideman, 1959), and the use of tests has come under considerable criticism (Barclay, 1964, 1968), it appears to me that the use of multiple testing instruments, computer reporting systems, and the development of testing devices related to the measurement of the environmental press constitutes an ally to counseling. In recent years we have been able to construct testing devices that will tap multiple dimensions of the environmental "press" and that will provide aid in determining specific treatment objectives in counseling. One example of this is a testing device measuring self-competency judgments, peer judgments, reinforcers, vocational awareness and teacher judgments for the elementary school. I have worked on this instrumentation for nearly 12 years in an effort to pool various sources of the classroom environment (*Barclay Classroom Climate Inventory*, 1970). This instrument converts test scores into a written computer report that can be used by counselors and learning consultants to individualize both programs of instruction and counseling interventions (Forsyth and Jackson, 1966; Brown, 1967; Barclay, Arnold, Stilwell, Santoro, and Clark, 1971). There is a great need for further test development in the areas of counseling and interventions, since many of the tests that are currently used in counseling appear to be outdated or, at least, in need of revision. Testing can provide a basis for the evaluation of existing functional relationships. Cautela (1969) has presented a behavioral inventory that can be used by counselors and clinicians in determining which reinforcers can be used most effectively with individuals. This type of test information can be most valuable to behavioral counselors in knowing what potential activities may be useful in changing behavior.

A final issue that should be discussed here briefly is the problem of man's free will, his responsibility for his behavior, and the question of whether behaviorism is guilty of undue pressure in the shaping of behavior. It has often been argued in one way or another that a behavioral approach to counseling unduly influences the individual, abrogates his free will by a subtle shaping of his thinking, and constricts his ability to choose from a variety of alternatives. It is implied that behaviorism selects goals for the counselee and then uses behavioral techniques to push the client in that direction. This set of arguments should be outlawed! Krasner (1962) and Goldiamond (1963) have both discussed the matter admirably. Skinner in *Walden II* has also been concerned with this problem (1962).

Actually, there is no safeguard against manipulation by unethical counselors in either behavioral counseling or humanistic counseling. Humanistic counseling can be as subtle as behavior modification when it involves a conscious or unconscious shaping of responses on the part of the counselor. The very way agreement or disagreement is expressed by the counselor has a reinforcing value in shaping the direction of the verbal elaboration of the client. Behavioral counseling as outlined by Krumboltz, makes it very clear that criterion determination, the goals of the problem-solving process, are arrived at jointly by counselor and client. Once any one of us enters into a counseling relationship, or into any other human relationship, a few degrees of freedom are lost. For the interaction of human beings in any setting is a shaping experience. But this interaction does not militate against personal responsibility for behavior. The only safeguard against the possible tyranny of psychological conditioning— whether through behavior modification or intensive group "sensitivity" sessions—is an informed and ethical professional. For as our knowledge of learning increases, our potential power over individuals will also increase. With this, there must be a concern with ethics and social responsibility.

SUMMARY AND CONCLUSION

The future of psychology and education, in general, and of counseling, in particular, is tied to the need for personal and social accountability. Accountability in meeting the needs of others requires cognitive sophistication, sensitivity to human needs, and social conscience. Counselors no longer can think of themselves outside of the context of learning and development.

We are approximately 30 years from the turn of a new century. In 1940 how many of us might have forecast the developments in postwar clinical psychology training, the vast expansion of employment and vocational counselors into the schools, or the successive controversies between "directive" and "nondirective" approaches? How few counselor educators or counseling psychologists foresaw the development of sophisticated research methodologies, the increase of professional organizations, and the emergence of learning theory (an area opined by many to be irrelevant to human learning) as a key methodological approach? Nor could we have guessed that social psychology, education, and anthropology had much in common. Possibly in the next decades we may be able to substantiate the views now widely held in the field that there is an individual difference in counseling style and method that can be fitted to individual needs. In the future it is most likely that psychologists and counselors of the year 2000 will view with curiosity our focus on seeing people for long periods of time, often with vaguely defined bases for treatment and with generally nonspecific goals.

We can look forward to a continuation of group training and treatment procedures, an exploration of individual needs through work interaction, recreational therapy, the understanding of the problems of aging, and the possible establishment of intensive treatment centers for specific psychological and social disabilities. We can also look forward to increasing disillusionment with the continuing power of governmental influence and interventions, and to the alienation of human existence from primary and secondary sources of reinforcement. We can equally look forward to the expansion of technology as a potential aid to man.

But central to all of these developments is the need for the students of today to appreciate and to understand the heritage that they have obtained through the history of man's thinking about how to change human behavior. For this reason, it is hoped that this book will provide a cognitive synthesis for those who search—not for answers, but for relevant questions.

Questions for Discussion—Chapter I

1. Counseling has been considered as a generic term for professionals who engage in a helping relationship with others. Certain expectations are related to the role and function of counselors. What kind of expectations exist in your training program? Are these expectations identified in a consistent and clear manner? Are they congruent with your role expectations?

2. Some counselor and psychologist educators have disagreed strongly with the notion that the counselor is a type of extension of the role of the priest and/or minister as suggested by Halmos. What are some arguments for and against Halmos' thesis?

3. Do you think that everyone who enters into the field of counseling has some problems himself and is thereby explicitly or implicitly seeking the answer to his own problems? Should everyone who is a counselor be counseled first? Is it important to have experienced an encounter or t group? Is psychoanalysis necessary for real adjustment? Is it possible for a person to help others without himself first being helped?

4. Many individuals who enter counseling as a helping profession are unwilling to seek the help of a professional counselor themselves. If you had a professional problem where would you turn for help?

5. Why is epistemology important to counseling?

6. Make an operational list of what is meant by the term "adjustment." What are the characteristics that would be considered generally indicative of good personal and social adjustment: (1) in your immediate circle of friends, (2) elsewhere (specify the context)?

7. Make a list of alternative criteria that can be used in setting evaluation procedures and goals for the results of counseling. How would they be measured?

8. Give a critique of Krumboltz's contention that many clients do not desire "self-understanding" as a goal of counseling.

9. Make a list of your own views on the nature of man, the hierarchy of knowledge or epistemology, the nature of reality, and what you consider to be the ultimate purpose of man's existence. Now order them in terms of priority and value in terms of your own existence. Compare your ordering of these values to those of your classmates and see if it is possible for you to arrive at a consensus with your classmates regarding these items.

10. It has been said that unless a man acts the way he thinks, he will soon begin to think the way he acts. Give a critique of this saying.

Questions for Discussion—Chapter II

1. Judgments form the basis of expectations. Expectations in turn reflect various aspects of the cultural "press" or environmental transmission. Compare the various sets of expectations that have shaped your behavior: (1) within your home, (2) in school settings, (3) in work situations, (4) in dating, and (5) in college or university settings. Can you identify the ones that have been most powerful in maintaining your own behavior?

2. How many different role expectations do you feel others have concerning your thinking and behavior? How do they differ? How does an individual integrate all of the different expectations that others have for his behavior?

3. Discuss Boskoff's contention that mass communications have resulted in a multiple control mechanism that is as complex as the culture it mirrors and controls. Do you agree with the statement that mass media create "a superficial, but effective consensus reducing and insulating irritations, and imposing a kind of vague optimism about underlying conditions?"

4. If John Holland is correct regarding his contention that the choice of an occupation reflects a personality-oriented search by the individual, then how do most people learn whether an occupation fits their needs? Is this theory related in any way to students' decision making about alternate curricula in a university setting?

5. Peer group opinions and expectations are very important monitors of social behavior. What are some ways and means in which counselors can utilize peer group expectations positively? How do you react to negative criticism from your peers? Will you accept critical judgments from some peers, but not from others? Are there important differences between those you will accept criticism from and those from whom you will not accept such criticism?

6. Observational learning, modeling, and reinforcement are important determinants of behavior. Review the recent literature relating to observational learning, modeling, and imitation. Discuss your results with the class. To what extent are these forms of behavior susceptible to some use by counselors?

7. Recently, there has been a noticeable increase in interests relating to astrology, palmistry, theosophy, and other esoteric subjects. Why do you think, in an age of technology and education, that interests in occult and pseudo-psychological subjects are increasing? Perhaps they are not pseudo-psychological or pseudo-scientific?

Questions for Discussion—Chapter III

1. Aside from the theological aspects of religion, what are the psychological characteristics of religion? Is religion related to personal and social security?

2. Why are many ministers and priests disillusioned with organized religion? How does one explain the phenomenon of the "Jesus Freaks" or young individuals' community experience in religious phenomena? From your knowledge of history, how does the emergence of religious reform relate to cultural crises? Can you cite examples from other periods?

3. Give a critique of Protagoras' dictum "man is the measure of all things, of things that are, that they are, of things that are not, that they are not."

4. What parallels can you draw between Platonic idealism and Aristotelian realism, and humanism and behaviorism?

5. Do all individuals have an implicit metaphysical outlook or is such a stance a by-product of education? How would you test out your view?

6. One of the theses of the portion of this chapter that concerns the emergence of Christianity is that the events recorded in the New Testament are describing a series of intensive group experiences that were related to new forms of behavior. Reread some of these accounts and evaluate in your own mind whether a priority on behavior and intensive group experiences may be a sufficient explanation of these events.

7. If intensive group experiences might be one of the components of a dynamic religious identification, is it possible that the simultaneous decline of organized religion and the emergence of intensive group psychotherapy experiences are tied to an identity crisis?

Questions for Discussion—Chapter IV

1. Contrast the methodology of scholasticism with the methodology proposed by Descartes.

2. How did the Renaissance contribute to changes in man's conception of reality and values?

3. During the period of the Enlightenment, what did individuals who had a serious problem do for counseling?

4. How did Locke and Rousseau differ on the question of individual differences?

5. La Mettrie compared man to a machine; Freud described human brain functioning in terms of electrical circuits; more recently the analogy has been made comparing man to a computer. What do you think of these comparisons?

6. It has been said that man first lost his soul, then his will, and now his mind. Is there room in a technological society for concepts such as soul, will and mind? What do they represent?

7. A Scholastic postulate was that functioning is a necessary derivative of structure. For example, a computer operates in accordance with its circuits, capacities, and programming. What might the logic of this postulate hold for man's behavior? Does he function in accordance with some structural limitations or design? If so, what are these limitations and/or constraints?

Questions for Discussion—Chapter V

1. Aquinas and Scotus can be considered protagonists in a major conflict concerning the nature of reality and the approaches to adjustment in the medieval period. Aquinas clearly represented the objective environmentalist approach, and Scotus the subjective humanistic and mystical approach. What were the effects of this conflict in terms of the revolt against authority, the Renaissance, and the emergence of science? How did this influence behavior?

2. What were Locke's views about individual differences?

3. How does man's conception of the good life relate to "adequate" and "inadequate" notions according to Spinoza?

4. What does the phrase: "Paul's conception of Peter reveals more about Paul than Peter," mean in terms of intentionality and human relations?

5. Spinoza suggests that bodily responses to external objects or stimuli are indicative of emotions, feelings, and willing about these objects. What does this say about the observation of "body english" in interviewing or observation of behavior?

6. If mathematics is the basic set of principles underlying a scientific knowledge of reality and ethics, isn't it logical to look for the most advanced theory of man in mathematical models? Why or why not?

7. If "intuitive" knowledge is important to the real understanding of man and his reality, as Descartes, Spinoza, and Leibnitz all seem to indicate, is this an "innate" quality of some men or can it be developed as a skill in counselors? Does intuitive knowledge and the concept of empathy seem identical?

8. Leibnitz's concern for intuitive ideas may be simply another way of stating that the mind of man itself is structured in certain ways to receive information, very much as the computer is programmed. This is a preoccupying concern with the phenomenologists of later years. In recent times, also, Benjamin Whorf has suggested that different cultures structure knowledge and their epistemology in different ways. This is also a concern of Jean Piaget in terms of modes of logical thinking in children from stage to stage in development. What are some hypotheses that could be investigated regarding the role of possible intuitive structural variables in the interpretation and understanding of experience?

9. Leibnitz's concern for a prearranged harmony, and Spinoza's emphasis on self-knowledge all appear to suggest that a consistent goal of man is a reflective self-understanding that is one step removed from simple apprehension of ideas and is the product of reflective, and meditative thought and dialogue. How can man in a technological society arrive at some of these goals?

10. Both Leibnitz and Spinoza appear to believe that man's internal events, emotions, feelings, and the like, as stimulated by external objects, are the determining factors in the influence of that executive potency of man known as the will or ego. Lloyd Homme (1965) has suggested that internal events can be controlled and shaped through the proper use of contingency arrangements within the individual (See Chapter IX). This suggests that man may himself learn to control his own internal events by appropriate self-contracting. Does this type of internal control have any relevance for counseling?

11. Brentano maintained that experience helped to shape the nature of internal experiences, and that perception itself was a unique construction derived not only from that flow of experiencing but from certain integrating characteristics of perception that reflected inner needs as well as causal relations. What does this mean in terms of the formation of an adequate or inadequate self-concept? Is this position congruent with or contrary to modern social learning theory, which suggests that the self-concept is the integrated product of much experience and social interaction?

12. What arguments can you think of regarding the validity or nonvalidity of Brentano's statement positing perception rather than sensation as the basis of psychic experience? Do you agree with the notion that speech precedes grammar?

13. To what extent do you feel that psychologists have attempted to construct a valid science of mental experience through careful observa-

tion of the physical states of others, the deriving of testable hypotheses, and experimentation with these hypotheses?

14. Brentano suggested that laws of the association of ideas might be related to basic electrochemical neurological reactions. What do the studies of Kreschmer, Sheldon, and Eysenck regarding body temperament, response level to stimulation, and the like, contribute to this hypothesis? Does susceptibility to various kinds of reinforcers also fit into this problem?

15. Recent research in the area of expectation and learning would suggest that much social interaction is based on expectations which, in turn, are based on judgments. Does the phenomenon of expectation provide any confirmation of the intentionality hypothesis? If so, in what ways?

16. Some writers have thought that Brentano opened the door to complete ethical relativism in his contention that the judgment of rightness precedes the judgment of goodness. He suggested that the ultimate moral forum was related to the individual's mature judgment of what was right for him. Do people who seek counseling need help in arriving at some priority of judgment in terms of their behavior?

Questions for Discussion—Chapter VI

1. Discuss Freud's contention that true science begins with an adequate description of phenomena. Does it appear that Freud favored inductive or deductive reasoning in the development of his theory?

2. The unconscious was the target of many of Freud's observations. Review the concept of the unconscious in current literature and prepare a critique of Freud's arguments for and Brentano's arguments against the unconscious hypothesis.

3. Why did Freud drop his use of hypnosis? What does literature on the subject of hypnosis say about states of consciousness?

4. Needs, goals, psychic processes, and meaning are all involved in Freudian theory. The manner in which they are manifested in behavior is often related to a complex series of defense mechanisms. Describe some of the following defense mechanisms and illustrate them by examples: repression, suppression, sympathism, projection, displaced aggression, rationalization, sublimation, and participation without ego involvement.

5. Distinguish between primary and secondary processes in Freudian theory. How does the evolution of these processes relate to the emer-

gence of the reality principle as against the functioning of the pleasure principle?

6. What is Freud's theory of the evolution of psychic development in terms of object cathexes? Is there any physiological evidence from other sources that the early development of the human brain is related to objects?

7. Review some of the modern findings about dream research and relate them to Freud's theories about dreams.

8. The concepts of tension and anxiety have been derived from psychoanalytic theory. Review some of the modern findings regarding these concepts and relate them to processes of counseling.

9. What would you judge to be the lasting contribution of Freud's thought to psychotherapy? What is most relevant today?

10. Read several chapters from Otto Fenichel's *The Psychoanalytic Theory of Neurosis*, particularly the chapters that relate to organ neuroses and conversion phenomena. Discuss and give a critique of the evidence cited.

11. What would be Adler's stance on the "Women's Liberation" movement today?

12. Read some of Carl Gustaf Jung's works and give a critique of his use of the symbol in man's mental evolution.

13. Albert Ellis has identified some "irrational ideas" that often form the basis of personal identity crises and problems. How relevant are these ideas to counseling?

14. The words ego and will are often interchanged in discussions. Just what do these constructs mean and how are they differentiated?

Questions for Discussion—Chapter VII

1. In various periods of time, mention has been made of the equation theory, the correspondence theory, and isomorphism. All of these theories relate to the manner in which the external and internal world of reality are related to each other in the human brain. What relevance do these concepts have to the nature and function of perception, and thereby to interpersonal communication?

2. Music and art both have various forms and structures. Cattell at the University of Illinois has developed a personality test to evaluate individuals by their listening preferences in music. Stumpf also investigated the psychology of music. Ancient therapy utilized music and bathes. What roles can music and art play with respect to counseling?

3. Heidegger said that the present and the past are always monitored in terms of the future. What does this say to us in relationship to the mid-career depressions that often occur in men and women when they begin to realize that they will not meet the expectations of a glorious future?

4. Phenomenology and Existentialism require serious study. Read selections from the writings of Martin Buber, Viktor Frankl, Soren Kierke-gaard, or Paul Tillich and discuss their philosophy with class members.

5. Death has often been considered the only absolute of existentialism. Why is this so, and why is it relevant?

6. Rogers has often suggested that the only real learning is that which an individual does himself. This would tend to suggest that Ausubel's notion of receptor learning is incorrect. Contrast these ideas about learning. What does Rogers mean? Do some individuals need more structure in learning than others?

7. Phenomenology and Gestalt theory appear to have foundered on methodological problems relating to the investigation of internal phenomena. Are there new possibilities for research today? Develop in class discussion some new possibilities for phenomenologically oriented research.

Questions for Discussion—Chapter VIII and Chapter IX

1. What are some of the advantages of eclecticism and some of the disadvantages? Is a higher-order eclecticism, that is, a philosophy of behavioral-phenomenology, a possibility?

2. Select a reference from John Dewey or William James and read it. Does functionalism and/or experimentalism relate to eclecticism?

3. Read a reference from Thorndike. Thorndike's theory of individual differences is still the undergirding of much of social learning and behavioral theory. What is Thorndike's theory about the original nature of man?

4. How valid are the contentions of behaviorism about the subjective criteria of counseling effectiveness used in phenomenological research? Is there an epistemological hierarchy evident in all criteria?

5. Give a critique of Hosfords' article on behavioral counseling and discuss his contention that behavioral counseling does not supplant other forms of counseling. Consider operationally his suggestions about when reinforcement will work and the conditions need to utilize it effectively.

6. What do the views of Homme and Premack offer to the counselor who is confronted by a client who wishes to develop "will power."

7. If expectations are important determinants of behavior, how can we go about changing expectations?

8. What is the role of the computer in providing diagnostic information about individuals in decision making for counselors and clients? Review modern developments in vocational information-giving, measuring the social climate of the classroom, and the like.

9. How does a counselor decide whether a client wants information, needs, or insight?

10. Catterall has suggested that there are many techniques that can be used with clients. They are grouped into four major areas: (1) environmental interventions (program management, placement, positive and negative reinforcement), (2) installed interventions (such as counseling as a catylitic agent, arbitrating a time-out or moratorium in conflict situations), (3) assigned interventions (such as practice in role or attitude shifts and the development of new behaviors), and (4) transactional interventions (sensitization, group counseling, and personal dialogue with clients). How many of these techniques do you feel that you can use effectively?

References

Adams, L. *Christ and the Western Mind,* translated by E. Bullough. London: Sheed and Ward, 1930.

Adler, A. *The Individual Psychology of Alfred Adler,* edited by Heinz and Rowena Ansbacher. New York: Basic Books, 1956.

Adler, A. *Understanding Human Nature,* Greenwich, Conn.: Fawcett, 1957.

Allen, J. A. *Mind Studies for Young Teachers.* New York: E. L. Kellogg, 1893.

Allport, F. *Theories of Perception and the Concept of Structure.* New York: John Wiley, 1955.

Aquinas, St. Thomas. *Summa Contra Gentiles.* English translation by Joseph Rickaby S.J. Westminster, Maryland: Carroll Press, 1950.

Augustine. *City of God.* London: J.M. Dent and Sons, 1947.

Ausubel, D. P. *The Psychology of Meaningful Verbal Learning.* New York: Grune and Stratton, 1963.

Backman, C. W., & Secord, P. F. Liking, selective interaction, and misperception in congruent interpersonal relations. *Sociometry,* **25,** 1962, 321–325.

Backman, C. W., Secord, P. F., & Pierce, J. R. Resistance to change in the self-concept as a function of consensus among significant others. *Sociometry,* **26,** 1963, 102–111.

Baker, F. B. Computer-based instructional management systems: a first look. *Review of Educational Research,* **41** (1), 1971, 51–70.

Baker, M. C. *Foundations of John Dewey's Educational Theory.* New York: King's Crown Press, 1955.

Baldwin, J. *Psychology Applied to the Art of Teaching.* New York: Appleton, 1892.

Bandura, A., & Walters, R. *Social Learning and Personality Development*. New York: Holt, Rinehart, & Winston, 1963.

Bandura, A. *Principles of Behavior Modification*. New York: Holt, Rinehart, & Winston, 1969.

Barclay, J. R. *Franz Brentano and Sigmund Freud: A Comparative Study in the Evolution of Psychological Thought*. Unpublished doctoral dissertation, University of Michigan, 1959.

Barclay, J. R. Mobility, cultural change and educational leadership. *Family Life Coordinator*, **12** (3–4), 1963, 97–104.

Barclay, J. R. Franz Brentano and Sigmund Freud. *Journal of Existentialism*, **5** (17), 1964.

Barclay, J. R. *Studies in Sociometry and Teacher Ratings: A Diagnostic and Predictive Combination for School Psychology*. Pocatello, Idaho: Idaho State University, 1964, lithographed 220 pages.

Barclay, J. R. *Testing for Higher Education: Cultural Perspective and Future Focus*. ACPA Monograph Series, No. 6. Washington: American Personnel and Guidance Association, 1965.

Barclay, J. R. Interest patterns associated with measures of social desirability. *American Personnel and Guidance Journal*, **45** (1), 1966a, 56–60.

Barclay, J. R. Sociometric choices and teacher ratings as predictors of school dropout. *Journal of School Psychology*, **4** (2), 1966b, 40–41.

Barclay, J. R. Sociometry: rationale and technique for effecting behavior change in the elementary school. *American Personnel and Guidance Journal*, **44** (10), 1966c, 1067–1076.

Barclay, J. R. Variability in sociometric scores and teacher ratings as related to teacher age and sex. *Journal of School Psychology*, **5** (1), 1966d, 52–59.

Barclay, J. R. The Counselor's *Lebenswelt*, unpublished study, 1966.

Barclay, J. R. Approach to the measurement of teacher "press" in the secondary curriculum. Monograph. *Journal of Counseling Psychology*, November 1967, 550–567.

Barclay, J. R. Effecting behavior change in the elementary classroom: an exploratory study. *Journal of Counseling Psychology*, **14** (3), 240–247, 1967b.

Barclay, J. R. Changing the behavior of school psychologists: a training method and rationale. Final Report, United States Office of Education, Grants: OEG 4-7-120003-1952, and OEG 9-8-070098, California State College, Hayward, 1968.

Barclay, J. R. *Controversial Issues in Testing.* Boston: Houghton-Mifflin, 1968.

Barclay, J. R. *Counseling and Philosophy: a Theoretical Exposition.* Boston: Houghton-Mifflin, 1968.

Barclay, J. R. *Manual for the Use of the Barclay Classroom Climate Inventory* (University of Kentucky, 1970).

Barclay, J. R. Descriptive, theoretical and behavioral characteristics of subdoctoral school psychologists. *American Psychologist,* 1971, **26** (3), 257–280.

Barclay, J. R., Montgomery, R. & Barclay, L. K. Measuring the effectiveness of intensive teacher training in social learning and behavior modification techniques. *Measurement & Evaluation in Guidance,* July 1971, in press.

Barclay, L. K., & Barclay, J. R. Measured indices of perceptual distortion and impulsivity as related to sociometric scores and teacher ratings. *Psychology in the Schools,* 1965, **2** (4), 372–375.

Baruch, J. A. The relation between sin and disease in the old testament, *Janus,* **51,** 1964, 295–302.

Bateman, B. Learning Disorders, *Review of Educational Research* **36** (1), 1966.

Bear, H. The Theoretical Ethics of the Brentano School; a Psycho-Epistemological Approach. Unpublished doctoral dissertation, Columbia University, 1954.

Beck, C. E. *Philosophical Foundations of Guidance.* Englewood Cliffs, New Jersey: Prentice-Hall, 1963.

Bede (Venerable). *Historia Ecclesiastica Gentis Anglorum,* edited by Plummer. Oxford: Clarendon Press, 1896, I.

Beez, W. V. Influence of biased psychological reports on teacher behavior and pupil performance. APA Annual Meeting, 1968, San Francisco, California. Also reported in *Proceedings of the 76th Annual Convention of the American Psychological Association*, Vol. 3, American Psychological Association, Washington, D.C., 1968.

Bereiter, C., & Englemann, S. *Teaching Disadvantaged Children in the Preschool*, Englewood-Cliffs, Prentice-Hall, 1966.

Bergum, B., & Lehn, D. Prediction of Stimulus Approach: Core Measures Experiment II, III, IV, V, VI. July 1966–January 1967. Rochester, New York: Xerox Corporation.

Berlyne, D. E. *Conflict, Arousal and Curiosity*. New York: McGraw-Hill, 1960.

Bernfeld, S. Freud's Earliest Theories and the School of Helmholtz, *Psychoanalytic Quarterly*, vol. 13 (1944), 341–362.

Beshers, J. M., & Nishiura, E. N. A theory of internal migration differentials, *Social Forces*, **39** (3), 1961, 214–218.

Bidley, D. *Conflicts of Power and Culture*. Seventh Symposium of Conference on Science, Philosophy and Religion in a Relationship to the Democratic Way of Life. New York: Harper Bros., 1947, 183–197.

Bigge, M. Schema of Representative Theories of Learning, NEA *Journal*, March 1966, 18–19.

Bijou, S. W., & Baer, D. M. *Child Development I, II*. New York: Appleton-Century-Crofts, 1961.

Bixler, R. H. Counseling: eclectic or systematic? *Educational & Psychological Measurement* **8**, 1948, 211–214.

Blondheim, S. H. The first recorded epidemic of pneumonic plague: the Bible I. Sam. VI, *Bulletin of the History of Medicine*, **29**, 1955, 327–345.

Bloom, B. J. Learning for Mastery. *Evaluation Comment*, **1** (2), May 1968, Los Angeles, Cal.: Center for the Study of Evaluation of Instructional Programs.

Boring, E. G. *A History of Experimental Psychology* (1929) 1950, New York: Appleton-Century-Crofts.

Boskoff, A. Social indecision, a dysfunctional focus of transitional society. *Social Forces*, **37** (4), 1959, 305–311.

Bowen, H. C.   *Froebel and Education through Self-Activity.* New York: Scribners, 1894.

Boyd, W.   *The History of Western Education.* London: Adam & Charles Black, 1952.

Boyd, W.   *From Locke to Montessori.* New York: Holt, 1914.

Boyd, W.   *The History of Western Education.* London: Adam and Charles Black, 1952.

Boyd, W.   *Jean Jacques Rousseau.* London: Longmans Green, 1911.

Bradbury, D. E.   The contribution of the child study movement to child psychology, *Psychological Bulletin,* 1937, **34,** 21–38.

Brentano, F.   *Aristoteles Lehre vom Ursprung des Menschlichen Geistes.* Leipzig: Vert (1867), 1911.

Brentano, F.   *Die Lehre vom Richtigen Urteil.* Bern: Francke, 1956.

Brentano, F.   *Grundlegung und Aufbau der Ethik.* Edited by Franziska Mayer-Hillebrand. Bern: Francke, 1952.

Brentano, F.   *Origin of the Knowledge of Right and Wrong.* Translated by Cecil Hague and Archibald Constable. London: Westminster Press, 1902.

Brentano, F.   *Psychologie vom empirischen Standpunkt,* vol. I and II, Leipzig: Meiner, 1924. (Hamburg: Meiner, 1955).

Brentano, F.   *Von Ursprung sittlicher Erkenntnis.* Hamburg: Meiner, 1955.

Brentano, F.   *Wahrheit und Evidenz.* Leipzig: Meiner, 1930.

Brentano, F.   Unpublished manuscripts University of Minnesota: A 153 "Philosophie des Aristoteles" (1876); EL 72 "Plan fuer die Logikvorlesung" (1875); PS 62/62 "Fuer das Psychologiekolleg" (1872–1873); PS 63/63 "Fuer das Psychologiekolleg" (date unknown).

Brett, G. S.   *History of Psychology.* London: George Allen and Unwin Ltd., 1953.

Breuer, J., & Freud, S.   *Studies on Hysteria.* Translated by James Strachey in collaboration with Anna Freud. New York: Basic Books Inc., 1957.

Bronfenbrenner, U.   The Changing American Child, mimeographed speech, Golden Anniversary, White House Conference on Children and Youth, also delivered at American Psychological Association Convention, 1960, Chicago, Illinois.

Brophy, J. E., & Good, T. L.   Teachers' communication of differential expectations for children's classroom performance: some behavioral data. AERA National Meeting, Minneapolis, 1970.

Burgess, R. W.   *World Almanac,* 1961, New York World Telegram.

Burton, R. V., & Whiting, J. W. M.   The absent father: effects on the developing child, paper presented at the American Psychological Association Convention, 1960, Chicago, Illinois.

Campbell, D. T., & Fiske, D. W.   Convergent and discriminant validation by the multi-trait-multimethod matrix. *Psychological Bulletin,* 1959, **56**, 81–105.

Calkins, N. A.   *Manual of Object-Teaching.* New York, Harper, 1882.

Campbell, D. P.   *The Results of Counseling: Twenty-five Years Later.* Philadelphia: Saunders Co., 1965.

Carnegie, A.   Wealth, *North American Review,* 1889, **148**, 653–664.

Carroll, K. M.   Alienation, existentialism, and education. Paper read at the Sixteenth Annual Meeting, Philosophy of Education Society, *Annual Proceedings.* Lawrence, Kansas: University of Kansas Press, 1960.

Cassirer, E.   *The Question of Jean Jacques Rousseau,* translated by P. Gay, New York: Columbia University Press, 1954.

Castiglioni, A.   *A History of Medicine,* New York: Knopf, 1947.

Catterall, C.   *Taxonomy of Prescriptive Interventions.* Santa Clara Unified School District, Santa Clara, California, 1967.

Cautela, J. R.   Use of imagery in behavior modification. Paper presented to annual meeting of the Association for Advancement of Behavior Therapy, Washington, D.C., September 1969.

Cavanaugh, J. R.   *Fundamental Pastoral Counseling.* Milwaukee: Bruce Publishing Co., 1958.

Coan, R. W.   Dimensions of psychological theory. *American Psychologist,* 1968, **23**, 715–722.

Cobb, J. A.   The relationship of discrete classroom behaviors to fourth grade academic achievement. Oregon Research Bulletin, No. 10, Eugene, Oregon: 1970.

Cobb, J. A., Ray, R., & Patterson, G. R.   Direct intervention in the schools. Paper presented at APA Convention, Miami, 1970.

Cole, S. G.   *Perspectives on a Troubled Decade,* 10th Symposium of the Conference on Science, Philosophy and Religion, New York: Harper Brothers, 1947, 109–124.

Coleman, J. S. et. al.   *Equality of Educational Opportunity.* Washington, D. C., Office of Education, U.S. Department of Health, Education, and Welfare, 1966.

Combs, A. W., & Snygg, B.   *Individual Behavior: A New Frame of Reference for Psychology.* New York: Harper and Brothers, 1949.

Compayre, G.   *History of Pedagogy* 1886 (publisher data missing).

Condillac, E.   *Treatise on the Sensations,* translated by Geraldine Carr, University of Southern California Studies, Political Series No. 1, Los Angeles: University of Southern California Press, 1930.

Cronbach, L. J., & Meehl, P. E.   Construct validity in psychological tests, *Psychological Bulletin,* 1955, **52,** 281–302.

Davidson, T.   *Rousseau and Education According to Nature.* New York: Scribners, 1898.

Davis, H.   *The Works of Plato,* Vol. II. London: Henry G. Bohns Co., 1849.

Dawson, C.   *The Age of the Gods.* London: Sheed and Ward, 1934.

Descartes, R.   *Descartes Selections,* edited by Ralph M. Eaton. New York: Charles Scribners and Sons, 1927.

De Vaux, R.   *Ancient Israel: Its Life and Institutions.* New York: McGraw-Hill, 1961.

Dewey, J.   *Democracy and Education.* New York: Macmillan, 1916.

Dewey, J.   *Experience and Nature.* New York: Gover Publ. Inc., 1929.

Dewey, J.   *Experience and Education.* New York: Macmillan Co., 1938, 1959.

Dewey J.   *Intelligence in the Modern World.* New York: Modern Library, 1939.

Dittes, J., & Kelly, H.   Effects of different conditions of acceptance upon conformity of group norms, *Journal Abnormal and Social Psychology,* **53,** 1956.

Dost, S. A history of medicine in ancient Israel, unpublished paper, University of California, Berkeley, 1968.

Drexelius, J. *Heliotropium,* edited by Ferdinand E. Bogner, New York: Devin-Adair Company, 1912.

Driesch J., & Esterhues, J. *Geschichte der Erziehung und Bildung,* Band II, *Vom 17 Jahrhundert bis zur Gegenwart.* Paderborn: Schoningh, 1952.

Eaton, H. O. *The Austrian Philosophy of Values,* University of Oklahoma Press, 1930.

Eby, F. *The Development of Modern Education.* (2nd ed.) New York: Prentice-Hall, 1952.

Ellis, A. Rational psychotherapy, *Journal of General Psychology,* **59,** 1958, 36–49.

Erikson, E. H. The first psychoanalyst, in Benjamin Nelson (Ed.), *Freud and the Twentieth Century,* New York: Meridian Books, 1957.

Eysenck, H. J. (Ed.). *Behavior Therapy and the Neuroses,* New York, Pergamon Press, 1967.

Eysenck, H. J., & Rachman, S. *Causes and Cures of Neurosis.* San Diego: Robert Knapp, 1965.

Fairbairn, W. R. D. *An Object-Relations Theory of Personality.* New York: Basic Books Inc., 1954.

Farber, M. *The Foundations of Phenomenology.* Cambridge, Massachusetts: Harvard University Press, 1943.

Farber, M. *The Foundation of Phenomenology.* New York: Paine, Whitman, 1962.

Feigl, H. Aims of education for our age of science: reflections of a logical empiricist. In *Modern Philosophies and Education,* Fifty-fourth yearbook of the National Society for the Study of Education. Chicago: University of Chicago Press, 1955.

Feigl, H., & Seriven, M. *Minnesota Studies in the Philosophy of Science,* Minneapolis: University of Minnesota Press, 1956.

Fenichel, O. *The Psychoanalytic Theory of Neurosis,* New York: W. W. Norton & Company, 1945.

Fiedler, F. E. A comparison of therapeutic relationships in psychoanalytic, non-directive and Adlerian therapy, *Journal of Consulting Psychology,* 14, 1950b, 436–445.

Fiedler, F. E.   The concept of an ideal therapeutic relationship, *Journal of Consulting Psychology,* 14, 1950a, 239–245.

Fitch, J. G.   *Lectures on Teaching* (presented at Cambridge University in 1880). New York: L. Kellogg, 1897.

Flanders, N. A., & Havumaki, S.   The effect of teacher-pupil contacts involving praise on the sociometric choices of students, Chapter 40, *Educating for Mental Health,* edited by Jerome M. Seidman. New York: Thomas Y. Crowell Co., 1963.

Flavell, J. H.   *The Developmental Psychology of Jean Piaget.* Princeton, New Jersey: D. Van Nostrand Co., 1964.

Fodor, N., & Gaynor, F.   *Dictionary of Psychoanalysis.* New York: Philosophical Library, 1950.

Ford, D. H., & Urban, H. B.   *Systems of Psychotherapy,* New York: John Wiley, 1963.

Freud, S.   *Psychopathology of Everyday Life.* New York: Macmillan Co., 1914.

Freud, S.   *Interpretation of Dreams.* London: George Allen and Unwin Ltd., 1927.

Freud, S.   *Civilization and its Discontents,* New York: Jonathan Cape & Harrison Smith, 1930.

Freud, S.   *New Introductory Lectures on Psychoanalysis.* New York: W. W. Norton Co., 1933.

Freud, S.   *Group Psychology and the Analysis of the Ego.* London: Hogarth Press, 1949.

Freud, S.   *The Future of an Illusion,* London: Hogarth Press, 1949.

Freud, S.   *Gesammelte Werke,* Vols. 1–17. London: Imago Publishing Co., 1952.

Freud, S.   *Collected Papers,* Vols. I-VII. London: Hogarth Press, 1953–1956.

Froelich, C.   *Guidance Services in Schools.* New York: McGraw-Hill, 1958.

Fromm, E.   Selfishness and self-love. *Psychiatry,* 1939, 2, 507–523.

Gagne, R. M.   *The Conditions of Learning.* New York: Holt, Rinehart and Winston, 1965.

Georgiades, P.   *De Freud a Platon.* Paris: Fasquelle, 1934.

Gilbert, W. M., & Ewing, T. N. Counseling by teaching-machine procedures. Presentation to the American Psychological Association Annual Convention, Los Angeles, 1964.

Gilson, L. *La Psychologie Deschiptive Selon Franz Brentano.* Paris: Librairie Philosophique J. Vrin, 1955.

Gilson, L. *Mèthode et Metaphysique Selon Franz Brentano.* Paris: Librairie Philosophique J. Vrin, 1955.

Gimbel, B. E. Freud's Theory of Mind and Meaning. Unpublished doctoral dissertation, Bryn Mawr College, 1949.

Goldiamond, I. Justified and unjustified alarm over behavioral control. In a symposium on the social responsibilities of the psychologist, American Psychological Association Annual Convention. Philadelphia, 1963.

Goodenough, F. L. *Mental Testing: Its History, Principles and Applications.* New York: Rinehart, 1949.

Goodwin, D. L., Garvey, W. P., & Barclay, J. R. Microconsultation and behavior analysis: a method of training psychologists as behavioral consultants, *Journal of Consulting Psychology,* in press, 1971.

Gottschalk, L. *Understanding History.* New York: Alfred A. Knopf, 1951.

Green, A. W. The middle class male child and neurosis, *American Sociological Review,* **11,** 1946, 31–41.

Gronlund, N. E. *Sociometry in the Classroom.* New York: Harper Bros., 1959.

Grossberg, J. M. Behavior therapy: a review. *Psychological Bulletin,* **62,** 1964.

Guinouard, D. E., & Rychlak, J. F. Personality correlates of sociometric popularity in elementary school children. *Personnel and Guidance Journal,* **40,** 1962, 438–442.

Hagen, C. L. Changing concepts toward the child as a learner, unpublished doctoral dissertation, University of Utah, 1957.

Hall, C. S., & Lindzey, G. *Theories of Personality.* New York: John Wiley, 1957.

Hall, G. S. *Adolescence.* New York: Appleton, 1904. 2 vols.

Hall, G. S. *Life and Confessions of a Psychologist.* New York: Appleton, 1923.

Haller, A. O., & Butterworth, C. E. Peer influences on levels of occupational and educational aspiration. *Social Forces,* **38,** 1960, 289–295.

Halmos, Paul. *The Faith of the Counsellors.* New York: Schocken Books, 1966.

Halpern, Sidney. Free association in 423 BC. *The Psychoanalytic Review,* **50** (3), 1963, 69–87.

Hamerlynck, L. A., Martin, J. W., & Rolland, J. C. Systematic observation of behavior: a primary teacher skill. *Education and Training of the Mentally Retarded,* 1968, **3,** 39–42.

Harlow, H. F. William James and Instinct theory, in *William James: Unfinished Business,* Robert McLeod (Ed.), Washington: American Psychological Association, 1969.

Harper, R. A. *Psychoanalysis and Psychotherapy 36 Systems.* Englewood Cliffs, New Jersey: Prentice-Hall Inc., 1959.

Havighurst, R. J., & Davis, A. A comparison of the Chicago and Harvard studies of social class differences in child rearing, *American Sociological Review,* **20** (4), 438–442, 1955.

Hebb, D. O. Concerning imagery. *Psychological Review,* 1968, **6,** 7–12.

Heider, F. *The Psychology of Interpersonal Relations.* New York: John Wiley, 1958.

Hewitt, F. *The Emotionally Disturbed Child in the Classroom.* Boston: Allyn, Bacon, 1968.

Hilgard, E. R. The Place of Gestalt Psychology and Field Theories in Contemporary Learning Theory, Chapter III, in *Theories of Learning and Instruction,* the 63rd Yearbook of the National Society for the Study of Education, Part I., University of Chicago Press, 1964.

Hilgard, E. R. *Theories of Learning.* (2nd ed.) New York: Appleton-Century-Crofts, 1956.

Hobbs, N. Sources of gain in psychotherapy. *American Psychologist,* **17,** 1962.

Höffding, H. *A History of Modern Philosophy,* I, II. New York: Dover Publications, 1955.

Hofstadter, R. *Social Darwinism in American* Thought. Boston, Beacon Press, 1955.

Holland, J. L. A theory of vocational choice. *Journal of Counseling Psychology,* **6,** 1959.

Holland, J. L. Some explorations of theory of vocational choice. *Psychological Monographs,* **76,** (26), 1962.

Holland, J. L. *Psychology of Vocational Choice.* Boston: Ginn and Co., 1966.

Holland, J. L. A psychological classification scheme for vocations and major fields. Mimeographed, 1966.

Homme, L. Control of coverants, the operants of the mind. *Psychological Record,* 1965, **15,** 501–511.

Horney, K. *The Neurotic Personality of our Times.* New York: W. W. Norton, 1937.

Horney, K. *Our Inner Conflicts.* New York: W. W. Norton, 1945.

Horney, K. *Neurosis and Human Growth.* New York: W. W. Norton, 1950.

Hosford, R. E. Behavioral counseling—a contemporary overview, *The Counseling Psychologist,* **1,** (4), 1969.

Hosford, R. E., & Briskin, A. S. Changes through counseling, *Review of Educational Research,* **30** (2), 1969.

Howes, H. R., Jr. *An Evaluation of Short-Term School Counseling.* Unpublished doctoral dissertation, Northwestern University, 1961.

Hutson, P. W. *The Guidance Function in Education.* New York: Appleton-Century-Crofts Inc., 1958.

Hyman, L. H. Zoology. In *Encyclopedia Britannica,* 1955, **23,** 976–986.

Jakobovitz, I. *Jewish Medical Ethics.* New York: Philosophical Library, 1959.

Jacobson, E. *Anxiety and Tension Control.* Philadelphia: J. B. Lippincott, 1964.

Johnson, E. L. *The Relationship between Certain Propositions of Client-Centered Theory and Certain Tenets of the Philosophy.* Unpublished doctoral dissertation, Indiana University, 1961.

Jones, E. *Papers on Psychoanalysis*. New York: William Wood Co., 1922.

Jones, E. *Essays in Applied Psychoanalysis*. London-Vienna: International Psychoanalytic Press, 1923.

Jones, E. *Life and Work of Sigmund Freud*. Vols. 1–3. New York: Basic Books Inc., 1953–57.

Jung, C. G. *Two Essays on Analytical Psychology*. New York: Pantheon 1953.

Jung, C. *The Practice of Psychotherapy*. New York: Pantheon, 1954.

Jung, C. G. *Psyche and Symbol*. Garden City, New York: Doubleday & Co., Inc., 1958.

Kallen, H. M. *The Philosophy of William James*. New York: Modern Library, 1953.

Kaplan, A. Freud and modern philosophy, in Benjamin Nelson (Ed.), *Freud and the Twentieth Century*. New York: Meridian Books, 1957.

Kastil, A. *Die Philosophie Franz Brentanos*. Salzburg: Francke, 1951.

Kelly, G. A. *A Theory of Personality*. New York: W. W. Norton Co., 1963.

Kennedy, D. A. Sociometric assessment: a validity study (Barclay Technique). American Personnel and Guidance Association, National Meeting, Las Vegas, 1969.

Kluckhohn, C. The concept of culture. In Ralph Linton (Ed.), *The Science of Man in the World Crisis*. New York: Columbia University Press, 1945.

Kneller, G. F. *Existentialism and Education*. New York: Philosophical Library, 1958.

Knight, D. *Mysticism, Freudianism and Scientific Psychology*. St. Louis: C. V. Mosley Co., 1920.

Kohn, M. L. Social class and parental values. *American Journal of Sociology*, **64**, June 1959, 337–351.

Koff, R. H., & Hawkes, T. H. Sociometric choice: a study in pupillary responses. Paper presented at AERA National Meeting, Chicago, 1968.

Kolesnik, W. *Mental Discipline in Modern Education*. Madison: University of Wisconsin Press, 1958.

Krasner, L. Behavioral control and social responsibility. *American Psychologist*, **17**, 1962.

Krasner, L., & Ullmann, L. P.   *Research in Behavior Modification.* New York: Holt, Rinehart, and Winston, 1965.

Kraus, O.   *Franz Brentano zur Kenntnis seines Lebens und seiner Lehre.* Munich: Beck, 1919.

Krumboltz, J. D.   Behavioral goals for counseling. Mimeographed, 1964(a).

Krumboltz, J. D.   Parable of the good counselor. *Personnel and Guidance Journal,* 43, 1964(b).

Krumboltz, J. D.   Behavioral counseling: rationale and research. *Personnel and Guidance Journal,* 44, 1965.

Krumboltz, J. D. (Ed.).   *Revolution in Counseling.* Boston: Houghton-Mifflin, 1966.

Krumboltz, J. D.   *Stating the Goals of Counseling,* California Counseling and Guidance Association Monograph No. 1, 1966.

Krumboltz, J. D., & Goodwin, D. L.   *Increasing Task-Oriented Behavior: An Experimental Evaluation of Training Teachers in Reinforcement Techniques.* United States Office of Education, Department of Health, Education, and Welfare, Contract OE 5-85-095. Stanford University, Stanford, California, 1966.

Krumboltz, J. D., & Hosford, R. E.   *A Study to Determine How Counseling Procedures Can Be Used to Help Students Make Decisions and Plans More Effectively.* United States Office of Education, Department of Health, Education, and Welfare, Contract OE 5-10-363, Stanford University, Stanford, California, 1966.

Krumboltz, J. D., & Schroeder, W. W.   Promoting career planning through reinforcement and models. *Personnel and Guidance Journal,* 44, 1965.

Krumboltz, J. D., & Thoresen, C. E.   The effect of behavioral counseling in group and individual settings on information-seeking behavior. *Journal of Counseling Psychology*, 11, 1964.

Krumboltz, J. D., & Thoresen, C. E. *Behavioral Counseling: Cases and Techniques.* New York: Holt, Rinehart & Winston, 1969.

Külpe, O. *Introduction to Philosophy.* London: Swan Sonnenschein & Co., Ltd., 1897.

Kuo, Z. Y. *The Dynamics of Behavior Development.* New York: Random House, 1967.

La Mettrie, J. O. *Man a Machine,* translated by Margaret W. Calkins. LaSalle, Illinois: Open Court Publishing Co., 1943.

Landsman, T. Existentialism in counseling: the scientific view. *Personnel and Guidance Journal, 43,* 1965.

Lashley, K. The behavioristic interpretation of consciousness. *Psychological Review,* 1923, 30, 329–353.

Lee, G. C. *Education in Modern America* (Rev. ed.). New York: Henry Holt & Co., 1958.

Lee, R. S. *Freud and Christianity.* New York: A. A. Wyn Co., 1949.

Leibnitz, G. *New Essays Concerning Human Understanding.* LaSalle, Illinois: Open Court Publishing Co., 1949.

Levine, D. U. The integration-compensatory education controversy. *The Educational Forum,* 32, March 1968, 323–332.

Levine, I. *The Unconscious.* London: L. Parsons, 1923.

Lewin, K. *Principles of Topological Psychology.* New York: McGraw-Hill, 1936.

Locke, J. *The Works of John Locke* (10 vols.), III, *Of the Conduct of the Understanding.* London: Thomas Tegg, W. Sharpe & Son, 1823.

Locke, J. *Some Thoughts Concerning Education.* Cambridge, England: University Press, 1902.

Locke, J. *Selections from Locke.* In S. P. Lamprecht (Ed.). New York: Charles Scribners and Sons, 1928.

Lott, B. E., & Lott, A. J. The formation of positive attitudes towards group members. *Journal Abnormal Social Psychology,* 61, 1960, 297–300.

Luchins, A. S. Ego determinants in Gestalt theory. Paper presented at the Annual Convention of the American Psychological Association, Chicago, 1960.

Mager, R. F. *Preparing Instructional Objectives.* Palo Alto: Fearon Publishers, 1962.

McDaniel, J. E., Lallas, J. A., Saum, J. & Gilmore, J. L. *Readings in Guidance.* New York: Henry Holt & Co., 1959.

MacLeod, R. B. *William James Unfinished Business.* Washington, D.C.: American Psychological Association, 1969.

McHugh, M. A. The implications of interactive theory for counseling: an analysis of the relationship in four philosophical areas, unpublished master's thesis, Idaho State University, 1964.

McReynolds, W. T. "Bibliography on Behavior Therapy." Lithographed by the Psychology Department, University of Kentucky, 1969.

Mahrer, A. R. *The Goals of Psychotherapy.* New York: Meredith Publishing Co., 1967.

Mann, H. *Seventh Annual Report of the Board of Education,* 1843. Washington, D.C.: National Education Association, 1950.

Maritain, J. In *Freud and the Twentieth Century,* Benjamin Nelson (Ed.). New York: Meridian Books, 1957.

Maslow, A. H. *Motivation and Personality.* New York: Harper Bros., 1954.

May, R., Angel, E., & Ellenberger, H. F. *Existence.* New York: Basic Books, 1958.

Miller, J. G. *Unconscious.* New York: John Wiley, 1942.

Miller, W., & Swanson, S. *The Changing American Parent.* New York: John Wiley, 1958.

Merlan, P. Brentano and Freud. *Journal of the History of Ideas,* **6,** 1945, 375–377.

Merlan, P. Brentano and Freud—A Sequel. *Journal of the History of Ideas,* **10,** 1949, 451.

Meyerson, L., & Michael, J. A behavioral approach to counseling and guidance. *Harvard Educational Review,* **32,** Fall 1962.

Misiak, H., & Staudt, V. M. *Catholics in Psychology.* New York: McGraw Hill Co., 1954.

Montgomery, R.   Data collection systems for use by elementary counselors in direct classroom observation of maladaptive children. APGA Convention, Las Vegas, Nevada, 1969.

Munroe, R. L.   *Schools of Psychoanalytic Thought*. New York: Dryden Press, 1955.

Murphy, G.   In *Freud and the Twentieth Century*. Benjamin Nelson (Ed.). New York: Meridian Books, 1957.

Murray, E. R.   *Froebel as a Pioneer in Modern Psychology*. Baltimore: Warwick & York, 1914.

Nelson, B.   (Ed.), *Freud and the Twentieth Century*. New York: Meridian Books, 1957.

Newman, J. H.   *The Arians of the Fourth Century*. London: Lumely, 1871.

Newman, J. H.   *An Essay on the Development of Christian Doctrine*. Longman's, London, 1920.

Nixon, S. B.   *Ways by Which Overly-Active Students can be Taught to Concentrate on Study Activity*. Cooperative Research Project No. S-379. United States Office of Education, Department of Health, Education, and Welfare, Stanford University, Stanford, California, 1966.

Ohlsen, N. M., Proff, F. C., & Roeber, E. C.   Counseling and adjustment. *Review of Educational Research*, **26**, 1956.

O'Neil, W. F.   Philosophical analysis: a philosophical analysis. Paper presented to the Annual Convention of the Far Western Philosophy of Education Society, Hayward, California, 1964.

Osgood, C. E., Suci, G. J., & Tannenbaum, P. H.   *The Measurement of Meaning*. Champaign-Urbana, Illinois: University of Illinois Press, 1957.

Pace, C. R., & Stern, G. G.   An approach to the measurement of psychological characteristics of college environments. *Journal of Educational Psychology*, **49**, 1958, 269–277.

Patterson, C. H.   *Counseling and Psychotherapy: Theory and Practice*. New York: Harper and Bros., 1959.

Patterson, G. R., & Bechtel, G. C. Formulating the situational environment in relation to states and traits. Chapter in R. B. Cattell (Ed.), *Handbook of Modern Personality Study,* 1969, Aldine Publishing Company.

Patterson, G. R., & Harris, A. Some methodological considerations for observation procedures. Paper presented at the APA meeting, San Francisco, 1968.

Patterson, G. R., Ray, R. S., Shaw, D. A., & Cobb, J. A. Manual for coding of family interactions. Unpublished manuscript, Oregon Research Institute, Eugene, Oregon, 1969.

Patterson, G. R., & Reid, J. Reciprocity and Coercion: two facets of social systems. Paper presented for the Ninth Annual Institute for Research in Clinical Psychology sponsored by the University of Kansas, Department of Psychology: *Behavior Modification for Clinical Psychologists,* April 1967, Lawrence, Kansas.

Payne, J. *Lectures on the Science and Art of Education.* New York: E. L. Kellogg, 1887.

Pegis, A. C. *Introduction to Saint Thomas Aquinas,* Modern Library. New York: Random House, 1948.

Pepinsky, H. B. *Diagnostic Categories in Clinical Counseling.* Stanford: Stanford University Press, 1948.

Pestalozzi, J. H. *Leonard and Gertrude,* translated and abridged by Eva Channing. Boston: Heath, 1908.

Pestalozzi, J. H. *How Gertrude Teaches Her Children,* translated by Lucy Holland and F. C. Holland. London: George Allen & Unwin, 1915.

Peter, L. *Prescriptive Teaching.* New York: McGraw-Hill, 1965.

Peters, R. S. (Ed.) *Brett's History of Psychology.* London: Allen & Unwin, 1953.

Phenix, P. H.   *Philosophy of Education.* New York: Henry Holt and Co., 1958.

Piaget, J.   *Origin of Intelligence in Children.* New York: International Universities Press, 1952.

Pine, G. J., & Boy, A. V.   The counselor and the unmotivated client. *Personnel and Guidance Journal,* 44, 1965.

Plato.   *The Republic of Plato,* translated by Francis MacDonald Cornford. New York: Oxford University Press, 1957.

Premack, D.   Reinforcement theory. Paper presented at the Nebraska Motivation Symposium, 1965.

Ratner, J.   (Commentator) *The Philosophy of Spinoza.* Modern Library, New York: Random House, 1927.

Robinson, F.   *Principles and Practices in Student Counseling.* New York: Harper Bros., 1950.

Rogers, C. R.   *The Clinical Treatment of the Problem Child.* Boston: Houghton-Mifflin, 1939.

Rogers, C. R.   *Client-centered Therapy.* Boston: Houghton-Mifflin, 1951.

Rogers, C. R.   *On Becoming a Person.* Boston: Houghton-Mifflin, 1961.

Ross, D.   *The Nichomachean Ethics of Aristotle.* London: Oxford University Press, 1954.

Rousseau, J. J.   *Confessions. In the Great Confessions Five Sinners and a Saint.* New York: Tudor Press, 1934.

Rousseau, J. J.   *Emile,* translated and abridged by W. H. Payne. New York: Appleton, 1926.

Rousseau, J. J.   *Emile,* translated by Barbara Foxley. New York: Dutton, 1911 Everyman's Library, No. 518.

Ryan, T. A., & Krumboltz, J. D.   Effect of planned reinforcement counseling on client decision-making behavior. *Journal of Counseling Psychology,* 11, 1964.

Sartre, J. P.   *Existentialism.* Translated by B. Frechtman. New York: Philosophical Library, 1947.

Schaupp, Z.   *The Naturalism of Condillac.* University of Nebraska Studies in Language, Literature and Criticism, No. 7. Lincoln: University of Nebraska Press, 1926.

Schwartz, C.   *Neurotic Anxiety.* New York: Sheed & Ward, 1954.

Sewell, W. H., & Haller, A. O. Social status and the personality adjustment of the child, *Sociometry*, **19** (2), 1956, 114–125.

Shermis, S. S. Interaction in the writings of John Dewey, unpublished master's thesis, University of Kansas, 1960.

Shermis, S. S. John Dewey's social and political philosophy: its implications for social studies education, unpublished doctoral dissertation, University of Kansas, 1961.

Shoben, E. J., Jr. The counselor's theory as a personal trait. *Personnel and Guidance Journal*, **40**, 1962, 617–621.

Shulman, L. S. The multiple measurement of self-concept. Paper presented at the AERA National Meeting, Chicago, Illinois, 1968.

Skinner, B. F. *Walden Two*. New York: Macmillan Co., 1948.

Skinner, B. F. Behaviorism as a philosophy of psychology. In T. W. Wann (Ed.), *Behaviorism and Phenomenology*. Chicago: University of Chicago Press, 1964.

Snygg, D., & Combs, A. W. *Individual Behavior: A New Frame of Reference for Psychology*. New York: Harper, 1949.

Soares, A. T., & Soares, L. M. Self-perceptions of culturally disadvantaged children. *American Educational Research Journal*, 1969 **6** (1), 31–45.

Spiegelberg, H. *The Phenomenological Movement I, II*. The Hague: Martinjus Nijhoff, 1965.

Staats, A. *Learning, Language and Cognition*. New York: Holt, Rinehart & Winston, 1968.

Staats, A., & Staats, C. *Complex Human Behavior*. New York: Holt, Rinehart & Winston, 1963.

Standal, S. W., & Corsini, R. J. *Critical Incidents in Psychotherapy*. New Jersey: Prentice-Hall, Inc., 1960.

Stefflre, B., & Matheny, K. *The Function of Counseling Theory*. Boston: Houghton-Mifflin, 1968.

Sturt, H. *Condillac, Etienne, Bonnot de*. In *Encyclopaedia Britannica*, 1955, edition VI.

Sullivan, H. S. *The Interpersonal Theory of Psychiatry*. New York: Norton Co., 1953.

Sullivan, J. J.   Franz Brentano and the Problems of Intentionality, in *Historical Roots of Psychology* (Benjamin B. Wolman, Ed.). New York: Harper and Row, 1968, 248–274.

Sundland, D. M., & Barker, E. N.   The orientations of psychotherapists. *Journal of Consulting Psychology,* **26,** 1962, 201–212.

Susskind, D. J., Franks, C. M., & Lonoff, R.   Desensitization program with third and fourth grade teachers, a new application and a controlled study. Paper presented to Annual Meeting of the Association for Advancement of Behavior Therapy, Washington, D.C., September 1969.

Svalastoga, K.   *Prestige, Class and Mobility.* London: William Heinemann, Ltd., 1959.

Tarver, J. D.   Predicting migration. *Social Forces,* **39** (3), 1961, 207–213.

Taylor, J. G.   *The Behavioral Basis of Perception.* New Haven: Yale University Press, 1962.

Thorndike, E. L.   *Educational Psychology: Briefer Course.* New York: Teachers College, Columbia University Press, 1914 & 1922.

Thorndike, E. L.   *Educational Psychology. I. The Original Nature of Man. II. The Psychology of Learning.* New York: Teachers College, Columbia University Press, 1913.

Thevenaz, P.   *What is Phenomenology?* Chicago: Quadrangle Books, 1962.

Thorne, F. C.   *Six Approaches to Psychotherapy.* New York: Henry Holt, 1955.

Tiebout, H. M., Jr.   Philosophy and Psychoanalysis: Theories of Human Nature and Conduct in Freud's Psychology. Unpublished doctoral dissertation, Columbia University, 1952.

Tillich, P.   *Theology of Culture.* New York: Oxford University Press, 1964.

Titchener, E. B. *Lectures on the Experimental Psychology of the Thought Process.* New York: Macmillan Co., 1909.

Titchener, E. B. Prolegomena to a Study of Introspection. *American Journal of Psychology,* vol. 23 (1912), 427–446.

Titchener, E. B. The Schema of Introspection. *American Journal of Psychology,* vol. 23 (1912), 485–508.

Titchener, E. B. Functional Psychology and the Psychology of Act, part I. *American Journal of Psychology,* 32 (1921), 519–542.

Titchener, E. B. Functional Psychology and the Psychology of Act, part II. *American Journal of Psychology,* 33 (1922), 43–83.

Titchener, E. B. Experimental Psychology a Retrospect. *American Journal of Psychology,* 36 (1925), 313–323.

Trow, W. C. *Educational Psychology.* (2nd ed.) Boston: Houghton-Mifflin, 1950.

Trowbridge, N. T. Self-concept of disadvantaged and advantaged children. AERA National Meeting, Minneapolis, Minnesota, 1970.

Turner, F. J. *The Frontier in American History.* New York: Holt, 1958.

Turner, W. *History of Philosophy.* Boston: Ginn & Co., 1929.

Tyler, L. E. *The Work of the Counselor.* New York: Appleton-Century-Crofts, 1961.

Tylor, E. B. *Anthropology.* London: Watts & Co., 1881, 1946.

Ullmann, L. P., & Krasner, L. *Case Studies in Behavior Modification.* New York: Holt, Rinehart and Winston, Inc., 1965.

Van Kaam, A. Counseling from the viewpoint of existential psychology. *Harvard Educational Review,* 32, Fall 1962.

Vaughn, R. P. Existentialism in Counseling: the religious view. *Personnel and Guidance Journal,* 43, 1965.

Viney, L. Self, the history of a concept. *Journal of the History of the Behavioral Sciences,* 1969, 5 (4), 349–359.

Voss, G. S. Missionary accommodation, pamphlet printed by the American Press, New York, 1946.

Vygotsky, L. S. *Thought and Language.* Translated by E. Hanfmann and G. Vakar. Cambridge, Massachusetts: Massachusetts Institute of Technology Press, 1962.

Walker, D. E.   Carl Rogers and the nature of man. *Journal of Counseling Psychology* 3 (2), 1956, 89–92.

Wallach, M. S., & Strupp, H. H.   Dimensions of psychotherapists' activity, *Journal of Consulting Psychology*, **28**, 1964, 120–125.

Walsh, J. J.   *The Thirteenth, the Greatest of Centuries.* Washington, D.C.: Catholic Summer School Press. Catholic University, 1913.

Wann, T. W.   (Ed.), *Behaviorism and Phenomenology.* Chicago: University of Chicago Press, 1964.

Watson, A.   Freud the translator. *International Journal of Psychoanalysis*, **39**, Part V, 1958, 326–327.

Watson, R. L.   *The Great Psychologists.* Philadelphia and New York: J. B. Lippincott Co., 1963.

Way, L. M.   *Adler's Place in Psychology.* New York: Macmillan, 1959.

Weatherhead, L. D.   *Psychology, Religion and Healing.* Nashville: Abingdon Press, 1951.

White, A. D.   *A History of the Warfare of Science with Theology in Christendom.* New York: D. Appleton & Co., 1899, 1955. 2 vols.

White, L. A.   *The Science of Culture.* New York: Grove Press Inc., 1949.

Wild, J.   Educational and Human Society: a Realistic View, in *Modern Philosophies and Education,* fifty-fourth yearbook of the National Society for the Study of Education, Part I, Chicago, Ill.: University of Chicago Press, 1955.

Williamson, E. G.   *How to Counsel Students.* New York: McGraw-Hill, 1939.

Winkler, F. E.   *Man: The Bridge Between Two Worlds.* New York: Harper and Bros., 1960.

Wisdom, J.   *Philosophy and Psychoanalysis.* New York: Philosophical Library, 1953.

Wittels, F.   *Freud: His Personality, His Teaching and His School.* New York: Dodd, Mead, 1924.

Wylie, R. C.   *The Self Concept.* Lincoln: University of Nebraska Press, 1961.

Wundt, W.   *Grundzuge der Physiologischen Psychologie.* Leipzig: W. Engelmann. (5th ed.) Vol. 3, 1903.

Zax, N., & Klein, A. Measurement of personality and behavior changes following psychotherapy. *Psychological Bulletin,* **57,** 1960.

Zener, K., & Gaffron, J. Perceptual Experience: An Analysis of its Relations to the External World through Internal Processings. In Koch, S. (Ed.), *Psychology: A Study of Science.* New York: McGraw-Hill, 1962.

Zilboorg, G. *A History of Medical Psychology.* New York: Norton, 1941.

Zilboorg, G. *Sigmund Freud, His Explorations into the Mind of Man.* New York: Scribners, 1951.

Author Index

Abelard, 135
Abraham, K., 282
Adams, L., 114
Adler, A., 250, 281, 287-289
Adler, M. J., 381
Aesculapius, 124
Albert the Great, 135, 136, 139, 187
Alexander, F., 282
Allen, T. A., 178
Allport, F., 324
Almy, M., 327
Ambrose of Milan, 119, 122
Anaximander, 80
Anaximines, 80
Angell, T., 359
Anselm, 226, 308
Aquinas, T., 88, 114, 135, 136, 139, 158, 187-200, 218, 225, 226, 236, 237, 253, 260, 274, 305, 380, 417
Aristophanes, 65, 102
Arnold, D., 425
Arnold, M., 381
Aristotle, 82, 99, 114, 124, 133, 187, 196, 212, 218, 225, 226
   influence on Freud, 253, 254, 271, 274, 284, 304, 380, 417
Astin, A., 58
Augustine, 114, 115, 119, 127, 133
Aurelius, Marcus, 116
Ausubel, D., 139, 280, 327-329, 383, 384
Averroes, 134
Avicenna, 134

Backman, C., 57
Bacon, F., 142, 218, 226
Bacon, R., 135, 139, 150
Baer, D. M., 405
Bain, A., 149, 159, 164, 236
Baker, F. B., 349, 406
Baldwin, J., 178
Bandura, A., 60, 61, 376,

402, 404
Barclay, J., 18, 29, 57, 60, 252, 406, 425
Barclay, L., 57
Barrow, 142
Baruch, T. A., 73
Basedow, J. B., 171, 172
Bateman, B., 405
Bayles, E., 382
Bear, H., 228, 240
Beck, C., 331
Bede, Venerable, 116
Beez, W., 412
Bekhterev, V. M., 389
Benedict, 122
Bentham, T., 224, 254, 363
Bereiter, C., 405
Bergum, B., 411
Berkeley, G., 219
Berlyne, D., 47
Bernfeld, G., 261
Bernoulli, J., 356
Besher, T., 50
Bidley, D., 44
Bigge, M., 382, 383
Bijou, S. W., 405
Binet, A., 326, 355
Bixler, R., 375
Blondheim, S., 77
Bloom, B. T., 412
Bode, B. H., 382
Boniface, VIII, 115, 134
Borden, E. S., 419
Boring, E., 161, 162, 165, 179, 319, 350, 354
Boskoff, A., 54
Bowen, H., 173
Boy, A., 22
Boyd, W., 150, 168, 174, 175
Bradbury, D., 349
Braid, J., 285
Brentano, C., 221
Brentano, F., 133, 146, 149, 157, 185, 187, 218, 220-246, 249, 251-255, 260, 269, 274, 275, 303, 305, 306, 309-312, 318, 332, 359, 397, 421

and Freud, 276-280
Brentano, J., 237, 238, 250
Brentano, L., 221, 222
Brentano, P., 221
Breuer, T., 250, 260
Briskin, A., 419
Bronfenbrenner, U., 51
Brophy, J., 412
Brown, T., 406
Brown, P., 425
Bruecke, E., 180, 250, 252, 253, 255, 280, 285, 394
Bruner, J., 139, 320, 327, 383
Buber, M., 305, 309, 336
Burgess, R., 49
Burke, 167
Burton, R., 52

Calkins, N., 177
Campbell, D., 419, 423
Carnegie, A., 348
Carroll, K., 331
Cassirer, E., 167
Castiglioni, A., 73
Cattell, J., 106, 181, 353-356
Catterall, C., 10
Cautela, T., 412, 425
Cavanaugh, T., 198, 199
Charcot, 250, 255, 284-286
Chittenden, E., 325
Christ, 188
Cicero, 116
Claparede, E., 326
Clark, C., 425
Clement, Pope, 135
Clement of Alexandria, 118, 128
Coan, R., 30
Cobb, J. A., 405, 406
Cole, S., 50
Coleman, T., 424
Combs, A. W., 22, 311, 320, 323-325, 335, 337, 383, 423
Comenius, J. A., 150, 165,

463

169, 172
Compayre, G., 163, 164
Comte, A., 180, 181, 220, 225, 226, 254
Condillac, E., 149, 160, 161-165, 173, 175, 349
Copernicus, 140, 143, 145, 393
Cousin, V., 164, 176
Cronbach, L., 423
Cusa, N., 226

Darwin, C., 346, 357, 362
Davidson, T., 165
Davis, H., 52, 260
Dawson, C., 44
Democritus, 80, 212
Descartes, R., 133, 141, 143-146, 149, 159, 178, 187, 200-205, 210-215, 218, 219, 226, 227, 234, 246, 271, 281, 393, 398
Dewey, J., 18, 20, 166, 319, 320, 335, 342, 343, 348, 349, 351, 359, 360-371, 373, 377, 378, 383, 387, 389
De Vaux, R., 70, 76
Diderot, D., 162, 167
Dilthey, W., 318
Dittes, T., 58
Dollard, J. C., 258, 322, 384, 399, 400
Döllinger, J., 221, 222
Donders, F. C., 181
Drexelius, J., 129
Driesch, T., 172
DuBois-Reymond, E., 180, 224, 251, 252, 394

Eby, F., 148, 151
Edi, J. M., 302
Elkind, D., 327
Ellis, A., 281, 282, 294-295
Epicurus, 117
Epictetus, 116
Empedocles, 80, 104
Engelmann, S., 405
Erikson, E. H., 225
Eruigena, J. S., 133
Eysenck, H., 24, 106, 401-403, 411

Fairbairn, W., 270
Farber, M., 224, 304, 309, 318
Fechner, G., 179, 236, 237, 251, 252, 260, 356
Federn, P., 282
Feigl, H., 295, 394, 396
Fenichel, O., 283, 300
Ferenczi, S., 282

Ferster, C. B., 14, 376
Festinger, L., 320
Fichte, J. G., 179, 220
Fiedler, F. E., 34, 369
Fisher, R. A., 356
Fiske, D. W., 423
Fitch, J. C., 346
Flanders, N., 58
Flavell, T., 327, 383
Fodor, N., 266
Ford, D., 28
Forsythe, F., 425
Frazer, J. G., 62
Freud, S., 23, 133, 180, 187, 221, 225, 237, 248-284, 335, 337, 338, 365, 379, 384, 399
Froebel, F., 149, 157, 165, 173, 174, 346, 349
Froelich, C., 343, 375
Fromm, E., 282, 423

Gaffron, M., 398
Gagne, R. R., 379, 405
Galen, 105, 145, 284
Galileo, 140, 143, 145, 393
Galton, F., 353-356
Garvey, W., 406
Gauss, K., 356
Gay, P., 167
Georgiades, P., 252
Gilbert, W. M., 19, 142
Gilson, L., 224-226, 230
Gimbel, B., 262
Glasser, W., 10
Goddard, H. H., 355
Goethe, J. W., 165, 221
Goldiamond, I., 27, 426
Gomperz, T., 250
Goodwin, D. L., 406
Goodenough, F., 354
Gregory the Great, 115
Griesinger, W., 285
Green, A. W., 52
Gronlund, N., 57
Grossberg, T., 25, 402, 404
Guinouard, D. E., 52
Guthrie, E. R., 391
Guilford, J. P., 106

Haeckel, E. H., 349, 350
Hall, G. S., 173, 174, 177, 181, 266, 349, 350
Halmos, P., 5
Halpern, S., 102
Hamerlynck, L., 405
Hamilton, W., 304
Harlow, H. F., 386
Harper, R., 296, 332
Harris, W. T., 361, 405
Hartley, D., 100, 159
Hartmann, K., 236, 237, 304

Harvey, W., 145
Havighurst, R. J., 52
Havumaki, S., 58
Hebb, D. O., 411
Hegel, G., 179, 220, 224, 226, 304, 305
Heidegger, M., 305, 307-309, 315, 317, 318, 329, 330, 332, 416, 421
Heider, F., 320, 324, 333, 421
Helmholtz, H., 159, 179-181, 220, 224, 251, 252, 319, 389, 394
Helvetius, C., 153
Heraclitus, 81
Herbart, 133, 146, 149, 156, 172, 179, 220, 236, 237, 251, 349, 353, 356
Hewitt, F., 405
Highet, G., 381
Hilgard, E., 319, 321, 323, 386
Hippocrates, 103, 124, 145, 284, 352
Hobbes, T., 25, 167, 218
Hoffding, H., 203, 214
Hofstadter, R., 347
Holland, J. L., 5, 58
Homme, L., 411
Hosford, R. E., 406, 408, 409, 419
Horney, K., 281, 282, 295-297, 423
Howes, H., 25
Hull, C. L., 391, 394, 397, 399, 400
Hume, D., 133, 149, 158, 219, 224, 226, 238, 305, 393, 398
Husserl, E., 187, 221, 224, 251, 280, 302, 304-309, 311-314, 316, 318, 332, 421
Hutchins, R., 381
Hutson, P., 371
Hyman, L., 350

Inhelder, B., 326
Innocent III, 134
Irenaeus, 118, 128

Jackson, E., 425
Jacobson, E., 411
Jakobovitz, I., 74, 75
James, W., 221, 237, 311, 312, 335, 344, 348, 356-360, 382, 386, 397, 421
Janet, P., 260, 286, 291,

326
Jaspers, K., 318
Jerome, 119, 122, 133
John of the Cross, 130
Johnson, E. L., 21, 324,
    325, 336, 337
Jones, E., 180, 224, 249-
    253, 255, 261, 280,
    282, 404
Judd, C. H., 181, 359
Jung, C., 250, 260, 281,
    291-293
Justinian, 124

Kallen, H., 358, 359
Kant, I., 105, 138, 139, 179,
    186, 219, 220, 224,
    226, 304, 305, 356
Kaplan, A., 254, 271, 272
Kastil, A., 223, 224
Kelly, G., 58, 324, 421
Kepler, J., 140, 143, 232,
    393
Kilpatrick, W., 335, 374,
    389
Kierkegaard, S., 305, 330,
    332, 336
Klein, M., 24, 282
Kluckhohn, C., 44
Kneller, G., 331
Knight, P., 253
Koch, S., 333, 397
Koehler, W., 222, 304, 311,
    319, 320, 323, 382,
    421
Koff, R. H., 411, 412
Koffka, K., 311, 319, 320,
    382
Kohn, M., 424
Kolesnick, W., 98, 381
Korsakov, S., 285
Kraepelin, E., 284, 285
Kraft-Ebbing, R., 285
Krasner, L., 27, 402, 426
Kraus, O., 223, 224, 237
Krumboltz, J. D., 14, 23, 25,
    26, 371, 376, 406-408,
    420, 426
Külpe, O., 186, 303
Kuo, Z. Y., 9, 411

Lambert, J. H., 304
LaMettrie, T. O., 149, 159,
    160
Landsman, T., 331, 334
LaPlace, P., 356
Laroche, M., 221
Lashley, K., 163, 386, 389
Lee, G., 344
Leibnitz, G., 132, 133, 142,
    146, 157, 178, 184,
    200, 211-218, 226-228,

236, 237, 246, 260,
    279, 312
Levine, I., 237
Levine, D. V., 424
Lewin, K., 288, 311, 317,
    319, 320-323, 333, 335,
    337, 378, 383, 400
Lindzey, G., 266
Lipps, T., 312, 313
Locke, J., 132, 133, 138,
    142, 146-158, 159, 167,
    171, 175, 178, 192,
    200, 212, 218, 220,
    224, 226, 305, 393,
    398
Lott, A. J., 58
Lott, B. E., 58
Lotze, R., 133, 222, 236,
    312
Lucretius, 117
Ludwig, C., 180
Luke, 123
Lully, R., 226
Luther, M., 138

MacLeod, R. B., 315
Mager, R. F., 405
Mahrer, A. R., 28
Maimonides, M., 254
Maine, J., 167
Mann, H., 176, 177, 346
Maritain, J., 237
Marx, K., 305
Maslow, A., 335, 423
Matheney, K., 31
Mathers, C., 126
Maudsley, H., 159, 180,
    220, 224, 232
May, R., 15, 18, 22, 329,
    330
McClelland, D., 320
McDaniel, H. B., 376
McDougal, W., 384
McHugh, M., 19, 370
McReynolds, W., 405
Meehl, P., 423
Meinong, C., 221, 224, 324
Merlan, P., 224, 249, 251
Mesmer, F., 285
Meyer, Adolph, 298
Meyerson, 14, 26
Meynert, F., 251
Mill, J. S., 149, 157, 159,
    164, 180, 181, 222,
    224, 232, 236, 237,
    250, 253, 254, 312,
    313, 363
Miller, J., 258, 259
Miller, N. E., 384, 399, 400
Miller, W., 53
Milton, J., 150, 151
Misiak, H., 180

Mohler, J. A., 225
Montaigne, M., 154
Montessori, M., 149, 175
Montgomery, R., 405, 406
Moses, 71, 188
Mowrer, O., 404
Muller, J., 140, 159, 179-
    181, 285
Munroe, R., 282, 289,
    290, 292
Murphy, G., 248, 258

Nelson, B., 237, 258, 260
Newman, H., 113, 115,
    222
Newton, I., 142-145, 149,
    232
Nietzsche, F., 251, 305

Ohlsen, M., 419
Olson, W. C., 319
Origen, 114, 118, 128
Osgood, C., 421

Pace, E. A., 58, 181
Parsons, F., 371
Patterson, G., 15, 22, 402,
    405, 406
Paul, 110, 113, 126, 127
Pavlov, I. P., 389, 392
Payne, J., 171, 346
Pearson, K., 354, 356
Peirce, C. S., 304, 360,
    361, 363
Pepinsky, H., 373
Pestalozzi, J. H., 149, 157,
    165, 171-173, 176,
    177, 179, 349
Peter, L., 405
Philo, 78, 117
Piaget, J., 68, 139, 322,
    326, 327, 333, 379,
    383, 384
Pine, J. G., 22
Pinel, P., 285
Plato, 96, 98, 99, 133,
    191, 196, 212, 251,
    253, 254, 260, 274,
    284, 305, 308, 352,
    380, 417
Plotinus, 117, 118, 224,
    226, 253, 254
Poincare, R., 260
Porta, B., 285
Preyer, W., 174, 326
Prince, M., 260
Proff, F., 419
Protagoras, 81
Ptolemy, 140
Purbach, G., 140
Pythagoras, 80

Quetelet, L., 354, 356

Rachman, S., 106, 354, 401
Rank, O., 281, 289, 291,
    335, 337
Reich, W., 282
Reid, T., 226, 406
Rice, J. M., 355
Robinson, F., 343, 375
Rogers, C., 15, 18, 22, 26,
    324, 325, 331, 332,
    334-341, 371, 379, 423
Roscelin, 133
Ross, F., 101, 102
Rousseau, J. J., 149, 154,
    157, 164, 165-171, 285,
    349, 417
Rychlak, J., 52

Santoro, D., 425
Sartre, J. P., 318, 320, 331,
    332
Scheler, M., 314-315, 318
Schell, H., 222
Schelling, F., 220, 221
Schiller, F., 359
Schopenhauer, A., 237, 251,
    260
Schwartz, C., 253
Scotus, Duns, 135, 136,
    226, 305, 315, 417
Scripture, E. W., 181
Sears, R., 371
Sequin, E., 149, 175
Sheldon, E. A., 177
Shermis, S. S., 367
Shoben, E., 34
Shulman, L., 423, 424
Skinner, B. F., 14, 391,
    392, 394, 424, 426
Smith, W. R., 222
Snygg, D., 22, 311, 320,
    323-335, 337, 423
Socrates, 65, 82, 83, 133,
    191, 196
Spearman, C., 356
Spencer, H., 149, 164, 222,

236, 347-349, 353, 362,
    381, 388
Spiegelberg, H., 251, 302,
    303, 304, 310, 314,
    315, 316, 317, 318,
    324
Spinoza, B., 146, 187, 205-
    211, 215, 218, 227,
    246, 251, 254, 275,
    279, 309
Staats, A., 385, 405
Staats, C., 385, 405
Staudt, V., 180
Stefflre, B., 31
Stern, 58, 355
Stilwell, W., 425
Stumpf, C., 187, 221, 222,
    224, 225, 280, 305,
    310-311, 316, 320
Sullivan, H. S., 281, 282,
    298-299
Sullivan, J., 251

Terman, L. M., 355, 356
Tertullian, 107, 118, 119,
    127, 128
Thales, 80
Theresa of Avila, 130
Thévenez, P., 317
Thorndike, E. L., 18, 159,
    178, 319, 344, 351,
    355, 356, 359, 378,
    382, 386-391, 392
Thorne, F. C., 375
Thoresen, C., 406
Thurstone, L., 356
Tiebout, H., 21, 85, 86,
    253, 254, 271
Tillich, P., 15, 18, 309, 315,
    331, 332, 421
Titchener, E. B., 181, 233,
    320, 359
Tolman, E., 319, 358, 386
Trendelenberg, A., 221, 225
Trow, W. C., 388
Turner, F. J., 219, 344
Twardowski, K., 221

Tyler, L., 419

Ullman, L., 402, 404

Van Doren, M., 381
Van Kaam, A., 15, 331,
    332, 420
Vaughn, R. P., 331, 332
Von Ehrenfels, C., 221,
    224
Voss, G., 113
Vygotsky, L. S., 384

Walker, D., 336, 337,
    338
Walsh, J., 136, 137
Walters, R., 60
Wann, T., 21, 315, 398
Watson, A., 224, 254,
    319
Watson, J., 389-391, 394
Watson, R., 158, 159, 178
Weatherhead, L., 63, 109,
    123
Weber, E., 356
Wertheimer, M., 311, 319,
    320, 382
White, A. D., 125
White, L., 44
Whorf, B., 313
Williamson, E., 14, 18,
    343, 371-374, 377,
    419
Wild, J., 33
Winkler, F., 331
Wolff, L., 219, 304, 381
Wolpe, J., 24, 400-402,
    404
Wundt, W., 106, 179-181,
    220, 222, 236, 238,
    319, 320, 353, 354,
    356, 359
Wylie, R., 423

Zener, K., 397, 398
Zeno, 116
Zilboorg, G., 72, 253, 271

Subject Index

Abnormal psychology, 283
Act psychology, 157, 158, 186, 220, 359
Activity, 263
Actuality, 92
Adequation theory of scholasticism, 201, 202, 241
Adjustment, 371, 420
Adolescence, 350
Affective movements, 239-241, 244, 379, 384
Aggression, 60, 406
Alexandrian school, 133
Anaclitic characteristics, 266
Animistic thinking, 68
Anxiety, 317
Apologetical writings, 133
Apologists, 118
Aristotle, 87-95
    criticism of idealism, 88
    ethics and politics, 93
    metaphysics and physics, 92, 186
    psychology and theory of knowledge, 89
Assessment of behavior, 8, 9, 351-356, 381, 414
Association of words, 261
Associationism, 174, 176
    laws of, 100, 158, 380
    see also Wundt*
Associationists, 132, 149, 158
Attention, 264, 275
Authority, 56, 136, 139, 154, 171, 198
Axiology, 20

Behavior modification, 2, 24, 95, 123, 178, 378-415, 426
Behavioral engineers, 23, 276
Behaviorism, 14, 320, 340, 386, 389
    philosophical basis for, 393-399, 418, 420-422, 425
Being, 90, 315-317, 329,
*Author Index.

339, 398
Benedictines, 129
Birth trauma, 289, 290
Byzantine Empire, 134

Calvinists, 149
Carmelites, 130
Cartesian, see Descartes*
    Cartesian Cogito, 306, 312
Carthusians, 129
Catechumenate, 128
Cathexis, 254, 266, 267, 273, 275, 278, 279, 304
Causal concept, 228, 240, 267
Censorship, 96
Child as man in miniature, 164, 168
Child-centered approach, 165
Child development approaches, 165, 176
Child-rearing, 51, 149, 165, 424
Child-study method, 347, 348-349, 362
Christ, teaching, 108-110
Christianity, 107, 180
Client-centered counseling, 14, 165
Client-centered therapy, 334, 335, 337, 341, 425
Clinical approach to human behavior, 256, 258, 335
Clinical observation, 104
Concept formation, 328, 383, 384
Conceptualism, 138, 139
Concupiscible appetite, 191, 274
Conditioned response, 390
Conditioning, classical, 131, 390
Conditioning, operant, 131, 335, 369, 392, 423
Confession, 420
Configurationalism, 382
Conformity, 421
Connectionism, see

Thorndike*
Conscience, 246, 253
Consciousness, 203, 207, 234, 257, 261-265, 273, 277, 306, 313, 359, 365, 389
Contradiction, laws of, 91, 202
Control mechanisms, cultural, 45, 54, 56, 352
Cosmology, 141
Correspondence theory, 25, 225
Counseling, 198
    approaches, 14
    defined, 4, 12
    theory, 31
Criterion, 11, 18, 25
    determination, 419
Cultural transmission, 46, 68, 95, 101
Culture, defined, 43
    nature of, 43, 56
    purpose of, 48
Customs, 45, 136

Daseinanalysis, 15, 21, 316
Death, 316, 317, 330, 331, 413
Decision-making, 3, 102, 376
Defense mechanisms, 300, 384, 403
Dependability, 64
Desensitization, 24, 401
Determinism, 254, 279
Deviation, 353
Dialectic, 98, 133
Didactic methods, 175, 176
Discipline, mental, 100, 157
Disease, 75, 104, 145
Distribution, 371
Dominicans, 129, 138
Dreams, analysis of, 257, 281
    formation, 265

467

Dualism, 81, 142, 145, 155, 157, 178, 271

Eclecticism, 164, 343, 374-377
Education, 54, 96-100, 128, 149, 151, 153-155, 164, 168, 176, 177, 198, 199, 366-368
Ego, 85, 197, 220, 235, 253, 270, 273, 274, 278
Ego ideal, 86, 264, 271
Emotionality, 235, 246, 278
Empirical method, tradition, 132, 135, 189, 220
Empiricism, 159, 161, 162
Environmentalism, 21, 28, 37, 171, 218, 219, 417
Environmental press, 287, 410, 422, 425
Epicureanism, 116, 117, 226
Epistemology, 15, 25, 157, 195
Essenes, 75
Evolution, 180, 346-348, 387, 388, 391, 394
Existentialism, 317, 329-334, 418
Experimentalism, 21, 179, 342-377, 394, 397
Experimentalists, 23
Extinction, 385

Faculty psychology, 168, 176
Family, 45, 52, 288, 406
Fathers of the Church, 118, 134
Fear, 317
Field theory, 322, 333, 337, 378, 382, 383
Form, 93, 321, 396
Formal cause, 92
Formal discipline, 378, 381, 382, 390
Four humor theory, 104
Four phases of philosophy, 225
Franciscans, 129, 138
Free association, 102, 231, 243, 256, 267, 320
Freudian psychotherapy, 65, 280-283
Functionalism, 356-360, 384

Gemütsbewegung, 239
Gestalt psychology, 133, 146, 185, 221, 223, 228, 236, 247, 280, 288, 310, 318-329, 341, 359, 382, 384

Gestalten, 24
Goal determination, 101

Habits, 47, 101, 163, 391
Happiness of the soul, 217
Harmony, 172
Harmony of the soul, 217
Healing, 109, 123, 284
Health, 104
Hebrews, 69-75
Hedonism, 155, 165
Hostility, 297
Humanism, 28, 38, 147, 362, 417, 418, 420-422
Humanists, 21
Hypnosis, 281, 285
Hypotheses, unconscious, 258
forming of, 339, 340
Hysteria phenomena, 255, 257, 264

Id, 85, 86, 270, 278
Idealism, 81, 179, 219, 220, 224, 253, 306, 337, 361, 418
Identification, 267
Imitation, 61, 96, 101, 408
Individual differences, 152, 173, 176, 231, 346, 354, 355, 378, 388, 390
Individuality, 315, 347, 368, 417
Induction, 328, 384
Inferiority complex, 288
Innate ideas, 211, 213, 276
Instincts, 163, 191, 239; Freud 261-263, 265, 266, 274, 275, 281; Watson 390
Intentionality, 178, 185, 192-195, 218, 220, 234; Brentano 245, 246, 273, 302, 304, 363, 414; Freud 261, 267, 278, 283
Intentionalistic imagery, 411, 412
Interpersonal theory, 298
Introspection, 213, 232, 256, 257, 261, 310, 312, 320, 361, 389
Intuition, 303, 307, 313
Ipseity, 316
Irrascible appetite, 191, 274
Isomorphism, theory of, 304, 320, 321

Jesuits, 130, 149
Judgment, 265, 270, 275

Knowledge, theory of, 15

Aristotle, 89
Brentano, 225
Descartes, 201, 202
Leibnitz, 214
Scheler, 314
Scholastic, 195
Spinoza, 208
Thomistic, 199

Language, 173, 174, 328, 384
Law of the three stages, 181
Law, 134
natural, 196
Learning, 100, 321, 378-415
stimulus-response, 384, 385, 398, 409
conditioning, 385
classical, 380, 381
Learning, reception, 328, 383, 384
discovery, 328
Learning theory, 398-415, 419
Lebenswelt, 15, 303, 306
Libido, 291
Life space, 322
Logic, 90, 141, 188, 189, 200, 213, 216, 220, 225, 227, 228, 304, 307, 313
Love, 109-111, 171, 172, 290

Magic, 62
Manichaeism, 119
Mass communication, 54
Material cause, 92
Material sensism, 91
Materialism, 162, 254
Mathematics, 139, 143, 206, 213
Matter, 92, 118
McGuffey readers, 178
Measurement, 344, 351-356
Medicine, early, 75-79
Greek, 103
Mental discipline, 100, 382
Mentally retarded, 174, 175, 284
Metaphysics, 186
Missionary accommodation, 112-116
Mobility, 49
Modeling, 60, 131
Models, 109
Monads, 213, 214, 217
Monasteries, 122, 130
Monastic way of life, 122, 129

Motion, 93, 213
Mysticism, 133, 135, 138, 226, 271

Nature, 116, 145, 167, 170, 171, 206, 211, 213
Nature of man, Descartes, 202, 393
  Ellis, 295
  Freud, 271, 275
  Plato, 83
  Rogers, 337, 338
  Scholastic, 190
  Thorndike, 386
Naturphilosophie, 221, 224, 226
Neo-Freudians, 15, 281, 283, 288
Neo-Platonism, 114, 116, 117, 120, 133, 226
Neo-Psychoanalytic, 14
Neurosis, 283, 288, 296, 400, 401
Nicaea, Council of, 118, 188
Nominalism, 138, 139, 202
Notation, 265

Object-manipulative counseling, 14
Object-oriented counseling, 13
Object-relationship, 195, 208, 217, 218, 233, 241, 266, 300
Object teaching, 150, 177, 178
Objectivist tradition, 133
Observation, 101, 171, 257, 258
Observational learning, 60
Ontology, 331
Oswego system, 171, 177
Overt person, 298

Parable, 109
Perception, 264, 265, 273, 319, 320, 321, 323, 325, 327, 358, 380, 382
Personality, 86, 259, 281, 283, 289, 290, 300, 324, 341
Pestalozzianism, 171
Pharisees, 75
Phenomenologists, 139
Phenomenology, 15, 21, 181, 185, 280, 302-341
  axiological, 308
  epistemological, 306
  ontological, 308
Philosophy and counseling, 12
  beginnings of, 79
Physicians, 145

Plato, 81-87
  ethical values, 86
  laws, 87
  metaphysics, 82
  nature of man, 83
  religion and aesthetics, 87
Play, 174
Pleasure-pain principle, 263, 266, 267, 271, 273, 275, 388, 389
Pliny's letters, 113
Port royalists, 150
Positivism, 180, 181, 226, 227, 254, 304, 305
Potency, 92
Pragmatism, 304, 356-360
Preconsciousness, 263, 265, 273, 277, 307
Predictability, 48, 64, 353, 396
Problem-Solving, 342-377, 383
Process, 7, 24, 195, 379-384
Psychiatry, development of, 285
Psychic phenomena, 299, 230
Psychoanalytic theory, 248, 403, 425
Psychodynamics, 259
Psychologism, 312
Psychology, defined, 229
  abnormal, 283
  clinical, 9, 258, 280, 283, 284, 286, 336, 337, 424
  experimental, 14, 178
Psychotherapy, 248
  distinction between psychotherapy and counseling, 4
Purification, 72-74
Purity, 72

Quadrivium, 98

Rationalism, 135, 170, 219, 220, 363
Real self, 296, 297
Realism, 220, 361, 394, 397
  moderate, 138, 225, 389
  ultra, 138
Reality, 142, 144, 171, 209, 213
  Aquinas, 189
  behaviorism, 398
  Brentano, 235
  Dewey, 361, 365
  existentialism, 304, 306, 330
  experimentalism, 395
  Freud, 264, 268, 270, 271, 273
  James, 358

  principle, 393
Reason, 84, 147, 155, 156, 168, 171, 189, 220
  Brentano, 223, 347
  Freud, 259, 271
  Leibnitz, 215, 217, 307
Recapitulation theory, 164, 173, 174, 347, 349-351
Reflection, 156-158, 165, 219, 246
Reinforcement, 61, 100, 385, 392
  schedules of, 61, 392
Relaxation, 281
Religion, 62, 67, 68
Representation, 233, 236
  psychic, 268, 313, 327, 328
Repression, 264, 265, 267, 270, 281, 283, 384, 401, 403
Res Cogitans, 142, 393
Res *Extensa,* 142, 393
Revelation, 145, 188, 196, 217, 274

Scepticism, 116, 117, 225, 226, 230
Schedules of reinforcement, 61, 392
Schema, 383
Scholasticism, 132, 133-138, 141, 142, 187-200, 208, 218, 221, 225, 226, 269, 274, 318, 396
Self-acceptance, 341
Self-analysis, 262
Self-concept theory, 332, 334-341, 365, 369-370, 371, 406, 419, 423, 424
Self-understanding, 23, 26, 314, 334, 338, 341, 368, 374, 421
Sensations, 164, 165, 177, 179, 209, 219, 231, 235, 236, 292
Sensationalists, 132, 149, 155, 156, 159, 171
Senses, external, 191
  internal, 196
Sensory processes, 189, 204
Sexual motivation, Freud, 262
Shaping, 60
Slaves, 127
Sleep, 265, 273
Social control, 377
Social Darwinism, 347, 348

Social learning, 55, 109, 113, 116
    antecedents to, 385-393, 399, 408, 409, 413, 414
Sociometry, 57
Sophists, 81
Soul, 82, 83, 93, 144, 158, 160, 162, 190, 192, 194, 202, 207, 210, 269, 270; Adler 287; Brentano 299, 242; Freud 278; Jung 291, 292, 293; Leibnitz 214, 217
Spiritual advisement, 130
Stages of development, 168, 169
Statistics, 143, 356, 398
"Statue analogy", 162, 163
Stoicism, 114, 116, 226
Strategy-making, 8, 10
Stream of thought, 306, 359
Subject-manipulative counseling, 14

Subject-oriented counseling, 13, 15, 22
Superego, 85, 86, 253, 271, 272, 278
Superstition, 68
Syllogism, 91, 141, 201, 213, 216, 228

Tabula Rasa, 147, 149, 153, 158, 168, 212, 277
Teleological argument, 199, 200, 206
Temperaments, 105
Temporality, 317
Tokens, 131
Transfer of training, 382
Tribe, 45, 115

Unconscious, 236, 237, 246, 257, 258, 260-263, 265, 273, 281, 283; collective 292, 293; determination 254, 259, 262, 283

Universals, 138, 144, 202, 210, 308, 313, 357, 395
Utilitarianism, 362, 363

Values, 62, 145
Vérites de fait 227;
    Vérites de raison 227
Vicarious experience, 109
Virtue, 94, 101, 117, 157, 198, 210
Vorstellung, 233, 267
Vortex Theory, 142, 178

Wild boy of Aveyron, 175
Will, 138, 191, 196-198, 204, 205, 207; Leibnitz 216, 218; Brentano 239, 240, 241; Freud 252, 254, 278; Rank 290, 303, 426

Zeitgeist, 161, 165